A History of Seventeenth-Century English Literature

Thomas N. Corns

Blackwell Publishing

BLACKWELL PUBLISHING
350 Main Street, Malden, MA 02148-5020, USA
9600 Garsington Road, Oxford OX4 2DQ, UK
550 Swanston Street, Carlton, Victoria 3053, Australia

First published 2007 by Blackwell Publishing Ltd

1 2007

Library of Congress Cataloging-in-Publication Data

Corns, Thomas N.
  A history of seventeenth-century English literature / Thomas N. Corns.
    p. cm.—(Blackwell histories of literature)
  Includes bibliographical references and index.
  ISBN-13: 978-0-631-22169-2 (alk. paper)
  ISBN-10: 0-631-22169-7 (alk. paper)
    1. English literature—Early modern, 1500–1700—History and criticism.
  2. Great Britain—Intellectual life—17th century. I. Title. II. Series.

PR431.C67 2007
820.9'004—dc22

                                          2006004745

A catalogue record for this title is available from the British Library.

Set in 10.5pt/13pt Galliard
by SPI Publisher Services, Pondicherry, India
Printed and bound in Singapore
by Markono Print Media Pte Ltd

The publisher's policy is to use permanent paper from mills that operate a sustainable forestry
policy, and which has been manufactured from pulp processed using acid-free and elementary
chlorine-free practices. Furthermore, the publisher ensures that the text paper and cover
board used have met acceptable environmental accreditation standards.

For further information on
Blackwell Publishing, visit our website:
www.blackwellpublishing.com

5000844422

 University of
Hertfordshire

College Lane, Hatfield, Herts. AL10 9AB

Learning and Information Services

For renewal of Standard and One Week Loans,
please visit the web site **http://www.voyager.herts.ac.uk**

This item must be returned or the loan renewed by the due date.
The University reserves the right to recall items from loan at any time.
A fine will be charged for the late return of items.

A History of Seventeenth-Century English Literature

BLACKWELL HISTORIES OF LITERATURE

The books in this series renew and redefine a familiar form by recognizing that to write literary history involves more than placing texts in chronological sequence. Thus the emphasis within each volume falls both on plotting the significant literary developments of a given period, and on the wider cultural contexts within which they occurred. 'Cultural history' is construed in broad terms and authors address such issues as politics, society, the arts, ideologies, varieties of literary production and consumption, and dominant genres and modes. The effect of each volume is to give the reader a sense of possessing a crucial sector of literary terrain, of understanding the forces that give a period its distinctive cast and of seeing how writing of a given period impacts on, and is shaped by, its cultural circumstances.

General editor: Peter Brown, University of Kent, Canterbury

Published to date

Old English Literature	Robert Fulk
Seventeenth-Century English Literature	Thomas N. Corns

Forthcoming

Victorian Literature	James Eli Adams

To Pat, for even more patience

Contents

List of Illustrations

Preface

This is a history of English literature in the seventeenth century. It covers writing in English in England and Wales. Writing in English in Scotland and Ireland, like new composition in Latin, figures only marginally, where it relates to or illuminates the principal subject. Literatures produced in the other languages of Britain and Ireland are not considered, because they are both beyond my remit and outside my competence.

Other decisions in the selection or omission of texts are less clear-cut. Those authors who currently are most read and studied receive most attention. I have added some non-canonical works to throw light on the mainstream, together with some which, in my view, have literary merit that has been overlooked. Writers who were once influential or were otherwise perceived as important in their own day are generally included, even though they have substantially fallen from the canon. Translation, particularly from the classical languages, was a significant component of the seventeenth-century experience of literature. Here my treatment is selective and perhaps somewhat arbitrary, though works which proved influential, like Sylvester's rendition of Du Bartas, are included. Dryden's late, glorious translations seemed too good and too important a component of his oeuvre to omit. Populist genres such as ballads or works of popular piety for the most part are drawn on only as part of the larger cultural context. Writers in other genres outside those that are typically considered literary appear intermittently. Francis Bacon and Thomas Sprat, who have often figured in critical histories of non-fictional prose, are engaged with in literary terms; Thomas Hobbes and John Locke, despite their higher status as thinkers, are not considered, except as influences on or analogues to other writers. Though both write with persuasive power, their principal genius rests in their contribution to the tradition of western philosophy, and a proper appreciation of their work would have carried me beyond the concerns of literary history.

This study owes much to the kindness of others. Neville Davies, Paul Hammond, Neil Keeble, Robert Wilcher and David Womersley read and commented on large sections. Alastair Fowler read it in its entirety, and with extraordinary generosity met with me over two days to talk through matters of detail and some of the larger issues. More casual conversations with Gordon Campbell, David Loewenstein and Nigel Smith, particularly at the early stages, shaped the project more profoundly than they can have realized. The early modernists among my Bangor colleagues, Tony Claydon, Bruce Wood, Andrew Hiscock and Ceri Sullivan, have been a recurrent source of advice and assistance. The English department, by the sweat of its collective brow, made possible a semester of study leave at a critical point, and I am grateful, too, to Densil Morgan, who deputized for me as head of the School of Arts and Humanities over that period. Several people at Blackwell Publishing also deserve my thanks: Andrew McNeillie for encouraging me to take the commission on and Emma Bennett for encouraging me to finish it; and Karen Wilson and Sarah Dancy for seeing it through the final stages. The dedication acknowledges a more pervasive kind of debt.

Thomas N. Corns
Bangor, Gwynedd

1

The Last Years of Elizabeth I: Before March 1603

This chapter deals with the literary history of the concluding years of the Tudor era. In terms of the material circumstances of literary production and consumption, much that is described remained substantially unchanged from the 1590s, nor were there major discontinuities with literary life in the Jacobean decades. There were some highly significant shifts of emphasis, particularly in the structures of patronage, as the fall of Robert Devereux, second Earl of Essex, disrupted the complex web of protection and praise that had developed around his circle. The arrival of the Stuart court, with radically different cultural aspirations and a diverse and polycentric organization, would open new opportunities. Few of the writers who shaped the literary culture of the Elizabethan golden age lived into the new century. Sir Philip Sidney died in 1586, Edmund Spenser in 1599, Robert Greene in 1592, Christopher Marlowe in 1593, Thomas Kyd in 1594. The figures who dominate Jacobean literary culture, Francis Bacon (b. 1561), John Donne (b. ?1572), Ben Jonson (b. 1572), and William Shakespeare (b. 1564), were all writing, but only the last had achieved an eminence to match his Jacobean status. Sidney and Spenser, both available in print before 1600, offered a subtle and pervasive influence deep into the new century, and many earlier Elizabethan plays remained in the repertoire of London drama companies, but inevitably those deaths closed off some aspects of Elizabethan culture, despite the continuities, as surely as others with different aesthetic assumption and different strengths moved the tradition on. Yet late Elizabethan and Jacobean literary cultures shared much common ground.

Literary Consumption and Production

Literacy in the early modern period reflected gender, class (and more particularly profession) and geography. In all social groups, men were more likely to be more literate than women, reflecting, no doubt, assumptions about gender roles, though literacy rates among the upper classes were so high and among the very poorest so low that this factor lost its significance. Some professions required good literacy skills, though for others in the same social echelon the issue was less pressing. Once those factors are allowed for, it emerges that literacy rates in London were generally higher than elsewhere. Rates improve over the century, although, based on a simple test of whether people made a mark or signed their name, literacy levels were low. By 1640, 20 per cent of women and 40 per cent of men were signing official documents, rather than using a mark.

The test of literacy in this account, which rests entirely on David Cressy's classic study (1980), is undemanding, though social historians have often argued that the ability to read may have been enjoyed by some who were not able to write (see, for example, Spufford 1979 and Thomas 1986: 103, both discussed by Watt 1991: 7). This may well be the case; I can read modern Greek with facility, but find it exceptionally difficult to write. The skills needed to write one's name or indeed to make out the words in a simple text belong to a different order from those required to read, let alone write, literary English. Indeed, only tentatively may we surmise the literary experience of the poor and often unlettered majority of Elizabethan England. Certainly, we may identify a folk culture, resting in an oral tradition, of popular song, of dance and of tale-telling, most fully realized in seasonal festivals – pre-eminently Christmas, May Day, harvest-home – and the annual celebration of church-wakes, holidays commemorating the patron saints of parish churches. By the late Elizabethan period, some kinds of popular culture were to be found in print: ballads and chapbooks, sold by itinerants, have a place here, and the illiterate could still share some aspects of that print-mediated culture by learning songs from those who could read printed ballads, or listening to chapbooks read aloud. Arguably, popular ballads constituted one of the few points of cultural connection that transcended social division. As Tessa Watt puts it: 'Ballads were hawked in the alehouses and markets, but in the same period they were sung by minstrels in the households of the nobility

and gentry, who copied them carefully into manuscripts' (1991: 1).
The ballad tradition resonates widely across high-culture genres and
throughout the century. Ballad sellers and their songs figure in plays by
Shakespeare and Jonson; the political and social satires of Rochester
and his imitators were sometimes sung to their tunes. Indeed, estimates for the number of ballads printed in London in the half century
to 1600 range from 600,000 to more than 3 million.

The very poorest were substantially excluded from written literary
culture by indigence as well as illiteracy. A ploughman, a semi-skilled
agricultural day labourer, earned five or six old pence a day (5d or 6d:
about 2.5p) (Palliser 1983: 118). A penny would have got him into a
public theatre or bought him a couple of single printed sheets (Gurr
1980: 197; Bennett 1965: 299); both expenditures seem improbable
indulgences for a poor cottager, though the latter could have come to
him as a hand-me-down, and there is ample evidence of ballads being
posted decoratively in alehoues (Watt 1995: 253). Moreover, through
the 1590s the gap between rich and poor increased and the conditions
of the latter, through rural overpopulation and bad harvests, deteriorated very significantly (Sharpe 1995).

Yet among the middling sort, as they were contemporaneously
termed, there emerged a general readership and elements of a theatre
audience. In the rural context, the yeoman class and the lower gentry
and, in towns and cities, the tradesman class below the ranks of the
higher professions and prosperous burgesses bought and reflected on
printed matter and sometimes had access to plays in performance.
These consumer groups became more substantial over the Elizabethan
period, in part because their disposable income grew (Palliser 1983:
ch. 4), and in part because of growing literacy rates among them
(Cressy 1980). Tessa Watt, considering the role of itinerant booksellers
in disseminating print culture outside towns large enough to support
their own booksellers, has analysed disposable income and assessed
how this may have produced a market. Whereas a labouring man lived
close to subsistence level, a small farmer working 30 acres could
average 14d–18d surplus a week, sufficient to meet a taste for two-
penny pamphlets, though probably more substantial works would have
remained an infrequently purchased luxury (Watt 1995: 256).

The demand was reflected in publishing trends. The number of
extant titles recorded per annum averaged 125 between 1558 and
1560, rising to 202 per annum between 1580 and 1589, although
the figure slipped back a little thereafter (Bennett 1965: 271). Practical

and devotional works predominated, and recreational literary genres constituted a small but growing minority; among those, high literature was, quantitatively, slight. H. S. Bennett somewhat disdainfully observes:

> The increase in the number of books published ... fails to reflect the degree to which all classes of the public were being catered for, or that for one work such as the *Arcadia* there were a dozen ballads, or news pamphlets available for those whose ability to read and to reach any serious intellectual level was limited. (1965: 248)

Scarcely 'all classes', for the illiterate and penniless cottager had little stake in this culture. Nor should understanding and class be so readily equated. As we shall see, by the mid-seventeenth century, readers of modest attainment devoured texts aimed at a wide readership with a discerning and evident intelligence that alarmed their social superiors.

Indeed, among the most striking features of early modern literary culture is how profoundly fragmented it is. Apart from a pervasive interest in ballad ephemera, the only texts that all English men and women would have been exposed to were the instruments of institutionalized religion. The Elizabethan church settlement had returned England to Protestantism, and attendance at Sunday worship was legally required, under sanctions that sought to eliminate residual Catholicism and discourage the development of Puritanism. Such attendance brought even the illiterate into repeated contact with three texts: the Book of Common Prayer, the Bible readings it prescribed throughout the liturgical year, and the Book of Homilies. Here, and only here, may we identify a substantial and unified English literary culture in the early modern period.

Sunday worship was driven by the Book of Common Prayer, the 'sombrely magnificent prose' of which, in Eamon Duffy's eloquent summary, 'read week by week, entered and possessed [the] minds [of worshippers], and became the fabric of their prayer, the utterance of their most solemn and vulnerable moments' (Duffy 1992: 593; cited and discussed in Maltby 2000: 5). The concern for religious uniformity ensured that the child of a cottager and the heir to an earldom may have entered the Christian community hearing the same prayer. When marrying, they would have made the same pledge. They would have descended to their graves as the priest read the same office for the dead. By 1600 Protestant uniformity was something of an objective and aspiration of the Anglican hierarchy, threatened variously by adherents to the displaced Catholic faith and by Puritans for whom the prayer book itself was an obnoxious remnant of England's Catholic past. Yet the Book of Common Prayer, revised in 1559, permeated the collective consciousness of all English people. Its strengths were enormous. Founded, albeit somewhat covertly, on its Catholic predecessors, it drew on the psychological benefits of comforting ritual. As David Cressy and Lori Anne Ferrell shrewdly observe, it offered English worshippers 'an idiosyncratic form of Protestantism that was reformed in doctrine but traditional in liturgy' (1996: 40). It was endlessly reiterated. Cranmer and the team that produced the 1549 version from which, with significant changes of emphasis, subsequent editions derived, absorbed much of the vocabulary of the English Bible and recast that language into a balanced, sonorous style perfectly suited to ceremonious, ritualized delivery, producing a grave, eloquent and decorous prose. Moreover, the ceremonies it supported, requiring antiphonal exchange between minister and congregation, drew the laity into the act of corporate worship. The same service was conducted on the same day, at approximately the same time, in every English parish throughout the liturgical year. Many participants must have possessed their own text, both as an aid to participation and as a source of private solace and pious meditation. Judith Maltby estimates that 290 editions of the Book of Common Prayer were produced between 1549 and 1642, and more than half a million individual copies were in circulation by the end of that period, many in small print appropriate for personal use (Maltby 2000: 25). The Book of Common Prayer, though criticized by Puritans, in the phrase John Milton honed much later in the century, as 'the *Skeleton* of a *Masse-booke*' (Milton 1953–82: I, 597), assiduously asserted its Protestant faith, in its studied silences about the role of saints, in its explicitly Reformed eschatology (for example, in the Order for the Burial of the Dead), and in the symbolic, rather than mystical, interpretation of Holy Communion, though here the 1559 liturgy returned to some of the ambiguities of the 1549 which the more challengingly Protestant formulation of the 1552 version had excluded (Cressy and Ferrell 1996: 45). Moreover, its loyalty to the Crown is repeated explicitly: for example, the Order for the Administration of the Lord's Supper, or Holy Communion, includes prayers for the monarch.

The Church of England, like all Protestant churches of the early modern period, promoted the vernacular translation of the Bible. In

periods when Catholicism was the state religion, translators and pro-
moters of English Bibles faced considerable difficulty. William Tyndale
produced his translation of the New Testament in a cautiously self-
imposed exile in Lutheran Germany, while the Geneva Bible, first
published in 1560, was initiated by exiles from Marian persecution
working in Switzerland, where the first edition was produced. The
Elizabethan church settlement which returned England to Protestantism at first confirmed the official status of the so-called 'Great Bible'
(second edition, 1540, and subsequently reprinted), but a new translation, the 'Bishops' Bible' was shortly commissioned, and published
in 1568. At the start of our period, this was the version appointed for
use in churches. This version sought, in part, to oppose the Calvinist
theology inscribed in the translation and more explicitly in the head-
notes and marginal commentaries of the Geneva Bible, viewed by
Matthew Parker, then Archbishop of Canterbury, as 'bitter' (quoted
in Berry 1969: 12).

Whatever the aspirations of Parker and his episcopal colleagues, the
Bishops' Bible proved to be only a limited success in competition with
the Geneva. Certainly, in the services of the Church of England its
adoption was uniform. However, just as many worshippers had their
own prayer books, so too did they have their own Bibles as an aid to
personal devotion and study. While the Elizabethan settlement could
legislate for uniformity of belief and promote it in corporate worship,
the emphasis of the Protestant Reformation on believers' obligations
to their own piety empowered individuals outside the clergy to seek
their own interpretation of the primary text and understand his or her
own salvation. Here, in part because of its extreme utility in private
study by theological amateurs, the Geneva version routed the official
alternative (Corns 2000: 103). Each book has an abstract, as does each
chapter. Each page has a header. The margins are crammed with
glosses, interpretation, cross-references, and further pointers to context. Its evident concerns with personal salvation carry through to its
final motto, appended to its penultimate page:

IOSHUA CHAP. 1 VERS. 8. Let not this boke of the Law departe
out of thy mouth, but meditate therein daye and night, that thou
mayest obserue and do according to all that is written therein: so
shalt thou make thy way prosperous, and then shalt thou haue good
successe. (Berry 1969: sig. LLl3v)

Note the singular form: '*thou* make *thy* way'. This was a version tailored to the needs of single and private readers, not the corporate congregation, but those needs were met in ways that simultaneously drew them to a distinctively and polemically Calvinist interpretation, especially of the issue of salvation.

In statistical terms, the victory of the Geneva version is striking. Between 1560 and 1611, there were 7 editions of the Great Bible, 22 of the Bishops' Bible and more than 120 of the Geneva version. While statutory requirements sought to secure exposure to the state religion in acts of corporate worship, in the homes of the literate and godly another interpretation, unsupported by the Church, guided them through personal and private reflection.

The Church of England brought two other texts into nationwide familiarity: the books of homilies, the first instalment of which had been published in 1547 as *Certayne Sermones or Homelies, Appoynted by the Kynges Majestie to Be Declared and Redde by All Persones, Vicars, or Curates, Every Sondaye in Their Churches Where They Have Cure*, and John Foxe's *Actes and Monuments of these Latter and Perillous Dayes*, first published in 1563 and generally know as the 'Book of Martyrs'.

The homilies originated in the recognition in the earliest days of the English Reformation that the clergy required a preaching resource to carry the Protestant theology to newly converted or compliant congregations. At the restoration of Protestantism on the accession of Elizabeth, the first collection was reissued and a second collection was published in 1563, to which a final piece, *A Homily against Disobedience and Wilful Rebellion*, was added in 1570, against the background of the abortive Catholic uprising known as the Northern Rebellion. Elizabeth herself was the most enthusiastic promoter of the homilies as an instrument towards the confirmation of religious uniformity, and oversaw the second collection herself (Bond 1987: 11). Every church was charged with keeping a copy, and each minister, unless specially licensed to preach (as only a minority were), delivered by way of a sermon each Sunday the homily appointed for that day. Homilies dealt in Protestant fashion with the events of the liturgical year, with matters of popular morality and with the obligations of the congregation to the Church and state. The message was simple and usually uncompromising. The latest of them, against rebellion, solemnly traces oppositionalism to Lucifer, 'the first aucthour and founder of rebellion', and counsels the most passive obedience:

What shall subjectes do then? Shall they obey valiaunt, stoute, wyse and good princes, and contemne, disobey and rebell against children beying [being] their princes, or against undiscrete and evyll governours? God forbid. For first what a perilous thing were it to commit unto the subjectes the judgement which prince is wyse and godly and his government good, and whiche is otherwise, as though the foote must judge of the head – an enterprise very heynous, and must needes breede rebellion. (Bond 1987: 210, 213)

Such sentiments, proclaimed from the pulpit of most English churches on the appointed day each year, achieved a signal resonance after the Essex uprising of 1601 and set the official position against which contemporary discussions and depictions of sedition and rebellion should be placed.

Elizabeth's own commitment to the pulpit dissemination of her version of orthodoxy did not command the unanimous support even of her own church leaders, some of whom recognized that it inhibited the development of a preaching ministry and felt uneasy about its doctrinal crudeness, while those of more Puritan leanings regarded the homilies as obstacles to further reformation. Nor do we find much evidence of the laity's enthusiasm for them as aids to private devotion; only in 1687, as they were falling out of use in church services, does an edition appear apparently intended for the private use of families (Bond 1987: 9–13).

Foxe's *Actes and Monuments* was not appointed to be read aloud as part of church services, but the Elizabethan state certainly promoted its success, recommending, but not requiring, that each parish acquire a copy to be kept available for the godly. For a large and expensive book costing over £6, its circulation was evidently considerable and it went through numerous editions: 10,000 copies may have sold by 1603 (Palliser 1983: 355). It was the only extensively illustrated book to which all English people could have claimed access. Numerous woodcuts in the early editions depict graphically those sufferings of the godly under Catholicism which its text narrates. The enthusiasm of the Crown for its promotion no doubt reflected anxiety about Catholic insurrection and, as the reign continued, the war with Catholic Spain. Its legacy in terms of popular anti-Catholic sentiment was protracted and profound. But Foxe commemorated for the most part martyrs of faith who opposed their ruler's right to determine their religious belief. Implicitly, the rights claimed for Elizabeth by the homily of 1570 are irreconcilable with celebration of that heroism. When Anne Askew, a young provincial gentlewoman racked and burnt under Henry VIII for her plainly

Protestant critique of the Catholic faith, retorts to her interrogator, 'I had rather to reade five lines in the bible, than to heare five masses in the temple' (Beilin 1996: 166), she expounds Reformed values, but she also asserts the rights of the individual believer to defy the requirements of Church and state in ways that are ultimately subversive of the programme which was to develop under Elizabeth. Unsurprisingly, Foxe retained his influence longest on suffering and defiant Puritan writers like John Lilburne and John Bunyan, for whom the experiences of the early Protestant martyrs provided paradigms for their own conduct and the representation of their personal defiance.

Books of popular piety appeared in increasing numbers through the later sixteenth century to meet the demand from the godly and literate for supplementary study materials to aid devotion, to improve their prospects for salvation, to solace them with recognition of their justification (Bennett 1965: 156). Probably about 40 per cent of all publications in the late Tudor and early Stuart periods were religious, and the proportion remained large among those cheaper items available to the literate among the poorer sort. Ballads on moral or religious themes constituted a very sizeable minority of that genre (Watt 1991: 333–53). Foxe profoundly influenced popular piety, and undemanding derivatives of his martyrology appear in the broadsheet ballad tradition. Indeed, a ballad purportedly written by Askew while in Newgate awaiting immolation appeared in a brief allusion in Thomas Nashe's prose work *Have With You to Saffron Walden* (1596), though the first extant printed version dates from 1624 (Beilin 1996: xxxix). The gap between first mention and first extant printing may suggest some evidence of the relationship between oral performance and print culture, though earlier editions may simply not have survived. Though clumsily phrased, the ballad assiduously rehearsed the dangers to individual consciences and salvation that would have been posed by a national return to Catholicism within a framework of pious reflection on the speaker's own frailty and the mercy and salvation extended to those who turn from sin, here, of course, represented by her own earlier subscription to the Catholic faith:

> Strength me good Lord in thy truth to stand
> for the bloudy Butchers have me at their wil
> With there slaughter knives ready drawn in ther hand
> my simple carkas to devour and kill.
>
> (Beilin 1996: 197)

Opposition to Catholicism was profound and commonplace among English Protestants of all classes.

Pious dross like the Askew ballad is far removed from the achievements of high literary culture of the late Elizabethan period, although of course probably much better known to most English people alive in 1600. The uniform devotional culture inculcated by the state church touched everyone, even those who resisted it. In comparison the market for those texts that are now most valued was tiny and fragmented.

In part the problem was one of scale. In 1600 the total population of England stood at about four million. Of these, about 30 per cent were under 15 years of age (Palliser 1983: 45), and probably 70 per cent of adults were illiterate or had only very rudimentary reading skills. Effectively, the maximum adult reading public was about 900,000, though only a small fraction had the learning or opportunity to participate in high literary culture. Many of the writers to be considered in detail in the early Stuart period had matriculated at Oxford or Cambridge, and much of their writing assumes some familiarity with classical culture; typically, the combined annual cohort for both universities numbered about 750 (ibid.: 363). Metropolitan London, that is the City and immediately adjacent conurbations, had about 200,000 inhabitants, and, as Cressy has demonstrated, literacy rates among these were higher than in the rest of England. No other city had more than 15,000 inhabitants, and probably only three (Norwich, Bristol and York) had more than 10,000 (ibid.: 203). The demography has far-reaching implications for literary consumption.

Only London was sufficiently large to sustain a developed system of booksellers and printers, although printing was allowed in Oxford and Cambridge, provincial cities and towns supported occasional booksellers, and itinerant chapmen served the rest of the country after a fashion. There is evidence from the mid-seventeenth century of a developing system of mail-order trading. However, for non-academic writers to get into print, their manuscripts, from whatever source, had to be available to the London book trade because there were no appropriate presses elsewhere. Moreover, a print culture, with habitual readers seeking out literary publications from a range of suppliers, only developed in the metropolis.

Only London could sustain professional theatres on a permanent basis. Amateur dramatics played some role in the recreational life of schoolboys and Oxford and Cambridge students. The performance of

Latin plays combined both recreational and educational purposes. London companies and less formal bands of actors toured provincial towns and cities. Even quite modest houses sometimes provided performing spaces. Aristocratic households sometimes supported companies of actors, though the evidence comes from the sixteenth, rather than the seventeenth, century. Overwhelmingly, however, theatrical performance was a metropolitan phenomenon, and in 1600 there were almost certainly no purpose-built or dedicated performing spaces outside London.

But, again, that London market was fragmented by class, by profession, by generation, by gender and by geography. We may identify several cultural communities, though each in turn was subdivided.

Until her declining years Elizabeth frequently made summer 'progresses' through the shires (though never north of Stafford). But the royal court resided for most of the year in palaces around the Thames Valley, and predominately in the large complex of buildings in Whitehall, to the west of the City (Palliser 1983: 10). Here dwelt the queen and her household, and those closest to her in the administration of government had accommodation too. By the 1630s the royal household had grown to between 1,800 and 2,600, and with their dependents Whitehall probably had a population little short of that of Exeter or Norwich (Carlton 1995: 124). The population of Elizabeth's court, though certainly smaller, would still have been considerable. Aristocrats also kept substantial London households, with a hierarchy of retainers, from senior agents, 'secretaries' (in effect personal assistants), chaplains and advisers, down to domestic servants, again many with their dependents. Many, though not all, of these great houses lined the north bank of the Thames from the City to Whitehall. This social cluster of monarch and aristocrats supported a court culture, of which literature was a fairly important component, made up a highly literate and prosperous readership and acted as the principal source of patronage and protection. Court entertainments involved actors and musicians drawn from the professional companies, and court performances of plays from the repertoire of the companies were lucrative if infrequent.

All but one parish of the City was within the medieval walls in an area a little more than a mile from west to east, and less than that northward from the Thames. It had a complex system of local government, with a corporation dominated by prominent members of the more prosperous guilds, and a Lord Mayor, who was chosen annually.

Its principal businesses were organized through a series of guilds, 'the livery companies', each with a guildhall and its own system of governance. Among these, the Stationers' Company controlled and regulated the manufacture and sale of printed matter, and is given closer attention below. But guilds also commissioned writing, particularly texts for their corporate ceremonies, pre-eminently the pageant associated with the annual inauguration of the Lord Major. The corporation of the City exercised fairly strict control over all public activities, and towards the end of the Elizabethan period drama companies tended to establish themselves outside their jurisdiction.

Around the City, and particularly in Southwark, on the opposite bank of the Thames, and to the north and east of the City walls in a series of parishes extending along the north bank with its docks and quays and inland towards Hackney and Stepney, there rapidly developed a sprawling conurbation collectively known as the 'suburbs'. Indeed, as the metropolis more than quadrupled its population over the early modern period, nearly all the growth took place outside the City wall (Beier and Finlay 1986b: 8). Here, local government control was slacker, providing a more straightforward area of operation for London's theatres. Certainly, the suburbs contained some of the poorest areas, and plague lingered longer and took more victims than in the City itself. But here, too, manufacturing industry flourished outside the control of the guilds, and the enterprising, aspirational and literate, with some disposable income, lived here in their thousands (Beier 1986: 155), making, with similarly affluent citizens of the City, a large market for printed matter and a potential component of theatre audiences.

A strip of territory, about a quarter of a mile across and running from what is now High Holborn southwards to the north bank of the Thames, contained (as it still does) the four Inns of Court. These served (as they still do) the legal profession with an operational base and functioned as an educational institution for lawyers. Legal studies at Oxford and Cambridge were restricted to Civil Law, based on Roman Law, which was of limited application, being the basis of proceedings in the Chancery, the Admiralty Court, the Court of Requests and the ecclesiastical courts. Common Law operated in the rest of the judicial system. The Inns were governed by senior practitioners of the Common Law (usually termed 'benchers'), men (and only men) typically with two decades of experience, who practised law from their chambers and who regulated entry into and promotion through a profession which could be lucrative and which carried some prestige, though also, perhaps, some lingering taint of the social stigma which adhered to anyone in early modern England who had to work for a living (Prest 1972: 22, 61). The Inns were described during the Elizabethan period as England's 'third university', since they enrolled students, provided instruction and granted a higher education qualification, but as Wilfred Prest sagely observes, they 'were at once both more and less than a university' (ibid. 115).

They were much smaller. Membership was for life (as it still is) but actual residence was irregular, and while the records indicate the numbers entering each Inn, how many were living there at any point remains more speculative. Prest suggests that by the beginning of the seventeenth century there were probably about 1,000 members in all during term time, though with some fluctuations. Oxford and Cambridge probably had more than 2,000 undergraduates each, plus other categories of residents. However, the Inns were socially more exclusive, in part because no scholarships subsidized the expenses of more needy students, there was no scope for working one's way through by acting as servants to richer students (another option at the universities) and costs were high – about £40 per annum, at a time when the most wealthy yeomen farmers were typically drawing £100 from their lands (ibid.: 16, 27). Not only were the Inns' young members the children of the wealthy, they often showed very little interest in the law. Certainly, the legal profession had its attractions, not least because it could lead to a range of appointments and careers outside the law courts, as accountants, brokers, financiers, entrepreneurs and land agents (ibid.: 22). In such a litigious age, when men of property had frequent recourse to law, some familiarity with Common Law could prove a useful accomplishment. But significant numbers, by the late Elizabethan period, were attending the Inns as a sort of finishing school, and such a cluster of young men with time and disposable income had an impact on the economy and the cultural life of the capital disproportionate to their mere numbers.

The Inns directly patronized the professional theatre companies, hiring them for private performances, particularly over the Christmas festivities, and they intermittently staged masques, sometimes presenting them at the royal court. They also supported chaplains and a preaching ministry, adding to the diversity of religious life around the City. Most obtrusively, members of the Inns attended the professional theatres. At a time when performances were usually given in daylight in the afternoon, these men were more likely to have the leisure to attend than citizens engaged in business and trade. That leisure promoted their most significant, though less visible, literary activity: the writing, circulating and collecting of verse, particularly lyric poetry. This was predominately a manuscript culture, for which the most influential model and inspiration was John Donne, a member of Lincoln's Inn in residence in the early 1590s. But, of course, they also bought printed books.

Latin, Neo-Latin and English

The literary culture of early modern England was further fragmented along language divisions. Elite male education sought to produce people who could read, write and converse in Latin with facility. Latin was largely the medium of instruction in the grammar schools that prepared boys for the universities and learned professions, and, outside the Inns of Court, it dominated teaching and learning in higher education. It held a similar place in the private education favoured by the upper gentry and aristocracy for their children (sometimes including girls). Among the principal achievements of the pan-European humanist movement of the late fifteenth and early sixteenth centuries had been the major overhaul of Latin education. At its foundation was the re-establishment of spoken and written Latin on classical models, achieved by purging medieval neologisms from its lexis and replacing them with classical equivalents. To support this transformation, educational reformers placed fresh emphasis on learners' assimilation of the classical idiom through extensive reading and memorizing of approved authors from the classical canon. Almost as a by-product, the classical literary tradition became a central part of the educational experience of England's educational and social elite, through familiarity with Cicero (especially his letters), with Terence and with Virgil. Neo-Latin style was conceived as perfectible through imitation of such models, and the practice of Latin composition – that is, of literary production in neo-Latin – was concomitant with educational reform, though by 1600 schools were relying more heavily on a new generation of textbooks at the expense of early exposure to primary classical texts (Jensen 1996).

Such an education, for those with an aptitude for second-language acquisition, meant access to a fairly extensive literary culture available

in print, the literary culture of ancient Rome. But widespread competence in the Latin language also supported another cultural movement
of enormous importance in England as elsewhere in Europe, although
one whose extent and achievement are now largely forgotten: neo-
Latin writing. The cultural elite of England frequently produced in
Latin not only technical or administrative or academic prose, but also a
wide range of creative genres. New plays in Latin were performed in
the universities, sometimes in circumstances of great celebrity and
acclaim. Elizabeth attended such performances at least three times,
and James I at least four (Binns 1990: 136). Continental neo-Latin
poets were reprinted in England as part of a substantial print culture in
this medium, foreign-printed works were extensively imported, and, as
J. W. Binns has so comprehensively demonstrated, hundreds of items
were printed in England as part of a rich, varied and extensive print
culture (ibid.: 553–601).

On Binns's account, the Latin-medium material offered to its
readers an experience so fulfilling as to render vernacular literature
unnecessary and unsought for:

> [N]eo-Latin books furnished all the material needed for the creation of
> self-contained, self-sufficient, rich and satisfying, literary and intellectual
> culture. To those who moved freely within it in the age of Elizabeth and
> James I, there can have seemed little need to turn to popular vernacular
> writing. Virtually every taste was, after all, catered for in Latin. There
> were novels, poems and plays in profusion, books of history and travel,
> letters, tracts and treatises on a wide variety of topics. Neo-Latin could
> provide ample material for serious study, and for leisure reading too.
> This, perhaps, is why vernacular writing is so rarely referred to in neo-
> Latin works. Vernacular writing belongs, on the whole, to a different
> world; and much of the English vernacular writing of the time may have
> seemed crude, clumsy and uncouth to the average reader and writer of
> neo-Latin literature, apparently offering nothing which could not more
> agreeably be found in Latin. It is for this reason that Latin literature
> dominated the high intellectual culture of Elizabethan and Jacobean
> England. (1990: 393–4)

Binns is a stirring advocate for a largely forgotten literary culture, and
the case he makes for its range and currency is convincing. Moreover,
any alternative literary tradition, in competition for a readership already narrowly circumscribed by demography and social exclusion,
necessarily contracts further the demand for high-culture vernacular

literature. But the sharpness of the division may be questioned. Neo-Latin writing may not allude to vernacular literature, but among the most accomplished vernacular writers of the late Elizabethan and Stuart periods there are those whose oeuvre embraces both cultures: Donne, Bacon, Jonson, Milton and Marvell, for example, write in both languages. Neo-Latin and vernacular poems were sometimes published in the same books (see below, chapter 5). Neoclassicism develops across the seventeenth century as the most dynamic and pervasive cultural ideology in English vernacular literature. It is surely fed by an admiration for and familiarity with the classical literary tradition, both of which find parallel reflection in the production of and demand for neo-Latin writing.

Manuscript, Performance, Print

Most of the literary legacy of the late Elizabethan period began in manuscript. Songs may have had a rather different early life, as lyricist-composers may have performed new work experimentally before committing it to paper, though the lag may well have been trivial: manuscripts of lyrics with tablature are not rare. Generally and unsurprisingly, most works of literature, including play texts, were transmitted first as ink on paper.

Few working manuscripts of significance survive from this period. Perhaps the most famous – and most disputed – is the play text, *Sir Thomas More* (British Library, MS Harley 7368). The main part of the manuscript is a fair copy of a play sometimes assigned to 1600–1, into which, by way of revision, has been inserted pages in a hand that has been identified as William Shakespeare's (Schoenbaum 1975: 156–60). Yet here, though worked over with a few deletions and additions, the document appears to be a fair copy or late draft. The disappearance of first and early drafts, however, is unsurprising. Writing paper was expensive. Little was manufactured in England, where paper production was overwhelmingly directed to producing brown paper. Nearly all paper for both manuscript and print was imported from France and the Low Countries until very late in the seventeenth century. The two kinds were distinguished primarily by the finish given to them. Paper for pen and ink was sized (that is, sealed with a glutinous wash to render it less porous) more heavily than printing paper, which had a greater absorbency, a technical distinction that reflected the differing characteristics of the ink and modes of application (Love 1993: 105; Woudhuysen 1996: 21). White paper was made from bleached rags in a labour-intensive process that required each sheet to be formed in an individual tray, to be carefully dried, to be hand-treated with size and to be dried a second time. Its materials, its manufacture and the transport costs meant that paper remained expensive, a fact that shaped significantly the operations of the printing and bookselling industries. Allusions abound from the early modern period to rejected or spurned texts variously used to line pie-trays, wrap fish or wipe bottoms. The paper from rough drafts retained a utility and even a value: recycling precluded survival.

Numerous factors retarded the progress of literary texts from manuscript to print. Play texts belonged to theatre companies, which operated on a repertory system, reviving old plays as well as performing new ones. Some plays from the 1590s were performed late into the seventeenth century. That mode of operation meant that play texts constituted a major asset of the companies. But the right to that intellectual property was unguarded in a law, which, as we shall see, protected only the rights of manufacturers of printed books. Plays were traded, but they were not readily given away. Quite probably, the manuscript of *Sir Thomas More* (and the associated opportunity to perform it) was transferred from the Lord Admiral's Men to the Lord Chamberlain's Men as the former temporarily quit London (Schoenbaum 1975: 158).

Playwrights had no right to their work once they had delivered it to the companies that had bought or commissioned it. (Shakespeare stands outside these generalizations, since he was a part-owner of the company that produced his plays.) While the authors may have had an interest in selling to the press copies of plays that had succeeded in production, such a practice would have been professionally hazardous, since it would have forfeited the good will of the companies, which provided their primary source of income. Writing frequently for performance constituted the only way to secure a steady living. Certainly, publishers recognized a market for printed plays, and sometimes purchased manuscripts from companies, but the majority of works existed only in manuscript and performance, at least until they ceased to draw audiences.

The case of Henry Chettle is instructive. Chettle was among the most prolific dramatists of the late Elizabethan period, writing mainly for the companies managed by Philip Henslowe, whose diary records their dealings. Henslowe bought 13 plays written by Chettle and another 36 plays in which Chettle was a collaborator, usually for a couple of pounds each. Of the first group, only one is extant – in a corrupt edition of 1631, a quarter of a century after his death. Only four of the collaborations survive in print. Despite his seemingly frenzied activity, Chettle evidently experienced periods of extreme financial difficulty. The diary notes payments to support him during incarceration in the Marshalsea prison, Southwark, perhaps for debt (for example, see Henslowe 1904–8: I, 100). He was immensely popular in his own age. Yet the circumstances of literary production rendered him virtually invisible to posterity. By trade, curiously, he was a master printer (Schoenbaum 1975: 117).

The owners of play manuscripts had so obvious an interest in with-holding them from print that the emergence of a supply of printed plays needs some explanation. Piracy has long been recognized as an important component. Besides occasional indiscretions by the writers, some works became available to publishers through the memorial reconstructions by actors who had taken part. In the case of Shake-speare, the most printed dramatist of the late Elizabethan period, the presence of a pirated version in print seems to have stimulated his company to release manuscripts, in part because the damage was done and the risk sustained, in part perhaps to spite those responsible by displacing their publications with authorized editions, and no doubt in part at times to earn cash payments from publishers.

Though dramatists wrote primarily for performance, the theatre business stimulated the emergence of professional writers who diversi-fied into other genres that typically were print-based. Around the turn of the century, the London stage and the London publishers supported a literary culture of talented men, often of modest social standing, who lived off their writing (while seeking patronage and support on the basis of their cultural eminence). George Chapman published translations of passages from Homer and an edition of the epyllion *Hero and Leander*, seemingly left incomplete on Marlowe's death in 1593, but now con-cluded by Chapman himself. Thomas Dekker began in 1603 the first of his prose pamphlets depicting London life in the age of plague epidem-ics. Michael Drayton wrote narrative poems based on English history. John Marston penned plays for companies of boy actors and published verse satires that contributed to the tightening of censorship in 1599 (see below). Anthony Munday wrote for the press newsbooks, anti-Catholic propaganda and translations of French romances, and wrote the texts for civil pageants, while writing at least 18 plays, only four of which are printed and extant. Ben Jonson diversified his activities, as actor, dramatist and soon-to-be-printed author of pageants and masques, and Chettle also published pamphlets.

The pattern had been set in the early 1590s by Robert Greene, dramatist, prose-fiction writer and pamphleteer, John Lyly, dramatist, romance writer and political pamphleteer, Christopher Marlowe, dramatist and Ovidian imitator, and Thomas Nashe, dramatist, brilliant novelist and political pamphleteer. It is sometimes remarked that the professional writers of the late 1590s differed from the generation of Greene and Marlowe in social and educational terms. For the most part the older men were university-educated and technically gentlemen, whereas Shakespeare, Jonson, Chettle and Munday came from a tradesman-class background and had little or no experience of higher education. The distinction has some merit, though there are numerous exceptions: Chapman studied at Oxford, Marston at Oxford and the Middle Temple, for example. The London stage and the London press were content-hungry and driven by a competitive market of readers and audiences that had plenty of alternative ways to spend their money. The writing they supported was performed or printed because it was in demand. The size of the market, especially for print, remained too small to produce for its authors the kinds of rewards they could live off, and the organization of stage and press served the interests of entrepreneurs, rather than creative writers. Yet together these alternative income-streams supported an emerging class of professionals who, while often seeking preferment through patronage, and while sometimes pursuing other professions in parallel, could after a fashion live off their writing, and who sought out working relationships with printers and booksellers as well as theatrical managers.

Poets who were not professional writers took a different view of print culture, from which they had little to gain materially (relative to their typical personal wealth). Certainly there was a demand for printed verse. Shakespeare's *Venus and Adonis* had been a publishing sensation since its first appearance in 1593; there were 16 editions before 1640. By the second edition, its publishers surely had a good sense of the market for it, and print runs were probably longer than the usual 250 or 500 copies, though few copies of each individual edition survive, perhaps supporting the conclusion that their owners read them to pieces (Schoenbaum 1975: 131). But Sir Philip Sidney proved a more influential model for poetic conduct.

Sidney was a unique figure in Elizabethan literary history. His eminence derived in part from his political and social status. He was a prominent figure in the court faction most implacably hostile to peaceful coexistence with Catholicism at home or abroad, and a fierce advocate of open hostility to Spain. He manifested little political acumen, but his sister was the Countess of Pembroke and, more significantly, the Earl of Leicester, for a time the most influential of Elizabeth's counsellors, was his uncle. Though his own influence at court did not survive once he was banished for his overly vehement opposition to the (subsequently unrealized) match between the Queen and the catholic Duke d'Alençon, internal banishment to his sister's home, Wilton House, can scarcely have been a hardship. His political commitment led to his participation in the English campaign in the Low Countries, in support of Dutch Protestants in arms against the Spanish. Death at the battle of Zutphen, documented and carefully related, secured his status as heroic martyr in the Protestant cause, and his lavish funeral attracted large crowds of mourners, becoming in effect a state funeral of almost regal proportions. Those on whom his wide influence was felt for the most part had little in common with a writer connected closely with the peerage, a glittering figure of immense distinction and – almost a new phenomenon for an English writer – celebrity.

Collecting poems emerged strongly from the 1590s onwards as a major cultural activity of the universities and Inns of Court, and the practice perhaps acquired there had currency among the gentry class and aristocratic families even in provincial England. Manuscript collections, usually termed 'miscellanies', were sometimes the collective project of a family, an Inn of Court or a university college, though often individuals copied into booklets or loose leaves poems that they had encountered, most commonly in manuscript circulation, constructing a kind of personal and incremental anthology. As H. R. Woudhuysen observes, 'some miscellanies were undoubtedly very private collections', whereas others were 'social documents, shared among fellow students, passed between family and friends, who might be invited to contribute to them, so that they may be written in several different hands' (1996: 157).

The practice of miscellany-building certainly reflected the paucity of printed poetry. Once an author was available in print, the number of manuscript copies of his poems tended to decline. Most strikingly, the posthumous printing of Sidney's works eroded their status as treasured

manuscript items that presumably had been acquired with some difficulty (Woudhuysen 1996: 386). Again, the excess of demand over
supply is evident in the marked-up price of printed poetry. In 1598,
the Stationers' Company, the guild representing the book trade,
attempted to regulate maximum prices per printed sheet; books of
poetry (like lawbooks) commanded a higher price than other kinds of
publication (Bennett 1965: 300).

Manuscript circulation brought with it an informed and appropriate
readership whose earliest access poets could control by withholding or
vouchsafing access to their writing. In the search for patronage (see
below), the gift of a poem, particularly an occasional poem addressed
to a named individual, represented as valuable a present as a writer
could bestow on a potential benefactor. If the benefactor allowed
others access to it, to read and indeed to copy, then the panegyric
achieved currency, the patron celebration and the poet a degree of
celebrity. Eventually, such circulation spread far beyond authors' control, and sometimes resulted in unwelcome and unauthorized publication in print. Woudhuysen vividly describes the social circumstance
for the enjoyment of contemporary poetry in manuscript circulation in
terms of its fashion among the young, leisured and wealthy and of the
evident enthusiasm of such aficionados. No doubt, but the experience
of some poetry-lovers in late Elizabethan England must often have
been a frustrating one, excluded from access to texts still circulating
only in the tightest coteries defined by social networks, by consan-
guinity, by structures of patronage. Such circulation also inhibited the
development of authorship as an element in interpretation. We have
noted the celebrity of Sidney. But the work of most poets was infrequently encountered in any quantity in any one location, and individual poems frequently occur in miscellanies under a false ascription.
Most readers could have formed only the most imperfect sense of the
characteristic style or themes of particular authors, let alone any idea of
their development. Miscellanies are sometimes organized thematically,
though eclectically, and a distinct enthusiasm emerges for juxtaposing
poems which in some sense answer other poems. But typically, each
poem must have been read as an autonomous text, rather than a
component of something more complex. This is profoundly limiting
for both author and reader, though it may usefully inform our own
interpretative strategies in engaging with internally inconsistent works
such as Donne's 'Songs and Sonnets' (see below, chapter 2). Yet it may
in part explain the most significant exception to the predominance of

manuscript circulation in late Elizabethan poetry: the sonnet sequence. Woudhuysen argues that the sudden availability in print of Sidney's *Astrophil to Stella* may have stimulated imitation and a sense that public exposure in print was not so demeaning after all (1996: 386). The kind of larger structure that Sidney built from his 108 sonnets and 11 songs, with its intricate numerological symbolism premised on its totality (Fowler 1970: 174–80), cannot be communicated in the piecemeal assemblage of the miscellanies; even its more evident thematic development would be lost.

The Press and its Controls

All printing in England, except for single presses at Oxford and Cambridge, was controlled by the Stationers' Company, a guild invested with very considerable powers and responsibilities through a series of government measures. Its earliest history was as the trade association for those engaged in the production of manuscript documents, the scriveners or copyists, the lymners or illustrators, the bookbinders and the manuscript sellers. In the late fourteenth century, scribes specializing in the production of legal documents separated to form the Scriveners' Company, and in time diversified to include activities like financial advice, money-lending and brokering loans. Milton's father is now perhaps the most renowned scrivener active in that business from the late Elizabethan period. The Stationers' Company developed to incorporate participants in the book trade, and included printers as well as bookbinders and those engaged in both retail and wholesale bookselling. The craft of the lymner was displaced by print illustration and as the trade in manuscripts substantially halted.

To the Company fell the usual restrictive practices that characterized early modern capitalism in London. Its internal organization invested most of the power in coteries of master craftsmen and leading entrepreneurs, who acted to control prices and wages and regulated an apprenticeship system that ensured a convenient excess of trained journeymen. But a unique relationship between the stationers and late-Tudor government distinguished them from all other London guilds.

While numerous problems confronted anyone attempting to do business in the City of London without full membership of a guild recognized by the Corporation, generally, if one had achieved that 'freeman' status, one could diversify into activities outside the sphere of one's own guild. Not so with the book trade. Although there is strong evidence that stationers themselves diversified into other businesses (Bennett 1965: 271), by 1600 only stationers could print books, and the Company had powers to police the industry to ensure there were no violations – and to ensure that seditious writing had no currency.

Much of this special status can be traced to its Charter of incorporation, granted by Philip and Mary in 1557. Its preamble declares that the king and queen, wishing to provide a suitable remedy against the seditious and heretical books that were daily printed and published, gave certain privileges to the stationers. Specifically, the Company had a monopoly of printing, except for holders of particular royal permission, and was commissioned to search for, seize and confiscate any material printed contrary to any statute or proclamation. An assumption that press control fell within the royal prerogative was much older. By a proclamation of 1538, for example, pre-publication censorship had been introduced into England for the first time through a requirement that no book could be printed without the approval of a royal licenser (Blagden 1960: 20–1, 30).

It was in Elizabeth's reign, however, that, in the judgement of Siebert's classic account, 'the high point' of control was reached, measured by 'the number and variety of controls, stringency of enforcement, and general compliance with regulations' (1952: 2). Elizabeth had confirmed the Charter granted by her late sister shortly after accession, and began a fruitful working relationship with the more powerful figures in the book trade. Under her reign, and particularly from the Ordinances of the Company of 1562, a notion of copyright developed which invested ownership not in the authors who wrote works, but in the printers or booksellers who registered with the Stationers' Company their ownership of the title. Such registration followed scrutiny by an appointed censor (initially a Warden of the Company) and in effect protected the officers of the Company from any general responsibility for the circulation of forbidden books. The right to reprint was frequently traded among stationers; authors had no part of such transactions (Blagden 1960: 42–5). At the same time, Elizabeth secured close support from leading printers by selectively granting monopolies to individuals which gave them the privilege of producing particularly lucrative classes of publication, such as bibles, psalters and alphabet books; increasingly large areas of the market were parcelled out to loyal clients whose continued compliance was ensured both by the easy income it secured and the recognition that monopolies could be withdrawn as easily as they were granted. The practice produced deep disparities across the trade, impoverishing some and ensuring that new start-ups often floundered (Siebert 1952: 39–40).

Government control of the intellectual life of England certainly tightened in the latter half of the reign. As Jim Sharpe comments:

> The Tudor period was one in which the treason laws were constantly elaborated, one step in this process being the statute of 1581 against seditious works. This legislation, which, *inter alia*, prescribed that first offenders unable to pay a £200 fine should be stood on the pillory and have their ears cut off, was fairly comprehensive. (1995: 199)

As laws against oppositional discourse were made more severe, so too were the mechanisms of press control refined. The Star Chamber Decree of 1586 assumed that the best way to control the book trade was to scrutinize especially closely the earliest phase of book production: the work of printers. The Company's rights and obligations of search and control were strengthened, while, most significantly, the actual number of printing presses and of their operatives was reduced. A census of presses and materials was expeditiously instituted, and no new presses were to be permitted until the number of master printers had been reduced by natural wastage to a total to be determined by the Archbishop of Canterbury and the Bishop of London, who emerged as powerful figures in the control of the trade. All presses had to be 'openly displayed' and accessible to the officers of the Company; presses used in any way illicitly could be 'defaced, sawn to pieces, battered or broken at the smith's forge' (Greg 1967: 41). No presses could be set up outside London. In Blagden's telling phrase, the Decree 'does not make pleasant reading' (1960: 71–3).

In 1599 the final significant Elizabethan measure of control, the so-called 'Bishops' Ban', amounted to a decree from the Archbishop of Canterbury and the Bishop of London instructing the Stationers' Company to address five issues. The decree required the calling in, and in some cases the burning, of recent satires, presumably in an initiative to control the spirit of too-free witty censure. It announced similar measures against the erotic verse of Sir John Davies and the late Marlowe. It demanded a total ban on publishing any works by Gabriel Harvey and Thomas Nashe, and the confiscation of their titles already in print; again, both were active satirists. It required that 'noe Englishe historyes be printed excepte they be allowed by some of her maiesties privie Counsell'. Finally, it required 'that noe playes be printed excepte they bee allowed by suche as have aucthorytie' (Arber 1875–94: III, 316). At a stroke, the authorities sought to reform morals, limit oppositional writing and perhaps even prevent the acrimony and social friction satire could engender. How effective the measures were may be questioned, though certainly Harvey, who lived on until the 1630s in provincial retirement, was effectively silenced; no later work by him appears in print. Nashe lived to see the publication of *Summers Last Will and Testament* in the following year. He died in 1601, and so conclusions are harder to draw. Plays were subject to pre-performance censorship, and the ordinary rules applied if they were to be printed; the measure here no more than insists on the strict observation of current procedures. The Ban targets specifically literary genres, in the case of satires, presumably because of their topicality; in the case of erotic verse, on grounds of decency. Book burning had precedents in England, though typically for works of religion; suddenly, literary criticism had assumed a militant and repressive form. The new procedures for English histories – it is unclear whether it means books about England or books in English; perhaps both – whether implemented or not, demonstrate the extraordinary attention deemed appropriate for politically sensitive material. The Privy Council, in effect the executive wing of the crown and the highest council in the land, was, in theory at least, impanelled as licensers. Elizabeth's reign closed on a book trade more mindful than ever of its subservient and client role within the power structure.

How well did the stationers serve late Elizabethan literature? Certainly, as Bennett has demonstrated and argued, there was a copious supply of reading material in the London bookshops and stalls at the turn of the century. But such evident success requires qualification. English books were poorly printed in comparison with the best products of continental Europe. They were poorly designed, sometimes scarcely designed at all. They relied on copy that was sometimes unauthorized and unreliable. Their sloppy standards reflected the cosy security of the guild that produced them. The investment of all legal and financial advantage relating to intellectual property in stationers rather than in authors inhibited the development of professional writers, ensuring that those who lived by their pens worked frantically and dissipated energies in necessary diversification.

Moreover, the arrangement meant there was little commercial incentive to persuade writers with a secure income from elsewhere to seek exposure in print, and thus the trade was starved of appropriate content. The privileged and monopolistic retention of lucrative parts of the trade by a favoured few produced disparities that made it difficult for new publishers, perhaps better attuned to the market or closer to authors, to break in. The Company's willingness to police the trade in return for privileges encouraged every government of the seventeenth century to entertain the notion that press control was a feasible project that could be achieved using a seemingly effective structure that required no funding. As government and industry collaborated, to their apparent mutual advantage, the implications for the reading public and for authors were malign.

The Final Years of Elizabethan Theatre

The London theatres were closed during the final illness of Elizabeth in March 1603, and remained closed through a period of mourning. Thereafter, the long and devastating plague of 1603 required a further period of closure, which kept them shut till April 1604 and brought about a major crisis of viability (see below, chapter 2). Before those reversals, the stage was for the most part in quite good health, if somewhat cowed by recent events. Five companies played regularly in the City. The three adult companies, the Lord Chamberlain's Men, the Lord Admiral's Men and the Earl of Worcester's Men, securely occupied new and purpose-built theatres outside the City itself. The Lord Chamberlain's Men played at the Globe on the south bank of the Thames, owned by a partnership which included Shakespeare. They were technically the servants of George Carey, Lord Hunsdon, the duty of whose royal office included the highest responsibility for the regulation of the English stage and the provision of theatrical entertainment for the monarch. As a privy councillor, he was plainly a powerful patron and protector. The Globe itself was a polygonal amphitheatre, open to the sky and made in part from the timber frame of the theatre in Shoreditch, quit by the company in 1598 and subsequently dismantled. Three tiers of galleries provided the more expensive accommodation, and there was standing in the 'pit' around the stage itself. Its capacity, based on late Jacobean evidence, is usually estimated at about 3,000, considerable by the standards of any period of English theatre history. The Fortune, the home of the company patronized by the Lord Admiral, Lord Howard of Effingham, Earl of Nottingham and also a privy councillor, opened in 1600 outside the City wall on the north-west side. Square rather than polygonal, though in other respects broadly resembling the Globe, this too was a considerable venue. The company itself had a long history, and its migration north across the river from its earlier Bankside site may have reflected anxieties about competing with the Globe in such close proximity. Both companies were competently managed and were established on a sound legal and financial basis. The third adult company was newer and less stable. Its patron, Edward Somerset, Earl of Worcester, had recently been advanced to some of the court offices stripped from the Earl of Essex (see below). However, his company had been established with difficulty at a time when there was pressure to limit to two the number of adult troupes. Its performing space was built within a courtyard of the sprawling and ancient Boar's Head Inn, in Whitechapel, close to the City wall on the east side. When in 1598 it became a theatre, it ceased to be an inn. Though its location was fairly propitious, the theatre was smaller than the rival amphitheatres, its design seems to have been somewhat improvised, and its owners dissipated much energy and expense in legal squabbles among themselves. The Earl of Worcester's Men were not properly sanctioned to play till 1602. (This account and what follows rest largely on Wickham et al. 2000: Pt III, which in turn draws on earlier work; and Gurr 1996: Pt II.)

Two companies of boy actors performed within the City itself. The adult companies had located in the suburbs because of the long-standing antipathy of the authorities of the City to theatres. Their petitions typically cite threats to civil order, the 'lewdness' of the theatrical business and the vice trade it allegedly attracted to its locations, and the idleness it promoted among employees lured from work by its afternoon performances. Suburb dwellers often shared these objections, though in the case of the Fortune their powerful patron intervened swiftly and effectively to protect the project (Wickham et al. 2000: 537–9). The City authorities were evidently, though rather mysteriously, more tolerant of the boy companies. Paul's Boys, founded on the participation of choristers of St Paul's Cathedral, performed in an indoor theatre accommodated within its precinct. The company was revived in 1599 after a long interruption. The other, the Blackfriars Boys, appeared in 1600 as a revival of a much earlier company based on child choristers of the Chapel Royal. They performed at Blackfriars in a venue adapted from earlier buildings by entrepreneurs associated with the Lord Chamberlain's Men, who were themselves forbidden to use it, because of its situation within the City, until 1609. Boy companies performed a repertoire as adult in its content as the public theatres, but theirs were smaller venues, technically 'private' (as opposed to the 'public' amphitheatres) and it is customarily surmised that their audience may have been drawn from a narrower social range. Both venues were indoors, an obvious advantage for much of the year.

The boy actors in their 'private' performing spaces may have enjoyed some immunity from the controls which governed the public theatres. In general, though, that regime was comprehensive and effective. It emanated directly from the crown, where an ambiguous attitude to the stage prevailed. The Lord Chamberlain was responsible for royal entertainment, most significantly during the protracted festivities around Christmas. To this end, a flourishing London stage was necessary to provide command performances in temporary performing spaces at court. All early Privy Council discussions of stage control prioritize the provision of entertainment at court, which constitutes its primary *raison d'être*. Yet the court evidently shared some of the City authorities' concerns and there was a recurrent anxiety lest the stage were to foment sedition through hostile depiction of the political establishment. Legislation was tightened over the late Elizabethan period. Edmund Tilney became Master of the Revels in 1579, with the combined responsibilities of regulating the theatre and securing performances at court. By the end of the reign, those powers included licensing powers over the companies and over the plays they performed, which had to be approved after his inspection.

The professional theatre in 1603 was still mindful of its own dependence on protection and its susceptibility to sudden and potentially very punitive intervention. A scandal of 1597 had starkly asserted their powerlessness before the will of the regime. The Earl of Pembroke's Men performed a comedy, *Isle of Dogs*, co-authored by Thomas Nashe and Ben Jonson. The content of this lost play has been the subject of some speculation. However, it seems likeliest that, in the spirit of contemporary satire, it approached too closely the critical representation of living persons. The Isle of Dogs, a muddy spit in the Thames downriver from the City, confronts from the north shore the royal complex at Greenwich along the south shore, and the probability must be that it included some allusion to or reflection on the court.

The Privy Council's response sharply reminded theatrical companies of their dependence and vulnerability. The play contained 'very seditious and slanderous matter' constituting 'lewd and mutinous behaviour'. Those terms are a stark reminder that, for all the interest of literary historians in the statutory framework of censorship, far more draconian measures became available once a transgressive text strayed into what could be represented as blasphemy or sedition, which carried a range of spectacular corporal and capital punishments. Jonson and some of the leading actors of the company were arrested and imprisoned, while Nashe escaped, to live on the run till the storm passed (Nicholl 1984: ch. 16; Wickham et al. 2000). Chillingly, the Privy Council instructed 'Mr Topcliffe' 'to examine ... those of the players that are committed ... what is become of the rest of their fellows that either had their parts in the devising of that seditious matter, or that were actors or players in the same; what copies they have given forth of the said play and to whom; and such other points as your shall think meet to be demanded of them' (Wickham et al. 2000: 102). Richard Topcliffe was the notorious chief inquisitor of recusants, a man licensed to use torture in extracting information. Indeed, his involvement leads Charles Nicholl to speculate that the objectionable play had some recusant elements within it (1984: 254), though there would seem to be no supporting evidence. In the event, nobody seems to have been interrogated by rack or strappado, or sentenced to be branded, mutilated or flogged, and certainly nobody was executed.

But the stage had had its lesson. At the same time, the regime took action against the other adult companies, ordering their immediate though temporary suppression. When the theatres reopened in London, only the Lord Admiral's and the Lord Chamberlain's Men were licensed. Pembroke's Men reformed only as a company permitted to tour the provinces. 'Playhouse owners and acting companies had learned that ... they must either accept the Court as their master or forfeit the right to work in their chosen profession' (Wickham et al. 2000: 104).

A major brush with authority, though more limited in its impact, resulted from the peripheral involvement of the Lord Chamberlain's Men in the abortive Essex coup of 1601. The larger intentions of the earl remain as uncertain to modern historians as they were among his contemporaries. To repair his political eclipse after the failure of his military expedition to Ireland and his rash response to that, he had assembled a small private army in his London mansion and attempted to take over both the Tower of London and the royal court. Even on the scaffold he maintained his innocence of any attempt to hurt or kill the queen. On the eve of the uprising, he entertained his followers at the Globe with a performance of 'the play of the deposing and killing of King Richard the Second' (evidence of a player in the company to Chief Justice Popham and Justice Fenner – Wickham et al. 2000: 195). The event has posed problems and provoked varied speculation. Shakespeare's play, as we know it, seems like a text arguing against uprising: was it altered or was this some other play on the same theme? Perhaps Essex wanted to distinguish the intended coup from an act of sedition, like that depicted. Practically, using the Globe had advantages for conspirators in that it was perhaps the only venue where 3,000 people could meet without seeming like a riotous assembly. Theatres were closed later in the century at times of uncertainty about civil order, for a long period during the 1640s and 1650s and again during the Monmouth rebellion of 1685. Andrew Gurr, eschewing wider speculation, simply concludes that 'Essex's judges accepted their story [of their innocence of any larger involvement in and knowledge of the coup]. The players . . . got away lightly' (1996: 289). But, as the minor figures in the failed uprising followed Essex to execution, they had another reminder of the nature of power in the last years of Elizabeth and of their own lowly status.

Patronage and Court Culture

Elizabethan writers could rarely live well from the direct fruits of their labours. Those who were not privately wealthy needed employment, perhaps in the learned professions, or as a servant of the crown or an aristocrat, or as an office-holder of some sort. Competition for preferment was fierce, and men of letters offered limited attractions to potential benefactors, who may have wished to reward or advance people with rather different skills. Among leading writers of the period, Francis Bacon was the most successful in securing powerful aristocratic patronage, though the second Earl of Essex no doubt valued his shrewd legal mind at least as much as his prose style. At an early stage of his career, Bacon was engaged, for example, in 'drafting position papers' (Jardine and Stewart 1998: 131). Some great families had, over several generations, a record of offering protection and financial reward to creative writers, as we might call them. Over the

Tudor and early Stuart period the Herbert family, the Earls of Pembroke prominent among them, attracted tributes and dedications from more than 250 writers. In the late Elizabethan period, these included George Chapman, Samuel Daniel, Thomas Nashe and Edmund Spenser (Brennan 1988: xii). No doubt to some they extended some protection and largesse, though the second Earl of Pembroke could do little to protect his servants' theatrical company when crisis came (see above). Other great aristocratic families, the Dudleys, the Cecils and the Howards, were similarly courted. In the 1590s, Essex, assiduously building his retinue, was recognized as a major source of patronage and preferment. He was courted by numerous writers, and had a remarkable number of published works dedicated to him, which clearly reflected 'a perception that he was a likely source of preferment, protection or financial reward'. However, although dedications to the mighty, to the queen and her courtiers, flowed from the presses, 'there is no proof that a dedication ever secured for an author the desired reward, or even the benevolence of the patron to whom the work was addressed' (Fox 1995: 231). Essex, though, plainly did extend some small-scale rewards for artistic services. The Lord Chamberlain's Men, in the aftermath of the coup, may well have thought the two pounds they received to play *Richard II* a poor deal for the risks they ran. But he did pay for other performances in other contexts. For example, he hired a troupe of Oxford 'scholars' to put on an entertainment at an Ascension Day tilt (Hammer 1999: 202). His fall certainly disrupted a major network of dependency and protection.

Patronage in the early modern period functioned on principles other than kindness and charity. Typically, clients gave to patrons something they thought the patrons wanted – material goods or services, perhaps even sexual favours – and patrons gave to the clients something that cost them nothing but which was 'in their gift' – a court office, a nomination to a living or an academic appointment, perhaps. Of course, the rich and powerful needed servants, employed at their own charge, and hiring one, rather than another, constituted another kind of patronage. Where state appointments were concerned, a market in offices emerged. For a minor post £200 would be offered, with competitive bids of between £1,000 and £4,000 for lucrative offices such as the receivership of the Court of Wards or the treasurership at war (Guy 1995b: 8). In markets like this, dedicating a book or delivering a birthday ode did not carry much weight, although if that was all one had to offer, the persistence of the practices is understandable.

Setting the style for her leading aristocrats, Elizabeth was notoriously parsimonious in her support for creative artists. In fairness, as a monarch at war she was relatively hard up. She would accept dedications, 'but she gave nothing in return. An author might as well dedicate a book to the moon for all the benefit it brought' (Parry 2002: 125). Moreover, the wider cultural activity she supported appeared increasingly insular, stagnant and outmoded. While her great adversary, Philip II of Spain, was collecting the work of Titian and Bosch and building El Escorial, Elizabeth eschewed major expenditure and patronized portrait painters in the old iconic English tradition. As Sir Roy Strong puts it, 'Stylistically England was a backwater, for [Elizabeth's] reign [was] a rock against change' (1986: 87–8). (Elizabethan miniature painting should probably be exempted from the general censure.) But the queen demanded entertainment, and the theatre companies left standing after the *Isle of Dogs* scandal often played at court. They did so, in part, because it was much cheaper to hire them that to stage court entertainments, and 'most of the surviving Elizabethan entertainments were not performed at court, but were presented to the Queen on her progresses around the country' (Lindley 1995: xvi). The rich achievements of late Elizabethan literary culture, the work of Spenser and Marlowe, the early writing of Shakespeare, Bacon and Donne: all owe virtually nothing to Elizabeth herself or the cultural microclimate she inhabited.

2

From the Accession of James I to the Defenestration of Prague: March 1603 to May 1618

Changes and Continuities

Elizabeth I died on 24 March 1603, leaving a competent political administration, simplified and strengthened by the removal of the Earl of Essex. Her chief minister, Robert Cecil, had worked assiduously to ensure a peaceful transfer of the crown to James I, who since since his infancy had reigned as King James VI of Scotland (albeit, initially, with a regent). James retained Cecil, creating him Earl of Salisbury in 1605, and till shortly before his death in 1612 he guided quite effectively the political fortunes of his new royal master. James inherited a country at war with Spain, but moved quickly to end hostilities. Throughout the period covered by this chapter, England was at peace, which gave its monarch great advantages in domestic politics. Although James would have liked subsidies, and sought them from the parliaments of 1604 and 1614, he could manage without them, as long as he eschewed military adventures.

His parliamentary experiences disclosed distinct differences between his perception of the English political system, which saw the king as an autocratic and divinely sanctioned patriarch, and a nascent parliamentary tradition already thinking in terms of an 'ancient constitution', which invested citizens and their representatives with political and civil rights of a different order. However, James was clear that foreign policy remained wholly in the domain of his personal decision-making.

As long as he avoided wars, the political process could be kept substantially away from the public domain.

When James came to England, he already had two sons, Henry and Charles, as potential heirs, and a daughter, Elizabeth, who in due course would possibly engage in an advantageous marriage contract with a foreign prince. James brought with him a Scottish entourage, some of whom he allowed to waste away, returning to Scotland without finding employment. But he largely governed through English ministers, pre-eminently Cecil, which did something to mitigate resentment and to ensure continuities. Though he adopted the style of 'King of Britain', real unification, which would have required complex parliamentary legislation, remained elusive. England remained a separate kingdom, with its own distinctive literary culture, scarcely touched by Scottish influence. James continued as monarch of Scotland, ruling there through proxies, while governing his new kingdom from palaces in and around the Thames basin. The 'British' project remained largely an unrealized aspiration, though one frequently celebrated among writers looking to James for patronage and preferment.

Ecclesiastical affairs seemed calmer in his early years than in the reign of Elizabeth. A major assassination attempt, the Gunpowder Plot of 1605, plainly signalled that some in the disadvantaged Catholic community retained treasonous intent. But reprisals were limited to participants and the attempt was not repeated. Since the 1580s James had sought 'to persuade Catholics, both in Elizabeth's dominions and on the Continent, of . . . at least his leniency to the ancient faith' (Lee 1990: 100). His queen, Anne of Denmark, was a convert to Catholicism. James's own faith was Calvinist, though his preferences in church government were episcopal and English Presbyterianism received no encouragement. He watched carefully the disruption caused in the United Provinces by the Arminian schism, and his policy at the Synod of Dort was support for orthodox Calvinism against Arminian innovation. (On Arminianism and its consequences for literary culture, see below, chapters 3 and 4.)

Three principal disasters affected the literary history of these years. The plague of 1603, the worst for several years, brought with it, besides enormous loss of life, closure of London's theatres, posing major problems for its acting companies (see below, 'Early Jacobean Theatre'), and its frequent recurrence was also disruptive. The death of Prince Henry in 1612 killed off a significant, though still developing, patronage system. The Carr-Overbury scandal, which broke in 1615, certainly shaped perception of the royal court among outsiders and perhaps stimulated an enthusiasm for the popular representation of courtly corruption.

The Making of the Royal Courts

On his accession, and in some cases even earlier, James had been courted as both a political and a cultural patron. His formal entry into the City of London, in March 1604, allowed the corporation to make its most public show of welcome by drawing on the talents of Ben Jonson and Thomas Dekker, both established dramatists, and the architect and builder Stephen Harrison. Each has left a printed account, primarily of his own contribution (Dekker 1604; Harrison 1604; Jonson 1604). Most striking is the sureness with which collectively the endeavour hit the principal themes of early Jacobean rule, the king's role as peacemaker and his patriarchal view of government. Thus, at the last triumphal arch on the royal procession, Jonson's script for the speaker, Genius Urbis (that is, tutelary deity of the City), hails James as one who has 'brought / Sweet peace to sit in that bright state shee ought' (Jonson 1925–52: VII, 102). From the first arch to the last, London was styled the 'camera regia' or royal chamber, with a powerful suggestion that it is the bridal chamber of James and his kingdom. The notion chimed well with James's own words to his first parliament: 'I am the Husband, and the whole Isle is my lawfull Wife' (James VI and I 1994: 136). England's political and cultural elite thronged to tell the king what they believed he wished to hear.

But the court culture of the king himself took some while to assume a definitive shape. James was a competent poet and a confident political theorist. His *True Lawe of Free Monarchies* and *Basilikon Doron*, published in Edinburgh in 1598 and 1599, were reprinted in London in 1603. He also had a fair grasp of controversial theology, and to some extent he encouraged in his immediate circle respectful debate, though would respond quickly and implacably to insolence from outsiders, as theatre companies that attempted to ridicule the new regime soon discovered (see below, 'Early Jacobean Theatre'). Ben Jonson soon found a role as masque writer and in time emerged as James's laureate poet and his pensioner, though at the start of the reign his play *Sejanus* attracted government attention (see below, 'Other Drama'). Inigo

Jones became the favoured masque designer from early in the reign. Only later did he emerge as architect of significant royal buildings; prominent among his extant structures are the third and final Banqueting House at Whitehall (begun 1619, completed 1622) and the Queen's House at Greenwich (begun 1617, though not completed till 1635). James retained a considerable musical ensemble, though less ambitious than Charles I's.

James notoriously supported favourites, showering them with presents, titles and offices that were in his gift. Among those he most openly favoured in the early part of his reign was Robert Carr, a gentry-class Scot, who had entered England as his page but by 1611 was Viscount Rochester and a Knight of the Garter; in 1613 he was created Earl of Somerset. No obvious political talent or industry had secured his advancement. Quite why James rewarded him was a matter of salacious speculation then as now. Yet the king supported Carr's marital ambitions. He allowed the annulment of the marriage of his lover, Frances Howard, from the third Earl of Essex on the grounds of non-consummation, which in turn made possible a highly advantageous marriage. Frances, however, had somewhat overreached herself, securing the poisoning, while he was in prison, of her husband's erstwhile confidant Sir Thomas Overbury, who had tried to block the annulment and had been jailed for his pains. The scandal broke in all its gross complexity, compounded by James's evident insistence that Frances and Carr should escape the capital penalties their agents suffered. As Maurice Lee observes, 'Worse still, he did not even disgrace them.' Too many people outside the king's circle knew, or thought they knew, about events within it, and 'the reputation of the court never recovered from this scandal' (Lee 1990: 154). Carr's eclipse coincided with the rise of George Villiers, the future Duke of Buckingham, whose influence is explored more fully in chapter 3. By the time of his advancement, popular opinion about the Jacobean court in particular, and perhaps royal courts generally, was decidedly negative. Anti-court sentiment, couched in moral and religious terms, emerged as a dominant perspective among those excluded from the court itself.

Other royal courts gradually developed alongside that of the king, each with its own potential for patronage of the arts. The queen, Anne of Denmark, rapidly assembled a household which retained her closest companions from her Scottish days and added English aristocratic luminaries, among them, perhaps most significantly in cultural terms,

Lucy, Countess of Bedford, a patroness of both Ben Jonson and John Donne and a lady of the queen's bedchamber. Anne certainly extended some patronage to English writers, though probably the only one to be closely dependent on her was the relatively minor figure of Samuel Daniel, a modestly accomplished poet, skilled lyricist (much of his shorter verse was set by his brother John) and occasional masque writer. Anne had masqued in Scotland, and her arrival helped to revive aristocratic entertainments in England (see below, 'Masques and Other Court Entertainments'). Anne's cultural influence was felt more widely. She was an accomplished musician and kept a musical consort that was fairly large for a subsidiary royal household, and she also collected paintings, though her almost clandestine Catholicism excluded her from dispensing ecclesiastical patronage (*DNB* 2004). Visits were exchanged with Christian IV of Denmark, her brother, whose glittering court showed the Scots and English what patronage could achieve. After the decades of Elizabethan niggardliness, parochialism and isolation, Anne's was an important part in the advancement of English court culture, which reached its apogee in the personal rule of Charles I.

Similar claims have been advanced for the court of Prince Henry. He was only 9 at the time of his father's accession, and not until 1610 was he created Prince of Wales, receiving at the same time his own revenues, household and the palaces of Richmond and St James's (Strong 1986: 11). The two years before his death saw a flurry of cultural activity as he generated around himself a militantly Protestant, austere and yet creative court, patronizing artists, architects and garden designers, and extending very direct patronage to a small number of writers who seem not to have secured his father's favour, in particular Josuah Sylvester and Michael Drayton (see below, 'Non-dramatic Poetry'). Understandably, his sudden and untimely death in 1612 occasioned poetic lamentation, not least from those who depended on him, such as Sylvester's *Lachrimae Lachrimarum; or, The Distillation of Teares Shede for the Untimely Death of the Incomparable Prince Panaretus* (1612). It went rapidly into three editions.

Henry participated energetically in aristocratic entertainments, particularly those of a martial kind (see below), and, as Sir Roy Strong (1986) and David Norbrook (1984, 2002) have argued, the old, anti-Spanish, anti-Catholic, pro-war factions of the Elizabethan regime looked to him as a potential leader for their cause. Sir Walter Raleigh, incarcerated in 1604 for well-substantiated if marginal involvement in a conspiracy against James's accession, received his protection and support, for example.

It is difficult to assess the cultural impact of a royal adolescent who enjoyed a modest level of independence for only the last two years of his short life. For Strong, he 'takes his place as the final figure in a series of still-born renaissances', particularly associated with Sir Philip Sidney and the second Earl of Essex (1986: 224). Yet perhaps we should see his contribution as simply a distinctive component within a larger revival associated with the dynastic change. The Scottish royalty that descended on England may have left behind a minor court, but it was one in touch with European expectations. The Scottish crown had long-standing links with France. James's grandmother, Mary of Guise, was a French aristocrat. His mother had grown up in the French royal court. Anne was a sister of the Danish king and descended from the Hapsburgs. James was a poet and political theorist, who already felt comfortable in the company of poets and theologians. Henry's own nascent style had begun to establish his own cultural space. But England finally achieved a court culture to match, at least in aspiration, those of the Hapsburgs and Bourbons in the reign of Charles I in the 1630s, although its ideology differed sharply from the court of his brother.

Masques and Other Court Entertainments

The arrival of the Stuarts reanimated the tradition of court entertainment in England. Queen Anne of Denmark, initially, played the key role. She was a veteran of court entertainments, pageants and processions both in her native Denmark and as Scotland's queen. Between 1604 and 1611 she danced in six masques, which 'accounted for almost the entirety of the English Jacobean court's female performance in the first two decades of the seventeenth century' (McManus 2002: 3). In so doing, Barbara Lewalski claims, she 'affirmed the worth of women, and her court was perceived as a separate female community, marginalized yet powerful' (1994: 43). Certainly, these activities rapidly established a significant patronage network. Samuel Daniel, who wrote scripts for two of her masques, remained a beneficiary, and, more important, she secured Ben Jonson for the other four, thus founding a long-standing, though eventually acrimonious, working relationship with her chosen designer, Inigo Jones. Two years after arriving from Scotland she had largely determined the future trajectory of an important component of early Stuart court culture.

Her most challenging performance was the first collaboration between Jones and Jonson, *The Masque of Blackness*, danced on Twelfth Night, 1605. The queen and her ladies appeared dressed and made up as 'blackamores' (line 21; Orgel and Strong 1973: I, 90). Participants who had blacked up had featured in court entertainments in both Denmark and Scotland (McManus 2002: 76–7), but the English court was evidently bewildered by its strangeness and apparent ugliness. A contemporary correspondent observed: 'you cannot imagine a more ugly Sight, then a troop of lean-cheek'd Moors.' He elsewhere remarked upon the indecorous sexual display of the aristocratic dancers' costumes, which seemed 'too light and curtisan-like' (Orgel and Strong 1973: I, 89). Plainly, Anne was prepared to push the limits of a genre that, over the early Stuart period, was characterized by a searching for spectacular and surprising innovation.

The Masque of Blackness was contemporaneously recognized as a particularly expensive production, perhaps costing more than £3,000 to put on. Modern criticism has sought to identify in it a defiance of monarchical patriarchy, its 'perhaps partly subconscious . . . gestures of resistance' (Lewalski 1994: 43; see also McManus 2002: *passim*). But we should recognize, too, its clear surface significance. This is an overt celebration of the king's wealth and power, acted out in a closed rite that celebrated, in the uniting of Anne with masquers drawn for the most part from the highest ranks of the English aristocracy, the security with which the new dynasty had been established. Moreover, the action and the text endorse James's early enthusiasm for a real unification of Scotland and England. Thus, Jonson has Aethiopia remark: 'With that great name Britannia, this blessed isle / Hath won her ancient dignity and style' (ll.224–5; Orgel and Strong 1973: I, 92). Such an explicit and stately compliment to the king characterizes this and most other masques danced by Anne.

Anne danced in three further masques by Jonson: *The Masque of Beauty* (1608), a companion piece to *The Masque of Blackness*; *The Masque of Queens* (1609); and *Love Freed From Ignorance and Folly* (1611). *Tethys' Festival* (1610), her masque to celebrate the creation of her elder surviving son, Prince Henry, as Prince of Wales, marks a major transition in the cultural landscape of the royal courts. For the first time, Charles, Duke of York, the future Charles I, appeared significantly in a court entertainment, performing symbolic acts which confirm both James's status as supreme monarch of the British kingdoms and Henry's assumed role as the embodiment of English chivalry (Orgel and Strong 1973: I, 193).

Henry's own entertainments emphasize his potential for military glory, but they carefully include acts of formal submission to his father. Thus, *Oberon, The Fairy Prince*, the 1611 Christmas masque scripted by Jonson, displays Henry and his company as gentle knights in the Arthurian tradition. But it is unequivocal about where power ultimately rests:

> [These knights], for good they have deserved
> Of yond'high throne, are come of rights to pay
> Their annual vows; and all their glories lay
> At his feet, and tender to this only great
> True majesty ...
> (ll.258–62; Orgel and Strong 1973: I, 209)

Similarly, *Prince Henry's Barriers* (1610), a chivalric and martial entertainment scripted by Jonson to commemorate Henry's first bearing arms, concludes with a speech by Merlin which cautions the young prince to curb his militaristic impulses and observe the higher wisdom of James the peacemaker (Orgel and Strong 1973: I, 163).

The death of Henry in 1612, together with Anne's retirement from performance, led to a brief hiatus in royal masquing, though aristocratic masques were sometimes presented (for example, on the occasion of the marriage of Princess Elizabeth), as were masques produced by the Inns of Court. *The Vision of Delight*, the Twelfth Night masque in 1617 scripted by Jonson, was led by the newly created Earl of Buckingham, George Villiers. It marked his rise in the king's favour. His status was confirmed in 1618 when he danced again in another Jonson masque, *Pleasure Reconciled to Virtue*, for the first time led by Charles, Prince of Wales. It elicited the fullest surviving account of Jacobean masque, the report of Orazio Busino, chaplain to the Venetian Embassy and spectator at the event:

> Then there was such a crowd; for though they claim to admit only those favoured with invitations, nevertheless every box was full, especially with most noble and richly dressed ladies, 600 and more in number ... their clothes of such various styles and colours as to be indescribable. ... At about the 6th hour of the night his majesty appeared with his court. ... After his majesty had been seated under the canopy

alone . . . he had the ambassadors sit on two stools, and the great officers and magistrates sat on benches. . . . [After the prince and his company had descended from the stage set and approached the king] They did all sorts of ballets and dances . . . the King, who is by nature choleric, grew impatient and shouted loudly, 'Why don't they dance? What did you make me come here for? Devil take all of you, dance!' At once the Marquis of Buckingham [Villiers had been promoted again], his majesty's favourite minion, sprang forward, and danced a number of high and very tiny capers with such grace and lightness that he made everyone admire and love him, and also managed to calm the rage of his angry lord. . . . The Prince, however, surpassed them all in his bows, being very formal in doing his obeisance both to his majesty and to the lady with whom he was dancing. (Orgel and Strong 1973: I, 282–4)

Busino's account points up key characteristics of early Stuart masque. It has an important role in the diplomatic process. This is a closed, caste rite, a display of wealth and power, to which ambassadors are admitted in order that they may be impressed as well as entertained. The monarch is central: he has the best seat, indeed, probably the only seat from which all the visual effects of Inigo Jones's stage design appeared to work perfectly. The whole performance plays to and moves towards the king, though there is some doubt as to how entertaining its content would have seemed to the cerebral James, who did not himself masque in England. But Busino is alert, too, to how the masque discloses a significant shift of power within the royal circle. Buckingham's eminence and his future progress are plainly recognized. He picks up, too, on the personal style of Prince Charles, already evident here: this is a restrained, careful youth, with a strongly developed sense of decorum.

Indeed, the principal theme of the masque, well represented in the title, points away from the simpler chivalry of Prince Henry's entertainments and towards the court culture that emerged in the years of the personal rule (see below, chapter 4). However, Busino's account ends with a description of the feast that followed the performance, at which the banquet spread out for the wealthy and powerful was plundered so greedily that the tables collapsed and glassware was smashed. By then James had already gone to bed. (The court of Charles brought a more restrained tone to feasting.) The text and design were adapted for subsequent performance as part of the celebration of Charles's installation as Prince of Wales, now with a new antimasque of goats and funny Welshmen.

Early Jacobean Theatre

The economic, social and legal conditions for theatrical performance in the early Jacobean period were substantially similar to those that obtained in the final years of Elizabeth's reign. Companies were composed either of boys or of a mixture of adult males and boys. There were still two principal kinds of performing space: 'public' theatres, which were outdoor amphitheatres, with a capacity of about 3,000 spectators, many of whom stood in the courtyard around the stage; and 'private' theatres in halls, where all the audience were seated. Since the cheapest admission charge for the latter was higher than for the former, it is usually assumed that some who habitually attended the public theatres would have been excluded by price from the private theatres. There is no reason to suppose that the audience for the private theatres did not also attend performances in the public theatres. Indeed, from 1608 onward one company, the King's Men (formerly the Lord Chamberlain's Men) performed in both a private and a public theatre, drawing on the same repertoire in both venues. Theatre historians contend that the rise of the private theatres led to a fragmentation of a market that formerly had been broadly inclusive and to the emergence of an elite-culture drama, which, stripped of an animating vigour drawn from that wide social base, looked towards the court, whereas a low-culture audience developed for cruder forms of entertainment. The argument certainly has some merit in the Caroline period (see below, chapter 4), but it is less tenable earlier, although boy companies, the earliest occupants of the private theatres, as we shall see, developed a distinctive and politically challenging repertoire in the earliest years of the new reign.

At the reopening of the theatres in April 1604, the two companies of boy actors active at the close of Elizabeth's reign resumed at Blackfriars and St Paul's, the former renamed as the Children of the Queen's Revels under royal patent. The three adult companies which had survived more stringent controls formerly introduced were also revived. The Lord Chamberlain's Men, again under royal patent, became the King's Men, a privilege which probably acknowledged their status as the senior company in London and anticipated the special favour with which they would be held when players were commanded to perform at court. Shortly afterwards, also by royal patent, the Lord Admiral's Men became Prince Henry's, servants to the royal heir, and the Earl of Worcester's Men were similarly attached to the household of Queen Anne (Wickham et al. 2000: 260, 120–2). These developments signalled the resolve to keep close control over the playing companies. But the patents also carried protection: to obstruct the players in their legitimate business was to thwart the royal family. The patent for the King's Men, addressed to all magistrates and subjects alike, is unequivocal in:

> Willing and commanding you, and every of you, as you tender our pleasure, not only to permit and suffer them herein without any your lets, hindrances or molestations during our said pleasure, but also to be aiding and assisting to them, if any wrong be to them offered. . . . what further favour you shall show to these Our Servants for Our sake We shall take kindly at your hands. (Quoted in Wickham et al. 2000: 123)

Although weakened, as the whole sector had been, by the long closure of 1603–4, the King's Men now found themselves in a singularly strong position. The Globe gave them a major venue on the southern shore of the Thames, outside the control of the City but conveniently close to London Bridge (and to other leisure-industry activities). Through the Burbage family, the company had long had an interest in the private theatre at Blackfriars, which was only allowed to be used by a boys' company, whose weekly performances seemed less offensive to powerful City interests. But when it fell vacant on the disbanding of the Children of the Queen's Revels in 1608, Richard Burbage set up a new partnership that included six of the seven shareholders in the Globe, five of whom were members of the King's Men, and, after an enforced interruption for plague, the company opened there late in 1609. For the first time an adult troupe regularly played in a private playhouse. From then until 1642 the King's Men used both spaces, favouring the Globe in summer months (Wickham 2000: 502).

The move reflected the growing confidence the company had in its special relationship with the court and the protection that gave them. Indeed, from the opening of the reign they had performed very frequently at court, and the company contributed personnel to court masques. Its chief cause for assurance, however, and probably the key factor in its pre-eminence, was William Shakespeare's exclusive work for the company. The Christmas entertainments for 1604 were virtually a Shakespeare festival, including not only the new or recent *Othello* and *Measure for Measure* and the late Elizabethan *Merchant of Venice*, but also 'a chance to catch up' on his earlier work, 'going back as far as *The Comedy of Errors* and *Love's Labour's Lost*, and including also *Merry Wives* and *Henry V*' (Duncan-Jones 2001: 170). Shakespeare's relationship to the King's Men was unprecedented hitherto in English theatre history. He was a major shareholder in the Globe (and subsequently in the Blackfriars theatre), which secured his services for the company, and in the process his personal prosperity. The creativity and the commercial dynamism of the undertaking were uniquely aligned.

Other adult companies fared quite well in the early Jacobean period. In 1600 the company that became Prince Henry's Men, under the entrepreneurial leadership of Philip Henslowe and the actor Edward Alleyn, had shifted from proximity to the Globe to the Fortune, a substantial new theatre north of the river, northwest of the City boundary, where it continued to prosper once the theatres reopened (Wickham et al. 2000: 532). The Queen's Men used several venues before settling in another new theatre, the Red Bull, in the northern suburb of Clerkenwell, where it continued till the late 1610s. The latter especially became associated with rather populist entertainment, and theatre historians recount how, in the longer term, they were 'increasingly seen as in an unfashionable part of the City and lacking in the refinement of the private playhouses' (Wickham et al. 2000: 566). Yet at its creative peak, the Red Bull included in its repertoire the work of the competent Thomas Heywood and Thomas Dekker and saw the premiere of at least one work of genius: John Webster's *The White Devil*. Perhaps significantly, Webster's other masterpiece, *The Duchess of Malfi*, was performed by the King's Men, a surer platform for a testing, avant-gardist work.

The boys' companies, too, attracted writers of distinction. Ben Jonson and George Chapman wrote for the Children of the Queen's Revels, Thomas Middleton for the Children of St Paul's, Beaumont and perhaps Fletcher for both. John Marston, the writer probably most significant in the development of a smart, hard-edged dramatic idiom among the boys' companies, migrated from the latter to the former, although his finest play, *The Malcontent*, was soon taken over by the King's Men (see below). The boys' troupes continued to enjoy the privilege of playing within the City with relatively little interference from the corporation. However, they incited a very significant intervention from the court, which led to their discontinuation. The legislative framework for stage control continued little changed from the Elizabethan period. Ultimate responsibility rested with the Lord

Chamberlain, but everyday control fell to the Master of the Revels. Edmund Tilney continued in this office, though Sir George Buc, his eventual successor (in 1610), played an increasing part as deputy through the early Jacobean years. However well disposed the new regime evidently was towards the professional stage, it was not to be mocked, and the power of the state was soon asserted. At least four plays caused royal offence: *Eastward Ho!* (1605), *The Isle of Gulls* (1606), Chapman's *The Conspiracy and Tragedy of Charles, Duke of Biron* (1608) and 'a lost play about an ill-fated silver mining enterprise in Scotland' (1608). The third broke a taboo by commenting on recent history and attracted a protest from the French ambassador. The others were altogether too free in their glances at Scots in general and the king's court in particular. The silver mine was a royal enterprise. The Children of the Queen's Revels lost royal patronage and in 1608 were closed down by the Lord Chamberlain: 'his grace [the king] had vowed that they should never play more, but should first beg their bread' (Wickham et al. 2000: 126, 515). Several children were imprisoned for a while, though the group was later reconstituted after a fashion.

The lesson of 1608 was well learnt by all the companies of London. A theatre acceptable to the court had much to gain from the court; once it became transgressive, it had little to protect it. Not till the 1620s did a new spirit of oppositionalism and of simple curiosity about the processes of government stimulate a renewed and sustained critique on the London stage of a royal court that had become less monolithic ideologically and less sure of its own priorities and agenda (see below, chapter 3).

Jacobean Shakespeare

By the final years of Elizabeth's reign, Shakespeare's distinctive idiom was complete. Of course, even his earliest plays had shown, sometimes rather intermittently, an accomplishment as dramatic poet that altogether transcended that of his precursors. *The Two Gentlemen of Verona*, perhaps his first play, already showed a mastery of comic prose. (Dating the oeuvre remains notoriously controversial; this account adopts the dates postulated by Stanley Wells and Gary Taylor – see Shakespeare 1989.) Parts of the *Henry VI* plays and most of *Richard III* reached levels of expressive excellence rarely touched even by Christopher Marlowe at his most ambitious (in the final scene of *Dr Faustus*, for example).

But it was in the very late 1590s and early 1600s that Shakespeare achieved complete technical maturity. *Henry V* (1599) showed him picking open the nature of kingship and the limitations of incipient English nationalism with an attention to complexities and contradictions that makes earlier dramatization of political processes – even his own – seem naively unequivocal. In *Julius Caesar* (1599), for the first time, he offered in the reconstruction of Roman political life a fully realized world at sufficient cultural distance from his own to allow an exploration of those political processes uninhibited by the exigencies of observing the primitive orthodoxies of Tudor state ideology. Brutus's role as reluctant assassin illuminates the paradox of a conservative revolution and criminal conspiracy in defence of an ancient constitution. Again, Shakespeare used the freedom afforded by a setting remote in time and distance to juxtapose the public and private faces of political action. Thus, Antony, whose 'heart is in the coffin there with Caesar' (III.ii.108; Shakespeare 1989: 615), joins Octavius in a backroom conclave to decide 'who should be pricked to die / In our black sentence and proscription' (IV.i.16–17; Shakespeare 1989: 617).

Both plays showed a new quality in the representation of human personality, thought and feeling. Character study has long been driven from the forefront of critical approaches to Shakespeare. Yet the kinds of characterization he so brilliantly accomplished are central to the perennial appeal of his oeuvre. In the theatre, his plays – especially those from 1599 onwards – remain star vehicles because they challenge the actors that perform the leading roles in ways unparalleled in early modern drama in English. In a curious process of empathy, modern audiences seem to care about the apparent experiences of his heroes and heroines. Arguably, there are limitations in a critical tendency that excludes such affectiveness from recognition and consideration.

Shakespeare's distinctive characterization rested in the unprecedented interiority of the depictions and his exploration of the relationship between interior processes and external action. Of course, his characters are imaginative constructs within dramatic genres which were marked by a mature system of constraints and conventions, issues explored so effectively in M. C. Bradbrook's classic studies (1935, 1955). Yet Shakespeare vividly shows his characters feeling and thinking, expressing recognizable representations of ordinary human responses to the kinds of extraordinary circumstances which sometimes mark the crises of human life. He shows them balancing alternatives and identifying conflicts of interest and of values. Thus, Brutus ponders the horror of murder and the responsibilities of patrician republicanism in a long and meditative scene of interrupted soliloquy, which expresses a heightened state of agitated introversion: 'Between the acting of the dreadful thing / And the first motion, all the interim is / Like a phantasma or a hideous dream' (I.iii.63–5; Shakespeare 1989: 606). Mature Shakespeare was often drawn to depicting that interim.

Again, in a multilayered mimesis, Shakespeare has his actors playing characters who then both play roles and comment on the distinction between those roles and a depicted interiority that conflicts with them. Thus, before the battle of Agincourt, Henry V moves in disguise among the English common soldiery, defending his actions, before in soliloquy exposing a human frailty that defines the limitations of royal status: 'O be sick, great greatness, / And bid thy ceremony give thee cure' (IV.i.248–9; Shakespeare 1989: 586). Then he once more assumes a role, this time of the hero-king: 'We few, we happy few, we band of brothers' (IV.iii.60; Shakespeare 1989: 588). Shakespeare's representation of the king's role-playing is framed in turn by the speeches of the Chorus and his reiterated insistence that we are witnessing a representation of events, not events themselves, 'Minding true things by what their mock'ries be' (IV.0.53; Shakespeare 1989: 584). Uniquely among his contemporaries, Shakespeare placed questions about the nature of dramatic illusion and its relationship to external reality at the heart of his theatre. (For a classic account, see Righter 1962). It became a potent component in his critique of the integrity of the self.

Pre-Jacobean development culminated in *Hamlet* (1600) and *Troilus and Cressida* (?1601). The former offers Shakespeare's longest meditation on that interim before a 'dreadful thing'. In the latter, a distant mythic setting allowed him, as in *Julius Caesar*, to analyse the political animal in isolation from circumambient and facile state propaganda. In the process, he makes explicit a vein of cynicism latent in the earlier play.

Like other playwrights, Shakespeare had no work performed during the closure of the theatres that followed Elizabeth's death and a singularly savage visitation of the plague. He re-emerged as still the chief dramatist of London's best company, though now under the protection and patronage of James I. Thereafter followed an astonishing sequence of plays, among the finest dramatic texts in the western tradition: *Measure for Measure* (1604), *Othello* (1604), *All's Well That Ends Well* (dating problematic, but certainly early Jacobean), *King Lear* (first version before 1608), *Macbeth* (1606), *Antony and Cleopatra* (1606), *Coriolanus* (1608), *The Winter's Tale* (1609/10), *Cymbeline* (1610/11), *The Tempest* (1610/11), together with some works that were probably or certainly collaborations, *Timon of Athens* (?1604), *Pericles* (?1607), *All is True* (*Henry VIII*) (1613), and *The Two Noble Kinsmen* (1613). Much critical effort has been invested in a spurious taxonomic endeavour to cluster them into generally unhelpful categories – 'romances', 'the great tragedies', 'late plays', 'problem plays', 'tragi-comedies', and so on. I shall argue instead for seeing them as individual experiments at the edge of what was dramatically possible, each remarkable and distinctive in its own right, though sharing not only some community of themes and perspectives but also a grounding in the dramatic techniques and subtlety of representation mastered in the closing years of Elizabeth.

This approach is further informed by arguments drawn from Alastair Fowler's extended essay on realism in early modern literature and art:

> Shakespeare's realism is probably a good deal closer to Spenser's than is supposed within the world of Shakespearean criticism. ... Renaissance comedy tends to combine illusionistic representation with allegory. And it is full of multiple narrative; the unified structure of a single, fully developed plot is hardly to be found. ... Nowadays, novelistically minded directors tend to iron out Shakespeare's interwoven structures into a single, rationalized sequence, with at most a 'main plot' and 'subplot'. (Fowler 2003: 100)

As we shall see, the argument may be extended to Shakespeare's Jacobean tragedies, though Fowler himself hesitates: 'But the tragedies, it might be argued, are more naturalistic, and more unified. In *Othello* (1604) and *Macbeth* (1606) all plots are tributaries of the main stream: "causes are all contained"' (ibid., p. 101, quoting Kastan 1982: 26). Yet what of the narrative of Fleance and his dynastic destiny, interrupted in *Macbeth* III.iii and resumed in proleptic vision in IV.i? The tale of Brabanzio, left bereft of his daughter, is picked up with the report of his death – 'pure grief / Shore his old thread in twain' (V.ii.212–13; Shakespeare 1989: 851). His story seems more like an ox-bow lake, left behind by the mighty river of Othello's tragedy, than a tributary stream.

My approach to the multiple plots recognizes the intricacies of the coexistence in early modern cultural practices of literal and symbolic modes. To adapt Fowler's complex thesis (and to extend, though at the risk of vulgarizing it, an important concept latent in his account), I turn to the more tractable domain of portraiture. A painting may appear as a recognizable representation of the sitter. That image, necessarily, is to a degree life-like – there is no point in a portrait that is unrecognizable. However, it may well be idealized, cleaned up, purged of unwelcome elements evident in the sitter, whose warts may go unrecorded. Again, the posture that is struck may connote status, as may the associated accoutrements. These may reflect the sitter's habitual practice, though they are as likely to require symbolic reading.

Thus, like many early modern portraits, a familiar image of Elizabeth may be decoded through the simultaneous application of multiple and very different interpretative strategies. Consider the so-called 'Ditchley' portrait by Marcus Gheeraerts the Younger (*c*.1592) (National Portrait Gallery, London; conveniently reproduced in Duncan-Jones 2001: plate 1). We find at once a recognizable simulacrum and an idealized image of the queen, whose waist appears improbably thin, her breasts improbably high, her body improbably elongated. Her dress connotes wealth and power, but it also carries heraldic escutcheons. She wears a pink flower, which *may* reflect habitual or particular practice, but certainly invites identification as the Tudor rose and as such symbolizes her dynastic connections. The background, part stormy, part under blue skies, carries a Latin motto of explication, while her stance, on a globe displaying England, plainly allegorizes her regal status. In a more fine-grained explication, Katherine Duncan-Jones points out, 'her right toe point[s] to Ditchley Park, in Oxfordshire, the seat of her loyal Champion (and perhaps half-brother) Sir Henry Lee, while her heel rests on the adjacent county of Warwickshire. ... This posture symbolically declares her especially proud ownership of the English Midlands' (2001: 1).

Shakespeare's Jacobean plays demand a similar juxtaposition and coexistence of interpretative strategies, though the challenge is compounded by the dramatic coherence and a depth of characterization which is overwhelmingly rooted in a realistic depiction of personality. The characters are low mimetic, representations of ordinary people such as live in the everyday world, although the circumstances in which Shakespeare places them are often symbolic.

In *All's Well*, Shakespeare depicts with a considerable and realistic interiority two aspects of adolescent longing. On the one hand, we have the sexual desire of Helen for Bertram, the socially unapproachable son of her patroness; on the other, his youthful dreams of martial and masculine comradeship. But Helen's story assumes a folkloric quality as she stakes her life to regenerate an old and ailing king (and, by implication, an ailing state in a senescent world). Shakespeare marks the shift to a symbolic and indeed mystical mode by adding an almost incantatory quality to his dramatic verse:

> KING Art thou so confident? Within what space
>   Hop'st thou my cure?
> HELEN The great'st grace lending grace,
>   Ere twice the horses of the sun shall bring
>   Their fiery coacher his diurnal ring,
>   Ere twice in murk and occidental damp
>   Moist Hesperus hath quenched her sleepy lamp,
>   Of four-and-twenty times the pilot's glass
>   Hath told the thievish minutes how they pass,
>   What is infirm from your sound parts shall fly,
>   Health shall live free, and sickness freely die.
>   (II.ii.159–68; Shakespeare 1989: 863)

Note the rhythmic regularity, the endstopping of the lines and the insistent rhyming. This poetic idiom returns in the concluding scene where Helen's disclosure to the other characters of what the audience already knows, that she has engineered the consummation of her marriage to Bertram, liberates him from disgrace and punishment.

In between, however, the joint protagonists behave like real people trapped in a fairytale world. Once she has revived the king, Helen claims the wish he has granted her. There follows a highly symmetrical scene of a kind frequent in Jacobean Shakespeare (although he had developed it earlier in *The Merchant of Venice*). She considers and rejects four lords who would accept her before choosing Bertram, who rejects her partly on social grounds and partly because of his conflicting desire to join the wars. Both react as ordinary people in the real world would react. Helen, as if waking from a dream, is startled by the absurdity of the process. What, after all, has her curing the king to do with Bertram's choice of career or sexual partner? Thus, she comments: 'That you [the king] are well restored, my lord, I'm glad. Let the rest go.' Bertram feigns compliance while simply asserting:

'I cannot love her, nor will strive to do't' (II.iii.148–50, 146; Shakespeare 1989: 865). In so doing, he declines the role assigned him by the symbolic structure of the play.

He recovers it through Helen's next excursion into a non-mimetic mode, the so-called 'bed-trick', in which she substitutes herself for Diana, whom Bertram believes he has seduced. I suppose such events are possible in external reality in the dimly lit interiors of early modern England, though audiences and readers over recent centuries have found the ethical and aesthetic issues disconcerting. Bertram's sexual amorality is inconsistent with his heroic role. Why would Helen still want to marry such a scoundrel? But Bertram is tricked in turn and his rights are abused. If he behaved to a woman as Helen behaves to him, it would constitute sexual violation. Above all, there is a question of taste. Here are characters who show interior processes of longing, frustration, regret and ambition. Yet their stories intersect in a sexual act we are invited to imagine, an act so impersonal, so perfunctory, so devoid of affection that the male does not recognize the woman he is deflowering. Jacobean Shakespeare often poses his audience with such challenges to response and interpretation. In *All's Well*, the plot turns implausibly on a comedic device, the gift of a ring (as in two of the love stories in *The Merchant of Venice*). Bertram's conduct once more closely reflects ordinary human behaviour in embarrassing and disconcerting circumstances.

Even in the minor story line, the disgrace of Paroles, Shakespeare takes an ancient theatrical stock character, the *miles gloriosus* or braggart soldier, established in the western theatrical tradition at least since the time of Plautus. His showing up is again depicted in a highly symmetrical scene (IV.iii), in which, kidnapped and hooded, he methodically betrays and demeans his comrades, who stand around him. Despite the formal theatricality of the scene, he nevertheless responds with a realistic assessment of his loss of status, concluding in a powerfully resonant phrase: 'Simply the thing I am / Shall make me live' (ll.334–5; Shakespeare 1989: 877).

The 'France' of *All's Well* is a moral testing ground, strikingly ahistorical and atopical. It is obviously constructed to provide a platform for a challenging theatrical experiment, not a depiction of a real place at a specific time. So, too, is the Vienna of *Measure for Measure*, though this is a world not of senescence revived through the sexual vigour of youth, but of dysfunctional and pervasive sexuality and the corrupting power.

Uniquely within the Shakespeare oeuvre, the play develops from a biblical text: 'For with what iudgement ye iudge, ye shal be iudged, and with what measure ye mette, it shal be measured to you againe' (Matthew 7:2; see also Mark 4:42, Luke 6:38; Geneva Bible 1560 edition). As Isabella explains to Angelo, justice and mercy are at the heart of the doctrine of the atonement:

> Why, all the souls that were were forfeit once,
> And He that might the vantage best have took
> Found out the remedy. How would you be
> If He which is the top of judgement should
> But judge you as you are? O, think on that,
> And mercy then will breathe within your lips,
> Like man new made.
> (II.ii.75–81; Shakespeare 1989: 797–8)

Sinfulness is the common inheritance of humankind. The Duke, as he returns undisguised, enters into the seat of judgement in an *imitatio Christi*, anticipating Christ's role at Doomsday. The switch to a symbolic mode is signalled by blasts from trumpets and by the bewilderment of Escalus and Angelo at the extraordinary form the Duke has decreed for his entry (IV.iv). But the shift is sustained only briefly and the Duke soon seems less like a Christ-figure than a stage detective, disclosing a complex plot for the benefit of dim characters and the slower members of the audience.

That plot draws on challengingly disparate elements. At its centre lies another bed trick: the substitution of the presumably inert and silent body of Mariana for that of the novice nun whom Angelo desires. Once more, there are aesthetic and ethical problems. Again, the resolution hurtles towards the familiar Shakespearian closure of multiple marriages. But these are characters of a different kind from those that populate *As You Like It* or *Midsummer Night's Dream*. They have too much interiority for such a conclusion. We have seen too much of their anguish. Modern audiences or readers cannot feel comfortable with the Duke's sudden proposal of marriage to Isabella. We know too much about both of them to accept their incorporation into the dramatic symmetries of a well-worn comedic resolution.

Indeed, how much we know disconcerts us throughout. Angelo behaves disgracefully, yet he has an almost tragic potential. Isabella needs to be militantly celibate for the plot to work, but sexual repression emerges as a perverse masochism:

> were I under the terms of death,
> Th'impression of keen whips I'd wear as rubies,
> And strip myself to death as to a bed
> That longing have been sick for, ere I'd yield
> My body up to shame.
> (II.iv.100–4: Shakespeare 1989: 800)

Claudio is invited to play the heroic victim, but the role disintegrates into a vividly depicted terror that, transhistorically, seems frighteningly real:

> Ay, but to die, and go we know not where;
> To lie in cold obstruction, and to rot;
> This sensible warm motion to become
> A kneaded clod
> . . .
> The weariest and most loathed worldly life
> That age, ache, penury, and imprisonment
> Can lay on nature is a paradise
> To what we fear of death.
> ISABELLA Alas, alas!
> CLAUDIO Sweet sister, let me live.
> (III.i.118–21, 129–34; Shakespeare 1989: 802)

Nor does the Duke's disguised presence really underpin expectations of comedic resolution. This is no Oberon, dispatching Puck to control the lives of mortals, nor, to anticipate, a Prospero drawing on the supernatural capabilities of Ariel. The Duke's motivation originates in an admission of his fallibility as a ruler (I.iii) and his control of the plots slips when he underestimates Angelo's criminality. He is surprised when his deputy confirms the sentence on Claudio (IV. ii).

Measure for Measure redefined Shakespearian comedy for a new age. *Othello* marked a different kind of departure and played a part in establishing domestic tragedy as a major subgenre of early Stuart theatre. Uniquely in his tragic oeuvre, it deals with characters below regal status. Only here does Shakespeare locate his characters' motivation in sexual anxiety divorced from political aspirations.

He sets the scene with careful precision. Here indeed there is a strong sense of place. Venice has a mature political system, different from Jacobean England's, but at least as functional. The Duke and senators are depicted making a difficult choice between unattractive alternatives. Either they must support the claim of Brabanzio and thus lose Othello's participation in the intended defence of Cyprus, or they have to allow the marriage to be lawful. Mindful of what is most expedient for the state, they are easily persuaded and move on to the next business (I.iii). Urgency comes from a real and familiar historical process, the Ottomans' persistent threats to Venetian control of Cyprus. The island fell finally in 1571, though *Othello* depicts an earlier and abortive assault. The Venetian Duke and senators talk of a Turkish feint towards Rhodes, which fell in 1526. But the Ottoman threat to Christendom was well known and carefully followed in England. In the 1600s, the thrust had switched to the Slavic underbelly of Europe, while the remaining possessions in Venice's eastern empire remained in danger.

The plot incorporates two stock narratives. Desdemona's story is premised on the motif of defying an interdictive father and eloping with a lover, familiar from several of Shakespeare's comedies of the 1590s and one to which he turns again in *Cymbeline*. Here, of course, the outcome proves tragic for both father and daughter. Again, the interpretation of events which Iago persuades Othello to adopt, as Catherine Bates observes, resembles 'a hackneyed city play whose plot is just waiting to happen: "the knave [Cassio] is handsome, young, and hath all those requisites in him that folly and green minds look after. A pestilent complete knave; and the woman hath found him already"' (Bates 2002: 190–1, quoting Iago). But this is also the basis of a traditional and much older storyline, available to Shakespeare from Chaucer, among others, for example in *The Merchant's Tale* or *The Franklin's Tale*. A tragic, not comic, outcome ensues.

Sexual anxiety drives the motivation. Iago appears fascinated and awed by the Moor's alleged potency. He is 'an old black ram' and 'a Barbary horse' (I.i.88, 113; Shakespeare 1989: 821, 822). Iago also dreads that Othello has cuckolded him or at least that his reputation has been damaged by such a rumour (II.i). Othello's anxiety is in part generational. Passing comments disclose a concern that he is significantly older than his wife. But the most powerful factor is his sense that he is an outsider to Venetian society.

The issue crystallizes around the plot detail of Desdemona's handkerchief, which is planted in Cassio's lodging. For Iago, it functions much as any spuriously introduced evidence would in a low mimetic account: 'Trifles light as air / Are to the jealous confirmations strong / As proofs of holy writ' (III.iii.326–8; Shakespeare 1989: 837). Certainly for Othello the 'trifle' works as it was intended. But he slips into a different mode, in effect into a different symbolic universe, in the process:

> OTHELLO ... That handkerchief
>   Did an Egyptian to my mother give.
>   She was a charmer, and could almost read
>   The thoughts of people. She told her, while she kept it
>   'Twould make her amiable, and subdue my father
>   Entirely to her love; but if she lost it,
>   Or made a gift of it, my father's eye
>   Should hold her loathed, and his spirits should hunt
>   After new fancies. She, dying, gave it me,
>   And bid me, when my fate would have me wived,
>   To give it her. I did so, and take heed on't.
>   Make it a darling, like your precious eye.
>   To lose't or give't away were such perdition
>   As nothing else could match.
> DESDEMONA Is't possible?
> OTHELLO 'Tis true. There's magic in the web of it.
>   A sybil that had numbered in the world
>   The sun to course two hundred compasses
>   In her prophetic fury sewed the work.
>   The worms were hallowed that did breed the silk,
>   And it was dyed in mummy, which the skilful
>   Conserved of maidens' hearts.
>   (III.iv.55–74: Shakespeare 1989: 839–40)

Desdemona, obliged to find a magical hankie, responds with a rational incredulity: 'I'faith, is't true?' (line 75). But Othello's attribution of a different kind of signified to the trivial and arbitrary signifier – Iago evidently was unconcerned what piece of evidence he fabricated – defines his cultural difference. Here is a way of perceiving that is mystical and spiritual. It contrasts sharply with the fierce and material rationalism, established by the Venetian senators' dismissal of Brabanzio's suit, and manifest again in Desdemona's bewilderment.

Iago has already persuaded Othello of what is plainly the case, that he knows little of the Venetian world. Specifically, he affirms that 'In Venice they [married women] do let God see the pranks / They dare not show their husbands' (III.iii.206–7; Shakespeare 1989: 836). However inapplicable to the case of Desdemona, this is a generalization about the lax morals of Venice to which many of Shakespeare's contemporaries would probably have subscribed.

The nightmare of the closing scenes ends with the intervention of Lodovico and Graziano, whose exchanges with Othello again both point up cultural difference and indeed modal distinctions. The Venetians ask questions, form judgements and make decisions. Othello occupies instead a universe of demons, of heroic recollection and of an honour code that has served him badly.

Othello remained Shakespeare's most intimate and domestic tragedy, his most detailed exploration of sexuality and its discontents, and his most continuous in its naturalistic realism. It contrasts sharply with *Timon of Athens*, where motivation is generally depicted in starkly simple terms and where the sense of place and period is very tentatively established. This play is set in Athens, but it is Athens in name only. Its iconic buildings and institutions are scarcely alluded to. The historical figure of the politician and general Alcibiades (*c*.450–404 BC) troops across the stage and fragments of his remarkable career are woven into the plot. His treatment by an ungrateful state parallels Timon's experience, though his martial response provides a contrast to Timon's retreat into the wilderness. But this, emphatically, is Timon's play, and he is based on a semi-mythical figure found in an anecdote in Plutarch's life of Mark Antony. The play has a highly schematic structure. The first half shows Timon in a giving mood; the second matches this with his misanthropism after his financial ruin and the desertion of his friends.

For a long time, the critical and editorial tradition was uncertain how to treat the play. Variously, it has been seen as an incomplete work, a work printed from an early draft and a work of collaboration. A consensus has now emerged that Shakespeare wrote the play with the young Thomas Middleton. (The issues are valuably considered in Vickers 2002: ch. 4.) We should beware of the implicit devaluation of a play as a work of collaboration, as though it were a great pity that Shakespeare, for whatever reason, didn't write it all himself. Collaborative working had a very significant place in late Tudor and early Stuart theatre and, in the rather special form of revisions and reworkings of earlier plays, it contributed vitally to the repertoire of the Restoration stage. Without Middleton, the play would not exist, and his engagement with the senior dramatist has produced a work of distinction within Shakespeare's oeuvre (and Middleton's).

It fuses a starkness of structure and characterization with vivid
diatribes that anticipate the idiom of *King Lear*. Unusually among
Shakespeare's plays, most of the characters have no name and are
simply designated by their roles – 'first Lord', 'Poet', 'Painter', and
so on. Even the Steward, perhaps the only straightforwardly decent
character in the play, and a figure who rises to choric status, has no
name. Yet out of this undetailed background emerge passages of
astonishing power, like Timon's speech to Alcibiades and the camp-
followers who accompany him:

> I know thee too, and more than that I know thee
> I desire not to know. Follow thy drum.
> With man's blood paint the ground gules, gules.
> Religious canons, civil laws, are cruel;
> Then what should war be? This fell whore of thine
> Hath in her more destruction than thy sword,
> For all her cherubin look.
>   (IV.iii.57–63; Shakespeare 1989: 899)

The systematic social satire that is central to the conception of the play
thus supports passages of disconcerting vividness in the mature Shakespearian fashion.

The play probably seems simpler to modern audiences than it would
have done to Shakespeare's contemporaries. Timon appears to respond
understandably to the ingratitude of those he has formerly befriended.
But, seen in a Jacobean context, his behaviour is less straightforward.
In elite social circles and among those who looked to such echelons for
advancement, giving was regulated by the conventions of patronage
(see above, chapter 1). The client gave services, presents, loyalty and
support; the patron gave the client his patronage, in the form of
protection or perhaps an office or living that was 'in his gift'. The
system made for a kind of reciprocity and was for the most part
sustainable. What Timon does is outside the structure of reciprocity
and is not sustainable. As the Steward realizes all along, he is depleting
his estate, his patrimony, to give presents to friends who recognize no
social obligation to reciprocate. In so doing, he violates another social
taboo, the responsibility of an heir to maintain and pass on the estate
he has inherited. When a critical point is reached, Timon's actions are
judged rather differently. His ruling-class status, while it lasts, exempts
him from financial scrutiny. Once his credit worthiness wobbles,

however, he is evaluated against the criteria by which the mercantile classes were judged – whether he can meet debts – and the catastrophe then comes quickly. (On the ethics of credit in early modern England, see Sullivan 2002: chs 1–4.)

King Lear sits curiously among the mature tragedies, in that its plot mechanisms include elements more customary in drama with a comedic resolution. Disguise plays an important part. Lear's faithful companion, the Earl of Kent, dismissed for opposing his bizarre behaviour in the opening scene, returns to his service as a much humbler retainer, unrecognized by Lear. As if anxious about plausibility, Shakespeare gives him a short soliloquy explaining how he is borrowing 'other accents . . . / That can my speech diffuse' (I.iv.1–2; Shakespeare 1989: 949). When Gloucester's spurned son, Edgar, assumes the role of Poor Tom, a Bedlam beggar, Shakespeare again offers a soliloquy which describes in some detail the method and rationale for his disguise.

The play opens with a fairytale ritual marked by the kinds of symmetry we have noted elsewhere in Jacobean Shakespeare. Its vehicle is a symbolic action. Using a map of his kingdom, Lear divides his lands among his daughters and their partners. The scene, in Jacobean terms, is deeply shocking. Lear is what James aspired to be, King of Britain (rather than King of England and King of Scotland, which was James's actual constitutional position). In the late twentieth century the United Kingdom moved with little difficulty to substantial levels of devolution for Wales and Scotland. But integrity of the realm was a high priority for early modern monarchs and especially for the early Stuarts. When Charles I commissioned Rubens to decorate the Banqueting House at Whitehall, the wholly misleading celebration of the union of England and Scotland was given prominence. We may recall Elizabeth's Ditchley portrait, considered above. Yet Lear, far from controlling his realm and protecting its integrity, tears up the political map and thus abdicates, not merely from power, but from the responsibilities that power brings.

Cordelia, rather like Bertram, declines to participate in the fairytale Lear would construct. Here the gift of territory rewards protestations of filial love: 'Unhappy that I am, I cannot heave / My heart into my mouth' (I.i.91–2; Shakespeare 1989: 945). Her insistence on responding in a way that suggests an emotional interiority inappropriate to a non-naturalistic mode diverts the narrative into a tragic trajectory, though the role of her 'wicked sisters' suggests vestigial elements from a folktale.

Shakespeare shows his audience a great deal of the inner workings of the innocent victims in the play, from Cordelia's asides in the opening scenes, through Gloucester's agony on what he mistakes for the cliffs of Dover, to Lear's lamentation over the corpse of Cordelia. Audiences care about what happens to them, and Shakespeare tests their response to an unprecedented – and perhaps unrepeated – degree. Of course, in *Titus Andronicus* we see Lavinia with 'her hands cut off and her tongue cut out, and ravished', while Chiron and Demetrius make a final appearance 'baked in this pie, / Whereof their mother directly hath fed' (II.iv. s.d.; V.iii.59–60; Shakespeare 1989: 136, 150). But that play, with its breathless sensationalism and glittering exuberance, cannot be mistaken for a mimesis of life as we know it. In *Lear*, characters of a palpable decency with a plausible interiority are pushed into comparable horrors. Gloucester's blinding is unflinchingly portrayed: 'Out, vile jelly!' (III.vii.81; Shakespeare 1989: 963). His absurd attempt at suicide makes even greater demands: 'Is wretchedness deprived that benefit / To end itself by death?' (IV.iv.61–2; Shakespeare 1989: 966).

Indeed, we have some good evidence that at least in the later seventeenth century audiences found the final tragedy, Lear's death while grieving over the corpse of Cordelia, unbearable. When Nahum Tate reworked the play in 1681 he changed the end. His Lear retires with Kent to some happy monastic cell to contemplate the golden realm under the rule of Edgar and Cordelia. As Dr Johnson noted, audiences preferred that resolution: 'In the present case the publick has decided' (Clark 1997: 371–2, lxv; see below, chapter 6). Jacobean Shakespeare made sterner demands of his audience.

Macbeth offers a more comforting resolution. Macbeth and his wife have an obvious culpability and their end is represented by the new King of Scotland in simple terms: they are 'this dead butcher and his fiend-like queen' (V.xi.35; Shakespeare 1989: 999), a tenable if incomplete summary. Certainly, the innocent suffer in the course of the play, but they are minor characters: Banquo (albeit the progenitor of the Stuart dynasty), Macduff's family and the vague, passive figure of Duncan. The deaths of Macbeth and Lady Macbeth both come as a kind of relief, from their own evident turmoil, to which we are intimately privy, and from the malaise that blights Scotland. At the end, the realm, now governed legitimately by Duncan's son and nominated heir, seems unequivocally secure in a way that Britain at the end of *King Lear* does not. Macduff leads all those still standing in a unanimous cry of 'Hail, King of Scotland' (V.xi.24–5; Shakespeare 1989: 999).

Unlike Ben Jonson, Shakespeare contributed nothing to the celebration of James's accession to the English throne. *Macbeth* makes amends for the omission. It is premised on a credulity about witchcraft, a crime which James was known to find particularly fascinating. He had published his own treatise, *Daemonologie*, in 1587, and his Scottish reign was marked by an evident enthusiasm for witch-hunting. The coup that overthrows Macbeth endorses James's unrealized vision of the union of England and Scotland, in that it shows the legitimate governments of both working harmoniously to achieve moral and political success. Moreover, *Macbeth* explicitly celebrates James's lineage in Act IV, scene 1 (Shakespeare 1989: 975), where a series of apparitions conclude in 'a show of eight kings', presided over by Banquo: 'eight Stuart kings were said to have preceded James'. The theme may seem to a modern reader somewhat marginal. However, in the early modern theatre it could have been performed as a stately and even splendid pageant. It marks a shift towards a symbolic mode and incorporates in its silent grandeur a kind of staging more appropriate to court masque. It constitutes in some ways the real climax of the play as Macbeth recognizes in it the termination of his own dynastic ambitions: 'Let this pernicious hour / Stand aye accursed in the calendar' (IV.i.149–50; Shakespeare 1989: 992). History, destiny and stagecraft are nudging Macbeth aside.

Yet Jacobean Shakespeare is never so straightforward. Against the grand narrative of Stuart achievement, he pitches an extraordinary exploration of abnormal psychopathology. The guilt-ridden Lady Macbeth, delusionally and obsessionally washing Duncan's blood from her hands, has even given her name to a modern clinical syndrome. For Hamlet, the status of his father's ghost is problematic: is he an authentic revenant or a demonic imposter? In the case of Macbeth, paranormal manifestations are much more like delusions externalizing his inner turmoil. Before he kills Duncan, he sees and clutches at 'a dagger of the mind', 'a false creation / Proceeding from the heat-oppressed brain' (II.i.38–9; Shakespeare 1989: 982). Shakespeare carefully establishes that, when the dead Banquo turns up at the banquet, only Macbeth can see him (III.iv).

In the characterization of Macbeth, Shakespeare achieves the kind of interiority established in the role of Hamlet, though more succinctly. Once more, he models the 'phantasma or a hideous dream' that precedes action. Thus, Macbeth vividly rehearses the cogent arguments against killing Duncan: 'He's here in double trust'; 'his virtues / Will plead like angels . . . against / The deep damnation of his taking-off'; 'If we should fail?' (I.vii.12, 18–20, 58; Shakespeare 1989: 981). Yet still he does it.

The world of *Macbeth* roughly resembles that of *King Lear*, a rather indeterminate period of British history in a landscape of almost unrelieved gloom. Scenes on bleak moors blasted by foul weather alternate with gory events acted out in grim castles. Only the hapless Duncan mistakes Macbeth's stronghold for a pleasant place (I.vi). The plot jumbles the chronicle narrative of two quite separate Scottish reigns into a generalized depiction of an early medieval dark age. In *Antony and Cleopatra*, Shakespeare ends his play at a precise and crucial point in western history, the establishment of the Roman empire under Octavius Caesar, the future Augustus. Shakespeare syncopates events, but their epochal significance is not compromised. However, he represents more than just the closing years of republican Rome. Rather, he produces a studied contrast between two discrete societies at this time of crisis and transformation. Thus, he depicts the austere world of Roman realpolitik and the sensual incompetence of late Ptolemaic Egypt. In doing this, he makes great technical demands of its performers and directors, requiring more than 40 scene changes and frequent doubling of parts.

The play shows Antony's vacillation between the two worlds, before he opts, disastrously, for Egypt. Shakespeare represents this as a choice between a harsh realism and irrational emotion, culminating at Actium, where he quits the battle to follow the fleeing Cleopatra. Yet, ingeniously, a second set of binary opposites shapes the drama. Throughout, a contrast is established between the images of Antony and Cleopatra believed in and expressed by themselves and their supporters and their often disgraceful behaviour, their duplicity, their cowardice and their disloyalty. It is as though there are Platonic ideals of the protagonists, whose presence and conduct in the world contrast with their essential selves.

Thus Antony is described in the opening lines of the play as one whose 'good eyes / . . . o'er the files and musters of the war / Have glowed like plated Mars' (I.i.2–4; Shakespeare 1989: 1003), though clearly he falls off from that Roman ideal. His subsequent conduct opens further the distance between repute and reality. His rehabilitation begins dubiously, with a bungled suicide attempt which recalls the theatrical embarrassment of Gloucester's. 'I will be / A bridegroom in my death' is followed by the bewildered 'How, not dead? Not dead?' (IV.xv.99–100, 103; Shakespeare 1989: 1029). Yet the poignancy of his death effects a transformation approaching apotheosis. In Cleopatra's recollection, 'His legs bestrid the ocean; his reared arm / Crested the world' (V.ii.81–2; Shakespeare 1989: 1032).

Cleopatra manifests a similar distinction between how she is spoken of and how she behaves. The semi-choric figure, Enobarbus, in one of the great anthology pieces of Shakespearian dramatic verse, lengthily celebrates her playful sensuality and 'infinite variety' (II.v). Yet her cowardice causes the catastrophe at the battle of Actium and thereafter – even in her death scene – Shakespeare shows her in negotiation with Caesar. But her own suicide unites the mortal Cleopatra with the essential Cleopatra established in the consciousness of her admirers:

> Give me my robe. Put on my crown. I have
> Immortal longings in me. Now no more
> The juice of Egypt's grape shall moist this lip.
> (V.ii.275–7; Shakespeare 1989: 1034)

In terms of the dramatic conventions relating to characterization, Shakespeare is attempting a very bold experiment, juxtaposing the depiction of conduct and the commentary of others on the legendary status of his joint protagonists. He places in jeopardy that most uncontroversial of dramatic unities, the requirement that the characters of tragedy 'should be consistent' (Aristotle et al. 1965: 51), although in the conclusion essence and existence triumphantly merge.

Pericles resembles *Timon of Athens* in that a consensus has emerged that it is a work of collaboration, though dissenting voices remain. (For a review of the issues, see Vickers 2002; the editors of Shakespeare 1998 argue strongly for Shakespeare's single authorship.) The likeliest collaborator is George Wilkins, 'a hack-writer of small account, whose work and career are rendered of interest by professional association with greater writers of the day' (*DNB*: 1975). He worked on other projects for the King's Men in the early Jacobean period. There are other similarities with *Timon*. The cast list is long – at least 48 characters, which must have tested the King's Men's skills at doubling and trebling up. But once more, many are undeveloped and anonymous roles played out in scenes of marked dramatic symmetry. Even among named characters, motivation is little explored. Antiochus simply is cruel, libidinous, incestuous and corrupt. Thaliart simply is a villain. Cleon simply is weak and incompetent. Dioniza simply is cruel and vindictive.

Nor is motivation explored more deeply in the good characters. Helicanus of Tyre replicates the honest loyalty of Timon's Steward. Marina has an aura of inviolable chastity that can discourage successive whoremongers from deflowering her. As the Bawd observes, 'she is able to freeze the god Priapus and undo the whole of generation' (sc. 18, ll.11–12; Shakespeare 1989: 1058). Pericles himself merely responds honourably and practically to the contrasting circumstances in which his largely random peregrinations place him. Unusually for a play from Shakespeare's hand, several pivotal scenes are depicted in dumbshow. In these we do not hear what the characters say, let alone overhear in soliloquy their verbalized thoughts. The issue of shallow characterization is most acute in the case of Lysimachus. The audience is required to accept his transformation from a corrupt statesman, who frequents brothels on the look out for sex slaves to deflower, into a fit husband for Marina.

Technically, however, the play takes on a number of challenges. This is highly polyphonic storytelling, as Thaisa, Marina and Pericles are separated to experience their disparate adventures across the eastern Mediterranean. What ties the stories together is the choric figure of the fourteenth-century poet John Gower, from whose *Confessio Amantis* the tale in part derives. In a fascinating experiment, Gower speaks in a poetic idiom generally alien to Jacobean theatre. Several of his speeches are in the eight-syllabled couplets used in the *Confessio Amantis*. Moreover, his idiolect is marked by archaisms, as in 'Now sleep y-slacked hath the rout' (sc. 10, l.1; Shakespeare 1989: 1051), as though further to distance the world of the play from Jacobean England. External reality as the audience knows it is scarcely engaged. This is a fantastic tale set in fantastic lands, mediated through an ancient and remote narrator.

Coriolanus constitutes Shakespeare's most detailed representation of class struggle. Like *Julius Caesar* or *Antony and Cleopatra* it depicts an epochal shift in Roman history, though from an earlier period. Early in the fifth century BC Roman government developed from an aristocratic oligarchy to a more complex constitution in which the plebeians had their spokesmen.

Coriolanus champions the extreme wing of the patricians, a position on the edge of extinction. The plebeians are no more sympathetically represented than in *Julius Caesar*. Yet Coriolanus's abrasive dismissal of them appears impolitic and counter-productive, as wiser figures among the patricians appreciate. Early in the play, Shakespeare establishes Menenius as representative of what may be misperceived as a rational middle way between unruly proletarians and uncompromising aristocrats. He is certainly rational, but 'middle way' scarcely describes his political philosophy, which is wholly patrician in its assumptions. He offers a lengthy parable of the belly (the senators) and the limbs (the proletariat), a lucid image of a Rome where classes are mutually dependent.

Coriolanus's tragedy is that of a primitive warrior incompetent in a politically complex and dynamic state. Menenius maintains a dialogue with the proletarians' tribunes; Coriolanus cannot. For all his talk of honour, he behaves disgracefully. He commits what is, unequivocally, treason against the Roman republic. Then he betrays the martial *Brüderschaft* he establishes with Aufidius. At no point does he seem aware of his own limitations and culpability. His volte-face outside Rome, prompted by his mother's pleading, contains no word of apology or self-reproach. His is a kind of monolithic simplicity, a terminal naivety in a politic world. He discloses no partially hidden interiority because nothing intervenes between his emotions and the articulation of those emotions. Once more, Shakespeare is experimenting with characterization. Here we have a hero who is palpably simpler and dimmer than both the audience and the other characters with whom he is juxtaposed.

The Winter's Tale, like *Measure for Measure*, depicts the kinds of passionate interiority more characteristic of Shakespeare's Jacobean tragedies. Leontes' pathological jealousy, more sudden and even more puzzling than Othello's, has the destructive potential of Angelo's lust. In terms of the Shakespeare oeuvre, the play looks backwards thematically, while technically it innovates, anticipating features more fully realised in *Cymbeline* and *The Tempest*. Its larger symbolic structure shows the reanimation of an aging and repressive court by a pastoral sojourn in a landscape peopled by young lovers. Analogies with *As You Like It* and *A Midsummer Night's Dream* are obvious. The theme appears again as a minor motif in *Cymbeline*, where the problems engendered in the court scenes are resolved in the healing wilderness of wild Wales. It shapes more fully the process of reconciliation in *The Tempest*.

Technically, the play is challenging. The 16-year gap between the winter world of acts one, two and three and the springtime of acts four and five is actually helpful to modern productions, the perfect place for an interval. But there is nothing to suggest that theatrical custom in Shakespeare's age allowed for a protracted intermission, although musical interludes were sometimes introduced. Indeed, Shakespeare feels constrained to introduce 'Time, a Chorus' (IV.i), to soften the surprise and ease comprehension: 'I turn my glass, and give my scene such growing / As you had slept between' (ll.16–17; Shakespeare 1989: 1116). The usual continuities of Jacobean drama, where scene follows scene with an assumption of causality and close sequence, are violently fractured.

As in *All's Well* and *Measure for Measure*, a modal shift ushers in the resolution, though here the movement to a mythic and symbolic mode is spectacular. Hermione, who seemingly died 16 years earlier, reappears as a statue, lifelike but showing the aging process. As music plays, it comes to life. Paulina, widow of the courtier Antigonus, evidently organizes events, though she and Shakespeare are evasive about quite how the apparent miracle has been effected: 'you'll think – / Which I protest against – I am assisted by wicked powers' (V.iii.89–91; Shakespeare 1989: 1130). But Shakespeare leaves a bitter-sweet edge to the story. The lost years cannot be recovered. Antigonus, mauled by a bear while leaving Perdita in Bohemia, cannot be revived. Florizel's arrival reminds Leontes of his own dead son, Mamillius. Reconciliation may be the dominant note of the closing scene, but the wastefulness of pathologically misdirected emotion is scarcely mitigated.

Cymbeline shares with *Lear* a vaguer kind of historicity. Shakespeare draws on the legendary early history of Britain. In that it celebrates the *British* achievement of independence from Roman dominion, it is both patriotic and an endorsement of James's British aspiration. Yet Cymbeline, the king of Britain, is not represented wholly sympathetically. He emerges as an overbearing father with poor judgement in the people he favours. Indeed, there are possibilities for reading this character as a critique of James's own performance. Yet the play antedates the Overbury scandal, and the most nearly contemporary royal marriage was that of his daughter to the apparently unexceptional Elector Palatine, early in 1613. The concluding scene has a 'Soothsayer' celebrate the universal peace that has been established, in a ringing endorsement that echoes that of court entertainments, where figures of authority yet again praise James as a peacemaker. For example, the Soothsayer's praise of 'the radiant Cymbeline, / Which shines here in the west' (V.vi.476–7; Shakespeare 1989: 1165) chimes with Merlin's reconciliation of Prince Henry's youthful bellicosity to James's irenic wisdom at the end of *Prince Henry's Barriers* (1610), written by Ben Jonson:

> Nay, stay your valour; 'tis a wisdom high
> In princes to use fortune reverently.
> He that in deeds of arms obeys his blood
> Doth often tempt his destiny beyond good.
> Look on this throne, and in his temper view
> The light of all that must have grace in you:
> His equal justice, upright fortitude
> And settled prudence, with that peace endued
> Of face, as mind, always himself and even.
> (ll.396–404; Orgel and Strong 1973: 163; see above)

War has its place in the history of nations, but peace is the good for which wise monarchs strive. Shakespeare endorses in the figure of Cymbeline James's values and hopes while – unlike the masque-writer – accepting that kings, too, may err.

As in *Lear*, a folkloric element initiates much of the plot. The lover's reckless boast of his mistress's fidelity has a long pedigree in western narrative, in which a tale from Boccacccio's *Decamaron* is key. This plot element culminates in probably the most erotically charged scene in Shakespeare as the Italian Giacomo emerges from concealment to view the naked Innogen, asleep in her bed. (This account, following Shakespeare 1989, uses the form 'Innogen'; 'Imogen' is found only in the Folio edition, where it 'appears to be a misprint' – Shakespeare 1989: 1131.) In a 40-line soliloquy, Giacomo recalls Lucrece, the victim of an earlier analogue to Posthumus's boast: 'Our Tarquin thus / Did softly press the rushes ere he wakened / The chastity he wounded' (II.ii.12–14; Shakespeare 1989: 1140). Innogen herself had been reading the tale of Philomela, a mythological rape victim whose fate closely parallels Lavinia's in *Titus Andronicus*. Giacomo listens to her breathing, he smells her, he slips off her bracelet as a trophy, he bares and scrutinizes her body, fixing his gaze on 'On her left breast / A mole, cinque-spotted, like the crimson drops / I'th' bottom of cowslip' (ll. 37–9).

'*Our* Tarquin': presumably he says this because, Tarquin, like himself, was Italian. Yet the scene plays disturbingly with the sensibilities of the audience, for Giacomo is *our* surrogate. In a way he responds for us, reporting his sensations and reflections – the rapist's stealth, what he hears, smells and sees. Somewhat uncomfortably, we experience the victim through his agency. We are voyeurs, watching an act of voyeurism.

Elsewhere, in its juxtaposition of horror, pathos and absurdity, the play poses challenges to its audience's reception that are analogous to those in *Lear*. Consider the funeral rites for Cloten and Innogen (IV.ii), the one a would-be rapist, the other his intended victim. Over their bodies, Guiderius and Arviragus sing 'perhaps the most exquisite lyric in the language ... , whose serene beauty has brought consolation to many a real-life funeral' (Shakespeare 1997: 1):

> Fear no more the heat o'th' sun,
>   Nor the furious winter's rages.
> Thou thy wordly task hast done,
>   Home art gone and ta'en thy wages.
> Golden lads and girls all must,
> As chimney-sweepers, come to dust.
> (IV.ii.259–64; Shakespeare 1989: 1154)

Even for readers, the effect is stunning; as a theatrical moment, amid the chaos that surrounds the characters of the play, it is extraordinary. It challenges any easy moralizing. One of the singers has murdered Cloten, who deserved his fate, as he plotted murder and rape. Yet Cloten finds his place alongside an intended victim, both seemingly reconciled by that great leveller, death. But Innogen is not dead. She revives to embrace the headless corpse, believing it to be her husband's, smearing her face with his blood after a poignant and intimate soliloquy: 'I know the shape of 's leg; this is his hand ... ' (IV.ii.311; p. 1155). But we know, though her grief is in earnest, she is mistaken. She bathes in the blood of a man who would have raped her, rendering grotesque a moment of unbearable tenderness. As Roger Warren observes, the scene, 'combining the extremes of lyrical beauty and psychological and physical horror, presents the technique of the play in its most dramatic form' (Shakespeare 1997: 1).

Cymbeline is a spectacular play. Like *The Winter's Tale*, it has an extraordinary *coup de théâtre*, as 'Jupiter descends in thunder and lightning, sitting upon an eagle. He throws a thunderbolt' (V.v. s.d.; Shakespeare 1989: 1159). His appearance ends a ritualized dream sequence and anticipates the scene of reconciliation, with which the play ends. Its masque-like quality has often been remarked on and is sometimes associated with the King's Men's earliest years in their second venue, the indoor Blackfriars theatre. Yet the play in repertory probably appeared also at the Globe and was certainly performed at court. Warren notes that, contemporaneously, a *deus ex machina* device was used at the outdoor Red Bull theatre.

The Tempest was almost certainly the last play Shakespeare wrote unaided. Thematically, it draws on the concerns present elsewhere in his Jacobean comedies – a general celebration of reconciliation and forgiveness, together with the mythical power of youth, sexual love and a pastoral setting to revive a senescent and corrupt society. But he adds a pervasive tone of valediction. Prospero abjures his extraordinary powers, through which 'graves . . . / Have waked their sleepers, oped, and let 'em forth' (V.i.48–9). Shakespeare, too, has raised the dead in the form of the English kings and Roman statesmen he has animated to strut his stage. The critical tradition has long been drawn to the equation of Prospero and Shakespeare. The actor playing Prospero, in the kind of epilogue Shakespeare wrote only infrequently, appears to crave release: 'As you from crimes would pardoned be, / Let your indulgence set me free' (Epilogue, 19–20; Shakespeare 1989: 1189). Yet this is no mere retirement speech. Shakespeare has had Prospero set his exit in a context of universal mutability:

> Our revels now are ended. These our actors,
> As I foretold you, were all spirits, and
> Are melted into air, into thin air;
> And like the baseless fabric of this vision,
> The cloud-capped towers, the gorgeous palaces,
> The solemn temples, the great globe itself,
> Yea, all which it inherit, shall dissolve;
> And, like this insubstantial pageant faded,
> Leave not a rack behind. We are such stuff
> As dreams are made on, and our little life
> Is rounded with a sleep.
>   (IV.i.148–58; Shakespeare 1989: 1184)

Inevitably, 'the globe' seems an allusion to the King's Men's theatre, the venue where at least sometimes *The Tempest* would have played.

Jacobean Shakespeare plainly felt uneasy with doing over what he had achieved before, and *The Tempest* marks some of his boldest theatrical experiments. If *The Winter's Tale* had challenged notions of dramatic unity with its binary structure and *Antony and Cleopatra* with its frantic multiplicity of scenes and locations, *The Tempest* takes on the challenge of the classical unities, depicting the events of just a few hours in a single location. He meets with consummate mastery the technical problem of nesting a complex back story in the developing dramatic exposition. The obsession with the passing of time, most strongly expressed in Ariel's frequent reminders that soon he, too, will be released, lends an urgency to the imminent closure.

Masque-like elements appeared in the living statuary of *The Winter's Tale* and the *deus ex machina* in *Cymbeline*. *The Tempest* contains a fully realized hymeneal masque (IV.i), evidently using stage machinery and culminating in 'a graceful dance' (s.d.; Shakespeare 1989: 1184). Ariel and other spirits fly and the opening storm scene requires elaborate stage effects. Thus this is the most spectacular of his plays.

But Shakespeare did not retire. The oeuvre concludes with two works of collaboration with John Fletcher: *All is True* (or *Henry VIII*, as the First Folio terms it) and *The Two Noble Kinsmen*. Neither stands comparison with the Jacobean plays Shakespeare wrote alone, and, compared with *Pericles* and *Timon*, they seem curiously backward-looking.

All is True completes the great arc of English political history which Shakespeare had dramatized for the Elizabethan stage, bringing events up to the eve of the English reformation, celebrating the birth of the future Elizabeth I and anticipating the happy reign of James I. Cranmer prophesies:

> Peace, plenty, love, truth, terror,
> That were the servants to this chosen infant,
> Shall then be his, and, like a vine, grow to him.
> Wherever the bright sun of heaven shall shine,
> His honour and the greatness of his name
> Shall be, and make new nations.
> (V.iv.47–52; Shakespeare 1989: 1223)

The speech constitutes the most explicitly royal panegyric in the Shakespearean oeuvre. How curious that it should have appeared so long after the accession and so late into his own career.

The dramatic exposition is reminiscent, perhaps, of that in *Richard III*. Political action is part of a world of intrigue in which powerful figures pursue, often ineptly, their own ends, in scenes of dramatic irony, where the audience and some of the characters know what is really happening, but the doomed do not. But in common with his other late plays, this too is spectacular, with a dream vision, court masque and ceremonial, and, at one point, the discharge of a cannon. This, in June 1613, signalled the end of the greatest phase of English drama: it caused the thatched roof of the Globe to catch fire, and the whole structure rapidly burned. The King's Men still had their Black-friars venue, and the Globe was soon rebuilt, but Shakespeare was no longer a shareholder (Duncan-Jones 2001: 254).

The Two Noble Kinsmen shares some of its characters with *A Midsummer Night's Dream*. The setting again is the realm of Theseus and Hippolyta, though here the play adheres more closely to its source in Chaucer's *Knight's Tale*. It even has an inset entertainment by comic proletarians, roughly equivalent to Bottom's amateur dramatics, in the form of a morris dance of countrymen and women under the direction of a comic schoolmaster (III.v). The play is organized around a simple opposition of two rival lovers, with little to distinguish them and not much by way of psychological interiority. Nevertheless, the play has a final experimental component: one of the youthful heroes actually dies: not a false death like Hermione or Innogen, but a final expiration on stage. A bland epilogue follows, though with a perfect curtain line for the most remarkable writing career in the English literary tradition: 'Gentlemen, good night' (l.18; Shakespeare 1989: 1256).

Other Drama

John Marston's early contribution to the Elizabethan and Jacobean stage was primarily for the children's companies. He had been educated in the Middle Temple and 'resided there, off and on . . . throughout his dramatic career' (Marston 1999: xix), and he brings to his plays the kinds of youthful cynicism associated with that milieu. His best-known play, *The Malcontent*, reflects and confirms a significant development in the characteristic repertoire of the King's Men, manifest both in the Jacobean plays of Shakespeare and in the increasingly prominent role of Ben Jonson as a writer for that company.

As is often the case in the history of the early modern stage, much of the detail has not been recovered. However, *The Malcontent* evidently began in performance at the Blackfriars Theatre, home of the Children of the Chapel Royal, who became after 1604 the Children of the Queen's Revels (see above). Its premiere was probably no earlier than 1602, though 1603 or 1604 are likelier dates. Shortly afterwards it was acquired by the King's Men, perhaps through theft, perhaps through purchase, and performed with a new and ingenious induction, which acknowledges that the play had its origins elsewhere and pre-emptively makes light of it. An actor in the role of a theatre-goer addresses members of the cast, appearing as themselves, about the reasons for the transfer. Henry Condell, actor, shareholder and future editor of Shakespeare's First Folio (see below, chapter 3), responds: 'the [prompt-] book was lost; and because 'twas pity so good a play should be lost, we found it, and play it' ('Induction', ll.74–5; Marston 1999: 13). Whatever the events that prompted the transfer, the King's Men now had something of a keynote drama.

Marston, much as Shakespeare does in his Jacobean plays, situates his actions in a foreign location so remote from England and from actuality as to be almost hypothetical. Here, we have the depiction of three dukes of Genoa, though, as his epistle acknowledges, Genoa had no duke, and the family names he attributes to them belong to the ruling elites of other Italian city-states. His rejoinder claims: 'it was my care to write so far from reasonable offence that even strangers in whose state I laid my scene should not from thence draw any disgrace to any, dead or living' ('To the Reader', ll.9–12; p. 4).

The plot has often been compared with that of *Measure for Measure*, in that a duke, Altofronto, disguised as the eponymous malcontent, in this case deposed, haunts his former court unrecognized, observing sourly the conduct of the courtiers. Marston nudges this world a further step from a plausible representation of actuality by having his successor, deposed in turn, join him in disguise. He anticipates some of the more spectacular dramatic effects of late Shakespeare, in that the resolution, a counter coup, takes place under the pretence of a court masque. Thematically, its concerns are more uniformly satirical than Shakespeare's. Marston had written verse satire in the late Elizabethan period, and his targets are familiar ones from that genre. Indeed, they recur in the Jacobean epigrams of Ben Jonson and in the character tradition. Braggarts, voluptuaries and time-serving courtiers people the stage and play the lackey to successive dukes. Under the guidance of Maquerelle (a French term for a bawd, borrowed already into English; see *OED* s.v. 'Mackerel'[2]), Emilia and Bianca, the Duchess Aurelia's ladies in waiting, develop strongly into the role of what

Jonson, in a later epigram, would term '*court pucelle*', more courtesan than courtier. Though the anti-court sentiment is almost unrelenting, it is systemic, rather than particularized. In timely fashion, though, its primary concern is with the responses to regime change. When Bilioso, 'an old choleric marshal', is asked what he would do if Altofronto were restored – 'What religion will you be of now?' – he replies, 'Of the Duke's religion, when I know what it is' (IV.v.93–4; p. 125). Perhaps the facility with which James assumed power in England was not so surprising.

Marston's career as a dramatist in a significant respect followed a pattern which was to become more frequent as the century progressed, whereby rich men's sons wrote for the stage in their bohemian youth before retiring to respectability. Marston's father was a successful lawyer and the dramatist himself flirted, evidently half-heartedly, with a legal training while creating his plays. About 1608 he took holy orders and spent the rest of his life as a moderately successful provincial clergyman. 'His only activity connected with his former literary career was to lobby . . . to have his name removed from the title-page of the 1633 collected edition of his plays' (*DNB* 2004).

Ben Jonson's best and currently most studied plays date from the first part of the Jacobean period: *Sejanus* (1603), *Volpone* (1606), *Epicoene* (1609), *The Alchemist* (1610), *Catiline* (1611), *Bartholomew Fair* (1614) and *The Devil is an Ass* (1616). Although at the same time he had established himself as the principal writer of court masque, his plays are markedly less spectacular than Shakespeare's, rarely using theatrical effects, dance and music in a major way. His is a very verbal drama, of great speeches marked by high rhetoric and of dialogue shaped into distinctive idioms to differentiate character, class and cultural background. At its best, his plotting is intricate and precise. He brings to the stage a display of learning and indeed scholarship remarkable in any age.

At the outset, Jonson did not write exclusively for the King's Men. The ill-judged collaborative work, *Eastward Ho!*, had been performed by the Children of the Queen's Revels. *Sejanus*, however, was staged by the King's Men at the Globe. (Shakespeare, it is often observed, probably played the role of Tiberius.) Yet it fared badly in the theatre. In the epistle affixed to the printed version in which Jonson dedicates it to his currently most important patron Lord Aubigny, he remarks, 'It is a poeme that (if I well remember) in your Lo[rdship]'s sight, suffer'd no lesse violence from our people here, then the subject of it did from the rage of the people of Rome' (Jonson 1925–52: IV, 349). The play *Sejanus* was torn to pieces by the mob. An amphitheatre performing space, with its large audience in close proximity, must have been a terrifying place if a play went seriously wrong.

Whereas Shakespeare based his own plays about classical history on single sources available in translation, Jonson drew on Tacitus, Suetonius and Dio Cassius, together with 'multitudes of scattered passages in other writers', and he provided extensive marginal notes in the first printed version, making this 'probably the first time that a work of imaginative literature had come forth buttressed with all the apparatus of critical scholarship' (Jonson 1965: 7–8). But annotation is irrelevant in performance.

The play itself lacks the depiction of action. Following the conventions of classical theatre, Jonson relegates the many blood-curdling events to reportage, restricting the play to an exchange of speeches, some of which are unrewardingly long. Nor does he accomplish the psychological interiority that Shakespeare had brought to the stage. Sejanus neither develops as a character nor really explains his motivation beyond a ruthless and remorseless individualism. The catastrophe comes in a meeting of the senate, where a letter from the emperor, indicting Sejanus, is simply read. His supporters fall off, he is arrested, and sentenced, scarcely speaking a word in his own defence. Jonson shies away from dramatic conflict, almost disdaining the established and current aesthetic of the genre within which he was writing. Yet the play had some topicality for his contemporaries. The Privy Council, jittery in a period of dynastic transition, evidently thought some aspects of the play treasonable, perhaps seeing in the fall of an over-ambitious favourite some allusion to the disastrous rebellion of the Earl of Essex a couple of years before. For a man hungry for preferment, Jonson sometimes showed an imperfect grasp of the nature of power and the rules of patronage.

Perhaps unsurprisingly, Jonson did not risk another Roman history till 1611. *Catiline* depicts another crisis, the failed insurrection of a patrician faction late in the history of republican Rome. This is a play with a hero, Cicero, currently consul, and there is genuine dramatic tension in his personal struggle against Catiline. Jonson opposes the former's intelligence, learning, civility and culture to the latter's reactionary and primitive assertion of the privileges of his birth. Catiline's conspirators kill a slave and swear their treasonous oath in his blood. Cicero asserts his difference clearly and challengingly, as a 'new man', not a patrician. This is the voice of a new age and a new political culture, though we recognize, too, its attraction for Jonson, the bricklayer's stepson and autodidact, taking on a world dominated by inherited wealth and power.

Once more, however, he declined to fulfil the genre expectations of his audience. The speeches are long and sometimes heavily rhetorical. Cicero is given orations in the Ciceronian manner. Catiline may indeed die 'A brave bad death' (v.688; Jonson 1925–52: IV, 548), but it is offstage and merely reported. The King's Men, no doubt, tried their best. Yet once again Jonson had failed to carry an audience with him. His epistle dedicatory to another patron, William Herbert, third Earl of Pembroke, attributes the failure to populist taste among theatre audiences. It marked his last attempt at non-comic drama.

The comedies constitute unequivocal testimony that Jonson could indeed craft a play well, despite the untheatrical nature of his Roman excursions. *Volpone* is a bold experiment that worked. Written for the King's Men, it allowed them access to the kinds of unsentimental and satirical comedy more typical of the repertoire of the boys' companies (Bevington 2000: 73). At the same time, he organizes his drama around an informing motif in the idiom of Aesopian animal fable: Volpone (the fox), aided by Mosca (the flesh-fly), feigns terminal illness to attract to him carrion eaters Corbaccio and Corvino (crows) and Voltore (the vulture), so he can prey on them. They bring him gifts in expectation of becoming his heir; but he's not dying. Allusions to the animal equivalents of the characters recur throughout, holding the plot quite tightly together. A parallel plot, concerning the humiliation of Sir Politic Wouldbe, an English knight abroad, aligns a different kind of metamorphosis as, in a ritual humiliation, he hides himself in a large tortoise shell, 'Creeping, with house, on backe' (V.iv.88; Jonson 1925–52: V, 121).

Yet, for all its apparent formalism, Jonson's play overflows with vivid vitality. Volpone himself develops into an almost Marlovian overreacher. His opening lines sound like a lover in a Donne poem, though the subject of the aubade is his wealth, not his mistress: 'Good morning to the day; and, next, my gold: / Open the shrine, that I may see my *saint*' (I.i.1–2; Jonson 1925–52: V, 24). Nor does he stay on mission. Once he sees Celia, he conceives a sexual desire at least as strong as his lust for gold. Left alone with her by her husband Corvino, he tries, after a brief and unsuccessful seduction attempt, to rape her: 'Thou, like EUROPA, and I like IOVE. ... Yeeld, or Ile force thee' (III.vii.222. 266; Jonson 1925–52: V, 84–5).

Celia's role is one of solitary, abandoned victimhood, a frequent one for heroines in early Stuart drama, from which she is saved by Bonario's heroic intervention. Yet Volpone's attempted violation is surpassed in its violence by the threats of her husband. When he suspects her of looking favourably on Volpone as he appears in disguise beneath her window, Corvino manifests a pathological jealousy that outstrips Othello's or Leontes'. He threatens to 'make [her] an anatomie' (II.v.70; Jonson 1925–52: V, 62). When Mosca persuades him that Volpone would find it a tonic if she would sleep in his bed, he bullies her to the task with a similar vehemence:

> I will drag thee hence, home, by the haire;
> Cry thee a strumpet, through the streets; rip up
> Thy mouth, unto thine eares; and slit thy nose,
> Like a raw rotchet.
> (III.vii.96–9; Jonson 1925–52: V, 80)

The rochet (or rotchet), the red gurnard, is a spiny fish, well liked in early modern cuisine, though obviously one that needs careful filleting in the preparation (OED; see cited examples of the word). Corvino proposes to give his wife's face the same treatment. The image and the vile threat it embodies shock modern audiences and perhaps Jacobean ones too, though it has some of the unflinching precision they would have found, a little earlier, in the prose of Thomas Nashe. Jonson himself had come close to judicial mutilation in the form of ear-cropping and nose-slitting for his part in writing *Eastward Ho!* (Riggs 1989: 126).

Volpone is a metropolitan play, though its setting is Venice, which both resembles London and differs from it. No doubt its larger theme, that greed and legacy-hunting corrode traditional family ties of husband to wife and father to son, may be applied to his view of London life, but the foreign setting allows the secondary satire on the Englishman abroad. Again, by placing it in Italy, Jonson may depict a venal judicial system without risking the wrath of the judicial system under which he lived and had already suffered. His remaining early Jacobean comedies more straightforwardly have a London setting.

Volpone plainly achieved some success. The King's Men toured the universities of Oxford and Cambridge with it. Yet Jonson still refused his audience an easy gratification. He could easily have married Celia off to Bonario. Instead, he grants her a divorce and returns her to her father's house with her dowry reimbursed threefold.

Epicoene, or The Silent Woman marked a return to writing for a boys' company, the Children of the Queen's Revels. Though the basis of the action, a young man securing his inheritance from an ageing but whimsical relative, is ancient, the play emphatically anticipates major developments in English drama after the Restoration. John Dryden fittingly told his contemporaries its depiction of 'the conversation of Gentlemen' was exemplary (*Essay in Dramatic Poetry*, quoted and discussed by Riggs 1989: 160). Indeed, were one unaware of its provenance, the opening scene could as easily be ascribed to William Wycherley (see below, chapter 6). It gained immediate popularity once the theatres reopened, four performances taking place in 1660, and more in 1661 (Clark 2001: 288).

It depicts generational conflict – an old and eccentric dupe (Morose) and a cluster of wealthy young toughs. Among the young, there is a further distinction of a kind dear to the Restoration stage between those who are young and witty (Dauphine, Clerimont and, above all, Truewit) and those who are young and either affected, stupid or both (John Daw, Amorous La Foole). A delicacy of wit characterizes the plan to have Morose marry a 'silent woman' and then give part of his fortune and pledge the rest to his nephew in return for an annulment – unnecessary in the event, since the 'woman' is actually a boy. Of course, this is an affectionless world, without pity for the defeated, but the skilful plotting, observing unities of time and place, and the facility of the bantering dialogue, all noted and praised by Dryden, carry it pleasingly through.

It shares some of its spirit with *The Alchemist*, though that is a far richer play thematically and in its characterization and the stagecraft shows Jonson at his most accomplished. As in *Volpone*, a pair of rogues, Subtle and Face, expose the cupidity of an array of gulls. This time they are aided by Dol Common, their 'stale', or prostitute, used to lure and entrap the victims of crime. The part calls for good timing, for precise stagecraft and for versatility in assuming a number of guises; so much so that the earliest Restoration actresses shied away from it as being too demanding technically (Clark 2001: 288). Subtle sets up as an alchemist in a house that Lovewit has quit for the duration of the plague, leaving it in care of Face, an evidently dishonest housekeeper. Through the door in search of quick rewards comes a succession of types and characters, marked each by their own styles of speaking. Thus, Sir Epicure Mammon soars into wildly overreaching erotic fantasies of how he will live once Subtle's alchemy has made his fortune:

> My mists
> I'le have of perfume, vapor'd 'bout the roome,
> To loose our selves in; and my baths, like pits
> To fall into: from whence, we will come forth,
> And rowle us drie in gossamour, and roses.
> (II.ii.48–52; Jonson 1925–52: V, 319)

Kastril, 'the Angry Boy', has his own brutal idiom: 'Gods lid, you shall love him, or Ile kick you', he cautions his sister (IV.iv.34; Jonson 1925–52: V, 373). And so on, through an aspirational tradesman, a would-be man-about-town and a 'gamester' appropriately named Surley. Meanwhile, at every turn, Face and Subtle keep up a constant babble of alchemical jargon to delude the gulls:

> SUB[TLE] Looke well to the register,
>   And let your heat, still, lessen by degrees.
>   To the *Aludels*.
> FAC[E] Yes, sir.
> SUB[TLE] Did you looke
>   O'the *Bolts-head* yet?
> FAC[E] Which, on *D.* sir?
> SUB[TLE] I.
>   What's the complexion?
> FAC[E] Whitish.
> SUB[TLE] Infuse vinegar,
>   To draw his *volatile substance*, and his *tincture* . . .
>   (II.iii.33–8; Jonson 1925–52: V, 322)

Of course, there are no bolt-heads or aludels. But note the flavour of the language. 'Aludel' looks like what it is, an Arabic loanword, carrying associations of the recondite and exotic. 'Bolt-head' is first recorded here in this sense; a new word for a new technology and baffling to the inexpert. Surley, the only character not really taken in, remarks with some justice, 'What a brave language here is? next to canting?' (line 42).

Besides his familiar concern – the exposure of the pervasive and corrosive effects of greed on metropolitan life in early modern England – Jonson develops in *The Alchemist* a potent satire on Puritanism in his picture of Tribulation, a pastor of Amsterdam, and Ananias, his deacon. Professional writers had been used to attack Puritanism since the late 1580s, when John Lyly, Thomas Nashe and Robert Greene were enlisted to counter the effective satirical prose of the pseudonymous Martin Marprelate (see Milward 1977: ch. 4). A complex, hostile stereotype had developed, on which Jonson freely draws. He ridicules the Puritans' preposterous linguistic affectations, particularly the absorption of biblical phrases into their ways of perceiving and discussing the world they live in, and their endless celebration of their own 'zeal', which Jonson equates with fanaticism: 'In pure zeale, I doe not like the man [Subtle]: He is a *heathen*. / And speakes the language of *Canaan* ...' (III.i.4–6; Jonson 1925–52: V, 340–1). Jonson picks up on other elements of the stereotype: these are relatively uneducated men; they are from outside the classes that traditionally supplied the clergy; they are hypocrites; and they are as grasping as the other dupes. Most significantly, they are subversive. Their grand plan is to finance the overthrow of the state. Jonson, by this time a lapsed Catholic convert reconciled to the Church of England, carefully places them at the outer extremity of the spectrum of Puritan opinion. They are 'brethren of the separation', believers who have withdrawn from the national church and gone into exile, rather than the more moderate Puritans seeking a new reformation from within the church. Thus, they are a safe target, and one which the Jacobean establishment would have been happy to see ridiculed. Of course, what Jonson has to say about extremists serves to taint the mainstream of moderate Puritan opinion. But that game is an old one in reactionary polemic.

Bartholomew Fair was written, not for the King's Men, but for Princess Elizabeth's Men, a rival troupe also performing in a Bankside amphitheatre, the Hope. It appeared while the Globe was under reconstruction and may have been a clever piece of opportunism by the proprietors of the Hope, though the advantage was soon lost. No other major works were premiered there, leaving this as 'the Hope's one brush with literary fame', and its alternative use, as a bear- and bull-baiting arena, largely took over (Wickham et al. 2000: 596).

The play teems with London life. The annual fair brought rogues and twisters together with citizens and visiting provincials across generational, ideological and social divides in a vaguely carnivalesque atmosphere. Jonson adapts several plot mechanisms already familiar in Jacobean comedy. The rivalry among suitors seeking marriage with a wealthy heiress recurs frequently in city comedy (see below). He uses, too, a disguised magistrate, who, like the Duke in *Measure for Measure*, develops, undercover, a better understanding of the corruptions under his jurisdiction. Appropriately in the spirit of carnivalesque inversion, the magistrate spends some of the play in the stocks. It ends with a 'play within the play', rather closer in tone and purpose to 'Pyramus and Thisbe' in *A Midsummer Night's Dream* than 'The Mousetrap' in *Hamlet*, though with an added twist: this is performed by puppets.

Once more Jonson offers a satirical caricature of a rabid Puritan in the person of Zeal-of-the-Land Busy. The familiar components are present: Busy is a hypocrite, fiercely critical of indulgence by others while himself a glutton, a seemingly upright figure but an embezzler. His idiom, a limited pastiche of biblical phrases often of a prophetic kind, discloses an insistent transformation of the world as it is into the world as his preconceptions require it to be – the scene of a constant struggle between zealous purity and a Babylonian corruption. Yet he uses this idiom casuistically. Asked to find good reason for going to the fair and eating its delicacy, roast pork, he abandons his original view (that the pig is idolatrous since its nomenclature as a 'Bartholomew-pig' popishly commemorates a saint). He argues instead that 'we may be religious in midst of the prophane, so it be eaten with a reformed mouth, with *sobriety*, and humblenesse' (I.vi.72–4; Jonson 1925–52: VI, 38).

Jonson uses him, too, to ridicule Puritan opposition to the stage, a minor anxiety for the profession in the early Jacobean period, though one that grows through the early Stuart period. He bursts in on the puppet show in a whirlwind of iconoclastic self-righteousness: 'Downe with *Dagon*, downe with *Dagon*; 'tis I, will no longer endure your prophanations' (V.v.1–2; Jonson 1925–52: VI, 133). But he makes the irretrievable tactical error of debating the morality of theatrical repre-sentation with one of the puppets – and losing. Cross-dressing, inev-itable in an all-male theatrical profession, is at the centre of Busy's case against the stage: 'my maine argument against you, is, that you are an *abomination:* for the Male, among you, putteth on the apparel of the *Female*, and the *Female* of the Male' (ll.98–100; p. 135). He is easily confuted as the puppet pulls up its garment to disclose its sexless body. Of course, a boy actor in drag could scarcely have used this response. Busy concedes the case, but, significantly, he remains with the rest of the company to watch the show, a surprisingly genial and inclusive ending to the play.

Jonson's last play before his temporary retirement from the theatre, *The Devil is an Ass*, marked a return to the King's Men. In some ways a play on a more modest scale, it develops through a clever and, for Jonson, rare excursion into the supernatural. Pug, a minor devil, persuades Satan to allow him a day on earth to prove his capacity for evil. But he finds London life already so appetitive and corrupt that he is marginalized and ineffectual. As Satan chides him, 'whom thou hast dealt with, / Woman or man, this day, but have out-done thee / Some way, and most have prov'd the better fiends?' (V.vi.60–3; Jonson 1925–52: VI, 261–2).

Jonson's fascinated and vivid perception of metropolitan life retained a clear-eyed and unflinching recognition that virtue was often not rewarded, that the good did not always prosper, and that the unwary were at risk from the cunning and ruthless. The city is a place of danger and disease. *The Alchemist*, performed shortly after the theatres reopened following a major visitation of the plague, takes as its premise the flight of the rich from the city at such times.

Jonson stands adjacent to the mainstream of low-mimetic Jacobean comedy depicting city life, usually termed 'city comedies'. The progenitor of the form was Thomas Dekker's late Elizabethan play, *The Shoemakers Holiday*. That differs, however, from the favoured premises of its Jacobean successors in that it celebrates a relatively unprestigious manufacturing guild, rather than the goldsmiths and merchant adventurers, whose breathtaking wealth motivates most characters. Dekker's play is retrospective. Set in the late Middle Ages, it shows the origins of London's institutions and celebrates the ancient loyalism of citizens to the crown.

More typically, city comedies are set in the present. Often they have a love story or perhaps parallel and contrasting love stories, in which heiresses are competed for. The worthy make good marriages; the greedy and idle tend to get what they deserve. Sometimes the ancient love triangles of aged husband, young wife and lustful gallant are explored. As civic hostility towards the theatres eased in the early Stuart period, a drama that was more sympathetic to mercantile value systems seems to have emerged, although the companies of boy actors fostered a dramatic idiom that was coolly cynical towards the institutions of city and of state. Indeed, in *Eastward Ho!* the authors took the reckless step of tying their depiction of London society very closely to immediately contemporary circumstances. Their London shows the usual cast of goldsmiths, apprentices, citizens and their wives, heiresses and their suitors. But the figure of Sir Petronel Flash, 'a new-made knight', hits at James's policy of creating and selling many such honours, and the encounter with a Scottish 'gentleman' on the Isle of Dogs, opposite the palace of Greenwich, where James and his entourage were contemporaneously living, was injudicious impudence that provoked 'his Majesty's high displeasure' and a punitive response for both the company and the dramatists (IV.i; Jonson et al. 1973: 74 and appendix 3; see above, 'Early Jacobean Theatre').

The authorities' response to *Eastward Ho!* set limits to what city comedies could do in reflecting London life. Yet at their best, they retain something of the clear-eyed moral judgement of Jonson's own oeuvre. Thomas Middleton, Shakespeare's collaborator in *Timon of Athens* and arguably the most accomplished dramatist of the 1620s, wrote for the boy actors in the earliest years of the Jacobean period. Among several plays of his staged by the Children of St Paul's, *A Mad World, My Masters* (?1604–6) well illustrates his controlled and rather jaundiced perspective on London life. One plot explores the ancient storyline of the young and profligate heir, seeking premature access to the wealth of a relative of inconvenient longevity. The other principal story has the old triangle of citizen / young wife / gallant. Nobody behaves well. Duplicity characterizes all relationships, and tricksters are themselves duped. Yet, curiously, Middleton admits the possibility of moral reformation. In an excursion into the paranormal unusual in this genre, he confronts Master Penitent Brothel, the lecherous gallant, with a succubus that has assumed the form of Mistress Harebrain, the woman he would debauch. But by the time she appears, he has begun a process of spiritual meditation which already points towards his regeneration (IV.1.1–29; Middleton 1965: 63), and he goes on both to redeem the woman he covets from her own lascivious impulses and to effect a reconciliation with her husband. In the other storyline, the would-be heir, Follywit, is duped into marrying the courtesan of his grandsire, Sir Bounteous Progress, though the latter compensates him with a wedding gift in celebration of the trickster being tricked. Thus one plot ends in spiritual regeneration and the other in a genial reconciliation of sorts. Jonson rarely has his characters escape so well the consequences of their folly.

A jaundiced perspective and moralizing conclusion recur in Middleton's later city comedy, *A Chaste Maid in Cheapside* (?1613). It was performed by the adult actors of a company under the patronage of the Princess Elizabeth, the king's daughter, which occupied the Swan for a while in the early 1610s. With a neater symmetry than often characterized the genre, the good daughter of Yellowhammer, a goldsmith, and his stupid son enter into marriages that are appropriate to their moral status. The son's is to a Welsh whore he has mistaken for a gentlewoman. The daughter's is to an honourable suitor, Touchwood, who triumphs boldly over his inappropriate and corrupt rival, Sir Walter Whorehound. Again, corruption is widespread. Even Yellowhammer, by the end a judicious figure, has kept a whore, and he contemplates marrying his daughter to Sir Walter, whose depraved sexual life has become known to him. But the play ends by observing a kind of poetic justice and with a double wedding of the contrasting couples. Virtue is rewarded in a decidedly unJonsonian way. No wonder Jonson's comedies figured, as Middleton's did not, on the Restoration stage

City comedy generated the most sustained and successful literary joke of the early Stuart period, *The Knight of the Burning Pestle* (?1607), written by Francis Beaumont, perhaps with John Fletcher, for the Children of the Queen's Revels. The play shows extraordinary dramaturgical ingenuity. London citizens George, a grocer, and Nell, his wife, flushed with the confidence and aspirations – and cultural limitations – of their class, attend a performance of a city comedy with their apprentice Rafe. The play within the play, 'The London Merchant', broadly accords with the kind of drama the boys' company would perform, though George and Nell persistently interrupt, misunderstanding its plot, criticizing its values and comparing it disadvantageously with more naive and populist dramas staged elsewhere. The problem is further compounded by their insistence on Rafe's participation in the play as a grocer's boy suddenly transformed into the 'Right Courteous and Valiant Knight of the Burning Pestle' (I.273–4; Beaumont 1967: 24). George and Nell require his role to introduce an incoherent romance component into a radically different dramatic discourse:

[GEORGE] Let Rafe come in an fight with Jaspar [the apprentice role in *The London Merchant*].
[NELL] Ay, and beat him well; he's an unhappy boy.
BOY Sir, you must pardon us. The plot of our play lies contrary, and 'twill hazard the spoiling of our play.
[GEORGE] Plot me no plots. I'll ha' Rafe come out.

(II.263–7; p. 42)

Ingeniously, *The London Merchant* and Rafe's improvised chivalric romp run side by side until their complex resolution in a scene of reconciliation (in the former) and heroic death (in the latter): 'I die; fly, fly, my soul, to Grocers' Hall. / O, O, O, &c.' (V.332–3; p. 108).

But the play is not only a wonderfully sustained burlesque and a technical *tour de force*. It maps important terrain within the contemporary cultural landscape. Nell and George are seasoned theatre-goers, but this is not their theatre; they are bees in the wrong hive. The boys' company at Blackfriars offers something alien to their values and expectations. Though they leave well pleased with what they have seen, Nell's final words, as she invites the gentlemen of the audience back to her house for a pipe of tobacco, disclose a gaucheness that defines her social distance from the target audience of the boys' companies.

The revenge play, 'that relatively low form of tragedy' (Fowler 1985: 276), and variants on it substantially followed Elizabethan conventions. The society depicted in such plays is despotic. The acts requiring revenge are perpetrated by those in or close to supreme authority and no recourse to law is possible. (Necessarily, since England had a developed judicial system and a strong tradition that asserted the independence of legal process from government, the setting was generally foreign.) But whatever the circumstance, revenge requires the sin of murder. Christian patience always offers a better alternative. Moreover, since it sets the individual against the state, it disturbs the civic polity.

The Revenger's Tragedy (?1605–6) is probably the most accomplished and purest example of the genre in the early Jacobean period. Formerly attributed to Cyril Tourneur, currently it is thought most likely to be work of the astonishingly versatile Thomas Middleton. It was first performed by the King's Men, a company used to playing Shakespeare's tragedies and thus better suited for this sombre though pacy drama than the boy actors for whom Middleton was writing comedies at this time. Time and place are only vaguely indicated; the play seems to be set somewhere in Italy, in a ducal state dominated by a vicious and ruthless ruling family. Vindice and his grudge dominate the play from beginning to end. The first scene has him watching a ducal procession while holding the skull of his late girlfriend, poisoned by the Duke because she would not accede to 'his palsy-lust' (I.i.34; Tourneur [attrib.] 1966: 4). Vindice and his brother Hippolito, with wit and guile, work their way through the ducal family, killing them with various degrees of cruelty and ingenuity. The death's head, that grim emblem, reappears as a useful prop in killing the Duke. Vindice dresses the skull with wig and mask and presumably attaches it to something that could be mistaken for a body, and puts poison on its boney lips, which the Duke duly kisses. Hippolito warmly approves: 'I do applaud thy constant vengeance, / The quaintness of thy malice' (III.v.108–9; p. 73). The Duke not only endures agonies before expiring but also lives long enough to witness how his own bastard son, Spurio, cuckolds him with his duchess. The spirit of *Grand Guignol* continues to the final resolution, a 'masque of revengers' followed by a scene of absolute carnage in which all remaining members of the ducal family are put to the sword. A new order emerges, and Vindice and Hippolito resign themselves to the legal process: 'are we not reveng'd? / Is there one enemy left alive amongst those? / 'Tis time to die, when we are ourselves our foes' (V.iii.108–10; p. 128). The play ends with order restored, crime revenged and the disruptive process of revenge itself punished and eliminated, after an exhilarating but ultimately normative sequence of events.

The sensational murder, a feature of *The Revenger's Tragedy*, finds perfect expression in the work of John Webster. In *The White Devil* (?1612), first performed to little acclaim in the populist theatre of the Red Bull at Clerkenwell, Webster offers a lurid account of infidelity, murder and judicial malpractice. Much of his repertoire is on display. He offers in the character of Vittoria Corombona the frisson of an isolated woman surrounded by powerful men who may treat her much as they wish. He offers, too, deaths of an ingenious and sometimes prolonged kind. Most spectacularly, Bracciano, the male lead, is afflicted by poison placed inside his tournament helmet. Despite his agony, he survives through almost 200 lines, before he is strangled, though not before he has received the last rites from his assassins, who disclose themselves to be no priests and thus gloat over his probable damnation (V.iii; Webster 1972: 141–4).

The King's Men performed *The Duchess of Malfi* (1614) at the Blackfriars and the second Globe. Like *The White Devil*, it depicts in extreme form the vulnerability of an isolated woman deprived of the male support so important in a patriarchal society, a recurrent theme in many early Stuart plays. Once more, deaths are cruel and unusual. The Duchess herself dies after a prolonged and macabre episode of psychological torture, tormented by madmen and subjected to a harrowing encounter apparently with the bodies of her husband and children, though these subsequently are identified as mere waxwork simulacra. She dies by strangulation, though not without making, somewhat improbably, a brief recovery. The remaining characters of the play, or at least those who have any significant culpability, die in an exchange of stabbings. Motivation for the crimes against the Duchess is perverse.

Her brothers have some material advantage in her remaining unmarried, but Ferdinand's fascination with imagining her sex life more than hints at an incestuous impulse. That, however, cannot explain the curiously gothic development in his depiction as he acts out the role of werewolf.

Cyril Tourneur wrote *The Atheist's Tragedy* (?1611) for the King's Men, who evidently played it with some success, taking it twice to court in the early 1610s and retaining it in their repertoire for 30 years (Tourneur 1964: xx). Generically, it resembles *Hamlet*; it is a providential variant on the conventions of the revenge play. The hero and heroine, Charlemont and Castabella, are certainly much sinned against: a father murdered, a forced marriage to an unsavoury child of the villain D'Amville, a rape attempt and a fraudulent trial leading to a capital sentence. Yet, though the state is unrelentingly hostile, Charlemont piously eschews revenge, preferring instead the patience of Christian fortitude. He and Castabella are rewarded for their suffering by an extraordinary sequence of providential acts, culminating in their trial and escape from execution. D'Amville, the eponymous atheist, asserts there is no force above nature and seeks to counter their piety by insisting on executing them himself. In the event, 'As he raises up the axe [he] strikes out his own brains, [and then] staggers off the scaffold' (Tourneur 1964: 116, s.d.). He survives long enough to expatiate on the significance of the outcome and his recognition of his own error:

> D'AM   What murderer was he
>   That lifted up my hand against my head?
> 1 JUDGE None but yourself, my lord.
> D'AM   I thought he was
>   A murderer that did it.
> 1 JUDGE   God forbid.
> D'AM Forbid? You lie, judge; he commanded it
>   To tell thee that man's wisdom is a fool.
>   (V.ii.243–7; Tourneur 1964: 116).

Of course, on the printed page and to a modern reader this concluding scene probably seems more than a little ridiculous. Yet, like the mainstream of revenge tragedy, it is theatrically arresting, a moment of great peril to the good characters suddenly and violently reversed.

Revenge tragedy and its variants plainly retained popularity. But they constitute an undemanding kind of entertainment. Certainly, they present a vision of continental, often Italianate, corruption and cruelty, and offer a frisson of outlandish deviousness and cruelty. Death and suffering are often protracted, sensational and exotic. Ultimately, however, this is a conservative art form. Even in *The Atheist's Tragedy* its assumptions pass unchallenged. Order is restored to the commonwealth, and the guilty, including those who have taken the law into their own hands, are duly punished. Larger questions, about the appropriate relationship between government and the governed and between the law and the state, implicit in their typical plots, are not addressed. Nor, indeed, are the plays innovative in terms of dramatic technique, though certainly they often allow a great deal of noisy action on stage. In their lack of ambition they throw into sharp relief the accomplishment of Jonson and, more especially, Shakespeare in the challenges they posed to their audiences. Jacobean drama was a component of high literary culture in the sense that social elites (as well as the middling sort) had access to it and evidently valued it. But without Jonson and Shakespeare its achievements would appear modest.

Outside the conventions of the professional stage, Elizabeth Cary wrote *The Tragedy of Mariam*, a closet drama depicting events among the highest circles in the court of King Herod. It is usually regarded as the first English play by a woman to have appeared in print (in 1613). Cary, wife of the first Viscount Falkland and mother of Lucius Cary, the second Viscount and patron of many writers and thinkers in the Caroline period, had nothing to gain from the publication of her work, and so its appearance in print is the more remarkable, given the compounding factors of her sex and class. Formally, this is both a history play and a careful simulation of the conventions of Senecan drama, drawing on a late Elizabethan translation of Josephus's *History of the Jewish People*, and producing a play which, though lacking in spectacle and dramatic tension, supports lengthy and psychologically complex speeches, for the most part in alternately rhymed pentameter. But it is its themes, particularly about gender politics, that have stimulated most critical debate. Its heroine, the second wife of the tyrannical Herod, attempts to negotiate a modus vivendi that would allow her to speak the truth on her own behalf while satisfying the demands for subordination made by a patriarchal society. Yet she is a victim not only of the caprice of Herod but also of the duplicity of Salome, his sister, and of the implacable resentment of Doris, his first wife. Her final encounter on her way to execution is with Doris, whose parting curse extends to the next generation: 'I do hope this boy of mine, / Shall one day come to be the death of thine' (ll.1836–7; Purkiss 1994: 62). Herod is a monarchical as well as a domestic tyrant, and the play engages, however tangentially, with those old but still pertinent questions of how subjects should respond to unjust government and what resistance is permissible. Herod himself, though, takes so firm a grip on his regime that real resistance, as opposed to verbal opposition, scarcely appears an option.

Non-Dramatic Poetry

In a letter possibly addressed to Henry Wotton and tentatively dated 1600 John Donne warned its recipient thus:

> Yet, Sir, though I know their low price, except I receive by your next letter an assurance upon the religion of your friendship that no copy shall be taken for any respect of these or any other my compositions sent to you, I shall sin against my conscience if I send you any more. I speak that in plainness which becomes (methinks) our honesties, and therefore call not this a distrustful but a free spirit. I mean to acquaint you with all mine, and to my Satires there belongs some fear, and to some Elegies, and these, perhaps, shame. Against both which affections although I be tough enough, yet I have a riddling disposition to be ashamed of fear and afraid of shame. Therefore I am desirous to hide them, without any over-reckoning of them or their maker. (Donne 1990: 65)

Donne's late Elizabethan career constituted an almost perfect essay in ambition (Carey 1990: *passim*). He had a legal training, which equipped him well for the role of civil servant or aide to a powerful magnate. He had changed his religion, giving up Catholicism, in the cause of which both his maternal uncle and his younger brother had died. He had served with the Earl of Essex as a gentleman volunteer on the successful Cadiz expedition and the rather less successful attempt to intercept the Spanish treasure fleet in the Azores. He had moved nimbly to widen his base of patronage. By the time of Essex's eclipse he was well established as secretary to Sir Thomas Egerton, a privy councillor and senior law officer, who had the queen's confidence. In 1603 an injudicious and clandestine marriage to Egerton's niece occasioned Donne's dismissal and relative impoverishment. Through most of the period till his ordination in 1615 Donne with intermittent success sought new patrons to help him to a public or private office lucrative enough to repair his fortunes. The letter makes clear how little a wide readership meant to a creative writer of Donne's class and aspirations. Professional writers, including Shakespeare, had vouch-safed poetry to the press in the late Elizabethan period, as they would in the Jacobean. Donne sees no advantage even in wide circulation in manuscript. His is an art to be enjoyed by the closest of coteries (although inevitably, despite his efforts, poems leaked into wider circulation and were to be found in numerous manuscript anthologies). After all, in late Elizabethan England satirists attracted official censure of a kind he could not risk, and his early erotic verse scarcely fashioned the image of a serious man of business.

The letter also shows how Donne perceived his previous literary achievement. He writes about his elegies and his satires as if he regarded them (wholly appropriately) as complete, substantial and generically distinct bodies of work. He knows they will be valued by contemporaries who have privileged access to them.

The satires are the more conventional. They rehearse familiar complaints against rather generalized and threadbare targets such as Puritans, courtiers, corrupt politicians and lecherous, promiscuous women. Juvenal and Horace hover in the background, but affinities are closer with English satirists of the late 1590s. The elegies, in a neo-Ovidian fashion that widely characterized Elizabethan literature, manifest a cool, libertine, sometimes cynical persona combined with an eye for erotic detail and a telling turn of phrase. Ovidian situations are sometimes rehearsed. In 'Elegy 6: The Perfume', the lover dodges a father's watchfulness and a 'grim eight-foot-high iron-bound serving-man', only to be betrayed by his 'loud perfume, which at my entrance cried / Even at thy father's nose' (ll. 31, 41–2; Donne 1990: 20–1).

The most vivid elegy, 'Elegy 2: To his Mistress Going to Bed' (Donne 1990: 12–13), plainly poses difficulties for a modern sensibility. It appears voyeuristic, intrusive to the point of morbid scopophilia. Its equation of sexual 'conquest' and colonial exploitation readily invites political readings. There is some evidence that its indelicate libertinism, with its witty wordplay about tumescence, shocked at least some contemporaries. It was omitted when his poems were first published in 1633. Yet it shows, too, a principal strength of Donne's mature verse, an extraordinary capacity to write as if within the moment the poem describes. The lyric voice speaks with immediacy: he is aroused, his mistress undresses, he urges her to admit his fumbling fingers and to present herself 'as to a midwife', while, presumably in the course of the speech act which the poem simulates, the speaker himself undresses.

The dating of Donne's mature poetry for the most part remains highly uncertain. No evidence places the composition of the 'Songs and Sonnets' earlier than 1602 (Donne 1990: 88). The *terminus ad quem* is open to dispute. The argument that he must have finished them before entering holy orders lacks substance. Robert Herrick's *Hesperides* (considered in chapter 4) demonstrates that one could be a clergyman of the Church of England, celebrant in devotional verse of its values and practices, and simultaneously a libertine and highly erotic poet.

The collective title was not given, nor were the poems assembled as a group, till the second edition of Donne's poems (1635). The 53 poems (or 54 if 'The Dream', originally printed as an elegy, is included) are thematically and emotionally disparate, even contradictory, though technically they share some common ground. They are atopical and anonymous. The mistresses are never named, a deviation from a convention that stretched from Elizabethan lyricists, most influentially Sidney, through to Richard Lovelace and Abraham Cowley. The only place specially identified is the eponymous Twickenham Garden, from 1607 in the possession of Lucy, Countess of Bedford, one of Donne's patrons, though nothing suggests that the poem is about her. Contemporary references are very rare. 'The Sun Rising' alludes to James I's enthusiasm for hunting (l.8; Donne 1990: 93). Sometimes the *mise en scène* is a bedchamber, a graveside, a saint's vigil, but usually it is unspecified.

The lyrical 'I's are disconcertingly diverse. Sometimes the speaker expresses the tenderness of confidently reciprocated affection:

> Sweetest love, I do not go,
>   For weariness of thee,
> Nor in hope the world can show
>   A fitter love for me . . .
> . . . .
>   But think that we
> Are but turned aside to sleep;
> They who one another keep
>   Alive, ne'er parted be.
> ('Song", ll.1–4, 37–40; Donne 1990: 99)

Sometimes there is an anxiety that the relationship is transient, as in 'A Valediction: of my Name in the Window' (Donne 1990: 103–5), where all that may remain may be a name shallowly etched in the glass of a bedroom window. Elsewhere, the lover speaks with a warm, languidly post-coital voice, as in 'The Good Morrow' and 'The Sun Rising' (Donne 1990: 89–90, 92–3). (After sex, Donne's lovers, contrary to the received Lucretian wisdom, usually seem quite pleased with themselves and the world around them.) But sometimes sexual contact, in hindsight, seems repulsive, as in 'Love's Alchemy' (Donne 1990: 113–24). Even the implied intelligence of the lover changes, from the sportive logicality of 'The Flea' or 'Air and Angels' (Donne 1990: 89, 101), to the vituperative incoherence of 'The Apparition' (Donne 1990: 118–19), where he imagines himself as a revenant slain by a mistress who won't sleep with him but who is, after his death, sexually insatiable. In human terms, his resolve not to say while living what he will say once dead makes no sense. Elsewhere the gender of the speaker is unstable. 'Break of Day' (Donne 1990: 102) certainly has a woman speaking. So, perhaps, does 'Woman's Constancy' (Donne 1990: 91).

Of course, modern readers, like readers of the 1635 edition, see the poems as a whole in a way in which, most probably, very few readers did in Donne's lifetime. We seek a coherence when what he offers us is a myriad of voices in a myriad of circumstances, articulating a range of values, affections and assumptions. Yet collectively they constitute an anatomy of heterosexual relations in early modern England – and perhaps beyond. These are poems largely detached from social context. We have little sense of the relative status of the lovers. What distinguishes Jacobean sexual mores from those of our own age is substantially missing. These poems are silent about the risks of unwanted pregnancy in an age without reliable contraception, of sexually transmitted diseases in an age before antibiotics, and of social disgrace and danger at a time when chastity was valued in unmarried women and fidelity after marriage. What remains at the core of the work is probably transhistorical and cross-cultural in human desire and affection.

Collectively, too, the poems constitute a technical *tour de force*. They frequently exhibit the immediacy of 'Elegy 2'. Readers are seemingly overhearing bedroom conversations, seduction routines and acts of valediction. Imaginatively, they are invited to project future scenes of dying, of post-mortem examination, of exhumation, of ghostly visitation, and of the resurrection of the dead. The poems pose some of the stiffest challenges to interpretation (and even comprehension) to be found in high literary culture across the century. Working out what a poem like 'Air and Angels' means is a tricky brain-teaser for an experienced and elite reader. The poems exude an encyclopedic knowledge (although the encyclopedia was shorter then, and better known). For example, 'The Good Morrow' (Donne 1990: 89–90) bounces through a witty appropriation of Platonism into a testing analogy between love and cartography and ends with an allusion to Galenic medicine.

But the challenge Donne poses is profounder still, testing to near breaking point readers' tolerance for the polymorphous sensibility implied, especially in the imagery of the poems. Sex persistently is associated with death, with decomposition, with dissection and with torture, and poems teeter on the brink of blasphemy. Twice a lover ponders how a bracelet of braided hair would be perceived by people handling his corpse. In 'The Funeral' (Donne 1990: 127), where the lover speaks to those who will come to lay out his body, the love token is an enigmatic sign, an ineffective talisman and a fragment from an unobtainable object of desire to be carried to the grave. 'The Relic' relocates the conceit to an exhumation in a distant age, when gravediggers, looking to accommodate another corpse, break open his grave and notice 'A bracelet of bright hair about the bone' (l.6; Donne 1990: 130), which is at once a resonant phrase and a gruesome image. The poet has them wonder whether the keepsake was a ruse to secure a short meeting at the last judgement, since the mistress, to be resurrected whole, would need to collect the lock from him, which makes the relationship seem singularly fragile and delicate, an embrace beneath the towering finality of last things. But the poem plays for a frisson of blasphemy. If the exhumation takes place in a superstitious age, perhaps the gravediggers will think the bracelet to be a relic of Mary Magdalen, whose iconography traditionally depicts her with long blonde hair. If the bracelet is from her, who does that make the lover? The poem is studiedly and playfully evasive: the lover is 'A something else thereby' (l.130). Perhaps a former client from her days as a prostitute. But perhaps her legendary lover, Jesus Christ – although Christ, of course, is not physically present in any tomb. But then Donne sets the fancy in an age of 'mis-devotion' (l.13).

The associations are sometimes more appalling. In 'Love's Alchemy' the speaker likens a woman who has been 'possessed' to 'mummy', a vile medicament made from grinding to paste the embalmed bodies of ancient Egyptians (or else some presumably inferior substitute), typically taken orally. Again, 'Love's Exchange' ends:

> . . . Love is enraged with me,
> Yet kills not. If I must example be
> To future rebels; if th'unborn
> Must learn, by my being cut up, and torn:
> Kill, and dissect me, Love; for this
> Torture against thine own end is,
> Racked carcases make ill anatomies.
> (ll.36–42; Donne 1990: 110–11)

The principal image is macabre enough, but the conclusion has a gruesome precision. I suppose heavy racking may reduce the usefulness of a cadaver for anatomical purposes since the articulation of the spine and perhaps the shoulders would be damaged.

Donne's most important religious poems are the 'Holy Sonnets'. Careful study of the extant manuscripts has established that these form less coherent a cluster than their appearance together since the early editions would seem to suggest (Donne 1978: xxxvi–liii). However, the primary and secondary groups, sonnets 1–6 and 7–16, offer series of meditations on salvation (and damnation) by a speaker who variously appears anxious, guilt-ridden or triumphantly aware of his own justification. The other three are more difficult to incorporate in that schema. Sonnet 17 is an elegy for a loved one, perhaps his wife. Sonnet 18 is evidently late and makes allusion to the Thirty Years War. Sonnet 19, with its conclusion, 'Those are my best days, when I shake with fear' (Donne 1990: 289), fits more easily with the rest.

Theologically, the poems are in the Protestant tradition. On the nascent division within the Church of England between Calvinist and Arminian theories of salvation, they seem disengaged and evasive. The last rites of Catholicism have no place. Yet, as a long critical tradition recognizes, they take from the Counter-Reformation some of the intensity of the meditational practices it encouraged. The speaker projects himself into pivotal moments, to the point of death, to the very moment of Christ's second coming:

> Oh my black soul! now thou art summoned . . .
>
> This is my play's last scene . . .
>
> What if this present were the world's last night?
> (first lines, sonnets 2, 3, 9; Donne 1990: 174, 177)

The poems often share the immediacy of the 'Songs and Sonnets'. The reader seemingly overhears the interior monologue of a believer animated by a heightened sense of his own mortality and of the imminence of judgement. Though generally simpler, the poems sometimes pose intellectual challenges, as in 'At the round earth's imagined corners, blow / Your trumpets, angels' (sonnet 4, ll.1–2; Donne 1990: 175). The 'imagined corners' recollects Revelation 7:1: 'I saw four angels standing on the four corners of the earth. . . . ' But Donne knows the earth is round and in cartographical terms best represented as a globe, not a map. He points up the contradiction, leaving it only partially resolved (why would the holy ghost or Saint John the Divine want to imagine the world erroneously as rectangular?), before hurling the reader into contemplating the resurrection of the dead:

> . . . and arise, arise
> From death, you numberless infinities
> Of souls, and to your scattered bodies go . . .
> (sonnet 4, ll.2–4)

'Numberless infinities': again a game, a brain-teaser – can infinities be plural? does 'numberless' mean there are so many infinities they can't be counted or that each infinity defies computation? But the logical, indeed mathematical, conundrum is swept aside in contemplation of that far greater mystery, as vast multitudes of souls reunite with their long decayed bodies, which are physically resurrected and rejuvenated.

As in the 'Songs and Sonnets', though more straightforwardly, given the rather different subject matter, images of death and decay proliferate. The poems share, too, that disturbing sensibility. Sometimes it seems sado-masochistic, as when the speaker urges, 'Spit in my face you Jews, and pierce my side, / Buffet, and scoff, scourge, and crucify me' (sonnet 7, ll.1–2; Donne 1990: 176). Sonnet 10 represents the speaker as a woman en prise, like the heroine of a Webster tragedy, there to be taken. It moves to a remarkable conclusion:

> But [I] am betrothed unto your enemy,
> Divorce me, untie, or break that knot again,
> Take me to you, imprison me, for I
> Except you enthral me, never shall be free,
> Nor ever chaste, except you ravish me.
>   (ll.10–14; Donne 1990: 178)

'Ravish' could mean no more than 'seize', though its paradoxical juxtaposition with the word 'chaste' surely excludes all but its narrowest, sexual meaning.

Many of Donne's remaining poems are verse epistles to friends and potential patrons, together with occasional poems arising out of those relationships. Two projects, however, stand out from these, 'Good Friday, 1613. Riding Westward' and the *Anniversaries*, the only book of verse to be published in his lifetime. The former is an astonishing poem. Its title fixes it more precisely in time and space than Donne's other devotional poetry, and we know from external evidence that it grew out of a social context, the journey from one friend and patron, Sir Henry Goodyer, to another, Sir Edward Herbert. Both the day and the direction are central to the poem, but this is work of interiority, of meditation while in transit. Like much of his best poetry, it has a sort of immediacy, as though we are overhearing a process and expression of thought in real time. In this case a surviving manuscript copy indicates that it may well have been completed and sent back to Goodyer before his journey's end (Carey 1990: 106). It starts with an intellectual challenge, a familiar kind of brain-teaser, sounding like an algebraic proposition: 'Let man's soul be a sphere' (l.1; Donne 1990: 241). An elaborate analogy is then worked through to a simple conclusion: Donne is constrained to move westward physically while meditationally he inclines eastward, to where Christ was crucified and where, at this point of the liturgical year, he symbolically is crucified again. Christ rises as a towering figure, equated with the sun, which also rises. Suddenly the stark simplicity of that image is incorporated into the cosmic conceit with which the poem started. In the western Christian tradition Christ is identified as the person of the godhead who effected creation: 'Could I behold those hands which span the poles, / And tune all spheres at once, pierced with those holes?' (ll.21–2; Donne 1990: 242) The paradox of power and suffering is affectingly developed till the poem concludes, rather like the more violent of the 'Holy Sonnets' but with a further reiteration of the journey westward as an informing symbol:

> O Saviour, as thou hang'st upon the tree;
> I turn my back to thee, but to receive
> Corrections, till thy mercies bid thee leave.
> O think me worth thine anger, punish me,
> Burn off my rusts, and my deformity,
> Restore thine image, so much, by thy grace.
> That thou mayst know me, and I'll turn my face.
> (ll.36–42; Donne 1990: 242)

John Carey observes, correctly, that the landscape through which Donne passes is excluded from the poem, which is peopled by just two figures: the poet and the crucified Christ (Carey 1990: 106–7). But the purpose of meditation is as much to exclude what is not relevant as to focus on what is. Donne takes from the context two vital givens, date and direction, and excludes the rest, in what is a triumph of devotional intensity.

Patronage provides the context for his *Anniversaries*. In 1610 he wrote a funeral elegy for Elizabeth Drury, the daughter of Sir Robert Drury, who had died at the age of 14. Sir Robert was to take Donne into his entourage on his European travels in 1611–12, and on their return he provided Donne and his family with a London house gratis. Besides a funeral elegy, Donne wrote two long and ambitious poems. The elegy and the first of these were published in 1611; and then reissued with the second in 1612. Donne evidently felt uneasy about this, and a letter of 1612 shows him remorseful that he '*descended* to print anything in verse . . . and do not pardon myself' (quoted and discussed in Beal 2002: 122). The poems are problematic and a little embarrassing for modern readers, too, who find perplexing the disparity between the hyperbolic celebration and the diminutive achievements of the person celebrated. Yet taken together, the poems share some common ground with other major funeral elegies of the early Stuart period. Like Jonson's Cary-Morison ode (see below, chapter 3) and Milton's 'Lycidas' (see below, chapter 4), the untimeliness of the death of a young person provides the platform for a much larger exploration of the human condition and the imperfection and fragility of the world:

> She, after whom, what form soe'er we see,
> Is discord, and rude incongruity;
> She, she is dead, she's dead; when thou know'st this
> Thou know'st how ugly a monster this world is . . .
> ('The First Anniversary', l.322–6; Donne 1990: 214–15)

Carey remarks on the 'dizzy cadenzas of praise' which make up these poems (1990: 89), but a brutal precision and a darker sensibility intermittently intrude:

> ... as sometimes in a beheaded man,
> Though at those two red seas, which freely ran,
> One from the trunk, another from the head,
> His soul be sailed, to her eternal bed,
> His eyes will twinkle, and his tongue will roll,
> As though he beckoned, and called back his soul,
> He grasps his hands, and he pulls up his feet,
> And seems to reach, and to step forth to meet
> His soul ...
>
>   ...
>
> So struggles this dead world now she is gone ...
>   (ll.9–17, 22; Donne 1990: 218–19)

When the poem is over, I suspect most readers remember the twitching decollated cadaver and forget the idealized girl.

How widely read and how influential was this poet who, for the most part, eschewed print and fretted about limiting the circulation of his work in manuscript? Peter Beal is unequivocal: 'the sheer quantity of manuscript copies of poems by him which still survive (4,000-odd texts in upwards of 260 manuscripts) – and which must be only a fraction of the number once in existence – indicates beyond doubt that Donne was the most popular English poet from the 1590s until at least the middle of the seventeenth century' (2002: 122). A substantial collection of early musical settings has recently been rediscovered (Alberge 2005). In terms of literary taste, the success, despite an absence of printed collections, points to an elite audience, unsqueamish, intelligent and ready for the challenges his verse so often poses. He substantially redefines English love poetry, moving past classical and Petrarchan models. Yet when Caroline love poets like Carew and Herrick follow him, they take the situations, the assumptions, the occasional playfulness and the libertine toughness, though they restrain the demands they make on their readers' interpretative skills, and they lack his emotional intensity. His influence is more decisively evident on religious verse. Single-handedly he revived devotional and meditational poetry in English, which had languished since the days of the late Middle English lyric. George Herbert, whose mother and brother were among his patrons and friends, takes his intensity and at times his obscurity, and Vaughan and Crashaw perhaps follow, the former aspiring to that cosmic view we noted in 'Good Friday, 1613', the latter not flinching to challenge his readers' responses with images approaching the grotesque.

Ben Jonson knew Donne and read his poetry in manuscript. They shared some patrons and moved in overlapping social circles. Jonson, however, depended on his writing for his status and income. We have considered above his texts for court masques and entertainments and his early Jacobean drama, for which, of course, he was paid. He was readier than most to commit his plays to print publication, though he seems to have been aware that some were better than others and that they could be revised as he prepared them for the press. We know this because he was selective about including play texts in his collected works of 1616, and comparison with quarto versions, where they exist, show he evidently continued to work on them in varying degrees since their performance and earliest printing (Riggs 1989: 222–4). That collection also includes the earliest substantial publication of his non-dramatic verse.

The Workes of Beniamin Jonson (Jonson 1616) is rightly regarded as a landmark volume in the history of English literary culture in general and more specifically in the history of the book. It is a lavish folio publication of just over 1,000 pages, mostly with generous margins, which sometimes carry learned annotations by the author, and a fine engraved titlepage, depicting a façade of Corinthian columns, niches, allegorical statuary and a picture of a Roman theatre, which proclaims the neoclassical ambitions of the contents (see plate 1). Harold Love and Arthur Marotti not unfairly term the work 'self-advertising' (Love and Marotti 2002: 67). It marks, too, Jonson's new status; shortly before, James I had granted him an annual pension of 100 marks. The 'catalogue' to the *Workes* lists not only the contents but also the people to whom the works are dedicated. It includes the inns of court, the universities, Lady Wroth, the most creative Sidney of her generation, William, third Earl of Pembroke, Lord Aubigny, a cousin of the king and Jonson's most generous patron, in whose house he lived for much of the early Jacobean period, and the antiquarian, William Camden, among the finest early modern scholars. The list makes impressive reading, connecting Jonson with the seats of learning and, more significantly perhaps, suggesting the protection he may enjoy from people very close the royal seat of power. It strikes a blow for the

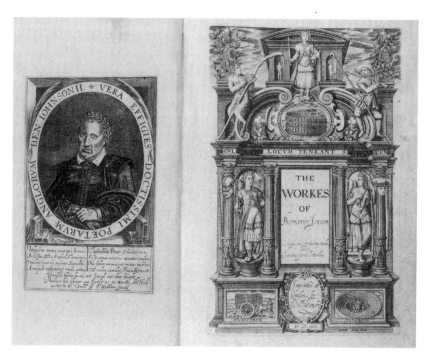

Plate 1 Ben Jonson, *The Workes of Beniamin Jonson* (1616), portrait frontispiece and title page. Reproduced by permission of the British Library G.11630.

status of the profession of creative writing and print culture. Moreover, the juxtaposition of play texts and poetry addresses head-on the low status of the former in contemporary cultural ideology. Jonson himself was to rail against the lamentable taste of theatre audiences (see below, chapter 3), a theme adumbrated even here in the dedicatory material to *Sejanus* and *Catiline*. But to treat plays as 'works' meriting collection, revision and luxury publication certainly struck some contemporaries as at least provocative and perhaps affected and silly (Jonson 1976: Introduction). Again, the presence of the poems both distinguishes his perspective on the so-called stigma of print from that of the anxious Donne and declared his claims to be regarded as a poet and a playwright. The collection was also a finely accomplished publishing project. In a context where play texts could still be pirated and were often quite fiercely guarded by the companies that owned them and where publishers found it difficult to acquire manuscripts of the work of living, elite-culture poets, Jonson and his printer William Stansby, scored an extraordinary victory. In so doing, they pushed open the door for two other significant publications, the first folio of the collected plays of Beaumont and Fletcher and, seen in a longer perspective, the single most important book in the English literary tradition, the first folio of Shakespeare (1623; see below, chapter 3).

The poems fall into two sections, the epigrams and the 'forest'. The former formally share common ground, for example, with Donne's own epigrams, though Jonson seems more frequently than Donne to invite recollection of classical precursors, above all the poetry of Martial. The latter, which translates the Latin '*silva*', the usual word for 'wood', also invokes classical models and a classical genre. The original *silvae* were 'occasional pieces, rapid effusions … in a great variety of forms', and neoclassical writers across western Europe who adopted the term, both for neo-Latin and vernacular writing, retained the criteria of multifariousness and of apparent spontaneity (Fowler 1985: 220–1). Jonson, in selecting the term and anglicizing it, invites comparison with Statius and other Latin writers of such miscellanies.

The epigrams themselves are strikingly diverse. The hostile, satirical ones deal with 'types' rather than individuals, although the editorial and critical traditions have in some cases attempted identification. Figures on the periphery of court society are frequent, such as 'Courtling' or 'Court-Parrot' or 'Mill, My Lady's Woman' or 'English Monsieur' (Jonson 1985: 246, 251–3). We meet the bawds, lechers, gulls, cheats and swaggerers that people his city comedies, like 'Cashiered Captain Surly', whose whore 'keeps him', or Captain Hazard the Cheater, or Captain Hungry, a braggart (ibid., pp. 250–1, 263–4).

The poems of compliment fall into two categories. Those to patrons are straightforward and sometimes rather vague panegyric. For example, 'To William, Earl of Pembroke' opens declamatorily with 'I do but name thee, Pembroke, and I find / It is an epigram on all mankind' and ends 'they that hope to see / The commonwealth still safe must study thee' (ll.1–2, 19–20; pp. 260–1). 'To Mary, Lady Wroth' concludes, 'My praise is plain, and wheresoe'er professed / Becomes none more than you, who need it least' (ll.13–14; p. 261).

The poems of praise rehearse the virtues of the patronage circles he courted and include those aristocrats cited in the 'catalogue'. Several poems address the king himself, the great prize for patronage-hunters. In the first, 'To King James', the 'best of kings' is also celebrated as 'best of poets' (ibid., p. 223). Yet what are we to make of 'To the Ghost of Martial'?

> Martial, thou gav'st far nobler epigrams
> To thy Domitian, than I can my James;
> But in my royal subject I pass thee:
> Thou flattered'st thine, mine cannot flattered be.
>
> (Ibid., p. 233)

The superiority of Martial over Jonson has a pleasing modesty; but James exceeds Domitian so emphatically that he cannot be flattered; the wildest of Jonson's panegyric merely reflects accurately his astonishing virtues. The poem, self-reflectively, lays on the flattery by denying that flattery is possible. In conjuring the ghost of Martial, he has raised, too, that of Domitian, whose reign ended in a seven-year orgy of terror, fuelled by the extensive use of informers, before assassins killed him. It seems a hazardous kind of praise to place James in comparison with a Roman tyrant, but Jonson, even at his most obsequious, remains a risk taker.

Martial's spirit flits through many poems, his topoi recur and his phrasing is echoed. Ideologically, the effect is destabilizing. Yet Jonson genuinely does share a problem with Martial: both are moralists, strict satirists, unflinching observers of a corrupt and corrupting society, but at the same time they are panegyrists of the authoritarian rulers ultimately responsible for that world. The issues even emerge in so engaging a poem as 'Inviting a Friend to Supper' – indeed, rather more strikingly in Jonson than in the three Martial analogues it invokes and in the longer tradition that stand behind them (Jonson 1985: 660–1). The poem develops a powerful image of a warm, secure intimacy, lubricated by 'rich Canary wine, / Which is the the Mermaid's now, but shall be mine', enlivened by readings from the classics, frankly discussed. The bounty of farms, fields and foreshores provides the feast. Yet explicitly this is a temporary and private space in a threatening world:

> And we shall have no Poley or Parrot by;
> Nor shall our cups make any guilty men,
> But at our parting we will be as when
> We innocently met. No simple word
> That shall be uttered at our mirthful board
> Shall make us sad next morning, or affright
> The liberty that we'll enjoy tonight.
>
> (ll.29–30, 36–42; p. 260)

Poley and Parrot are spies feeding information to the government. In their absence, Jonson and his friend enjoy 'liberty', a word that had then more or less its current semantic range; but for tonight only.

The 15 items of the *silvae*, 'The Forest', show an extraordinary technical range across a miscellany of subgenres. There are songs, including two recycled from *Volpone*, evidently in Jonson's view untainted by that association. (Volpone sang them as part of his attempt on the virtue of Celia.) The best, 'To Celia', seemingly embodies a quintessential Englishness of simple, sincere expression:

> Drink to me only with thine eyes,
>   And I will pledge with mine;
> Or leave kiss but in the cup,
>   And I'll not look for wine.
>   (ll.1–4; p. 293)

Syntactically simple, the opening sentence apparently offers a plain, predominately monosyllabic, expression of affection. Yet Jonson is rarely plain or simple. The informing metaphor is, on reflection, quite challenging: how may one exchange drinking pledges with one's eyes? or leave a kiss in a cup? Behind the poem, as the commentary tradition has long recognized, stand close echoes of the *Epistles* of Philostratus, a shadowy, late Greek author. This work serves as a particularly good example of much that characterizes Jonson's poetry. The vocabulary, direct, English, straightforward, articulates an intellectually complex idea; it demonstrates that in some sense classical models may be matched by vernacular poets; and beneath its surface lies a world of erudite cultural reference.

The same qualities mark 'To Penshurst', 'the seminal early estate poem, and easily the most discussed example of the genre'. Epigrams by Martial, praising the villas and estates of his circle, are discernible influences, as too is Virgil's *Georgics* (Fowler 1994: 58). But this remains an English poem about an English estate, reflecting contemporary and very personal social anxieties. The panegyric strategy of the country house poem, taken up in a series of fine exemplars that extend through Carew's 'To Saxham' (see below, chapter 4) and Marvell's 'Upon Appleton House' (see below, chapter 5), is here already established. Jonson praises the house owner and his family by praising his house and its estate. Penshurst was owned by Robert Sidney, Viscount Lisle, younger brother of Sir Philip Sidney and a patron of Jonson's.

Penshurst emerges as the embodiment of moderation and responsibility. Unlike prodigy houses contemporaneously favoured by aristocratic grandees, this is not 'built to envious show' (l.1; p. 282). Indeed, Jonson may be a neoclassicist in literary culture, but here Penhurst's exemplification of a native architectural tradition is celebrated as a physical manifestation of its owner's avoidance of expensive rebuilding on Palladian lines. Instead, this estate honours its role as the centre of a mutually supportive social structure. The 'farmer and the clown' bring in their wholesome rural gifts, and are hospitably received (ll.48–60; pp. 283–4).

At the equivalent point in 'To Saxham', Carew rehearses the charity topos: the household offers succour to the rural poor in hard times. Jonson prefers to celebrate his own reception, and he does so in a socially insecure manner. He contrasts his treatment here with how other grandees receive those who, whatever their merits, are their social inferiors. Here he may eat the same food as Lisle and the servants don't begrudge him food and drink. As it happens, the house rules at Penshurst forbade servants to eat from the poor tub. They know they have sufficient provision without relying on the leftovers from the hall table. Telling how he is treated at Penshurst becomes, in effect, a lament for how he is treated elsewhere.

The poem offers detailed celebration of Lisle, noting the family's commitment to innovations in orchard management and commemorating the only occasion that James I and Prince Henry visited the house. Other poems in 'The Forest' similarly tie Jonson very publicly to his multiple patronage networks. There is a long poem to Sir Robert Wroth, Lisle's son-in-law and husband of the writer Lady Mary. Verse epistles address the Countess of Rutland and Lady Aubigny, wife of his currently most valuable patron, and there is a birthday ode to Sir William Sidney, Lisle's son.

The only printed poetry collection to rival Jonson's in accomplishment in the early Stuart period is as riddlingly bereft of circumstantiality as Jonson's is suffused with it. *Shake-Speares Sonnets. Never before Imprinted* appeared in 1609. *Venus and Adonis* and *The Rape of Lucrece*, published in the 1590s, went into numerous early editions. No second edition of the sonnets appeared until 1640. Love sonnet cycles were commoner in the late Elizabethan period, and by 1609 the project had a decidedly retrospective feel to it, perhaps surprisingly in the context of the constant innovation which characterized Shakespeare's Jacobean drama. The volume, like Spenser's *Amoretti and*

Epithalamion published in 1595, concludes with a longer poem in a different genre, in this case *A Lover's Complaint*, a rather leisurely pastoral dialogue, the Shakespearean provenance of which has been questioned (Shakespeare 2002: 138–9).

Dating the composition of these poems has proved difficult and controversial. Some were circulating in manuscript and two appeared in print in the 1590s. Colin Burrow, drawing on recent stylometry, postulates a division of the sonnets over a period extending from about 1591 to perhaps 1604, though 'there are many grey areas in these approximate findings ... there is not certainty when Shakespeare began to write sonnets, and there is no certainty that his revisions and rewritings continued beyond about 1604–5' (Shakespeare 2002: 105), though some evidence suggests a later date for *A Lover's Complaint*.

However backward-looking the volume may be formally, its relationship to the Petrarchan tradition that predominated among Elizabethan sonneteers shows very significant differences. Many of the poems seemingly address a young man, whose physical beauty is explored in a subtle appropriation of the Petrarchan idiom. Thus, sonnet 18, 'Shall I compare thee to a summer's day?', picks open a delicate conceit in which the loved one emerges favourably in the comparison, before the poem modulates into a delicate and self-referential exploration of the power of art to resist mutability: 'So long as men can breathe or eyes can see, / So long lives this, and this gives life to thee' (ll.1, 13–14; Shakespeare 1989: 753). Nothing indicates the gender of the 'thou'. Elsewhere the implied relationship does emerge more clearly, as in the sequence of sonnets urging a young man to wed and breed. There are remarkable nuances: the poet is older, wiser, yet not only less physically attractive but also socially inferior. It is inherently curious to read poems seemingly urging the loved one to sleep with someone else. Nor does Shakespeare work towards the sort of fashionable homoerotic frisson that Marlowe carried off so brilliantly in sections of *Hero and Leander*, first printed in 1598, or indeed he himself produced in *Venus and Adonis*. Indeed, one of the most playful of the sonnets, 'A woman's face with nature's own hand painted', ends with double entendres that mix sexual uncertainty with a show of paradoxical resolution:

> ... nature as she wrought thee fell a-doting,
> And by addition me of thee defeated

> By adding one thing to my purpose nothing.
> But since she pricked thee out for women's pleasure,
> Mine be thy love and thy love's use their treasure.
> (sonnet 20, ll.10–14; p. 753)

The indecorous quibbles work in Jacobean English much as they do today: 'prick' and 'thing', then as now, meant genitalia, and they are unstably juxtaposed with the declamatory decorousness of the last line. The clash of registers signals a suppressed unease or regret at an uneasy resignation, which acknowledges that the loved one will mate with women, that the speaker apparently excludes the alternatives of homosexual congress, and that this relationship is imperfect in that it lacks the consummation that is the usual objective of erotic desire.

A smaller number of sonnets are addressed to or are about the so-called Dark Lady. In the simplest, Shakespeare takes the commonplace compliments of Petrarchanism and inverts or subverts them, as in the *blason*, sonnet 130, 'My mistress' eyes are nothing like the sun'. For 12 lines the physical characteristics of the woman are differentiated from those of the stereotypical and idealized mistress of the tradition. The final couplet, as often in Shakespeare's sonnets, cuts against the grain of what has gone before: 'And yet, by heaven, I think my love as rare / As any she belied with false compare' (ll.13–14; p. 767). Burlesquing the *blason* has Elizabethan, pre-Shakespearean precedents (Fowler 1985: 176). However, we should search in vain for poems that anticipate sonnets like 129, 'Th'expense of spirit in a waste of shame', as challenging reflections on the sexual act in human relationships:

> Enjoyed no sooner but despised straight,
> Past reason hunted, and no sooner had
> Past reason hated as a swallowed bait
> On purpose laid to make the taker mad;
> Mad in pursuit and in possession so,
> Had, having, and in quest to have, extreme;
> A bliss in proof and proved, a very woe;
> Before, a joy proposed; behind, a dream.
> (ll.5–12; p. 767)

There is a depth and subtlety here that stands outside the crudity of the western misogynistic tradition. This is a hatred not of women but of an irrational, irresistible impulse that brings people level with other animals and sets at nothing social costs and health risks for a moment-ary bliss, a joy in prospect and in retrospect a dream. Donne, as we saw, developed the English sonnet as a fit medium for intense religious meditation; later in the century, Milton uses it for two-edged political comment and praise (see below, chapter 5). Shakespeare, however, pursues a different and even more ambitious direction.

Aemilia Lanyer has been associated very closely with Shakespeare. A. L. Rowse, in an argument that finds no support among more recent biographers, identified her as the original 'Dark Lady' of Shakespeare's sonnets (Rowse 1974, 1978; for responses, see, for example, Lewalski 1994: 213–15; Purkiss 1994: xxx–xl; Woods 2002; *DNB* 2004). The principal connection between them is likely to have been much more tangential: Lanyer was for a while mistress to Henry Cary, Lord Hunsdon, the Lord Chamberlain who patronized and protected Sha-kespeare's acting company, the future King's Men. In purely literary terms, there are more points of comparison and connection with the work of Donne and Jonson.

Lanyer's solitary publication is her only extant work, *Salve Deus Rex Judaeorum*, published in 1611 (as others have noted, the same year that Donne published his first *Anniversary*). Like Donne's poem (above), it is a sustained exercise in panegyric directed to a patron whose sole claim to modern fame is the patronage extended to or at least sought by the poet. Lanyer arguably belonged to a lower social class than Donne, though she moved on the fringes of court circles, both as a grandee's mistress and as the daughter and wife of court musicians. (A contemporary account, frequently cited, suggests Huns-don passed her on to Alfonso Lanyer once she was pregnant.) At the time of publication, her primary source of patronage was Margaret Clifford, the Dowager Duchess of Cumberland, whose companion she was. Though print publication by women was relatively rare, Lanyer's family status, among those who entertain for remuneration, perhaps precluded the kind of squeamishness Donne chose to manifest. Like Jonson and Shakespeare, her principal milieu was among those who were paid to amuse.

The volume is a curious one, more so, perhaps, in modern editions than in the original. In the former, about a third of it is taken up with front matter in the form of dedicatory epistles, mostly in verse. Strik-ingly, all the dedicatory poems are addressed to women, which points to what is perhaps most remarkable about the volume, Lanyer's as-sembly of what Barbara Lewalski calls 'a defense and celebration of the enduring community of good women that reaches from Eve to contemporary Jacobean patronesses' (1994: 213). The core text is a verse retelling of a Bible story, a genre that becomes increasingly popular in the following decades. In this case, the narrative depicts the passion and resurrection of Christ, in a broadly Protestant theological idiom. But Lanyer ties the poem closely to the praise of virtuous women with which the volume opened. Repeatedly, she turns from contemplation of the suffering of Christ to the celebration of the piety of the Duchess of Cumberland. Indeed, at times within the poem Lanyer seems to debate with herself about who is the real subject. Thus, in an aside to the Duchess, she urges:

> Pardon (good madam) though I have digressed
> From what I do intend to write of thee,
> To set his glory forth whom thou lov'st best,
> Whose wondrous works no mortal eye can see . . .
> (ll.145–8; Purkiss 1994: 275)

Furthermore, her narrative selects and emphasizes feminine responses to the events. An 'apology' from Eve counters the facile misogyny of a long western tradition. Other digressions, which are listed on the title page as if they were separate poems, articulate the sufferings of the mother of Christ and the lamentations of the women of Jerusalem. Thus, they confirm the feminine – indeed, feminist – orientation of the account.

The book concludes with 'The Description of Cooke-ham', a poem that is often said to be the first country house or estate poem in the English tradition, a claim formerly advanced for Ben Jonson's 'To Penshurst' (see above). It remains uncertain which was composed first, though certainly Lanyer's was the first to appear in print. There is no evidence that one may have influenced the other, though they share a common ancestry in the classical literary tradition. Lanyer's poem has less than Jonson's to say about the house and the estate on which it stands. Cookeham, rather, figures as a symbol for a lost happiness, when Lanyer enjoyed a closer proximity to Margaret Clifford, who is the primary subject for praise within the poem. It functions as a kind of paradise lost, where once the poet experienced a subordinate but intimate involvement in what is represented as an exclusively female social group. The Duchess herself walks the grounds in communion with God, much as Eve may have done in the original garden. The house itself goes undescribed, while the landscape features mainly as part of an extended poetic conceit, mirroring, in its love at the Duchess's presence and grief at her imminent departure, the feelings of the poet. But the compliment is elaborately and delicately turned:

> The trees with leaves, with fruits, with flowers clad,
> Embraced each other, seeming to be glad,
> Turning themselves to beauteous canopies
> To shade the sun from your brighter eyes.
> (ll.22–5; Purkiss 1994: 327)

Lanyer's own perspective matches the deferential tone of the front matter with which the book opens, pulling a seemingly very disparate assembly of diverse genres into a kind of unity.

Michael Drayton, among the most rewarding of the second-rank poets of the early Jacobean period, justifiably described his major work, *Poly-Olbion* (1612, 1622), as a 'Herculean labour' (Drayton 1931–41: IV, 391). Over the two parts, he offers a tour of England and Wales, describing the topography, freely mythologizing about the landscape of rivers and hills, and tying an occasionally fanciful historical narrative to a precisely realized sense of place (see plates 2 and 3). En route, he incorporates a great amount of serious history and politics. He had intended a third part, a description of Scotland, though that never appeared in print and nothing of it survives in manuscript, if indeed he wrote any of it.

Superficially, Drayton's seems a thoroughly Jacobean project, a celebration of the *Britain* over which James claimed sovereignty. Indeed, Drayton had early sought the patronage of the king, but he soon became alienated, and gravitated to the circle of Prince Henry, in whose household he was employed (Norbrook 1984: 197; *DNB* 2004), and to whom the first part was dedicated. A full-length portrait of the young prince, engaged in a martial exercise, is among its front matter. Henry's death and the loss of that patronage left Drayton unprotected. The dedication of the second part to Henry's younger brother, Charles, Prince of Wales, the future Charles I, seeks an ideological continuity that never emerged.

From the epistle to the second part it is evident that the first part sold poorly, though it is an attractive book, with a splendid engraved title page, allegorical maps drawn to fit each 'song', and notes by John Selden, the most learned Englishman of his generation. Yet the reasons may lie in the fundamental concept of the project. The England and

Plate 2 Michael Drayton, *Poly-Olbion* (1612), title page and facing text. Reproduced by permission of The Huntington Library, San Marino, California 59144.

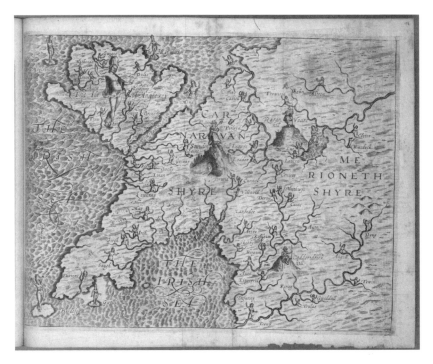

Plate 3 Michael Drayton, *Poly-Olbion* (1612), map of 'Carnarvanshire'. Reproduced by permission of The Huntington Library, San Marino, California 59144.

Wales he celebrates are overwhelmingly rural; cities, where mentioned, are much more briefly treated than the rivers that run through them. Even his account of London has more to say about the Lee and the Thames than about the city itself. English culture in the early modern period was overwhelmingly metropolitan. By implication, Drayton turns his back on the court and the city, the 'Marchants long train'd up in Gayn's deceitfull schoole' (song XVI, l.354; IV, 322). He addresses the England (and Wales) of the counties and their gentry-class hierarchies. This in part may explain its commercial failure, since there is little to interest the Londoner, while regionalism tends to fragment the potential readership. Even now, the passages that treat the landscape each modern reader is familiar with are surely more fascinating than the rest.

William Browne's two volumes of *Britannia's Pastorals* (1613, 1616) are often regarded as companion pieces to *Poly-Olbion*. Browne and Drayton moved in some of the same circles, and the project evidently owed much to him in its conception. Like *Poly-Olbion* it celebrates 'Britain', though once more it is scarcely a panegyric to James's grand design. In this view, the allegorical figure of 'Famine' intermittently terrorizes the land. There are, moreover, other anti-court sentiments developed with various levels of obliqueness, as in the digression on '*Delayes*, the *stones* that waiting *Suiters* grinde, / By whom at *Court* the poore mans cause is signed' (Browne 1616: 105). An Inner Templar, Browne anticipates the sharper critique of royal policy that develops, particularly among writers associated with the Inns of Court, in the years following the inception of the Thirty Years War (below, chapter 3). More immediately, Browne had shared Drayton's enthusiasm for the more militant Protestantism associated with Prince Henry's entourage. His first published poem had been a funeral elegy for the prince, and he incorporated it into the last song of the first volume (Browne 1613: 89–93).

The two volumes of *Britannia's Pastorals* are represented by Drayton as defiantly old-fashioned: 'Drive forth thy Flocke, you Pastor, to that Plaine, / Where our old Shepheards wont their flocks to feed' ('To his Friend the AUTHOR'; Browne 1613: sig. A4v). Ideologically, neo-Spenserianism signalled a return to the militantly anti-Catholic Protestantism of Elizabethan England, 'given that the new regime had rejected the Elizabethan ideals of Protestant chivalry' (Norbrook 2002: 177). Yet Browne's work is innovative, and anticipates (and influences) the new interest in Caroline verse in the pastoral mode. It draws actively on *Poly-Olbion*, peopling the landscape with those quasi-allegorical figures, nymphs, shepherds and river gods, which Drayton attributes to topographical features and which recur alluringly in the maps that accompany each song. At times Browne draws so closely on Drayton that he cross-references his own annotation with Selden's notes to *Poly-Olbion* (Browne 1616: 67, marginal note). Though there are some excursions – the first song of the second volume has an outing to Anglesey, for example – the strongest sense of place relates to the Tavy, the river of his native Tavistock, and to south Devon more generally. While Browne's current connections were metropolitan, he nevertheless articulates a provincial perspective and country values. Culturally, although allusions to and echoes of classical pastoral abound, he roots his work in English soil. Technically the two volumes show a high competence, a facility in the ten-syllable couplets in which most of the poetry is written, and he incorporates into it elegies, lyric pieces, pastoral dialogues, epigrams and one singularly ornate poem in the shape of a love-knot (Browne 1613: 61). In his later career, he became closely dependent on the Herbert family, writing elegies for family members, most of which 'appear to have had a very limited circulation, and may have been confined to the family itself' (*DNB* 2004).

Browne had probably aspired to join the coterie around the court of Prince Henry, and Drayton received direct patronage from the prince, a pension of £10 per annum (*DNB* 2004); so, too, did Josuah Sylvester, author of the most popular and influential long poem of the early Jacobean period, completed in 1608 as *Bartas his Devine Weekes and Workes*. Guillaume de Salluste, sieur du Bartas, a French Protestant, had published two works 'that brought him national and international attention' (Sylvester 1979: I, 1), *La Semaine ou Création du monde* (1578) and *La Seconde Semaine* (1584). Du Bartas was a devout Protestant and rapidly acquired a wide Protestant readership. Sir Philip Sidney apparently translated at least part, though the work is not extant. Six other writers, of minor status, had published sections by 1604. Perhaps most significantly for Sylvester's own aspirations, James I had made verse translations of three parts, two of which had appeared in print in his *Poeticall Exercises at Vacant Houres* published in Edinburgh in 1591. Sylvester's own involvement with Du Bartas was of long standing. He had published instalments of his translation since 1590, and had for long sought out wealthy patronage to allow him to leave his profession of 'merchant adventurer', a cloth trader privileged by membership of an elite mercantile guild, and to concentrate on the massive task of translating a poem twice as long as *Paradise Lost*. He had courted the Earl of Essex before his fall, and, though wooing the king proved unprofitable, from 1608 he was a pensioner (at twice Drayton's rate) of Prince Henry. His personal fortunes never recovered from the devastating impact of the prince's death. By the time of his own death in 1617 he had returned to his old trade, working as Secretary of the Merchant Adventurers at Middelburg in Zeeland (Sylvester 1979: I, 70–1, 4–32; *DNB* 2004).

Du Bartas had produced an ambitious work that, in its first 'divine week', relates the events of the week of creation and, in the second, events from the Old Testament from the fall to the Babylonian captivity of Zedekiah, before his efforts were interrupted by his death. Sylvester worked patiently through du Bartas's text, though he added about 2,000 lines of his own, usually putting this material in italics (Sylvester 1979: I, 55, 102). Protestant poetics had agitated for a doctrinally and culturally appropriate literature, at least since the age of Sidney. Sylvester offered that with some accomplishment. His generally competent couplets are often assembled into a swelling verse of controlled power. Compare his description of the creation of the globe with the analogous passage from Milton's *Paradise Lost*:

> This was not then the World, 'twas but the matter,
> The Nurcerie, whence it should issue after:
> Or rather th'*Embryon* that within a *Weeke*
> Was to be borne: for that huge lumpe was like
> The shape-lesse burthen in the Mothers wombe,
> Which yet in Time doth into fashion come:
> Eyes, eares, and nose, mouth, fingers, hand, and feete,
> And every member in proportion meete;
> Round, large, and long, there of it selfe it thrives,
> And (*Little-World*) into the World arrives.
> But that becomes (by Natures set direction)
> From foule and dead, to beauty, life, perfection
> But this dull Heape of undigested stuffe,
> Had doubtlesse never come to shape or proofe,
> Had not th'Almighty with his quick'ning breath
> Blowne life and spirit into this Lump of death.
>
> (Sylvester 1979: I, 119)
>
> The earth was formed, but in the womb as yet
> Of waters, embryon immature involved,
> Appeared not: over all the face of earth
> Main ocean flowed, not idle, but with warm
> Prolific humour softening all her globe,
> Fermented the great mother to conceive,
> Satiate with genial moisture . . .
>
> (*Paradise Lost* VII.277–82; Milton 1999: 406)

Milton's, of course, is a much richer account, and it modulates to invoke resonances of Neoplatonic cosmology (Milton 1999: 406, n. to 279–82) and probably alchemical process (Abraham 1998: s.v. 'prima materia' and 'womb'). Again, his lexical felicity is of a different order from that of the earlier work. But the principal image is already there in Du Bartas-Sylvester. Certainly, it is developed in leisurely fashion – do we really need the list of the embryonic parts? – yet a vivid antithesis emerges between the life processes at work and 'this Lump of death'.

Sylvester's work was valued highly in his life time and in the decades that followed. Substantial sections were printed intermittently through the late Elizabethan and early Jacobean periods. After the first publication of the complete translation in quarto in 1608, further quarto printings appeared in 1611 and 1613, followed by a lavish posthumous folio of his complete works in 1621, which was in turn reprinted in 1633 and 1641. His influence on the next generations of devotional poets in the English Protestant tradition is easily demonstrated. References to parallels and echoes of Sylvester abound in any scholarly edition of *Paradise Lost*. Lucy Hutchinson's modern editor rightly observes that, in terms of structure and content, in *Order and Disorder* she approaches much closer to Du Bartas-Sylvester than to Milton (Hutchinson 2001: xxv). The influence is plainly evident in the biblical narrative poems of Francis Quarles (see below, chapter 3).

Yet *Bartas his Devine Weekes and Workes* has all but disappeared from the corpus of seventeenth-century texts which are read today, and it is rarely anthologized. Fowler (1991) prints fewer than 80 lines; it is not represented in Abrams et al. (2000) or Cummings (2000). Sylvester's decline in popularity was rapid and complete. By 1681 John Dryden could observe: 'I remember, when I was a boy, I thought inimitable Spenser a mean poet, in comparison of Sylvester's *Dubartas*, and was rapt into an ecstasy when I read these lines. ... I am much deceived if this be not abominable fustian' (quoted in Sylvester 1979: I, 72). Possibly it would have retained some place as the most substantial poem of English Protestantism were it not for the astonishing achievement of *Paradise Lost*, a poem it had helped in some measure to shape. Milton does everything that Sylvester does, but much more briskly. He brings, too, character, narrative skill, an ear for rhetoric as a function of oratory rather than syntactical patterning, prosodic innovation, brilliant imagery, learning, an engagement with the longer literary tradition of western Europe, almost a manifesto for neoclassical cultural ideology, political and theological nuance, extraordinary stylistic genius, and more. England may well have needed a serious poem to be appreciated by the predominant faith community, but Milton displaced Sylvester as surely as Dr Johnson's dictionary replaced Nathan Bailey's or *Homo sapiens* nudged aside Neanderthal man.

Non-Fictional Prose

Francis Bacon had established a limited literary reputation with the first edition of his *Essays*, published in 1597. (For subsequent extended editions, see below, chapter 3.) But his principal ambitions lay elsewhere, in seeking preferment in the legal profession, though publication no doubt functioned also to advance these aspirations. The late Elizabethan period proved singularly trying for him in that he was a protégé and client of the second Earl of Essex, and indeed his brother, Anthony, probably remained associated with the earl until catastrophe befell him. After the abortive coup Anthony was perhaps lucky to escape prosecution alongside others of the earl's supporters and retainers (Jardine and Stewart 1998: 252–53). Francis had already repositioned himself within the political factions of the Elizabethan court, and he shone as a prosecuting council at the earl's trial for treason, after which he produced for the press an official version of the proceedings.

To some contemporaries, Bacon's conduct in the last years of Elizabeth and the opening years of James's reign seemed at the least unedifying, and perhaps it seems so still. Certainly, shortly after James's accession he felt constrained to write and send to press his *Apology, In certain imputations concerning the late earl of Essex* (1604), perhaps prompted by recollection that 'James himself had had a soft spot for Essex' (Jardine and Stewart 1998: 265). On several fronts he plainly strove assiduously to elbow his way into the king's notice and favour.

His *Twoo Bookes of the Proficience and Advancement of Learning* (1605), the first great prose work of the Stuart age, may be mistaken as little more than part of his campaign for personal advancement. Certainly, it is addressed to the king and opens with a long passage of sustained panegyric, praising 'The largenesse of your capacitie, the faithfulnesse of your memorie, the swiftnesse of your apprehension, the penetration of your Judgement, and the facility and order of your elocution' (Bacon 1605: sig. A2v). But he soon settles to his real task, which is a broad and challenging one.

James was bright, learned, and intellectually confident. Bacon offers him a strikingly comprehensive review of the state of learning in England, of its institutional and philosophical basis, its deficiencies and its scope for improvement and advancement. While plainly demonstrating his own astonishing range and brilliance, he presents to the king a sort of uncommissioned report on how patronage could be extended in ways that would stimulate academic endeavour. In the process, he writes a manifesto for secular, rational enquiry that is to prove deeply influential in English philosophical and scientific circles through the mid-century and into the Restoration.

Bacon concedes some role for intellectual enquiry in theology, but, in an argument which anticipates the core proposition of Sir Thomas Browne's *Religio Medici* (1642, 1643) (see below, chapter 5), faith and reason on his account are opposed: 'The prerogative of God extendeth as well to the reason as to the will of Man; So that as we are to obey his law though we finde a reluctance in our will, So we are to believe his word, though we finde a reluctance in our reason' (book II, 108). Issues of church government, already divisive within English Protestantism, are carefully evaded. Thinking deeply about the material world without making persistent reference to divine first causes was probably the most crucial development in the history of ideas across the century in England. On it depended the political philosophy of Thomas Hobbes and John Locke, and the scientific movements which culminated in the founding of the Royal Society.

Bacon's dependence on the longer humanist tradition has often been demonstrated. His principal targets include Ciceronian copiousness in prose style; the shortcomings of established educational provision; scholastic philosophy, with its obsessive emphasis on refining the Aristotelian legacy; pseudo-sciences that depend on magic and deception, like alchemy; and unquestioning deference to the authority of earlier thinkers. These had been attacked in the previous century by influential humanist thinkers, pre-eminently Desiderius Erasmus.

His achievements in the philosophy of science are limited by his commitment to the method of induction, rather than the experimental process of observation, hypothesis and testing which subsequently dominated the physical sciences. Induction on the Baconian model require the assembling of 'histories', observations of the characteristics of phenomena from which more general propositions may be derived. Bacon thus invested heavily in what turned out to be a minor tradition in the history of western science. Bertrand Russell concludes his inductive method is flawed through this insufficient emphasis on hypothesis: 'He hoped that mere orderly arrangement of data would make the right hypothesis obvious, but this is seldom the case' (Russell 1946: 566).

Yet, despite these devaluative comments, Bacon brought a new excitement to the philosophy of science and the advancement of learning. His indictment of old thinking is unrelenting in its forensic genius, and often a vivid simile clinches the argument. Thus, the project of the Schoolmen, laboriously annotating Aristotle 'their Dictator', was hopelessly sterile because:

the wit and mind of man, if it work upon matter, which is the contemplacion of the creatures of God, worketh according to the stuffe, and is limited thereby; but if it worke upon it selfe, as the Spider worketh his webbe, then it is endless, and brings forth indeed Copwebs [*sic*; a common variant spelling] of learning, admirable for the finesse of thread and worke, but of no substance and profite. (Book I, fol. 20r)

Consider how many points are made in this passage. He offers a view of sound intellectual process as an engagement with external reality which is shaped by that external reality, the stuff the mind works on. External reality is the proper matter for such engagement. Otherwise, like the spider, the unsound thinker merely generates worthless analysis from within himself, however nuanced that product may be.

In contrast with the morbid images of introspection, vital, organic imagery masses around the new philosophy, as though its inception marks a springtime for western civilization. For example, Bacon engages with great insight the issue of how learning should be communicated, and, in an acute discussion that anticipates the pedagogic theory of our own day, he attacks the 'Contract of Errour, betweene the Deliverer, and the Receiver: for he that delivereth knowledge, desireth rather present satisfaction, than expectant Enquirie, & so rather not to doubt, than not to erre: glorie making the Author not to lay open his weaknesse, and sloth making the Disciple not to knowe his strength'. The argument, as so often in his *Essays* begins in a shrewd understanding of human frailties, but he sums it up in a vivid simile of fertile georgic endeavour:

For it is in Knowledges, as it is in Plantes; if you mean to use the Plant, it is no matter for the Rootes: But if you meane to remoove it to growe, then it is more assured to rest uppon rootes, than Slippes [that is, hardwood cuttings]: So the deliverie of Knowledges (as it is nowe used) is as of faire bodies of Trees without the Rootes: good for the carpenter, but not for the Planter: But if you will have Sciences growe; it is lesse matter for the shafte, or bodie of the Tree, so you looke well to the takinge up of the Rootes. (Book II, fol. 62r and v)

Instinctively, I suppose, we side with the planter against the carpenter. Bacon probably thought more deeply about English style and the purposes of writing than any English writer before him. No doubt he was aware of the paradox of employing persuasive eloquence in defence of transparency, functional simplicity and openness.

Character-writing, a minor but popular genre throughout the early Stuart period, shared some ground with the essay as developed by Bacon. Formally, characters, too, were short, smartly written and acutely observed, often with a certain worldly scepticism. They sought to generalize about the behaviour of the human animal by depicting supposed types of character or behaviour or profession. Their most significant precursor, however, was much more ancient, the classical Greek writer Theophrastus, a friend and pupil of Aristotle. His 30 sketches depicted deviations from a highly socialized model of normal behaviour. They contain witty observations of contemporary life. The boorish man 'sits down with his cloak hitched up above his knee, thereby revealing his nakedness' (character 4; Theophrastus 2002: 61). The man with bad timing, 'When a slave is being beaten . . . stands watching and tells the story of how a slave of his once hanged himself after being beaten in just this way' (character 12; p. 89).

Theophrastus offered an interesting model to satirical sensibilities frustrated by the state discouragement of verse satire, and his first and most influential imitator in English was Joseph Hall, whose own verse satires had been burnt in the Bishops' Ban of 1599 (see above, chapter 1). Hall's *Virgidemiarum* appeared in 1597 and 1598 and the parts were reprinted in 1599. Like Theophrastus he turns a sceptical and observant eye on society around him, producing brilliant vignettes of Jacobean behaviour.

By far the most successful collection of characters started life in 1614 as a makeweight to Sir Thomas Overbury's poem, *Sir Thomas Overbury his Wife*, a dull account of the purposes of marriage and how ideally they can be realized. No doubt its immediate impact owed much to Overbury's central role in the most prominent sexual scandal of the Jacobean period (see above). The poem itself is traditionally interpreted as part of Overbury's attempt to dissuade his patron, the Earl of Somerset, from marrying Frances Howard. But the characters plainly proved extremely popular. More were added by several hands and editions proliferated as the volume expanded. The sixteenth edition appeared in 1638. What had been a *succès de scandal* had plainly hit the taste of a considerable proportion of the book-buying population.

Writers like John Webster and Thomas Dekker, highly skilled professionals, are among those who swelled the contents of Overbury's posthumous volumes. Yet, read through, the collection is singularly dispiriting. Here, of course, is crude stereotyping almost at the inception of those cultural constructs which pollute the English literary tradition over the century and in some ways for longer. Thus, we find them: commonplace ones like the inns of court man, the would-be courtier, the bawd; then the embodiments of class prejudice in portraits of the tailor, the serving man, the ostler, the pedant, the chamber maid; the slanderous representations of Puritanism and Catholicism; and the racial stereotypes of the Frenchman, the Dutchman and the 'Braggadochio Welshman' who 'accounts none well descended, that call him not cousin' (Overbury 1890: 68). More dispiriting still is the reflection that this material found such an eager readership.

3

From the Defenestration of Prague to the Personal Rule: May 1618 to March 1629

At the start of this period, England was governed by a Stuart monarch of generally autocratic inclination committed to an irenic foreign policy and deeply disinclined to call and consult with parliaments; at the end, the same principal features characterized the regime. But the years between were marked by major disruptions of the patronage system, by political and fiscal crises which redefined the relationship between government and the governed and radically shifted the discourse of power, by an epidemic of plague on a scale comparable with those of 1603 and 1665, and by the disastrous prosecution of wars with two of the major powers of continental Europe. Against this background, the most innovative new drama achieved an unprecedentedly close mimesis of social distinction and interaction and of psychological and particularly sexual impulse; everyday life, especially of a Londoner, was depicted with a new vividness; poems of state and the earliest English newspapers, somewhat falteringly, made their first appearance; the formal sermon reached the acme of eloquence; and a new idiom developed for the celebration of a new court with new values.

Continental Wars

Bohemia, separated by some 700 miles (as the crow flies) from London and for the most part in what is now the Czech Republic, seemed an improbable flashpoint for the chaos that descended on James I's foreign and domestic policies. Indeed, so unfamiliar and remote was that country that Shakespeare less than ten years earlier had attributed to it a coastline (*The Winter's Tale*, III.iii). Unlike most of the states of early modern Europe, it followed a tolerationist religious policy, and its population contained Catholics as well as Lutherans, Calvinists, and members of other Protestant groups. However, this anomaly proved a source of conflict, rather than stability. Bohemia was a constituent element of the Holy Roman Empire, and the Counter Reformation, newly animating Hapsburg ambitions for a closer control of their territories, led to confrontation between Vienna and Prague. In May 1618 a stormy meeting of Protestant activists and Catholic deputies appointed to govern in the name of Ferdinand, the newly appointed Hapsburg king of Bohemia (and future Holy Roman Emperor), culminated in the deputies' forcible ejection from a first-floor window. A modern historian sardonically notes: 'The drop was a considerable one, but only [one deputy] was injured. Catholic witnesses saw the falling Regents supported by angels, but Protestant writers attributed their escape from death to the heap of paper and rubbish in the basement into which they fell' (Ogg 1965: 117). Those alternative narratives point to the immediate incorporation of the event into a rapid widening of the conflict among the major faith communities of Europe, a process in which the Protestant grouping most ably established the image of Bohemia as in the frontline against a sustained assault on the Reformation by a revived Catholicism driven on by ignorance, cruelty and superstition (Polisensky 1974: 104).

Although parts of northern England still had a significant Catholic population, anti-Catholic sentiment generally predominated among the English propertied classes (and indeed more widely), and so their instinctive sympathies lay with the Bohemian Protestants. But a crucial development transformed a vague support for co-religionists in a remote country into an obsessive fervour. The Bohemian rebels deposed Ferdinand, and installed in his stead Frederick V, the Elector Palatine, whose marriage to James's daughter Elizabeth had been so elaborately celebrated in 1612. Frederick's actions, while staunch to international Protestantism, connived at subjects' deposition of a legitimate monarch and ran counter to key principles in James's theory of kingship, however well they may have been perceived by others in England. But James's problems were compounded by his long-standing ambition to secure a marriage alliance with a major power of Catholic Europe, preferably Spain, which was ruled by another branch of the house of Hapsburg, and by the military disasters that befell his son-in-law. By 1620, Bohemia was overrun by Imperial forces; a bloody persecution of Protestants followed, to the virtual extirpation of the religion. An English expeditionary force, commanded by Sir Horace Vere and supported by public subscription, assisted in the defence of the Palatinate, taking a severe mauling as the three cities it defended fell to siege or assault. By 1623 the Palatinate was in the hands of the Imperial forces; Frederick's lands were given in trust to the ruler of Bavaria, who had actively supported the Emperor; the Elector and his English queen were in exile and his Protestant subjects were powerless against sustained persecution (Ogg 1965: 128–9, 133). Moreover, there was a widely current 'domino theory', in which 'the fall of Prague and Heidelberg represented the first major pieces in a chain that led inexorably to the United Provinces and England' (Cogswell 1989: 70).

Political opinion in England, in so far as it can be judged, favoured an active support for the Protestant cause in continental Europe and feared and loathed a rampant Catholicism, which 'exercised a powerful grip on the imaginations of many Englishmen': 'The English crown's personal link with the suffering Protestants of the Palatinate ... brought the conflicts of the Thirty Years War into every English parish church, where prayers for the Elector and his family were regularly read' (A. Milton 1995: 42–3). The Marquis of Buckingham, James's chief minister and soon to be created a duke, explained to Gondomar, the Spanish ambassador to London, that to deprive James's grandchildren of their legitimate right to the Palatinate was intolerable (Cogswell 1989: 18–19). Some sort of English support for the continental Protestants was inevitable. Yet simultaneously, and no doubt bewilderingly for politically conscious Englishmen outside the royal circle, James pursued 'the Spanish Match' through the years of the disaster in the Palatinate; the *arcana imperii*, the secrets of rule that James assiduously invoked and guarded, can never have seemed more arcane. In February 1623 Charles, Prince of Wales, and Buckingham made a sudden and clandestine journey to Madrid to press the prince's suit for the Infanta, in circumstances that remain uncertain and perplexing (Cogswell 1989: 36). Their failure to secure a marriage contract on terms that would not have been humiliating to a Protestant prince and outrageous to his subjects inadvertently occasioned the greatest public relations success of the early Stuart period. Pandemonium greeted the empty-handed return of prince and duke in October: fireworks, bonfires, peals of bells and much inebriation characterized the festivities across the country (Cogswell 1989: 6–9).

The failure of the Spanish strategy led to a French match and to war with Spain. The former seemed wise to the royal circle at the time. Louis XIII was minded to support Frederick, not least out of anxieties about the balance of power in the areas immediately adjacent to his own borders (Cogswell 1989: 121). But Charles's betrothal to Henrietta Maria, the king's youngest sister, carried some disadvantages. She, too, was a Catholic princess, and proved to be devout and resolute in the observation of her religion, and her religion remained central to negative representations of her; John Milton still thought the point worth making in 1660 (Milton 1953–82: VII; rev. edn: 425). A sense that the Spanish royal family had shown them too little respect probably catalysed the royal circle's increased enthusiasm for armed conflict with the Hapsburg axis, which led in due course to a sea-borne campaign designed to inflict damage on Spanish port cities and perhaps to intercept the Spanish treasure fleet, which was essential for financing both Spanish and Imperial military activity.

In the event, neither objective was achieved, but the necessity to fund the project and to raise revenue to support proxy armies in continental Europe initiated a series of fairly short-lived parliaments. Those financial exigencies were soon to be exacerbated. Despite the French marriage, Charles, shortly after his accession in 1625, found himself drawn into a second sea-borne campaign, against his new brother-in-law in defence of the Protestant Huguenots concentrated around La Rochelle. In this campaign, as in that against Spain, Buckingham played the leading role, taking personal command of the desperate and inept venture to relieve La Rochelle using the Isle of Ré as a bridgehead. Such activity had three immensely significant effects on the political consciousness of propertied Englishmen. The frequently convoked and dismissed parliaments functioned as a forum for a more searching critique of government policy, both domestic and foreign. As the campaigns foundered, the demonization of Buckingham gathered pace, and, in the longer term more significantly, a new discourse of anti-court constitutionalism emerged. Finally, repeated parliamentary elections, like the general anxiety about the threat to Protestantism, sharpened propertied Englishmen's sense of the need to know what was happening, a process arguably keener still in the hiatus between parliaments, especially when the monarch resorted to dubious methods of raising revenue unsanctioned by parliament.

Hence arose a new hunger for news and a closer engagement with the political process. As James recognized, and Charles and Buckingham did not, working through parliaments had made 'a rod for their own backs' (Sharpe 1992: 7).

Three Funerals and a Wedding

Anne of Denmark died in March 1619, predeceasing by less than a year Samuel Daniel, who had been among the earliest beneficiaries of her literary patronage in England (Barroll 2001: 66). Her funeral, a contemporary noted, 'was better than Prince Henry's, but fell short of Queen Elizabeth's' (quoted in *DNB* 1975), though the former's was impaired by lack of royal funds after the excesses of the wedding of Princess Elizabeth and Frederick V. Anne's position in the patronage system had declined over the previous decade. Barroll has demonstrated her role in shaping the late Prince Henry's cultural milieu, but he had died seven years before, and while she had been central to the promotion of the early Stuart masque, she had last danced in 1611; Charles (and Buckingham) had superseded her in that court ritual. However, her death did leave the Queen's Men in want of a protector, which can scarcely have helped them in what proved to be a difficult and probably terminal phase for the company. By the end of the year, its players seem to have been dispersed among other companies (Bentley 1941–68: I, 165).

The theatres were closed for the ten weeks between her death and her funeral, the delay proving a 'great hindrance of our players, which are forbidden to play so long as her body is above ground' (quoted in Bentley 1941–68: I, 6). Despite her contribution to producing a 'rich and hospitable climate' for the arts in Jacobean England (Barroll 2001: 161), the literary response to her death was relatively muted and notably learned. The universities produced similar collections of predominately Latin elegies, with a sprinkling of Greek and the occasional Hebrew composition (*Academiæ Oxoniensis Funebria* 1619; *Lacrymæ Cantabrigienses* 1619). One James Anne-son (*sic*), 'Antiquarie and Maister of Arts', produced a commemorative volume in which the 'poeme in honour' is much overshadowed by an elaborate and ultimately implausible genealogy of the late queen (Anne-son: n.d.). Perhaps most impressive is *Threnodia* by her quondam chaplain William Slatier, again in Latin, Greek and Hebrew, but predominately made up of English acrostics, mostly on Anne's name, though sometimes on his own, together with poems shaped like columns, pyramids, and the dial of a compass, which are doggedly ingenious though not otherwise distinguished:

I

am

not

though

ABLE

to shew

how divine

her Royall Grace,

In heaven doth shine.

Where a Cherubs place,

Or a Seraphique height

Exceeds the thoughts of Men,

As far as heavenly towers fraile sight.

Wisely, the collection opens with a poem to James and ends with one to Charles: dead patrons are of dubious value compared to living ones (Slatier 1619: sig. C4r, B1r, D3r). Slatier, already a fellow of Brasenose College, Oxford, and holder of a decent living, prospered through the 1620s, receiving a further benefice, which he held pluralistically (*DNB* 1975). I am unaware of commemorative verse of a more abiding significance to the late queen.

James I died in March 1625, and was buried early in May. Buckingham and Charles walked in the funeral procession. The literary response broadly followed that to the death of the queen, though on a grander scale. There were collections of learned Latin and Greek verse from the universities, pious sermons and the tributes of minor poets. As in the case of Anne, the most distinguished writers remained surprisingly silent. From Jonson, who had frequently praised him living, both in poems and masques, and who would write poems to the new king, his queen and his burgeoning family, no elegy survives.

Panegyrists, in general, had three problems to negotiate. First, James's death had occasioned rumour and gossip that it had been caused or hastened by Buckingham, perhaps aided by Charles (Ashton 1969: 271–5; Lockyer 1981: 233–5). Second, since 1603 James had been figured in English panegyric as the blessed peacemaker, but his reign ended with England locked in a Spanish war of uncertain outcome. And finally, he was replaced by a ruler whose own larger agenda was decidedly uncertain, as the would-be wooer of the Infanta became the would-be hammer of Spain. John Williams, Bishop of Lincoln, Privy Councillor and a politically astute cleric, preached the funeral sermon. His influence at that time was at its height, and he could scarcely have anticipated his imminent eclipse by William Laud in the favours of the new king, though belatedly his own ecclesiastical fortunes revived with his appointment to the Archbishopric of York in 1642. Williams's sermon, twice printed as *Great Britains Salomon*, negotiated the first two difficulties with considerable dexterity. The sermon, while scarcely matching Donne in eloquence, is a masterpiece of tact, though the issues it foregrounds indicate the anxieties of the new court. It develops an extended comparison of James and Solomon. Their 'wisdom' provides the primary point of the analogy, but so, too, does their death. The notion of a 'good death' as indicator of spiritual health and confidence in personal salvation pervades early modern thinking (Houlbrooke 2000: esp. 147–219), but in this case Williams risks protesting too much. Solomon has died a good death: 'his *Death* is resembled to slumbring and *sleeping. And Solomon slept*' (Williams 1625: 30). James's closing hours are described in detail, and the duke and prince, far from hurrying him on with poison, stand by him to hear his last words of piety. Again, like Solomon, James followed the nobler course of the peacemaker, though he showed himself heroic when constrained to do so, as in resisting internal rebellion in Scotland. Yet that part of the account ends celebrating the benefits England enjoyed through avoiding war: 'all kinde of *learning* improved, *manufactures* at home daily invented, *Trading* abroad exceedingly multiplied', and so on (ibid.: 57–8).

However, not even the agile Williams could confidently characterize the new king. In a delicate if evasive trope he offers him as a replica of James, a '*breathing Statue* of all his *Vertues*' (ibid.: 75–6), not really yet distinctive from his predecessor. That uncertainty, in contrast with the long-established image of James, found expression in the title of the Cambridge collection of elegies, *Cantabrigiensium Dolor et Solamen: seu Decessio Beatissimi Regis Jacobi Pacifici: et Successio Augustissimi Regis Caroli* (1625). While James is 'the most blessed peacemaker', Charles has the much vaguer epithet 'most august' or 'majestic, venerable, worthy of honour' (L&S: s.v. 'augustus'). It was the least panegyrists could have said of a new king.

Charles's own coronation and his marriage to Henrietta Maria could have provided the occasion for a more definitive enunciation of the values and priorities of his government, though in the event neither afforded the platform James had enjoyed in his entry of 1604. Circumstances combined to maim those rites of state by which a new monarch could present himself to a broader gaze. Cautiously, perhaps, the marriage was effected by proxy: the new queen's Catholicism would no doubt have been otherwise so publicly expressed as to stimulate a wave of anti-popery reminiscent of the Spanish Match. The couple effected an entry into London in some state. But a major outbreak of plague contributed to the postponement until 1626 of the coronation. When it occurred, the event was deeply unsatisfactory as a display of power and unanimity. The queen declined to attend on the grounds that she would only be crowned by a Catholic clergyman. Buckingham turned the procession to Westminster Abbey into an exercise in factional feuding. Charles gave to William Laud the major clerical role in the proceedings, which, while it marked to any knowing observer the rise of both that individual and Arminian ceremonialism, ensured that the ceremony itself was the manifestation of division within the Church rather than of confessional unity. Civic celebrations were cancelled out of fear of plague (Corns 1999b: 14–15; Lockyer 1981: 308; Carlton 1995: 76–8).

Odes for the coronation displayed the uncertainties which gripped even those well disposed to Charles: does he bring peace or war? stability or adventurism? defence of the faith or a rapprochement with Catholicism? Hence, probably, arose the evasive emptiness of odes like Sir John Beaumont's 'Panagyrick at the Coronation of our Soveraigne Lord King Charles':

> Shine forth great *Charles*, accept our loyall words,
> Throw from your pleasing eies those conqu'ring swords,
> That when upon your Name our voyces call,
> The Birds may feele our thund'ring noise, and fall ...
>   (Beaumont 1629: 117)

The poem continues with aspirations that he may enjoy 'large Honour, happy Conquest, boundless Wealth / Long Life, sweete Children, unafflicted Health' – a comprehensive if significantly contradictory wish-list; in the English context, conquest and wealth usually proved to be alternatives (Corns 1999b: 17–19).

As with the death of Anne, James's demise caused some disruption of the major cultural patronage systems. Donne and Jonson, the towering figures of the late Jacobean age, continued to enjoy royal favour. Thomas Carew was already in royal employ as a court officer, and remained so to become a defining voice of court poetry in the 1630s. But Caroline culture was to give to literary achievement a secondary role. Since his earliest days as Prince of Wales, Charles, an accomplished performer himself, had established a considerable ensemble as part of his household, with a particular emphasis on string consort music. On the death of his father, he simply added this group to the already considerable ensemble, the King's Music, that he inherited, retaining all but a handful of performers (Wainwright 1999: 162–3). However, his patronage of the stage showed no such commitment. On his accession, the evidence suggests that the company he formerly patronized broke up as the new king took over his father's role as patron of the King's Men, though plague no doubt played a part in the ensemble's disbandment. However, a new company formed under the patronage of Henrietta Maria and played from the reopening of the theatres in late 1625, achieving considerable success in the early and mid-1630s (Bentley 1941–68: I, 209–10, 218–39; see below, chapter 4).

Buckingham died at the hand of John Felton, an army officer and solitary malcontent disappointed by his lack of promotion, in late August 1628. So great was his odium, that the funeral was without elaborate ceremony and care was taken to limit the public demonstration of hostility. The event severed Charles's last considerable tie to the Jacobean age. Buckingham had danced with him when first he performed the role of principal masquer. He had been his comrade in the wild and strange adventure of the Spanish Match, and had negotiated his marriage to his French princess. There were few poems of commemoration, though Edmund Waller's 'Of his Majesties receiving the newes of the Duke of Buckinghams death' is precise, tender and tactful, diverting the reader's gaze from the problematic life of Villiers to the pious image of the king. Charles was at a divine service when the news arrived. According to the Earl of Clarendon's much later account,

> [the king] continued unmoved, and without the least change in his countenance, till prayers were ended; when he suddenly departed to his chamber, and threw himself upon his bed, lamenting with much

passion and with abundance of tears the loss he had of an excellent servant and the horrid manner in which he had been deprived of him. (Quoted in Lockyer 1981: 454)

Waller is drawn to his peculiar public behaviour and silent on his later, more conventional grief once he had withdrawn:

> So earnest with thy God, can no new care,
> No sense of danger interrupt thy prayer?
> The sacred Wrestler till a blessing given
> Quits not his hold, but halting conquers heaven:
> Nor was the stream of thy devotion stopp'd
> When from the body such a limb was lopp'd
> (Waller 1645: sig. B1r).

Waller perhaps discloses some uncertainty about quite how the king is best to be represented – the poem is a list of what his conduct was not like: not like Hector's over Patroclus, or Apollo's over Hyacinthus or David's for Absalom. But it reflects a sense that here is a different kind of kingship, marked by a piety, restraint and a curious interiority – 'God-like unmov'd, and yet like woman kinde' (ibid.: 2). Waller, still in his early twenties, anticipated sooner than others the subtle fashioning of that royal sensibility in the years of the personal rule of Charles I.

But Buckingham's status outside the immediate circle of the court, the evident hatred felt for him across the political nation and more widely, found full and frequent expression in satirical or more straightforwardly critical verse, usually anonymous, rarely accomplished, that constituted an important phase in the development of what we may term 'poems of state'. (Hammond 1990: 57–66 discusses them well, with generous quotation.)

Buckingham's ability to dominate English public life for a decade depended largely on the vast network of patronage which depended on him. It extended to the judiciary, to court offices, to financial favouritism and to the operations of the church. Though the promotion of the interests of contemporary creative writers probably figured as a low priority, he was widely perceived as a patron worth seeking. Most certainly he secured the immediate ecclesiastical advancement of John Donne to the deanery of St Paul's (Lockyer 1981: 115). Robert Herrick, a chaplain on the Isle of Ré expedition, took up his living in Dean Prior in the month after the duke's funeral. The post was in the gift of the king, and may well have been an act of posthumous patron-age arranged earlier by his dead benefactor (Moorman 1910: 87). Francis Bacon, too, owed immediate debts to his patronage (ibid.: 70–1). At the duke's death, the king himself appeared much more straightforwardly as the ultimate source of influence and advancement. More subtly, too, the duke's massive pre-eminence among the grandees of the 1620s produced a climate in which the ambitious looked to the royal court for preferment. Already, by 1629, the key figures of the court culture of the personal rule – Carew, Waller, Davenant, Townshend – were in varying degrees attached to the royal sphere. Whatever the considerable justice of the popular strictures he attracted, Buckingham left as his cultural legacy the foundation of that glittering age.

Masques and Pageants

Pleasure Reconciled to Virtue (1618), written by Ben Jonson and designed by Inigo Jones, marked the maturation of Prince Charles as focus of court masque and heir to the tradition his mother had so enthusiastically established. All the extant masques of the late Jacobean period show the political centrality of Charles and Buckingham and the continuing creative domination of Jonson and Jones. *News from the New World Discovered in the Moon* (1620) offered in its antimasque a portrayal of gossiping purveyors of 'news'. The next in the series, *Pan's Anniversary, or the Shepherds' Holiday*, danced as a birthday gift to James at the more rural palace of Greenwich in June 1620, had a less abrasive antimasque of nymphs and shepherds. James was celebrated in the figure of great Pan:

> Pan is our all, by him we breathe, we live,
> We move, we are; 'tis he our lambs doth rear,
> The warm and finer fleeces that we wear.
>
>   . . .
> The rites are due to him, who doth all right for us
>   (Orgel and Strong 1973: I, 318)

This is a landscape of pastoral plenty and stability, the product of a benign and pacific regime. The theme was rehearsed more explicitly in *The Masque of Augurs*, again written by Jonson, designed by Jones and performed by Charles and attendant lords as the Twelfth Night's masque of 1622. Apollo leads the masquers to James with the song,

> Behold the love and ease of all the gods,
> King of the ocean and the happy isles,
> That whilst the world about him is at odds,
> Sits crowned lord here of himself, and smiles.
> The Chorus immediately adds,
> To see the erring mazes of mankind,
> Who seek for that doth punish them to find.
> (Orgel and Strong 1973: I, 337)

'*Dulce bellum inexpertis*', 'war is sweet to those who haven't tried it', James's old dictum, is echoed in this explicit rebuke to advocates of a belligerent foreign policy, whereas the blessings of peace are material and evident; the literary culture of the court is establishing a repertoire of responses that will serve through much of the 1630s.

James's horror of public scrutiny recurred as a theme in *Time Vindicated to Himself and to His Honours*, the Twelfth Night's masque for 1623, danced by Charles 'and the Lords', designed by Jones and scripted by Jonson. The organs of sense depicted in the antimasque represent the intrusive and inappropriate probing of a wider public into the king's business:

> EYES ... I had now a fancy
>   We might have talked o' the King.
> EARS Or state.
> NOSE Or all the world.

Fame chides them, 'They that censure those / They ought to reverence, meet they that old curse, / To beg their bread and feel eternal winter', adding, 'There's difference 'twixt liberty and license' (Orgel and Strong 1973: I, 351). The masque ends with a choric endorsement of James's irenic alternative to war, the blood sports he had so eagerly pursued: 'Hunting it is the noblest exercise, / Makes men laborious, active, wise.' The noble pastime of the chase serves the ends of peace: 'Men should not hunt mankind to death' (I, 354). Though the audience for masque was severely limited and controlled, it included among its most significant members ambassadors of major nations. The message, that James sought peaceful coexistence, not familial revenge nor regional conflict, was explicitly articulated in the scripts Jonson wrote in the early 1620s.

Sadly, James's hunting days and his irenic policies were drawing to a close. The masque written for Twelfth Night, 1624, was not performed 'because of a dispute over ambassadorial precedence' (Orgel and Strong 1973: I, 363). The last extant masque of his reign, *The Fortunate Isles, and Their Union* (Jonson and Jones, Twelfth Night, 1625) contained in its title a poignant misrepresentation. The union of England and Scotland, an objective of James from the earliest years of his reign, had not been achieved except in the sense that one king ruled both kingdoms. The masque marked a transition from the celebration of peace to the prosecution of war, the attack on Spain which ended in the inept assault on Cadiz in late 1625 (Lockyer 1981: 281–5). Jonson's script, though it ends once more with a panegyric to James's 'golden gifts of peace', knowingly stresses Britain's insularity and the importance of 'Neptune's strength': Buckingham's and Charles's enrolment in Hispanophobic populism pointed inexorably to naval adventures for the island race.

Masquing thereafter fell into desuetude through the mid- and late 1620s as political and financial crises occasioned by the Spanish and French campaign disrupted government, as James and Buckingham expired, and as the family life of Charles and Henrietta Maria staggered through early years of apparent incompatibility. Records, but not scripts, survive for some kind of court entertainment, and indeed the new queen presented and performed in an elaborately staged pastoral play, *Artenice* (1626), contemporaneously misperceived as 'of her own composition' (Orgel and Strong 1973: I, 384). But not till 1631 did a new and assured masquing idiom emerge.

Thomas Middleton replaced Anthony Munday as the favourite pageant writer from 1619 onwards, at a time when the genre achieved a singular significance in English literary history. He wrote the scripts for the mayoral inaugurations of 1619, 1620, 1621, 1622, 1623 and 1626. There was no pageant in the plague year of 1625, 'Tryumph was not in season (Deaths Pageants being onely advanc'st upon the shoulders of man)' (Middleton 1626: sig. B2r). In 1624, in the aftermath of *A Game at Chess* and Middleton's own flight, possible imprisonment and certain notoriety, the commission went to John Webster

Middleton's contribution to the event focused on the mayor's triumphant return from Westminster. Munday evidently retained responsibility for the opening component, the water pageant that took the new mayor upriver, when 'squibs and volleys of ordnance combined with jostling for priority among the company barges to produce a scene so chaotic that Middleton usually declined to lay his hand to [it]' (Manley 1995: 283). But Middleton substantially followed the formula Munday had perfected for the rest of the event, including his characteristic obsessions with the antiquity of London, of the guilds and of the patronage extended by the crown to the city and its institutions. In 1619 the history of royal and aristocratic support for the Skinners' Company from 1329 was patiently rehearsed (Middleton 1619: sig. C2r-v). In 1622, the Grocers' turn, he writes a speech for 'Antiquitie a grave and reverend Personage, with a golden Register-boke in his hand' (Middleton 1622: sig. B3v): famous Grocer Lord Mayors were duly listed (sig. B4r-v). In 1623, 'the Never-dying Names of many memorable and remarkable' Drapers got a hearing (Middleton 1623: sig. B1r). In 1626, the medieval figure of Sir Henry Fitz-Alwin, a favourite in Munday's Draper pageants, made another appearance, together with Sir Francis Drake, evidently also a member of the Drapers' Company, though more famous in other capacities (Middleton 1626: sig. A4v-B1v).

The inclusion of Drake, icon of Elizabethan maritime adventurism, marked the restrained but knowing ideological shifts Middleton introduced into the pageants. It is no coincidence that Philip Nichols published in the same year *Sir Francis Drake Revived Calling on this dull and effeminate age, to follow his noble steps* (Nichols 1626). The Lord Mayor was the King's Lieutenant, 'his Majesties great substitute' in the City of London (Middleton 1626: sig. A3r). The pageant writer was paid by the incumbent's guild, and a continuity of employment was both desirable and achievable. What Middleton had his pageant actors say reflected close control by patrons fully aware that London had a surfeit of indigent playwrights should he prove unsatisfactory. Royal panegyric was central to the form, and Middleton rehearsed James's merits in terms not radically different from the 1604 royal entry (see above, chapter 2). London remains the *camera regia*, the royal chamber of a wise and pacific king, who reigns '*with* Salomons *brest*' (Middleton 1622: sig. B3v), while 'Neighbouring Kingdoms grone' (Middleton 1621: sig. B3r). In 1623, at Wood Street, a tableau represented the beatitude '*Beati Pacifici*, being the Kings word or *Motto* ... set in faire great Letters .... so is it comely and requisite ... that some remembrance of Honour should reflect upon his

Majesty, by whose peacefull Government under Heaven we enjoy the Solemnity' (Middleton 1623: sig. B4v). But the pageant reflected, too, the Hispanophobic euphoria occasioned by the collapse of the Spanish Match: '*we have the Crowne of* Britttaines *Hope agen, / Illustrious* Charles *our Prince,) which all will say, / Addes the chiefe Ioy and Honor to this Day*' (sig. C1r). Middleton picked up and perhaps promoted the evident mood of the City. In similar fashion, his pageant for the inauguration of Sir William Cokayne, his first since the commencement of continental hostilities, had a martial patina, incorporating a parade of the City militia and 'Gentlemen of the Artillery Garden' (Middleton 1619: sig. C1v).

Plays and Players

The King's Men, Shakespeare's old colleagues, dominated the 1620s even more emphatically than they did the 1610s (see above, chapter 2). Theirs was the only troupe to survive the eight-month closure in the plague year of 1625, though even they needed a direct cash subsidy from the new king to keep them going (Bentley 1941–68: I, 20; Wickham et al. 2000: 639). Their most illustrious actor, Richard Burbage, who had created many Shakespearian roles, died in 1619. But the strength both of their repertoire and of the new plays they commissioned ensured their continuing domination. They continued to perform the plays of Jonson, Beaumont and Fletcher, and Shakespeare, and most of Middleton's best plays were written for them, and they performed frequently at court, negotiating with evident facility the change of patron on the succession of Charles (Bentley 1941–68: I, 23). They retained two playhouses, the second Blackfriars and the second Globe, as in the previous decade. The latter, however, plainly declined in importance. Typically, they used the open-air public theatre only for relatively short summer seasons (Wickham et al. 2000: 609). No other company managed to operate over the whole decade, and those who played only in public theatres were among the most short-lived.

The Phoenix playhouse (also known as the Cockpit), a private playhouse and the first in what is now termed the West End of London, was home to the Lady Elizabeth's Men (also known as the Queen of Bohemia's Men). The history of troupe is somewhat uncertain in the late 1610s, but it evidently formed again in 1621 or 1622.

It did not survive the hiatus of 1625, though it enjoyed some success in its short career. *The Changeling* was first staged there, probably in 1622. The reopening of the theatres coincided with the arrival of Henrietta Maria as potential patron, and her company occupied the Phoenix from late 1625, assembling an impressive repertoire of new plays and performing from time to time at court. Its dramatists included Thomas Heywood and Philip Massinger, and James Shirley established himself as their principal writer, continuing with them in the years of the personal rule (Bentley 1941–68: I, 218, 223; Wickham et al. 2000: 625).

The Palsgrave's (or King of Bohemia's) Men were probably the most significant ensemble to play the public theatres. However, the burning of the first Fortune in 1621 left them temporarily homeless until its replacement with the second Fortune in 1623. The group did not survive after 1625, but for a while it classically embodied the practices of the public theatres. Their venue stood outside the city limits (to the north-west), and few of their known repertoire of plays, usually either anonymous or by undistinguished writers, have survived. Rather shadowy groups lacking patronage and protection intermittently operated in the Fortune once the theatres reopened (Bentley 1941–68: I, 156–7; Wickham et al. 2000: 639).

The Red Bull at Clerkenwell dated back to about 1605, and seems to have been substantially unchanged from its rather primitive design, until well into the 1620s. Queen Anne's Men had used it formerly and returned to it after 1617. Partially reconstituted from that company, the Revels company occupied it till 1623, when Prince Charles's Men, in a venture that did not survive the migration of his patronage to the King's Men, took it over. After the plague, an obscure group, the Red Bull Company, played there intermittently. Prince Charles's Men secured some good writers – Dekker, Ford, Rowley and Middleton worked sometimes for them – though the repertoire of the Red Bull Company resembles that staged at the second Fortune (Bentley 1941–68: I, 174, 282; Wickham et al. 2000: 564–7).

The highly conservative nature of London theatre should once more be emphasized. These were repertory companies whose stock in trade was revivals of plays in their ownership. The Shakespearian canon remained at the heart of the King's Men's operation, even when it played at court. Plays by Marlowe and Robert Greene may still have been playing in the public theatres in the 1620s (Bentley 1941–68: I,

156–7, 174). The best new plays were staged by the most successful companies, for the most part, but not exclusively, in the private theatres. Above all, this is the period in which Middleton, so often promising, finally achieved his potential.

Middleton collaborated with William Rowley on the script of *The Changeling*. He worked alone on *Women Beware Women*, probably first performed in 1621. Both plays have retained a popularity in our own period, and have secured their place in contemporary canon formation. Indeed, Alastair Fowler, noting that in 1978 there were three London productions of *The Changeling*, tartly asks 'Who can tell how many Jacobean plays may not be better than the very few that happen to have been put on in our time?' (Fowler 1985: 215). A Welsh translation of the play was premiered in 2003 (Middleton and Rowley 2003). The abiding fascination of both plays remains clear, and it rests largely in their chilling observation and representation of abnormal psychology in the context of extreme social stress – with an added frisson: the focus is on the sexual behaviour of young women. Neither conforms to the expectations of domestic tragedy, in that essentially they depict the perpetration of criminal or dishonest behaviour and its condign punishment. The low mimesis of morally limited and emotionally stunted characters blundering into desperately self-destructive actions resembles a novel by Georges Simenon rather than *Othello*. But the social problems they engage with belong firmly to early modern England.

Over the course of the seventeenth century among propertied English people, the role of the paterfamilias in determining the marriage contracts of his children was gradually displaced by the emergence of love matches and companionate marriage. Indeed, it was 'the accepted wisdom' at the start of that period that 'marriage based on personal selection, and thus inevitably influenced by such ephemeral factors as sexual attraction or romantic love, was if anything less likely to produce lasting happiness than one arranged by more prudent and more mature heads' (Stone 1979: 128). Of course, in the literary context patriarchal interdiction confronted true love, producing both tragic and comic outcomes. Middleton's version is more closely grounded in early modern social reality than *Romeo and Juliet* or *A Midsummer-Night's Dream*. In *The Changeling*, the issues are established with brutal clarity in a scene between Beatrice, her father Vermandero, and Alsemero, the male lead she has just met and whom she prefers to Alonzo, her father's choice:

> VERMANDERO ... I should ha' told thee news,
>   I saw Alonzo lately.
> BEATRICE [*aside*] That's ill news.
> VERMANDERO He's hot preparing for this day of triumph:
>   Thou must be a bride within this sevennight.
> ALSEMERO [*aside*] Ha!
> BEATRICE Nay, good sir, be not so violent; with speed
>   I cannot render satisfaction
>   Unto the dear companion of my soul,
>   Virginity, whom I thus long have liv'd with,
>   And part with it so rude and suddenly;
>   Can such friends divide, never to meet again,
>   Without a solemn farewell?
> VERMANDERO Tush, tush! There's a toy.
>   (Middleton and Rowley 1964: 1.1.188–97; p. 12)

Vermadero is rightly dismissive of Beatrice's concern to retain her virginity, for she loses it soon enough to De Flores. Beatrice's choices are simple. She could have obeyed – Alsemero's initial response is to give up any hope of the relationship and quit Alicante (1.1.198) – and married Alonzo. The road not taken remains an element in the play. Compliance with patriarchal authority would have retained honour, and secured prosperity and lawful procreation; the alternative leads to disgrace, suicide and murder.

Women Beware Women opens after Leantio, a man of modest means, a mere 'factor', an agent in the service of a mercantile master, has already clandestinely married Bianca, the daughter of rich Venetians, 'parents great in wealth, more now in rage' (Middleton 1975: 7; 1.1.50). He articulates the voice of romantic love, as customarily depicted in plays: 'Little money sh'has brought me; / View but her face, you may see all her dowry' (ll.53–4). But his mother explains that he has acquired a woman who entertains expectations that cannot be met on his income without an advantageous marriage settlement. She observes, 'to draw her from her fortune ... You know not what you have done' (ll.59–61). He soon discovers.

Bianca's capitulation to the Duke after her mother-in-law's dereliction of her chaperon role betrays her into his power is usually termed a rape. However, while morally indistinguishable, the incident is more complex. Bianca has no hope of defence, but she has a choice: she may resist, in which case she will be held down and violated; or she may accede, and be rewarded. As the Duke tells her:

> I can command,
> Think upon that. Yet if thou truly knewest
> The infinite pleasure my affection takes
> In gentle, fair entreatings, when love's businesses
> Are carried courteously 'twixt heart and heart,
> You'd make more haste to please me.
>
> (2.2.362–7; p. 65)

Bianca says very little in this exchange because she recognizes, as soon as she is left alone in a confined space with the duke, that there are no good options, that the game is lost. The courtroom experiences of women in early Stuart England demonstrate repeatedly that a woman accusing a social superior of rape was unlikely to succeed. As Laura Gowing concludes:

> The legal and social culture of early modern society accorded less credit to women's words than to men's. In the sphere of sexual conduct this was particularly so; women, especially young women and servants, found it hard to make accusations of seduction, assault, or rape stick against men. Some of their accusations, indeed, ended up being cited as slander. (1998: 251; see also p. 75)

Even if the duke were not the head of the Florentine city-state, if he were merely a Jacobean grandee, the possibility of justice through a judicial process would have been slight. Middleton's characters function within a milieu close to the social conditions of seventeenth-century London. Bianca's only honourable recourse is to the dagger of Lucrece, an option she never considers.

Leantio and De Flores manifest the powerlessness that comes of social dependency. The cuckold was the most despised figure in early modern Europe, universally derided and blamed not only for the sexual humiliation he incurred but for betraying the responsibilities of patriarchy, on which society depended, in failing 'to maintain household order' (Gowing 1998: 94). Though Leantio is compensated with the reward of a military command in the gift of the duke and is kept as a sexual plaything by the socialite Livia, a residual sense of shame prompts him to indiscreet displays of new-found wealth and eventually to a fatal duel with Livia's brother, an act of belated male honour which he enters into as an act of social and sexual redemption: 'Slave, I turn this to thee / To call thee to account, for a wound lately / Of a base stamp upon me' (4.2.35–7; p. 135).

Because he is her father's dependent, Beatrice may treat De Flores with disgust and contempt. Her revulsion is of a sexual nature. When he picks up a glove she drops, she discards it rather than have again something he has fingered. Even a pre-Freudian audience would have been alert to the symbolism. When the notoriously promiscuous Frances Howard dropped a glove for the fastidious Prince Henry, he declined to retrieve it on the grounds that 'it is *stretcht* by another' (Strong 1986: 55). What Middleton does extremely well is to chart the difference between audience expectations of dramatic heroines and the chilling calculation of these earthier characters. Thus, the non-Lucrece, Bianca, becomes the 'glist'ring whore shin[ing] like a serpent / Now the court sun's upon her' (4.2.20–1; Middleton 1975: 134). Thus, too, the non-Juliet, Beatrice, allows De Flores to deflower her in recompense for his murder of Alonzo. She does so with little protestation.

I have noted the conservative nature of the Jacobean stage, and indeed Middleton's stark, fresh engagement with the world of his audience rests on the old improbabilities of earlier decades. *The Changeling* has a conscience-pricking ghost and another run-out for the bedtrick as the deflowered Beatrice bribes her virginal waiting-woman to take her place in the bridal bed. *Women Beware Women* ends with a murderous masque that kills off all the principal characters still standing; its genealogy descends from *The Spanish Tragedy* through the exhibition bout of sword-play that ends *Hamlet*. Yet aside from those creaking conventions, the Inns of Court men of the original audiences, lustful, ravenous for preferment and patronage, and terrified of losing them once achieved, would have recognized as their own the world of Middleton's plays. Perhaps we should recall the fate of John Donne, whose clandestine marriage to the ward of Sir Thomas Egerton, whom he served as secretary, was met with disgrace, dismissal and impoverishment. Or Thomas Carew, a former Middle Templar, whose imprudent and disloyal comments on his first employer, Sir Dudley Carleton, cost him his place in his household. Middleton's plays assume that sexual mores relate to class and that hierarchical structures may breed corruption; he was scarcely telling his audience anything they didn't already know. These plays are neither satire nor gestures towards social reform. When in 1624 *The Changeling* was played at court, the royal family could have viewed it with equanimity as the portrayal of weak people making poor choices in a world little different from how the world had always been and for which no early modern English ruler would have recognized or acknowledged a responsibility.

Middleton's *A Game at Chess*, first performed in August 1624, has rarely been revived, nor indeed was it, in all probability, intended as a repertory piece for the company that delivered it, the King's Men, at their usual summer venue, the Globe. Among pre-Restoration plays that have survived, it is by some way the closest depiction of contemporary political events on the public stage. Within the lightly sustained political allegory of a game of chess, Middleton depicts three clusters of events: the defection back to the Church of Rome by Marcus Antonius de Dominis; the eclipse of the Spanish party (that is, the anti-war party) at the English court; and the return of Buckingham and Charles from the aborted attempt to secure the Spanish Match. The first motif seems to have been added some time after the play was first performed, and adds a comic dimension somewhat inappropriate to the high seriousness of its subject. De Dominis, born in Venetian Dalmatia, was a former Jesuit, a former archbishop of Split, a leading theologian and a major theoretician on the relationship of secular and ecclesiastical power. His had been a high-profile career in which he had accepted Anglicanism and gained access to the most powerful levels of the Jacobean patronage system. In part through the agency of Gondomar, he had reverted to Rome, in the event a disastrous move. He died of natural causes while incarcerated and under investigation for residual heresies. (For the best account, see Malcolm 1984.) The complexity of the case and the personal tragedy it constituted were, of course, brushed aside in contemporary pamphlet attacks in the rush to present a devious and ambitious papist cleric, a perspective Middleton substantially followed. A modern editor speculates that Middleton may have added this theme to provide a role for William Rowley, his former collaborator and a somewhat overweight actor gifted in the representation of comic fat men (Middleton 1993: 29–31), but there were real enough connections with the Jesuits and with Gondomar. The impeachment of Lionel Cranfield, Earl of Middlesex, seems alluded to in the perfidy of the White King's Pawn, though the figure has been otherwise identified by some commentators (Middleton 1993: 89, 116), and functions perhaps as a combined representation not only of Cranfield but of the whole court faction hostile to war with Spain. (Cranfield, as Lord Treasurer, had a very sure sense of its fiscal implications.)

But the representation of the White Duke (Buckingham) and the White Knight (Charles) in their outwitting of the Black Knight

(Gondomar, formerly Spanish ambassador and principal Spanish archi-tect of the match) is at the centre of the play. Middleton's depiction is a species of panegyric. Charles and Buckingham in private conversation are represented discussing how their purpose is simply to disclose the 'gins, traps and alluring snares' of Spain, and thus to secure 'truth's triumph' (4.4.5, 8; Middleton 1993: 160–1). As others have noted, Charles adopts a stratagem adapted from Malcolm's testing of Macduff in *Macbeth*. He feigns vicious appetites. When Gondomar tempts him with the promise of satisfying those vices once he joins their ranks, he reveals his true character, in effect leaping out of the way, which allows the Black King to be given 'checkmate by / Discovery . . . the noblest mate of all' (5.3.160–1; ibid.: 186).

In this endgame, a piece that has blocked a line of check moves out of the way of another piece of the same colour, thus exposing the opposing king. Charles, by showing himself not be what the Spaniards thinks he is, conclusively discloses their real nature. The chess analogy here works quite well. Throughout the play, though, Middleton struggles to sus-tain the conceit. Even the premier drama company had limited mem-bership and he cannot deploy enough chessmen – at most he manages 22, probably achieved through some doubling up. Moreover the case he wants to make is only fitfully consonant with the rules of chess. One pawn changes sides. The Fat Bishop (and his Pawn) belongs to neither side. And the pieces enter and exit in ways that bear no relationship to the pattern of the actual game. Nobody moves the chessmen; they move of their own volition; there are no players. Why, then, bother with an allegory that proves so problematic? The obvious answer, perhaps, has to do with an attempt to put a little fictive distance between the events of the play and those to which they allude. But the game also allows Middleton to negotiate the difficulty of representing events that made very little sense to those outside the highest royal circles. Why did James want such proximity to Spain? Why did Buckingham and Charles, now so hot for war with Spain, compromise themselves with a clandestine mission? Chess is generally perceived as a pastime of deep policy played by powerful minds, and thus it offered a way of representing events that served particularly well Charles, Buckingham – and James, whose fre-quent assertion that foreign policy belongs among the *arcana imperii*, the secrets of government, seems confirmed by the depiction of a game too complex for outsiders to comprehend or anticipate.

Though approved by the Master of Revels, *A Game at Chess* violated the custom that precluded the representation of living people on stage.

It proved immensely successful, playing for ten days in the largest playhouse in London to a packed audience that was estimated in total at about 30,000 people (though some may well have seen it more than once). It rested heavily on the anti-Catholic and Hispano-phobic prose tracts produced in profusion in the early 1620s, but it transformed their vitriolic commonplaces into a striking theatrical experience (Cogswell 1989: 281–301). Perhaps Midddleton was uniquely suited to the task, in that he had recently assumed the role of chief script writer for mayoral pageants, and was used to the allegorical representation of contemporary figures and events in that rather different context. The play prompted a protest to James from the Spanish ambassador, and he ordered the Privy Council to suppress it. The Master of the Revels was questioned, the players were bound over for their future conduct, and Middleton may briefly have been imprisoned, but the lenity of the royal response suggests that the King's Men still enjoyed royal protection, and no doubt were assured too of the favour of the duke and the prince (Cogwell 1989: 306–7). But then Middleton and the company, far from articulating the voice of opposition, served the ends of the new war party, which had come into alignment with the widely and fiercely held prejudices of much of the political nation. No wonder they got away with it.

The plague of 1625 that devastated the viability of London theatre companies carried off one of the finest survivors from the age of Shakespearean drama: John Fletcher. He perished, on a seventeenth-century account, because he delayed his planned flight to the country until a new suit of clothes was ready from his tailor (*DNB* 1975). Several highly accomplished plays for the King's Men date from this period, including *The Pilgrim* (?1621/2), an adaptation of Lope de Vega's recently translated comedy *El Peregrino en su Patria*, *The Wild-Goose Chase* (?1621), *A Wife for a Month* (?1624) and *Rule a Wife and Have a Wife* (?1624), the last also from a Spanish source (Beaumont and Fletcher 1966–94: VI, 113–14, 227–8, 357–8, 485–6). The late flowering of a master craftsman, these plays evidently enjoyed immediate popularity. Most were presented at court, and they remained in the repertoire till the closure of the theatres.

They negotiate a complex relationship with late Jacobean London. The settings are foreign – perverse, exotic, 'oriental' in the manner of *Measure for Measure* or *The Duchess of Malfi*. The rules of English common law are often strikingly absent. In *A Wife for a Month*, Frederick, the 'unnatural and libidinous' king of Naples ('Persons represented in the play'; p. 368), out of lust for the virginal Evanthe, allows her to marry Valerio, her beloved, on condition that he be executed after a month – and then, wickeder still, forbids Valerio to consummate the marriage on pain of Evanthe's immediate death, a threat which he was also charged to conceal from his bride. Contemporaneously, Naples had no king; it was a Spanish dependency with a Spanish viceroy (Ogg 1965: 48). But the anachronism matches the vaguely atopical setting: this is a generalized Italy of bawds, poisoners, absolutists and the 'necessary creatures' who perform their will. There is no recourse to legal process. However, among the array of impossibly wicked villains and impossibly resolute heroes, Fletcher amazingly achieves some delicacy of characterization, particularly in his depiction of Evanthe's sexual frustration as the decent characters in the play celebrate the bedding of the bride, which she eagerly anticipates, while we and her husband and her tormentor know that Valerio may not deflower her. (In the event, he pretends to be suffering from sexual dysfunction that renders his willingness to die for a month of married life somewhat puzzling, not least to his bride: 'Tis hard to dye for nothing' – 3.3.238; p. 412.) The play would have made a decent Puccini libretto. Fletcher works the audience's expectations with persistent adroitness. First we think Valerio and Evanthe will enjoy an intense married life under urgent time pressure. Frederick's second arbitrary ruling eliminates that. Then we think the king's decent but melancholy brother, the only possible source of external intervention, is poisoned. Then we think Evanthe or Valerio will die and someone will avenge the death. In the event, Fletcher saves Valerio from execution through a cruder version of the mechanism that saves Claudio in *Measure for Measure* – a decent officer charged with the task pretends to have flung his corpse in the sea 'To feed the fishes' (5.3.12; p. 440). A *coup d'état* replaces Frederick with his brother. We anticipate his condign punishment, but in yet another surprise Fletcher dismisses him to the monastery where his brother had been dwelling, a commutation secured through a surprising – and very brief – act of contrition. Fletcher achieves an engaging work of immense pace, but also the most intimate depiction of female desire to be accomplished on the early Stuart stage.

A prologue to *Rule a Wife and Have a Wife*, presumably added for a court performance, explicitly distances the setting and the events depicted from Jacobean England: '*still tis* Spaine, / *No such grosse errors in your Kingdome raigne*' (Prologue, ll.11–12; p. 502). The main plot tells how Margarita, a virginal but libidinous heiress, marries Leon, a seeming buffoon, to give a specious respectability to the life of debauchery she intends for herself. The buffoon, however, rapidly emerges as a Petrucchio figure in disguise, asserting his role within the patriarchal household, making himself master of her fortune, and in the process saving her honour and winning her love. The play hovers around the disgrace of cuckoldry but produces instead an orthodox celebration of masculinity and male dominance in marriage, although the secondary plot, in which the heiress's maid, Estifania, gets the better of her duped husband, Perez, precludes too simple a schematization, for this is a play, as the prologue announces, designed to appeal to both sexes. Again, though unequivocally a comedy, the play reflects the changed direction of Jacobean foreign policy. Its opening remarks seek to allay anti-Spanish sentiment: '*Now we present their* [Spanish] *wit and not their state*' (Prologue, l.8; p. 502). Moreover, the background to the action is mobilization for war, which gives an urgency to the mating game. Margarita anticipates Leon's embarkation, and while the gallants accept her colours, they acknowledge they will 'Weare em before the bullet, and in bloud too' (5.5.176–7; p. 576). Moreover, Estifania's depiction of her hunt for her husband has an immediately pertinent resonance:

> I went to twenty Taverns.
> . . .
> Where I saw twenty drunk, most of em souldiers,
> . . .
> From hence to'th dicing house, there I found
> Quarrels needlesse, and senselesse, swords, and pots, and candlesticks,
> Tables, and stooles, and all in one confusion,
> And no man knew his friend.
>
> (4.1.28–35; p. 548)

Fletcher looks unflinchingly on the less glorious side of military adventurism, in the civil disorder associated with the muster of young and riotous men. The seaports on England's south coast would be habituated to such scenes in the years to come.

The Wild-Goose Chase was first printed in 1653, most fittingly with a prefatory poem by Richard Lovelace, that paradigmatic royalist poet and, as we shall see, a decisive figure in the fashioning of the cavalier image. In terms of plot, Fletcher's play owes something to early

Shakespeare. Like *Love's Labour's Lost* or *Much Ado about Nothing* or *Twelfth Night*, it is a multiple mating story, in which disguises, games and tricks are used to bring together characters that the audience perceive as mutually compatible. But Shakespeare's world of playful, witty courtiers to whom no hint of grossness adheres is superseded by a milieu peopled by rich young toughs, for whom the backstory, plainly established in their libertine banter, is one of riot and debauchery. The audience is never invited to ponder the previous sex life of Benedick or Orsino. But Mirabell and his fellow-travellers Pinac and Bellure, returned to Paris, explicitly rehearse their past fornication and their current intentions:

> MIRABELL Welcom to *Paris* once more, Gentlemen:
>   We have had a merry, and a lusty Ord'nary,
>   And wine, and good meat, and a bounsing Reckning;
>   And let it go for once; 'Tis a good physick:
>   Only the wenches are not for my dyet,
>   They are too lean and thin; their embraces brawn-fall'n.
>   Give me the plump Venetian, fat, and lusty,
>   That meets me soft and supple; smiles upon me,
>   As if a cup of full wine leap'd to kiss me;
>   These slight things I affect not.
> PINAC They are ill built;
>   Pin-buttockt, like your dainty Barbaries,
>   And weak i'th' pasterns; they'l endure no hardness
>   (1.2.1–12; p. 256)

Fletcher's heroes probably approximate more closely in their appetites and values to the rich, young and unmarried men of the Inns of Court than Shakespeare's more ethereal lovers. The play ends with a dirty joke. Bellure, about to wed and forswearing further travels, vows, 'No more for *Italy*, for the *Low-Countries*, I' (5.6.108; p. 335). Fletcher revivals proved immensely popular in the early years after the reopening of the theatres in 1660 (Clark 2001: 284); characters like these anticipate the earthiness of the Restoration rake.

Ben Jonson fared less well with his late plays, though modern critical opinion has attempted a revaluation. He had last composed for the theatre in 1616 (*The Devil is an Ass*). In 1626 *The Staple of News* was performed by the King's Men, significantly first at court, and then at the Blackfriars Theatre. Since his previous play, his dramatic output had been confined to writing masques. *The Staple of News*, in an audacious baroque interrogation of genre boundaries, shifts city comedy into the allegorical mode. The premise is a familiar one, a plot that exposes, in part through the use of disguise, the appetitiveness of contemporary society, in effect Jonson's standard fare since his late Elizabethan plays. Chiselling, turning a dishonest penny and conspicuous consumption drive the action in a milieu of frauds and gulls. The wealthy but aged Pennyboy Canter, in improbably successful disguise, breaks to his son and heir, Pennyboy Junior, the false news of his death and Junior's sudden accession to vast wealth. Junior runs a prodigal's course, squandering resources on, inter alia, investment in the eponymous 'staple of news', from which a news service is operated. In the process, in a curious modal shift, Junior is encouraged by his usurer uncle, Pennyboy Senior, to pursue the Lady Pecunia (= 'Money' [Latin]), an heiress who is 'The *Venus* of time, and state' – Jonson 1925–52: V, 319; 2.5.34). The allegory functions rather fitfully, although, as the plot runs its course, she returns to enunciate the moral:

> And so *Pecunia* her selfe doth wish,
> That shee may still be ayde vnto their vses,
> Not slave vnto their pleasures, or a Tyrant
> Ouer their faire desires; but teach them all
> The golden meane: the *Prodigall* how to liue,
> The sordid, and the *couetous*, how to dye:
> That with sound mind; this, safe frugality.
>
> (5.6.60–7; p. 382)

Jonson's conclusion may strike but a glancing blow at the early Caroline court. Presumably nobody would have interpreted words written by the favoured masque-writer of the 1620s as a reproach to a court expenditure, the lavishness of which was to its supporters and participants merely a decorum of state. However, the intergenerational conflict at the centre of the play, resolved in the shaming of the young man, could scarcely have struck a sympathetic chord among those scions of the propertied, wasting their fathers' money in feigned study at the Inns of Court, who may well have made up a significant proportion of the audience at Blackfriars. Moreover, Jonson's secondary target contains a further ill-judged reproach. In 1620 Jonson had scripted a Twelfth Night masque, *News from the New World Discovered in the Moon*, which had found such favour that it was repeated a few weeks later (Orgel and Strong 1973: 307). In it, the antimasque had satirically represented 'a factor of news for all the shires of England', whose enterprise supplied the political nation with spurious reports (pp. 308–11). No doubt James, increasingly concerned with intrusive gazes into the *arcana imperii*, relished the deprecatory depiction and savoured the antimasque's dismissal at the disclosure of the Prince of Wales, Buckingham and their masquing companions. In the printed version of *The Staple of News*, Jonson inserted a note 'TO THE READERS', making explicit his purpose in repeating the attack on news distribution. What he depicts is:

> *Newes* made like the times *Newes*, (a weekly cheat to draw mony) and could not be fitter reprehended, then in raising this ridiculous *Office* of the *Staple*, wherin the age may see her owne folly, or hunger and thirst after publish'd pamphlets of *Newes*, set out euery Saturday, but made all at home, no syllable of truth in them . . .   (p. 325)

The audience, who had paid their 6d to watch the performance, may well have taken a different view of their appetite for news. After all, many – indeed, probably most – of them would have been among the multitudes who had seen *A Game at Chess* at the Globe. *The Staple of News* is in many ways an ingeniously crafted and theatrically challenging play, artfully self-referential, marked by modal instabilities and distancing ironies. But its contentions that young men should respect their parents and, more significantly, that the ordinary Englishman should keep his nose out of the king's business, showed a dramatist too much at odds with his audience. Jonson, evidently, had been away too long.

The Staple of News was received unenthusiastically and did little to revive Jonson's career away from court. His next play, *The New Inn*, was performed in 1629 by the King's Men, a year after a severe stroke had physically incapacitated him. The play proved an instant disaster. He vouchsafed it to the press in 1632, hedged around with attacks not only on the audience, a familiar target for Jonson's anger, but also the acting company with which he had been associated through the best years of his playwriting career. Even the title page is a howl of complaint: this is the text of a comedy 'As it was neuer acted, but most negligently played, by some, the King Seruants. And more squeamishly beheld, and censured by others, the Kings Subiects' (Jonson 1925–52: V, 395). No corroboration is extant, though Jonson perhaps reports accurately the limitations of the single performance the play received. Yet there are other evident explanations for its failure. Richard Harp notes that the plot, with its improbable reunion of lovers long separated, recalls Shakespeare's 'late romances' (Harp 2000: 94). But Jonson, once more bending genre conventions, transposes those improbabilities from Shakespeare's remote and exotic locations to an English country inn, a setting carefully established in realistic detail. This is Barnet, not Bohemia. But the location would be merely a challenge to the audience's suspension of disbelief, were the problems not compounded by the extreme complexities that the plot develops. Indeed, the printed version appeared with a 1,000-word 'Argument' and a 'short Characterisme', a pen portrait, of each principal character (Jonson 1925–52: V, 398–404), indicative, surely, of some entirely reasonable anxiety about its comprehensibility even in its printed version. As in the disaster of his Roman tragedies (see above, chapter 2), Jonson realized too late the limitations of what can be communicated theatrically. To the printed text he added a poem, 'The iust indication the Author tooke at the vulgar censure of his Play, by some malicious spectators' (Jonson 1925–52: V, 492–4), though his farewell to the 'lothed stage' (l.1) smacks rather of Coriolanus banishing Rome. It was not, however, his last theatrical venture.

Philip Massinger's brilliant comedy, *A New Way to Pay Old Debts* (?1621–5), negotiated the urgent issues of its own age as nimbly as Jonson blundered. The date and circumstances of its earliest performances are unclear. The title page to its first edition (1633) alludes to a performance by the Queen's Men at the Phoenix in Drury Lane, but that company took up residence there in late 1625, and perhaps the play had an earlier stage history. Certainly, it engaged deeply with matters of widespread interest and concern across the first half of the decade. The love plot involves the mating through trickery of a young hero, Alworth, with Margaret, the daughter of a cruel and interdictive usurer. It has an obvious affinity with *The Merchant of Venice*, but in place of a villainous Jew (at a time when almost no Jews lived in England) Massinger offers the instantly recognizable figure of Sir Giles Overreach, whom critics unanimously identify as Sir Giles Mompesson (1584–1651?), as no doubt the earliest audiences did. Mompesson was a very safe target. His wife's sister had married the half-brother of Buckingham. This gave him a route to the heart of government where his development of schemes for the licensing of public houses and of the production of luxury textiles allowed him to accumulate a considerable fortune very quickly. Parliament in 1621 had stripped him of his knighthood and passed a sentence of massive fines and lifetime incarceration, which he escaped by bolting (*DNB* 1975). Massinger's depiction misses much of the detail, though his misconduct in the licensing of unsuitable public houses seems to be alluded to. But Overreach becomes, rather, a composite figure of mercantile greed and corruption. The play develops a larger symbolic structure as Massinger opposes the ancient values of what modern historians call 'the county community' to the ruthless individualism of the city.

In the main plot, Overreach's nephew Welborne, born to the brother of his former wife, has through his own profligacy and his uncle's usurious guile fallen into extreme indigence. He reminds Lady Alworth, a rich widow, of his former kindness to her late husband: 'Wants, debts, and quarrels / Lay heavy on him: let it not be thought / A boast in me, though I say, I reliev'd him' (Massinger 1964a: 22; 1.3.100–2). Furnace, Order and Amble, the servants of her country house, function almost as a chorus, to assert the values of gentry society, and one duly remarks, 'Are we not base rogues / That could forget this?' (ll.108–9). Lady Alworth connives in a plot to deceive Overreach into thinking she is about to marry Welborne. In the resolution, Overreach is betrayed by his creature Marrall, who in turn is rejected for his violation of the code of personal loyalty the county community requires:

> WELBORNE You are a rascal, he that dares be false
> To a master, though unjust, will ne'er be true
> To any other: look not for reward,
> Or favour from me . . .
> . . .
>   not a word
> But instantly begone.
> ORDER Take this kick with you.
> AMBLE And this.
> FURNACE If that I had my cleaver here
> I would divide your knave's head.
> MARRALL This is the haven
> False servants still arrive at.
>   (Massinger 1964a: 89; 5.1.338–41, 346–9)

Massinger dedicated the printed edition to Robert Dormer, Earl of Caernarfon, in terms that asserted the loyal retainership of his lineage:

'I was born a devoted servant, to the thrice noble family of your incomparable Lady' (1964a: 3). His father had been an estate manager in the Wilton household of William Herbert, third Earl of Pembroke. The daughter of his brother, Philip, Earl of Montgomery and eventually fourth Earl of Pembroke, had married Caernarfon. While the dedication chimed with the theme of old values and county community, it also picks up the martial dimension Massinger gives the play. Alworth is page to Lord Lovell, who participates in the country plot against Overreach and ends by marrying Lady Alworth. Lovell is briefly back in England from the continental wars, where his role roughly resembles that of Sir Horace Vere, leader of the ill-fated English expeditionary force. At the end of the play, Welborne asks for and is granted command of a company in Lovell's service, and the assumption clearly is that they will all return to the continental wars. The larger ideological structure of the play opposes selfish and appetitive mercantilism, the sort of thing Buckingham's cronies get up to, with not only country values but also selfless courage in the Protestant cause. Massinger's is a text for his times.

In November 1623, the month in which Ben Jonson's own library and accumulated manuscripts were accidentally destroyed by fire, Shakespeare's First Folio appeared. Many of his plays had remained staples in the repertoire of the King's Men, frequently revived in their theatres and performed in court, as they continued to be till 1642 (Bentley 1941–68: 1, 127–30), a practice which reflected not only an abiding enthusiasm for an extraordinary dramatist but also the evident conservatism of dramatic literary taste. About half the oeuvre had appeared piecemeal as quarto editions of single plays. *Mr. William Shakespeares Comedies, Histories, & Tragedies* marked an innovation in English publishing (see plate 4). Jonson had offered his *Works* in 1616, but that had mixed drama with poetry. The new volume offered a definitive collection of a wholly dramatic corpus 'Published according to the True Originall Copies' (Shakespeare 1623: title page).

In a singularly barren period for printed poetry, Shakespeare's dramatic verse must have seemed extraordinarily rewarding to aficionados. But the collection appeared hedged around with evidence of caution and anxiety. Its editors, Henry Condell and John Heminge, formerly colleagues of Shakespeare and still shareholders in the King's Men, placed the collection in that same patronage network that Massinger had courted in *A New Way to Pay Old Debts*. Here the dedication is to William, third Earl of Pembroke, and Philip, Earl of

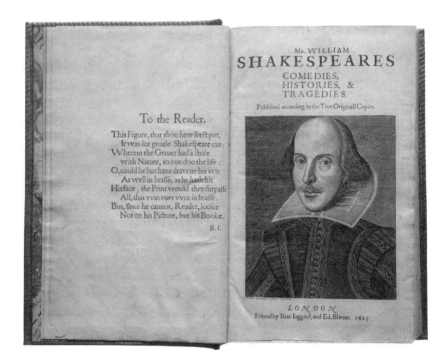

Plate 4 William Shakespeare, *Mr. William Shakespeares Comedies, Histories, & Tragedies* (1623), portrait frontispiece and titlepage. Reproduced by permission of the Folger Shakespeare Library.

Montgomery. More interesting is Heminge and Condell's epistle 'To the great variety of Readers', which urges the browser to be a buyer of the book: 'the fate of all Bookes depends on your capacities: and not your heads alone, but of your purses. Well! It is now publique, you wil stand for your priviledges: to read, and censure. Do so, but buy it first' (Shakespeare 1623: sig. A4r). This was, indeed, a luxury item, typically sold for 15s. unbound, 16s. to £1 bound (depending on the quality of the binding), a price which may be contextualized by reference to the 6d a day paid to seventeenth-century agricultural labourers, and expenditure of a different order from the 6d usually charged for a single play. Recent estimates of the print run vary from 750 to 1,500 copies, of which about 230 copies are extant (West 2001: vi, 4). The capital invested in the project may well have been without precedent in the publishing of creative writing in English, though comparisons with incunabula are necessarily speculative. But its appearance was timely. John Pitcher, setting it against the other now canonical works available to the late Jacobean readership, has sagely concluded they 'urgently needed, as its heart and mind, something less upper-crust than Sidney, less trashy than the newsletter, less erudite than Spenser, and less hard to understand than Chaucer'. Shakespeare's collected plays appeared 'arranged in traditional generic groups, rather than in some order of performance or composition that purported to trace the author's development (as with Chaucer and Jonson)', a feature John Pitcher judges to be 'rather old-fashioned' (2002: 373–4). Yet it reflects how Shakespeare's plays were contemporaneously perceived and encountered, as central to a living theatrical experience in which the order of their first appearance had little significance. *Richard III* and *The Taming of the Shrew* were still performed at court in the 1630s (Bentley 1941–68: I, 97). Ben Jonson's prefatory poem recognizes Shakespeare's historical impact on English drama, as he outshines '*our* Lily...*or sporting* Kid, *or* Marlowes *mighty line*'. But Jonson works towards an assertion of Shakespeare's transhistorical significance. If he is, indeed, '*not of an age, but for all time*', an appreciation of his development has little part in the general reader's experience of the text (Shakespeare 1623: sig. A4r-v).

Poetry and Prose Romance

Donne and Jonson wrote significant verse during this period, though the former vouchsafed none to the press and the latter's poetry appeared piecemeal and infrequently. We have considered some items in passing, such as his dedicatory poem to the First Folio and his farewell to the stage printed with the quarto of *The New Inn*. However, further consideration of their late verse is reserved until the next chapter, as is the early writing of Thomas Carew, George Herbert, John Milton and Robert Herrick, though again they were writing important verse in the late 1620s. In terms of what could be bought, rather than culled from manuscripts in circulation, this was a relatively unrewarding period, though with some fascinating developments, particularly in the published work of Francis Quarles, George Wither and Lady Mary Wroth.

Quarles is best remembered as the author of *Emblemes* (1635), probably the most successful emblem book in the English tradition (considered in chapter 4). But his busy career as a religious poet began in 1620 with *A Feast for Wormes* (Quarles 1620), a narrative poem about Jonah, in effect a sort of sacred epyllion. Quarles's early writing demonstrates readers' demands both for religiously improving writing (the masses of which are largely unconsidered in this history) and for printed verse; neither need was met by those who are, from a modern perspective, the major writers of the period. *A Feast for Wormes* demonstrates a fairly competent if evidently unexciting command of the heroic couplet:

> Why? what are men? But quicken'd lumps of earth?
> A feast for wormes, A bubble full of mirth.
> A looking-glasse for griefe, A flash, A minnit,
> A painted Toombe, with putrefaction in it.
> (Quarles 1620: sig. C3r-v)

The narrative frequently provides a platform for such religious meditation. This is a strictly and explicitly functional piety: the volume concludes with 'The Generall Use of this History', enjoining, 'reade it often, or else reade it not: / Once read, is not observ'd, or soone forgot' (sig. L1r).

Quarles rapidly followed the story of Jonah with other narrative poems, on Esther, Job and Samson (Quarles 1621, 1624, and 1631). Milton's own great narrative (and dramatic) accounts of Bible stories should be set against this rather homespun domestic tradition as surely as against the models of Homer, Virgil and Sophocles he more evidently emulates. Indeed, Quarles made Milton's own point, about the superiority of godly heroism over pagan heroism, as the subject for verse, while invoking Urania as his explicitly Christian muse (Quarles 1621: sig. B1r-v). He also favoured the occasional epic simile, sometimes flagging them up with a marginal note, '*simile*'.

The case of Quarles also serves as a caution against over-schematic accounts of late Jacobean and early Caroline ideological formations. He had held a minor court office as a cupbearer in the entourage of Princess Elizabeth, Queen of Bohemia, and had dedicated *A Feast for Wormes* to Robert Sidney, first Earl of Leicester, which would place him on the side of (or at least under the patronage of) the advocates of continental intervention in the Thirty Years War (though later publications are dedicated to King James and Charles, Prince of Wales, among others). His career, through the 1620s and early 1630s, was as secretary to James Ussher, Archbishop of Armagh, who, among critics of episcopacy, emerged in the early 1640s as the most acceptable of prelates, and evidently Quarles shared his master's objections to

Laudianism (Norbrook 1984: 235). Yet he proved loyal to the king's cause in the early 1640s. (See *DNB* 1975.)

Quarles figures in a minor way in some modern anthologies; Wither rather less so, though his role as a significant oppositional writer in the 1610s and his later career as defender of parliament and republic give him a prominence in the cultural ideology of those periods. (See also Norbrook 1999; both are in Fowler 1991; Quarles alone in Cummings 2000; neither is in Abrams et al. 2000). In the 1620s Wither attempted to position himself as independent of the patronage system. In practical terms, this required a radical shift in authorial relations with the Stationers' Company. As long as copyright belonged with its members, rather than with authors, the emergence of a class of professionals able to live from non-dramatic dissemination of their writing was constrained. Indeed, Wither's early work was reissued in a pirated edition in 1620 (*DNB* 1975). As Wither incisively put it, 'the Bookeseller hath not onely made the Printer, the Binder, and the Claspmaker a slave to him: but hath brought Authors, yea the whole Commonwealth, and all liberall Sciences into bondage' (n.d.: 10). Wither, who recognized as surely as Quarles the demand for devotional writing of some literary accomplishment, in 1623 sought to take on the stationers by publishing himself his *Hymnes and Songs of the Church* under letters patent issued by royal prerogative. The collection presumably seemed unexceptionable to James, who may well have relished the penultimate hymn, 'for the *Kings* day', with its fulsome acknowledgement of the *arcana imperii*:

> Make us (that placed are below)
>   Our callings to apply,
> Not over-curious be to know,
>   What he intends on high.
>   (Wither 1623: 53)

When the stationers declined to handle it, he issued a prose pamphlet, *The Schollers Purgatory, discovered in the Stationers Commonwealth*, excoriating the book trade for its 'contempt of his Maiesties powre, the hindrance of devotion, the prejudice of the Authors estate, & the disparagment of his best endeavors' (Wither n.d.: title page, verso).

Wither's strongest poetry of the period came in *Withers Motto* (1621), an extended celebration in heroic couplets of the poet's sense of his own independence of spirit. Wither inflects the genre characteristics of early modern satire by placing himself – or, rather, a construct composed of Horatian values and Christianized stoicism – at the centre of his poem. The usual targets recur, from 'Hispaniolized *English men*' (Wither 1621: sig. B5r) to court parasites and patronage brokers (sig. D5r), the latter perhaps supporting a vague attack on Buckingham. Wither is careful to exempt his poem from the kinds of close attention more specific topicality would have attracted: 'You are deceiv'd, if the *Bohemian* state / You thinke I touch; or the *Palatinate*' (sig. A6v). Wither's recurrent concern is the nature of literary production in late Jacobean England and the part played by patronage. By writing alone one can scarcely live: 'Men aske me what Preferment I have gained? / What riches, by my Studies are attain'd?' (sig. C3r). His response is to differentiate his truth-telling from flattery, in ways which plainly found a sympathetic readership. The STC (Short Title Catalogue) distinguishes seven editions in its first year of publication. Yet, since his great coup of publishing under letters patent depended on a regal generosity, the claims he makes for himself may have seemed to some as more aspirational than real.

Wither and Quarles inhabited a world of financial insecurity and social dependence familiar to many of the early Stuart writers, for whom the material circumstances of literary production had scarcely changed since the Elizabethan period. Lady Mary Wroth, who had masqued with Queen Anne of Denmark, was an aristocrat with the finest social and literary credentials, proclaiming her 'strong sense of identity as a Sidney author' (Lewalski 1994: 243). Her father was Robert Sidney, first Earl of Leicester and brother of Sir Philip, and her long-term lover and father of her children was her cousin William Herbert, third Earl of Pembroke. Again, the connections – kinship rather than patronage – were nominally with the advocates of continental military adventurism, and, in ways that reflect the nostalgia for Elizabethan prowess, her literary aesthetic was retrospective, despite her evident achievement of publishing the first work of English prose fiction written by a woman. Perhaps equally remarkable is the lifetime publication of a work of creative writing by an aristocrat.

The title page of *The Countesse of Mountgomeries Urania* (Wroth 1621a) proclaimed the author's status as niece to Mary Herbert, recently deceased widow of the second Earl of Pembroke and 'the ever famous, and renowned Sr Phillips [*sic*] Sidney knight'. The latter, plainly, was profoundly influential. His *Arcadia* provided the generic model, and to the romance was appended a sequence of poems,

Pamphilia to Amphilanthus, unequivocally inspired by *Astrophil and Stella*. The romance, some 558 pages, breaks off (in some copies) mid-sentence, possibly indicative – though some have doubted this – that the copy which the printer used was fragmentary and unprepared by its author for the press, and a large manuscript, evidently not ready for the press, containing a second and concluding part is extant and has recently been published (Lewalski 1994: 264). Wroth herself wrote to Buckingham a letter of disclaimer, claiming that the printed copies 'were solde against my minde I never purposing to have had them published' (Wroth 1996: ix).

The prose romance has in recent years attracted considerable critical attention. In its own age, its apparent allusions to the manners and conduct of some Jacobean courtiers rendered it mildly notorious. More recently, the critical focus has been on gender issues and its differences from romances by male writers. Thus, Paul Salzman concludes: '*Urania* has its valiant heroes, but the reader's attention is directed to the women who are left behind by the questing men, or whose paths cross the heroes' with invariably miserable results' (Salzman 1985: 141; see also Lewalski 1994: 244, 266–8 and 2002: 611–12). More obvious and utterly unrelenting are its social assumptions. This is a tale of male and female shepherds and aristocrats – and aristocrats transiently disguised as shepherds: 'How came this fortune to you, said he, for no doubt but you were borne of better ranke then the estate you appeare in shewes you to be' (Wroth 1621a: 356). The characters are rarely more than (improbable) names, the landscapes they pass through bear no relation to the Balkan and eastern Mediterranean countries in which the stories are supposedly set, and the style is elegantly unremarkable: '*Amphilanthus*, and *Ollorandus* with *Dolorindus* passed farther into the countrie, and tooke their way by *Amphilanthus* direction towards *Neapolis*, where they were to visit the faire *Musalina*, who by meanes made by *Allimarlus* was reconciled to *Amphilanthus*, betweene whom an ancient quarrell ceased thus' (ibid.: 341).

Wroth's poetic oeuvre consists of the lyrics and sonnets inset in the romance itself and its poetic supplement. Once more, the current critical objective is the identification of a woman's distinctive voice within a customarily male idiom, here English appropriation of Petrarchanism. As Barbara Lewalski notes:

Wroth does not simply reverse the usual sonnet roles. Pamphilia addresses very few sonnets to Amphilanthus: there are no praises of his over-powering physical beauty or charms, no narratives of kisses or other favours...no blazons scattering his parts as a gesture of aggrandisement or control, no promises to eternise him through the poet's songs. (2002: 611; see also Lewalski 1994: 252 and Masten 1998: 34–6)

Yet while the gender values and politics are identifiably new, poetic technique is studiedly conservative. The dense ambiguities of Shakespeare's sonnets and the extraordinary metrical confidence and imaginative potency of Donne's holy sonnets are displaced in favour of the restrained elegance of Sidney's idiom:

> You blessed Starres, which doe Heauen's glory show,
>   And at your brightnesse makes our eyes admire:
>   Yet enuy not, though I on earth below,
>   Injoy a sight which mouese in me more fire.
> I doe confesse such beauty breeds desire
>   You shine, and clearest light on vs bestow:
>   Yet doth a sight on Earth more warmth inspire
>   Into my louing soule his grace to know.
> Cleare, bright, and shining, as you are, in this
>   Light of my ioy: fix't, stedfast, nor will moue
>   His light from me, nor I change from his loue;
>   But still increase as th'earth of all my blisse.
> His sight giue life vnto my loue-rould eyes
> My loue content, because in his loue lies.
>   (Wroth 1621b: 24)

Non-Fictional Prose

In 1620 Bacon published the *Novum Organum*, a substantial Latin treatise intended to place his mature reflections on the advancement of learning before an educated and international readership. He was already Baron Verulam, Lord Chancellor, the most senior lawyer in England, and, as his father had been, Keeper of the Great Seal. In the week before the first meeting of the parliament of 1621 he was promoted Viscount St Albans. The success that had come to him reflected not only his evident abilities – he remained as clever, cunning and energetic as ever – but also his seemingly secure place as a major beneficiary of Buckingham's patronage. That apparent strength proved an evident weakness. Once parliament had dealt with Mompesson, it turned to Bacon, who had, in an official capacity, supported Mompesson's patent for the licensing of inns (see above). Parliament tried him on well-substantiated charges of corruption. A convincing array of evidence established that he had accepted bribes from those whose law cases he was adjudicating on, and he could not be saved by Buckingham or by the king without a degree of exposure they were unwilling to accept. He was stripped of his offices, imprisoned in the Tower of London and heavily fined. Buckingham ensured his incarceration was short-lived, and through the king he wriggled out of paying the fines (an impossibility, anyway, for someone already, through his own profligacy, massively in debt). He was, however, effectively banished from court and parliament, and never regained the access he had enjoyed to the highest circles of power (*DNB* 1975; Jardine and Stewart 1998: 448–69).

He assiduously fashioned an image of himself in those five years of enforced rural retreat, as a sage and scholar withdrawn to complete the literary, historical, philosophical and scientific projects that he had pursued but fitfully in his years of power and prominence. But, as his most recent biographers have demonstrated, that image belies his fervid attempts to regain, primarily through courtship of Buckingham, the pre-eminence he had lost. That project was disrupted by the adventure of the Spanish Match and by James's recognition that his presence at or close to court while the parliament of 1624 was sitting would have been a provocative display of royal prerogative in defiance of the determination of the previous parliament (Jardine and Stewart 1998: 473–501).

Yet his final years allowed an extraordinary flurry of diverse activity. His crowning literary achievement, the third and final major edition of his *Essays* (1625), revises the essays of the second edition of 1612, and adds 19 new essays, justifying the claim he makes in the dedication to Buckingham that 'they are indeed a new Worke' (Bacon 2000: 5). Michael Kiernan, a modern editor, demonstrates the continued transition from the voice of the first edition, written 'essentially from the suitor's point of view', to the persona, present in 1612 but dominant in 1625, of Bacon as sage counsellor of princes (ibid.: xix–xxxi). Bacon was contemporaneously writing what were in effect briefing papers for Charles and Buckingham, and the new edition can be perceived as constituting a more oblique attempt to convince of his indispensability those who could redeem his fortunes. But some of the new essays also give the collection a tone of autumnal melancholy. The Baconian perspective is still unflinching and clear-eyed, although it seems, here, cast backwards.

'Of Truth', the new essay which opens the volume, begins with an image of paradigmatic judicial malpractice: '*What is Truth*; said jesting *Pilate*; And would not stay for an Answer.' It develops into a recognition of the limited attractions for most people of truth over fancy, and ends with a contemplation of 'the last Peale' and 'the Judgements of God' (ibid.: 7–9). Some essays work to adjust the authorial image produced in the earlier editions by suggesting a hitherto unsuspected cultural hinterland in a Bacon who is sagacious not only about the affairs of state and the world of business but also about foreign travel (ibid.: 56–7), masques (ibid.: 117–18), architecture (ibid.: 135–8) and gardens (ibid.: 139–45). Others seem coloured by his recent disgrace. 'Of Envie', read in context, offers an anatomy of where he went wrong:

> those are most subject to *Envy*, which carry the Greatnesses of their fortunes, in an insolent and proud Manner…publique *envy*, seemeth to beat chiefly, upon principall Officers, or Ministers, rather then upon Kings, and Estates themselves. But this is a sure Rule, that if the *Envy* upon the Minister, be great, when the cause of it, in him, is smal;…then the *Envy* (though hidden) is truly upon the State it selfe. (Ibid.: 29–31)

Bacon no doubt well knew that his prosecution originated both in personal resentments of those who prepared that case against him and in the larger odium occasioned by Buckingham's de facto management of the realm.

Of the essays newly added in 1625, the most remarkable, 'Of Vicissitude of Things', concludes the volume. As Bacon added material to the 1612 edition, he developed the collection from 'advice to the esurient' into 'advice to the prince', a shift that adds a sort of Machiavellian statecraft to more intimate counsel. But it still functioned as a conduct book replete with hints on how to succeed in the early Stuart state. The 1625 edition remains a consummate expression of individualism, guiding the reader on his watchful and solitary paths through the anterooms and privy chambers of power. It concludes:

> In the Youth of a *State*, *Armes* do flourish; In the *Middle Age* of a *State*, *Learning*; And then both of them together for a time: In the *Declining*

Age of a *State*, *Mechanicall Arts* and Merchandize. *Learning* hath his Infancy, when it is but beginning, and almost Childish: then his Youth, when it is Luxuriant and Juvenile: then his Strength of yeares, when it is Solide and Reduced: And lastly, his old Age, when it waxeth Dry and Exhaust. But it not good, to looke too long, upon these turning Wheeles of *Vicissitude*, lest we become Giddy. As for the *Philology* of them, that is but a Circle of Tales, and therefore not fit for this Writing.   (Ibid.: 176)

Bacon's has been an engagement with the exigencies of personal struggle, but he ends with a long perspective in which individual endeavour appears puny against the larger cycles of maturation and decay which seem to afflict all hitherto existing societies. He vouchsafes no opinion as to which phase Jacobean England had reached, and he recognizes that his is an idiom and a mindset that cannot sustain such a long view, 'lest we become Giddy'. He breaks off and turns away.

Robert Burton's *Anatomy of Melancholy* was first published in 1621. Rather like Sir Thomas Browne's *Pseudodoxia Epidemica* (see below, chapter 5), this was to remain a life's work. It appeared in four further lifetime editions and a posthumous one, and, principally in the second, third and fourth editions, it was much augmented by the author. It was, at the outset, a very long book of about 350,000 words; by the end, it was half as long again (Burton 1989–2000: I, xxxviii). Structurally and thematically, it changed relatively little. Rather, Burton, as he continued his own reading, found new material to supplement the examples and authorities already included.

Plainly, this was a relatively popular work. All these early editions were printed at Oxford. Burton was a career academic, a senior 'student', that is a fellow, of Christ Church, at that time Oxford's richest college, and his income was increased by the lucrative ecclesiastical livings which he held from time to time. His recurrent concern with 'the miseries of scholars' (apparently, they are not paid enough and not respected enough) both reflects his own preoccupations and perhaps indicates where his strongest readership may have been. This is, indeed, a very scholarly work, a vast assembly of much of the learning of the ancient world and of subsequent investigation into human physiology, the aetiology of melancholy and its supposed cures, as well as a wide review of history and philosophy. He bluntly tells his readers, 'Thou thy selfe art the subject of my Discourse' (ibid.: I, 1). Yet his views on the human animal are endlessly refracted through the cumulative but often contradictory wisdom of centuries of European thought and speculation.

In genre terms, the book poses difficulties. At one level, it may seem merely a scholarly redaction. No doubt J. B. Bamborough is right in his surmise that 'he seems to have felt the need to "cover the ground" and give the reader the benefit of every particle of knowledge which he himself had gleaned' (Burton 1989–2000: I, xxvi). Yet that inclusiveness virtually neutralizes the value of the work even as a self-help guide, let alone a treatise on the causes, diagnosis and treatment of a malady. As he considers the role of diet, for example, almost every plant and animal has been adduced by someone as a cause of melancholy, leaving almost nothing on the menu (ibid.: I, 211–20). When he considers surgery, procedures proliferate: '*Montalus cap. 35.* would have the thighes to bee cauterised, *Mercurialis* prescribes beneath the knees; *Laelius Eugubinus consul. 77* for an Hypocondriacall Dutchman, will have the cautery made in the right thigh, so *Montanus consil. 55*' (ibid.: II, 263). And the list continues through another half dozen alternatives, leaving the practising surgeon facing a perplexing range of options for his first incision.

Yet despite its endless presentation of facts and theories from a myriad of predominantly academic sources, this is a masterpiece of literary creativity. Burton recognizes a good anecdote, and he retells them well, incorporating them briskly and ingeniously into his own exposition:

> And as that great captaine *Zisca* would have a drumme made of his skinne when he was dead, because he thought the very noise of it would put his enimies to flight, I doubt not, but that these following lines, when they shall be recited, or heareafter reade, will drive away Melancholy (though I be gone) as much as *Zisca's* drumme could terrify his foes.   (Ibid.: I, 24)

His own style is exuberant, and he uses a riotous juxtaposition of discordant discourses to stunning effect. Though he endlessly synthesizes the voices of others, Burton carefully controls the dominant voice that emerges. It is not, straightforwardly, his own. Rather, in a long prefatory epistle, 'Democritus Junior to the Reader', some 50,000 words in the later editions, he explicitly constructs as his persona, his alter ego, within the text a figure based on Democritus of Abdera, styled in his own age the laughing philosopher, a contradictory and unstable character, 'sometimes sad & sometimes againe profusely merry' (ibid.: I, 63). This figure well suits the labile narrator. Thus, in quick succession, we find him rounding belligerently on his readers: 'I owe thee nothing, (Reader) I looke for no favour at thy hands, I am independent, I feare not', before collapsing into an apology: 'No, I recant, I will not, I care, I confesse my fault . . . I have anatomized mine own folly' (ibid.: I, 112). That is, in his instability he has represented and exemplified the instability of the pathologically melancholy. Of course, this is a trick, a game. If Burton himself were worried about what he had written, he could easily have redrafted it. After all, the passage survives through multiple editions. But the stratagem serves him, allowing him to pre-empt a hostile response with a sudden reversal. For example, a pervasive misogyny, an interest in female sexual frustration and an unhealthy fascination with the melancholy effects of menstrual dysfunction recur over large sections of the book. As if anticipating a charge of morbid obsession, he pulls himself up: 'Into what subject have I rushed? What have I to doe with Nunnes, Maids, Virgins, Widowes? I am a bacheler my selfe, and leade a Monasticke life in a College . . . though my subject necessarily require it, I will say no more.' That paragraph ends thus; the next begins: 'And yet I must and will say something more . . .' (ibid.: I, 416). Burton remains a moving target.

Sermons formed a significant part of the cultural, intellectual and spiritual life of the cultural elite in early Stuart England. Certainly during the 1630s, Archbishop Laud discouraged a preaching ministry, to the chagrin of his Puritan critics for whom the pulpit allowed alternative perspectives to be developed. But celebrity preachers, pre-eminently John Donne, featured significantly in Jacobean London.

Donne entered holy orders in 1615, and the patronage of the king and leading aristocrats secured his rapid preferment. From 1621 he was Dean of St Paul's, a post he held pluralistically with other benefices and offices (*DNB* 2004). Several pulpits were open to him, and he preached frequently at court before the royal household. He had already begun to preach from time to time from the Paul's Cross sermons. Until 1633 these were delivered from a pulpit in the church-yard of the cathedral; thereafter the venue moved inside. Large audi-ences attended, among them aristocrats and the leading citizens. The preachers were carefully selected for their orthodoxy. The duty of appointment rested with the Bishop of London. Sermons clustered around Eastertide and Whitsun week and the major anniversaries of the royal calendar, such as accession day and the Gunpowder Plot (Maclure 1958, passim). Donne's own sermons mark most of these occasions.

Donne's sermons were sporadically printed during his own lifetime. The first dates from 1622, a Paul's Cross sermon preached to endorse and support a recent royal decree, 'Directions concerning Preachers', which was intended to rein in more speculative and oppositional sermons. The sermon was printed on the king's command. We know something of Donne's ways of working. He preached from notes, which he expanded significantly into a written text (Love 2002: 100–1). The large collections of his sermons, three impressive folios, are posthumous, published in 1640, 1649 and 1661. In their own age, each must have had a poignancy, as celebrations of the finest achievements of an episcopal church that was challenged, abolished and eventually restored.

Donne's most acclaimed sermon, in his age and ours, falls slightly outside the period of this chapter: *Deaths Duell, or, A Consolation to the Soule, against the dying Life, and living Death of the Body* (Donne 1953–62: VII, 229–48). Preached before Charles I in 1631 at the start of Lent, it was his last sermon, and one delivered under dramatic and vivid circumstances, which render it, to an extent, atypical of his sermons more generally. Donne was palpably very ill, appearing terribly emaciated, quite probably as a result of stomach cancer. He had returned to London after an unsuccessful attempt at rural recuperation, amid rumours that he had already died. The first edition carried a headnote: '*preached not many dayes before his death; as if, having done this, there remained nothing for him to doe, but die: And the matter is, of Death*' (ibid.: 229). Yet in many ways it is simply a fine example of Donne's preaching art. The printed version – presumably he used some of his remaining time to work it up for the press – is carefully annotated and tied intricately to Bible texts in a manner resembling formal exegesis. The principal themes differentiate human mortality from the death of Christ and they examine the implications of the death of Christ for human mortality. But what makes Donne's sermons extraordinary is not the quality of the theology, but the exhilarating vividness with which a sometimes disconcerting sensibility is produced and expressed within the text. It is a quality shared with his verse (see above, chapter 2), and it proves disturbingly appropriate for his themes in *Deaths Duell*:

> Wee have a winding sheete in our Mothers wombe, which growes with us from our conception, and wee come into the world, wound up in that *winding sheet,* for wee come to *seeke a grave;* And as prisoners discharg'd of actions may lye for fees; so when the *wombe* hath discharg'd us, yet we are bound to it by *cordes* of flesh, by such a *string*, as that wee cannot goes thence, nor stay there. We celebrate our owne funeralls with cryes, even at our birth.   (ibid.: 233)

The informing notion, that birth and death are intricately connected, is commonplace, but Donne reanimates it with the details, a caul as winding sheet, an umbilical as a bond or fetter tying the newborn to the womb like a felon to his cell.

Donne had rehearsed some of the issues in what is now his most quoted prose work, his *Devotions upon Emergent Occasions, and sever-all steps to my Sickness*, first published in 1624, and evidently popular in his own day since it went through five seventeenth-century editions. Donne produces an experimental form: each of 23 sections describes a stage in a developing, life-threatening illness; responds to it emotionally and spiritually; and ends with a prayer fashioned to match the context. The schema is encouraging, a sort of *in vita* purgatorial experience that ends with the patient returned to life both chastened and spiritually cleansed. The relapse he finally fears is a moral, not a physical, one, 'a *relapse* into those *sinnes*, which I have truely *repented*, and thou hast *fully pardoned*' (Donne 1975: 127). As in *Deaths Duell*, Donne's practical theology leads him to generalize from his experience to that of his audience, so that they may the more vividly visualize their own demise and seek a saving faith. It is a mission that extends back to medieval sermons, though the tradition owes a recent debt to the Catholic Counter-Reformation, a movement which had shaped Donne's own early religious experience. The text has retained its resonance. The 17th meditation, which cautions that 'No man is an *Iland*, intire of it selfe' and urges 'never send to know for whom the *bell* tolls; It tolls for *thee*' (ibid.: 87) probably matches the song from *Cymbeline* as a consoling reading for modern funerals. Yet familiarity perhaps dulls the awareness of how challenging, both emotionally and intellectually, Donne's prose really is. The critical part of the argument is carried by a puzzling analogy: 'if a *Clod* bee washed away by the *Sea, Europe* is the lesse, as well as if a *Promontorie* were, as well as if a *Mannor* of thy *friends*, or of *thine owne* were; Any Mans *death* diminishes *me*, because I am involved in *Mankinde*.' In what sense may losing a tiny fragment be equivalent to losing a large portion? Presumably in the sense that both are losses. In the same way, any person's death carries the implication of loss. The reader needs to work at Donne's prose, and understanding it, closely, clearly, unambiguously, sometimes comes a long way behind feeling it more vaguely as comfort or counsel.

News

The first newspaper printed in English appeared in 1620, the same year that the first newspapers were printed in French. Both series were produced in Amsterdam, primarily for export, and their appearance reflected a Europe-wide concern with the international crises at the outset of the Thirty Years War. There had long been manuscript correspondence carrying financial, social and political news. Earlier non-serial newsbooks dealing with particular events had been intermittently printed in English since the 1580s. But the new genre – perhaps the only really new genre to emerge in the 1620s – was distinguished by an expectation of regular and frequent publication in print (Frank 1961: 1).

The first paper, usually termed the *Corrant out of Italy, Germany, &c.*, was published by Pieter van den Keere at least 15 times between December 1620 and September 1621, though there may have been earlier issues that have not survived. As Joseph Frank observes in his classic history of the earliest English newspapers (on which this account substantially depends), its 'coverage of the Thirty Years War during this period left no large gaps, and it was this war that was the major stimulus to the growth of the newspaper in western Europe' (1961: 3).

James's government regarded this wide dissemination of news with concern, and persuaded the States General of the United Provinces to ban the export of corantos to Britain. However, shortly afterwards London-produced corantos appeared, largely based on foreign gazettes. Official hostility gave way to a subtler form of control, and publication continued under a government patent through the early and mid-1620s. Anxious, presumably, to retain this privilege, editors carefully eschewed English domestic news and explicit comment and interpretation of the course of the war, although the circulation of accounts of Protestant victories and Catholic atrocities gave support to the case for English participation in the continental land campaigns. Despite their tact and evasiveness – the Isle of Ré expedition passed virtually unreported – in 1632 newspapers were banned and success-fully suppressed by the Privy Council.

It would be difficult to claim any literary merit for these early publications. Not until the revival of the news periodical in the 1640s did authors and editors of wit, élan and guile emerge. In many ways, printed newspapers were less informative to their readers (and modern historians) than manuscript alternatives. But they were cheap: 2d, when a manuscript report cost from 6d to 3s. (Cust 1986: 64; Frank 1961: 12). The provision of manuscript reports by London agencies provided provincial England with detailed information, for example, about late Jacobean and early Caroline parliaments, and even insider gossip about Privy Council politics in a form that, in county society, trickled down to independent yeoman level. The manuscript newsletter shared with the political ballad and the rudimentary poems of state the responsibility for opening up the business of government to wider scrutiny and, more significantly, wider evaluation (Cust 1986). By 1626, Charles I appeared in the eyes of some gentry as irrevocably tainted by association with Buckingham. As Cust con-cludes, 'the widespread dissemination of a portrait [of Charles I] so much at odds with the contemporary ideal inevitably undermined the prestige of the crown and confidence in the status quo' (ibid.: 75).

In terms of literary history, this national hunger for news explains the success of *A Game at Chess* and provides a context for Jonson's depiction of the staple of news. But it also demonstrates the probably growing gap between the image of the state entertained more widely and that presented in an elite literary culture. That culture looked to the highest circles for protection and patronage, remaining always susceptible to easy suppression, to prosecution, to ruin – or, more, mundanely, to the withholding of preferment. Court poets, theatres under the patronage of the royal family, and publishers controlled by the Stationers' Company had an interest in self-censorship which did not obtain among, for example, provincial MPs writing home to their constituency supporters about their parliamentary experiences and the shortcomings of the monarch and his creatures. Moreover, as Bacon had sardonically observed to Buckingham in 1620, 'nowadays there is no vulgar, but all statesmen' (quoted Jardine and Stewart 1998: 446).

The deaths of James and Buckingham significantly shaped the cul-tural history of this period, though it was the Protestant disaster in continental Europe that animated propertied and educated English-men at the outset, raised anti-Catholic sentiment, rendered the Span-ish Match odious in prospect and politically impossible, and paved the way for the disastrous wars with Spain and France. Patronage, flowing from the court, most conspicuously through the channel of the duke, supported a court culture of sorts, from which the most accomplished writers, Bacon, Donne and Jonson, evidently benefited. Others, such as Herrick and Carew, who would contribute so much to elite literary culture in the next decade, were already associated with that network and already active. But literary production reflected, too, a wider audience with a probably unprecedented interest in the affairs of state. James's ideal of government as royal prerogative, conducted with an appropriate secrecy, proved unsustainable once wars required frequent recurrence to the parliamentary process necessary for raising taxation. Charles and Buckingham, on their return from Spain, had tentatively mounted the unbroken stallion of public opinion; they kept that saddle only briefly. As successive parliaments were called, con-sulted and dismissed, so a reading and theatre-going public came to value a literary experience that looked, or seemed to look, at the real world. Middleton is the paradigmatic writer of the 1620s.

On 2 March 1629, Charles, now personally and directly in control of the state without the mediating presence of Buckingham, dismissed parliament. He was still at war with two European superpowers, still, it would seem, unhappy in his marriage, still childless. A beleaguered ruler of a beleaguered realm, engaged in military conflicts he could not afford, alienated from a country increasingly critical of his policies in church as well as state, he evidently intended to rule for a little while without recourse to parliaments: his proclamation of 27 March, sup-pressing false rumours, made it clear that none was to meet immi-nently, but it proved in the event a renunciation of parliamentary government. That it did so until 1640 could scarcely have been antici-pated. Nor, indeed, would a review of the writing of the 1620s have given much indication of the extraordinary cultural achievement, in literature as in the performance and visual arts, of what we now know as the personal rule of Charles I.

4

The Literature of the Personal Rule: March 1629 to April 1640

The Making of the Caroline Court

Surprisingly for institutions that apparently embody in extreme form tradition and continuity, English royal courts, even into our own age, have proved singularly responsive to the preferences and priorities of reigning monarchs. Kevin Sharpe's magisterial study, on which this section substantially depends, has demonstrated the immediacy of Charles I's transformation of the conduct of the court he inherited from James. Even before his father's funeral, the Venetian ambassador reported:

> [T]he king observes a rule of great decorum. The nobles do not enter his apartments in confusion as heretofore, but each rank has its appointed place. . . . The king has also drawn up rules for himself, dividing the day from his very early rising, for prayers, exercises, audiences, business, eating and sleeping. It is said that he will set apart a day for public audience and he does not wish anyone to be introduced to him unless sent for. (Quoted in Sharpe 1992: 210–11)

The relative ease of entrée that characterized his father's court gave way to careful regulation of admission from the entrance gate through to the royal bedchamber. Charles's own sexual conduct, over the whole reign and indeed before his succession, occasioned relatively little adverse comment, even from parliamentarian and regicide apologists in the 1640s and 1650s. In his *Defensio pro populo Anglicano* (1651), John Milton, viewing sceptically the cultural agenda of the court, asserted that 'even in the theatre [Charles] kisses women wantonly, enfolds their waists and . . . plays with the breasts of maids and mothers' (IV.i; Milton 1953–82: 408). Probably he was alluding to the eroticizing of court entertainments, to which we turn shortly. But in sharp contrast, Lucy Hutchinson, another republican and the spouse of a regicide and Cromwellian officer, praised Charles's transformation of his court explicitly in terms of his correction of the sexual mores of the Jacobean period: 'The face of the court was much changed in the king, for King Charles was temperate and chaste and serious, so that the fools and bawds, mimics and catamites of the former court grew out of fashion' (Hutchinson 1995: 67).

Such changes could be effected without significant expenditure and with the household members already in post. Yet while Buckingham lived, he retained his obvious control of a complex system of patronage, which flowed ultimately from the throne, though its origins were occluded by the mighty presence of the duke. Buckingham also kept out of the king's immediate circle some significant figures of the personal rule. The Earl of Arundel, for example, avoided the court till after Buckingham's death, when his enormous influence on the king's artistic taste and enthusiasms developed fully. Most accounts attribute to Buckingham some role in the relative estrangement between Charles and Henrietta Maria in the early years of their marriage. Three months after his death, the poet Thomas Carew, whose duties as a gentleman of the bedchamber included lighting the king's way on nocturnal visits to the queen's bedchamber, noted that 'we find their master and mistress at such a degree of kindness as he would imagine him a wooer again and her gladder to receive his caresses than he to make them' (quoted in Sharpe 1992: 170–1).

The most tangible manifestation of this new affection was their abundant fertility: four sons and five daughters, born in 1629, 1630, 1631, 1633, 1636, 1637, 1639, 1640 and 1644. Throughout the personal rule, Henrietta Maria was 'almost constantly gravid or recovering from childbirth'; 'the paradigm at the centre of Caroline culture', pervasively, obtrusively and inescapably, was 'highly sexual, prolific marriage' (Coiro 1999: 26–7). The 'royal pair' were celebrated as a couple and as consorts in monarchy in ways that wholly eluded James I and Anne of Denmark. Politically, the phenomenon adjusted the balance of power; the queen shaped the careers of courtiers. She influenced foreign policy to a limited degree: her first pregnancy in January 1629 was said to have made the king 'very forward to have a peace' with France (Wilcher 2001: 9). She established her own networks of patronage, and secured some freedom of worship for her Catholic co-religionists. In terms of cultural ideology, the celebration of the royal couple set the agenda for masque-writers and court poets.

By the mid-1630s, Charles had overseen the development of the most vibrant and coherent court culture in the post-medieval history of England. The process was eased by the political breathing space he won through the cessation of hostilities with Spain and France. Richard Weston, Earl of Portland, steered the Treasury from the bankruptcy of the late 1620s to a position where the king could live comfortably within his means without recourse to calling parliaments with their concomitant disputes. As long as Charles eschewed resort to arms he could survive without engagement in popular politics, though he remained concerned with the Palatinate question and closely observant of the shifting fortunes in the Thirty Years War. Once France entered in 1635, an active alliance seemed for a while quite likely (Sharpe 1992: 598), though in the event England never became embroiled in a conflict that would continue till 1648. That England was a country privileged among nations by its peace became the second theme of court ideology.

Charles was an aesthete rather than an intellectual, though his interests were varied – indeed, almost comprehensive – and some predated his accession by a considerable time. He dropped from the repertoire of kingship its vestigial machismo. Unlike his late and lamented brother, Charles as a young man had found martial display rather challenging. At the age of 16, at the tilt to commemorate his creation as Prince of Wales, he 'was not strong enough to put on an impressive display, so his opponents had to hold back lest they outshone him' (Carlton 1995: 17). Though he trained hard and appeared to great acclaim in the tilts of 1620, these neo-medieval jousts, traditionally though not exclusively held to mark the anniversary of royal accessions, were gradually discontinued in the last years of James's reign, and no further accession-day tilts were held after the accession of Charles I. In J. S. A. Adamson's phrase, 'The tournament knight had had his day' (1994: 165). In its place, Charles developed a rather different image of chivalry, one that placed the monarch more centrally. Of course, in the tiltyard, the king or his sons were supposed to look good, though the illusion (or reality) was hard won.

Charles, however, radically reformed another medieval legacy, the Garter Festival held on St George's Day, removing it from London to Windsor and in the process rendering it less a public spectacle and more a closed caste-ritual with the figure of the monarch surrounded by the most senior of his loyal subjects. In the process, he invested it with a new piety and ceremonialism (Strong 1972: 59–63; see also Corns 1992: 74). Thus, it became a bonding exercise with the king as its focus. The Garter cult and the celebration of the 'royal pair' intersect ingeniously in the *Landscape with St George and the Dragon*, a product of Peter Paul Rubens's first visit to England and painted circa 1630 (and variously well discussed by Howarth 1997: 72–4; Strong 1972; 60–1; and Veevers 1989: 189–90). At the centre of a sombre landscape of devastation and suffering, brilliantly illuminated and attended by putti, stand Charles in the figure of St George and Henrietta Maria as the maiden newly delivered from the dragon that lies slain at his feet. The Caroline inflection of chivalry has generated an island of love, light and peace in a world manifesting horrors akin to those contemporaneously suffered in much of continental Europe. Strong calls it 'a fairy-tale picture', but within the symbolic mode it represents honestly enough the irenic aspirations realized at the height of the personal rule: an England at peace could indeed be distinguished by a stable court culture centred on the royal couple.

Painting, however, was Charles's second artistic enthusiasm. Music was his first. He was a skilled performer on the bass viol. (This account rests on the summary in Wainwright 1999; see also Holman 1993; Spink 1986; and Walls 1996). After he was created Prince of Wales, he established an ensemble of seventeen musicians within his household and employed four of the most eminent composers of consort music: Alfonso Ferrabosco the younger, John Coprario, Orlando Gibbons and Thomas Lupo. In 1622 he formed a violin and viol ensemble. Within his household there developed innovations in instrumental music, of which Jonathan Wainwright concludes: 'The importance of these court consort pieces cannot be overestimated, for they stand at the head of a tradition that was to culminate in the trio sonatas of Purcell, and, as such, perhaps herald the beginnings of the English musical Baroque' (1999: 163). James, too, had kept a relatively large musical ensemble, which Charles merged with his own on his accession, retaining all but a handful of his own musicians. Though the composers he had first patronized died in the late 1620s, the retention of Nicholas Lanier, Robert Johnson and William Lawes and the emergence and development of Henry Lawes safeguarded the place of the King's Music at the leading edge of English performance and composition. Charles also invested liberally in the music of the Chapel Royal. Its prestige and attractive rates of pay ensured the retention of excellent singers served by fine composers and provided in both repertoire and performance standards 'a model for cathedrals and collegiate establishments to follow' (Wainwright 1999: 167).

Music was at the heart of the cultural life of Charles's court, part of the daily experience of the king, his consort and their courtiers. Choral work was performed on a limited scale in the ceremonies of morning and evening worship and on a grander scale on Sundays and major festivals. Secular music provided intimate song for private chambers, more complex pieces for larger occasions and a regular supply of instrumental music, not least for dance. Of course, the royal composers, musicians and singers, supplemented with performers from the London waits and theatres, played a central part in masques. In terms of cultural production, the King's Music was distinctive because it was a permanent part of the royal household; these were paid retainers, recipients, not just of fitful rewards and intermittent patronage, but of a regular and reliable salary.

Charles's interest in the visual arts was complex and developed more slowly. The English elite came late to connoisseurship and art collecting. While Italian and princely courts, and thereafter the several courts of the Habsburg dynasty, had acquired large collections by the late sixteenth century, Protestant English aristocrats found continental travel, and especially visiting Rome, too vexed and thus could not enjoy exposure to the genius of elsewhere much-prized artists, especially of the cinquecento (see Brown 1995: esp. chs 1 and 2). English connoisseurship begins no earlier than the 1610s with Thomas Howard, Earl of Arundel, a Catholic whose continental travels and immense wealth, brought to him by a lucrative marriage, stimulated the accumulation of large numbers of major works:

> According to the 1655 inventory – which of course reflects a mid-seventeenth-century view of attributions, many of which would now be considered excessively optimistic – there were some thirty-six paintings by Titian, nineteen Tintorettos, seventeen Veroneses, sixteen paintings attributed to Giorgione, a dozen or so Raphaels, eleven Correggios, and a remarkable twenty-five pieces by Parmigianino, five Leonardos ... and forty-three paintings by Holbein.   (Parry 1981: 117)

The Duke of Buckingham, perhaps unsurprisingly, entered the market in a competitive vein, assembling a network of agents to put together a major collection with extraordinary alacrity. Jonathan Brown surmises, 'Unlike Arundel, who was steeped in knowledge and imbued with the love of art, Buckingham seems, at least initially, to have regarded collecting as one among other attributes of noble status' (Brown 1995: 24; Howarth 1997: esp. ch. 7).

Charles developed, I think, something of Arundel's connoisseurship, his genuine enthusiasm if not his depth of knowledge, combined with Buckingham's ambition and organizational awareness. Moreover, in pursuit of the Spanish Match, he had visited with Buckingham the greatest collection of them all at the court of Philip IV of Spain, where 'they had arranged for a team of experts to join them' (Brown 1995: 35). That group included the principal agents used by both Buckingham and Charles. In 1627 Charles seized the opportunity to overtake both rivals through the purchase, for about £16,000, of a sizeable part of the collection of the Gonzaga family, Dukes of Mantua, both quantitatively and qualitatively a turning point in the management of his collection. Through the 1630s, the rate of acquisition slowed markedly, though Charles continued to purchase particularly sixteenth-century art selectively. By 1649, when the republican government of the Rump Parliament in its ignorant venality dumped the now confiscated collection on the art market, the inventory totalled 1,570 pictures.

That number also included new works of art commissioned by the king. He understood well the role of celebrity painters at the Habsburg courts and their importance in establishing an appropriate royal image. Indeed, Titian's imposing full-length portrait, *Charles V with a Hound*, was among the gifts he brought home with him from Madrid (Brown 1995: 37). As John Peacock puts it, 'It was important to secure the services of artists whose portrayal of the ruler would be powerful and persuasive, who could command a visual language which would be intelligible on a European scale. In early seventeenth-century England this meant employing foreigners' (1999: 220). The accomplished Dutch portraitist, Daniel Mytens, had worked in London since 1618, in part under the patronage of Arundel, and had been taken up by Charles while still Prince of Wales. James had awarded him a pension, and in all Charles spent almost £1,800 on his services (Peacock 1999: 221; Smuts 1996b: 104), mainly for portraits of himself and his queen. He was nudged aside early in the personal rule by

Anthony Van Dyck, a pupil of Rubens's whose 'prodigious talent had been enhanced by his cosmopolitan experience' (Peacock 1999: 226); Mytens had been in England too long. Van Dyck definitively fixed the image of Charles and his family in all its complexity. Thus, *Charles I riding through a triumphal arch* and *Charles I on horseback* show an imperious figure, controlling a mighty horse much as he controlled his people, at once in armour but poised and restrained, capable of striking but aloof and loath to do so, while a more relaxed figure, poised but at ease, appears in *Charles I à la chasse*. The royal pair are celebrated in *Charles I and Henrietta Maria*, where, in a motif first used by Mytens, she hands him the victor's laurels while herself holding the olive of peace (Strong 1972: 72–3). Group portraits, like *Charles I and family* or *Children of Charles I*, record their fecundity. In all, Charles spent about £2,500 on Van Dyck, whom he also knighted (Smuts 1996b: 104).

The largest single purchase from a living artist was the set of panels for the third Banqueting House at Whitehall, still arguably the finest painted surface in England, for which Rubens received £3,000. The commission, which may have been to a plan drawn up by Inigo Jones, the architect of the building, was placed while Rubens was in England in 1629–30. The ideological implications of the ceiling are sometimes misunderstood: though the central panel depicts James hymned to his celestial rest, these pictures are, for the most part, depictions of struggle, not triumph. The union of England and Scotland, the subject of the panel nearest the staircase and an objective that had been high on James's agenda, remained unaccomplished at the level of governance and constitution (though, of course, one monarch ruled both countries and claimed the title of King of Britain). It appears as an aspiration and a challenge to subsequent Stuart monarchs who pass beneath it. Again, the depiction of the benefits of peace acknowledges that James as *rex pacificus*, was right (and, by implication, Buckingham and Charles in their aggressive foreign policy had been wrong), that blessings do flow from peace and fill the national cornucopia. But once more, it is a scene of struggle. James casts down the forces of discord but they are not destroyed, a theme repeated in the allegorical depictions in the corner paintings. The state art of the personal rule depicts struggle, not triumph; adversarial forces must be met with eternal vigilance.

It is a mark of the relative importance of the visual arts in Charles's value system that the rich vein of masquing which he and the queen engaged in during the early 1630s came abruptly to a halt during 1636–7 explicitly to protect the panels from smoke and condensation during the performances, though Jones's wooden masquing house, ready by 1638, was a mighty structure and itself cost £2,500 (Orrell 1985: 149–59).

Charles's patronage of the visual arts shows a competitive edge, a desire to outshine the aristocratic collectors, whose efforts stimulated his own enthusiasm. It shows, too, the international element within Caroline court culture. Organized, systematic and utterly elitist, these activities involved a very few participants, though of the highest calibre. The agents he employed had an expertise rare in England; sometimes they were diplomats, who were also art historians and critics; sometimes they were art historians and critics, who also functioned on occasion as diplomats. He employed only the finest living artists he could engage, recognizing that the journeymen who had worked in the early Jacobean court served ill the establishment and celebration of the royal image, and he rewarded them handsomely. But the services of the agents and artists he chose were competed for in a highly lucrative international market.

Most probably in an attempt to second Henrietta Maria's efforts on behalf of English Roman Catholics, Pope Urban VIII allowed her to commission from Gian Lorenzo Bernini, by some way the greatest living sculptor and exclusively contracted to the Pope, a bust of Charles I, which he modelled from Van Dyck's *Triple Portrait of Charles I*, painted for the purpose. Significantly, when eventually it arrived in 1637, Inigo Jones was on hand as it was unpacked, exclaiming, accurately enough, that it was 'a miracle' (Parry 1981: 223–4; Peacock 1999: 217). Jones held a unique place within the complex structure of Caroline court culture, and actually lived in Somerset House, a royal palace.

Since the second decade of James I's rule, he had been the favoured architect of the royal family and, as Surveyor-General of the Works, a salaried servant of the king. For long, to the virtual exclusion of all others, he had designed the sets and costumes of court masques and had evidently played a part in their conception; 'his "personal rule" over the masque productions began after the displacement of Ben Jonson in 1631' (Peacock 1995: 325; and see below). John Peacock has latterly vindicated him from the customary charge of plagiarizing continental models, effectively demonstrating how his vigorous synthesis of the high culture, particularly of Italy and France, educated the Caroline court in new ways of representation and interpretation in the visual arts. He was astonishingly accomplished, perhaps most enduringly as an architect. The exterior of his late Jacobean triumph, the third (and still extant) Banqueting House at Whitehall seems diminished by the ministerial buildings that now surround it, though the carefully proportioned 'double cube' of its interior perfectly complements the Rubens ceiling. His best work of the personal rule is the Queen's House at Greenwich, restrained, with a striking unity of design and, in its own day, an obvious utility; so many accounts labour the pomp of the Caroline court, but this is a building on a human scale. In both projects his claims as the major influence in the development of English Palladianism are amply substantiated. In Graham Parry's phrase, he contributed 'a serene dignity' to the early Stuart monarchy (1981: 163). Extraordinarily, Ben Jonson apparently thought that Charles, constrained to choose for retention between himself and Jones, would choose him, for the latter's role was pivotal to the king's cultural agenda.

Writers relate rather differently to the economy of cultural production in court circles. Jonson had been salaried by James, a pension of almost £67, which Charles increased to £100 in 1630, and he succeeded Middleton as City Chronologer, the remuneration for which was paid only fitfully. In the years before his death (in 1637) he looked increasingly to the patronage of the Earl of Newcastle. Among the later generation of court writers, none was directly salaried for work in that role, though Thomas Carew became a gentleman of the king's privy chamber in 1628 and subsequently Sewer in Ordinary, a member of staff responsible for overseeing the ceremonies and protocols when the king dined. Charles, apparently, quite liked his company, holding 'a high opinion of his wit and abilities' (*DNB* 1975). Robert Herrick had accompanied Buckingham as chaplain on the Isle of Ré expedition, and the living he held from 1629 at Dean Prior, Devon, and on which he depended, was in the gift of the king (Moorman 1910: 87). William Davenant, who wrote for the professional theatre, seems to have secured no court office during the personal rule, despite being 'a hanger about court' and the intimate of such prominent court officials as Henry Jermyn, the queen's vice-chamberlain (*DNB* 1975). Aurelian Townsend (or Townshend) may perhaps have been a gentleman of the privy chamber (*DNB* 1975) though he seems mostly to have depended on the patronage of the Earl of Bridgewater, with whose household he was connected (Townsend 1983: 13). Sir John Suckling's father had assembled a fortune, which he inherited in 1627, and Edmund Waller not only inherited a considerable fortune but also in 1630 made a highly lucrative marriage (*DNB* 1975).

The production of literature was not funded and institutionalized like other aspects of Caroline court culture. Rather, it originated within a social grouping probably unique within English literary history, a cluster of poets who either looked to the court for preferment or associated themselves with the court as the fit setting for youngish men of extravagant means. They shared the values of the king. They perceived his role as central to their view of the world, and they viewed their own status as dependent on their proximity to the monarch. Theirs, however, was a second-rank cultural activity, less pervasive than music, less evidently valued and promoted by the king and queen. Certainly, they knew each other, wrote to and against each other and were sometimes, evidently, friends, but they belonged to a more than literary cultural system in which they were generally the junior partners. Masque and song, those essentially collaborative and interdisciplinary forms, were their finest achievements, and much of their other writing, at its best, was occasional, social or dialogic.

Masques of the Personal Rule

At least nine royal masques were staged during the personal rule, four danced by each of the royal pair and a final masque danced by them both: in 1631 *Love's Triumph through Callipolis* (the king's masque) and *Chloridia* (the queen's masque), both scripted by Jonson; in 1632 *Albion's Triumph* (the king's masque) and *Tempe Restored* (the queen's masque), both scripted by Townsend; in 1634 *Coelum Britannicum* (the king's masque), scripted by Carew; in 1635 *The Temple of Love* (the queen's masque); in 1638 *Britannia Triumphans* (the king's masque) and *Luminalia* (the queen's masque); and in 1640 *Salmacida Spolia* (danced by both the king and the queen). Of these, Davenant scripted the last four.

Innovation within an established format characterized this series. There are three pairs of responding masques, in 1631, 1632 and 1638. The king's and queen's masques are subtly gendered, differentiating the manly heroism of Charles, who variously 'triumphs', from the gentler manifestation of Henrietta Maria. Erica Veevers analyses the contrast perceptively:

In the King's masques, the discovery of the masquers is associated with images of civic order, or with the rugged 'earthy' aspects of nature: the 'stately temple' in *Albion's Triumph*, a cave in the Mountain of the Three Kingdoms in *Coelum Britannicum*, the Palace of Fame in *Britannia Triumphans*, and the throne in *Salmacida Spolia*, which is placed in a setting of 'craggy rocks and inaccessible mountains' representing 'the difficult way which heroes are to pass ere they come to the Throne of Honour'.... In the Queen's masques the discovery is associated with pleasant aspects of nature or with 'heavenly' scenes.... Jones's complementary sets of stage images reinforced visually the basic dualities of Neoplatonism, of masculine and feminine, body and spirit, earth and heaven. The uniting of these complementary qualities at the end of each masque represented an ideal unity, which was reinforced by the harmonious union of King and Queen. (Veevers 1989: 119)

Jones and his series of collaborators work with a different palette for each royal masquer. The pairing of masques occasioned changes in scheduling: the king danced on Twelfth Night, the favoured masquing day for earlier Stuart masques, whereas the queen danced at Shrovetide, a feast recognized in English custom but no doubt familiar to her as Carnival. (In 1634 when there was only one masque, the king danced at Shrovetide; in 1640 they danced together on Twelfth Night.) The schedule of nine masques may have been shaped in part by the queen's eight confinements during the personal rule; only in two calendar years did she both masque and give birth, and on both occasions at least six months intervened. This is a new kind of masquing ethos, one of studied and affectionate reciprocity between the king and queen and their respective households.

Technical innovations abounded as Jones ceaselessly refreshed the genre. In *Albion's Triumph*, instead of retiring with his company at the end of the masque, Charles joined Henrietta Maria on a double throne (Orgel and Strong 1973: I, 457). In *Tempe Restored*, women singers appeared on the English stage apparently for the first time (ibid.: II, 479). For *Britannia Triumphans* and the masques that followed, the new purpose-built masquing house was used, which 'gave scope for the development of scenic machines more elaborate than any that had been used in London' (Orrell 1985: 150). In *Luminalia* the range of non-professionals involved in the performance was extended to include non-aristocratic members of the queen's household: Jeffrey Hudson, her dwarf and various 'gentlemen of quality' presented some of the antimasques (Orgel and Strong 1973: II, 707). *Salmacida Spolia* was the only Stuart masque danced by both king and consort.

Thematically, one concept dominates: the celebration of the profoundly and explicitly eroticized version of married chastity which is at the centre of Caroline court culture. *Chloridia*, the queen's first masque, ends with Chloris-Henrietta Maria commended to Charles in a song acclaiming her as,

> the queen of flowers,
> The sweetness of all showers,
> The ornament of bowers,
> The top of paramours.
> (ll.269–72; Orgel and Strong 1973: II, 422)

'Paramour' had long since developed its rather dubious connotations, and the *OED* cites this as its last occurrence in the sense of 'the object of chivalric admiration and attachment' (s.v. 'Paramour' sb. 2.c. and 3; Corns 1998: 61). Jonson no doubt knew exactly how he was redefining sexual love in Caroline terms.

But most masques of the personal rule close in the same way, with a final song ushering the royal pair to their fecund bed. The 'last general chorus' blesses

> Mary-Charles, whose minds within
> And bodies make but Hymen's twin,
> Long live they so, and breast to breast,
> May angels sing them to their rest.
> (ll.443–8; Orgel and Strong 1973: II, 458)

'Breast to breast' invited the audience to imagine the royal couple in an intimate embrace. Townsend's presumably inadvertent but still ominous echo of Horatio's farewell to the dead Hamlet (V.ii.374) perhaps passed unremarked. The closing exchange of *Coelum Britannicum* dwells on 'the ripe fruits of your chaste bed, / Those sacred seeds of love' (ll.1128–9; Orgel and Strong 1973: II, 580). The final song of *Britannia Triumphans* beds not only king and queen, but the whole court in a paroxysm of conjugal coupling:

> Wise Nature, that the dew of sleep prepares
> To intermit our joys and ease our cares,
> Invites you from these triumphs to your rest.

May every whisper that is made be chaste,
Each lady slowly yield, yet yield at last,
Her heart a prisoner to her lover's breast!

To wish our royal lover more
Of youthful blessings than he had before
Were but to tempt old Nature 'bove her might,
Since all the odour, music, beauteous fire
We in the spring, the spheres, the stars admire
Is his renewed, and bettered every night!

To bed, to bed, may every lady dream
From that chief beauty she hath stolen a beam
Which will amaze her lover's curious eyes!
Each lawful lover to advance his youth
Dream he hath stol'n his vigour, love and truth,
Then all will haste to bed, but none to rise!
          (ll.627–44; Orgel and Strong 1973: II, 667)

King and queen function as an aphrodisiac paradigm for other couples, who may revive themselves by 'stealing' some of the youthful vigour of the royal pair. (Charles by now was approaching 40!)

Jonson's quarrel with Jones, probably an area of tension since their earliest collaborations, had at its source the relative precedence of spectacle and script, though the immediate *casus belli* was Jones's protest at his name appearing second on the title page of *Love's Triumph through Callipolis* and the subsequent omission of his name altogether from the title page of *Chloridia* (Jonson 1985: 721). Jonson wrote three verse satires, which, though unprinted in his lifetime, presumably enjoyed a manuscript circulation in influential circles where both were familiar. They mix an argument about content over performance with a personal vindictiveness:

O Showes! Showes! Mighty Showes!
The Eloquence of Masques! What need of prose
Or Verse, or Sense t'expresse Immortal you?
You are ye Spectacles of State!
('An Expostulac[i]on w[it]h Inigo Jones', ll.39–42; Jonson 1925–52: VIII,
                                                                    403)

But spectacle is at the core of masque, which shares some of its key characteristics with those other essentially symbolic and visual genres, the triumph, the pageant, the entry and the show. After Jonson, Jones increased the pyrotechnics, elaborating the scene design and the stage machinery. In the new masquing house, for example, in *Britannia Triumphans* the actor in the role of the mythological hero Bellerophon rode Pegasus 'with large white wings' into the middle of the room, while hell disappeared, a forest with a castle appeared, a palace was disclosed and then sank, to be replaced with a seascape (Orgel and Strong 1973: II, 664–7). There was considerable justice in Davenant's prefatory comment on *Luminalia*:

> the Queen commanded Inigo Jones, surveyor of her majesty's works, to make a new subject of a masque for herself, that with high and hearty invention might give occasion for variety of scenes, strange apparitions, songs, music, and dancing of several kinds, from whence doth result the true pleasure peculiar to our English masques, which by strangers and travelers of judgement are held to be as noble and ingenious as those of any other nations.   (ll.1–9; Orgel and Strong 1973: II, 706).

In spectacle inhered the principal pleasure for spectators and much of the pleasure for royal and aristocratic participants. Modern responses to Stuart masques have concentrated on wringing from them their ideological significance. Yes, *of course*, masque was a celebration of power, it proclaimed the centrality of the monarch, it showed his wealth to his subjects and impressed foreign ambassadors. Its political content and values were certainly not trivial. But primarily it functioned as part of a festive season. It afforded the king or queen the opportunity to bond with a close circle of aristocratic courtiers, not least in the time-consuming rehearsal of their dance routines. Charles and Henrietta Maria masqued because they enjoyed it.

Caroline masque differed little from Jacobean in terms of its political thesis: the regal and heroic virtue of the masquers dismisses, but does not destroy, the riotous threat usually posed by the antimasque. The point is both optimistic – goodness wins with little struggle, in a sense just by turning up – and realistic – the forces of evil are always there to be engaged with and neutralized; we see a principal theme of the Rubens ceiling given a dramatic expression. Jonson's antimasques sometimes veered towards low mimesis or political satire, and his last script showed him at his most wordy. In the scripts of his successors, the antimasquers usually pose a vaguer sort of threat, as when, in *Salmacida Spolia*, 'Discord, a malicious fury, appears in a storm and by the invocation of malignant spirits, proper to her evil use, having already put most of the world into disorder, endeavours to disturb these parts, envying the blessings and tranquillity we have long enjoyed' (ll.1–5; Orgel and Strong 1973: II, 730). The theme restates the Caroline appropriation of Jacobean irenicism, though, appropriately in an England already in conflict with the king's Scottish subjects, it does so in a rather beleaguered way. Charles and his aristocratic companions well knew by then that regal virtue, to prevail, needed to do rather more than merely disclose itself.

Did masquing shape the course of Caroline politics? Almost certainly not. To the enemies of the court and especially to some of a Puritan disposition it could be represented as conspicuous and wasteful consumption and as indecorous or scandalous. As late as 1660, John Milton, whose own masque we shall turn to shortly, was frightening Puritan backsliders with a nightmare vision of a restored Stuart court, 'a dissolute and haughtie court . . . , of vast expence and luxurie, masks and revels, to the debaushing of our prime gentry both male and female' (Milton 1953–82: VII; rev. edn: 425). But the morality and aesthetics of early Stuart court entertainments probably outraged nobody who had not already taken a hostile view of more pivotal issues like religious policy or foreign affairs or the raising of revenue without recourse to parliament. I doubt that anyone took up arms in 1642 because they disliked the queen's décolletage. Nor should the impact of masquing on the royal budget be overstated. Demonstrating that Caroline masques typically cost in the range of £900–1,200, Stephen Orgel and Sir Roy Strong sternly remark, 'After the gaiety and revelry, the dancing and feasting, came the reckoning' (1973: 46–7). But latterly Kevin Sharpe and Malcolm Smuts have set the cost of the Caroline cultural agenda in a rather different perspective. By the mid-1630s, the king's costs totalled annually about £600,000, with £135,000 going on the royal households, £130,000 on pensions and even £26,000 on the royal wardrobe. As Sharpe notes, 'In the big picture of Caroline finance, the annual sums spent on the allegedly profligate expense of masques . . . cannot be said to loom large' (1992: 127–8). The cost of masques pale into insignificance in comparison with other kinds of regal display: the funeral of James I, for example, cost about £40,000. But the most unbearable cost for a Stuart king was the cost of going to war. The Spanish conflict cost about £1,000,000 in 1625 (Smuts 1996b: 94, 103). Putting an expeditionary force into the field or launching the fleet cost a thousand times more than putting on a masque (though, in the interests of balance, we should reflect that an agricultural day-labourer would have had to work about 130 years of six-day weeks to recoup the cost of a single masque).

Other Entertainments

Four other entertainments, not strictly royal masques, require some comment: *A Masque Presented at Ludlow Castle* (1634), considered below in the section 'Early Milton'; *The Triumph of Peace* (1634) by Inigo Jones and James Shirley; and Ben Jonson's two entertainments written for the Earl of Newcastle, *The Kings Entertainment at Welbeck* (1633) and *Loves Welcome at Bolsover* (1634).

Jonson's texts formed part of the hospitality offered by the earl to the king on his way to Scotland and on a second occasion when he was entertained with the queen. Both strongly reflect the regionality of the production at major country estates of a very significant magnate. According to the Earl of Clarendon, writing in the Restoration, Newcastle spent £20,000 on the two events (*DNB* 1975), though it is difficult to believe that the entertainments themselves accounted for much of that, insofar as we may judge from the extant texts. Together, they show the flexibility of the courtly entertainment. In the former, Charles is entertained by a sung 'Dialogue betweene the *Passions*, *Doubt* and *Love*', before being waylaid by a sort of antimasque en route to his horse. In the latter, the king and queen are entertained at a banquet by a three-part song; they then retire to watch an anti-masque, and are served a 'second Banquet set downe before them from the Cloudes by two Loves', who entertain them with a dialogue that is finally interrupted by a long prose speech from Philalethes ('love of truth' or 'lover of truth').

Both texts are true to Jonson's late Jacobean style of masque-writing: there are sweet lyrics, a great deal of long prose speeches and both low mimesis and satire in the antimasques. Spectacle would seem to have been in fairly short supply, though there are fantastic costumes and wild dancing. Jonson remains unrestrained in the demonstration of learning. The Welbeck script has as an inkhorn character, a Mansfield schoolmaster called Mr Accidence. We have a sense of the road not taken in Caroline court masque, of what the later masques of the personal rule might have been like if Jonson, not Jones, had emerged as the favourite of the king and queen for making masques. In most respects, however, the writer remained as scrupulous as ever in respecting the values and aspirations of the monarch. The king, on his way to his very belated Scottish coronation, is represented as reviving, in some sense, the old Jacobean design for union:

> O Sister *Scotland!* what hast thou deserv'd
> Of joyfull *England*, giving us this *King!*
> What Union (if thou lik'st) hast though not made
> In knitting for great *Britaine* such a Garland?
> And letting him, to weare it?
>   (ll.314–18; Jonson 1925–52: VII, 802)

Love's Welcome at Bolsover has Eros and Anteros celebrate love as central to the style of the royal couple:

> EROS It is the place, sure breeds it, where wee are,
> ANTEROS The King, and Queenes Court, which is circular,
>   And perfect.
> EROS   The pure schoole that we live in,
>   And is of purer Love, the Discipline
>   (ll.135–8; Jonson 1925–52: VII, 812)

Yet Jonson was unforgiving of Inigo Jones, and the antimasque at Bolsover is led by the figure of 'Iniquo Vitruvius', 'a Surveyour', 'An Overseer', 'A busie man! And yet I must seeme busier than I am' (Jonson 1925–52: VII, 809). Under the protection of Newcastle, whose own partiality for the poet over the designer was evident, Jonson plainly felt licensed to question at least one decision of the king.

The Triumph of Peace, the most expensively staged masque of the period, was given by the four Inns of Court to the king and queen, nominally to celebrate the birth, in October 1633, of James, Duke of York. Early accounts link it to the recent scandal occasioned by *Histriomastix* (1633) by the Puritan and lawyer William Prynne, an attack on theatrical performance which was deemed to have slandered the queen. Possibly the masque functioned as a sort of lesson to the Inns in subservience, as an expensive gift required by the court that acknowledged the transcendent power of the monarch. But for the leaders of the legal profession there were plain advantages in making a declaration of loyalty and distancing themselves from their disgraced colleague. At the same time, the obvious and conspicuous wealth of the Inns of Court made a memorable display. Cooperation between the court and the Inns is evident in the use freely made of Inigo Jones and royal retainers from the King's Music and the Queen's Chapel (Orgel and Strong 1973: II, 537–45), though the choice of James Shirley to write the script shows some independence in their thinking. Shirley was a professional dramatist, not a courtier, and he had launched his career while resident in Gray's Inn (*DNB* 1975). The antimasque represents, satirically, patent holders, the subject of complaint since the Jacobean period (see chapter 3), but the principal theme of the masque is wholly in accord with that of Caroline court masques. At the climax of the performance, 'the whole train of musicians' approach the royal thrones and sing:

> To you great King and Queen, whose smile
> Doth scatter blessings through this isle,
> To make it best
> And wonder of the rest,
> We pay the duty of our birth,
> Proud to wait upon that earth
> Whereon you move,
> Which shall be named,
> And by your chaste embraces famed,
> The paradise of love.
> (ll.609–18; Orgel and Strong 1973: II, 551–2)

Charles liked the masque so much that he ordered it to be played again to a predominately civic audience in Merchant Taylors' Hall.

Music and Literature at the Caroline Court

Masques posed the most stimulating challenge to the King's Music and the composers who wrote for it. But the 1630s was also the golden age of early modern English song, and Henry Lawes was its finest exponent. More than 430 of Lawes's songs survive, and he set more than 40 poems by Carew and at least 14 by Herrick, as well as poems by Suckling, Waller and Lovelace (Spink 1986: 76, 94). With Nicholas Lanier, Lawes consolidated a transformation of English song, characterized by less obtrusive instrumentalism and a more declamatory singing style, approaching recitative. Thus, they completed a process Thomas Campion and others had begun earlier in the century. That renegotiation of the relationship of song to the rhythms of ordinary speech permitted the setting of poems while retaining the directness and clarity which characterize the verse of the Caroline court (ibid.: 76; see also Corns 1998: 58). As Milton claimed in his sonnet to Lawes, he 'taught our English music how to span / Words with just note and accent' ('Sonnet XIII. To Mr H. Lawes, on his Airs', ll.2–3; Milton 1997: 294–5).

After the exhilarating challenge posed by the love poetry of Shakespeare or Donne, Caroline verse can seem insipid and a little pedestrian, but poems that are to be set to music require metrical regularity and a straightforward comprehensibility. They need to be understandable when sung. They lend themselves to simulating a small number of familiar speech acts: the lover appeals to his mistress, the lover laments, the lover leaves his mistress, the lover recalls an erotic episode, the lover rehearses his mistress's merits. Often the singer, in effect, assumes dramatically the role of the lover. A regular stanzaic form of no great complexity may facilitate the setting. 'The Night-piece, to Julia' (Herrick 1956: 217) may seem a trivial little poem, but in performance its latent drama and genuine charm are readily apparent (Lawes 1993).

Similarly, on the printed page, Carew's 'A Pastorall Dialogue' appears at best a dull manifestation of the influence of French pastoralism and at worst aimless and confusing:

> SHEP[HERD] Harke!
> NY[MPH] Aye me stay!
> SHEP For ever.
> NY No, arise,
>   Wee must be gone.
> SHEP My nest of spice.
> NY My soule.
> SHEP My Paradise.
> CHO[RUS] Neither could say farewell, but through their eyes
>   Greife, interrupted speach with teares supplyes.
>   (Carew 1964: 46)

The poem was set by Henry Lawes (1669: 114–17; for a transcription, see Corns 1998: 68–71) and it has in recent times been plangently and affectingly recorded (Lawes 1988). In performance, the considerable structural ingenuity of the poem is apparent (Corns 1998: 59–60). It begins as if *in medias res*, as Nymph and Shepherd visit the scene of a lovers' tryst. Singing together, they frame a dialogue within the dialogue, in which they act out the roles of the unknown lovers whose lives they parallel and whose sensibility they assume. The narrative component of the embedded scene is carried by a choric section where they sing together, and the framing is concluded by a final choric section, which offers a musical closure to match the dramatic closure. Lawes and Carew presumably worked together, and the composer's contribution to the success of the piece is at least as great at the poet's.

Themes, Occasions and Conversations

Poems of complement, directed to the king or queen, and presented variously as New Year gifts, commemorations of births and birthdays, or greetings on specific events, conform to the panegyric agenda of Caroline masque. Thus, references to the marriage bed and childbirth recur as the poets focus on the royal pair, their fertility and on the 'chastity' of their union. Waller's 'Puerperium' ('childbed') hails Henrietta Maria as 'Great *Gloriana*; fair *Gloriana*, / Bright as high Heaven is, and fertile as Earth' (1645: 70). In Carew's 'To the Queene', she

> shewes us the path
> Of Modestie, and constant faith,
> Which makes the rude Male satisfied
> With one faire Female by his side;
> Doth either sex to each unite,
> And forme loves pure Hermophradite [*sic*].
> (ll.13–18; Carew 1964: 90–1)

The symbolic economy of the court postulates a polarity between monogamous regal sexuality and sexual anarchy. Where a libertine note is struck, it is unsustained. Herrick's 'A Vine' on the unlikely topic of matutinal tumescence records a transient reverie: 'with the fancie I awok' (l.21; Herrick 1956: 17). Many of his more erotic poems rehearse a voyeuristic sensibility of looking but not touching. Carew's most extensive libertine exercise, 'A Rapture', is again, explicitly, a fantasy set in 'Loves Elizium', remote from 'the world' as he and his readers know it (ll.2, 165; Carew 1964: 49–53; see Corns 1993b: 210–11), and it is balanced by poems moralizing on the importance of sexual continence among women, warning against 'Snaring Poems . . . spred, / All to catch thy maidenhead' ('Good counsel to a young Maid', ll.11–12; Carew 1964: 13).

In terms of international politics, the prevailing tendency is an endorsement of the king's irenic policy. Davenant, in 'Madagascar', while praising the military exuberance of Charles's nephew, Prince Rupert, sought also to emphasize Charles's own restraint: 'I saw thy Uncles anger in thy brow: / Which, like Heavens fire, doth seldom force assume' (ll.244–5; Davenant 1972: 16). In a remarkable exchange of poems, Townsend's 'Elegy on the death of the King of Sweden: sent to Thomas Carew', urges him to join in lamenting the recent death of the King of Sweden, Gustavus Adolphus, in effect the leader in arms of continental Protestantism. It suggests, somewhat obliquely, that the role he leaves vacant is an appropriate one for a Protestant prince, like Charles, to assume:

> Princes ambitious of renowne shall still
> Strive for his spurres to helpe them up the hill;
> His glorious gauntlets shall unquestioned lie
> Till hands are found fit for a Monarchie . . .
>   (ll.33–6; Townsend 1983: 48)

The death of Gustavus was widely mourned among many of the English people who were trying to follow the course of the war, and it certainly exposed further the territories of Charles's brother-in-law. But to those in the inner circles of government it was not without its compensations. Charles had permitted levies to be raised to aid him. Yet the Swedish king's intransigence raised the suspicion that, if once he liberated the Palatinate, he would be reluctant to hand it over. As Sharpe summarizes the position, 'When Gustavus Adolphus met his end at the battle of Lutzen in November 1632, his death may have been mourned by the populace as that of a Protestant saint; for others it ended the threat of uncontrolled Swedish ambitions' (Sharpe 1992: 82).

Carew responded with 'In answer of an Elegiacall Letter upon the death of the King of Sweden from Aurelian Townsend, inviting me to write on that subject', the definitive poetic account of the blessings of peace during the personal rule (1964: 74–7). So vivid and comprehensive is the reply that Townsend's statement seems rather like a ball tossed up for Carew to hit – or like an antimasque to be dismissed by the disclosure of the masquers. He reviews Gustavus's victories but both reflects on the cost in human suffering – 'all her ["the whole *German* continents"] Cities doe but make his Tombe' (ll.33–34) – and ponders that God's providential working in the war is proving difficult to understand and is more powerful than any human agency – 'Let us to the supreame providence commit / The fate of Monarchs' (ll.35–6). Meanwhile, in England,

> let us that in myrtle bowers sit
> Vnder secure shades, use the benefit
> Of peace and plenty, which the blessed hand
> Of our good King gives his obdurate Land
> . . .
> Tourneyes, Masques, Theaters, better become
> Our *Halcyon* dayes; what though the German Drum
> Bellow for freedome and revenge, the noyse
> Concernes not us, nor should divert our joyes.
>   (ll.45–8, 95–8)

That resonant phrase, 'Our *Halcyon* days', and its allusion to days so calm that the halycon could brood upon the sea, had a wider currency ('Puerperium', Waller 1645: 70; see also Sharpe 1992: 610). Behind it lies James I's favoured apophthegm, borrowed from Erasmus, '*Dulce bellum inexpertis*', 'war is sweet to those who haven't tried it'.

That Carew should have written so important a poem as part of an apparent dialogue or exchange is wholly typical of court poetry in the 1630s, where there are numerous exchanges of various degrees of seriousness between poets within the coterie (Corns 1998: 56–7). Scores of other poems assume the form of speech acts directed to brother poets, sometimes in a spirit of literary rough play. Suckling's effort among the prefatory poems to *Madagascar: with Other Poems* congratulates Davenant on the curious achievement of celebrating a victory in a context where the expedition has not yet been launched:

> Thou (*Will*) do'st not stay
> So much as for a Wind, but go'st away,
> Land'st, View'st the Country, fight'st, put'st all to rout,
> Before another cou'd be putting out!
>   (Davenant 1972: 7)

Suckling is the master of this idiom, scoring his most telling points against the rather sober and restrained figure of Carew, a reformed rogue. 'Upon T[homas] C[arew] having the P[ox]' is an intimate, though scarcely friendly poem: 'Troth, *Tom*, I must confess I much admire / Thy water should find passage through the fire' (ll.1–2; Suckling 1971a: 32). The amusing aspects of what sounds like gonococcal urethritis perhaps eluded the sufferer. Suckling's most sustained sally against Carew, 'Upon my Lady Carliles walking in Hampton-Court garden' (ibid.: 30–2), simulates a dialogue between the poets. Carew had addressed two lyrics to Lucy Hay, Countess of Carlisle, in an elevated idiom: 'Gums nor spice bring from the East, / For the Phenix in Her brest / Builds his funerall pile, and nest' ('To the New-yeare, for the Countesse of Carlile', ll.4–6; Carew 1964: 91; see also p. 32; also Suckling 1971a: 238). In his poem, Suckling has 'T. C.' speak in a similar idiom, while 'J. S.' cuts him down with a brutal simplicity: 'I must confesse those perfumes (*Tom*) / I did not smell' (ll.10–11). In the process he interrogates both Carew's idealizing sensibility and his poetic idiom.

Many occasional poems were written to or about aristocrats and courtiers who were not poets, often with great felicity. Carew's well-judged epitaph for Maria Wentworth was adapted and inscribed on her tomb (1964: 56, 243). Slighter occasions also found commemoration, as in Suckling's epigram 'Upon Sir John Laurence's bringing Water over the hills to my Lord Middlesex his House at Wiston' (1971a: 28). Jonson, of course, had written many poems to patrons, and continued to do so through the 1630s; Caroline court poets, however, eschewed the mixture of resentment and hungry edginess that sometimes characterized Jonson's work. The point is eloquently made in a comparison of Carew's 'To Saxham' (1964: 27–9) and Jonson's 'To Penshurst', considered above (chapter 2). Both owe much to the Latin epigrammatist Martial, and particularly to poem lviii in his second book of epigrams, although Carew also knew Jonson's poem (Carew 1964: 225). What is most significant, socially, is that Jonson adds to Martial's genial poem of praise for an evident friend a sardonic account of how badly Jonson has been snubbed elsewhere, unlike at Penshurst, where the servants don't mind what he eats and drinks. Carew, younger son of a knight, staying at the family home of an old friend John Crofts, also the younger son of a knight, like Martial simply writes like someone comfortable with his role; of course, the servants don't treat him rudely.

From Manuscript to Print

Performance plainly had a central role in the delivery of the literary culture of the Caroline court. Song and masque remained its defining genres. As in the Jacobean period, the latter quickly found its way into print in the production of booklets, typically in quarto, that include the words sung and spoken, a list of the aristocratic participants, and a description of costumes, sets, machinery and actions. Those who succeeded Jonson as script writers usually continued his practice of taking responsibility for the printed text. No doubt these publications both gave to the elite participants and their audience a record of the event and allowed those outside that circle, courtiers not at court, country gentlemen, citizens, a window into that privileged world.

The court poetry we have been considering remained almost exclusively in manuscript circulation during the personal rule. Even when set to music, it remained within the performance repertoire of court musicians. Only William Davenant's *Madagascar: with Other Poems*, was printed before 1640, probably both to praise publicly the recently arrived Prince Rupert and to talk up the planned colonial adventure to the island, in which he wished to play a leading part, and which was anticipated in the heroic title-poem (see Davenant 1972: 342–5 on the circumstances of its composition and publication). Caroline court poetry was writing by a coterie, for a coterie, and often about a coterie, though the works of Carew and Herrick, for example, leaked out into manuscript anthologies kept by outsiders (Love and Marotti 2002: 72–3).

Carew died in 1640 or thereabouts, and Suckling in 1641 or 1642. Waller was banished in 1643, though by then the king had long since left Whitehall, the war had begun and the court was itinerant and partially dispersed. In the context of this diaspora, poetry migrated from performance and manuscript circulation to the more portable medium of print. In the process, poems written in and about the personal rule, celebrations of those halcyon days, became incorporated in a new construct: Cavalier culture. Herrick, who remained in England and who continued to write, eschewed print until the publication of his mighty collection, *Hesperides* (1648), in which the verse of the personal rule was purposefully juxtaposed with later work suffused with the royalist experiences of the 1640s. But Carew, Suckling and even Waller had lost editorial control; as bookseller Humphrey

Moseley, who published much of the best poetry to appear in print in the mid-century, observed of his edition of Waller, 'like the present condition of the Author himselfe, [his poems] are expos'd to the wide world, to travell, and try their fortunes' (Waller 1645: sig. A4v).

The title page of Suckling's collected works (1646), published by Moseley, shows how the cultural life of the 1630s was reassessed and repositioned in the following decades: *Fragmenta Aurea. A collection of all the Incomparable Peeces, Written by Sir John Suckling. And published by a Friend to perpetuate His Memory. Printed by his owne Copies.* 'Fragmenta Aurea', that is, 'Golden Pieces', are the broken, discontinuous remains both of a writer and of a culture which to its participants and admirers by the mid-1640s must have seemed lost for ever. 'Published by a Friend' rehearses a topos of contemporary royalist ideology, the celebration of friendship and generosity towards those whose personal sacrifice mean they can never repay. Moseley's edition of Waller (1645) recalls his place in court culture: the title page reminds browsers, '*all the Lyrick Poems in this Booke were set by Mr. HENRY LAWES Gent. of the Kings Chappell, and one of his Majesties Private Musick*'. The title page of his '*third edition revised and enlarged*' of Carew (1651) – the first was in 1640 – notes he was '*Sewer in Ordinary to His late Majesty*' and that '*The Songs were set . . . by Mr. Henry Lawes Gent: of the Kings Chappell, and one of his late Majesties Private Musick*', thus recalling the dead king twice. In the 1640s and 1650s buying and reading these works was a political action, a defiant resistance to the domination of parliamentarian and republican ideologies and a perfectly safe way to manifest one's loyalty. Moseley seems to have published the works of his list without censorship or prosecution. The critical task is to resist that tendency, which bundles the court poetry of the personal rule with the works of Lovelace and the later poems of Herrick into the 'movement' or 'school' of 'Cavalier poets', separating them off from the vivid, singing world of the 1630s, the world of Jones, Lawes, Rubens and Van Dyck (Corns 1993b: 200–2; 1998: 51–4, 64–5).

But other verse was printed in the 1630s. Donne's poetry had circulated in manuscript since the Elizabethan period and had been avidly collected over his long writing career. After his death, in 1631, a collected edition was prepared and published in 1633, with seven further editions by 1669. As a posthumous edition, the 1633 Donne volume continued a tradition which can be traced from John Skelton (died 1529; published 1568), through Sidney, Spenser, Shakespeare and Daniel, in an age when collected editions of living authors were 'the exception rather than the rule' (Marotti 1993: 70). Donne's influence had been widely felt over the first quarter of the century, and he remained a formidable shaping presence in devotional poetry, both directly and more mutedly through his influence on Herbert (see below). Carew's 'An Elegie upon the death of the Deane of Pauls, Dr. Iohn Donne' (Carew 1964: 71–4) is as shrewd a critical essay as the seventeenth century produced on an English poet, but while Carew and his colleagues took from his secular verse attitudes, values and numerous topoi, theirs was a less challenging poetic idiom. Herbert's poetry is considered below.

Plays and Players

The theatre history of the 1630s in part mirrored that of the 1620s. The King's Men retained their pre-eminence and a major visitation of the plague closed theatres for a substantial period, after which some significant changes occurred among their rivals.

The King's Men had, besides the patronage of the king, another material advantage. They alone had two venues. Mainly in the winter months, they used the smaller, 'private' indoor theatre, the second Blackfriars, which they had occupied since the first decade of the century. It emerged as a place of fashionable (if sometimes rather disorderly) resort, and Henrietta Maria attended at least four performances there between 1634 and 1638 (Wickham et al. 2000: 527–8). In the summer, they favoured the second Globe, the larger 'public' open-air theatre on the South Bank. The Queen's Men remained at the Phoenix (or Cockpit, as it is sometimes called) in Drury Lane, a house owned and run until his death in 1638 by Christopher Beeston, a redoubtable entrepreneur who evidently secured his own position and probably continuing royal patronage through 'gift after gift' to Sir Henry Herbert, the Master of the Revels. During the plague of 1636–7, when London theatres were closed, he displaced the Queen's Men and replaced them with the King and Queen's Young Company, again securing royal patronage. Unlike the earlier companies of boy actors, this was a regular adult company with a large number of boys, and 'part of its purpose was to train the boys as players' (ibid.: 625). A third private playhouse, Salisbury Court, somewhat smaller than the other two indoor houses, opened in 1630 in an expensively converted barn. Significantly, this was the first and only playhouse substantially owned by court officers and courtiers: William Blagrave, deputy to Sir Henry Herbert, part owned the house, and, it has been surmised, Herbert himself may have had a share. The Queen's Chamberlain was its landlord. Before the interruption for the plague, it was occupied in turn by 'the King's Revels', then the Prince of Wales's Men, and then again the Revels. After the plague, the theatre was home to the reformed Queen Henrietta Maria's Men, merging actors displaced from the Phoenix with some from the Revels (ibid.: 649–51).

These four theatres staged all of the new drama of the personal rule that attained critical acclaim in its own age or in ours. A fifth should be added: the Cockpit-at-Court, often the venue for command performances. Of outdoor, 'public' theatres, other than the Globe, only the second Fortune and Red Bull seem to have functioned exclusively as playhouses through the 1630s, though the latter 'was increasingly seen as in an unfashionable part of the City and lacking the refinement of the private playhouses' and the former 'housed a series of "shadowy" and undistinguished companies' (ibid.: 566–7, 639).

The creative theatre certainly drew closer to the court in the 1630s. At its simplest, the royal pair enjoyed theatrical performance. Neither shrank, as James I had done, from the theatricality of performing in court masques, and the queen staged and acted in three amateur pastoral dramas to the sorts of audience that would have attended those masques. Their patronage of the major companies and the energetic efforts of their Master of the Revels ensured a frequency of court performances high enough to justify building their own – literally 'private' – theatre in the burgeoning leisure complex that the palace at Whitehall became. Performance in the companies' regular playhouses remained their core business, and the audiences there no doubt included very many from social classes that had patronized the King's Men and the private theatres in the late Jacobean period. There is no evidence that Inns of Court men or prosperous citizens or visiting gentry changed their pattern of entertainment in the personal rule, and I see no evidence to counter Martin Butler's influential argument that elements which, by 1640, proved opponents of the king or indeed, by 1642, enemies in arms against the king, may well have been in the audience of the Blackfriars or Salisbury Court or the Phoenix in the 1630s (Butler 1987, especially Appendix II). Nevertheless, the critical edge, the thirst for news, the anxieties and insecurities that were so characteristic of the drama of the 1620s (see above, chapter 3) were generally absent.

Thomas Middleton, who best exemplified those traits, had died in 1627. Jonson's last two plays, *The Magnetic Lady* (1632) and *a Tale of a Tub* (1633), though currently subject to a revaluation that recognizes a continuing innovation remarkable under the tragic circumstances of their composition, did little to rehabilitate the author with contemporary audiences as an active and creative force in the Caroline theatre, though the early 1630s witnessed a renewed interest in some of his Jacobean plays, revived by the King's Men (van den Berg 2000: 10). Of Jonson's generation of dramatists, Philip Massinger lived on till 1640 and remained successful. His best-known play from the 1630s, *The City-Madam*, premiered by the King's Men in 1632, invites comparison with *A New Way to Pay Old Debts* (1626; considered above, chapter 3). The earlier play constructs a country ethic of reciprocal loyalties that is opposed to the appetitive immorality of the prosperous citizen, whose lust for social advancement is explicitly associated with the scandals surrounding Sir Giles Mompesson. In the later play, good men from the country aristocracy and gentry and from the prosperous merchant class combine to teach salutary lessons to rogues like Luke Frugal, a merchant who has squandered his own resource, and to spendthrift, snobbish social climbers like Lady Frugal and her daughters. Sir John Frugal concludes the play by admonishing his wife to know her place and to exemplify that moral:

> Make you good
> Your promis'd reformation, and instruct
> Our city dames, whom wealth makes proud, to move
> In their own spheres, and willingly to confess
> In their habits, manners, and their highest port,
> A distance 'twixt the city, and the court.
>   (5.3.150–5; Massinger 1964b: 88)

The distance between court and city may be confirmed, but that between country and city is eroded as Frugal's daughters, with a new humility, accept marriage to a country gentleman and an aristocrat's relatively impoverished son, leaving an altogether less tendentious social construct at the heart of the play than that posed in *A New Way to Pay Old Debts*.

The most striking newcomers to writing for the stage were indeed courtiers themselves, most significantly William Davenant, the royal pair's favourite masque-writer, and Sir John Suckling. Suckling had started and abandoned a tragedy, *The Sad One* (published posthumously in 1659), and, though expensively staged, his first complete play, *Aglaura* (1638), retained a highly experimental quality. Indeed, though it first appeared as a tragedy, Suckling later supplied a radically different final act to turn it into a rather erotic tragi-comedy ('*A bed put out: THERSAMES and AGLAURA on it*', s.d., Suckling 1971b: 108). Unlike other dramatists, Suckling evidently expected to lose, rather than make, money by his endeavours. The play, which was staged at court, no doubt in the Cockpit-at-Court, as well as at Blackfriars, was distinguished by its sumptuous costumes and – most unusually — by its scenery, perhaps designed by Inigo Jones, at a time when plays in the public and private theatres characteristically used a stage no more adorned than that which Shakespeare had known (Suckling 1971b: 261). Richard Brome, a professional writer to whom we turn shortly, hunted out the extravagance, which, of course, made little sense in terms of the usual economics of theatrical presentation, and in the prologue to his *The Antipodes* (1638) censured Suckling's prodigality in subventing the production of his play:

> Opinion, which our author cannot court
> For the dear daintines of it, has of late
> From the old way of plays possessed a sort
> Only to run to those that carry state
> In scene magnificent and language high,
> And clothes worth all the rest, except the action.
> ('The Prologue', ll.1–5; Parr 1995: 221)

Suckling's text was sought after among courtiers and their wider circle (Suckling 1971b: 253), and soon saw print, not as a typical playbook in densely printed quarto, but as an elegant presentation folio (Suckling 1638); again, I suspect Suckling may have subvented the printing. The play itself is sometimes regarded as a precursor to the heroic dramas of the Restoration. Atopical and ahistorical, it mixes an admirable paciness with extremes of implausibility, a deficiency Suckling probably recognizes and attempts to excuse:

THERSAMES That *Ziriff* was thy brother, brave *Zorannes*
  Preserv'd by miracle in that sad day
  Thy father fell, and since thus in disguise,
  Waiting his just revenge.
AGLAURA   You doe amaze me, Sir.
THERSAMES And must doe more, when I tell all the Storie.
  The King ...

                    (III.ii.27–32; Suckling 1971b: 64–5)

John Dryden credited Suckling with one significant dramatic innovation, and surprisingly it is a very technical one: 'almost every scene
begins in the midst of a discourse, as if talk had been going on for some
time before the actors walked on stage' (Suckling 1971b: 256).

Davenant's theatrical credentials were altogether more secure, and
his later career carried him into a theatrical management before the
Civil Wars, in the late 1650s, and after the Restoration (see below,
chapters 5 and 6). Though his social aspirations were unremittingly
towards the court, he had sometimes written plays through the late
1620s and 1630s. *The Wits* (1634) shows his considerable strengths.
The play, a city comedy, endorses a major concern of early Stuart
monarchs, and one that currently exercised Charles considerably, the
drift of the heads of gentry and aristocratic families away from their
provincial responsibilities and towards London abode:

> To one proclamation Charles attached especial importance as a measure
> central to his quest for reform of local society by a reinvigoration of
> traditional modes of government. The proclamation, first published in
> 1626 and reissued in 1627 and 1632, commanded the nobility and
> gentry to leave London within forty days ... It referred to the waste of
> gentry estates in the capital ..., to the desirability of their maintaining
> wealth and power in the localities, most of all to the need for resident
> gentry governors in the counties.   (Sharpe 1992: 414–15)

James had issued at least six such proclamations; the concern was of long
standing. In *The Wits*, two heads of families, Palatine the Elder and Sir
Morglay Thwack, who should be at home securing the wealth and
governance of the nation, come up to London; as the former puts it:

      O to live here, i'th fair Metropolis
      Of our great Isle, a free Inheritor
      Of ev'ry modest, or voluptuous wish,

> Thy young desires can breathe; and not oblig'd
> To'th Plough-mans toyls, or lazie Reapers swet...
> (IV.i; Davenant 1665: 51)

Palatine's younger brother, with the help of a mixed crew of heiresses, soldiers and watchmen, reduces them to their senses through a series of well-contrived practical jokes that produce salutary humiliations. But the play, more obliquely, endorses another concern of Caroline court ideology in its casual and dismissive perspective on the continental wars, developed in the dialogue between Young Palatine and Pert and Meager, two soldiers 'newly come from Holland':

> Yo[UNG] PALLAT[INE] . . . Could . . .
>> A stiffe Iron Doublet . . .
>> Tempt thee from Cambrick sheets, fine active Thighs . . . ?
> PERT Faith, we have been to kill, we know not whom,
>> Nor why: Led on to break a Commandement,
>> With the consent of Custom and the Laws.
>> . . . .
>> It was Sir, nor Geographical fancie
>> (Cause in our Maps, I lik'd this Regioun here
>> More than that Country lying there) made me
>> Partial which to fight for.
> Yo. PALLAT True, sage *Pert.*
>> What is't to thee whether one *Don Diego*
>> A Prince, or *Hans van Holm*, Fritter-seller
>> Of *Bombel*, do conquer that Parapet,
>> Redout, or Town, which thou nere saw'st before?
> PERT Not a brass Thimble to me . . .
> (I.i; Davenant 1665: 1–2)

English troops had served with various Protestant armies throughout the period of the Thirty Years War, amid intermittent enthusiasm for committing the country to all-out war. Pert and Young Palatine echo in a satiric idiom some of the values and concerns of Carew's response to Townsend: this is not England's war, and who wins or loses doesn't have a direct impact on English national interests. It is not mere pusillanimity (and Davenant in the 1640s was to have the most active war of any Caroline writer); a moral horror at the profession of killing strangers lurks beneath the tough façade of the dialogue.

In terms of theatre history, *The Wits* shows more strongly than *Aglaura* an anticipation of key elements of Restoration theatre, most particularly in the tone and idiom of youthful wits, who speak a tough, unsentimental but vivid language. Young Palatine tells his mates that his mistress, Lucy, is so chaste that she declines to sleep with him until he marries her: 'This baggage sleeps / Cross-legg'd, and the Devil has no more power / O'r that charm, then dead men ore their lewd Heirs' (I.i; Davenant 1665: 7). Even in the decorous court of Charles and Henrietta Maria, the attitude, if not the world view, of Aphra Behn or Sir George Etherege was in the making.

James Shirley and Richard Brome wrote the most successful plays of the 1630s. Both were closely connected with particular playhouses and companies. Their plays, both in themes and in terms of their high dramaturgical competence, show considerable similarities. Both writers had evidently thought hard about the staging of multiple plots, about fine-grained engagement with contemporary events, and about refreshing the depiction of London life with a new attention to topographical detail. Typically, their principal characters are drawn from the leisured classes of an emerging beau monde, though Brome ranges more widely. Both had evidently studied vintage Jonson to considerable advantage.

Shirley had worked for the Phoenix in Drury Lane since the mid-1620s and remained associated with the Queen's Men till the theatres closed in 1636 when he moved to Dublin where the Werbergh Street theatre had recently opened, returning to London to join the King's Men in 1640 (Shirley 1987: xii–xiii). *Hyde Park* (1632) is wonderfully structured. Like *The Alchemist*, it keeps multiple plots ingeniously intertwined, and like *Bartholomew Fair* it brings them together at a scene of social resort for a wide mix of people, in this case the Hyde Park race course where the beau monde could meet the demi-monde. In a *coup de théâtre*, a horse race is represented as taking place just off stage, while characters exit to place bets, to watch it, to return with reports and to respond to the result. Pepys saw a Restoration revival in which horses were actually brought on stage (Shirley 1987: xii). It is a play of courtship, the wooing of Mistress Carol and the testing of Julietta, to which he adds an old theme, the return of the long-lost husband in disguise, refreshed by a new social poise. Bonavent, the Odysseus figure, reappears just as his wife is about to marry the inoffensive Lacy, but far from killing him, he joins him in amicable reconciliation: 'BONAVENT: ... Master Lacy, / Droop not'; 'LACY: I was not ripe for such a blessing; take her, / And with an honest heart I wish you joys' (Shirley 1987: 45). Shirley was supremely the dramatist of urbane restraint. The Master of the Revels particularly commended him for his avoidance of 'oaths, profaneness or obsceneness' (quoted in Butler 2002: 593).

The Lady of Pleasure (1635), sometimes claimed as his best play (Shirley 1973: Introductory Note), offers a matched pair of eloquent and strong-willed women of property, Aretina and Celestina. The former, the wife of a knight of the shires newly come to London, is on a path of increasing depravity, from which she is saved by her husband's ingenious demonstration of how they and their family would be ruined if he were to behave as extravagantly as she does. Duly chastened, she concludes, 'Already / I feele a cure upon my soule, and promises / My after life to vertue' (Shirley 1637: sig. H4r). Meanwhile, Celestina, a young and attractive widow, has resisted the attempts of an unnamed lord to debauch her, in the process reforming him and winning his love. As Celestina tells him, it should be relatively easy to find the way to the life of truth and innocence, 'which shine / So bright in the two royal luminaries / At Court, you cannot lose your way to chastitie' (ibid.: sig. K2v).

Brome had been a servant to Ben Jonson, though it is unclear in what capacity; the title page of the 1658 edition of *The Weeding of the Covent-Garden* still styles him 'an Ingenious Servant, and Imitator of his Master' Jonson. Jonson wrote a prefatory poem for his first significant work, *The Northern Lasse*, though it sounds more of a protest at the displacement of honest professional dramatists (like himself): 'Now each court-Hobby-horse will wince in rime; / Both learned, and unlearned, all write Playes' (Brome 1980a: 6). Like Shirley, Brome refined Jonson's strong sense of location and mastered the multiple plot, though his plays depict in some detail a wider social range. Their resolutions remain soberly moral. *The Weeding of the Covent-Garden* has prostitutes and roaring boys among its dramatis personae, as well as Gabriel Crosswill, a stage Puritan, whose depiction owes something to Jonson's early plays, though the satire is gentler and he is eventually redeemed from his folly. *The Sparagus Garden* (1635), an astounding success in its own day, for the most part depicts a familiar Jonsonian cast of citizens and country gentry of two generations, together with rogues and aggressive servants. Asparagus was regarded as an aphrodisiac, and the Asparagus Garden, which is thought to have been over the river from Whitehall, not only sold cooked asparagus but also provided a place of resort and assignation, where one may 'take a room, call for a feast and satisfy your wife' (or lover) (III.vii.7–8;

Brome 1980b: 292). Curiously, Brome interposes an episode to praise the chaste morals of the court (III.vi.; ibid.: 289). In *The Antipodes* (1638) Brome attempted an exceptionally ambitious plot, in which Peregrine, a young man so distempered by his obsession with travel that he ignores his wife, is brought to his senses through a complex stratagem in which he is induced to thinking he has been transported to the Antipodes, where the institutions and manners that characterize contemporary England are reversed, in Butler's judicious phrase, 'teasingly and ambiguously revers[ing] the order of home' (2002: 597). Quite what we are to make of the loutish Antipodean courtiers and the courtly Antipodean waterman, carman and sedanman remains elusive (IV.iv.166–257; Parr 1995: 291–6).

Brome enjoyed a singularly secure career among professional writers. He had migrated from the King's Men, who staged his earliest plays, including *The Northern Lasse* and probably *The Weeding of the Covent-Garden*, to the Salisbury Court in 1635, where he contracted over the next three years to provide three new plays a year for 15s. a week and the profits of the first day. The arrangement broke down during the closure for plague, and when plays resumed he migrated once more, this time to the Phoenix, which had recently lost Shirley to Dublin. A subsequent lawsuit included the accusation that he had been 'tampered withal', presumably poached, by William Beeston. Brome's defence included the remarkable claim that the Salisbury Court had made £1,000 out of *The Spargus Garden* (the story is frequently narrated, for example in Brome 1980b: 7; for the documents, see Wickham et al. 2000: 657–64). Literary production for the elite professional theatre had plainly moved some way from the days of Henry Chettle, languishing for debt in the Marshalsea (see chapter 1).

Shirley and Brome have rightly attracted interest over recent decades not only from academic critics, but also from the professional theatre, and revivals of their plays are relatively frequent. John Ford's critical and theatrical standing has been higher and for longer. *'Tis Pity She's a Whore*, no doubt aided by the catch-penny title, is played quite frequently and has even been filmed (Ford 1975: lix–lxii). *The Broken Heart* and *Perkin Warbeck* have some critical currency. Dating is problematic, but Butler, for example, provisionally assigns all three to the period 1631–4 (Butler 2002: 595). Ford seems not to have been retained by a particular playhouse. He was a lawyer by training, and, as Arthur Bullen observed, 'He was not dependent on the stage for his livelihood and his plays show few signs of haste in composition' (*DNB*

1975). Peter Ure tentatively suggests that the pattern of his career may have been that, once he devoted himself to non-collaborative composition, he had a period of writing for the King's Men before going over to their rivals (Ford 1968: xxix). The title pages of their quarto editions associate *Perkin Warbeck* and *'Tis Pity She's a Whore* with the Queen's Men at the Phoenix and *The Broken Heart* with the King's Men at Blackfriars.

Those circumstances may be significant in that Ford shows, along with a formidable level of dramatic competence and some poetic flair, a remarkable independence from the fashions driving new drama in the years of the personal rule, as he brings to the private theatres and their presumably genteel audiences some of the rawer obsessions of Elizabethan and early Jacobean theatre.

Ford was certainly conscious of his creative atavism. The Prologue to *Perkin Warbeck* observes, 'Studies have of this nature been of late / So out of fashion, so unfollowed' (ll.1–2; Ford 1968: 11), and indeed it is sometimes called the last English history play, a genre thoroughly out of fashion in the Caroline age. Yet the play itself, like Shakespeare's paradigmatic chronicle plays, does speak to the age of its composition, in effect counselling acceptance of wise government and showing the disruptions of civil wars. It depicts events relating to the attempt to install, in place of Henry VII, Perkin Warbeck, an imposter claiming to be 'Richard the Fourth', one of the princes supposedly killed in the Tower by Richard III, but miraculously escaped to lead the Yorkist cause. Events depict a Scottish invasion and two Cornish uprisings, the first of those in protest against the sudden levying of taxation, an issue of some contemporary resonance, given Charles's dubious fiscal innovations. But the rebels come off badly. The first Cornish uprising ends with its aristocratic leader dragged on a hurdle to decollation and its other prominent figures, a lawyer and a blacksmith, 'hanged, / Quartered, their quarters into Cornwall sent, / Examples to the rest' (III.i.99–101, Ford 1968: 66). In the final scene, the captured Warbeck is humiliated in the stocks before being led off to execution while his supporters are paraded wearing the halters with which they are to be hanged (V.iii; Ford 1968: 130–40). Thus, the play rehearses those familiar early Stuart themes of the blessings of peace and of the necessity of controlling those forces, ever present, that would threaten it.

In the other two plays, a Websterian, rather than Shakespearean, aesthetic predominates. Both depict numerous deaths, most of them

painful, violent, prolonged and curiously loquacious, though sometimes sudden and inexplicable. *The Broken Heart* is set in classical
Sparta, though no classical text informs the play nor is antiquarian
verisimilitude a priority. This is a land of fantasy, where English
common law has no place. Orgilus, outraged that his beloved Penthea
has been compelled to marry Bassanes, resists the marriage of his
sister Euphranea to Prophilus while resenting that Ithocles had sanctioned the marriage of *his* sister, Penthea. Meanwhile Calantha, the
king's daughter, is to marry Nearchus, prince of Argos. Orgilus's
vengeful actions occasion the death of most of the principals. He
himself traps Ithocles in a trick chair and then kills him fairly slowly
by stabbing; in punishment, he is required to bleed himself to death, a
process that allows him to engage in 35 lines of surprisingly animated
conversation (Ford 1965: 83–4). Inexplicably, but unsurprisingly,
Calantha drops dead: 'Her heart is broke indeed' (V.ii.95; Ford
1965: 88).

Of course, the plot is as sensational and as implausible as *Aglaura*,
but Ford carries it off with great elan, as he does the steamier tale of
sibling incest in *'Tis Pity She's a Whore*. Giovanni and Annabella are
siblings and lovers; she becomes pregnant; she marries Soranzo to
cover it up; Soranzo, who has abandoned his promise to marry his
former mistress Hippolita, despite the apparent death of her husband,
intends their brutal murder, but is forestalled by Giovanni, who kills
Annabella, cuts out her heart, presents it to Soranzo on a dagger and
then kills him with that dagger, before being stabbed to death by
Soranzo's hired 'banditti'; Florio, father to Giovanni and Annabella,
inexplicably, but unsurprisingly, drops dead. In a nasty little coda,
Putana, Annabella's 'tutress', who has already been kidnapped and
blinded by the banditti, is carried off to be burnt. Along the way,
Hippolita inadvertently poisons herself while trying to kill Soranzo at
his wedding feast and a simpleton courting Annabella is stabbed
through mistaken identity. We are in the landscape and the moral
universe of *The Duchess of Malfi* and *The White Devil*. Indeed, Vasques,
who has been Soranzo's agent throughout, exits to his banishment
with 'I rejoice that a / Spaniard outwent an Italian in revenge'
(V.vi.145–6; Ford 1975: 122). Yet again, though the play feels as if
it were written 20 years earlier, Ford gets away with it, largely through
the felicity of his verse. Certainly there are ripping rants, but at key
moments he masters a different tone, as in the final exchanges of
Annabella and Giovanni:

> GIO   ...yet look
>   What see you in mine eyes?
> ANN   Methinks you weep.
> GIO I do indeed: these are the funeral tears
>   Shed on your grave; these furrowed up my cheeks
>   When first I loved and knew not how to woo.
>   (V.V.47–51; Ford 1975: 112–13)

Just occasionally, his verse seems redolent of Dante's tender account of Paolo and Francesca, doomed lovers in the second circle of hell, a tone which Webster never achieved and probably never aspired to.

Literature and Laudianism

At least since the publication of Nicholas Tyacke's seminal essay (1973), Caroline ecclesiastical history has been among the most active fields of early modern historiography. (See, particularly, Davies 1992; Fincham 1993; A. Milton 1995; Sharpe 1992: esp. ch. 6; and Tyacke 1987.) The relationship between Charles and his archbishop, the nature of doctrinal change and the significance of such change in the origins of the conflicts of the 1640s remain controversial. This account largely rests on the work of Peter Lake and Kenneth Fincham and to other contributors to Fincham's influential collection of essays (Fincham 1993).

The Jacobean church, though certainly not so free from dissent and disharmony as was once assumed (Fielding 1993), reflected the king's careful attempts to steer clear of avoidable conflict. Theologians critical of Calvinist theories of salvation were constrained in the dissemination of their views. Indeed, some continuities of policy characterize the opening years of Charles's rule, especially when parliament was sitting; in the personal rule the situation changed very rapidly (Fincham and Lake 1993: 38–9). The Church of England in the 1630s was dominated by 'Laudianism', a word I use much as Peter Lake defines it, as a 'handy shorthand term for the policies and religious temper of the personal rule' and 'a coherent, distinctive and polemically aggressive vision of the Church, the divine presence in the world and the appropriate ritual response to that presence' (Lake 1993: 162).

Laud was both an agent and a symptom of those changes. From the accession of Charles I, his ecclesiastical (and political) career developed rapidly. He migrated from the see of St David's to Bath and Wells in 1626, joined the Privy Council in 1627, migrated to London and became Chancellor of the University of Oxford in 1628, and was promoted to the archepiscopacy of Canterbury in 1633, a preferment postponed by the longevity of the previous incumbent. By the time the Long Parliament assembled in 1640, he had become a focus of hatred among the godly of anti-ceremonial, Calvinist and Puritan inclinations, and his career ended in impeachment, incarceration and, in 1645, trial and execution.

What were the characteristics of Laudianism? At the level of doctrine, most significant was its theology of grace, which rejected the Calvinist notion of predestined salvation of the elect, particularly in its extremer form of double predestination, which posited the predestined damnation of the reprobate. Laudianism tolerated and promoted a peculiarly Anglican inflection of Arminianism. Early in the century Jacobus Arminius had shattered the Calvinist consensus of the Dutch reformed church with an alternative soteriology that attributed to fallen humankind a role in their own salvation, though one that depends on an active and widely merciful exercise of divine grace:

> In this [fallen] state, the free will of man towards the true good is not only wounded, maimed, infirm, bent, and weakened; but it is also imprisoned, destroyed, and lost. And its powers are not only debilitated and useless unless they be assisted by grace, but it has no powers whatsoever except such as are excited by divine grace. For Christ has said, 'Without me ye can do nothing'.   (Arminius; quoted in Bangs 1971: 341)

To fallen humankind, grace actively extends the invitation to align their impaired but residual free will in a synergy that leads to spiritual regeneration.

Arminianism is a psychologically liberating theology, repositioning the process of salvation on the human scale and contextualizing it in personal struggle, rather than leaving it in the unfathomable process of divine determination. Mid-century, it was incorporated into the theology of some of the most radical sectaries, and it was central to Milton's mature theology. In Caroline Anglicanism a significantly different emphasis evolved which attributed a vital function to the church itself in promoting the spiritual well-being of the individual by acting as a catalyst in the synergy of grace and free will.

To this end, the clergy had a role that distinguished them from the laity in a way closer to Catholicism than previous English practice. Indeed, 'priest' was Charles's preferred term for the ministers of his church (Fincham and Lake 1993: 42).

Numerous measures converged in this project to make the priesthood special and to separate them off from the laity. The location, orientation and protection of the communion table became Laudian obsessions. Sacerdotalism combined with a mystic valorizing of the place and instruments of worship in an extraordinary cultural transformation that edged the Church of England further still from the reformed churches of continental Europe. The priesthood were marked off by their distinctive vestments, the adoption and elaboration of which accompanied their increased incorporation into the rituals – the blessings and crossings – of the church. This was a movement that demanded uniformity of implementation. Liturgy was deemed holy because it served the end of carrying each believer towards potential salvation, but it also provided a framework to control variation and ensure the quality of priestly practice. We have noted how the royal court increasingly developed a detailed ceremonialism; here Charles found a spiritual echo of that programme, sharing the same discipline, decorum and precision.

Laudianism required careful conformity with the Book of Common Prayer, which emphasized the liturgical year as the template for the spiritual life. Laud's critics generally devalued the cycle of holy days and Christian festivals which make up that year because of twin impulses, towards sabbatarianism and the weekly holiness of the Sabbath, and towards a pervasiveness of religious consciousness. In contrast, for Laudians:

> [T]he great festivals of the Christian year both figured and extended to all believers the benefits conferred on fallen humanity by Christ's life, passion and resurrection. 'They which come to God's house upon the day of Christ's nativity (coming in faith and love as they ought) are', argued Robert Shelford [a Cambridge-educated anti-Calvinist divine], 'partakers of Christ's birth; they which come upon the day of circumcision are with him circumcised from the dominion of the flesh ...'. (Lake 1993: 175)

Such a concern aimed at an orderly meditation stimulated by the sequence of festivals, rather than devotional spontaneity. This was not primarily a preaching ministry, though its concern with religious drill was not with ceremony for its own sake but as a stimulus to regeneration, the principal vehicle for which was prayer.

The religious writers of the 1630s experienced Christianity through a church dominated by the cultural, doctrinal and spiritual agenda of Laudianism, and it shaped, too, the perceptions and expectations of those who in the 1640s either triumphed over or lamented its demise. To understand George Herbert or Herrick's religious verse or Henry Vaughan or the Caroline verse of Quarles or Wither or, indeed, both the early and rather ceremonious verse of Milton and his later anti-prelatical polemic we must set them against this most sustained trans-formation of the Church of England since the Elizabethan settlement. We begin with Herbert.

George Herbert

Except perhaps for Sir Philip Sidney, no major creative writer of the early modern period was better connected than George Herbert. His family was a cadet line of a mighty aristocratic clan headed by the Earls of Pembroke (for this and other biographical information, see Charles 1977). His eldest brother Edward, first Baron Herbert of Cherbury, was a distinguished diplomat and minor poet, and another brother, Sir Henry, was the energetic Master of the Revels, whose efforts we have noted above. His mother's social circle included John Donne and Francis Bacon, whom George had known since his youth; Bacon dedicated his translation of *Certaine Psalmes* (1625) to him. He sat in a parliament for a constituency under family control and held the high-profile office of Orator over the final years of a Cambridge career that had extended unfashionably long for one of his social class. His transition to an ecclesiastical career was under the patronage of John Williams, Bishop of Lincoln and Lord Keeper of the Seal, a major figure in church and secular politics in the mid-1620s. The living of Bemerton was in the gift of the Earls of Pembroke, though his pre-sentation may have fallen to King Charles himself. Though Bemerton is sometimes sentimentalized as a modest backwater, a retreat from the ecclesiastical rat-race, its previous incumbent had been appointed Bishop of Bath and Wells in succession to Laud himself; Herbert's career thus far certainly did not preclude considerable advancement

within the church, had he lived into middle age. As Michael Schoenfeldt astringently notes:

> Bemerton is...located midway between the ecclesiastical splendors of
> Salisbury Cathedral, where Herbert was ordained, and the aristocratic
> magnificance of Wilton House, inhabited by Herbert's powerful
> kinsman, Philip Herbert, the fourth earl of Pembroke; it is, further-
> more, in walking distance to both....Bemerton was geographically
> on the diagonal connecting political and religious power in the
> period. (Schoenfeldt 1991: 37)

His rectory at Bemerton had six servants (Charles 1977: 156).

Like his elder contemporary and acquaintance, John Donne, Herbert vouchsafed almost no poetry to the press in his lifetime; unlike
Donne, he would seem to have circulated little in manuscript, since few
manuscripts survive and the life records make no early reference to his
vernacular compositions. His greatest work, *The Temple* (1633), was
posthumously published by Nicholas Ferrar, a devout lay Anglican and
leader of an informal reclusive and meditative religious group, with
whom Herbert had collaborated in his lifetime (Valdes 1638: sig.
****4r-v). Its success was immediate and considerable. There were
six editions, all printed by the printers at the Cambridge University
Press, by 1641, and his earliest biographer reported that it sold more
than 20,000 copies during the 40 years to 1675 (Patrides 1983: 127).
Moreover, in recent decades, only Shakespeare and Milton, among
seventeenth-century writers, have stimulated more critical activity
and controversy and a richer scholarly response. (See, especially, the
classic studies by Doerksen 1997; Fish 1978; Nuttall 1980; Schoenfeldt 1991; Strier 1983; and Vendler 1975).

Herbert's piety recommended him to his earliest readers: 'scarcely
any surviving opinion values [the] poetry [of *The Temple*] as poetry'.
Moreover, that piety evidently appealed across a wide range of Protestant denominations (Patrides 1983: 1, 2–14). We shall return to
Herbert's relationship to popular piety shortly. His broad appeal runs
curiously counter to recent critical endeavour, which has laboured
definitively to place Herbert, as Ilona Bell observes, 'at every point
along the spectrum of English Protestantism, from ceremonial Anglo-
Catholicism to radical Puritanism', and indeed Bell's own thesis relates
his theological outlook to that of the somewhat heterodox Catholic
meditational writer Juan de Valdes, whose work he had commented on

at Ferrar's request (1987: 304). Finally fixing Herbert in contemporary terms proves elusive for at least three powerful reasons. As Bell notes, he died before Laudianism had reached its defining moments in the suppression of dissenting voices and the enforcement of its agenda. We do not know how Herbert would have lined up on issues like the placement of the altar. Secondly, a complex and extensive collection of lyric expostulations, each articulated as if at a discrete moment of heightened spirituality, poses an interpretative problem to its readers, who must tentatively and speculatively attempt a synthesis: as we shall see, the experience of reading *The Temple* is a challenging one. Finally, Herbert left no systematic theology of his own. The nearest he came are the notes on Valdes, fragmentary comments on a work that is itself ruminative and unsystematic. His notes on Christian ministry, *A Priest to the Temple, or, The Country Parson*, also published posthumously as part of *Herberts Remains or, Sundry Pieces* (Herbert 1652), are practical in orientation, though of course indicative of his value system and of his thoughts about ministry.

Yet Herbert's poetry certainly demonstrates a cluster of characteristics that chime with Laudianism. It stresses the value of ritual:

> When once thy foot enters the church, be bare.
> God is more there, then thou: for thou art there
> Onely by his permission. Then beware,
> And make thy self all reverence and fear.
>   Kneeling ne're spoil'd silk stocking: quit thy state.
>   All equall are within the churches gate.
> ('The Church-porch', ll.403–8; Herbert 1941: 22)

The poem urges the erosion of distinctions among the laity in the place of worship and in the sight of God. Meanwhile, in ways that Laud would have approved, the specialness of the clergy is rehearsed in terms which tie the ministers of the Caroline church to Aaron, the founding Levite consecrated by Moses to the service of the temple (Leviticus 8):

> Holinesse on the head,
> Light and perfections on the breast,
> Harmonious bells below, raising the dead
> To leade them unto life and rest:
> Thus are true Aarons drest.

> Profanesse in my head,
> Defects and darknesse in my breast,
> A noise of passions ring me for dead
> Unto a place where is no rest:
> Poore priest thus am I drest.
>
>   . . .
>
> So holy in my head,
> Perfect and light in my deare breast,
> My doctrine tun'd by Christ, (who is not dead,
> But lives in me while I do rest)
> Come people; Aaron's drest.
>   ('Aaron', ll.1–10, 21–5; ibid.: 174)

Priests – Herbert's word as well as Charles's – as agents promoting the operation of grace and divinely ordained for that purpose can lead believers to a salvation which may not otherwise be theirs. Moreover, the power to do so comes not from the personal merit of the individual priest but through his induction into the ancient sacerdotal order. Vestments, so prized and insisted upon by Laud, are at once the metaphor for the assumption of that power and its external and distinguishing mark.

Herbert drew on his own resources to refurbish his parish church (Charles 1977: 154), and in a rare autobiographical detail the poet speaks of 'all my wealth and familie' combining 'To set [God's] honour up' ('The Crosse', ll.5–6; Herbert 1941: 164). The division of the volume into 'The Church-porch' and 'The Church', in adopting those architectural distinctions as the shaping metaphor of the book, asserts the centrality of the church itself as a physical location for Christian worship. He observes in *A Priest to the Temple*:

> The Countrey Parson hath a speciall care of his Church, that all things there be decent, and benefitting his Name by which it is called. Therefore first he takes order, that all things be in good repair; as walls plaistered, windows glazed, floore paved, seats whole, firm, and uniform, especially that the Pulpit, and Deck, and Communion Table, and Font be as they ought, for those great duties that are performed in them. (1652: 57)

These things are rendered holy and thus to be treated reverently by association with the service they perform.

The liturgical year figures very prominently in *The Temple*. Poems commemorate Good Friday, Easter, Whitsunday, Trinity Sunday, Christmas, and Lent (Herbert 1941: 39, 41, 43, 60, 68, 81, 87), as, too, the great weekly rituals of the church. While both in his poetry and prose Herbert speaks positively about a preaching ministry, in both the object of preaching is prayer, and the best prayer is not private but a communal and public witness: 'Though private prayer be a brave designe, / Yet publicke hath more promises, more love'; 'Resort to sermons, but to prayers most: / Praying's the end of preaching' ('The Church-porch', ll.397–8, 409–10; ibid.: 22, 23). Though Laud's deep scepticism about the role of preaching was not shared by Herbert, the liturgical emphasis and the style of worship would have seemed to him acceptable and appropriate.

The soteriology of *The Temple*, its doctrine of salvation, takes some teasing out. Predestinate reprobation has no place in it. Christ's Atonement was for all humankind, and salvation, and holy communion, as celebration of that sacrifice, stands open to all, no matter how evidently sinful:

> Lord I have invited all [to communion],
>   And I shall
> Still invite, still call to thee:
> For it seems but just and right
>   In my sight,
> Where is All, there All should be.
>   ('The Invitation', ll.31–6; ibid.: 180)

Strier (1983) argues for the centrality in Herbert's thought of the Lutheran doctrine of the irresistibility of grace, the notion that those to whom grace is extended may not resist or avoid the salvation it brings. Indeed, in poems like 'A Parodie', or the climactic poem 'Love (III)', the poet's apparent resistance to accepting his worthiness for salvation are swept aside: 'but while I grieve, / Thou com'st and dost relieve' ('A Parodie', ll.29–30; ibid.: 184). The godly's sense of his or her own unworthiness shows a humble acknowledgement of universal and personal sinfulness, and may be broken by the accession of grace, while that same grace, though available to all, may indeed be rejected by those who decline the invitation: 'all may certainly conclude, that God loves them, till either they despise that Love, or despaire of his Mercy: not any sin else, but is within his Love; but the despising of

Love must needs be without it. The thrusting away of his arme makes us onely not embraced' (*A Priest to the Temple*, Herbert 1652: 156). To despise love is to commit the blasphemy against the holy ghost which shall not be forgiven (Matthew 12:31). In contrast, those whose damaged and imperfect freedom of choice, through God's aid, aligns them with proffered grace are led onwards: 'Enrich my heart, mouth, hands in me, / With faith, with hope, with charitie; / That I may runne, rise, rest with thee' ('Trinitie Sunday', ll.7–9; Herbert 1941: 68).

The author of *The Temple* and *A Priest to the Temple* was a child of his times, sharing the Laudians' reservations about Calvinist soteriology and recognizing the place of the priesthood and the liturgy and the beauty of holiness in steering all who share the inherited sin of Adam towards an acceptance of God's love and sacrifice and the grace extended to them. But Herbert's text is neither doctrinaire nor overtly controversial. When *The Temple* moves into potentially divisive areas, as in the somewhat enigmatic 'Church-rents and schismes', an anticipation of 'The Church Militant', rather more is said about Christianity abroad than about the problems within the Church of England (Herbert 1941: 140). Moreover, his writing advocates a kind of interiority, of meditation and reflection on personal sinfulness, that evidently appealed across the Protestant spectrum: 'Tumble thy breast, and turn thy book. . . . / Then once more pray' ('The Method', ll.9, 29; ibid.: 133–4): no wonder Richard Baxter, a prominent, mid-century Presbyterian, valued him so highly (Patrides 1983: 137).

The modern experience of reading Herbert differs sharply from that of his contemporaries. Typically he is first encountered in anthologies which, wholly reasonably, select his most distinctive, technically astonishing and emotionally intense lyrics: neither Fowler (1991) nor Cummings (2000) nor Abrams et al. (2000) draws from 'The Church-porch' or 'The Church Militant'. Quite probably, the discerning among his early readers also valued the frequently anthologized favourites the most. But the preaching, catechizing, didactic Herbert, the plain speaker (rather than the *faux-naif* speaker of some of the anthology pieces) is rarely heard. We lose, too, the sense of quite how much *The Temple* demands of its readers. Izaak Walton's phrase, 'this little book', often repeated, may reflect the small format, duodecimo, in which it appeared. Yet its 164 poems, including one of more than 400 lines and another of nearly 300 lines, constitute a volume that is almost as challenging to read through as *Paradise Lost*; indeed, more challenging in some ways, since it has no narrative structure. Like

Paradise Lost, taking it on calls for hours of close attention, and it leads
the reader through an emotional and physical experience that is both
exhausting and rewarding. Like Milton's closing image of Adam and
Eve, reconciled to God and each other, taking their leave of Eden, the
final poem of 'The Church' offers an assurance, a confirmation of faith,
and a sense of peace that have been hard won:

> Love bade me welcome: yet my soul drew back,
>   Guiltie of dust and sinne.
> But quick-ey'd Love, observing me grow slack
>   From my first entrance in,
> Drew nearer to me, sweetly questioning,
>   If I lack'd any thing.
>
> A guest, I answer'd worthy to be here:
>   Love said, You shall be he.
> I the unkinde, ungratefull? Ah my deare,
>   I cannot look on thee.
> Love took my hand, and smiling did reply,
>   Who made the eyes but I?
>
> Truth Lord, but I have marr'd them: let my shame
>   Go where it doth deserve.
> And know you not, sayes Love, who bore the blame?
>   My deare, then I will serve.
> You must sit down, sayes Love, and taste my meat:
>   So I did sit and eat. (1–18)
>   ('Love (III)'; Herbert 1941: 188–9)

The metaphor is of an arrival after a journey, which reader and poet
have made together, and of an undeserved but desired reward
extended by 'Love', a figure to be identified as the atoning Christ.
The meal is at once a feast and a communion.

Getting there has been difficult. 'The Church-porch' through which
the reader enters the volume is – altogether without irony – explicitly
and unrelievedly didactic:

> Hearken unto a Verser, who may chance
> Ryme thee to good, and make a bait of pleasure.
>   A verse may finde him, who a sermon flies,
>   And turn delight into a sacrifice.
>   ('The Church-porch', ll.3–6; ibid.: 6)

What follows, *pace* the poet, offers less delight and pleasure and more the kind of hectoring that would have met and satisfied the appetite of readers accustomed to works of popular piety. The poem carries a subtitle, 'Perirrhanterium', the Greek term for the instrument for sprinkling holy water (ibid.: 477): what the preacher sprinkles is sound advice about moral conduct, much of it couched in the imperative mood, and it often has a proverbial resonance:

'Drink not the third glass . . .'
'Flie idlenesse . . .'
'Never exceed thy income.'
'Play not for gain, but sport.'
'Pitch thy behaviour low, thy projects high;
So shalt thou humble and magnanimous be . . .'
'Restore to God his due in tithe and time . . .'
('The Church-porch', ll.25, 79, 156, 193, 331–2, 385; ibid.: 7, 9, 13, 14, 19, 22)

Thus cajoled into Christian neighbourliness, 'sprinkled and taught' by 'the former precepts' ('Superliminare', ll.1–2; ibid.: 25), the reader crosses the threshold into 'The Church'. His or her gaze is immediately arrested by the two most obvious objects in a well-kept Caroline church, the altar and the crucifix. The former, however, is '[a] broken ALTAR . . . Made of a heart, and cemented with teares' ('The Altar, ll.10–12; ibid.: 26), a site for penitence and, potentially, redemption. 'The Sacrifice', the only poem in the collection spoken throughout in the voice of Christ, functions as both cross and platform from which to address '*all ye, who passe by*' for some 250 lines: 'Was ever grief like mine?' ('The Sacrifice', ll.1 and passim; ibid.: 26–34). The topos is an ancient one, in the English tradition particularly favoured in the poetry of late medieval devotionalism, as in lyrics like 'Woefully Arrayed':

Wofully araide,
My blode, man, ffor the[e] ran
. . .
Thus nakid am I nailed, O man, for thi sake.
I love the[e], thenne love me. Why slepist thu? awake!
(Anon., 'Woefully Arrayed', ll.1–2, 10–11; Brown 1939: 156–7)

Indeed, the classic anthology of fifteenth-century religious lyrics has a whole section of 'appeals to man from the cross' (Brown 1939:

151–62). Softened up by the encounter with a time-honoured devotional practice, and, more significantly, aligned to a spirituality of the most profound and unswerving Christocentricity, Herbert's reader overhears the poet in a range of speech acts that simulate prayer, meditation, penitial reflection, praise and celebration.

Herbert's robust didactic practices, so like those of works of popular and practical piety, may well have led into reading lyric poetry a non-traditional readership, drawn much wider than the ranks of connoisseurs who dabbled themselves or made their own manuscript anthologies; hence, surely, the extraordinary early publishing history of *The Temple*. Here, finally, are delight and pleasure, in poems of an extraordinary accomplishment, some of which challenge interpretation and even understanding in the manner of Donne's denser poetry. Yet, though these poems simulate overheard devotional exercises, Herbert retains a clear sense of readership. His hardest poems end in at least an apparent transparency. Thus, the sonnet 'Prayer (I)' (Herbert 1941: 51) offers a list of fanciful and provocative synonyms for prayer: 'the Churches banquet' – how so?; 'Engine against th'Almightie'?; 'The milkie way'? The competent reader takes up the challenge: milky way, presumably, because that celestial configuration was thought of as a glittering pathway leading to heaven. For the bewildered, the poem resolves itself in a final phrase of apparent simplicity: prayer is 'something understood' (though the more knowing reader will recognize that phrase as in some ways the most enigmatic of them all). Often, the resolution comes in a phrase of biblical resonance. Thus, 'The Collar' ends with an echo of God calling Samuel (1 Sam. 3): 'Me thoughts I heard one calling, *Child!* / And I reply'd, *My Lord*' (ll.35–6; Herbert 1941: 154). 'Love (III)', the climactic poem of the collection, ends with an allusion to the Last Supper (Matt. 26:20) and the sacrament of Holy Communion. The most demanding poems, perhaps the most demanding literary experience some of Herbert's readers would ever encounter, end in what is familiar and reassuring.

After 'The Church' comes the curious extended coda of 'the Church Militant', almost 300 lines in couplets describing the progress of Christianity on a global scale, from east to west. Successively, the glory of each church is overwhelmed by 'sin' in the form of Catholicism and the real enough challenge of Islam: only in the final years of the century were Ottoman ambitions on the Holy Roman Empire finally defeated. It is a poem that has few modern admirers, nor do I fully understand quite how it relates to the rest of the volume.

I suppose it sends the reader, now spiritually exercised and justified in faith, back into an external reality of conflict and threat which requires a militant support for the godly cause. The poem contains lines that evidently caught the licenser's eye – 'Religion stands on tip-toe in our land, / Readie to passe to the *American* strand' (ll.235–6; Herbert 1941: 196 and 547n.) – though Herbert, I suspect, writes as the stepson of an enthusiastic investor in the American colonies, rather than as a supporter of the Pilgrim Fathers. Yet the new American church will be as susceptible to decline as its predecessors (ll.260–2). The poem returns the reader to the world of popular piety through its anti-Catholic sentiment and plain-spoken prejudice. The Orthodox church and the church of Rome are 'hells land-marks, Satans double crest: / They are Sinnes nipples, feeding th'east and west' (ll. 219–20). Herbert can do much better than this, but he chooses not to. Laud, too, saw the advantages of distancing his version of Christianity from the Pope's.

The Emblem Books of Quarles and Wither

Though the culture of the Caroline court, like that of its aristocratic imitators, was rich in visual as well as musical stimulation and its finest achievements often synthesized the arts, outside elite circles the English experience of painting and sculpture was arguably among the most impoverished of the major European states. In Florence, the citizens' daily round took them past some of Michelangelo's greatest civic sculptures to churches replete with paintings and murals of a century of astonishing accomplishment. In Rome, the citizen could step into churches and see the new and challenging art of Caravaggio, depicting the lives of Christ, of the Virgin and of saints, or into St Peter's to be astounded by sacred art from Michelangelo to Bernini. In Antwerp, Madrid and Seville, the devout knelt before altarpieces by Rubens, Murillo and Zurbarán. Nor was the experience denominationally determined in a simple way. The Dutch School, glittering with the varied talents of Rembrandt and Hals, and in mid-century Vermeer, Hobbema and Cuyp, served a complex marketplace that was in part aristocratic, in part civic and corporate, in part ecclesiastical, and in part bourgeois and fairly broadly based, for which it produced not only individual portraits and devotional works, but also seascapes, landscapes, townscapes, genre paintings, still lives, battle scenes and group portraits of militias, merchant guilds and the like. There were great paintings and great sculptures, particularly from classical antiquity, in Caroline England. The Earl of Arundel and the Duke of Buckingham collected assiduously from the late Jacobean period, and Charles as king made major investments, as we have noted earlier in this chapter, and work of the highest order was produced under royal and aristocratic patronage, most significantly by Van Dyck and Rubens. But these were the work of foreign artists and hung in private collections, though those collections were sometimes open to visitors (Brown 1995: ch. 1). Milton spent much of his early life within strolling distance of the king's galleries at Whitehall or Buckingham's at York House, but Graham Parry is probably right in his surmise that 'there was virtually no baroque painting in England that [he] could have seen' (Parry 2001: 60).

High art relates intricately to minor forms like engraving. Quite possibly, the limited English achievement in this field in the early modern period reflects the lack of a vibrant tradition of working painters seeking out a larger audience. Moreover, in England that potential audience was limited by the visual under-stimulation in its broader cultural life. Although the immensely talented Bohemian, Wenceslas Hollar, worked in England from the mid-1630s, partly under the patronage of the Earl of Arundel, the dominant illustrator in the London book trade throughout the '30s and '40s was William Marshall. Milton ridiculed his inability to capture his likeness in the portrait frontispiece Marshall made for his first collection of poetry (Milton 1645: poem appended to the frontispiece). Wither was scathing about his inability to follow instructions for the illuminated title page to his emblem book (Wither 1635: poem facing the title page). He couldn't draw, his texturing was crude, his sense of design limited; despite the availability of better engravers, he was Caroline England's most prolific source of visual images, a symptom and a cause of cultural impoverishment in the visual arts, outside the royal and aristocratic elite.

Emblem books originated in cinquecento Italy, and spread rapidly across continental Europe, appearing most frequently, I suggest, in those countries with a developed indigenous tradition in the visual arts. The first, Andrea Alciato's Latin *Emblematum liber* (1531), frequently translated and annotated, went into 90 editions in the sixteenth century and its popularity 'in no measure decreased in the seventeenth century' (Freeman 1948: 42). Alciato established the first paradigm for the genre: a visual image often of an allegorical sort is labelled by a tag line or proverb and glossed, usually by a poem, most frequently an epigram. Emblem books are exercises in the symbolic mode and share much common ground with the kinds of allegorical expression favoured in high culture across Europe. We see an obvious analogue, in terms of semiotic structure, in early Stuart masque.

The first printed emblem book by an English author dates from 1586, rather late in the history of the genre, and, in the judgement of Rosemary Freeman, the pioneer historian of the English emblem book, 'The work of the English emblem writers is not in itself of any great bulk or merit. Compared with that of Continental authors their output was small and, if judged by absolute standards, rarely of any permanent value'; few English examples went even into a second edition (Freeman 1948: 1, 43). By 1600, there were 'only half a dozen' English-produced emblem books, including manuscripts with drawings by hand (Bath 1994: 57). Yet in one year, 1635, presumably by coincidence, two works of considerable impact and abiding import-ance appeared: Francis Quarles's *Emblemes* and George Wither's *Col-lection of Emblemes, Ancient and Moderne*. They differ greatly, vividly demonstrating the range and variety that the genre achieved in its mature phase.

Quarles's is a modest little book printed in octavo. It is deeply derivative of two Jesuit works of morality and devotion, Herman Hugo's *Pia Desideria* (1624) and the anonymous *Typus Mundi* (1627) (see Freeman 1948: 117). Like Ferrar's and Herbert's engage-ment with Valdes, it shows an openness to take what seemed devo-tionally useful and doctrinally inoffensive from the Catholic tradition. Quarles evidently had William Marshall and associated engravers, some of them distinctly more able than Marshall, copy the plates of those texts, though 'he felt free to go his own poetic way' (Manning 2002: 179). The illustrations, though technically clumsy, are ingeniously conceived, and no doubt contributed much to the immense popularity of the work. The pictures illustrate a moment from a story of allegor-ical significance. Quarles stresses the narrative component when, in the epistle to the reader, he observes, 'An Embleme is but a silent Parable' (Quarles 1635: sig. A3r). Each section has a biblical text in lieu of a proverbial tag, and in some sections the engraving closely follows that text, almost like a plate from an illustrated bible. Thus emblem 3.12, which has the text 'O that thou wouldst hide me in the grave, and thou wouldst keepe me secret untill thy wrath be past'(Job 14:13), depicts a cowering figure sheltering in a cave or perhaps a sepulchre from lightning flashes that emanate from a large black cloud and a minatory flying angel. Quarles's poem on the scene is more moralizing than allegorical (ibid.: 168–71). In other sections, the action is unequivocally allegorical. Emblem 1.10 depicts a puzzling scene that challenges understanding and interpretation. On a pleasant bowling green, a male figure, distinctive only in that a purse hangs from his belt, bends to bowl, while Cupid stands by waiting his turn (see plate 5). In the mid-distance, a diabolic figure is pointing out the line he should take, while by the jack a female figure extends a cap and bells. The biblical text relates only tangentially to the scene: 'Yee are of your father the Devill, and the lusts of your father yee will doe' (John 8:44), but the poem explicates the allegory:

> The world's the Iack; The Gamsters that contend,
>   Are *Cupid*, *Mammon*: That judicious Friend,
> That gives the ground, is *Sathan*; and the Boules
>   Are sinfull Thoughts: The Prize, a Crowne for Fooles.

Yet the moralizing imperative is rarely still. His opening lines reflect a general disapproval of playing bowls: 'Brave pastime, Readers, to consume that day'; while the allegory receives an immediate application for his readers: 'Who breathes that boules not? what bold tongue can say / Without a blush, he hath not bould to day?' (ibid.: 40–3).

Quarles followed the success of *Emblemes* with *Hieroglyphikes of the life of Man* (1638), which retains a similar structure in each section, though it achieves a higher coherence in that each plate depicts 'life's taper', a candle variously blown out or burnt down. The engravings, in my view, represent the best product of Marshall's limited talent. The volume was subsequently reprinted and reissued with *Emblemes* ten times between 1639 and 1700.

Wither positioned his own emblem book rather differently within the book market. This was a luxury volume in folio, distributed in four early issues, each by a different bookseller. Wither acquired a set of Crispijn van de Passe's plates, first used to illustrate Gabriel Rollenhagen's *Nucleus Emblematum Selectissimorum* more than 20 years earlier. These were exceptional examples of Dutch engraving, that gave to the book 'the rare distinction [in England] of illustrations by a highly skilled professional engraver.... the pictures are uniformly excellent'

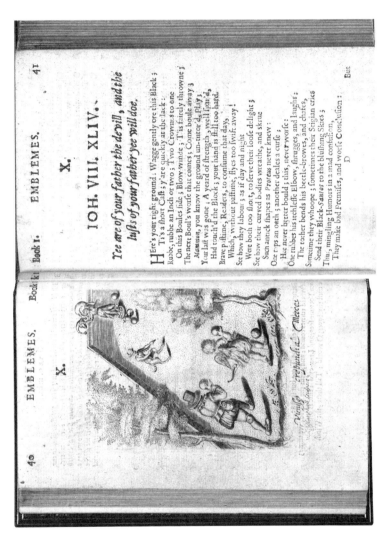

Plate 5 Francis Quarles, *Emblemes* (1635), Emblem X. Reproduced by permission of The Huntington Library, San Marino, California 69010.

(Freeman 1948: 142). Indeed, they offered a rare treat to the vast majority of educated English people who did not have access to masterpieces like Titian's *Pardo Venus* or Veronese's *Mars and Venus*, both hanging in the king's collections (Brown 1995: 36–8). I suspect that the lissom figure of Occasion was the first well-executed study of the female nude many of them had encountered (Wither 1635: 4; see plate 6).

Wither's approach to his source material was uninhibited. The plates were cut to remove Rollenhagen's text. In its place, in letterpress he produced for each plate a 30-line poem of allegorical explication. Sometimes he seems bewildered by his task. Emblem 2.49 shows three crescents intertwined, crowned and hovering over a rural scene, within a motto that reads (in Latin) 'may he [or she or it] fill the whole world'. He begins his commentary:

Plate 6 George Wither, *A Collection of Emblemes* (1635), pp. 4–5. Reproduced by permission of the British Library G. 11603 OR C.70.h.5.

> What in the *Emblem*, that mans meanings were,
> Who made it first, I neither know nor care;
> For, whatsoere, he purposed, or thought,
> To serve my *purpose*, now it shall be taught.
>   (Wither 1635: 111)

Once more, his persistent impulse is to moralize, sometimes lapsing into a satirical mode (discussed above, chapter 3). Thus, emblem 1.5, with the tag 'Virtue is contrived by labour, glory by virtue', has a 25-line attack on 'Drabbs and Playes . . . sleeping, drinking, and Tobacco-fuming', before, in the concluding line he deigns to explicate the *impresa* (ibid.: 5). Wither deals uneasily with abstractions, and intends his book should have a direct relevance to his intended readership. It includes at the back a curious little gadget made out of printed cardboard, and consisting of two dials, each with a pointer, by which the user may by chance select an emblem – and a moral – to meet any urgent occasion. Spin one pointer to pick a book within the volume; spin the other to find the number of an emblem. The accompanying instructions piously observe that thus a choice may be made by lot without the use of dice, the sight of which could tempt the user into 'worse *Gaming*'.

Together, the emblem books of Quarles and Wither mark the greatest *English* achievements in the genre. They show the potency of the allegorical mode in early modern ways of thinking about and representing the world, and bridge the gap between high literary culture and popular piety.

Early Milton

John Milton's first collection of poetry, *The Poems of Mr John Milton, Both English and Latin*, was published by Humphrey Moseley (see below, chapter 5) in 1645 (see plate 7). It contained little written after 1639. Why he chose the mid-1640s to deliver it to the press remains the subject of speculation. It has been argued that its appearance after his prose pamphlets had won for him a radical notoriety may have been intended to correct hostile stereotyping that was certainly produced by his political enemies (Corns 1982). But its publication could also reflect the influence of Moseley on the development of a print culture for creative writing in verse. Some poems had already been printed.

Plate 7 John Milton, *Poems* (1645), portrait frontispiece and title page. Reproduced by permission of the British Library C.12.d.20.

Henry Lawes, who had composed the music for *A Masque Presented at Ludlow Castle* (also known as *Comus*), took responsibility for having it printed in 1637. His prefatory epistle suggests the text had circulated widely in manuscript: 'the often copying of it hath tired my pen to give my several friends satisfaction' (Milton 1997: 174). 'On Shakespeare' appeared in the front matter of the 1632 folio. Part of one of his comic poems on the university carrier appeared in a jest book of 1640. 'Lycidas' was the concluding poem of a commemorative volume for Edward King, composed by Cambridge contemporaries and published by the University Press, *Justa Edouardo King naufrago, ab Amicis moerentibus* (1638).

Milton's early verse is marked by its extraordinary diversity. Most obviously, it is written in an array of languages: English, Italian, Latin and Greek. It has, at its most recondite, a translation from Hebrew into Greek ('Psalm cxiv'). The 1645 volume, like the volume for

Edward King, is a double volume, separating the poems in classical languages from those in contemporary vernaculars. We considered above J. W. Binns's argument that neo-Latin literary culture in early modern Europe allowed its enthusiasts to be effectively independent of vernacular traditions (see above, chapter 1). That may need some qualification in the context of English poetry of the early Stuart period. Certainly in both these collections a relationship of complementarity and equality seems to exist between the two parts.

But there is diversity, too, of genre. Just among the English poems, we find elegies for the dead, two aristocratic entertainments, a pair of poems responding to each other and drawing on the character-writing tradition, comic verse in the form of spoof elegies, and three poems linked to the liturgical calendar, among others. Several of the best poems, among them 'Lycidas' and *A Masque*, are occasional pieces, written to celebrate or commemorate particular moments. Remarkable, too, is the range of poetic and cultural idiom. Humphrey Moseley, in his preface to the 1645 volume, identified Milton as a neo-Spenserian. Certainly, some of his poems have a Spenserian texture, drawn particularly from his pastoral verse. In 'L'Allegro' his descriptions of the English rural landscape fits within the tradition of Spenser and his later imitators; so, too, does the lists of flowers invoked to strew the hearse of Lydicas. The 'rathe primrose' even takes its epithet, a dialect word, from *The Shepheardes Calender* (l.142; Milton 1997: 253 and note). But other poems draw on different poetic movements. Critics often note that 'An Epitaph on the Marchioness of Winchester' approaches Ben Jonson's lapidary style. The three divine poems share some common ground with the incipient culture of Laudianism, which harboured an enthusiasm for commemorating the great events of the liturgical year. The dialogue set up between 'L'Allegro' and 'Il Penseroso' suggests the sort of games played among Caroline court poets (see above). The implied cultural milieus range from priestly devotionalism, through the witty playfulness of contemporary Cambridge, to service to the lofty gentility of an aristocratic household. William R. Parker (1968, 1996) and Barbara Lewalski (2000) offer detailed accounts of the years from Milton's matriculation at Cambridge to his emergence as an assailant of episcopacy in 1641. Both accounts trace his vacillations of the time: should he accept holy orders? Was he attempting and failing to launch an academic career? or to find a patron and perhaps an employer among the ranks of the aristocracy? The sorts of poetry he was writing suggest a similar kind of casting around, without fixed engagement.

Yet he produced some of the most extraordinary poetry of his age, excelling over an astonishing range: the finest aristocratic entertainment, better than Carew or Davenant wrote; the best funeral elegy, better even than Jonson (see above, chapter 2); and the finest poem commemorating a Christian festival, better even than Herbert (see above) or Donne (see above, chapter 2). In a sense, his 1645 collection presents a summation of English poetry in the first four decades of the Stuart age. Robert Cummings perceptively observes: 'The 1645 volume parades difficulty and excess of manner over a remarkable range of minor genres, as if its author's originality consisted in going over what had already been done. Familiarity has rendered charming what was once only nearly so' (Cummings 2000: 253). Milton, in a sense, is taking on those 'minor' genres as practised by eminent Stuart poets and extending their range in challenging ways that would have been more apparent to his early readers than to those whose principal encounter with those genres is through the Milton oeuvre. Milton's masque, for example, is certainly the masque modern readers are likeliest to read first (and perhaps the only masque most ever read).

'On the Morning of Christ's Nativity' probably surprises the modern reader for the wrong reasons. In celebrating the nativity, it engages primarily with the incarnation, and it anticipates the crucifixion. It looks back to the creation and anticipates Christ's second coming. But such connections are familiar in other nativity poems in the early modern period (Corns 2001b: 221). Moreover, as Diane McColley notes, 'The readings for the communion service on Christmas Day, Hebrews 1 and John 1, concern the identity, exaltation, and kingship of the Son as creating Word and Redeemer' (1997: 186). While the making of connections between these events is commonplace, Milton perhaps uniquely brings them all together in one poem. He does so with extraordinary elan. As H. Neville Davies has demonstrated (Davies 1975), the poem has a quite complex numerological structure, in effect with two central points (depending on whether the proem of four stanzas is included in the calculation). Between these two centres, at a symbolically doubly potent middle, fall the most remarkable stanzas of the whole work, stanzas XII–XIV. A declarative voice cries out to the crystal spheres which sounded at the creation of the world. That voice is Milton's own, crying out in his own age, and invoking the time the music of the spheres will again ring out, at the creation and at the second coming. The beginning and end of the world are brought forcefully together in the middle of his poem.

Two other motifs familiar from contemporary treatments are pushed a little further. The idea of the poem as gift was a common topos. Milton gives it a new vigour. His poem is not simply handed over. The poet does not join the queue behind the Magi and the shepherds presenting their more humble gifts. His muse is urged to barge her way through; to beat the others to the manger of the Christ-child: 'O run, prevent them with thy humble ode, / . . . / Have thou the honour first, thy Lord to greet' (ll.24, 26; Milton 1645: 105). The competitive edge is obvious. Again, it was widely believed that the oracles of the ancient world were silenced on the incarnation of the true and living God, whose disclosure finally discredited the deities of the pagan world. As I have noted elsewhere (Corns 2001b: 228–9), Milton develops the expulsion of the gods into a protracted ceremony of power based on spectacular punishment (stanzas XVIII–XXV). Nymphs are turned off from the locations they haunt like camp-followers and collaborators stripped and shorn in the rough justice of liberation. The zoomorphic deities of the Middle East are blinded, humbled and symbolically castrated. Christ's potency appears inexorable and irresistible, anticipating the depiction of the Son, mounted in the Father's chariot, which appears at the very centre of *Paradise Lost*. Of course, in the epic fallen angels assume the guise and names of pagan gods.

Thus, the Nativity Ode transcends the scope, vision and power of contemporary analogues. *The Masque* negotiates a curious relationship with the masque tradition. This is a provincial and aristocratic entertainment, performed at Ludlow for the celebration of the Earl of Bridgewater's installation as President of the Council of Wales and Lord Lieutenant of Wales and the marches. While the event originated in a royal decree, the masque is not courtly, and the king was not present. Our expectation is that it should be relatively modest, compared, for example, with the court masques of the 1630s, and no doubt staging was fairly unambitious, though the incidental music and song-settings were the work of Henry Lawes. Certainly, the aristocratic masquers are limited in number and the opportunities for formal choreography are limited. But Milton more than compensates for what is lacking in spectacle with his innovations in the dialogue, in which he adds elements from pastoral drama and, indeed, from the professional theatre.

The aristocratic or royal masquers in court masque are wholly silent, leaving the speaking and the singing to hired professionals, and concentrating on processing and dancing. In Milton's drama, the two brothers and the Lady, played by children of the earl, speak, and the Lady even sings. Moreover, the antimasque, led by Comus, interacts directly with the masquers in situations of some dramatic tension. The brothers keenly debate with each other. They take on an aggressive and heroic role, routing Comus's crew. But the dramatic centre of the work is the exchange between Comus and the Lady, a scene of failed seduction and physical threat that perhaps stimulates recollection of the analogous exchange in *Volpone* between Celia and Volpone himself, a scene interrupted by the sudden arrival of Bonario, her liberator, who bursts in much as the brothers do. The Lady's plight matches that of many Jacobean or Caroline dramatic heroines, abandoned, unprotected and the object of a plainly sexual threat. The dialogue has a richness of a kind rarely found in Carew and Davenant, in its felicity of phrasing and its imaginative power, showing a poet who has absorbed the achievements of Shakespeare:

> [Wherefore did Nature] set to work millions of spinning worms,
> That in their green shops weave the smooth-haired silk
> To deck her sons, and that no corner might
> Be vacant of her plenty, in her own loins
> She hutched the all-worshipped ore . . .
> (ll.714–18; Milton 1645: 217)

Detailed, vividly imagined, lexically brilliant, playful in its metaphoric transformation of the silk-worms: this is a different voice from that usually found in aristocratic and courtly entertainments.

The masque serves its obvious functions. It entertains, it compliments the earl through the compliment to the heroism of his sons and the bold chastity of his daughter, and it leads into some kind of dancing. But Milton gives it a larger perspective. It begins and ends with speeches from the Attendant Spirit, whose description of his mission, couched in Neoplatonic terms, invites a more allegorical interpretation of the action. He saves the Lady, but his mission is a more general one, to save all godly souls, who, though incapable of making their own way there, can do so aided by the intercession of some external agency.

'Lycidas' is the concluding poem of the *Justa*, where it appears without its headnote, which was added in the 1645 volume: 'In this monody the author bewails a learned friend, unfortunately drowned in his passage from Chester on the Irish Seas, 1637. And by occasion foretells the ruin of our corrupted clergy then in their height' (Milton 1645: 243). With the headnote, and with the recognition of Milton's anti-prelatical activities in the 1640s, the poem can be read unambiguously as an assault on the Laudian Church. It reflects creditably on Moseley's own tolerance that he allowed its inclusion. In 1638, the issues would have seemed less clear. Certainly there is a passage on ecclesiastical malpractice, albeit couched in heavily metaphorical language. But all points on the religious spectrum in the early modern period thought of themselves as engaged in a process of church reform. Laud believed he himself was a reformer, as in some ways he was. So, too, did the likes of John Cosin or even Richard Crashaw (see below, chapter 5). Moreover, the others who appear with Milton in the collaborative volume include several in holy orders or in academic posts from which they would, in the 1640s, be expelled. For example, Michael Honywood, a Fellow of Christ's College, Milton's own and Edward King's, may well have been a key figure in promoting the project. He spent the late 1640s and '50s in exile in Utrecht before returning to be Dean of Lincoln (*DNB* 2004). It seems inherently improbable that men looking to patrons among the Laudian ascendancy for preferment would welcome at the key point of their prestigious project an expression of opposition so explicit as to forfeit their good will.

The political component is a relatively small part of the whole. Certainly, there is a minatory millenarianism implied in the dread voice of St Peter, who warns that 'that two-handed engine at the door, / Stands ready to smite once, and smite no more' (ll.131–2; Milton 1645: 252). Yet quite what he is referring to has provoked endless critical speculation, which at the least points to a studied evasiveness. From the perspective of 1645 it may seem prophetic of the fall of the bishops; but in 1638 it probably seemed unclear.

The rest of the poem brings together topoi of lamentation and Christian consolation that figured in other poems in the collection. This is an old, rich tradition. Milton, however, gathers a surprising number of them together in one poem, and he organizes them in a logical and emotionally effective way. Thus, for example, the bewildered lament, 'What boots it with uncessant care / To tend the homely slighted shepherd's trade' (ll.64–5; ibid.: 247) is met by the Christian consolation that 'all-judging Jove' notes meritorious conduct and rewards it in heaven (ll.82–84; ibid.: 249). The poem drives on to the final consolation of the penultimate verse paragraph, which shows Lycidas resurrected to a heaven where 'the saints above . . . wipe the tears for ever from his eyes' (ll.178, 181; ibid.: 256). There is an obvious echo of the biblical phrase, 'God shall wipe away all tears from their eyes' (Revelation 7:17 and 21:4). Where first it occurs, it is the consolation extended to people who 'came out of great tribulation' (verse 14), as, I suppose, in the context of the *Justa*, Milton and his colleagues may be said to have done. Its second occurrence offers a broader promise, of a resurrection of the dead in which 'there shall be no more death, neither sorrow, nor crying' (verse 4). Milton's poem works to free his readers from the grief and bewilderment of King's undeserved and untimely death by leading them all, and his fellow-elegists, into the security of the longer, Christian perspective. The final paragraph offers a structural surprise: evidently we have not been listening to Milton in pastoral guise, but to an overheard 'uncouth swain', who twitches his 'mantle blue', a symbol of hope, before departing: 'Tomorrow to fresh woods, and pastures new' (ll.192–3; 1645: 256). These lines close both the poem and the volume, and they bring a sense of emotional closure to the *Justa* contributors; the swain becomes a representative of them all. The maimed ritual of mourning, frustrated because as many including Milton noted no body was found to be buried, is made complete.

Milton's early verse, in its diversity, demonstrates what could be achieved within the literary culture of Caroline England. But it pushes the conventions of that culture to an extreme. His major work of the Restoration (see below, chapter 6) marks a shift to and the triumph of a new cultural agenda.

5

From the Short Parliament to the Restoration: April 1640 to May 1660

Events and Consequences

The middle decades of the century witnessed extraordinary developments in English literary history. In terms of achievement, of works that figure prominently in the literary canon, however that may be defined or understood, the output is relatively modest. This is the age of Milton's prose, not his major poetry. Marvell's early poetry, though plainly much read and appreciated now, was mostly unpublished and unknown to a wider readership around the time of its composition. For obvious reasons, few new plays were written and the masque almost disappeared as a cultural form, although aristocratic entertainments were sometimes presented to the itinerant royal courts. Some of the most remarkable publications belong to the minor genres on the margins of what is traditionally regarded as literature, while the most rewarding examples of high literary culture, the volumes of poetry by Richard Lovelace, Abraham Cowley, Robert Herrick and Richard Crashaw, invite from the modern reader disadvantageous comparison with John Donne, Ben Jonson and George Herbert, their acknowledged precursors. Yet these are decades of abiding fascination for the literary historian. The structure of literary production and consumption changed more rapidly than at any other time in early modern England. In these decades, old patronage systems disintegrated and new emerged. The relative status of performance, manuscript circulation and print publication was radically – and irreversibly – realigned.

News media arrived at a sort of maturity. New genres, especially the many forms of pamphleteering, emerged with astonishing rapidity and frequency, others which had developed in a less troubled age were adapted to changed circumstances and imperatives, and creative writing found a fresh and much closer engagement with the domain of politics, redefining notions of what was possible or appropriate for the writer to attempt.

Such changes were in a complex relationship with contemporary conflicts and crises in the state. The concerns of the literary historian are much less with the origins of such discord than with its cultural consequences, but some engagement with the events, especially of high politics, is necessary to establish the larger ideological landscape, to understand the principal shifts in the circumstances of literary production, and to understand the issues that so frequently make up the subject matter of the writing we shall consider.

Charles I's resort to the military option to reduce the recalcitrance of his Scottish kingdom precipitated the end of the personal rule. This was 'the first occasion since 1323 when England had gone to war without a Parliament' (Russell 1995: 82). Had the campaign, known now as the First Bishops' War, gone well for the king, his favoured style of government could perhaps have been continued. But military failure and the need to pay for his English army and to buy off the Scottish force raised to oppose it led to the calling of the Short Parliament, the failure of which to grant the necessary supply which he desperately sought seemed to repeat the impasses of the parliaments of the 1620s, with his opponents deferring consideration of the fiscal issues till matters of governance and religion had been addressed. The Short Parliament soon showed the capacity of godly opponents of the king, led by John Pym, to organize the business of the lower house. It was dissolved after three weeks, though the renewed military initiative against the Scots, the Second Bishops' War, which ended in the minor military disaster of the battle of Newburn and the subsequent Scottish occupation of Newcastle, brought Charles back to parliamentary government: the Long Parliament opened in November 1640 with the king's position significantly weakened. As Conrad Russell sagely observes:

> To go to war in the face of a Parliament and half the Council is a decision which only success can justify, and success had not come. Such defeats demanded scapegoats.... Kings who lost quite so discreditably could

expect to have their power reduced, and Newburn...meant that the
King who lost it could never hope to recover all the power he had had
before. Kings who had proved themselves so incapable tended to be
hedged around with restrictions. (1995: 146)

Charles never really appreciated the extremity his boldness had led him
to, and the road to civil war was marked by stratagems to regain the
sort of control he had enjoyed during the personal rule, while a
parliament for the most part managed and controlled by his opponents
worked inexorably against his closest supporters. William Laud and
Thomas Wentworth, Earl of Strafford, his most important political
supporters, were impeached and the latter executed in May 1641.
An abortive coup, the so-called 'Army Plot', to free Strafford and
bring parliament to heel, was in part orchestrated by Sir John Suckling,
who fled to exile. When later in 1641 sections of the indigenous
Irish population rose against Scottish and English settlers, neither
king nor parliament had a practical response, though the accounts of
atrocities against fellow Protestants both outraged English opinion
and fed the growing mood of anti-Catholic sentiment. Charles gradually lost control of London. He withdrew to York, and eventually,
in August 1642, raised an army to displace parliament. Once more
he failed.

The fortunes of war determined the remaining events of the 1640s.
After the stalemate of Edgehill, the royalist army marched on London,
though turned back when confronted by the trained bands at Turnham Green; Milton has a curious sonnet on the event ('When the
assault was intended to the City'; Milton 1997: 288–9). Marston
Moor (1644) destroyed the king's northern army under William
Cavendish, Marquis (and later Duke) of Newcastle, quondam gentleman dramatist and poet and Ben Jonson's old patron. He left for exile,
during which he subsequently met and married Margaret, the future
Duchess of Newcastle. Naseby (1645), the decisive battle, left Charles
without a major army, while marking the emergence of the reformed
parliamentary force, the New Model Army, as ultimately the real power
in the land, under the command of Sir Thomas Fairfax, seconded by
Oliver Cromwell; both in turn were to be Marvell's patrons. Meanwhile, Edmund Waller, who had remained in a parliament largely
deserted by the king's supporters, apparently devised 'the Waller
Plot', a failed *coup d'état*, from which he was lucky to be released
into exile with his life.

Parliament fell into conflict with its army once the king was beaten. In late 1648, that army, now controlled by an officer corps dominated by Cromwell, marched on London and removed those members inimical to its designs in a bloodless coup ('Pride's Purge', so called after the colonel who effected the task). Charles I had surrendered to the Scottish forces in England, but he had been handed over to the English parliament. The army had taken him into its own custody, and parliament, once purged of those who would resist the project, brought him to trial and, in January 1649, to execution.

Thereafter, England was a republic (though Charles II had been immediately declared king by his supporters). Power nominally rested with the Rump Parliament, that is, the part of the Long Parliament still sitting, though this body was eventually dismissed in April 1653. From the end of that year, Cromwell, as 'Lord Protector', ruled as a sort of constitutional monarch, though the constitutional framework itself remained unsettled and there were few real checks on his power. David Scott memorably concludes: 'For sheer spectacle and violence there are few decades in British or Irish history to rival the 1640s' (2003: 311). The 1650s were quieter. Hostilities had broken out again in the late 1640s, and for a while Stuart hopes were invested in Irish and Scottish support for the crown. By 1649, Cromwell's expeditionary force had effectively crushed the former; the storming of Drogheda and Wexford (1649) and subsequent massacres proved pivotal, though the final settlement took a little longer. Through a remarkable series of battles, Preston (1648), Dunbar (1650) and Worcester (1651), he crushed Scottish opposition. Yet at his death in 1658 no real ordered constitution had been settled and the improbable stratagem of appointing his son Richard in succession soon foundered. Divisions within the New Model Army saw the emergence of George Monck, military commander in Scotland, as a rather enigmatic strong man, and his negotiations with the exiled Charles II ushered in the Restoration.

The war intensely and almost pervasively touched the English propertied classes. Parliament was constrained to raise revenue through a necessarily ruthless fiscal policy. John Morrill helpfully summarizes the burdens imposed:

> [T]he conflict . . . imposed unparalleled fiscal burdens and hardships. . . .
> There is no counting the cost of the civil war. The records are too patchy
> and ambiguous. But some sense of the scale can be offered. Kent was
> paying more in assessments every month by 1645–6 than it had paid in

any one year for ship money; the Weekly Assessment Ordinance of February 1643 was equivalent to a parliamentary subsidy every fortnight; the treasurer of the Eastern Association handled in 1644 a sum equivalent to the annual revenue of the Crown before the war.... The assessment was inexorable. It ground on, year in, year out. Arrears were never written off. (1976: 84–5)

Impositions were compounded through the practice of 'free quarter', the billeting of soldiers on private householders, an unpleasant and intrusive violation of property rights, and often made worse by the soldierly practice of stealing from one's host (ibid.: 86). Royalist activists faced further problems. Ideologically unacceptable academics, like Abraham Cowley and Richard Crashaw, were purged from the universities. Many priests, like Herrick, were ejected from their livings. Those who were in arms for the king faced exile, imprisonment, occasionally execution, massive fines, the confiscation of all their property or a combination of these penalties, like Waller, or Suckling, or William Davenant, or Richard Lovelace (Hardacre 1956). Moreover, the civil wars brought to England a taste of the horrors that had stalked central Europe since 1618. Besides actual casualties among those in arms, like William Lawes the composer, and the much admired Lord Falkland, a widely influential patron of scholars and writers once celebrated by Ben Jonson, there were inevitable griefs and anxieties about friends and families. Lovelace's younger brother died at the siege of Carmarthen. Henry Vaughan's brother was also killed in the wars. In 1643, Milton's father and his royalist brother were in Reading when it fell to parliament, while the king's army stood between him and his young bride (Parker 1996: II, 234). Though neutralism or an indifference to all sides may have characterized many Englishmen's perspective on the mid-century conflicts (Morrill 1976: 97–8), nearly all the writers we shall consider in this chapter were in those years committed and partisan, adding a deep engagement, a profound concern for the fate of one's own party, to the concerns and miseries felt more widely by their countrymen. Generally, they were to be found among the 'militant minorities [who] did believe that there were issues worth fighting for' (Morrill 1993: 8), even when they didn't actually do the fighting themselves.

Chapter 4 considered the characteristics of the Church of England under Archbishop Laud. The reaction to Laudian ceremonialism constituted a principal motivation among those who in 1640–2 and beyond opposed the king. In Morrill's influential formula, 'The

English civil war was not the first European revolution: it was the last of the Wars of Religion' (Morrill 1993: 68). But the nature of that conflict was more complex than most continental analogues. Certainly, a broad spectrum of godly opinion, to whom the term 'Puritan' may appropriately but rather unfashionably be applied, believed that at the very least Laud's innovations needed to be reversed. Within parliament and in the country more widely a very significant group advocated a more sweeping reform, no less than a second Reformation, which would refashion the Church of England on Presbyterian, rather than Episcopalian, lines, bringing it into approximate conformity with the Scottish Kirk and the model of the Genevan Church. Militant Presbyterianism was Janus-faced, offering a radical critique of prelacy while looking to reduce more radical groups to conformity with a reformed national church. Congregational independency offered an alternative model, and by 1643 its advocates were defending a church government that allowed considerable diversity of doctrine and discipline between congregations (see, for example, Goodwin et al. 1643)). Such diversity, on the Presbyterian account, provided the necessary conditions for the development of radical sects holding heterodox and indeed heretical beliefs. In the mid-1640s, controlling these groups became an obsession of the Presbyterian opinion that prevailed within the unpurged Long Parliament, though the objective proved unrealisable. Thus, increasingly, radical groups prospered. Baptists, themselves suspect, developed a kind of radical Arminian wing, the General Baptists, who argued that salvation stood open to all. Antinomianism, the rather sensational and potentially subversive notion that those who have the spirit of God within them are unbounded by the Ten Commandments, animated several sects, most interestingly that rather shadowy grouping the Ranters, though it is present, too, in early Quakerism. Radical religion was intertwined with radical politics. Gerrard Winstanley's Digger movement was founded on a singularly bold interpretation of millenarianism. The most significant development in the political realm originated in the radicalization of some elements of the New Model Army, in association with primarily metropolitan confrères, particularly among apprentices and petty masters. These, the Levellers were, in H. N. Brailsford's telling phrase, 'the first Englishmen to conceive the idea of a political party as a secular organisation, whose affairs were managed on a democratic model . . . the first party in the modern world to call for a secular republic' (1983: 550). Their conflict with the emerging Cromwellian ascendancy at once allowed the latter to seem a bulwark against anarchy and produced controversial writing of an abiding fascination. The political and religious landscape of the 1630s had been much simpler.

The events shaped both the circumstances of literary production and its subject matter. The king's preoccupations rendered inappropriate and impractical the seasonal culture of the royal court. Neither he nor Henrietta Maria danced masques after 1640. Pressing affairs took him far from the royal palaces of the Thames valley, once more into the field against the Scots, into Scotland itself for a relatively long sojourn in Edinburgh, and, as relations with the Long Parliament deteriorated, to York and eventually to Oxford, which became in effect his seat of government through the first civil war. The larger cultural framework, that astonishing association of architecture, painting, stage design, music and the literary arts, substantially fell apart. Carew died of natural causes in 1640 or thereabouts, Van Dyck in 1641, Suckling, perhaps by his own hand, in 1641 or 1642, William Lawes by a sniper's shot in 1645. But more telling than individual deaths was the systemic disruption occasioned by geographical displacement and dispersal. The court culture of the 1630s had at its core the royal pair surrounded by a coterie of aristocratic families, some of whom sided with parliament or sought a kind of safe neutrality; men who had danced masques with the king took up arms against him. The royal court reached a low point of depletion in its early days in York, where Charles's entourage was reduced to '39 gentlemen and 17 guards' (Russell 1995: 495). In the custody of the New Model Army his household was reduced to a mere handful. A literary culture of performance and the coterie circulation of manuscripts among tight groups of friends and associates could not survive this sort of disturbance. Certainly, in a fragmentary fashion royalist coteries did re-form. While Oxford held the royal court, it held, too, a significant group of royalist writers, reinforced by scholars fleeing from Cambridge before or shortly after it fell into parliamentary hands and felt the force of an academic purge: Oxford's turn came later. Smaller groupings emerged, sometimes perhaps little more than discrete acts of patronage. Thus, Herrick and Mildmay Fane may have made up a coterie, as did Richard Lovelace and Charles Cotton, though perhaps in each case just a coterie of two. However, in the eclipse of the royal cause, a more extensive though less closely integrated network developed around Henry Lawes, who had stabilized his fortunes as a teacher of music and an early promoter of musical concerts of a more or less public nature (Philips 1990: 5–6). Though the manuscript circulation of creative writing does not disappear, certainly the circumstances favoured a movement towards a print culture. So, too, did the closure of the theatres in 1642 (see 'Mid-Century Drama', below).

Throughout the early part of the seventeenth century the demand for both plays and poetry in print exceeded supply. In the case of the former, plays were almost always the intellectual property of acting companies, and releasing them to the press while they still had a life and value within their repertoires made poor business sense. Once the companies had in effect been put out of business, the case was altered. Again, a court poet, writing within a secure context of patronage and esteem, had little reason to share with a larger public his poems of compliment addressed to the sources of advancement within that circle. The courtly diaspora of the early 1640s further shifted the balance in favour of publication. Posthumous publication of poetry had long been a convention, as in the case of Donne and Herbert. We have noted already the political reson-ance given to the posthumous appearance of the works of Carew and Suckling (see above, chapter 4). Lifetime publication became more customary. Most of the more significant poets writing in the 1640s and 1650s appeared in printed volumes of their collected verse during that period: Katherine Philips and Andrew Marvell, probably for very different motives, were the major exceptions.

The pressure of demand and the freeing up, however expensively in terms of a larger cultural audit, of supply would, by themselves, have produced a shift in the production and distribution of literature towards the medium of print. But one bookseller, Humphrey Moseley, stood out as both the beneficiary and finest exponent of the changed circum-stances of literary production (see Reed 1927–30, on which this ac-count largely depends). Moseley acquired the rights to many of the plays of the early Stuart period, sometimes from the acting companies, sometimes from other stationers who had already published them, among them works by Davenant, Beaumont and Fletcher, Jonson, Massinger, Middleton, Shirley and Webster. His poetry list was as impressive. As a poem 'To the Stationer', prefixed to his 1651 edition of William Cartwright, observes, it included 'melting CAREW... WALLER'S Muse... DAVENANT... *Pastor Fido* (cloath'd by FAN-SHAW's Pen)... hopefull STANLEY... learned CRASHAW... rare CARTWRIGHT... CLEVELAND, all his gallant lines... [and] COW-LEY' (ibid.: 65–6): the poet seemed to run out of epithets by the end.

A notable omission was Milton, whose first collection of verse Moseley had published in 1645. Moseley's own ideological orientation was royalist, evidenced both by occasional comments in his prefatory material, in the predominance of royalists in his list, and in the evident patronage he extended to James Howell, a loyal supporter of the king and in the 1640s a long-term prisoner in the Fleet, whose works he assiduously published. By 1651 the author of *Eikonoklastes* could scarcely have found favour with an aficionado of the verse of Cleveland and Cartwright. Moseley was at the cutting edge of English publishing. He often asserts that he has sought out true copy, and generally seems to have done so. Currently, there is some movement in editing early modern texts away from early printed versions towards manuscript sources. Moseley, though, did much to establish the primary texts of very many early modern authors for generations of readers, and, as Nigel Smith perceptively notes, by establishing the canons of pre-war dramatists, he had 'a profound impact upon the development of the drama and drama criticism, once the theatres were again opened after the Restoration' (2002: 718). He was expert not only in securing copy but also in marketing his publications. Numerous printed issues of his backlists are extant, usually bound in with his own publications. Yet they give us some indication of the relative enthusiasm for some high literature at that time: Milton's *Poems*, published probably in a print run of no more than a thousand and quite possibly considerably less than that, had not sold out in the mid-1650s. Even in print, this was substantially an elite culture.

Alongside the genres of that high culture occurred a rapid overall expansion in the output of the press, though quantification remains problematic, estimates do vary, and the reasons for that growth remain controversial. Steven Zwicker, following the work of Maureen Bell and John Barnard (1992, 1998), summarizes the statistics thus:

> If we track London imprints through the 1620s, the approximate number of individual titles for any given year stays well below 500; 1630 itself is marked by over 500 imprints, and through the 1630s these numbers remain above 400. Then in 1640 the number reaches 800; in 1641 there are over 2,500 imprints, and in 1642 the number reaches 4,000. From that high, the numbers begin to drop: 2,000 in 1643, 1,300 in 1644, down to a low for the decade of 900 in 1645 and then above 1,000 for each year through the rest of the decade. (2002: 189)

In a command economy in times of crisis, such as the Soviet Union in manufacturing tanks in 1941–2, or in very new technologies, such as some aspects of electronic engineering in our own time, a threefold increase, followed the next year by a twofold increase, is easily explicable. In this case, however, the technology was mature and was delivered, for the most part, by under-capitalized petty masters controlling small workshops or retail outlets in a fairly competitive environment. So how may the figures be explained? Quite probably, the total output of print did not expand at the same rate as the total number of separate titles; that is, publications may well have become, on average, shorter. Some genres tend to be shorter than others, and the kinds of news-related or controversial genres are among the shorter and are much in evidence in 1640–2 (see Corns 1986). In particular, 1642 was a news-hungry year, with much to report. But in the late 1630s there was certainly some surplus capacity, in the form of a pool of unemployed journeymen-printers, who had been recognized in the Star Chamber Decree of 1637 as the likeliest agencies for 'secret printing in corners' (clauses 20 and 21; the decree and the 1643 Licensing Order are helpfully reprinted in Milton 1953–82: II, 793–9). Moreover, in an industry which is labour-intensive, output can often be increased simply by working longer. Politically diverse contemporary accounts remarked on the heightened levels of press activity. The preface to the 1643 Licensing Order speaks specifically of those who have set up 'sundry private Printing Presses . . . to print, vend, publish and disperse Books, pamphlets and papers in such multitudes, that no industry could be sufficient to discover, to bring to punishment, all the severall abounding delinquents' (ibid.: II, 797).

The final years of the personal rule saw a sustained attempt to tighten up press control, principally through the agency of the Star Chamber court, and on its abolition in July 1641 the press was left 'virtually without legal regulation' (ibid.: II, 160). Scholarly opinion varies widely on how significant this interruption in censorship was for the sudden increase in the number of titles printed. There had been and there continued to be other legal frameworks under which authors and their publishers could be controlled, often offering sharper sentencing options than either the Star Chamber decree or the parliamentary orders that superseded it. The effect of legislative measures depended on enforcement and compliance, and the developing crises of 1640–2 greatly militated against their success. Indeed, between the abolition of the Star Chamber and the new licensing order, Long Parliament had tinkered with a number of other stopgap measures, and, legally if not in effect, press controls had remained in place (ibid.: II, 160–1). D. F. McKenzie, disputing the 'undue emphasis on censorship as a constraint on printing before the abolition of the Court of Star Chamber... and an equally misplaced celebration of the trade's new-found but short-lived freeedom from licensing', may well be right in his conclusion that 'fear of the courts' played little part in the changes in production between the 1630s and the very early 1640s (McKenzie 2002). Most certainly, such constraint played little part in the publication of the higher literary genres, irrespective of their ideological orientation, over the mid-century decades. Yet successive governments all subscribed to the view that the press could be controlled through licensing. Hence, not only the order of 1643, but further orders in 1647, 1648, 1649, 1653 and 1655. These enjoyed rather mixed success. Only supporters of the 1643 measure seem to have observed its precise requirements; the people it aimed to control openly flouted it (Corns 1986). The news press was sometimes temporarily reined in, as, for example, in 1649 (Nelson and Seccombe 2002: 541), and the Cromwellian control of the press worked quite ruthlessly. But different genres received different treatment. Though there is evidence that Richard Lovelace's first *Lucasta* was held up in the press, John Cleveland's works went through multiple editions.

Royalist Poetry

A singularly rich and surprisingly diverse corpus of verse was produced by writers loyal to the king in the mid-century decades. A singularly rich critical response has latterly developed. (See especially Miner 1971; Anselment 1988; Potter 1989; Loxley 1997; Wilcher 2001; there are shrewd discussions also in Hammond 1990 and Smith 1994.) The poets held in common a perspective on the events which shaped the royalist destiny over that period. For them, the personal rule was a lost paradise of peace and culture; the Long Parliament was a nest of rebellious sectaries, and Presbyterians were scarcely to be distinguished from the wilder heretics whose success was premised on the destruction of the episcopal government of the Church of England; the trial and execution of Strafford was a martyrdom and the betrayal of a heroic and deserted figure by men who should have shared his resolution; the first civil war was a rebellion and an act of treason; the military disasters of the mid-1640s were a tragedy inexplicable in terms of a divine providence, producing a terrible waste both of life and property; the death of the king was murder, treason and a deeply perplexing event; and the second civil war, at least till the battle of Worcester, a time of anxious hope. After 1653, as the Rump was displaced by the Protectorate and Cromwell emerged as a stabilizing figure safeguarding the realm against extremists, that royalist consensus fragmented.

Several themes recurred. There was a nostalgic invocation of life before the war. The failure of providence was met with bewilderment. The metaphorical death of Caroline England and the literal death of the king were treated with the familiar emotions of mourning: denial, anger, grief and an eventual resignation. Coping strategies included celebrations of libertine eroticism and political intransigence and a revaluation of the contemplative life, of retreat and retirement, and of friendship. Few poets manifested all of these concerns, but most engaged with several.

Some of these issues are more complex in their construction than others and require further comment. The evocation of nostalgia for the old regime is shaped by the multiple timescales of composition, early response and interpretation and eventual publication and, with it, wider circulation and appreciation. The collected poems of Suckling and Carew, reprinted through the 1640s and 1650s, reflected the court society about which and for which they were written, though in a context in which the court was dispersed and the king was displaced or, by the time of later editions, dead. Herrick's *Noble Numbers*, the shorter collection of religious verse that makes up a double volume with his *Hesperides*, thus presented in print 'To God: an Anthem, sung in the Chappell at White-Hall, before the King', 'A Christmas Caroll, sung to the King in the Presence [that is, the royal presence chamber] at Whitehall', and 'The New-yeeres Gift, or Circumcision Song, sung to the King in the Presence at White-hall' (1 January is the Feast of the Circumcision). For those hearing them performed in the 1630s, they would have seemed, straightforwardly, elegant components of sacred song delivered no doubt by members of the finest ensemble in England. In the 1640s, the music was silenced, and the printed record of 1648 memorialized a lost culture and a displaced value system.

Laudian ceremonialism had especially encouraged celebration of the major feasts of the liturgical year, an emphasis reflected by Anglican poets of the seventeenth century (Lake 1993:175; Corns 2001b: 215–17). Herrick, in publishing his poems, reasserted those priorities in the context of their political eclipse: Laud had been executed in 1645, episcopalian government was no longer functional and its ministers had been expelled, among them Herrick himself, driven from his Devonshire living in 1647. Moreover, the celebration of the special days of the liturgical year had been explicitly banned under the parliamentary ordinance of June 1647 'for Abolishing of Festivals', under which had been forbidden 'the Feasts of the Nativity of Christ, Easter and Whitsuntide, and other Festivals commonly called Holy-Dayes ...heretofore superstitiously used and observ'd' (Firth and Rait 1911: I, 580; Corns 1992: 104–7). Indeed, in 1647 itself, there were widespread disturbances as local communities resisted the intended ban. In Canterbury, 3,000 militia were needed to restore order (Gardiner 1889: III, 281–2; Underdown 1985: 260–1). Herrick has also about a dozen poems, charming evocations of the traditional rites of Christmas as observed in rural England, which again, by 1648, were describing time-honoured practices under immediate threat, though the composition, which seems premised on the poet speaking to members of his own rural household, may well have been much earlier: 'Come, bring with a noise, / My merrie merrie boyes, / The Christmas Log to the firing' ('Ceremonies for Christmas', ll.1–3; Herrick 1956: 263).

Nostalgia can be a posture of defiance and well as mourning. As Herrick puts it:

> But if that golden Age wo'd come again,
> And *Charles* here Rule, as he before did Raign;
> If smooth and unperplext the Seasons were,
> As when the *Sweet Maria* lived here:
> I sho'd delight to have my Curles halfe drown'd
> In *Tyrian Dewes*, and Head with Roses crown'd.
> ('The bad season makes the Poet sad', ll.8–11; ibid.: 214)

He writes, of course, before the regicide. Sometimes, re-reading a poem in changed circumstances must have produced a simpler sort of poignancy, even when the time-lag is relatively short. Herrick, for example, has occasional poems welcoming positive developments in the civil wars, such as the king's capture of Leicester in May 1645, a fortnight before the disaster of Naseby: 'This Day is Yours *Great*

CHARLES! and in this War / Your Fate, and Ours, alike Victorious are./ . . . / Fortune is now Your Captive . . . ' ('TO THE KING, Upon his taking of *Leicester*, ll.1–2, 5; ibid.: 271). I am uncertain how such a poem would have been read in 1648, on publication, let alone in 1649. Perhaps a curious honesty, an impulse to recognize how aspiration and reality had differed, prompted Herrick to retain it in the collection. Royalism, in its eclipse, was sometimes a deeply conflicted ideology.

English love poetry since Donne had developed the significant libertine component already present in the epyllia of Marlowe and Shakespeare. Donne's elegies, considered in chapter 2, demonstrated how high art could assimilate the sometimes witty depiction of human sexuality, and his influence was discernible in the chaste (but deeply eroticized) world of Charles and Henrietta Maria. Thus, Carew's reverie, 'A Rapture', mock-heroically described in some detail the docking of 'my tall Pine' in 'Loves channell', where it may 'unlade her fraight' (ll.85–90; Carew 1964: 51). The libertine component appeared more strongly in Suckling, who depicted a society not only of romantic transactions between equals but more mercenary relationships between demi-mondaines and gallants: 'I offered Forty crowns / To lie with her a night or so' ('Proferred Love Rejected', ll.2–3; Suckling 1971a: 54–5). In the 1640s, this element became both politicized and integrated in the production of an image of the cavalier that engaged with the hostile stereotyping of the parliamentarian press.

A powerful body of opinion within the broad spectrum of English Puritanism had for long advocated a draconian strengthening of the legislative measures available against extra-marital sexuality. Indeed, as if to demonstrate its puritanical bona fides to those solid Presbyterians and the like who may have felt unrepresented since Pride's Purge, the Rump Parliament included among its earliest legislation an ordinance, which 'epitomized the triumph of Puritanism in England', providing for execution for adultery and three months in gaol for fornication (though, in the event, penalties of such severity were rarely exacted) (Thomas 1978: 257–82; Corns 1992: 75–6). Royalist poetry abounds in depictions of illicit liaisons, seductions, deflorations, fetishism, the depiction of sexual acts and occasionally auto-eroticism. Lovelace followed closely on Suckling's model in poems like 'La Bella Bona Roba': 'I cannot tell who loves the Skeleton / Of a poor Marmoset, nought but boan, boan [that is, bone]. / Give me a nakednesse with her cloath's on' (Lovelace 1930: 96), or again, in 'The faire Begger', where in the context of offering charity for sexual favours the poet-lover with mannered indecency proposes:

> Thou shalt be cloath'd above all prise,
>   If thou wilt promise me imbrac't;
> Wee'l ransack neither Chest nor Shelfe,
> I'll cover thee with mine owne selfe.
>   (Lovelace 1930: 99)

'Her Muffe' has him anticipating an intrusive gaze at his mistress's genitalia: 'But I . . . still contemplate must the hidden Muffe' (ibid.: 129; for a discussion, see Hammond 1985: 228–9 and Corns 1992: 248). Lovelace's sometime patron, Charles Cotton the younger, represented himself as drawn to a woman cross-dressed as a man, perceptively concluding, since he was aroused by the figure and since he loathed 'the foul *Italian* sin' of homosexuality, it must have been a woman's, with 'a pair of thighs, / 'Twixt whose Iv'ry Columns is / Th'Ebon folding door to bliss' ('Amoret *in Masquerade*', ll.49–51; Cotton 1958: 213). 'Ebon', that is, ebony, may seem a curious word, though it was sometimes used erroneously for ivory (*OED*, s.v. 'Ebon' 4). Herrick recurrently represented himself as peering at bits of female anatomy and describing them with precision. Thus, Julia's leg is 'as white and hair-less as an egge' ('Her Legs', l.2; Herrick 1956: 139); Anthea's 'Hands, and thighs, and legs, are all / Richly Aromaticall' ('Love perfumes all parts', ll.5–6; ibid.: 59); Dianeme's *mons Veneris* is 'that Hill (where smiling Love doth sit) / Having a living Fountain under it' ('To Dianeme', ll.3–4; ibid.: 154); and each of Julia's nipples presents itself like 'A Strawberry shewes halfe drown'd in Creame' ('Upon the Nipples of Julia's Breast', l.6; ibid.: 164).

Such ludic (and, let it be said, intermittently puerile) verse displayed an indifference to the victories of Puritanism and the legislation that followed them, declaring that royalists unrelentingly, unashamedly and irredeemably remained committed to the pursuit and celebration of carnality. It showed, too, a disdainful indifference to the hostile stereotyping of the parliamentarian press, which, since very early in the 1640s had represented 'cavaliers' as pox-ridden rakehells and rapists, much handicapped by 'the French troubled stradling of the legges', and insatiable even after 20 whores (Corns 1992: 3–5, drawing on parliamentary pamphlets of the early 1640s).

But erotic poetry carried another component of royalist ideology. The Caroline court had, in its depiction of the royal pair, its own love story. In the 1640s, royalist poets often, in a spirit of nostalgia, remark upon the separation of Charles and Henrietta Maria, as in Herrick's 'The bad season', discussed above, or Tom Weaver's more militant aspiration, 'May *Charles* and she [Henrietta Maria] meet, / And tread under feet / Both Anabaptist and Independent' (1654: 12). The topoi of separation had been brilliantly explored by Donne, but they return in a military variant; when the cavalier leaves his mistress, he does so pressed by the exigencies of war, loyalty and honour. Weaver, whose verse often reads like a rough draft of Lovelace's, has 'A Dialogue Betwixt a Cavalier and a Lady, Upon Occasion of a sudden Alarm in the night', in which the former is called from bed by a trumpet call just on the point of deflowering his mistress. She urges him, 'dispatch my pain, / Leave not a Maiden-head half slain', but he defers consummation: 'Great Honour, bids me use my might, / For Reputation first, and then delight' (ibid.: 54–5). Lovelace gave definitive expression to the politicizing of erotic separation in 'To Lucasta, Going to the Warres': 'I could not love thee (deare) so much, / Lov'd I not Honour more' (Lovelace 1930: 18). Stoic resolution in the face of adversity added a further theme, and the topos of imprisonment allowed its purest statement, that one is freer in prison and still committed to the king's cause than at liberty and collaborating with the enemy. Weaver put it simply: 'I am no captive, I, I find, / My soul still free and unconfin'd' (Weaver 1654: 6). Again, definitively, Lovelace eroticized the topos:

> When Love with unconfined wings
>   Hovers within my Gates;
> And my divine *Althea* brings
>   To whisper at the Grates:
> When I lye tangled in her haire,
>   And fettered to her eye;
> The *Gods* that wanton in the Aire,
>   Know no such Liberty.
>   . . .
> Stone Walls doe not a Prison make,
>   Nor I'ron bars a Cage;
> Mindes innocent and quiet take
>   That for an Hermitage;

> If I have freedome in my Love,
>   And in my soule am free;
> Angels alone that sore above,
>   Injoy such Liberty.
>   (Lovelace 1930: 78–9)

Conditions for confinement of aristocratic and higher-gentry cavaliers compared favourably with those experienced by some parliamentarians in royalist hands.

Captured royalists were obliged to promise, as part of the terms of release, not to bear arms against parliament. Those who did so, in the second civil war, sometimes received exemplary punishment. There were numerous ill-conceived conspiracies, though after the battle of Worcester military opposition to the Cromwellian ascendancy was little more than a defiant gesture (Underdown 1960). That powerlessness set the context for another complex theme of royalist poetry: retirement. The opposition between the contemplative and the active life is ancient, and while the advantages of both had been rehearsed, the former plainly lacks the possibilities for civic virtue of the latter. Horace, after all, carefully opposed the joys of his Sabine farm with a depiction of the responsibilities and sacrifices demanded of a citizen of Augustan Rome. As James Loxley succinctly puts it: 'The classical and Renaissance constructions of retirement or *otium*, which provided the imagined space for all such cavalier engagements, were not as uniformly celebratory as has sometimes been assumed' (1997: 202). Yet in purely practical terms, retirement to a country estate must have seemed bliss compared with incarceration (even with visits from Althea) or the hardships of exile, the sudden poverty, the poor food, the damp and verminous beds, the bone-jarring journeys detailed in the autobiography of Ann, Lady Fanshawe, the wife of Sir Richard (Loftis 1979: 101–92). Moreover, changing sides was an easy option, and especially after 1649 when republican governments sought to minimize opposition through a process of incorporation. Lady Fanshawe recorded that, even after her husband had been captured in arms for the new king at the battle of Worcester, 'Generall Cromwell...would have bought him off to his servise upon any termes' (ibid.: 135). As we shall see, ideological reconciliation to the new order proved increasingly easy and frequent after the protectorate was established. Simply declining to come over constituted an oppositional act. Lady Halkett, a diehard and active royalist, noted a pertinent anecdote from Scotland in the aftermath of the battle of Dunbar, about her first encounter with her future husband:

> I wentt…to aske one of my Lord D[unfermline]'s servantts what gentlemen that was with his lord, who told mee itt was Sir James Halkett. I said, 'If hee had nott come with your Lord, I would nott have beene so civill as I am to him, because hee hath a sword aboutt him'; for all the nobility and gentry had that marke of slavery upon them that none had liberty to weare a sword, only such as served there interest and disowned the King, which made mee hate to see a Scotch man with a sword.   (Ibid.: 65)

In the event, Halkett was carrying only a stick 'that stucke outt like a sword, for hee was too honest a gentleman to weare one now', and the writer in due course married him. The symbolism, however, is deeply suggestive: pacifism betokens political purity, a refusal to change sides. The text that ends Izaak Walton's *Compleat Angler*, '*Study to be quiet*, I Thes. 4.11.', is explicitly linked to the retention of virtue by those who 'dare trust in [God's] *providence*, and be *quiet*, and go a *Angling*' (Walton 1983: 371; the text was added to the second edition of 1655). A cluster of recurrent concerns marked the royalist tradition during the eclipse of the Stuart monarchy: country living; a shared cultural life founded on a sometimes bibulous hospitality and the appreciation of poetry, as depicted paradigmatically in Herrick's 'To live merrily, and to trust to Good Verses' (1956: 80–1); and a revaluation upwards of friendship and personal loyalty as more formal systems of dependency and patronage collapsed.

Yet despite having so much in common in terms of ideology and symbolic structures, royalist poets manifested a considerable diversity of emphasis and technique. Nearly all Robert Herrick's extant verse was published, probably early in 1648 (Corns 1992: 307–8), in the double volume *Hesperides: or, The Works both Humane & Divine of Robert Herrick Esq.*, in which the first part, a collection of 1,130 almost entirely secular poems, are followed by the second, 273 divine poems, which has its own title page, *His Noble Numbers, or, His Pious Pieces*. John Williams and Francis Eglesfield, not Humphrey Moseley, were the booksellers. Neither was particularly energetic, seemingly registering no other titles in 1647 and 1648, but their shop sign, 'the Crown and Marygold' (the latter a familiar emblem of Henrietta Maria: see Corns 1998: 64), like the large printer's ornament of a royal crown on the title page, suggest their royalist affiliation. The collection is a huge retrospective, with poems that are datable stretching from the 1610s down to August 1647. Yet Herrick evidently excluded quite a few items since a number of poems extant in song settings are missing (Schleiner 1976: 77–8), and the volume we have has been shaped to reflect, in a balanced way, current anxieties and the recollection of happier times, the merits of resistance in arms and perseverance in retirement, and secular joys and values and the consolations of divine meditation. The cultural triumphs of the Caroline court in the personal rule figure at least as prominently as the disasters of the mid-1640s, with some suggestion that what has been may return again:

What though the Heaven be lowering now,
And look with a contracted brow?
We shall discover, by and by,
A Repurgation of the Skie:
And when those clouds away are driven,
Then will appeare a cheerfull Heaven.
('Hope well and Have well: or, Faire after Foule weather'; Herrick 1956: 188)

Technically, Herrick owed much to Carew and Jonson, the former for his lyricism, his tractability to musical setting, the latter for a hard-edged neoclassicism in imitation, particularly, of Martial, though he drew too on the topoi of Donne's love poetry. Hence his range stretches from what is now perhaps the best-known song of the early seventeenth century, 'Gather ye Rose-buds while ye may / Old Time is still a flying' ('To the Virgins, to make much of Time'; ibid.: 85; set by William Lawes), to spiky and risqué epigrams like:

> Scobble for Whoredome whips his wife; and cryes,
> He'll slit her nose; But blubb'ring, she replyes,
> Good Sir, make no more cuts i'th'outward skin,
> One slit's enough to let Adultry in.
>   ('Upon Scobble. Epig.'; ibid.: 44)

His comic epigrams are populated by proletarians and the middling sort, served up with a gentlemanly disdain, or else kept firmly in their place.

'The Hock-cart, or Harvest home: To the Right Honourable, Mild-may, Earle of Westmorland' qualitatively stands alongside Jonson's 'To

Penshurst' (see chapter 2), Carew's 'To Saxham' (see chapter 4), and Marvell's 'Upon Appleton House' (see below), as one of the finest country-house poems of the early modern period. It is distinguished, too, by the way it pulls together so many themes of royalist writing. Mildmay Fane, to whom we turn shortly, had been imprisoned in 1643, but retired thereafter to his estates, and may well have supported Herrick after his ejection. The poem commemorates a country custom, decorating the last cart to be filled at harvest, followed by a feast laid on by the landowner. As such, like several other poems by Herrick, it fixes in a literary context a country tradition under active and immediate threat from parliamentary legislation and Puritan magistracy, the '*May-poles,... Wassails, Wakes*' announced among his themes at the beginning of *Hesperides* ('The Argument of his Book', l.3; Herrick 1956: 5). The poem is located in a world untouched by the war and by the urgent questioning of traditional social relationships that followed it: 'Come Sons of Summer, by whose toile, / *We* are the Lords of Wine and Oile' (ll.1–2; Herrick 1956: 101; my italics). For the agricultural labourers in their ragged breeches (l.25) there is the prospect only of 'stout Beere' and renewed hard work (ll.37, 54–5). The poet – perhaps it's a priestly role– stands between landlord and workers, urging the latter to a proper appreciation of their relative roles: 'Feed him ye must, whose food fils you' (l.52).

Fane functions both as lord and friend and his estate represents a place that stands outside the exigencies of the bad season. Fane himself wrote a number of poems on adjacent themes, including his own celebration of harvest home, 'My Hock-Cart or Reaping Day' (Fowler 1994: 224–5). Fane, in general, seems to have entered a kindlier perspective on his peasantry, praising 'the brown lusty lass' that reaps his corn (l.29) and 'the wholesome maid... this bonny lass', who, singing, milks his cows ('My Happy Life'; ibid.: 211). Certainly, retirement is celebrated by Fane as, literally, a liberation; it is the 'Great patron of my liberty', freeing him from prison and from the 'fears, or noise of war' ('To Retiredness', ll.4, 61; ibid.: 216). But, again more generously than Herrick, he tried to use the celebration of rural friendship as a platform for horizontal social integration with potentially alienated former friends, as in his country-house poems 'Thorp Palace: a Miracle', on the country seat of Oliver St John, a leading parliamentarian close to Cromwell, and 'To Sir John Wentworth, upon His Curiosities and Courteous Entertainment at Summerly in Lovingland', the home of another supporter of parliament, whose friendship to Fane is expressed in 'such humanity, and press / Of crowded favours, and heaped courtesies' (ibid.: 220–2, 227–32). Fane's later verse remained – as it remained until very recently (Fane 2001) – in manuscript only, though the somewhat enforced retirement of the 1640s saw the publication in 1648 of what would seem to have been a privately published collection, *Otia Sacra*, the sacred fruits of leisure. Nigel Smith argues that 'Fane published his poems of retreat and devotion...but his political poetry was reserved for a private manuscript' (Smith 1994: 279). But at least some of that unpublished verse was an irenic celebration of the bonds of kinship and an attempt to revive the spirit of country society.

Richard Lovelace's poems appeared in two volumes, *Lucasta* (1649) and *Lucasta: Posthume Poems* (1659), neither published by Moseley. The immediate context for the former was the outbreak of the second civil war, which included at an early stage a significant insurrection in his home county of Kent in May and June 1648. He himself was a high-profile Kentish royalist, and had been imprisoned in 1642; from June 1648 to April 1649 he was again detained, which may have delayed publication; the volume had been licensed in February 1648 (Wilcher 2001: 308). Certainly, the collection has an unmistakably martial air. Many of the commendatory poems affixed to it are by soldiers, and Lovelace, who was addressed in them as 'Colonel', referred frequently and without much regret to a life in arms. (He probably did not serve in the English civil wars, though he certainly fought as an expatriate in continental Europe, where he was wounded in 1646 at the siege of Dunkirk; his non-combat role in England could have originated in the terms of his release in 1642; see Wilcher 2001: 308 and Corns 1993b: 213–14; he did take part in the Bishops' Wars.) There are paradigmatic celebrations of going to the wars and of incarceration in the king's cause, considered above, and even the imagery has a martial and chivalric patina, projecting his carefully constructed self-image as diehard cavalier. Yet these poems of resistance are often premised on an awareness of past failure and of the stratagems necessary to resist such reverses. 'The Grasse-hopper, to my Noble Friend, Mr. Charles Cotton' (it is uncertain whether the poet is addressed or his father) contrasts the vulnerability of the grasshopper to changes in the seasons with their own ability to ride out 'this cold Time and frosen Fate' at a warm fireside with friends and some good literature. It ends in a recurrent sentiment of royalist Stoicism: 'he / That wants himselfe, is poore indeed' (Lovelace 1930: 38–40); compare, for example, Fane's 'he who doth himself possess / Makes all things pass him seem far less' ('To Retiredness', ll.9–10; Fowler 1994: 216).

Yet Lovelace's first volume shows a feature that will be stronger still in his second, a sense of bewilderment and an associated tendency towards self-contradiction as he rehearses the royalist position. Whereas *Hesperides* looked Janus-faced at a lost paradise and a current tragedy, Lovelace's poems suggest no timeline, no development; they seemingly speak to a single moment, and they do so uncertainly. His remarkable poem on Peter Lely's portrait of Charles and the Duke of York, 'drawne by him at Hampton-Court', is an image of an image. The painting seems to have been commissioned by the Earl of Northumberland, who was to one of Lovelace's orientation a traitor to the king, to whom he owed an almost feudal debt of honour and loyalty. Northumberland was a supporter of the Long Parliament and, in effect, gaoler of those of the king's children that had fallen into parliamentary hands; his motives in commissioning the work invite interpretation (Loxley1997: 155–61 and plate 2). Lely drew Charles at Hampton court because that was where he was being held, and the picture shows a gravely pensive king against a background of funereal drapery, and his youthful son, looking uncertain and ill at ease, standing before a landscape dominated by a storm cloud. No wonder Lovelace speaks of 'clouded Majesty' and 'humble bravery' and 'grief triumphant' ('To my Worthy Friend Mr. Peter Lilly: on that excellent Picture of his Majesty, and the Duke of Yorke, drawne by him at Hampton-Court'; Lovelace 1930: 57), for the painting, ultimately, is of two captives, made at the instigation of their captors, a record of impotence, not a celebration of majesty, and, in its obvious recollection of the portraits of Van Dyck, it is both poignant and ironic. The first *Lucasta* ends with 'Aramantha. A Pastoral', which is sometimes interpreted as marking a shift towards pacifism and retirement. The hero, Alexis, hangs up his arms and breaks his sword, betaking himself 'unto the humble Crook' (Lovelace 1930: 118).

His posthumously published collection is marked by a fascinating technical development, first hinted at in 'The Grasse-hopper': poems about the natural world, often minutely and precisely observed, but resonating with the values of defeated and eclipsed royalism, as in his two poems on 'The Snayl', 'The Ant', 'The Falcon', 'A Fly caught in a Cobweb' and 'A Fly about a Glasse of Burnt Claret'. Sometimes they offer the opportunity for an almost Olympian perspective on the creatures' suffering and the futility of their endeavours. 'The Falcon', for example, describes in chivalric terms the death of the noble bird, spiked by the bill of a heron against which it has been loosed. The falcon is an aristocrat, a chivalrous cavalier, charging at a humbler target and perishing on 'the stand of Pikes', the heron's mighty bill, to the lamentation of other noble raptors at the wastefulness of a 'Victory, unhap'ly wonne' (Lovelace 1930: 141–5). As Raymond Anselment perceptively remarks, 'From this emblem of mortal conflict, Lovelace understands with considerable sympathy and remarkable detachment the elegiac lesson of civil war' (1988: 119). 'The Snayl' offers a moral to the defeated on how to move cautiously through a hostile world:

> Wise Emblem of our Politick World,
> Sage Snayl, within thine own self curl'd;
> Instruct me softly to make hast,
> Whilst these my Feet go slowly fast.

The poem ponders the advantages and limitations of retirement:

> ...when to rest, each calls the bell,
> Thou sleep'st within thy Marble Cell;
> Where in dark contemplation plac'd,
> The sweets of Nature thou dost tast...
> (Lovelace 1930: 136–7)

The first *Lucasta* had produced an image of the poet as an active and vigorous agent, who goes out, to war, to exile, and makes decisions that shape his own destiny. In the posthumous collection, though a construction of the poet remains at the centre of most of the poems, it is as a passive figure, someone who depends on the decisions of others and on the generally unfortunate outcomes of chance. Even in his most accomplished occasional poem, 'The Triumphs of Philamore and Amoret', in celebration of the marriage of Charles Cotton the younger, a fellow poet and a patron, is explicitly sent 'FROM London' to Staffordshire. He thinks of his friend but does not join the festivity, and he writes as if from a dungeon and from a position of indigent dependence in which his sense of his own temporary loss overwhelms the process of celebration: 'Sir your long absence I complain... / So I unthrifty, to my self untrue, / Rise cloath'd with real wants, 'cause wanting you' (ibid.: 169, 174).

Charles Cotton the younger, however, would seem to have been rarely in a London that had little to recommend it to a country-loving cavalier squire. Cotton published little before the Restoration, and his principal collection was printed posthumously in 1689. Dating of individual poems can be problematic, and he certainly remained actively engaged in writing well into the 1680s. His royalism was clear and uncompromising. Edmund Waller, one of many royalist activists minded to make his peace with the Cromwellian protectorate, was treated with a memorable robustness for his *Panegyrick to my Lord Protector*, first published in 1655:

> Feare not thy memory, that cannot dye,
> This Panegerick is thy elegie,
> Which shal be when, or wheresoever read,
> A Liveing Poem to upbrayed thee dead.
> ('To Poet E[dmund] W[aller], ll.33–6; Cotton 1958: 114)

His elegy for Lovelace, printed among the prefatory material of the second *Lucasta*, offers the opposite term to the turncoat Waller in a figure who was 'In fortune humble, constant in Mischance, / Expert of both' ('To the Memory of my worthy Friend, Colonel Richard Lovelace', ll.21–2; ibid.: 112). His elegy for the seventh Earl of Derby, executed after the battle of Worcester for his part in the second civil war, sets his own resolution in the context of the devastation occasioned by 'this prodigious beast Rebellion' that has carried off the king and the earl among a 'throng of Martyrs' ('On the Lord Derby', ll.2, 25; ibid.: 129–30).

Like most royalist poetry of retirement, Cotton's valorizes the countryside as the locus of integrity and of a bibulous friendship, a place to let the storms pass over. Personifying Old Winter, he comes closer to Horatian epicureanism than to Stoicism:

> Then let Old Winter take his course,
> And howle abroad till he be hoarse,
> Though his Lungs crack in fruitless ire,
> It shall but serve to blow our Fire.
> . . . .
> Or, let him *Scotland* take, and there
> Confine the plotting Presbyter;
> His Zeal may Freeze, whilst we kept warm
> By Love and Wine, can take no harm.
> ('Winter Quatrains', ll.201–4, 209–12; ibid.: 23)

Distinctively, though, Cotton's verse seems much closer to the working countryside. Not for him Fane's idealized and sometimes sentimental view nor Herrick's disengaged perspective from the steps of the great house; he writes as one who attentively walks his own estate. His 'wonderfully crisp quatrains on the times of day' (Fowler 1994: 370) abound in detail. He knows that dairy farming does not end with bonny lasses singing as they milk. He notes, at the end of the day, 'the Pans and Bowls clean scalded all, / Rear'd up against the Milkhouse Wall' ('Evening Quatrains', ll.35–6; Cotton 1958: 8).

John Denham (knighted in 1661) had a complicated war, in arms for the king from 1642, in exile at the court of Charles II, and in the mid- and late 1650s back in England, seemingly under the protection of a Cromwelliam sympathizer, Philip Herbert, fifth Earl of Pembroke, though actively engaged as an agent (or, just possibly, a double or even treble agent) in the royalist underground, living a shadowy life in a rather unsubstantial political universe (O Hehir 1968: esp. chs 3, 4 and 5). *Cooper's Hill*, which in quality far surpasses the rest of his oeuvre, remained something of a life work. Brendan O Hehir, its modern editor, has distinguished two principal states, what he terms 'the "A" Text' and 'the "B" Text'. The former is extant in two early manuscripts and appeared in print in 1642, published by Thomas Walkeley, who had recently published Carew's posthumous collected poems. In a way that exemplifies the print history of royalist high culture, it was reprinted in 1643 in Oxford, the provisional capital of the king, and thereafter became the intellectual property of Humphrey Moseley, who first published it in 1650. The B text first appeared in 1655, again under Moseley's imprint, but in a radically revised form, reflecting not only changed political circumstance but also Denham's considerable technical improvement. It was reprinted, with minor changes, in his collected works in 1668 and again, posthumously, in 1676.

The earlier printed edition, while plainly reflecting the anxieties and uncertainties of the months following the execution of Strafford and before the open hostilities of the first civil war, is excitingly adventurous in its avant-gardist extension of topographical poetry from describing an estate or country house and complimenting its owners to a much wider landscape and to more expansive themes. The poet takes as his vantage point Cooper's Hill, from which he can see (or perhaps imagine) – in one direction the City of London, in the other Windsor, and before him the flood plain of the Thames. Each is variously engaged with in ways that disclose political values and comment obliquely on immediate developments. The description of London supports a panegyric gesture towards Charles I for his restoration of St Paul's, that great Laudian project so deprecated by his enemies. In passing, there is a word of praise for Edmund Waller, who had celebrated that project in a memorable poem, 'Upon his Majesties repairing of Pauls', available only in manuscript before Moseley's 1645 edition. London, however, is the site of greed and luxury, where 'men like Ants / Toyle to prevent imaginarie wants' and where 'Some study plots, and some those plots t'undoe' (ll.29–30, 41; O Hehir 1969: 111–12). In an embryonic rehearsal of the royalist poetry of retirement, he turns his gaze to Windsor ('Oh happinesse of sweete retir'd content! / To be at once secure, and innocent': ll.47–48; ibid.: 113), the symbolic role of which, in opposition to the city, is sharpened by its role in January 1642 as the palace to which Charles withdrew his court in response to the tumults which followed his aborted attempt to arrest the Five Members. The passage supports a more developed panegyric to a long line of English kings, in his own century widened to embrace the royal houses of France and Scotland in the 'Royall paire' of Charles Stuart and the Bourbon Henrietta Maria. The poet's eye then turns to Chertsey Abbey, ruined in the Henrician reformation, which is represented as a symbol of the destructive impact of political impact on the church and as a warning to his own age of the dangers of too zealous a reformation: 'Is there no temperate Region can be knowne, / Betwixt their [the Catholic church's] frigid, and our Torrid Zone?' (ll.173–4; ibid.: 121), a question that carries an implied endorsement of a middle way to be equated with ceremonial Anglicanism.

Three scenes heavy with political symbolism then follow. Windsor Forest is the scene of a stag hunt, which commentators confidently identify as a complex negotiation of the trial and execution of Strafford. The stag, 'Like a declining Statesman, left forlorne / To his freinds pitty, and pursuers scorne', bravely resists as best he can 'Till *Charles* from his unerring hand lets flie / A mortall shaft' (ll.275–6, 297–8; ibid.: 129–30), which accurately enough reflects the sequence of events in Strafford's tragedy, deserted by those he may reasonably have expected to support him and finally condemned by Charles's decision to sign the bill of attainder. Conrad Russell's stark phrase, 'the King's courage failed him' (1995: 300), was the obvious judgement at the time and ever since. Denham's narrative, which eludes the relative simplicities of allegory, at once commemorates the resolution of Strafford and presents Charles's conduct, a little enigmatically, as a noble act in the context of an inevitable disaster for the quarry; if the king's arrow had not killed him, the dogs would have torn him to pieces. (Indeed, at one stage, Strafford's enemies were pressing for his hanging, drawing and quartering – ibid.: 288). The poem turns next to Runnymead, and celebrates Magna Carta as a compact through which monarch and subject arrived at a balanced relationship of mutual (but differing) respect, a relationship of greatest benefit 'When Kings give liberty, and Subjects love' (l.318; O Hehir 1969: 131). Flood management provides the concluding metaphor for the interdependence and mutuality of kings and subjects and a pious observation on how excess on either side threatens the property of both.

Denham wrote as a careful royalist, hoping, though perhaps not expecting, to find a way out of the conflicts of 1641 without further bloodshed. Wilcher perceptively links the poem to the formation of a constitutionally scrupulous royalism, appealing for moderation on all sides, and in its way as concerned to rein in the likes of Suckling as to calm the militancy of the king's enemies. As a long critical tradition has explored, the adjustments he made in the 1655 edition reflect changed political circumstances. Yet at the level of ideology we should not overstate how radically such tinkering transforms the poem. References to the dead Charles I are made vaguer – no longer is the slayer of the stag named; rather he is 'the King' (l.319; ibid.: 158). The hunt scene is elaborated and the end quite radically rewritten. Nigel Smith summarizes thus the significance of the changes:

> In the closing passages, Denham swaps sets of lines so that the poem ends with the Thames bursting its banks. The mutually controlling pressures of monarch and people in the 1642 version . . . are replaced by one of chaos and anarchy in a deluge. Indeed, what has happened is worse than any regal tyranny. Charles (now obviously represented in the stag, rather than Strafford) is hunted by a lawless mob. (Smith 1994: 324)

Yet what we are left with epitomizes the incoherence of mid-1650s royalism. There was, indeed, 'the king' of England, Charles II, yet it was difficult to see how he would be hunting in Windsor forest in the foreseeable future. The details of the hunt cannot be schematized into a coherent allegory; if Charles I is the stag, who is this 'king' that kills him? Moreover, the constitutional-royalist position is still apparent in the section of Magna Carta, and its immediate abandonment in the unredeemable pessimism of the concluding flood seems not to follow.

Technically, the B text shows a poet in much closer control of his medium. He eliminates the occasional cheap quibble. '[P]roud to dye / By such a wound, he fals, the Christall floud/ Dying he dies, and purples with his bloud' becomes 'Proud of the wound, to it resigns his bloud, / And stains the Crystal with a Purple floud' (A text, ll.298–300; B text ll.321–2; O Hehir 1969: 130, 159). A plainer aesthetic of closer artistic control is emerging. In the later version the closed, balanced couplet replaces a looser structure. Compare, again:

> And he might thinke it must, the cause, and time
> Considered well; for none commits a crime,
> Appearing such, but as 'tis understood,
> A reall, or at least a seeming good.
> 　　　　　　　　　(A text, ll.161–4; ibid.: 120–1)

and:

> No Crime so bold, but would be understood
> A real, or at least a seeming good.
> 　　　　　　　　　(B text, ll.127–8; ibid.: 146)

The revision is obviously briefer, but it is also balanced – Denham has evidently developed some assurance in the use of the caesura – and, contained within the closed couplet, it approximates to a sententia generalized effectively from the particular. It is no wonder that Dryden commended *Cooper's Hill* as 'the exact standard of Good Writing' (quoted in O Hehir 1969: 295).

Denham in exile wrote occasional and satirical verses to order, on topics, as he recalled, that the king was 'pleased sometimes to give me . . . to divert and put off the evil hours of our banishment' (quoted in O Hehir 1968: 91). Royalist poets had, since the early 1640s, been thus engaged, probably as much to keep up morale as to serve any larger polemical purpose. Such efforts often drew on a long tradition of anti-Puritan stereotyping that stretched through Ben Jonson's drama back to those playwrights who had been drafted into the Episcopalian campaign against Martin Marprelate (see above, chapter 2). Perhaps the most vigorous was John Taylor the Water Poet (to use his usual soubriquet; he had, for a while, been a working ferryman and generally styled himself thus, no doubt to assert his close connection with what our own age calls 'the real world'). His populist and robust rehearsal of essentially high Anglican and fiercely monarchical values long antedated the beginning of hostilities, but in the early 1640s he rallied to the royalist cause, joining the court in Oxford. Taylor well understood his own cultural antecedents, and explicitly invoked the spirit of Thomas Nashe, who had been one of the anti-Marprelate writers, in his prose tract *Crop-Eare Curried, or, Tom Nash His Ghost* (1644; discussed by Smith 1994: 297). The old stereotype of Puritans suggested that they were ignorant, low-class sectaries, opportunistically seeking to improve their own position while jeopardizing the fabric of the state. Taylor was comfortable working with that, adding a gleeful recollection of the punishments once dealt out to them (with an evident hope that such possibilities would return again). Hence in his *Rebells Anathematized, And anatomized: or, A Satyricall Salutation to the Rabble of seditous, pestiferous pulpit-praters, with their Brethren the Weekly Libellers*, a title that with singular explicitness reflects the content, he happily lashes 'the Cobling, Tub, pernicious Preacher, / With *Prinne* and *Burton*, (sweet-fac'd crop-ear'd Curres)' (Taylor 1645: 3). Taylor kept going till his death in 1653. Bernard Capp notes some caution in the texts that actually carried his name, though emphatically 'he never turned his back on politics' (1994: 183–4).

The adoption of that idiom and that range of cultural assumptions by John Cleveland produced some of the more fascinating satirical poetry of the 1640s. Cleveland was a hitherto successful, mid-career academic, who probably quit his Cambridge fellowship before parliament's purging visitation of 1643, joining the king in Oxford and writing for the royalist cause. His prose satire, *The Character of a London-Diurnall*, was immediately successful, going into at least five early editions, and his poems certainly circulated widely in manuscript before their print publication in 1647. There were 25 editions of his poems printed between then and 1700. (For both a life and a publishing history, see Cleveland 1967: xv–lv.) Cleveland, however, wrote an allusive, witty verse, more demanding of its readers than Taylor, though in his more aggressive poems he shares Taylor's offensive repertoire. He accepts the stereotype of the Puritan as the appetitive, hypocritical killjoy, but pushes it in new directions. 'The Rebell Scot', written on Scotland's entry into the English civil war on parliament's side, extends the denominational stereotype to become a racial one.

Scots are 'Citizens o'th World; they're all in all, / Scotland's a Nation Epidemicall', though they travel, not to learn foreign manners, but to fill their pockets. With a strange kind of optimism and in a precise, indecent and suggestive metaphor that probably comes closer to Jonson than Donne, he notes:

> Sure *England* hath the Hemerods, and these
> On the North Posterne of the patient seize,
> Like Leeches: thus they physically thirst
> After our blood, but in the cure shall burst.
> (ll.69–70, 83–6; ibid.: 31)

The imagery is dense and complex: the northern border is England's backdoor or postern; but the anus is a sort of backdoor, too; and around it, there are manifestations of national disorder, analogous to haemorrhoids, and haemorrhoids, like medicinal leeches, swell with blood, until they burst; as may the Scots.

He pushes the stereotype again in 'The Mixt Assembly', on the Westminster Assembly of Divines, convoked by the Long Parliament to reform the Church of England from its Laudian errors. The Assembly was mixed in that it included lay as well as clerical members, and, among the former, some of the parliament-supporting aristocrats who formerly had been prominent courtiers. So the poem offers us this curious society, in which the usual grasping anti-Laudian clergy dance a jig with William Herbert, the fourth Earl of Pembroke and formerly a close associate of the king, and Algernon Percy, tenth Earl of Northumberland and since 1638 Charles's Lord High Admiral. These make up a strange company, and a ludicrous one for the turncoat aristocrats to find themselves in: 'Hee that the Noble *Percyes* blood inherits, / Will he strike up a *Hotspur* of the spirits?' (ll.57–8; ibid.: 27).

Cleveland, like Lovelace and Herrick, took the hostile representation of royalists and made from it a positive image of daredevil defiance. Through the early years of the war Prince Rupert (Charles I's nephew) had been a particular target for parliamentarian attack, and even his pets attracted clumsy censure. Thus, an anonymous tract, *An exact description of Prince Ruperts Malignant She-Monkey*, ponderously claimed, 'Pr. *Ruperts* Monkey is . . . the little whore of Babylon in a green coat, that sometimes rides upon the beast that is Prince *Ruperts* dog, that tempts the Prince by her lascivious gestures, to think oftner on a woman than he would do' (Anon. 1645: sig. A4r).

The dog in question, a poodle called Boy, 'that four-legg'd *Cavalier*', had two well-known tricks that Cleveland, far from avoiding, chose to celebrate: sitting up at the name of Charles and cocking 'his Malignant leg at *Pym*'. Cleveland apologizes for nothing, praising Rupert as an aggressive martial figure that confirms parliament's fears of him: 'In fine, the name of *Rupert* thunders so, / *Kimbolton's* [i.e. the Earl of Manchester, the parliamentary commander] but a rumbling Wheel-barrow' ('To P. Rupert', ll.122, 126, 179–80; Cleveland 1967: 36).

Poor Boy was summarily executed after his capture at the battle of Marston Moor, an event gloatingly described in a parliamentarian pamphlet, *A Dogs Elegy, or Rupert's Tears* (Anon. 1644), a grubby action shamingly recounted. But Cleveland had a double problem: not only was his side losing, he was too perceptive and too honest not to recognize it. His elegy on Laud, finally tried and executed in 1645, expresses bewilderment that providence has served them so badly and that the king's cause has been a long process of continuous and irreversible defeat: 'How could successe such villanies applaud? / The state in *Strafford* fell, the Church in *Laud*' ('On the Archbishop of Canterbury', ll.41–2; Cleveland 1967: 39). The problem is most acutely explored in his finest poem, 'The Kings Disguise', which starts with a description of Charles's flight dressed as a servant to surrender to the Scottish army in 1646. Lois Potter in an intelligent reading summarizes thus: 'The first part of the poem is devoted to developing the paradox that the king, by voluntarily assuming this uncouth and humiliating disguise, has become a traitor to himself, performing all the sacrilegious acts of which Parliament has already been guilty' (Potter 1989: 63). But Cleveland's discourse never achieves the status of paradox because it is obviously and literally true that the king has disgraced himself, that his flight is shameful, and that he has fallen from high degree to a posture of abject dependency. With an alarming vividness, Cleveland piles up witty images of the king 'coffin'd in this vile disguise', like a 'martyr'd Abbeys courser [that is, coarser] doome, / Devoutly alter'd to a Pigeon roome', 'The Sun wears Midnight'. This is a most appalling ritual, itself emblematic of the total failure of the cause, in Cleveland's resonant phrase, 'Majestick twilight' (ll.1, 29–30, 45, 44, 41; Cleveland 1967: 6–7). Staring at this inversion of the royal image, finding metaphors for it, accentuates its poignancy; it does not make it go away. Through the rest of the poem, Cleveland tries to round on the king's enemies; he 'twists and turns' in his 'determination to prove that, despite all the evidence to the contrary, the mystical ruler of royalist devotion is still real' (Potter 1989: 64). But the final images represent the king on his 'strange journey' (l.117), a suppliant to his defiant and hostile Scottish subjects.

Abraham Cowley's first collection of poetry, *Poetical Blossomes*, appeared in 1633 when he was a schoolboy of 13 years. The portrait frontispiece represents him as a diminutive figure, dwarfed by the frame that surrounds him and by a cartouche, on which an inscription asserts 'for ought I can see / *Cowley* may youngest sonne of *Phoebus* bee' (Cowley 1989–: I, 12). A glittering early career followed, in which he continued to write verse, often in a fiercely loyalist spirit, and a play, *The Guardian*, which was staged by Trinity College, Cambridge, as an entertainment for Charles, Prince of Wales, in 1642. By the time the Earl of Manchester entered Cambridge to administer the Solemn League and Covenant (and thus, in effect, to eject royalist academics), he had withdrawn to Oxford, where he would seem to have entered the service of Henry Jermyn, secretary and aide to Henrietta Maria, whom he followed into exile. In the late 1640s he worked as a cipher clerk to the Louvre group of exiles (and, as such, perhaps attracted the enmity, later manifest, of the future Earl of Clarendon, the dominant figure in the group around Charles, both as Prince of Wales and king). He returned to England during the Protectorate. It was a route already trodden by Davenant, Waller and Thomas Hobbes in the years since the Act of Oblivion of 1652, though Cowley may have established contacts with the royalist underground at the same time. In 1655 he was arrested and interrogated, and then released on terms which remain the subject of speculation. Possibly he had become a double agent. A contemporary anecdote, frequently cited, tells of his attempts to secure preferment at the Restoration, when Clarendon, it was reported, dismissed him with 'Mr. Cowley, your pardon is your reward' (Nethercot 1931; Underdown 1960: 318).

His first significant publication, if we leave aside the product of his youthful precosity, was *The Mistresse*, first published by Humphrey Moseley, whose preface explains, somewhat vaguely, that the author had not been directly involved in the final stages of preparing the text. It is an accomplished example of restrained, late Caroline libertinism, in which the author figures himself rather like a civilian version of the Lovelace produced in the first *Lucasta*. These poems acquired and retained a considerable popularity, and some continued to be set to music through the later seventeenth century by composers, including

John Blow and his pupil Henry Purcell, who composed at least 16 settings to Cowley's lyrics (Cowley 1989–: II, 311–555).

The Mistresse is a nostalgic collection, looking back to the culture of the personal rule. But Cowley was also an innovative writer, arguably the most significant literary neoclassicist of the period between Ben Jonson and the post-1660 writings of Milton and John Dryden, both as a composer of Pindaric odes and as a narrative poet. Early in the first civil war he began a poem, modelled on Lucan (Smith 1994: 207), relating in heroic terms the triumphs of the armies of the king against 'the rebels', as he habitually terms them. Even for a partisan audience, the heroic tone must often have been uncomfortable. For example, the burning of Birmingham, a city known for its armament industry, by Prince Rupert's army emerged as a major atrocity of the opening years of the conflict, widely censured by parliamentarian writers and handled with care by other royalist apologists. Cowley turns it into a vengeful gesture couched in terms redolent of Homer or Virgil:

Goe burne the wicked *Towne*, and let it all
Bee one bright *Pire* for his [the Earl of Denbigh's, killed in the attack] great
    Funerall.
Into one glowing *Forge* the whole streets turne;
Soe *AEtna*, *Vulcans* other *Shop*, does burne.
Too late the foolish Rebells peace desire;
Like *Paris* Lust quencht when his *Troyes* on fire.
            (*The Civil War*, book 2, ll.85–90; Cowley 1989–: I, 132)

The triumphalism, the wishful thinking and the cultural indulgence of the neoclassical mode made this poem a difficult undertaking to sustain, and impossible once the royalists had evidently started to lose. The poem, abandoned incomplete, was not printed in his lifetime.

Smith concludes, 'Cowley's *Civil War* is not a great poem, but it is nonetheless remarkable for its attempt to address a contemporary reality in epic terms' (1994: 211). But it is not, strictly, epic, if we adopt the distinction Dryden makes in the prefatory material to his own *Annus Mirabilis*, a poem that, in genre terms, is close to Cowley's: 'I have called my poem historical, not epic . . . since the action is not properly one, nor that accomplished in the last successes. . . . I am apt to agree with those who rank Lucan [a model for Dryden as for Cowley] rather among historians in verse than epic poets' (Dryden

1995–2005: I, 114–15). For his second narrative poem, *Davideis*, Cowley adopts a genuinely epic genre, which allows a much more mediated engagement with the crises of his own age. This is a retelling of the struggle of the youthful David against Saul. Uncertainties shroud its date of composition and indeed its interpretation. Moseley published it in his collected works, *Poems: I. Miscellanies. II. The Mistress, or Love Verses. III. Pindarique Odes. And IV. Davideis* (1656). Cowley's prefatory remarks on this second abandoned narrative poem describe how its projected 12 books would have culminated in David's victory over the fallen Saul (Cowley 1656: sig. b1v). The poem certainly cannot be read as a detailed *roman-à-clef* in the manner of Dryden's own retelling of Davidic history in *Absalom and Achitophel* (see below, chapter 6). Yet as the story develops it depicts an agreeable fantasy of youthful elan defying crabbed militarism, perhaps much as the royalist underground entertained the aspiration of overthrowing the Cromwellian ascendancy. Abandoning the poem would have been consonant with the ideological surrender which Cowley committed in the preface to his 1656 collection: 'it is so uncustomary, as to become almost *ridiculous*, to make *Lawrels* for the *Conquered*' (ibid.: sig. a4r).

Cowley's Pindaric odes, first published in that volume, are technically accomplished and a significant contribution to the history of a genre, a vital link between Jonson's early experimentation and the achievements of, for example, Thomas Gray. Several of the odes closely render Pindar's poems, though he often turns the lyric freedom of the form to original compositions. Pindar's lofty and declarative idiom is adapted not for celebration, but for a generalized and pessimistic meditation. In his most resonant ode, 'Destinie', two angels play at chess, moving the human pieces with an Olympian indifference, among them 'the *Mated King*'. Cowley depicts himself withdrawing from the active life into the world of poets, marginalised though they may be:

> No Matter, *Cowley*, let proud *Fortune* see,
> That *thou* canst *her* despise no less then *she* does *Thee*.
>   Let all her gifts the portion be
>   Of Folly, Lust, and flattery,
>   Fraud, Extortion, Calumnie,
>   Murder, Infidelitie,

> Rebellion and Hypocrisie.
> Do thou nor *grieve* nor *blush* to be,
> As all th'inspired *tuneful Men,*
> And all thy great *Forefathers* were from *Homer* down to *Ben.*
> (Cowley 1905: 193–4)

Jonson appears both as a touchstone of integrity and as a precursor of Cowley's own neoclassical aspirations.

Sir William Davenant, active in arms for the king and like Cowley an adherent of the Louvre party, worked on his most ambitious narrative poem, *Gondibert,* while in captivity and for a while in danger of execution. Five books were projected, but like Cowley's verse narratives, it was left incomplete. Three books were published in 1651; the others were never written (Davenant 1971: ix). It is a curious work, and its eccentricity was certainly remarked on by contemporaries, several of whom collaborated in satirical observations, *Certain Verses Written by Several of the Author's Friends* (1653; Davenant 1971: 274–86). The poem is a heroic romance set in medieval Lombardy. Its modern editor notes, as did contemporaries, that it 'plays about the fringes of the *roman-à-clef*', though he adds, 'One is on fascinating but shaky ground in trying to construct a "key" to the characters'. There are analogies here with the *Davideis,* and once more royalist values and aspirations can be teased out (ibid.: xiii, xv). The poem is significant in that, in its version of what constitutes heroism, it points forward to the heroic drama of the 1660s (ibid.: xii; Wilcher 2001: 320). Its prosody reflects an interesting theory. Davenant explains in his preface that he has chosen what he terms 'my interwoven *Stanza* of foure' to give his reader a 'respite or pause' between stanzas. He thinks of reading poetry as essentially a voiced or indeed sung experience. Couplets in a long poem run the reader 'out of breath'. Davenant's alternative rhyme scheme is analogous to 'a plaine and stately composing of Musick'; 'the brevity of the *Stanza* renders it … more easy to the singer; which in *stilo recitativo,* when the Story is long, is cheefly requisite' (Davenant 1971: 17). The four-lined stanza, rhyming *abab,* was adopted by Dryden for *Annus Mirabilis,* in explicit imitation of Davenant (Dryden 1995–2005: I, 116–17).

Discussion of the early writing of Katherine Philips and Margaret Cavendish is reserved for chapter 6.

Crashaw and Vaughan

The doctrinal, ecclesiastical and cultural policies of Archbishop Laud (see above, chapter 4) had always invited the charge of popery, and among his enemies the assertion that he sought to return England to Roman Catholicism was commonplace. Laud himself both fiercely denied the assertion and sought actively to develop and promulgate a critique of the failings of Catholicism. Among the earliest triumphs of his career was the requirement by James I that he publicly debate with and confute Father Fisher, a successful Jesuit missionary, who had fallen into government hands. The confutation had been published, and he reissued it in the late 1630s (Trevor-Roper 1962: 60, 370–1). Yet Laud's insistence on repositioning altars and on the special status of the clergy, his enthusiasm for ceremonial, his belief in the centrality of the Eucharist, and his support for the decorous renovation of churches and chapels ensured that something of the allegations always adhered to him. After Long Parliament met and he was arrested and indicted for treason, he was charged 'with usurping "a papal and tyrannical power"', of seeking to introduce Popery, of preferring men of unsound doctrines and silencing and persecuting the "learned and orthodox", and of holding secret communication with the Court of Rome' (ibid.: 405).

Laud was tried for treason and executed early in 1645, by which time the royalist cause was substantially lost and many of the men he had preferred had lost posts and livings. The University of Cambridge, purged by the Earl of Manchester of its Laudian dons, had been the setting for a particular ceremonial manifestation of the Laudian pro-gramme, and as such had both nurtured Richard Crashaw and wit-nessed his ejection (though he had absented himself well in advance of the formal process).

Crashaw died a convert to Catholicism, and for long the critical tradition stressed his cultural affinities with the poetry of the Catholic Counter-Reformation and his role as 'the most un-English of all the English poets' (Crashaw 1972: xv). Certainly, he read, was influenced by and indeed adapted the baroque poetry of Giambattista Marino and his followers, bringing to his religious aesthetic an intense kind of devotional and sensational pietism not found in George Herbert. More recently, however, Thomas Healy (1986; also see *DNB* 2004) has demonstrated how in accord Crashaw was with the Cambridge circles in which he moved in the late 1630s and early 1640s. John Cosin, his sometime patron, was the key figure. Cosin had been an important figure in the Laudian revolution, a significant advocate for his agenda of ceremonial reform. Appointed Master of Peterhouse, Cambridge, in 1635, the year in which Crashaw took up his fellowship there, Cosin actively promoted the adoption of new liturgical practices and a new polyphonic choral tradition, and he refashioned the college chapel, refurbished its altar, and installed a window based on a painting by Rubens. Crashaw's attempts to write liturgical and processional hymns followed Cosin's own attempts to refashion church services in ways which seemed papistical to his enemies.

Yet the case of Cosin defines with some precision Crashaw's own religious sensibility (*DNB* 2004). Both went into exile, but Cosin remained in the holy orders of the Church of England, returning in 1660 to become Bishop of Durham and an influential force in the reconstruction of the Episcopalian Church. Crashaw, like some others in his circle, turned to Rome. Certainly, the poetry that he probably wrote while a fellow of Peterhouse would not have outraged the Cambridge Laudians with whom he associated. Yet, obviously, it is the poetry of a future convert, and, since stricter points of doctrine are displaced by its devotionalism, it is difficult to identify any significant element which would have contradicted Catholic belief or practice.

The Crawshaw oeuvre poses some textual problems, and its publishing history mirrors its author's own theological and ideological trajectory. His first book, a neo-Latin collection, was *Epigrammatum Sacrorum Liber*, published by Cambridge University Press in 1634. It showed a high level of competence within the demanding form of brief epigrams, some of which were reworked into English in subsequent publications. Three collections of predominately vernacular poetry are in a complicated relationship to each other. *Steps to the Temple. Sacred Poems, With other Delights of the Muses* was published by Humphrey Moseley (see above) in 1646, by which time Crashaw was already in exile. Moseley performed a similar service for Abraham Cowley (see above), a Cambridge friend and contemporary of Crashaw, whose first collection of poetry was also published after he had left for exile. Like Herrick's *Hesperides* (see above), it is a dual volume of sacred and profane verse, each with its own title page, though both the order and the significance of the sections is reversed. Moseley brought out a second edition in 1648 'wherein are added divers pieces not before extant', as the title page proclaims. Besides the new poems, several others were revised and supplemented. L. C. Martin, a modern editor, concludes that 'though some of the material appearing here for the first time no doubt represents gleanings from the Cambridge period... the religious and devotional verse now first published seems likely to have been very largely of recent composition' (Crashaw 1957: xlvii), that is, after his formal conversion to Rome. The final book, *Carmen Deo Nostro*, was prepared for the press by an émigré English Catholic priest, Miles Pinkney, who has assumed the name 'Thomas Carre' (*DNB* 2004, s.n. Pinkney, Miles). Pinkney was a significant figure in recusant circles abroad, and, like Crashaw, he had been drawn to the court in exile of Henrietta Maria. By the time of the publication, Crashaw had been dead for four years, in circumstances that seemed fitting for a martyr for the faith. He had expired shortly after assuming a post at the pilgrimage shrine to the Virgin at Loreto. Pinkney dropped the secular poems and rebranded the divine section in unequivocally Catholic terms. He was probably responsible for changing the titles of some poems and adding several engravings of a plainly Catholic provenance.

The Delights of the Muses, the secular poems of the first two books, has stimulated a limited critical response. Many are occasional poems, including elegies on the recently deceased, a panegyric on the birth of the Duke of York, a Latin poem to Henrietta Maria, and poems designed for the front matter of other authors' books. The erotic lyric, the staple of most Caroline secular poetry, is vestigially present in 'Wishes. To his (supposed) Mistresse' (Crashaw 1957: 195–8). The theme may have seemed less melancholy to an original Cambridge readership of supposedly celibate staff and students than it seems to a modern audience.

Graham Parry among others has made higher claims for the opening poem, 'Musicks Duell'. This relates a dialogue between a lutenist and a nightingale in ways designed to reflect the characteristic musical idiom of each. The poem is a reworking of a neo-Latin original by the Jesuit Famianus Strada, which had inspired several English imitators. Parry concludes that 'Crashaw far exceeds his poetic model in the evocation of the rival virtuosi [bird and musician], translating musical effects into verbal terms with prodigious facility' (1985: 126). Crashaw's version is much longer than the lines it adapts from its model, though perhaps that copiousness is just a celebration of the variety exhibited by bird and lutenist. Yet the technical mastery is unsupported by a developed argument or discernible schema within the poem. Crashaw's longer verse often seems to be a stringing together of local brilliances.

The title of the divine poetry, *Steps to the Temple*, seemingly claims some affinity with *The Temple* of George Herbert. For an extreme Laudian still claiming membership of the Church of England, this stratagem may have had obvious advantages. By the 1640s Herbert was read and admired by a wide spectrum of English Protestants, and Puritans found his seeming plainness attractive (see above, chapter 4). The Preface to *Steps to the Temple* proclaims '*Here's* Herbert' *s second, but equall*' (Crashaw 1957: 75). But Crashaw's and Herbert's collection have little in common. Crashaw's seems shapeless; Herbert's carefully structured. Crashaw scarcely uses the motif of the temple; for Herbert it is the key metaphor. Moreover, each poet produces a radically different image of himself within the text. Herbert appears priestly, modest, purposefully naive. Crashaw's best poems spectacularly proclaim his brilliance.

Nor does their subject matter coincide closely. Herbert writes *about* religious ceremony. A considerable part of the Crashaw oeuvre offers texts *for* liturgical practice. Herbert's work is Christocentric. So, too, is Crashaw's though he diversifies into celebration of women saints, particularly the Virgin Mary, Mary Magdalene and Theresa of Avila.

Crashaw's best divine verse has a vivid sensationalism of a disturbing kind. In 'On the wounds of our crucified Lord', he ponders whether the gashes are mouths or eyes. If the former, they may be kissed by the faithful; if the latter, they are bloodshot and they weep bloody tears. He takes the images to the edge of grotesqueness or absurdity: 'This foot hath got a Mouth and lippes, / To pay the sweet summe of thy kisses' (ll.13–14; Crashaw 1957: 99). It hints, too, at an undertone of repressed homoerotic desire. But he concludes with a baroque metamorphosis that transforms the bleeding wounds and bloodied eye into a bejewelled artefact: the foot now weeps '*Ruby*-Teares', while the penitent's own are now 'Pearles' (ll.20–1).

The transformation is effected more startlingly still in his most remarkable poem, 'On our crucified Lord Naked, and bloody':

> Th'have left thee naked Lord, O that they had;
> This Garment too I would they had deny'd.
> Thee with thy selfe they have too richly clad,
> Opening the purple wardrobe of thy side.
> O never could bee found Garments too good
> For thee to weare, but these, of thine owne blood.
>
> (Ibid.:100)

268 Fro... .... , ...

The notion of Christ's body as a wardrobe opened up by the centurion's spear may strike modern readers as approaching the surreal. It probably seemed as powerful to Crashaw's contemporaries. 'Purple' is complex word. Primarily, it functions as a transferred epithet. It is what issues from it that is purple, though I suppose it could also apply to the interior of the thoracic cavity itself. The word was used of a larger range of colours in early modern English, and could certainly have described flesh, blood or indeed internal organs (*OED*). It is also, of course, the word applied to the clothing of Roman emperors, and points up the paradox of Christ's regal status and tortured, incarnate body. But once that conceit is, easily enough, absorbed by readers, they are left with that shocking recognition that the garment is no other than a massive effusion of blood, covering an otherwise naked torso.

Saint Theresa is the subject of three poems (ibid.: 317–27). The choice is deeply expressive of Crashaw's representation of love towards Christ as emotionally powerful, like the profoundest erotic desire. Crashaw was by no means without parallel in his sexual reading of Theresa's narrative, a story of divine ecstasies brought on by the manifestation to her of a seraph who pierced her body with his dart. Gian Lorenzo Bernini's statue of her in the Cornaro Chapel in Rome, the iconic work of Roman Counter-Reformation art, habitually strikes viewers as the representation of a woman in orgasmic arousal. For Crashaw, as perhaps for Bernini, the redirected sexual frenzy has a sado-masochistic edge:

> O how oft shalt thou complain
> Of a sweet subtle PAIN.
> Of intolerable IOYES;
> Of a DEATH, in which who dyes
> Loues his death, and dyes again.
> And would for euer so be slain.
> And liues, & dyes; and knowes no why
> To liue, But that he thus may neuer leaue to DY.
> (ll.97–104; ibid.: 319)

This is a curiously textured passage, with its rapid alternations of dying and loving and its prosodic defectiveness in the context of a primarily octosyllabic metre, which suggests panting.

From the perspective of mid-century Puritanism, Crashaw is the perfect Counter-Reformation poet, an apostate from the Protestant faith, whose defection confirmed what the likes of William Prynne had for long argued: scratch a Laudian and you find a papist. But the stereotype should not obscure what is really distinctive and significant about his poetry. Here is a fascinating religious sensibility, an openness to the alternative aesthetic offered by the baroque art of continental Europe, and a confident, innovative and sometimes brilliant artistry.

Henry Vaughan, the finest Welsh writer in English of the early modern period, shared some common ground with Crashaw. He, too, gestures towards Herbert as his precursor, though in his case the influence runs much deeper. He is primarily a divine poet, though with a minor commitment to secular verse. His political allegiances were close to Crashaw's, and he, too, suffered personally for the royalist cause. Like Crashaw, he published with Humphrey Moseley, though, like Crashaw, his publishing history is not unproblematic.

But socially and in terms of cultural milieu he was closer to Katherine Philips and Thomas St Nicholas (see below) than to the tight coteries of Cambridge. We are at a relatively early stage of understanding the literary culture of the provincial gentry in early modern England and Wales. He knew Philips since her childhood, and celebrated her achievements as a 'wittie fair one' (Vaughan 1957: 61; see Wilcher 2001: 335). Vaughan was very probably in arms for the king in the closing months of the first civil war, fighting at the emphatic defeat at Rowton Heath, just outside Chester, and withdrawing with the shattered army to the fastness of Beeston Castle, which eventually surrendered on honourable terms. Though on the other side from St Nicholas, he has one rather fine poem in that spirit of ironized Stoicism that characterizes the parliamentarian's own prison writing. 'Upon a Cloke lent him by Mr. J. *Ridsley*' describes a disreputable garment pressed into service *in extremis* 'when wee / Left craggie *Biston*, and the fatall *Dee*':

> beaten with fresh storms, and late mishap
> It shar'd the office of a *Cloke*, and *Cap*,
> To see how 'bout my clouded head it stood
> Like a thick *Turband*, or some Lawyers *Hood*,
> While the stiffe, hollow pletes on ev'ry side
> Like *conduit-pipes* rain'd from the *Bearded hide*
> (ll.19–26; Vaughan 1957: 52)

Social, personal and comic, like St Nicholas's verse it negotiates reflection on suffering and defeat with resilience and a flair for surprising and apposite imagery. Such verse, however, is a minor component in the Vaughan oeuvre.

Vaughan published a small collection of poems in 1646, of which a translation of Jurvenal's tenth satire is the major piece. A more substantial collection, *Olor Iscanus* ('The Swan of Usk', Vaughan's native river), including the poems discussed above, appeared in 1651. Most of the poems to which an approximate date can be attributed were probably written no later than 1647 and Vaughan's epistle dedicatory is dated December 1647. Yet the volume did not appear until 1651, printed for Moseley, and endorsed on the title page 'Published by a Friend'. An epistle from the 'publisher', either Moseley or this anonymous friend (perhaps they were the same), asserts that they have been saved from obscurity against the poet's own judgement. By the time they appeared, Vaughan had brought out, not with Moseley, the first part of the collection on which his major status depends, *Silex Scintillans: or Sacred Poems and Private Eiaculations* (1650). In 1655, a 'second Edition, in two Books' appeared, consisting of unsold copies of the first edition, to which a second section was added. His last collection, *Thalia Rediviva: The Pass-Times and Diversion of a Countrey-Muse*, did not appear until 1678, though once more it seemed made up from much earlier material, some most probably antedating most of the poems in *Silex Scintillans*. All of this poses problems of interpretation. An obvious hypothesis is that, as he turned to religious verse, he found a kind of high seriousness that made him reluctant to vouchsafe his secular verse to the press (much as the posthumous collection from Crashaw was stripped of his secular verse). Poetry-writing seems substantially to have halted after 1655, and the final collection may be a nostalgic gesture.

The critical tradition has sometimes reflected on the changes in the ways Vaughan represented himself (or was represented) between *Olor Iscanus* and *Silex Scintillans*, though the distinctions can perhaps be overstated. Certainly, the 'Swan of Usk' proclaims a rural and provincial predisposition, and an illustrated title page depicts a swimming swan surrounded with paraphernalia appropriate for pastoral lyric, bees, trees, flowers. He appears, perhaps, as a sort of Cymric version of Charles Cotton, adopting, in political eclipse, the purity of rural retirement. On the 1650 and 1655 title pages of *Silex Scintillans* he is styled 'Henry Vaughan Silurist'. Again, it is a regional marker, and presumably an assertion of provincial purity: the Silures were the Celtic tribe that inhabited south-east Wales. But it may imply a different kind of resistance. Jonathan Post suggests it marks an invocation of the pristine primitivism of the British church flourishing before the Anglo-Saxon invasion, a kind of ancient godliness that antedated Britain's subsequent Roman conversion (1982: esp. ch. 5).

Silex Scintillans owes far more to Herbert's *The Temple* than Crashaw's *Steps to the Temple* does. His secondary title, *Sacred Poems and Private Eiaculations*, echoes precisely the secondary title of Herbert's volume. The debt is specifically acknowledged in his preface, dated 1654, to the 1655 collection (Vaughan 1957: 391). But it is pervasive both in the thematic concerns and the prosodic innovations of his divine poetry. Vaughan experiments repeatedly with line lengths and rhyme schemes with a freedom licensed by Herbert's practice (well considered by Post 1982, especially chapter 4). Sometimes his proximity to his model constitutes a kind of homage. Thus, in 'Prayer (I)' (considered above, chapter 4), Herbert assembles, in a series of noun phrases in apposition to the opening word 'prayer', a range of sometimes brilliant images to represent its characteristics. In 'Son-dayes' (that is, Sundays), Vaughan repeats the trick. The Sabbath is 'Gods walking houre; / The Cool o'th'day; / The Creatures *Jubile*' (ll.11–13; ibid.: 447), and so on. Occasionally, he matches the priestly imperatives of 'The Church-Porch: Perirrhanterium'. Using the same stanzaic structure, in 'Rules and Lessons' he adjures his readers to rise and pray early, to resist peer pressure, remember the poor, to stay true to God, country and friends, and to close the day by listing and evaluating one's deeds (ibid.: 436–9).

As in the case of *The Temple*, the experience of reading through the two parts of *Silex Scintillans* differs from expectations raised by a familiarity with the usual anthology pieces. This is a very substantial body of verse, some of it didactic, much of it quite stark, its plain style carrying argument and meditation on sacred themes. But it lacks the strong structural sense of Herbert's collection, which drives its readers through a process of penitential reflection to an assurance of grace. Vaughan returns persistently to a small number of themes, predominately the relationships between life and death and the living and the dead. Robert Wilcher has sought, with some success, to distinguish the 'grief and political despair' of the 1650 part from the 'renewed sense of historical purpose' of the 1655, which in turn may be related to a process of accommodation in royalist ideology (Wilcher 2001: 336).

Yet we should not understate how much the parts have in common, both in their core concerns and poetic technique.

A number of elegies, poems apparently occasioned by the death of unidentified individuals, punctuate the collection, and their subject has occasioned some critical speculation. The circumstantial details often match the death of his youngest brother, probably from wounds sustained in military action on the royalist side. Though he draws on the usual repertoire of Christian consolation to manage emotional response to death, he seems much less comfortable with managing the problems of living. Jonathan Post concludes, 'The elegiac past often blends into a chiliastic future and shrinks the place of the present into an almost nonexistent moment between the two' (1982: 99). Certainly, the present is rendered unimportant under the view of eternity, but it doesn't really feel like a moment. Rather, in its drossy solitude it appears for Vaughan achingly long, wearisomely tedious.

Consider that astonishing poem, 'They are all gone into the world of light!' Vaughan places the dead in a superior but unknowable realm, of which the living have only imperfect hints. 'Mists ... blot and fill' the vision of the poet (l.37; Vaughan 1957: 484). Death is the subject of celebration, 'beauteous death! the Jewel of the Just' (l.17). Two images establish the unease of the living in contemplation of the rewards of the dead. Going up into the world of light has a naturalistic resonance; as Vaughan, who lived in hill country, well knew, around dawn and dusk, the tops hold the sunlight while the lower slopes are in shadow. In shadow is where the speaker of the poem really stays. The image of the soul as a liberated bird is traditional and familiar, but again Vaughan ties it closely to the countryman's experience of finding 'some fledg'd birds nest' (l.21). The sense of place, of rural provincialism, gives a contextualizing richness generally missing in Herbert's ascetic atopicality. Though Vaughan may dismiss the material world in which he must sojourn, he notices and describes it with precision and sensitivity.

His political affiliations are much more transparent than Herbert's. In his secular poetry, cavalier themes and engagement with specific events, battles and the deaths that they occasion, are explicit and unequivocal: this is the voice of a defeated royalist. The religious verse reflects that tendency, too, though generally more obliquely. Yet it is to be found even in his most transcendent poem, the extraordinary 'The World'. Post rightly terms its opening 'vertiginous' (Post 1999: 191):

> I saw Eternity the other night
> Like a great *Ring* of pure and endless light,
>   All calm, as it was bright,
> And round beneath it, Time in hours, days, years
>   Driv'n by the spheres
> Like a vast shadow mov'd, In which the world
>   And all her train were hurl'd'
>   (ll.1–7; Vaughan 1957: 466)

Vaughan had mastered Herbert's lesson, that seemingly simple language can communicate a vatic profundity. Here, it adds to the surprise, the shock, of the opening. He 'saw Eternity the other night', an idiom he could use for a random encounter on the village green. But eternity, a bewildering concept, cannot sustain the reification 'saw' implies. The poem slides quickly to simile – eternity is *like* a ring – and thence to a kind of dream allegory. With an apposite circularity the poem return to the image of the ring, now, with a breath-taking leap of the imagination, transformed into the ring Christ the bridegroom brings for the watching souls of his brides, the saved. The image, of course, is apocalyptic, present both in a parable in the gospel of Matthew (25:1–10) and in the Book of Revelation (19:7–9).

Vaughan caps the poem with a text from the first epistle of John (2:16–17), which asserts that 'All that is in the world . . . is of the world'. But most of the poem, between those glimpses of eternity, is about the world, an account of materialism and misconceptions on the part of exemplary figures, 'The doting Lover', 'The darksome States-man', 'The fearfull miser', and 'The down-right Epicure' (ll.8, 16, 31, 38; Vaughan 1957: 466–7. Even at the heart of a visionary engagement with the transcendence of eternity Vaughan's political loyalties are apparent. Something approaching a grim satire informs his account of the states-man, digging like a mole as he plunders 'Churches and altars': 'It rain'd about him bloud and tears, but he / Drank them as free' (ll.29–30).Vaughan may contend, like Wordsworth, that the world is too much with us, but his ideological engagement remains undiminished.

Mid-Century Drama

Theatre history in 1640–2 saw some intensification of trends observed through the 1630s (see above, chapter 4), together with an incipient engagement with the developing crisis. Sir John Suckling, who had been in arms for the king on his Scottish expeditions, brought home to the stage a perspective on rebellion at odds with the king's attempts to patch up an agreement of sorts with his northern subjects. His *Brennoralt*, performed by the King's Men probably no later than 1641, depicts a war between Poland and Lithuania, a subject nation in rebellion against the Polish crown. Analogies with Anglo-Scottish tension are obvious, and, as Wilcher observes, 'the eponymous hero . . . was a spokesman for those more headstrong Cavaliers who felt that a firmer line should be taken with the Scots' (2001: 39). Nor was Suckling's a lone initiative. On the death of Christopher Beeston, the veteran impressario of the Phoenix theatre, his son William replaced him as manager of the King's and Queen's Young Company. After some initial success, in which he attracted Richard Brome from Salisbury Court to write for his company, William overplayed his hand by allowing the performance of 'an unlicensed and now unknown play mocking some of the King's doings that led to the second bishops' war', for which he and two actors were jailed and the theatre briefly closed. The Master of the Revels recorded Charles's direct involvement in the affair: the play, the playbook for which was confiscated, 'was complained of by his majesty to me with command to punish the offenders'. William Davenant was appointed the company's new director, a decision that signalled the court's closest interest in what was performed on the London stage as the political crisis developed. It also anticipated Davenant's role in the Restoration theatre (Wickham et al. 2000: 625, 635–6).

Theatres reflected the tense, active, unpredictable days immediately preceding the inception of the first civil war, though they proved the most fragile of cultural institutions. Davenant and Suckling, royalist plotters, both fled to exile, and the theatres themselves were closed, leaving actors and professional dramatists to shift as best they could. The first and decisive piece of legislation, 'An Ordinance of the Lords and Commons concerning stage plays', was passed by the Long Parliament in September 1642:

> And whereas public sports do not well agree with public calamities, nor public stage plays with the seasons of humiliation, this being an exercise of sad and pious solemnity, and the other being spectacles of pleasure, too commonly expressing lascivious mirth and levity: it is therefore thought fit and ordained by the Lords and Commons in this Parliament

> assembled, that while these sad causes and set-times of humiliation do continue, public stage plays shall cease and be foreborne.   (Ibid.: 132)

Puritan animosity to plays and playhouses extended back to the previous century, and some of the order, particularly its concern with pleasure and lascivious mirth, reflects the old spirit of Zeal-of-the-Land Busy. Yet the legislation was introduced as a temporary measure, 'while these sad causes . . . do continue', and was presented as a matter of decorum, of what was fitting during the melancholy days of civil strife and at a time when a system of public fasting and prayer was under development as a kind of national atonement. Theatres had been closed temporarily before, as during the period of mourning for members of the royal family. But they had also been closed when civil order had been under threat, for example by the Essex conspiracy (see above, chapter 1). Theatres afforded probably the only confined public spaces in which large numbers of citizens could gather together, and as such, quite reasonably, attracted the attention of a prudent and nervous government. Moreover, in the years immediately before the war began, plays had become once more topical in ways that had worried the king and could well have worried parliament.

Recent scholarship has disputed the old orthodoxy that 'a gap' separates the late Caroline theatre from that of Restoration England (Wiseman 1998). Yet the development of plays in performance was certainly arrested by the 1642 ordinance. But the market for plays in print was stimulated – a market ably served by Humphrey Moseley among others – and some pamphlets had dialogue and resembled formal aspects of playbooks. Moreover, records indicate a continued use of theatres for performances both of plays and of other entertainments in the years following the ban. The old and unfashionable public theatre, the Red Bull, seems to have been the most persistent, though what was performed is unclear (Wickham et al. 2000: 588–90). The legislation was toughened up in February 1648, with 'An Ordinance of the Lords and Commons Assembled in Parliament, for, the utter suppression and abolishing of all Stage-Plays and Interludes. With the Penalties to be inflicted upon the Actors and Spectators, herein exprest'. As Wickham et al. observe, the wording 'has a triumphalist finality built into it'. Significantly, the actors, once protected by royal patents, now 'shall be taken to be Rogues', which exposed them to the rigours of old Elizabethan legislation against vagabonds, though some remained prepared to take the risk (ibid.: 133–5). 'Utter suppression and abolishing' removed the provisional and reactive characteristics of the 1642 measure.

Yet in the 1650s fascinating new developments emerged on the English stage. In 1653 James Shirley, who had supported himself as a schoolmaster since the interruption of his career as a dramatist, scripted a masque, *Cupid and Death*, for performance at the Protectorate court as part of the entertainment for a Portuguese embassy. (A treaty of alliance was signed in 1654.) Like a Caroline court masque, the performance was a synthesis of the performing arts. Luke Channen, a leading dancing master of the day, provided choreography, and the music was composed by Christopher Gibbons, son of the late Orlando Gibbons, and a teacher of John Blow, and Matthew Locke, a major influence on Henry Purcell, who commemorated his death with an elegy (Rooley 1990: accompanying notes, 18–19). A cultural generation after the golden age of the personal rule, metropolitan networks were forming again across the creative disciplines.

Cupid and Death resembles Caroline masque in its use of staging, music, dance, singing and dialogue. Yet it differs in that the masquers take part in the action and they do not dance with the audience at the end; the antimasque figures, working-class characters, engage directly with the mythological and symbolic figures – Death, Cupid, Mercury, Nature – and they also sing. The balance between spoken prose dialogue, recitative and song carries the performance away from masque and towards opera, a form Davenant planned to introduce to the London stage as early as 1639 (Wiseman 1998: 126). Qualitatively, the work must have been a revelation to anyone unfamiliar with Italian opera, as can be appreciated from its fine modern recording (Rooley 1990). As Anthony Rooley observes, 'Matthew Locke's long recitative for Mercury is some of the finest English recitative setting ever composed, surpassing in beauty and dramatic effectiveness most of the similar work up to the end of the 17th century' (ibid.: accompanying notes, 19). The action, which culminates in a vision of blessed souls in a vaguely pagan Elysium, is generally ecumenical and contains nothing offensive to Cromwell's Catholic guests, though quite what the Protector made of it is difficult to conjecture. For blind Milton, who produced official correspondence as part of the Portuguese negotiations, who had heard opera in Italy, and who had collaborated with Henry Lawes in the creation of *Comus* (see above, chapter 3; Campbell 1997: 64, 155), were he present, the experience may well have had a poignant complexity.

William Davenant, who had become reconciled to the Protectorate, resumed theatrical activity in the late 1650s in the production of plays that were ideologically acceptable to the government, 'embracing a mercantile nationalism that echoed the imperialist ambitions of Cromwell's regime' (Butler 2002: 601–2). In 1658–9 he returned to the Phoenix theatre, which he had managed briefly in the pre-war years. He developed a new theatrical idiom, combining elaborate scenery and stage machinery with music, song, dance and dialogue. *The Cruelty of the Spaniards in Peru. Exprest by Instrumentall and Vocall Musick, and by the Art of Perspective in Scenes, &c* (1658) endorses the Cromwellian campaign to dispute Spanish control of the West Indies. After tableaux depicting the Spaniards' unworthiness and cruelty as imperialists, a final song anticipates the arrival of the English army and a concluding scene has redcoats of the New Model Army dancing with grateful indigenous people 'in signe of their future amity' (Davenant 1658: 27). The published text functions as a sort of advertisement for performances, as the title page discloses: the drama will be 'Represented daily at the *Cockpit* [i.e., the Phoenix] in DRURY-LANE, At three after noone punctually'. Formerly, playhouses had fiercely guarded their scripts. Davenant happily publishes his because the theatrical experience rests so much on staging and music that the mere words can only encourage their readers to seek out the play in performance.

The theatre history of the 1650s is thin compared with that of the 1630s, but there is evidence enough that the beginnings of a new and radically innovative era were established before the return of the king.

Sir Thomas Browne

Thomas Browne (knighted in 1671) probably wrote most of his first significant work, *Religio Medici*, in the mid-1630s. The text contains personal details consonant with that dating, and its level of erudition falls well short of that shown in his publications of the mid-1640s and later, suggesting he still had a lot of reading to do. Its circumstances of publication reflect that general movement seen elsewhere among royalist writers from a manuscript circulation to print. Quite a few handwritten copies are still extant, and no doubt others have perished. From such a lost manuscript, the work was pirated, as he avers, appearing twice in 1642. Its success is well marked by the evident demand for a third, and this time authorized, edition in 1643.

Latterly, the critical tradition has highlighted its pertinence in the emerging crisis of the early 1640s. Michael Wilding puts the argument most uncompromisingly: 'To situate *Religio Medici* in the context of the pamphlet war at the time of its publication, rather than in the mid-1630s when it was hypothetically composed, is to realize its ideological significance, and to see Browne's participation in the socio-political debate of the English Revolution' (Wilding 1987: 90–1). While the internal evidence points primarily to the early date of composition, it certainly carries a patina of cavalier loyalism. His opening complaint about the 'perversion' of the press links the piracy of his text to the print campaigns that have seen *'the name of his Majesty defamed, the honour of Parliament depraved'* (Browne 1964: 1), quite a common sentiment in immediately contemporary royalist writing. Joseph Hall, a friend and patient of Browne's and the most accomplished apologist of episcopacy, makes similar points at the time (see below, 'Pamphlet Wars'). Again, there is an ideological transparency in Browne's attack on 'that great enemy of reason, vertue and religion, the multitude . . . a monstrosity more prodigious than Hydra', among whom, tellingly, he includes 'a rabble even amongst the Gentry' (ibid.: 55–6). This reflects a royalist perspective on the leadership of the king's opponents, a clear anxiety that the county hierarchies on whom order depended could no longer be trusted.

But subtler themes connect the text to its age of publication. By the early 1640s Browne was established in Norwich as a respected physician with a prestigious list of patients. Such provincial security, however, came after a highly progressive education which had taken him, after Oxford, to Montpellier, Leiden and Padua, bringing him into contact not only with medical science more developed than that in the English universities, but also with a range of religious cultures: Huguenot, Calvinist, Catholic and Jewish (*DNB* 2004). In reading *Religio Medici* as a sort of crypto-polemic, we are in danger of losing our sense of quite what a strange text it is. Browne offers not a systematic theology, but a relatively formless account of how he arrived at his own belief system. He stresses both his own scientific rationalism, to which we shall return, and his 'generall and indifferent temper' (ibid.: 56) that disinclines him from intolerance and persecution: 'Perseution is a bad and indirect way to plant Religion' (ibid.: 26). He tells us of his encounters with Jews and Catholics, and of his own worship among the latter. He lists heresies he has transiently entertained. There is an engaging generosity about his method. He, too, has erred, but the errors have passed, and he has found a secure place within the tradition of the Church of England.

But has not that church in recent years hounded, tortured and imprisoned English dissidents? Browne's account would scarcely suggest that. As Achsah Guibbory concludes, he demonstrates 'a particularly generous vision of a church that, rather than silencing the individual, allows for his or her eccentric beliefs, so long as they are not made the occasion for dissolving the community' (Guibbory 1999: 130–1). Browne seeks to take the heat out of religious controversy, indeed, to nudge religion out of politics. He is drawn to a favourite distinction of moderate Anglican discourse, between saving faith and matters of indifference, what were technically termed 'adiaphora'. It would be silly to persecute or to be persecuted about issues which do not really matter: 'I would not perish upon a Ceremony, Politick point, or indifferency: nor is my beleefe of that untractable temper, as not to bow at their obstacles, or connive at matters wherin there are not manifest impieties' (Browne 1964: 27). Of course, in the 1630s and 1640s there was no shortage of men who would kill or be killed over just such matters.

Depoliticizing religion had an obvious attraction for supporters of episcopacy once the political tide had turned against them. What Browne tried to do was reflected in attempts by non-Laudian prelates to establish a new modus vivendi with Puritanism. It was manifest in the rise of clergy like Joseph Hall, recently translated from Exeter to the more prestigious see of Norwich, and thus into Browne's immediate circle. Hall, too, tried to develop a more generous and inclusive kind of church, one in which a Protestant brotherhood, despite its diversity, could find common ground and spiritual community. Milton's response is considered below (see 'Pamphlet Wars').

By calling his text *Religio Medici*, Browne makes two claims: first, that this is the well-intentioned work of someone who is not a professional theologian, a civilian in the paper wars of religious controversy; second, that he is a scientist and a rationalist. The latter point is important for the Baconian argument he develops within it, that faith and reason are potentially in conflict (see above, chapter 2). Thus, in detail and in its largest mysteries, Christianity makes demands of its believers that are intractable to or incompatible with reason or with scientific knowledge. Because rational and informed Christians know such central propositions cannot be reconciled with what is known, the test of faith, and the triumph of faith, is greater for them than for the ignorant and superstitious. As Browne puts it, 'How shall the dead arise, is no question of my faith; to beleeve onely possibilities, is not faith, but meere Philosophy; many things are true in Divinity, which are neither inducible by reason, nor confirmable by sense' (ibid.: 45).

Religio Medici marks a first attempt at reconciling the scientific and rational impulse with issues of faith. The matter remains a major concern even in his most overtly Baconian publication, *Pseudodoxia Epidemica: or, Enquiries into Very many received Tenents, And commonly presumed Truths*, first published in 1646, and frequently reprinted with significant additions throughout his lifetime. Its primary purpose is to identify and confute widely held opinions that are not true in 'a frontal assault on the troops of error', in Robin Robbins's phrase (Browne 1981: I, xxx). Thus, he ranges from 'that Crystall is nothing else but Ice strongly congealed', 'That an Elephant hath no joynts' and 'That man hath onely an erect figure and that to looke up to Heaven', through to 'many historicall Tenents generally received, and some deduced from the history of holy Scripture' ('Contents'; ibid.: I, x-xvii)

The volume, a sort of encyclopedia of what is known asserted in confutation of what is demonstrably false, affords a treasure-chest of contemporary opinion. The third book, concerning animals, appears particularly whimsical, even charming, to a modern readership. But each constituent chapter, often perfectly crafted, shows Browne's capacity for synthesizing received wisdom with direct observation and a shrewd rationalism, while looking often to move beyond the observational to the ethical or religious level. Once more, he juxtaposes the discourses of religion and science.

Thus, his interrogation of the proposition that hares are all hermaphrodites (ibid.: I, 226–32) starts with the origins of the error, in tradition, in false anatomy (both sexes have organs that could be mistaken for male and female genitalia), and imperfect field observation (both sexes urinate backwards and they copulate without ascension). Each proposition is engaged with and confuted. But he opportunistically digresses to moralize. Hares can carry two litters; he notes occasional examples among women who thought, once they were pregnant, they could behave promiscuously, only to conceive a second child that resembles the lover, not the husband. At the same time, the hares' abundant fertility reflects the kindness of a wise creator to his favourite species, since it ensures people will always have plenty of hares to hunt. Browne drives on to end with a *tour de force*. There is a flurry of details describing the sexual postures of serpents, apes, shrimps, worms, cuttlefish, even porcupines and hedgehogs, and then a robust, moralizing conclusion:

> This is the constant Law of their Coition, this they observe and transgresse not: onely the vitiositie of man hath acted the varieties hereof; nor content with a digression from sex or species, hath in his own kinde runne thorow the Anomalies of venery, and been so bold, not onely to act, but represent to view, the Irregular wayes of lust.   (Ibid.: I, 232)

Browne's last major publication was *Hydriotaphia, Urne-Buriall, or, A Discourse of the Sepulchrall Urnes lately found in Norfolk. Together with The Garden of Cyrus, or the Quincunciall, Lozenge, or Net-work Plantations of the Ancients, Artificially, Naturally, Mystically Considered. With Sundry Observations* (1658). Despite the discouraging title page, it proved popular in his own age and was quickly twice reprinted. Moreover, at least its first text has found unqualified approval in the modern critical tradition. Its informing strategy loosely resembles the one analysed in his chapter on hares. Here, antiquarian research and field archaeology take the place of biology, but once more scholarship in the spirit of Baconian enquiry provides the platform for ethical digression and a transcendent conclusion in a radically different idiom. But it also resembles *Religio Medici* in its quiet endorsement of royalist perspectives and aspirations. Just as, in the eclipse of their cause, royalist poets turned to themes of retirement, of retreat to the country, so, too, 'In the 1650s, many royalist gentlemen up and down the country were inclined to take their minds off contemporary discomfiture by thinking about the remote past' (Parry 1995: 248). Graham Parry is surely right to place Browne's antiquarianism in this cultural context.

Hydriotaphia begin with an initial review of burial customs in antiquity and then turns to 'a Field of old *Walsingham*, not many moneths past' (Browne 1964: 94), where funeral urns have been discovered. Field archaeology was in its infancy in the seventeenth century, and Browne's careful recording of the urns, their bones and other contents, and of the site where they were discovered, is technically at the cutting edge. His eventual surmise, that the remains were Roman, has proved incorrect – they were Saxon – but contemporary limitations in knowledge about post-Roman pagan practices, rather than his method, were to blame.

Sometimes he returns to the concerns of *Pseudodoxia Epidemica*. That buried corpses are eaten by worms was and probably remains a popular assumption, 'But while we suppose common wormes in graves, 'tis not easie to finde any there; few in Church-yards above a foot deep, fewer or none in Churches, though in fresh decayed bodies' (ibid.: 110). Yet by the fifth and final chapter he is moving inexorably to his mighty resolution. Robin Robbins's phrase for the tract, 'solemn music', is felicitous (*DNB* 2004). So, too, is Parry's judgement that this last chapter 'must be the most sublime and richly orchestrated passage of English ever composed' (Parry 1995: 255). The musical allusions feel apt, though it is the music of Beethoven, Brahms or Mahler, not the restrained precision of the English or Italian baroque. Indeed, the ending seems overwhelming, like the closing bars of some mighty symphony. Burial custom after custom has been described, meditated on, but now they are recognized as spiritually bankrupt attempts to secure a specious kind of immortality. Even to be remembered eludes the vast majority of the dead, and to be remembered confers no real immortality: 'There is nothing strictly immortall, but immortality; whatever hath no beginning may be confident of no end. All others have a dependent being, and within the reach of destruction' (Browne 1964:123). His great themes are brought together in a grandiloquent final paragraph:

> To subsist in lasting Monuments, to live in their productions, to exist in their names, and praedicament of *Chymera's*, was large satisfaction unto old expectations, and made one part of their *Elyziums*. But all this is nothing in the Metaphysicks of true belief. To live indeed is to be again our selves, which being not only an hope but an evidence in noble beleevers; 'Tis all one to lye in St *Innocents* Church-yeard, as in the Sands of AEgypt: Ready to be any thing, in the extasie of being ever, and as content with six foot as the Moles of *Adrianus*. (Ibid.: 125)

Yet note how, amid the grandiloquence, Browne remains true to his method, still tying the lofty assertion of faith to the minutiae of antiquarian scholarship. His own notes gloss the details – St Innocent's in Paris, because there 'bodies soon consume', and the Mole of Adrianus, because that was a stately mausoleum, and he adds the necessary detail, that it stood in Rome where the Castel Sant'Angelo now stands. *The Garden of Cyrus* has received less critical attention, and it remains for the modern reader something of a challenge. A quincunx, its focus, is a group of five objects of which four are arranged in a rectangle and a fifth is positioned in the middle, like the five on a die. Browne begins by considering the significance of its adoption as a recurrent motif in the gardens of antiquity. But he ranges immensely wider, pondering its occurrence in animal and botanical anatomy, its adoption in the construction of nets and its appearance in some celestial formations. Yet this text differs less from *Hydriotaphia* than may superficially seem to be the case. Once more, Browne is driving towards a moral and, indeed, theological conclusion and with a contemplation of last things: 'All things began in order, so shall they end, and so shall they begin again; according to the ordainer of order and mystical Mathemmaticks of the City of Heaven' (ibid: 174).

Poetry for Parliament and Protectorate

This section considers that rather slighter corpus of poetry written by supporters of parliament and the Protectorate, and ends with a consideration of Cromwellian panegyric. Milton and Andrew Marvell nowadays are the most frequently read and responded to, though Milton's apparently small verse output from the mid-century was for the most part not printed till 1673, and two poems, the sonnets to Cromwell and Fairfax, appeared only posthumously, and nearly all of Marvell's early verse remained unprinted till after his death, nor is there much evidence of significant manuscript dissemination. I consider much more briefly the poetry of George Wither and Thomas May, whose status is evidently under current revision. I begin, though, with Thomas St Nicholas, a writer of some wit and charm, whose surviving poetry, extant in a single manuscript, appeared first in print as recently as 2002.

St Nicholas, a gentry-class, Cambridge-educated lawyer with business interests in the iron industry, was an activist in the cause of parliament and a supporter of the Protectorate. In the mid- and late 1640s he functioned as paymaster to the forces under Sir Thomas Fairfax, and in the 1650s he was a prominent local office-holder and intermittently sat in parliaments. Two principal clusters of his verse survive: that of the 1660s will be considered in chapter 6; that of the 1640s at its most interesting relates to his capture at the surrender of Rotherham and his experiences as a prisoner.

Neville Davies's annotation and commentary on St Nicholas disclose few debts to vernacular poems, though rather more debts to contemporary prose from newsbooks to works of popular piety, and an awareness of classical authors, especially Horace. The Bible, however, predominates as a source. His verse, prosodically, has an untutored, almost primitive quality. But he comes at the issues that interest him without the heroic and chivalric templates of Cowley or Lovelace. His own experience, recorded with ample circumstantial detail, rests at the centre of poetry, as he observes and remembers with a freshness of vision the forced intimacies, the discomforts, and indignities of a prison life which seem closer to the world of Alexander Solzhenitsyn than of Lovelace entertaining his Althea through the prison bars. Yet, *in extremis*, there is wit and precision:

> We did desire to see if we could get
> Some beds to rest on, and two things at last
> Like beds we got, whereon when we were cast
> Straightways an ambuscado we discovered.
> A numerous brood of grey-coats there that hovered,
> Expert old soldiers that had thoroughly lined
> The sheets and blankets, who, as if quite pined,
> Made such a fierce assault, not giving over,
> And stuck so close that ere we could recover
> It was at least a fortnight first. So these
> Made these our beds prove but a little ease.
> After that night I lay some eight nights more
> Where, though it made my bones a little sore
> At first: the top of a clean parlour table.
> ('For My Son', ll.292–305; St Nicholas 2002: 21)

In its extreme haecceity, the passage, in an almost Wordsworthian manner, teeters on the edge of banality. There are no parlour tables for Lovelace's cavalier to sleep on for one night, let alone eight (but, then, there are no 'bowers' in St Nicholas's verse). While Lovelace can ponder flies and spiders, the bedbug is not a topic for his meditation. St Nicholas, ingeniously, metamorphoses these most unpleasant of ectoparasites into 'greycoats', veteran infantry of the Earl of Newcastle, who line the edges of the bedding like musketeers lining a hedge or wall and attacking as if from ambush to take the sleeper by surprise.

'For My Son', endorsed 'Pontrefact Castle, July 7, 1643', is a social act, a fixing of experience in verse for the illumination of the poet's son, explicitly avoiding engagement with the large issues behind the conflict: 'I'll only leave a word or two, my son, / For thee, that thou mayst know when I am gone / What in these troubles did befall thy father' (ll.13–15; ibid.: 15). Several poems begin with episodes from his wartime experience and develop into a wider view as a starting point for larger meditation (for example, 'A Meditation on the Way towards York 'cross Marston Moor after the Great Battle there, July 16, 1644, being the Day of the Rendition of York to the Lord Fairfax'; ibid.: 37); others function as a kind of therapy. 'A Farewell to the Provost-Marshal of Pontefract Castle upon his Journey Homewards, September 18, 1643' sends off the hated gaoler, presumably in a text shared with other prisoners, in a poem of parting that ends with an epitaph they would like to bestow on his grave, preferably sooner rather than later, once the 'Provost-Marshal Mors [Death] / ... has put him i'the hole, and there, don' you see, / Will keep his fat corpse till the worms have their fee' (ll.21, 23–4; ibid.: 33). Another poem recounts the ingenious killing of a mouse that has been nibbling the prisoners' books, using an improvised trap, a 'Samson's post', that dropped Ralegh's weighty *History of the World* on it: 'So great a weight as needs contained must be / In such an universal history' ('Upon the sight of a Mouse, Taken by a Samson's Post, under Sir Walter Ralegh's *History*', ll.4–5; ibid.: 32).

Perhaps surprisingly, some of Milton's mid-century verse shares common ground with St Nicholas's. The volume published by Moseley contained the sonnet 'Daughter to that good Earl', to Lady Margaret Ley, which functions as a delicately turned compliment to a friend and neighbour, though it celebrates, too, her father, the Earl of Marlborough, as a good courtier in a corrupt court, a good judge in a corrupt judiciary ('Sonnet X'; Milton 1997: 289–91). 'Sonnet IX. Lady, that in the prime of earliest youth', again seems like a poem directed to an intimate, while 'Sonnet VIII. When the assault was intended to the City', shares St Nicholas's practice of taking his own experience, with a grain of irony, as a starting point for larger themes. Arguably those harrowing sonnets, on blindness and on the death of his second wife, share some of the devotional practices, common within the Puritan tradition, of making an account of one's standing and of looking for evidence of providential workings even in personal hardship. Sometimes, their uncompromisingly bleak resolutions are a shocking deviation from the expected consolation of divinity. 'Methought I saw my late espoused saint' recounts a dream in which his late wife appears to him *and he can see her*, but the dream vision brings no comfort, not even a promise of reunion in death: 'But O as to embrace me she inclined / I waked, she fled, and day brought back my night' ('Sonnet XIX', ll.13–14; ibid.: 348). When the poet asks, 'Doth God exact day-labour, light denied[?]', 'Patience', to be equated with Christian stoicism, counsels that all human endeavour is irrelevant to an omnipotent godhead. Rather like those unfallen angels in *Paradise Lost* posted by God to guard hell's gate but withdrawn as soon as there is anything for them to do, 'They also serve who only stand and wait' ('Sonnet XVI', ll.7, 14; ibid.: 333).

Milton's most innovative poems of the mid-century decades, his explicitly political sonnets, were not printed until much later. They fall into two groups: the anti-Presbyterian sonnets of the 1640s, printed in his 1673 collection of his minor verse; and the sonnets to Cromwell, Fairfax and Sir Henry Vane, the first two of which were not printed in Milton's lifetime. The third was printed in 1662 in a posthumous biography of Vane, a radical parliamentarian, who, though not a regicide, was prosecuted and decollated at the particular vindictiveness of Charles II (Hutton 1991: 171; Milton 1997: 329–30). Milton, whose own escape from similar treatment had been uncertain and recent, probably did not welcome the publication, presumably from Vane's private papers, and did not reprint it in 1673. Of course, he need not have felt any such reservation about the first group of poems: nobody in the 1670s would be punished for being unpleasant to Presbyterians.

Though Milton did not invent the political sonnet in English, previous examples are few. He brings to the form an extraordinary capacity to engage in miniature with complex issues. 'Sonnet XII. On the Detraction which followed upon my Writing Certain Treatises' (again a title in an idiom shared with St Nicholas), not only rehearses his response to his divorce tracts, but also defines the moral requirements for civic integrity, without which 'all this waste of wealth, and loss of blood' is futile (l.14; Milton 1997: 297). In 'On the New Forcers of Conscience under the Long Parliament', technically a *sonnetto caudato* or sonnet with a tail, he works through a series of disparaging allusions to leading English Presbyterians and their Scottish allies ('Scotch What-d'ye-call') to the witty climax of his final line: 'New *Presbyter* is but old *Priest* writ large' (ll.12, 20; ibid.: 299–300). (As editors all explain, 'priest' is etymologically cognate with 'presbyter'.) The sonnet to Vane shows Milton's alignment with the most militant wing of revolutionary Independency, asserting the role of civilians in government and advocating the separation of church and state, an argument 'thou hast learned, which few have done', which indicates a critical edge to Milton's endorsement of the republican English state (l.11; ibid.: 331). The sonnets to Cromwell and to Fairfax, while originating in a panegyric impulse, modulate into more critical advice. Cromwell's victories at Dunbar and Worcester are rehearsed, but their value is reduced: 'much remains / To conquer still; peace hath her victories / No less renowned than war', which once more take the form of the separation of church and state, linked now with an implied attack on a professional clergy supported by tithes ('To the Lord General Cromwell', ll.9–11; ibid.: 328–9). Similarly, 'On the Lord General Fairfax at the Siege of Colchester', written before the purging of parliament which ushered in the trial of the king, calls on him to carry into the civil realm the militancy he has shown in arms. Once more, martial achievement is questioned unless it is converted into political action: 'In vain doth valour bleed / While avarice, and rapine share the land' (ll.13–14; ibid.: 325). Rather later than these, a remarkable sonnet, 'On the late Massacre in Piedmont', densely rehearses the anteriority of the Vaudois' Protestantism over other churches. It describes the atrocities recently committed against them, vividly selecting the details (scattered bones on the bleak hillside, mothers and children rolled down the rocks), articulating the fitfully maintained Cromwellian fantasy of forming a Protestant international movement against popery ('Sonnet XV'; ibid.: 342–3).

Milton may have begun *Paradise Lost* in the 1650s; indeed he may, some speculate, have written *Samson Agonistes* in whole or part before 1660; both, however, are publications of the Restoration and we return to them in chapter 6.

Andrew Marvell's first English verse to be printed appeared among the prefatory poems to Lovelace's first *Lucasta*. It declares some common ground with the royalist poet and shows evident concerns about 'th'infection of our times' ('To his Noble Friend Mr. Richard Lovelace, upon his Poems', l.4; Marvell 2003a: 20). Indeed, not only does he excel in poetic subgenres favoured by the libertine tradition in Caroline and cavalier verse, but much of his overtly political poetry manifests a studied ambivalence. The Marvell oeuvre falls into two major groups, poems on affairs of state, predominantly in the satirical mode, written after 1660 and usually circulated in print; and other poems which either engage with issues of the late 1640s or the 1650s or else are usually attributed to the mid-century decades and which, with occasional exceptions, were not published till the posthumous collection of 1681, though some would seem to have had a limited circulation in manuscript. The former group belongs in chapter 6. (The poems celebrating Cromwell were cut from nearly all extant copies of the 1681 collection.)

The mid-century poems, though a relatively small corpus, show astonishing accomplishment across a considerable range of kinds. Though current critical enthusiasm for his later works has stressed their importance in establishing his seventeenth-century reputation (Chernaik and Dzelzainis 1999a), their revaluation should not be at the expense of those lyric poems so eagerly acclaimed in the early twentieth century. Indeed, 'To his Coy Mistress' certainly stands comparison with Donne's paradigmatic 'The Flea', and, though it lacks its intellectual playfulness, it more vividly realizes its principal themes, of the transience of human life and of the violence of human sexuality:

> But at my back I always hear
> Times winged chariot hurrying near:
> And yonder all before us lie
> Deserts of vast eternity.
> Thy beauty shall no more be found;
> Nor, in thy marble vault, shall sound
> My echoing song: then worms shall try
> That long preserved virginity:
> And your quaint honour turn to dust;
> And into ashes all my lust.
> The grave's a fine and private place,
> But none I think do there embrace.
>   (ll.21–32; Marvell 2003a: 83)

Its time-honoured place in the seduction repertoire of more bookish undergraduates must not obscure the extraordinary quality of this writing. He takes a familiar image, the emblem of time's chariot, and reanimates it with a plausible detail – the poet hears it behind him, like a dangerous vehicle threatening to run him over. That resonant image, of the deserts of vast eternity, is almost thrown away, its logical difficulty (how can that which is endless have an attribute of size?) left unexplored. Although 'vast' could be simply an intensifier (*OED*, signification 5), the spatiality of the image keeps its other meanings in play. '[E]choing song' proleptically but a little bewilderingly implies that already he sings as if in her tomb. Those intrusive worms are at once embarrassing, as invasive as a gynaecologist's fingers, and shocking, but the tone remains cool, controlled and somehow aloof, confirmed in the measured couplet that ends the verse paragraph. Yet the sexual experience he opposes to the sterility of continence is almost as alarming, though here there is no mitigating irony, as the lovers 'tear our pleasures with rough strife, / Thorough the iron gates of life' (ll.43–4; ibid.: 84), ripping them, destroying them, swallowing them down piecemeal.

Marvell was the last considerable seventeenth-century poet of the pastoral tradition, and he regenerates the mode with a new intellectualism and with a judicious admixture of the georgic. To his shepherdesses he opposes the complex figure of the mower, at once the embodiment of seasonal progression, mutability and death, and their victim:

> . . . Flow'rs, and grass, and I and all,
> Will in one common ruin fall.
> For *Juliana* comes, and she
> What I do to the grass, does to my thoughts and me.
> ('The Mower's Song', ll.21–4; ibid.: 145)

Simultaneously, the poem has the characteristics of a pleasant, rather courtly song and a larger engagement, undeveloped, unsustained, oblique, with human frailty and transience. Marvell takes English pastoral in its final phase into new territory. He renders it poignant, showing a world of idealized or escapist fantasy invaded by a sterner reality, as in 'The Nymph complaining for the Death of her Faun', in which 'wanton troopers' have killed a pet (l.1; ibid.: 69).

Similar intrusive melancholy threatens the serenity of his longest pre-Restoration poem and perhaps his most ambitious – 'Upon Appleton House, To My Lord Fairfax' – in Alastair Fowler's words, 'In sheer length . . . an innovative, brilliant example [of the country-house poem]' (1994: 295). Marvell describes a summer's day in the grounds and estate of Lord Fairfax, the former commander-in-chief of the New Model Army, though an opponent of the regicide, who followed that action with withdrawal to his Yorkshire properties, a move which initially appeared to be temporary, though in the event initiated a protracted retirement from public life. The house itself is depicted as an embodiment of Protestant virtue. Marvell recollects that much of it was built from material reclaimed from a nunnery, which in turn supports a panegyric family history that demonstrates Fairfacian hostility to abuses of the medieval church and its grasping secularism even before the Henrician Reformation. A precise and ingenious description of the garden, which seems to be laid out to reflect a military theme, leads to a meditation on England as a Paradise lost: 'But war all this doth overgrow: / We ordnance plant and powder sow' (ll.343–4; Marvell 2003: 226). The georgic scene of haymaking again recollects the civil wars:

> The mower now commands the field;
> In whose new traverse seemeth wrought
> A camp of battle newly fought:
> Where, as the meads with hay, the plain
> Lies quilted o'er with bodies slain:
> The women that with forks it fling,
> Do represent the pillaging.
> (ll.418–24; ibid.: 228)

The grim image momentarily transforms a scene of healthy rural endeavour into a landscape of devastation and defines the limitations of retirement in an age of internecine conflict; memory and imagination cannot retire. Another allusion addresses the threat posed by political radicalism. The mown meadow is 'this naked equal flat, / Which Levellers take pattern at' (ll.449–50; ibid.: 229). In all, the poem celebrates as orderly and hierarchical a rural community as that depicted in Herrick's 'The Hock-Cart', but order rests on responsibility and authority. As Fowler shrewdly observes, though the sensibility of the poet has an unusually central role in the poem, the house owner is felt as a pervasive presence: 'M[arvell] is only the priest of the patron cult: F[airfax] is the god' (1994: 295). Ideologically, this is a profoundly conservative poem, a reminder that, if the world is not to be turned upside down in an England without a king, then the natural leaders, like Fairfax, distinguished by birth, upbringing, family tradition and an austere morality, have an obligation to lead.

A dispute has arisen about the date at which Marvell composed what is perhaps his most finely crafted lyric, 'The Garden'. Echoes of other writers not in print till the Restoration period may point to a date about 1668, a view tentatively endorsed by Marvell's most recent editor (Marvell 2003a: 152). Yet it bears little similarity to the poems he was writing around that time. In tone and form, it resembles the early lyrics, and in its praise of a retirement over the active life it shares some themes with 'Upon Appleton House'.

The poem is characteristically evasive. At its centre lies a Platonic reverie in which a garden provides the appropriate condition for the soul temporarily to quit the body and to contemplate an eternal world only transiently and imperfectly reflected in the world accessible to the senses. That ecstasy is hedged around by images of mutability. But the level of seriousness is difficult to pin down. It ends with a description of a sundial, which marks the passage of the hours, but it is also in the form of a floral ornament, and a bee busily tells the time as it gathers nectar. The flowers that make it up are themselves emblems of an unsustainable beauty. Earlier, the line 'Insnared with flow'rs, I fall on grass' (l.40, ibid.: 157) reminds readers and editors of Job 18:10, 'The snare for him in the ground, and a trap for him in the way', and Isaiah 40:6, 'All flesh is grass'. Yet there is a playfulness that undercuts that high solemnity: the poet ends on the grass through stumbling on melons. The opening stanzas establish the advantages of retreat, but once more the high theme is subverted. The poet's love of trees is manifest in an intention to carve on them the names of his true loves – not mistresses but the trees themselves. Marvell leaves us with a perfectly formed but ultimately perplexing poem.

The idiom of Marvell's non-political lyrics suggests close affinity with royalist poets. Marvell was a beneficiary of patronage from Fairfax (as tutor to his daughter), and from Cromwell (as tutor to his ward), and eventually a civil servant of the English republic (as Latin secretary to the Council of State), a colleague of Milton and Nedham, but the values inscribed in his overtly political verse are not straightforwardly partisan. 'An Horatian Ode upon Cromwell's Return from Ireland' both commemorates the success of the Irish campaign and anticipates the advance towards Scotland, which culminated in the triumphant battle of Dunbar. Yet it opens with perhaps the most vivid contemporary portrait of the execution of Charles I, incongruously bowing his head to the block 'Down as upon a bed', in a description that does not shirk the horrors of decollation (l.64; ibid.: 276). On issues Milton raised in his slightly later sonnet, about religious liberty and associated domestic reform, the poem is silent. It sits curiously alongside what was probably an almost contemporary poem, his mock elegy, 'Tom May's Death'. May was a significant neoclassical poet, a verse translator and imitator of Lucan, whose revised edition of his *Continuation* of Lucan's *Pharsalia*, something of a publishing success like his translation, had been adjusted to reflect the impact of the regicide (Norbrook 1999: 227–8). Marvell contrasts his alleged ingratitude to Charles, who had extended some patronage to him formerly, with the integrity of the late Ben Jonson, the real founder of English literary neoclassicism. Yet Marvell's charge against May, that in a facile and venal way he found classical parallels to contemporary politics, is exactly how he had concluded his own explicitly neoclassical ('Horatian') ode when he asserts that Cromwell will be 'A Caesar... ere long to Gaul, / To Italy an Hannibal' (ll.101–1; Marvell 2003a: 278; cf. 'Tom May's Death', l.48; Marvell 2003a: 122; see also Corns 1992: 231–5). As Norbrook concludes, 'It is very hard... to see the two poems as easily compatible' (Norbrook 1999: 280).

But Marvell's praise for Cromwell, even as early as the ode, attributes to him a stabilizing and patriotic role. For Marvell, Cromwell's decisive intervention into politics is an end to revolutionary uncertainty. 'The First Anniversary of the Government under His Highness the Lord Protector', which was printed as a pamphlet by Thomas Newcomb, who regularly printed works for the Cromwellian regime, flirts unconvincingly with the notion that the Lord Protector may usher in the millennium with a noticeable tepidness (Corns 1992: 241–2), though its central perspective on Cromwell is that he functions as a remarkable and superior autocrat, like a king but much better than any current or former king. Also, as if by an irony of history, Cromwell can control dissident elements in a way that Charles I could not. The Fifth Monarchists, whose leaders had been recently imprisoned for preaching against Cromwell, are carefully traduced through the old stratagem of guilt by association (with Quakers, Ranters, Adamites, Muslims and others), leaving the reader relieved that 'the great captain' is around to make them 'tremble one fit more' (ll.321–2; Marvell 2003a: 296).

Marvell's early essays in the satirical mode share some of the strategies found in his panegyrics. 'The Character of Holland', written at the time of the first Anglo-Dutch War, figures the enemy land as the breeding ground for socially disruptive religious radicals, the 'Staple of sects and mint of schism' (l.72; ibid.: 253). The poem invites a range of interpretative approaches. Plainly it exemplifies an important stage in the construction both of the national image of England and, through devaluative stereotyping, of its differentiation from other nations. But its technical accomplishment and innovation should be recognized, too. Satire, since its late Elizabethan beginnings, had been designed to be enticingly amusing and purposefully wounding, objectives which John Taylor the Water Poet, the best known satirist at the start of the conflict, had carried over into his own royalist writing. In 'The Character of Holland', as in his anti-Catholic personality attack, 'Fleckno, an English Priest at Rome', and indeed as in 'Tom May's Death', Marvell showed what a writer of great technical control, of literary wit and imagination could do with heroic couplets written in the satirical mode: 'Holland, that scarce deserves the name of land, / As but th'off-scouring of the British sand' (ll.1–2; ibid.: 250). Marvell opens his poem with a series of witty reflections on the geomorphology of the United Provinces, serving a larger argument about their former dependency on English support and about their general wretchedness. He quibbles on Hol*land*. The emphatic and pleasing 'British sand' closes the couplet, providing the rhyme word, and equates the whole of Holland with the least of Britain. Marvell's later achievements in this idiom could be anticipated from his poems of the 1650s.

John Dryden's earliest major poem was an exercise in panegyric, 'Heroic Stanzas Consecrated to the Glorious Memory Of his most Serene and Renowned Highness Oliver, Late Lord Protector of this Commonwealth, etc. Written after the Celebration of his Funeral'. It stresses the role of Cromwell as a force for stability, bringing civil discord to an end: 'He fought to end our fighting, and essayed / To stanch the blood by breathing of the vein' (ll.47–8; Dryden 1995–2005: I, 21). Besides an obvious prosodic facility, the chief technical interest of the poem rests in its sustained neoclassical imperialism: the death of Dryden's Oliver is commemorated through allusion to the funeral rites of Roman emperors. It was printed in 1659 in *Three poems to the happy memory of the most renowned Oliver, late Lord Protector of this Commonwealth*, alongside poems by Thomas Sprat, future historian of the Royal Society and Bishop of Rochester, and Edmund Waller, formerly a royalist conspirator and encomiast. The volume constitutes an attempt at state art, a literary monument roughly equivalent to the elaborate state funeral bestowed on Cromwell. The imperial idiom pervades the collection. Waller had returned from exile in 1651 and by mid-decade completed his rehabilitation with the publication of a poem exemplary of the Augustan idiom, *A Panegyrick to my Lord Protector, by a Gentleman that Love the Peace, Union, and Prosperity of the English Nation*. Cromwellian government, like the empire of Augustus, is validated by its success in securing peace and stability and in subjugating other nations:

Your drooping Country torn with Civill Hate,
Restor'd by you [Cromwell], is made a glorious State;
The seat of Empire, where the *Irish* come,
And the unwilling *Scotch* to fetch their doome:
The Sea's our own, and now all Nations greet
With bending Sayles each Vessel of our Fleet...

(Waller 1655: 3–4)

Waller's *Panegyrick*, like Marvell's *First Anniversary* printed by Newcomb, aroused considerable contemporary attention, for Waller had been a high-profile royalist. Norbrook comments, 'Waller had deftly dissociated Augustan poetic culture from the Stuarts and found an idiom for supporting the Protectorate which could appeal to a traditional political elite that was weary of tumult' (1999: 307). Indeed so, and the model he developed found followers among that younger generation of writers among whom the tumults – and the aspirations – of the 1640s were experienced only vicariously.

By the mid-1650s an extensive Cromwellian establishment had emerged, supporting a system of patronage analogous to that of the 1620s or 1630s. Waller, who was connected to Cromwell by marriage, accepted office as a commissioner for trade. Dryden probably was a minor civil servant alongside Marvell, though the details are uncertain. Sprat was a protégé of John Wilkins, Master of Wadham College, Oxford, and Cromwell's brother-in-law. Of course, Milton and Marchamont Nedham respectively occupied the principal roles of Latin apologist and periodical propagandist. George Wither, whose widely read emblem book was considered in chapter 4, stood substantially outside the golden circle, though his writings of the mid-century decades show interesting development from individualism and eccentricity to a version of Cromwellian conformity. Briefly in arms for parliament, he published in 1643 his *Campo-musae, or The field-musings of Captain George Wither*, mixing rudimentary political philosophy with reflections on recent events, though keeping himself near the centre of the account. Wither generally appears as the hero of his own narrative, and Norbrook's suggestion, that the poem shows 'a commitment to setting personal experience in a wider political context', perhaps understates his self-obsession (Norbrook 1999: 89). By 1655 and *The Protector. A poem briefly illustrating the superminency of that dignity*, he seems to have accommodated himself to the predominant idiom, although the declarative mode seems strained. The poem begins, 'LORD, of the noblest of all Soveraign Stiles, / Of BRITAN'S Empire, Provinces, and Isles: / Bright Load-star of the North…' (Wither 1655: sig. A2v).

Pamphlet Wars

Intermittently since the Reformation, fiercely polemical exchanges had exercised professional theologians, eager amateurs and others recruited primarily for their writing abilities. In the Elizabethan period and into the reign of James I, Catholics, for the most part based in continental Europe, assailed the Protestant church settlement and celebrated the witness of their martyrs. Puritans, critical of what they saw as the residual popery of that settlement, berated episcopalian church government, ridiculed the Book of Common Prayer, vestments and rituals, and eventually squabbled among themselves. Meanwhile, apologists for the leadership of the Church of England attempted to meet attacks from both directions. The scale of such activity is significant but relatively small. Peter Milward's surveys of printed sources identify 630 works of religious controversy in the Elizabethan age and 764 in the Jacobean, which averages out, respectively, at 14 and 35 a year, though some periods saw much more heated and frequent exchanges than others (Milward 1977, 1978). These works manifested a considerable range both in tone and form, from the most sober, detailed and scholarly exchanges to the pungent and exuberant satire of the Marprelate controversy, which contains some of the brightest prose in Elizabethan literature. Broadly, the pattern continued through the years of the personal rule, and occasioned probably the most serious and ultimately destructive episodes in the martyrdom of Prynne, Burton and Bastwick in 1637. As the Long Parliament turned to the grievances raised against the Laudian church, these controversies, in some measure fuelled by the agitation and writings of Scottish Presbyterians, flared into vigorous life that continued into the mid-1640s as the frictions grew between mainstream Presbyterians and their allies and more radical groups from Congregational Independency to the most extreme sectaries. David Loewenstein and John Morrill calculate that, over the 220 months between the calling of the Long Parliament and the demise of the restored Rump, 'explicitly religious publication averaged between twenty and fifty titles *a month*' among the books collected by the bookseller George Thomason (2002: 671; my italics).

The rapidly developing discourse of controversial theology had a long tradition on which to draw. The language of political conflict, however, at least as it was shaped in the medium of print, was relatively rudimentary. Yet, as issues of religious controversy emerge as issues about where authority should reside within the state, that discourse develops too. But matters of principle, at least in the early years, are less often and less clearly articulated than the discussion of specific events, cases or grievances, and the construction of negative representations of political enemies and rivals. As the king is brought to trial, so the vocabulary of politics matures. Royalist apologetics, particularly in the hugely successful *Eikon Basilike* (1649; many editions), which purports to be the king's account of recent history and his part in it, works in unprecedented circumstances the old routine of celebrating a holy image of the monarch. The opposition needed to find explanations and justifications for dismissing a large section of the elected members of the Long Parliament and, after the regicide, for bringing the king to trial and execution. Rudimentary and oblique arguments about the characteristics and role of the ancient constitution, sometimes heard in the 1630s, were more frequently and freely articulated in the early years of the Long Parliament. There were vitally important documents widely produced and distributed, perhaps none more so than the Solemn League and Covenant, first promulgated in 1643 and widely circulated as a contract to which many citizens were required to subscribe. Often, political discourse drew upon the discourses of the law, both in thinking about political agreements as contractual and in the forensic skills of prosecution. As the decade progresses, debate is widened by more fundamental discussion of what the state is for, how it is to serve its citizens, what their rights and powers may be and what indeed is the contract between government and the governed. By the 1650s something approaching a mature republican theoretical position may be identified. Moreover, in the Levellers, England had its first modern political party, indeed, a party that probably more closely resembled the popular movements of the nineteenth and twentieth centuries than the Whigs and Tories of the late Stuart and early Hanoverian period. It was an explicitly secular organization, and its programme and objectives were formulated in successive versions of *The Agreement of the People* (first edition, 1647) as a sort of statement of the founding principles of a new constitution: '*These things we declare to be our* native Rights, *and therefore are agreed and resolved to maintain them*' (Morton 1975: 141). At about the same time,

Gerrard Winstanley, proposing social, economic and political change of a hitherto unconscionable kind, laboured to find a fit idiom, as we shall see, resolving his difficulties with great creative elan.

Two other forces were major stimuli to the development of a polemical pamphlet literature: public opinion and the market for news. Who cared what 'the public thought'? Increasingly, in the 1620s, 1630s and early 1640s, both the king and his supporters and those who opposed them cared. Elections traditionally had reflected the collaboration of local men of property to agree on a candidate who could be acclaimed unanimously as the representative of his community. Contested elections were extremely rare and were regarded not as indicators of political health, but of a distemper within the community, of failure on the part of county gentry or urban governors to control and lead the electorate. In the elections for the parliaments of 1640, local contests were more frequent, and reflected and anticipated the growing polarity of opinion within the political nation. Moreover, they were, arguably, conducted by an electorate that was not only more knowing and politically conscious, but also in some cases larger and a wider section of society (see Hirst 1975; Manning 1976; Kishlansky 1986; and useful summaries in Richardson 1977: ch. 8; Hughes 1991: ch. 2). In terms of political activity, it mattered considerably in 1640 what enfranchised Englishmen thought; once the war began, mobilization depended on a broad spectrum of society and the willingness of the middling and lower sorts to bear arms for king or parliament.

We noted in chapter 3 a growing market for those genres that carried news about national and international affairs to those literate and propertied sections of the population that were not privy to the highest circles of power, and we noted, too, governmental attempts to control or stop that flow of news, something that was more easily done with respect to print, rather than manuscript, circulation. The late 1630s and early 1640s stimulated demand afresh. Not only were there remarkable events unfolding, but they often had a direct significance for a population among whom there were a new political excitement and polarized partisanship. Hence there rapidly developed a periodical press, alongside the frequent publication of newsbooks reporting, for the most part, a single event. Almost all sides perceived the advantage in producing their own version, both in terms of controlling and selecting the factual content and in terms of the ideological perspective projected and encouraged. We shall turn shortly to the periodical press to consider the achievements of Marchamont Nedham, its first real master.

Thousands of titles were printed over the central decades of the seventeenth century. George Thomason managed to collect about 15,000 books and pamphlets and about 8,000 individual issues of periodicals, and, it is generally acknowledged, he missed many. Of the polemical items produced, the overwhelming majority contain little that would interest a student of literature in our own age; however, they may illuminate aspects of social, religious and political history. Typically, the prose style is at best functional and pedestrian, the imagery sparse and familiar, there is little humour and that usually of a jeering kind, and even the polemical strategies adopted are often clumsily transparent. Yet within the cluster of genres that rapidly developed work of real distinction and an abiding fascination of a literary, rather than merely evidential, kind can be found almost throughout the period, particularly in the work of radical sectaries, especially Ranters and Quakers, in the personal narratives of Leveller activists and, above all, in the astonishing achievements of John Milton and Gerrard Winstanley.

Milton's career as pamphleteer was distinctively fragmentary. Probably radicalized in his views on church government no later than 1637, he remained silent over the opening months of the Long Parliament, when matters of religion – and the failings of William Laud – were already hotly debated, though he may well have supplied some information to his future allies, the Smectymnuus writing consortium of leading Presbyterian divines, which they printed as a postscript to one of their antiprelatical publications (Hoover and Corns 2004). However, once launched into print in his own right, with *Of Reformation* (1641), he hammered the leading spokesmen of prelacy again and again over 1641–42, dismissing the evidence for church government by a hierarchy of bishops in *Of Prelatical Episcopacy* (1641) and *The Reason of Church-Government* (1642), defending the Smectymnuans from Joseph Hall, the most able apologist for prelacy, in *Animadversions upon the Remonstrants Defence* (1641), and defending himself from an anonymous confuter in *An Apology against a Pamphlet Call'd A Modest Confution* (1642).

The very title of some of those tracts indicates an important characteristic of much of Milton's polemical writing – and of much of the mid-century pamphlet wars: this is controversial literature, locked into exchanges in which tracts are written to second or to assail the publications of others or defend the work of oneself or an ally. This is not a medium, for the most part, for the calm exposition of argument as in an academic discourse. The imagery of warfare understandably informs much of the critical language used to describe this corpus just as surely as it was adopted by Milton and by others to represent their own polemical activities. Late in his career, in his Latin *Second Defence* (1654) he still represents himself metaphorically in arms to defend the cause: 'I met him [Salmasius, his immediate adversary] in single combat and plunged into his reviling throat this pen, the weapon of his own choice' (Milton 1953–82: IV.i.556). Of course, civil warfare and pamphlet exchanges don't really have a great deal in common: generally, nobody dies from a brusque confutation, however humiliating. But they do share a common basis in aggression, in the eschewing of compromise, and in ideological polarization.

Milton, however, probably thought that the medium did indeed admit of dialogue of sorts between those who were culturally and ideological adjacent. Anti-episcopal controversy died down as the shooting war began in 1642, leaving Laud imprisoned to await his eventual fate, and Milton fell silent for 16 months before he attempted his first constructive (rather than offensive or apologetic) pamphlet, *The Doctrine and Discipline of Divorce* (first edition, 1643; second edition, much revised, 1644). Milton argues for radical reform of the divorce laws, to allow divorce, with the possibility of remarriage, for couples who discover themselves to be emotionally or intellectually or ideologically incompatible. As the law then stood, the grounds for divorce all related to desertion, physical cruelty, sexual dysfunction or immorality. Milton's tract provoked a response which may well have accelerated his radicalization away from the Presbyterian agenda of a uniform national church towards the greater diversity afforded under the Congregationalist model. Milton found himself bracketed with sectaries and heretics regarded as dangerous dissidents by his former allies. Thrown on the defensive, he reissued his tract in extended form. He attempted in *The Judgement of Martin Bucer* (1644) to find precedents for his position among the founding fathers of Protestantism. He laid out the biblical arguments in *Tetrachordon* (1645), and he slashingly rounded on an anonymous assailant in *Colasterion* (1645). In the process, recognizing that the new political ascendancy sought the kinds of press control that had developed in the personal rule, he produced his currently most widely read pamphlet, *Areopagitica* (1644), in which he argues for the rights of heterodox Protestants to have their views printed without pre-publication licensing.

Colasterion and *Tetrachordon* appeared in March 1645. In the following autumn, Humphrey Moseley, publisher of many luminaries of
the royalist literary tradition, brought out *Poems of Mr. John Milton,
both English and Latin*. Much as in Moseley's editions of the poets of
the personal rule, the title page has a nostalgic invocation of a lost
golden age, presided over by the genius of Henry Lawes: 'The songs
were set in Musick by Mr. Henry Lawes Gentleman of the Kings
Chappel, and one of His Maiesties Private Musick'. We have considered Milton's early verse in chapter 4, and this volume, plainly, is
ideologically diverse, though the anti-Laudianism of 'Lycidas', which
the astute may possibly have surmised when first it appeared in the
Cambridge collection of 1638, is made explicit in its headnote: 'the
author... foretells the ruin of our corrupted clergy then in their
height' (Milton 1997: 243). Thereafter, until 1649, Milton's publishing career was once more interrupted. He ends on a curious note, in an
assertion of his own high culture. The ideological significance of the
1645 collection continues to provoke critical discussion in our own
day. (See, for example, Corns 1982, 2002b; Wilding 1987: ch. 1;
Norbrook 1984, 2002.)

But his political trajectory could easily be surmised from comparing
his second cluster of tracts with his first: Milton, like many of those
who supported the execution of the king, was evidently en route to
revolutionary Independency, which recognized that Presbyterianism
would be as constraining as episcopacy to those unwilling to subscribe
to its newly asserted orthodoxies. Unsurprisingly, when next he publishes, it is to defend the rights of citizens to bring their rulers to trial,
even if they are kings. Charles was beheaded on 30 January 1649; a
fortnight later Milton's *Tenure of Kings and Magistrates* appeared,
retrospectively justifying the proceedings that led to regicide. The
Rump Parliament and the republican administration that it supported
found itself almost bereft of polemicists who could assume the *gravitas*
desirable in their official spokesmen. Milton's appearance in their ranks
must have seemed especially welcome. In mid-March the Council of
State appointed him Secretary for Foreign Tongues at an annual salary
of almost £300. He remained in government employment till the
autumn of 1659, and despite his deteriorating eyesight and eventual
blindness, he continued to discharge his principal duties of translating
into Latin the state letters of the English state to foreign regimes
(Campbell 1997: 186, *et passim*). He also wrote propaganda on behalf
of the government. In 1649 *Articles of Peace, made and concluded with*

the Irish Rebels, and Papists… Upon all which are added Observations
disclosed the treaties, representations and correspondence of the royalist commander in Ireland and the Ulster Presbyterians newly in
league with him against the infant republic, in such a way as to
condemn the king's party for betraying English interests in Ireland,
to involve the Presbyterians in that treason and to set a context for
what would be Cromwell's bloody and triumphant reconquest of
Ireland. Milton wrote the *Observations* that explain the significance
of the reproduced documents at the specific instruction of the Council
of State. His major vernacular project for the republic also appeared in
1649: *Eikonoklastes*, his chapter-by-chapter response to *Eikon Basilike*.
In the 1650s, he defended the regime again in three Latin treatises, the
First and *Second Defences* and *The Defence of Himself* (1651, 1654,
1655), aimed at a continental European readership and contrived in
part to support diplomatic initiatives of the English government.
These last five tracts were explicitly official publications. In 1660, as
the regime collapsed, he published three vernacular tracts, his two
editions of *The Readie and Easie Way to Establish a Free Commonwealth* and a pugnacious little pamphlet, *Brief Notes upon a Late
Sermon*. These followed a late foray into his old territory of church
government in his *Treatise of Civil Power in Ecclesiastical Causes* and
*Considerations touching the Likeliest Means to Remove Hirelings out of
the Church*. They represent the logical conclusion of his anticlericalism
of the mid-1640s. They oppose the support of the church by the state,
dismissing the role of the civil magistrate in ecclesiastical discipline and
arguing against the state endorsement of compulsory church taxes, in
the form of tithes, to support the clergy. Both arguments put him on
the radical side of the argument within the political grouping for which
he worked.

Given his continental reputation, which was based on his Latin
defences, and his high profile as adversary to the martyred Charles I,
Milton was probably regarded as the foremost apologist for English
republicanism. That he escaped execution in 1660 surprised his contemporaries, and he was briefly imprisoned. *Eikonoklastes* and the *First
Defence* were burnt by the hangman at the Old Bailey (Campbell 1997:
191–2). His prose oeuvre merits a central place in the intellectual and
political history of the mid-century, but what are its claims to critical
consideration?

Of course, the road from *Comus* to *Samson Agonistes* inevitably runs
through the territory occupied by his polemical prose. Milton studies

have long recognized that any attempt to address his work in terms of its development, its coherence or indeed its diversity must engage with those pamphlets. Michael Wilding merely makes explicit what many accounts assume when he observes:

> *Paradise Lost* has immediately relevant and urgent things to communicate to us today about war, about militarism, about political manipulation, about authority, about equality. Rather than seeing Milton's years of writing propaganda for the Commonwealth as an impediment between his aim and the achievement of his great poetic work, let us rather look at the poetry in the context of that period of political engagement. (1987: 4)

Milton has historically been celebrated as an agent and advocate of human progress and liberation, though such claims are not without their difficulties. Indeed, Milton's republican writing demystified political authority and asserted the rights of citizens to hold to account those who govern them. But it also justified a legal process against the king which would not stand much scrutiny and it provided the justification for the Cromwellian campaign in Ireland, which brought with it the immediate horrors of the mass execution of prisoners of war, at Drogheda and Wexford, the expropriation of the land of an indigenous people, and a wretched history of Anglo-Irish relations whose malign effect is felt to this day. Again, Milton's divorce tracts assert that marriage should have at its core something more affective than sating male libidos and generating children to pass on property, but the arguments rest on assumptions of male superiority. As Mary Nyquist concludes: 'much as the dominant discourse of the academy might like to celebrate this praiseworthy attention to mutuality, there are very few passages of any length in the divorce tracts that can be dressed up for the occasion' (1988: 105). Milton's anticlericalism leads him to advance the rights of simple, plain men to displace the minister's role in leading congregations. But in *Colasterion* he tries to silence the critic of his first divorce tract by asserting that such an adversary, formerly he alleges a mere servant, has no part to play in discussing such matters: 'This is not for an unbutton'd fellow to discuss in the Garret, at his tressle' (Milton 1953–82: II, 746). Even *Areopagitica*, that iconic text of the western liberal tradition, is premised on an easy invocation of populist anti-Catholic sentiment. Not only is 'popery' excluded from toleration, but also licensing is condemned *because* it is, on Milton's account, a Catholic invention. Milton exploits and endorses a vicious intolerance that had fed the bonfires of Elizabethan England and would so again in the Popish Plot. Moreover, the tract endorses the right of the state to censor books after publication. His blueprint for a free commonwealth, while it fends off the return of monarchy, contains little that is recognizably democratic in its model for stable government by a suitably godly subset of the classes that had traditionally ruled provincial England. His *Second Defence* actually contains a panegyric to a hereditary monarch, the eccentric figure of Queen Christina of Sweden: 'With what honor, with what respect, O queen, ought I always to cherish you' (ibid.: IV.i.604). Of course, Milton is both a child of his age and a writer seeking to engage his contemporaries in terms they could understand, but to value him in an unqualified way as a precursor of currently dominant ideologies of toleration and democracy both edges literary evaluation towards moral criticism and simplifies the issues that shape his text.

Indeed, much of the critical engagement with Milton's prose, over recent years, has been with these apparent inconsistencies, because they open up an appreciation of the polemical ingenuity he brings to his pamphleteering. Thus, the extraordinary vehemence of his attack on episcopacy reflects his objective of pushing on the Puritan reformation through a root-and-branch extirpation of prelacy that would admit of no compromise. His recurrent and undeviating hostility to Catholicism allows him, from a fairly extreme position on the spectrum of Puritan belief, to maintain a dialogue with more moderate Puritans whose world view, shaped by accounts of the Marian martyrs, was largely dominated by a fear of a return to Catholicism. Again, his dismissive attack on the servant-turned-lawyer who engaged with his divorce tracts can be seen as his resistance to that anti-sectary stereotyping, which took from royalist propaganda the image of the religious radical as a low-class tub-preacher: Milton speaks as a gentleman to other gentlemen with an appropriate disdain. His Latin defences are part of how the republic represented itself to the states of continental Europe, and it had signed an important treaty with Sweden just before the publication of Milton's tract (Fallon 1993: 161). Propaganda aims to persuade, and Milton is expert in achieving those larger ends of rhetoric. The new republic did not choose him lightly.

Once the exigencies of the polemical moment have been allowed for, some recurrent concerns and principles can be identified in Milton's prose oeuvre. Milton returns persistently to the rights and obligations of individual Christians (within the Protestant tradition) to think about theological issues and to follow ways of Christian worship that seem appropriate to themselves. With this concept comes a rejection of tradition and authority in matters of religion – each individual must freely engage the issue, not merely follow the dictates of a church, a regime, a priest – and it leads to a pervasive anticlericalism. Milton moves inexorably towards the views most explicitly expressed in his pamphlets of 1659, that religious leaders need no professional training and should certainly receive no fee, that they should have no recourse to the civil magistrate to secure their position or require the compliance of others, and that church taxes, that is, tithes, should not be compulsory. At the centre of those arguments is a kind of individualism that leads unsurprisingly to support for English republicanism. Historically and in his own age, monarchy was an enforcer of conscience. Moreover, for a king to have power over the beliefs, practices and, indeed, property of the citizen, unless he is inherently superior both morally and intellectually to that citizen, is – in terms Aristotle would have understood – a tyranny. As Milton observes in a brilliant passage added to *Eikonoklastes* in its second edition:

> Indeed if the race of Kings were eminently the best of men, as the breed at *Tutburie* is of Horses, it would in some reason then be their part onely to command, ours always to obey. But Kings by generation no way excelling others, and most commonly not being the wisest or the worthiest by far of whom they claime to have the governing, that we should yeild them subjection to our own ruin, or hold of them the right of our common safety, and our natural freedom by meer gift, as when the Conduit pisses Wine at Coronations, from the superfluity of their royal grace and beneficence, we may be sure was never the intent of God, whose ways are just and equal; never the intent of Nature, whose works are also regular; never of any People not wholly barbarous, whom prudence, or no more but human sense would have better guided when they first created Kings, then so to nullifie and tread to durt the rest of mankind, by exalting one person and his Linage without other merit lookt after, but the meer contingencie of a begetting, into an absolute and unaccountable dominion over them and thir posterity.   (1953–82: III, 486–7)

Reductive details are carefully placed among the assertions of high principle. On one side stand arguments from God's intentions, from nature, from human rationality. Against, stands an absurd proposition

– what if, indeed, kings were 'better' than ordinary people in the same way that stallions from Tutbury, famed for its large draught horses, were 'better' than the coalman's nag? (Probably the modern reader's mind drifts forward to an image of exuberantly promiscuous Charles II as if standing at stud.) Again, at times of apparent national rejoicing, monarchs ordered wine to be put into the London water system; 'pissing', however, suggests it was probably not of the finest quality and makes its consumption appear distinctly unappetising – and demeaning.

As I have elsewhere concluded, Milton largely defines government without kings in terms of what it is not; it is not barbarous, it is not magical, it does not depend on the whim and permission of a single man, it is not irrational, it does not frustrate the reasonable interests of its citizens and it is not at odds with the principles of the Christian faith (Corns 1995: 37).

There is an obvious eloquence in this passage from *Eikonoklastes*. Milton stands above other mid-century pamphleteers in the imaginative brilliance and stylistic control of a genuinely gifted writer. In most of his prose (as in the prose of many of his contemporaries) there are many, very long sentences, like the second one in the quotation ('But Kings . . . and thir posterity'), but he writes them with far more control of these large syntactic structures (see Corns 1982, 1999c, 2001c). Here, he pulls together numerous elements of the arguments: what we may be sure of, how that is premised on an understanding of the real, not the illusory nature of kingship, how it rests on God, nature and reason, which point to the absurdities of monarchic government. He is also a great phrase-maker: there is a memorable felicity in 'as when the Conduit pisses Wine', as in the less colourful 'the meer contingencie of a begetting'. His earliest pamphlets are characterized by a high incidence of sometimes rather flamboyant imagery. Here, as often in his mature tracts, the imagery is more restrained, giving his prose a greater decorum and a high seriousness perhaps. Always, though, the style is conspicuously superior to the styles of those around him.

Milton wrote as one schooled in the finest accomplishments of the western literary tradition from Aeschylus to the poets of his own day. Gerrard Winstanley's writing makes reference to only one book besides the Bible – Foxe's *Actes and Monuments* – but his work abounds in notions appropriated from or shared with a wide range of radical groups and theologians (Hill 1978: 9–11). His personal development depended on the conventicles of the radical sects, where he would certainly have encountered the forceful promulgation of heterodoxies in a discourse fit for its purpose. His own thought carried those heterodoxies far further into a kind of liberation theology *avant la lettre*, which supported a political analysis and demanded direct action of a simultaneously practical and symbolic nature (Bradstock 1997).

Winstanley's theological writing developed a complex argument, resting on five principles. First, the millennium is not a single event in the future but a personal resurrection of a spiritual, not a physical, kind, which happens whenever the spirit of God enters a regenerate believer. Second, that spirit is especially active at the time of his writing and it is spreading epidemically through England. Third, God may be equated with Reason. Fourth, the fall of Adam represents the effect of private property on the moral health of individuals, not a single event 6,000 years ago, and it is played out in daily lives when selfishness prevails. Finally, the regeneration of England requires a renunciation of self-interest and the economic liberation of the propertyless through communal direct action.

The tracts in which Winstanley developed this materialist and politically charged theology present difficulties of interpretation and may seem impenetrable to most modern readers. Yet the theories sometimes find expression of great eloquence:

> Was the earth made for to preserve a few covetous, proud men, to live at ease, and for them to bag and barn up the treasures of the earth from others, that they might beg and starve in a fruitful Land, or was it made to preserve all her children, Let Reason, and the Prophets and Apostles writings be Judge, the earth is the Lords, it is not to be confined to particular interest. (*The New Law of Righteousnes*, Winstanley 1941: 196)

'Bag and barn' ties the high rhetoric back to the English earth, to the practicalities of agricultural production. Already the language of his theological tracts pointed towards the Digger experiment of 1649–50. As he later observed, though he had expounded the theory in *The New Law of Righteousnes*, 'my mind was not at rest, because nothing was acted, and thoughts run in me, that words and writings were all nothing, and must die, for action is the life of all, and if thou dost not act, thou dost nothing' (*A Watch-word to the City of London and the Armie*, ibid.: 315).

That action took the form of incursions into the common lands of Surrey to cultivate them on a communal model. As that experiment foundered under pressure from local landowners and their tenants, Winstanley produced a series of pamphlets of a rather more accessible kind, in which he reported the measures and injustices that had been perpetrated against his Digger colony. The task requires an idiom of plain simplicity: 'Mr. *Plat . . . Tho: Sutton*, of *Cobham*, have hired three men, to attend both night and day, to beat the Diggers, and to pull down their tents or houses. . . . ' But it is juxtaposed with passages resonating with the high symbolic language of his theological writing:

> This work of digging, being freedom, or the appearance of Christ in the earth, hath tried the Priests and professors to the uttermost, and hath ripped up the bottom of their Religion, and proves it meere witchcraft and cosonage; for self love and covetousnesse is their God, or ruling power. They have chosen the sword, and they refuse love; when the Lamb turnes into the Lion, they will remember what they have done, and mourne. (*An Humble Request to the Ministers of both Universities and to all Lawyers in Every Inns-a-Court*; ibid.: 437)

Most of Winstanley's tracts were published by the bookseller Giles Calvert, as significant a figure in the dissemination of radical tracts as Moseley was in publishing royalist creative writing. He published at least one tract for the colourful antinomian Richard Coppin, with a contribution from Abiezer Coppe, the most prominent of the grouping of extreme radicals to whom, in their own age and subsequently, the term 'Ranter' is usually applied. A short-lived phenomenon (like the Digger movement), Ranterism had neither a discernible organization nor a programme, causing J. C. Davies, somewhat controversially, to question whether it was ever more than a media 'sensation' (Davies 1986: 11, 83). Certainly, the most prominent Ranter writers achieved both immediate notoriety and uncomfortably close attention from the civil or military law. Jacob Bauthumley, the finest thinker among them, had his tongue burnt with a hot iron before being cashiered from the New Model Army. Coppe himself was imprisoned and most probably released only when he had issued a recantation.

Bauthumley, in his solitary publication, approaches Winstanley in his vivid but demanding exposition of an advanced and speculative theology:

> Now for that which we call Heaven, I cannot conceive it any locall place, because God is not confined, or hath his Being or station in our setled compasse.... For Heaven is nothing but god at large, or god making out himself in Spirit and glory. And so I really see, that then men are in Heaven, or Heaven in men, when God appears in his glorious and pure manifestations of himself, in Love and Grace, in Peace and rest in the Spirit. (*The Light and Dark Sides of God*; Smith 1983: 235–6)

This is a patient exposition of an irenic theology that parallels Winstanley's thinking. Coppe connects tenuously to the world of Bauthumley, though he shares the pervasive political radicalism of Winstanley. His is a sensational style, producing a vibrant image of himself as an irreverent, ludic swashbuckler, staring down the grandees of the new republican establishment. But his radicalism appears clearly enough through the rents in its garish linguistic garb:

> Do I take care of my horse, and doth the Lord take care of oxen?
>   And shall I hear poor rogues in Newgate, Ludgate, cry *bread, bread, bread, for the Lords sake*; and shall I not pitty them and relieve them?
>   Howl, howl, ye nobles, howl honourable, howl ye rich men for the miseries that are coming upon you. (Ibid.: 112)

It is hard to think of contemporary analogues to or precursors of Coppe's rhymic prose, simulating a kind of ecstatic utterance that privileges the speaker even as it separates him from ordinary, serious people, nor are his successors obvious.

The Diggers and the Ranters were variously finished by the early 1650s, silenced by failure and by persecution. But as they ended, another group emerged, much larger, better organized, and destined for a longevity that has carried them strongly into modern times: the Quakers. Early Quakerism was characterized both by its theology, which advanced the pre-eminence of the spirit within to its logical conclusion, and by its style of worship, which asserted the primacy of the spirit acting within the true believer and utterly denigrated the role of the professional clergy. Early Quakers certainly shared the anticlericalism of Winstanley – and of Milton. They had an organizational robustness that allowed them to ride out the episodes of sometimes quite severe persecution they endured in the 1650s. Theirs was a proselytizing movement that sent out pairs of missionaries through the British Isles and much further, to the Americas and even to Turkey. By the early 1660s English Quakers probably numbered between

35,000 and 40,000, though some estimates place the figure as high as 60,000 (Reay 1985: 27)

David Loewenstein has latterly advanced claims for the eloquence of some early Quaker writers, and has demonstrated the messianic intensity especially of the early writings of George Fox, who certainly produces a singularly menacing apocalyptic voice, closely engaging the world of the 1650s (1995; 2001: ch. 4). For me, though, the most fascinating Quaker publications of their earliest days were plainer testimonies drawn from immediate experience.

The press played a massive part in the Quaker campaigns, and once more the bookshop of Giles Calvert figured prominently in their publication. As Kate Peters has demonstrated, itinerant preachers carried and distributed tracts which often served particular missions to specified places (1995). In effect, authors reported their own adventurous defiance in the face of authority and persecution in terms that allow them to repeat in the fixed medium of print to an unlimited audience what they did and said in the sight of but few. Often the subject is an exchange between Quaker missionaries and local magistrates. Those missionaries were often people from outside the political nation and many of them were women, whose role in the early days of Quakerism was more active and prominent than after the Restoration. Women were the first Quaker preachers to reach London and the university cities and many parts of the Americas (Hobby 1988: ch. 1; 1995: 88). Thus, a group traditionally forbidden to speak in church not only spoke but recorded and distributed what they said, often making much of their innocence of the tricks of masculine rhetoric as taught to the males of the educated classes, and distinguishing their holy simplicity from the sophisticated mendacity of the professional clergy they faced down. (See, for example, the achievement of Priscilla Cotton and Mary Cole's *To the Priests and People of England, we discharge our consciences, and give them warning* (London, 1655), considered in Corns 2001d: 82–4.)

Eikon Basilike (1649), the final tract to be discussed, stands in a different tradition. In its own age, by the most obvious of indicators, it was immensely successful. It went into 35 editions in England and 25 abroad in its year of publication, was widely translated, produced spin-off publications including a collection of aphorisms drawn from it, and sections were even set to music. Its later history shows its perennial value to Stuart apologists, and it has been the subject of numerous, mostly judicious readings by modern critics (among them, Potter

1989: esp. ch. 5, and 1999; Zwicker 1993: ch. 2; Knoppers 1999; Wheeler 1999; Rivers 2001; and Wilcher 2001: ch. 10; see also Corns 1992: ch. 4). Its critical attractions are obvious: Milton engaged with it in *Eikonoklastes*, and thus gave it for the modern reader a distinction it would not otherwise possess. Its reception invites interpretation and would seem to disclose insights into a major section of the reading public. It is certainly a propaganda masterpiece, however unappealing its literary merits might now appear.

The text, often known in its own age simply as 'the King's book', purports to be Charles I's narrative of events since the calling of the Long Parliament, together with his associated pious meditations. Its authenticity has long been questioned, and the current consensus is that the work was written by John Gauden, an Anglican divine, who was promoted to the see of Exeter and subsequently Worcester in the early 1660s. Gauden almost certainly worked from drafts, possibly begun as early as 1643 (Wilcher 2001: 277), which Charles had worked on during his captivity, and he may have been aided by other divines. Its integrity and composition have not been investigated stylometrically. By beginning no earlier than the autumn of 1640, the royal narrative seals off from contemplation any of those long-standing grievances which so exercised the king's opponents in the opening years of the Long Parliament. Despite its seeming reflectiveness, it tells us little about Charles's feelings or motivations outside a carefully constructed image of the king as lover of his people, devoted to their well being, and resolutely committed to following his own conscience with no thought to the price that he may have to pay. The text is very light on detail; besides the king himself, only Henrietta Maria, the Prince of Wales and the predeceased Strafford and Sir John Hotham are identified by name. It is especially vague about the king's enemies, and I have speculated that the book was a product of a phase in which royalist politicians were paralysed by uncertainties about the relationship between the various elements within the opposition they faced (Corns 1992: 85).

Why did the book evidently find so eager a readership and what does its success tell us about royalist ideology? The answers are complex. Most obviously, it is an attractive physical object. Most early editions were neat, pocket-sized octavos, easy to carry around and dip into, and surprisingly well printed given the probably clandestine circumstances under which most of the English editions were produced. Many editions carry an allegorical frontispiece engraved by William Marshall, showing a praying Charles putting down an earthly crown to take up Christ's crown of thorns, making the implied thesis of the text explicit and ensuring the penetration of the message to the dimmest reader. Indeed, in general, this is a very accessible text, plainly structured with pertinent and precise chapter titles. It is skilfully designed, with the narrative sections in roman and the associated meditations in italic (Corns 2000: 100–2). It comes endorsed with the apparent authorship by the late king. It appears, in its concluding chapters, quite irenic, looking beyond the immediate nightmare of the regicide to a time when monarchy could come again into its own, with only a few miscreants reserved for condign punishment. Moreover, as Isabel Rivers cogently summarizes it, 'Throughout there is an antithesis between reason, moderation, discretion, honour, innocency, conscience, piety and religion on the King's side, and faction, passion, prejudice, partiality, madness, slavery and policy on that of his opponents' (2001: 205).

The book even negotiates the problem of providence: how could God have allowed a pious and anointed king to be brought to his death? The solution rests in its penitential structure. The meditations are largely drawn from the Psalms. Charles, like David, has sinned, is penitent and through suffering has improved. As the motto on the allegorical frontispiece puts it, 'Crescit sub pondere virtus', 'virtue grows under a burden'. David's sin had been to seduce Bathsheba and to plot the death of her husband; Charles's has been to accede to pressure and allow the execution of the Earl of Strafford, which appears rather less sinful, motivated by a momentary loss of faith and courage, encouraged and enjoined by others, rather than by a murderous lust.

Newspapers

The history of journalism often overlaps literary history, though by how much should not be overstated. My purposes in this section are to give some sense of what readers were reading alongside the canonical texts with which I am principally concerned. I want also to note the extraordinary growth and development of a genre, another manifestation of the extraordinary impact of political crisis on the production and consumption of text. Moreover, among the mountains of newsprint, much of it wholly ephemeral in literary terms, England had in

Marchamont Nedham its first journalist of genius, whose work was as distinguished in its own milieu as that of Swift or Addison in a later age. The history of early modern journalism has been well served, and this account rests heavily on the work of Joseph Frank (1961, 1980) and Joad Raymond (1993, 1996).

Chapter 3 described the earliest periodical publications in England, originating in an obvious appetite for news during the opening phases of the Thirty Years War. The earliest corantos were circumscribed in what they could cover, largely excluded from engagement with domestic politics and carefully monitored. From 1632 the Privy Council, irked apparently by the lionizing of Gustavus Adolphus in the English press, imposed a six-year ban. The impact of that order was mitigated to some extent by the publication of semi-annual digests of news and by the importation of English-language corantos from Amsterdam. A new patent issued in 1638 allowed publication to resume, though the Licensing Order of 1637 ensured even closer control (Frank 1961: ch. 1).

The meeting of the Long Parliament provided at once a stimulus to demand and the dissemination of information in terms favourable to one or other political interest. Frank explicitly links the origins of domestic news media to the circulation of parliamentary speeches. The first English-language weekly containing home news, *The Heads of Severall Proceedings In This Present Parliament*, appeared in November 1641. Frank evaluates its contents unappetisingly: 'In a dull and impersonal style and with some inaccuracies it summarized the news from Ireland, told briefly of Charles's reception on his return to London, and devoted most of its space to a bare narrative of events in Parliament' (ibid.: 21). But demand rapidly stimulated supply, and titles, albeit often rather shortlived, multiplied:

> [D]uring the first week of 1644 any Londoner who wanted to read his newspaper in English had a dozen to choose from. On Monday he could select *A Perfect Diurnall, Certaine Informations*, or [*Mercurius*] *Aulicus* – which despite its Sunday dateline probably came out in London on Monday. Tuesday he had *The Kingdomes Weekly Intelligencer*; Wednesday, *The Weekly Account* or the newly revived *A Continuation of certain Speciall and Remarkable Passages*; and Thursday a choice between [*Mercurius*] *Britanicus* and *Civicus*. Friday brought forth three papers: *The Parliament Scout, The Scottish Dove*, and a new weekly, *Occurrences of Certain Special and Remarkable Passages*. On Saturday the reader either acquired *The True Informer* or went newspaperless. (Ibid.: 56–7)

Distribution networks into distant parts of England and Wales had been established for manuscript newsletters for many years and printed periodical parts rapidly achieved a similar penetration of remoter markets (Raymond 1996: ch. 5). The catastrophes of civil war touched most parts, and so, too, did the associated accounts.

London held almost all the presses and parliamentarians held London, controlled the legislative process, the agencies that could suppress publications, and moreover were the major source of information on which journalists could draw. A spirited attempt by the royalists at Oxford, who of course controlled the university press, produced in *Mercurius Aulicus* (the 'court mercury') a distinctive newspaper, principally from the pen of John Berkenhead (knighted in 1662), an academic who had served Laud as his secretary. The business of *Mercurius Aulicus* was primarily rapid rebuttal of parliament-supporting newsbooks, which it did with enormous elan, often through dextrous application of the hostile stereotypes that were so much a part of the repertoire of royalist ideology.

Nedham, an Oxford graduate and young schoolteacher, emerged as co-editor of *Mercurius Britanicus*, a paper established 'to counter Berkenhead, to negate the negative', not least by matching its racy idiom (Frank 1980: 15–16). Nedham learnt his trade well, and by the end of the decade he was plainly the most hireable of journalists. A turncoat to Charles I in the late 1640s, he emerged from a sojourn in prison to edit for Charles's enemies *Mercurius Politicus*, which appeared weekly through the 1650s. This was his greatest achievement, some 8,000 pages of newsprint, nearly all of it from his own pen. In the late 1650s he also contributed significantly to *The Publick Intelligencer*, the Monday companion to Thursday's *Politicus* (ibid.: 87).

Commercially, he had an easy run. The new republic achieved a tightness of press control that silenced most other newspaper publications from late 1649. Frank, whose early study is plainly shaped by a fairly fresh recollection of McCarthyism, speaks of the official periodicals of the republic as 'the licensed pallbearers' of press freedom (Frank 1961: 198). Perhaps, but that ethical judgement should not disguise the achievement of *Mercurius Politicus*, that 'extraordinary multi-generic text' by 'one of the most widely read writers of the seventeenth century' (Raymond 1996: 79; 1993: 332).

In *Mercurius Politicus*, Nedham immediately established a distinctive voice, characterized by its effortless urbanity, unimpressed with all opposition, confident of victory, at once cynical and satirical. The earliest issues appeared in a difficult time for the new republic, with a Scottish army already mobilized and awaiting the arrival at its head of Charles II. Montrose, an accomplished royalist activist and general, had recently been hanged by the king's new friends and his head and quarters set up:

> And for his better entertainment when he comes to *Edinburgh*, there is *Montrose*'s head of the *Kirks* own dressing, provided for his *Break-fast*, and mounted on the *Town-house*, on purpose to bid him welcome, and many Thanks for the remembrance of his famous Services; which the yong man (having one quality of a King) hath learned already to forget; and it is like the next News (we hear) will tell us, his *gude Lads* have made him declare.　(Nedham 1650–60: no. 1, p. 3)

Nedham's tactics are complex. He knows that he writes to Englishmen, and, in the absence of other sources of news, there will be Presbyterians and royalists among them. The republic's primary anxiety in 1650 was that those groups would greet and join with Charles II once he entered England with a Scottish army. Nedham works to discourage that idea. Charles has learnt one thing about kingship – it requires the betrayal of one's supporters as expediency requires, much as, Nedham suggests, he views with equanimity the severed body parts of his erstwhile most glittering Scottish supporter. Why be loyal to a monarch who rewards loyalty thus? As he puts it, in the same paragraph: 'the *Roialists* may see, what comfort their *old Interest* is like to receive from the new *Scottish* combination'. Nedham makes much of the foreignness of Scotland; 'gude Lads' at once indicates their language and suggests the chameleon nature of the young king who now courts a people who had assiduously opposed his father. In the last days of the republic Nedham was to write an extraordinary pamphlet, *Interest will not Lie. Or, a View of England's True Interest* (1659), in which he addresses interest groups across the political and religious spectrum, convincing each in turn of the risks of welcoming back monarchy: 'onely the *Papist*' would gain by restoring the king (title page). Nedham's world view assumes that people act from a sometimes rather unenlightened sense of their own self-interest and that they can be manipulated by enlightening them. He knows, too, their fears and anxieties: those early issues offer a vision of Charles as 'young Tarquin', a ridiculous but still resonant soubriquet, the last of the monarchic line but nevertheless, potentially, a ravisher, just as the Scottish incursion poses a threat to the property of all Englishmen. But the quality of the writing is remarkable, particularly that almost Swiftean notion of Montrose's head prepared and served like a breakfast delicacy; kings consume their people, even their closest supporters.

Nedham from the outset obliquely inculcates republican principles and assumptions. Indeed, he had shared Milton's view that kings are just ordinary men, though often impaired examples of the species, long before Milton himself had vouchsafed such a heresy to print. *Mercurius Britanicus* had called down a storm of pious parliamentarian protests when it remarked that Charles I had a speech impediment (in *Mercurius Britanicus* 92, helpfully reprinted in Raymond 1993: 348; see also Frank 1980: 26). *Mercurius Politicus*, in David Norbrook's phrase, 'puts its readers through a crash course in republican education' (Norbrook 1999: 223). Indeed, over part of its long run, it contains explicit and theoretically aware expositions of ideological republicanism. Yet what sold the papers was its virtual monopoly in the dissemination of hard news and its recurrent verve. His mastery of tone and his political nous remained shrewd throughout. Consider one further passage. In mid-summer 1656 Lucy Walter, mother of Charles II's first-born child, the future Duke of Monmouth, and still his mistress, returned to England with her son on private business and was discovered with a royal document about her that made handsome provision for her, an annuity of 'Five thousand Livres' to be paid in Antwerp. Nedham prints the document and comments:

> By this those that hanker after him may see they are furnished already with an Heir apparent, and what a pious charitable Prince they have for their Master, and how well he disposeth of the Collections and Contributions which they make for him here, towards the maintenance of his Concubines and Royal Issue. Order is taken forthwith to send away his Lady of Pleasure and the young Heir, and set them on shoar in *Flanders*, which is no ordinary curtesie. (Nedham 1650–60: no. 318, p. 7108; the incident is discussed in Hutton 1991: 125)

Understatedly, Nedham eschews *faux* piety and outrage. To republicans, he has said enough. He can leave Presbyterians to wring their hands that the king they ostensibly seek to restore should manifest the morals of a Tutbury stallion. But royalist readers are perplexed; the court of the king depended on clandestine collections, and this is how he spends those funds. Everyone, I suppose, was meant to be a little alarmed that this is the future queen and her son, the heir apparent. Leaving aside the historical irony of that final point, we may see here how, in effect, Nedham lays down the prototype for hostile representation of Charles and his court in the 1660s and more particularly the 1670s.

6

The Literature of the Rule of Charles II: May 1660 to February 1685

Dissent, Popery and Arbitrary Government

The Restoration of Charles II to the thrones of England, Scotland and Ireland resulted from a realignment within English politics in which some of the dominant figures in the Interregnum political landscape changed allegiances. Crucially, George Monck, who in Scotland commanded an army of occupation, recognized the inherent instability of the republican regime after the death of Cromwell. His troops, like the legions of a Roman general descending from a remote province, had marched south to take the metropolis and with it the apparatus of government. Despite Milton's briefly held hopes to the contrary (Milton 1953–82: 7; rev. edn: 482), Monck achieved not imperial power but a new political consensus founded on a restored and reformed monarchy. Negotiations with Charles produced in early April 1660 a document which has come to be known as the Declaration of Breda, a statement of the terms under which the king would return to England. The text and terms are wonderfully guileful. Difficult decisions, about who should be punished and about how land confiscated and redistributed in the previous decades should be recouped, are deflected to a future parliament, whose rights are clearly asserted. Monck's soldiers, essential for the transfer of power, are promised their arrears of pay. Puritanical Protestantism is appeased with the promise of 'a liberty to tender consciences … that no man shall be disquieted or called in question for differences of opinion in matter of religion, which do not disturb the peace of the kingdom' (Gardiner 1979: 465–7). Perhaps Charles intended to settle his English kingdom thus, with a more irenic and less confrontational relationship with parliament, founded on a toleration of a broad range of Protestant belief and practice.

The blood-letting after his return was spectacular but narrowly focused on those regicides who were of no use to the new regime. The Convention Parliament, which met in late April, debated until August the Act of Indemnity and Oblivion, which excepted a list of victims from the general pardon. The House of Commons and the Lords drew up their own lists. As many as 60 were at risk during the process, among them the chief apologist of regicide John Milton, whose *Eikonoklastes* and *Defensio Prima* were ordered to be burnt and who was briefly imprisoned after he emerged from hiding once the Act had been sealed. Financially, the Restoration was ruinous to him, since he had lent money to the republican government, debts which were not honoured by the monarchical regime, although he retained enough to live reasonably well (Campbell 1997: 190–4). In the event, 29 regicides were indicted in October 1660, and 10 executed as traitors shortly thereafter, a grisly process that left bits and pieces of them displayed on spikes around the city of London. A further 19 escaped death but were variously punished by the penal system, among them 5 who were annually taken from prison to Tyburn on hurdles with ropes around their necks, as if to execution. In a similarly bizarre ritual, on the 1661 anniversary of the execution of Charles I, the bodies of Oliver Cromwell, his son-in-law Henry Ireton and the presiding judge of the trial of Charles I were exhumed from graves in Westminster Abbey, suspended from the Tyburn gallows, decapitated and turned into a pit dug on the site; the heads were then impaled on spikes fixed to the roof of Westminster Hall. Other waves of judicial killing followed an abortive Fifth Monarchist coup and a republican conspiracy (the so-called Venner Rising and the Northern Plot), which produced more heads and quarters to set up on London Bridge and town and city gates. Further executions followed sporadically over the early years of the decade as regicides were captured or surrendered and as the range of prosecution was extended (Keeble 2002a: 54–76).

These events had a literary resonance deep into the reign of Charles II, most signally in the late poetry of Milton (Knoppers 1994, esp. chs 4 and 5). They shaped the political consciousness of John Dryden and that astute observer Samuel Pepys, both hastily repositioning themselves as royalists. The exhumation of Cromwell had a pivotal place in the *Journal* of the Quaker George Fox, who by his own account witnessed it (Fox 1998: 292–3). For Thomas St Nicholas, the accompanying celebration constituted a 'triumphant cock-a-doodle-doo' from men who would not have faced Cromwell living (St Nicholas 2002: 135). Milton's own anxieties may have surged again when Sir Henry Vane was tried and beheaded. Milton's sonnet to him was first printed in an account of his life and trial (see above, chapter 5; see also Milton 1997: 329–30). The Northern Plot occasioned the arrest of Lucy Hutchinson's husband John, a regicide who had initially escaped prosecution, probably through family connections with leading royalists; he died shortly afterwards in prison (Hutchinson 1995: 326–34; Keeble 2002a: 73, 76).

The Convention Parliament, which had ushered in the king, gave way to new elections, and its successor, the Cavalier Parliament, assembled in May 1661 with a far less conciliatory complement of MPs. Through much of 1660 Presbyterians and Episcopalians had without success explored possible compromises in the church settlement based on a reduced role for episcopacy in church government. But the wholesale ejection of Puritan ministers installed in Church of England livings had been deferred by legislation confirming most incumbents in their places. Advocates and apologists for regicide and those holding livings from which non-Puritans, like Robert Herrick, had been ejected were excluded from this measure. Some 700 parishes witnessed a change of minister (Spurr 1991: 34), though Herrick himself seems not to have returned to Dean Prior till 1662 (*DNB* 1975). In the provinces, away from the delicate minuet of leading Presbyterians and Anglican conciliators, newly animated Episcopalians, lay as well as clerical, were carrying the debate away from the formulae of Breda and towards a more straightforwardly prelatical resolution. Meanwhile, the Venner Rising occasioned a wave of repression directed against groups more radical than the Presbyterians. The Cavalier Parliament took over the business of settling the church in the context of this drift from conciliation. In May 1662 the Act of Uniformity received the royal assent. It required from ministers acceptance of the Book of Common Prayer, that skeleton of the mass-book so obnoxious to the godly in the 1630s and 1640s. It required subscription to the Thirty-nine Articles of the Church of England, which included an endorsement of episcopal church government. It required the renunciation of the Solemn League and Covenant, that founding document of the Puritan reformation of the 1640s. Finally, it required ordination to be confirmed by a bishop. About a thousand ministers still in post

felt constrained to resign, with effect from the deadline of St Bartholomew's Day, 1662 (24 August). Others of a decidedly puritanical
orientation found they could in conscience conform, and a broader
church than that conceived by Laud and Charles I resulted (Spurr
1991: 45–48; Keeble 2002a: 117–20).

For the Nonconformist ministers, as for more radical Protestants,
the legislative process now worked against them with little compromise. The Act of Uniformity was supplemented by the Five Mile Act of
1665, which prohibited ordained men who had not assented to the
Prayer Book from coming within five miles of the location of their
former livings (though a clause allowed fairly easy escape from this
restriction through taking a sort of extra loyalty oath). The Conven-
ticle Act of 1662, beefed up in 1670, prohibited meetings of like-
minded religious radicals, with a range of penalties, among which the
ultimate sanction was transportation. These measures, the so-called
Clarendon Code, collectively allowed local magistrates to act with
whatever vigour they chose against dissenters from Anglican conformity under their jurisdiction. But implementation was patchy and inconsistent, and after initial stringency, effective persecution declined as
'the likelihood of any serious threat from subversion receded' (Keeble
2002a: 142). Certainly, Quakers were badly treated, and Fox was
intermittently imprisoned through the 1660s and into the 1670s.
So, too, were those Baptists who attracted the hostility of local magistrates. John Bunyan was arrested in November 1660, even ahead of the
anti-dissenter legislation, and he spent the next 12 years in prison.
Nonconformist writing is a broad and diverse tradition that includes
Milton, and the Independent Lucy Hutchinson and St Nicholas, as
well as Bunyan and Fox. Of course, it relates intricately to dissenters'
awareness of the threats to them throughout the reign of Charles II.

But not only was persecution uneven, at times it was suspended by
the return to the principles of toleration enunciated in the Declaration
of Breda. Indeed, the Declaration of Indulgence, the royal edict proclaimed by Charles II in 1672, allowed open worship and organization
by dissenters, suspending all penal laws, providing that preachers and
meeting houses were licensed. This short-lived measure, soon withdrawn under pressure from parliament, was designed both to secure
Nonconformist support for war against the United Provinces and to
establish a climate of toleration, which included the rescinding of
measures against Roman Catholicism (Spurr 2000: 29). Even without
this temporary relaxation, Protestant dissenters felt a change in their

circumstances in the second decade following the Restoration. At its simplest, they realized that, no matter how bleak matters had seemed in the early days of the Cavalier Parliament, they had survived with their religious and cultural ideology substantially uncompromised. Worship was more open and less frequently interfered with. Dissenting groups as radical as Bunyan's Baptists were starting to buy buildings and plan or even operate chapels. Moreover, a broad dialogue was emerging between the Protestant denominations, exemplified, perhaps, by Milton's last work of controversial prose, *Of True Religion, Heresy, and Schism, Toleration, And what best means may be us'd against the growth of Popery* (spring 1673), in which he argues that the areas of disagreement within the Protestant community are technical and 'not essential to belief' (Milton 1953–82: VIII, 436).

As N. H. Keeble notes, 'The Act of Uniformity distinguished only two categories of religious practice: conformist and nonconformist' (Keeble 2002a: 138). Milton's late pamphlet argues what most English Protestants probably believed: that, indeed, religious practice admitted only two principal categories, not Conformist and Nonconformist, but Protestant and Papist. We have considered several times the powerful impact of anti-Catholic sentiment on the political, religious and cultural ideology of Stuart England, variously manifest in the response to the Spanish Match, in the strong suspicion that Laudian ceremonialism approached too close to Catholic practices, and in the easy resort of parliamentarian writers to associating the royalist cause with popery in general or Irish popery in particular. In the late Stuart period the issue remained current, and served to reconstruct a larger alliance of godly Protestants of greater political significance than at any earlier time in the century.

Two closely related events brought popery to the forefront in the 1670s, the conversion of James, Duke of York, heir to the throne, and the series of anti-Catholic riots, demonstrations, trials and executions occasioned by the disclosure of the so-called Popish Plot. Charles II's own religious convictions were uncertain and much debated by his subjects. He was widely rumoured to have converted to Catholicism during his continental exile. The secret Treaty of Dover, signed with the French in 1670, had a clause that required him to be publicly reconciled with Rome 'as soon as the affairs of his kingdom allowed' (Keeble 2002a: 63, 170), an obligation postponed till his hugger-mugger reception into the Roman Catholic Church on the last evening of his life (Hutton 1991: 443). James, Duke of York, whose conversion may have reflected an enthusiasm for hierarchy but certainly showed no political guile, was received into the Roman Catholic Church in 1672. He had last taken the sacrament in an Anglican communion at Easter 1671, although he continued to accompany Charles to the chapel royal till 1676; 'by then his Catholicism was so notorious that his avowing it openly could do him little further harm' (Miller 2000: 59). Indeed, the Cavalier Parliament's wish in the aftermath of the Declaration of Indulgence to exclude the Catholic office-holders whom it suspected of playing an increasing part in government had produced in 1673 the Test Act, requiring an oath renouncing the Catholic dogma of transubstantiation. James, like several of his closest associates, had felt obliged to resign his public offices, rendering his conversion almost a matter of public record (ibid.: 69).

James became central to the surging campaign against English Catholics, which in turn provided the necessary conditions for the sensation and tragedy of the Popish Plot. Titus Oates, the principal informer, and a cluster of allies alleged to the Council of State a wide-ranging Catholic plot to kill the king, implicating James's secretary Edward Coleman, himself a Catholic. To Englishmen educated in the populist tradition of Protestant historiography, these disclosures must have adumbrated the return of the Marian persecutions. The revelation of the Plot, rumbling on into the next decade, carried off to trial and execution a number of Catholics, including Coleman, priests and eventually the Catholic Primate of Ireland. The issues provoked by the English obsession with Catholicism and with the growing uncertainties about the appropriateness of James's place as next in line to the throne, dominate the political and literary landscape of the 1670s and 1680s.

Foreign policy and the related matter of supply, the provision of resources to fight England's wars, further shaped the political climate and with it the course of literary history. Cromwell's navy had fought a successful war against the United Provinces over a cluster of issues that had arisen from tensions and trade rivalries between two adjacent, maritime nations (1652–4), events which were to be recalled admiringly by some as the debacles of Charles's campaigns developed (Keeble 2002a: 167). The first of his Anglo-Dutch wars (1664–7) originated in further frictions over trade and empire, particularly over new English initiatives towards West Africa, where the king, the Duke of York and most of the political grandees around them had personal interests as major shareholders in the Royal African Company.

Most of the English political nation probably regarded the Dutch as solid Protestants in the frontline against the territorial ambitions of Catholic France and Spain, and therefore natural allies, rather than enemies. But the conflict, which started well, received the support of parliament in the form of 'the greatest supply ever made to an English monarch' (Hutton 1991: 220). Yet the war soon went badly, culminating in the events of May 1667, when the Dutch overwhelmed outer defences, sailed up the Thames, burned three of the biggest vessels in the Royal Navy, carried off its flagship and then withdrew to establish a blockade at the mouth of the river. Peace was, inevitably, made on poor terms. Charles's second Dutch war (1672–4) was an opportunistic attempt to regain lost ground by aligning an English maritime attack with Louis XIV's invasion of the United Provinces. Once more, the war at sea went badly, compounded by a growing parliamentary reluctance to grant sufficient supply. Charles, by now in effect a client of the French monarch, disappointed his allies by making another disadvantageous peace, though less ignominious than that of 1667. As Hutton summarizes: 'Nobody . . . thought that the gains made had been worth the expenditure of lives, limbs, money, and commercial opportunities' (1991: 317).

The military and diplomatic crises of the 1660s and 1670s not only contributed to the political instabilities of the times, but also afforded subject matter for creative writers. From opposing positions, both Dryden and Marvell represented and commented on the conflicts. In parliamentary terms, the period from the inauguration of the Cavalier Parliament in 1661 to its eventual dismissal in 1679 should have been straightforward for the king and his government since it was dominated by Episcopalian monarchists with a predisposition towards a supportive loyalty. However, military disaster, sexual scandal and a suspicious hatred of Catholicism frequently alienated it and undid the careers of leading ministers from Edward Hyde, Earl of Clarendon, through Henry Bennett, Earl of Arlington, to Thomas Osborne, Earl of Danby. Managing parliament became central to government concern and was often effected through an extensive use of bribery, contributing to the general air of corruption.

But the rule of Charles II was most strongly characterized by the sexual scandals of the monarch and his court and a libertine and lawless lifestyle among the highest ranks of society, which the king seemed prepared to tolerate. John Wilmot, second Earl of Rochester, whose work is considered below, at once functions as exemplar of and commentator on court circles and the monarch, whom he characterizes, as many others did, as a man prepared to risk much for his sexual gratification. A poem, probably by Rochester, observes:

> [The King's] was the sauciest that did ever swive,
> The prowdest peremptory Prick alive:
> Tho Safety, Law, Religion, Life lay on't
> Twou'd breake thro all to make it's way to C–t.
> Restless he rowles about from Whore to Whore
> With Dogg and Bastard, always goeing before,
> A merry Monarch, scandalous and poore.
> ('Satyr', ll.A16–22; Rochester 1999: 86)

Charles's most thorough modern biographer rather doubts his involvement with whores in the strictest sense of the term: 'not a single professional whore ever boasted of the honour of royal patronage' (Hutton 1991: 262). 'Whore' may have been a vaguer term for a lascivious woman. But Charles's liaisons included the one from his years of exile that produced the Duke of Monmouth (see above, chapter 5), two quite prominent actresses, Moll Davies and Nell Gwyn, and two semi-official mistresses, Barbara Villiers, Countess of Castlemaine and Duchess of Cleveland, and Louise de Querouaille, Duchess of Portsmouth. To these was widely attributed some degree of influence on the king, even by insiders in a position to know the truth: 'His Scepter and his Prick were of a length, / And she may sway the one who plays with t'other' ('Satyr', ll.A11–12; Rochester 1999: 85–6). Portsmouth, a Catholic and a minor French aristocrat and probable agent of the French throne, was regarded with particular suspicion.

Though he sired no legitimate offspring, rumour attributed as many as 75 royal bastards to Charles; he acknowledged 14. In itself, his conduct shocked much of the political nation, for whom monogamy, leavened by occasional and discreet extramarital activity, was virtually universal. Marchamont Nedham in *Mercurius Politicus* had cranked the rumour mill in the 1650s, with his depiction of Charles as 'young Tarquin', but post-Restoration confirmation of his unrestrained promiscuity came quickly and vividly. Moreover, it was perceived and represented as causally related to government failure and incompetence. It was said in London that he had spent the evening of the disastrous Dutch raid on the English fleet at a party with his illegitimate son Monmouth and with Castlemaine (Hutton 1991: 248).

Compared with some of his bibulous companions, Charles himself was relatively abstemious. But the larger circle around him perpetrated numerous and highly visible outrages, both sexual and violent, for the most part in their cups. Sir Charles Sedley, courtier and minor drama-tist, in an episode frequently related in modern accounts, on the balcony of a house in Covent Garden, 'in open day ... showed his nakedness – acting all the postures of lust and buggery that could be imagined. ... And that being done, he took a glass of wine and washed his prick in it and then drank it off; and then took another and drank the King's health' (Pepys, quoted and discussed by Keeble 2002a: 177; Spurr 2000: 185). Rochester, a fine lyric poet, the heir to Suckling and Waller, besides writing some of the grossest obscenities in the English literary tradition, was a drunken brawler and sometime vandal (Spurr 2000: 81; Huttton 1991: 278). George Villiers, second Duke of Buckingham and co-author of probably the wittiest comedy of the period, 'destroyed his reputation in the nation at large by killing the Earl of Shrewsbury, husband of his mistress, in the most spectacular duel of the century' (Hutton 1991: 256). Rumour had it that his mistress had witnessed the fight disguised as a page and that the couple had copulated while his clothes were bloody from her dead husband. Charles generally protected his wider circle from the appropriate op-eration of the laws of the land; Buckingham, for example, was par-doned, though he lost favour with the king. It is something of a critical commonplace that Restoration literary culture, particularly in the theatre, reflects the promiscuity and lawlessness of those close to the king. I would add that surely more interesting is the guileful and imaginative ingenuity with which Dryden contrives to transform this tawdry phenomenon into something heroic (see below).

Charles managed to ride out most of the storms that buffeted his governments in the 1660s and 1670s. However, towards the end of the latter decade, anti-Catholic sentiment, screwed to a new pitch by the developing crisis of the Popish Plot, produced a concerted effort to exclude James, Duke of York, from succession, and to nominate the Duke of Monmouth in his place. Gradually, the Cavalier Parliament had polarized into those supportive of the court and government and those against it, typically because of its supposed leaning towards popery, though the ideology that emerged was broader than that. In the crisis of 1678–81, these groups became more distinctive and acquired names. Those who supported the king and the rights of his brother were called by their enemies 'Tories', after dispossessed Irish

Catholics turned bandits; his enemies were 'Whigs', named after the participants in a short-lived Scottish rebellion, though the word had a longer history as a term for Scottish Presbyterians (Hutton 1991: 391; *OED* s.v. 'Whig', 2). Recently, historians have cautioned against interpreting the loose and sometimes rather opportunistic alliances of 1678 and thereafter as 'parties' in anything approaching the modern sense and against interpreting the so-called 'Exclusion Crisis' as a discrete event separate from larger concerns and the broader sweep of Charles's reign (see, for example, Scott 1991; Hutton 1991, esp. chs. 13 and 14). As Jonathan Scott observes, 'When the words 'whig' and 'tory' appeared on the scene ... [t]hey were markers, not of party, but of belief' (1991: 48), although, as we shall see, Dryden recognized some advantage in fostering the misapprehension.

As the crisis deepened, Anthony Ashley Cooper, Earl of Shaftesbury, emerged as the most prominent advocate of exclusion. Charles lost control of the long-serving Cavalier Parliament and dissolved it, though the three short-lived parliaments that followed were as unhelpful to him, and the last was finally dismissed, in intimidating circumstances, after he had convoked it in Oxford, a loyalist city controlled by his troops, rather than London, where a traditionally radical population could have protected it and fed its dissidence. Once more, the responses of Dryden and Marvell define opposing literary responses to events. The latter, however, died before events ran their full course.

From 1681 to his death in 1685, Charles ruled without recourse to parliaments, much as his father had done in the 1630s, though with the obvious advantage that secret French subsidies eased any fiscal problems. It was a turbulent period, dangerous for both the king and his opponents. Monmouth was disgraced and banished, while Shaftesbury was prosecuted and acquitted of treason. He fled into exile, to die shortly later. Several prominent Whigs conspired to take Charles prisoner while old republicans simultaneously contrived an assassination attempt. The events were fused in the government's response into the so-called 'Rye-house Plot', and treason trials and executions followed. After Charles's sudden and terminal illness, perhaps surprisingly, 'James was proclaimed king without the slightest disturbance and there were many reports of spontaneous popular rejoicing' (Miller 2000: 121). No doubt in the English political nation, memories of the Civil War and the associated threat to property and social order outweighed the fear and loathing of Catholicism.

Theatre of the Rule of Charles II

Early Stuart theatre, while it certainly admitted innovation and was changing significantly in the final years before civil war broke out, was a conservative art form: old plays remained part of the active repertoire of the drama companies that owned them. When the theatrical life of London revived substantially in 1660, plays of the early Stuart period, and indeed some Elizabethan ones, were revived and adapted for performance, and remained an important part of the theatrical life of London for decades to come. Practically, until new plays were written, it could scarcely have been otherwise; whatever the attractions of the dramatic idiom for authors of the Interregnum, closet dramas written since the theatres more or less closed were not a significant component of the Restoration stage. But the mid-century decades had seen a confirmed interest in reading old plays, which were a significant part of the creative writing to appear in print. From 1660 those readers, or at least those at leisure in London, could see how Shakespeare, Jonson, Webster and Beaumont and Fletcher worked on the stage.

But the limited theatrical innovations specific to the late 1630s and early 1640s were also picked up in the 1660s. The development particularly of a new relationship between the court and the stage certainly continued in those early years of the Restoration. Before 1642, courtier dramatists, in particular Sir John Suckling, and dramatists close to the court, such as William Davenant, edged the elite theatre companies towards a more refined aesthetic and, more concretely, to a closer dependency on the crown. Suckling's proto-cavalier plays were frequently revived in the 1660s (Van Lennep et al. 1965). The witty, rather libertine idiom of Shirley and Brome (with their excellent roles for women characters) and the libertine dash of Suckling are certainly felt as powerful influences on the new drama of the Restoration.

Continuities extended to organization and personnel. Davenant, the favoured masque-writer of the 1630s, had under royal patent entered theatre management before the war. In 1660 two royal patents issued to Davenant and to Thomas Killigrew shaped English theatrical history till the 1690s. Killigrew, quondam page to Charles I and member of Thomas Carew's circle, had been an active royalist and part of Charles II's entourage in exile. Davenant's own reconciliation with the Cromwellian ascendancy (see above, chapter 5) evidently was not held against him. The patents established two companies, the King's Men, under Killigrew, and the Duke of York's Men, under Davenant. Members of the companies were servants of the royal households, as the old King's Men had been in Shakespeare's day. The patents and subsequent royal actions guaranteed an effective duopoly of the London stage from the late summer of 1660 (Thomas and Hare 1989: ch. 1). Other companies had attempted to set up as the republic and its controls collapsed. The Red Bull, still serviceable as a public (that is, open-air) theatre, and intermittently used illegally in the 1650s, was briefly the home to a group of old players. Two private theatres also had short-lived companies. But Charles or his advisers plainly favoured the re-establishment of theatrical culture on a narrower basis than that which had obtained before 1642, though one company, under the management of George Jolly, attempted to continue in defiance of legal constraints and the privileges of his rivals till 1668, after which Jolly capitulated and was rewarded with the management of a training company or 'nursery' for young actors. Davenant's company survived the death of its founder in 1668 under the management first of his widow and later his son, Charles. Killigrew, despite the advantages bestowed on him by the king's favour, proved as incompetent a manager as he had once proved, in the early 1650s, an inept diplomat (*DNB* 1975), and in 1682 his company was taken over by Charles Davenant, who merged the patents to form the United Company, retaining his rival's stock of plays and disbanding his troupe of players. London from then to 1695 had only one principal theatrical company, though it retained two venues.

The creative impact of the arrangements made in 1660 was complex. It effectively closed down the populist side of theatrical life; the old Red Bull audience for the earthier and older dramatic tradition was displaced now to such marginal areas as the puppeteers, rope-dancers and sideshows of London's seasonal fairs. Through the Tudor and early Stuart period, the Master of the Revels had controlled the stage, acting as licenser and censor as well as entrepreneur for performances at court. Charles's theatre managers were old loyalists connected to his court and effectively clients wholly dependent on his continuing patronage. At the outset at least, an overtly critical and oppositional drama was unlikely to develop. Moreover, the court could make its own arrangements for its entertainment with Killigrew and Davenant. Sir Henry Herbert, George Herbert's brother and Master of the Revels since 1623, was restored to his office, and continued to exercise his formerly lucrative but now substantially supererogatory role as licenser: 'With only two companies, under the full control of Davenant and Killigrew, who also had powers to censor plays, there was nothing left for Herbert to do as far as the London stage was concerned' (Bawcutt 1996: 91), though his office continued and was sporadically involved in various tasks, including licensing other kinds of performance. Davenant and Killigrew's decisions, where they coincided, effectively determined how late Stuart drama would develop. Two issues were crucial: the design of playhouses and the composition of the acting companies.

Killigrew and Davenant's rivals thought in terms of reactivating the pre-1642 playhouses, and in the earliest months of their operation they also briefly used them. But none of these had proper wings affording the width outside the performing space to accommodate the new technical apparatus that was to characterize the Restoration stage, namely, changeable backdrops. These were, at their simplest, painted shutters, moved across an inclined stage on grooves cut parallel to its front edge, allowing a change of backdrop to match the change of scene. Elaborate mechanisms of spectacular effect had characterized the early Stuart masques designed by Inigo Jones and had sometimes been used in the amateur theatricals of Henrietta Maria (see above, chapters 3 and 4). Similarly astounding effects were achieved in the professional theatre of the late Stuart period, though more usually in musical plays and operas. Yet early in the history of the Restoration, stage backdrops, combined with some scenery, could contribute crucially to powerful dramaturgic effects unprecedented in the pre-1642 theatre, as in Sir Samuel Tuke's *The Adventures of Five Hours* (1662), to which I turn shortly.

In the various venues developed over the late Stuart period, performing spaces were designed with much of the stage protruding beyond the line of the curtain, another innovation since 1642, which was operated in conjunction with a proscenium arch. Though stages were deep, the action generally took place in the front part, close to the audience and often on the apron or forestage in front of the line of the arch and curtain, a proximity that promoted an intimate playing relationship between actors and audience and certainly called for courage and boldness. To use the back part of the stage would have compromised the effectiveness of the backdrops and the illusion of depth and perspective they were designed to create (on theatre design, see Langhans 2000: 3–12). Changing the backdrop was relatively easy, but it was noisy and took time. One result of these changes in presentation is in the structure of plays, which typically have fewer and longer scenes set in specifically established locations, rather than the fluid, rapidly shifting atopicality that, for example, characterizes much of Shakespeare's oeuvre. But the theatre of the 1660s builds on some of the technical developments that were happening in the late 1630s, for example in the plays of Shirley, such as *Hyde Park*, which in turn was innovatively revived by the King's Company in 1668, with the use of real horses on stage (see above, chapter 4; Van Lennep et al. 1965: 139). Salisbury Court and the Cockpit in Drury Lane were private houses and, unlike the Red Bull, in their heyday had not been patronized by a socially diverse clientele. The theatres developed by Killigrew and Davenant were all-seater, at prices that were similarly exclusive. Audiences were by no means wholly from the courtier class; civil servants, the learned professions, Inns of Court men and prosperous citizens could certainly have afforded to attend, and the servant class were noted as familiar occupants of the uppermost gallery, which typically cost a shilling. In place of the standing space in front of the stage was the pit, furnished with benches and typically separated from the stage by a sunken compartment for musicians, corresponding to a modern orchestra pit. Sitting on the pit benches typically cost 2s. 6d, boxes 4s., and the lower gallery 1s. 6d (Van Lennep et al. 1965: lxx). Pepys sometimes moans to his diary about the presence in numbers of his social inferiors, and theatre histories do usually point to some widening of the social range of the audience later in the century and especially in the last decade. But the servants in the gallery did not determine the ethos and aesthetic of a theatre that was, throughout the reigns of Charles II and James II, a place of fashionable resort, dominated by social display of the wealthy, patronized directly by royalty, who sometimes attended the playhouse as well as command performances in the private performing space at Whitehall, and where an outsider, in the wrong seat, in the wrong clothes, in the wrong company, would have felt decidedly uncomfortable. Plays were performed in the mid-afternoon, which again was a constraint. For Pepys, who could work in the morning, take 'dinner' at lunchtime and perhaps return to the office in the evening, the time suited quite well. For tradesmen and day-labourers, it would usually have precluded attendance. Servants could be present because they attended their employers to the theatre.

Since Killigrew and Davenant exercised a virtual cartel, controlling their players' terms of employment in uniform manner, no doubt aligning ticket prices, and respecting each other's intellectual property rights, they were evidently more relaxed about the publication of plays than any Jacobean company would have been. Piracy between companies was apparently not an issue.

The history of the Restoration playhouses is in broad outline well known (Van Lennep et al. 1965: xxxi–xliv provides the plainest narrative; Thomas and Hare 1989: ch. 2, prints both documents and plans). Killigrew created a playhouse for the King's Company through the reconstruction of Gibbons' Tennis Court, which became the Vere Street Theatre, staging plays there from late 1660 to mid-1663, by which time a completely new building, the Theatre Royal in Bridges Street, near Drury Lane, was ready. Davenant proceeded more cautiously, converting Lisle's Tennis Court into the Lincoln's Inn Fields Theatre, which the Duke's Company occupied till its move in 1671 into the newly purpose-built Duke's Theatre in Dorset Garden. All of these sites are conveniently placed at the west of the City, handy for both Whitehall and the Inns of Court. The Bridges Street venue was destroyed by fire in 1672, leaving the King's Company to find temporary accommodation in the Lincoln's Inn Fields Theatre, which had been dark since the Duke's Company left it the previous year. By 1674, they had moved to the second Theatre Royal, this time in Drury Lane itself, which was their home till their merger in 1682 when the United Company was formed. Thereafter, that group used the Drury Lane venue primarily for drama and presented more spectacular productions in the theatre at Dorset Garden. No other significant performing spaces were developed till 1695.

Within a matter of months after the Restoration, actresses appeared in the major companies, displacing boy actors from the women's roles, though one or two able female impersonators continued into the mid-1660s. At its simplest, the development met an obvious problem in human resources, since boys had not been apprenticed to the work since 1642. Its wider implications have been much debated (see, for example, Howe 1992 and, for overviews, Roach 2000 and Fisk 2001). The emergence of the actress allowed the full development of something approximating to a star system. Some adult actors, from the Elizabethan period, had developed star status with acting companies over many seasons. But boy actors were turned over relatively quickly as their voices broke, rather like boy choristers, though some, no doubt, were retained as adult actors. The leading actresses of the late Stuart theatre shared star status with their more prominent male colleagues, enjoying and perhaps enduring celebrity and sometimes notoriety. Elizabeth Howe (1992) shows how the prominence enjoyed, for example, by Elizabeth Barry, Rebecca Marshall, Elizabeth Boutell, Anne Bracegirdle and perhaps half a dozen other actresses probably influenced the newly emerging dramatic repertoire as authors shaped their plays to the particular strengths of the leading ladies.

It would be difficult to argue that the emergence of women on the professional stage had an immediate impact on theme and content of the plays performed. After all, most plays, in the early years, were revivals and adaptations of works written when boys played the female roles. Strong, articulate and sexually attractive women were frequently depicted, from Shakespeare's Cleopatra to the heroines of Brome and Shirley. Plots often had an erotic motif, from the celebration of sexual love that ends so many Shakespearean comedies to the representation of sexual violence and female powerlessness in the face of male threat, as when the Duchess of Malfi is leered over by her brother and tormented by Bosola or Celia assaulted by Volpone. In the comic ending of *Aglaura*, Suckling had a bed trundled onto the stage with his heroine displayed upon it.

But new modes of eroticism do emerge on the Restoration stage, in ways determined by the involvement of women actors. The work of the boy-actor begins with an act of cross-dressing, though in Shakespeare a transgressive arabesque may follow, as when in *As You Like It* a boy plays Rosalind, who dresses as a man, who role-plays a woman (IV.i). But Restoration theatre saw a different potential in cross-dressing. Actresses playing 'breeches roles' – and evidently these were the speciality of certain leading ladies – allowed a frisson of sexual display. As Howe remarks, 'The breeches role titillated both by the mere fact of a woman's being boldly and indecorously dressed in male costume and, of course, by the costume suggestively outlining the actress's hips, buttocks and legs, usually concealed by a skirt' (Howe 1992: 56). Again, rape and sexual violence, statistically more frequently depicted after 1660 than on the Jacobean stage, allowed exploitation of the actress's sexuality, not least as the 'most effective means of exposing female flesh' (ibid.: 43–5).

But the eroticism actresses brought to the stage was surely more pervasive. Necessarily bold, courageous and usually attractive, they rapidly required a reputation for sexual availability: 'Society assumed that a woman who displayed herself on the public stage was probably a whore' (ibid.: 32). To some contemporary commentators, there was a moral advantage in employing women, rather than male transvestites, since theatrical cross-dressing had been a point of moral concern since the late 1570s (Levine 1994: ch. 1; Roach 2000: 31). But counter-arguments of some substance were soon to be found: 'Of the eighty or so actresses we know by name on the Restoration stage between 1660 and 1689, apparently about a mere one-quarter of this number led what were considered to be respectable lives' (Howe 1992: 33). Among the best-known cases of sexual impropriety were Moll Davis, highly regarded for her breeches roles, and Nell Gwyn, principally a comedienne, both of whom left the stage as acknowledged and kept mistresses of Charles II, who openly recognized the offspring of their relationships as his own. Gwyn returned to acting shortly before the king's death; Davis did not, though she participated in at least one court entertainment. For an ordinary member of the English propertied classes there may well have been something inherently exciting about sitting almost within touching distance of a boldly displayed woman who was currently sleeping with the king. Moreover, in the peculiar intimacy of the Restoration theatre, such issues were openly alluded to, particularly in prologues and epilogues. The epic vein to which Dryden aspired in the two parts of *The Conquest of Granada* is somewhat subverted by the arch epilogue to part one, apologizing for the late appearance of the play, through the absence of actresses through a 'sickness' in which 'nine whole Mon'ths are lost', a reference to the recent confinement of Gwyn (who played Almahide, queen of Granada) with her first child by Charles (ll.28, 32; Dryden 1956–2000: XI, 99). Gwyn certainly spoke the prologue to that play and may well have spoken the epilogue. Nor were the actresses exclusively a royal preserve. Favoured patrons mingled in the tiring rooms and the 'green room'. Pepys, who was friendly with Elizabeth Knepp of the King's Company, was plainly thrilled by such access, and such intimacies persisted into the performing space. Theatres acquired some notoriety as haunts of prostitutes, quite apart from the actresses, though the epilogue to Wycherley's *The Plain Dealer* seems to suggest a broad homology between their trades: 'while we [actresses] Baul, and you [the audience] in Judgment sit, / The Visor-Mask sells Linnen too i'th'Pit' (that is, the prostitute solicits; Womersley 2000: 286, n.392).

The professional stage was the defining medium of the high culture of Restoration England, much as court masque had been in the personal rule. Its ethos was largely determined by the rich louts who were its most influential patrons, who strutted its theatres, bedded its actresses, intimidated its actors and at times fell to deadly quarrelling among themselves. The section of the audience that had to be satisfied was nostalgically cavalier and fiercely hostile to the values attributed to the Puritan regimes of the mid-century decades; it was courtly but not genteel, and effectively unshockable. Shakespearean comedy carefully crafted those moments of disclosure when female characters dressed as men reveal the deception. In Wycherley's *The Plain Dealer* the villain Vernish confirms Fidelia's revelation by pulling off her peruke wig and feeling her breasts (Womersley 2000: 273); Fidelia does not protest. When *Romeo and Juliet* was revived by the Duke's Company in 1662, the high point for the audience, according to a contemporary witness, was an obscene slip of the tongue by the actress speaking the line 'O my Dear Count!' (Van Lennep et al. 1965: 48).

The genuine achievements of Restoration theatre, to which we turn shortly, are accomplished almost in spite of the market it addressed, from Dryden's elegantly turned couplets and heroic attempts at heroic drama to the precise control of tone and neatly turned wit of even the grossest comedies. An extraordinary mastery of stagecraft characterizes almost all the plays that retain the interest of the modern audience or scholarship. Those rich louts got rather more than they deserved (though, of course, some of the authors could be thus classified themselves).

The Restoration repertoire was slow in forming. Michael Dobson helpfully summarizes the statistics:

> Two years into the new era, in the 1661–62 theatrical season, records show only 4 new plays being performed, as opposed to 54 written before the Interregnum, and though the proportion of new plays had greatly increased by 1667–68 – when there were 12 recorded premieres alongside revivals of 20 plays written since 1660 and 33 written before 1640 – there was little significant change thereafter . . . . Although these figures are neither exhaustive nor definitive . . . they are accurate in their suggestion that Restoration theatre companies usually spent only about half of their time performing strictly Restoration drama. (2000: 41)

Early plays, particularly I suspect those that were performed most successfully on the Restoration stage, were sometimes quite carefully reworked, so that the distinction between revivals and premieres is an uncertain one. Sometimes Shakespearean adaptation, though of course never really comparable to the original, both vividly defines the changes in cultural expectation and demonstrates a considerable degree of ingenuity. Nahum Tate reworked *King Lear* (1681), radically changing the ending so that Lear lives on to witness the happy restoration of order after rebellion and to anticipate a continuing old age spent in pious reflection, while England is to be governed by Cordelia and Edgar under 'the prosperous Reign / Of this celestial Pair'. Edgar has the last word: 'Thy [Cordelia's] bright Example shall convince the World / (Whatever Storms of Fortune are decreed) / That Truth and Vertue shall at last succeed' (*The History of King Lear*, V.vi.151–2, 159–61; Clark 1997: 371–2). As Sandra Clark observes, Tate writes up all three female parts to match the availability of actresses, and the role of Cordelia is something of a star vehicle for Elizabeth Barry, then the leading lady of the Duke's Company. Moreover, Tate turns the play from a tragedy into a sort of political adventure story and in so doing takes out the dark and disturbing sense of the cosmic injustice which Shakespeare could engage with but which scarcely suited the aesthetic of Tate's own age. As Clark notes, the term 'poetic justice' had been coined by Thomas Rymer three years earlier. Indeed, Samuel Johnson found the Shakespeare version unbearably painful to read, preferring the rewards of virtue that Tate's offered over the capricious cruelty of the original (Clark 1997: lxv–lxx).

Taking *Antony and Cleopatra* as his starting point, Dryden created in effect a wholly new play in *All for Love*, first performed in 1677. The blank verse is completely reworked; as Clark notes, he expands 'imaginatively into similes where Shakespeare is more typically metaphorical and compressed' (1997: lxi). The result is a much plainer style, more easily comprehended on first encounter. The dramatic structure is much tighter, more securely designed to point up contrasts and rivalries, between Alexas, Cleopatra's servant, who often speaks in her interest, and Ventidius, the voice of Roman duty, and between Octavia, Antony's abandoned wife, and Cleopatra. The time scheme is much condensed. As in some Greek tragedies, Sophocles's *Oedipus at Colonus* for example, Dryden locates the action after the pivotal catastrophe, in this case the defeat at Actium. The result again is a more rigorously structured play. He introduces Octavia into these closing episodes of Antony's life. Generally, Dryden cuts the number of roles to something manageable by the usual complement of the King's Company; in Shakespeare's theatre, doubling up of roles had been much more acceptable. Similarly, writing up the part of Octavia gave a second developed role for an actress.

Dryden has produced a play that suffers only in comparison with its Shakespearean precursor, and arguably it is his most accomplished tragedy, lacking the psychological incongruities of his rhymed heroic plays (see below). Besides his extraordinary prosodic facility, it demonstrates his command of stagecraft. That is evident, too, in his revision, in collaboration with Davenant, of *The Tempest*, where the simple expedient of retaining Trinculo and Stephano but making them members of the ship's crew once more reduces the dramatis personae.

That play is most distinguished, however, for its place in the history of musical theatre, and indeed Restoration theatre both shares common ground with the refounding of the musical establishment that flourished in the 1630s and marks an important advance in the history of music appreciation in the English context. Charles II reformed the King's Music, the resident consort of the royal household. There is evidence that his players may have supplemented the theatrical ensembles for spectacular performances. Most significantly, however, the theatre companies themselves considerably extended the size of their resident musical complement. As Killigrew remarked to Pepys, comparing the theatre music of the 1660s with that of his pre-war experience, 'Then, two or three fiddles; now, nine or ten of the best' (Pepys 1970–83: VIII, 55).

Song, dance and incidental music were important components of early Stuart theatre, and remained so after 1660. But music had a more pervasive role. Ensembles typically of half a dozen musicians, predominantly string players, also performed before the play began and in the entr'actes. Every Restoration play had such complementary music, typically two suites and an overture before the performance as well as musical interludes. Matthew Locke, Pelham Humfrey and Henry Purcell, among other popular and successful composers, wrote this kind of music. In the history of English culture, this represents the first time that an audience outside the closed circle of the royal court or, occasionally, the household of an aristocratic grandee would have had regular and open access to secular music by distinguished contemporary composers performed by accomplished, professional ensembles. Here we have, in an English context, the first public concerts.

Among the most highly regarded of the new plays written early in the 1660s was Sir Samuel Tuke's *Adventures of Five Hours*, a translation and adaptation of a Spanish original undertaken, so 'The Prologue at Court' affirms, at the wish of the king. It probably had its premiere at court before opening at Lincoln's Inn Fields theatre of the

Duke's Company in 1663. It was a favourite of Pepys, who saw it several times and who thought it made *Othello* seem 'a mean thing' (Womersley 2000: 2–4).

Tuke was a recent convert to Catholicism, a courtier and minor diplomat, a favourite of Charles II, who had fought for his father and had gone into exile after the fall of Colchester (*DNB* 1975). His play is replete with cavalier values. The upper-class characters manifest a murderous commitment to concepts like honour, friendship and loyalty, at the expense of sometimes acting absurdly. Thus, Antonio at one moment fights with Octavio over an apparent slight to Porcia, and at the next switches to join him in a fight with Porcia's brother Henrique, who seems understandably puzzled:

> HEN. Why were not you *Antonio* fighting with him?
>   Were you not doing all you could to Kill him?
> ANT. *Henrique*, 'tis true; but finding in my breast
>   An equal strife 'twixt Honor, and Revenge;
>   I do in just compliance with them both
>   Preserve him from your Rage, to Fall by mine.
>   (V.iii.363–8; Womersley 2000: 39)

Possibly the scene is meant to be comic, though I suspect not. Sword-fights in this play are frequently in deadly earnest. Before the events depicted, Octavio has killed a friend of Henrique. In the course of the play, Antonio, while committing a trespass, disdainfully kills Henrique's servant Sylvio: 'How I despise these slaves' (III.ii.8; ibid.: 17). Both murders are committed with the impunity Charles's own favourites came to expect.

While the social values are clearly evident, politically the play is studiedly indifferent to the Protestant cause in continental Europe. Events are set in Seville but depend on an incident in the Spanish Netherlands, in which Antonio saved Camilla from rape by a Dutch soldier. The Dutch, plainly, are contemptible villains, and the upper-class Spanish characters embody cavalier virtues. Womersley observes:

> It is clear ... that the play is set in the period of the Spanish Wars of Religion in the Netherlands, a conflict which at the time in England had for some assumed the proportions and dignity of a crusade, but which has now dwindled in significance until it provides the largely neutral backdrop to a series of romantic escapades. It would be a mistake to overlook the provocative shallowness of this. (2000: 2)

Quite so. The broad and long-term perspectives of Protestant inter-
nationalism, so often an ideological stimulus to the court's enemies
over the century, are almost impudently set aside. The conflict with
Dutch Protestantism becomes an arena for cavalier display, 'The King's
Fencing-School', while the Dutch themselves are traduced in terms
that echo the propaganda of Cromwell's Dutch war of 1652–4 as gin-
swilling rebels 'made up of Turf, and Butter' (I.i.400–65; ibid.: 8–9).
Of course, Protectorate propaganda, while hostile locally to the Dutch,
never subordinated their image or interests to those of Spain.

The dramatic qualities of the play are considerable. Certainly, as
'The Epilogue' boasts, it is tightly structured, in contrast with most
older plays in the English tradition, laying the scene 'In three Houses
of the same Town' and, like its model, *Los Empeños de Seis Horas*,
emphasizing its intense time scheme in the title (though with a certain
audacity pulling the span down from six hours). This is an exercise
observing the unities of time and place. More interesting, it is a play
superbly crafted to exploit the technical capabilities of the new performing space. Scenes frequently take place in what are represented as
locked rooms. The relationship within households and between adjacent households is vividly realized and shapes the development of the
plot; backstairs, balconies and connecting doorways play an important
part in intrigues and escapades. Act III starts with the two heroines
appearing on a balcony above a street which the two heroes enter; it
continues with their ingress through a door, into a garden, where a
fight ensues; 'the scene changes to a garden, out of which they issue
fighting'; 'The Rising Moon appears in the Scene'; meanwhile their
servant observes and comments on the actions from a tree outside the
garden wall but overlooking its interior. 'The Scene Changes to the
City of Sevil' and then 'to Don Henrique's House', where the heroine
and her maid are depicted first on a balcony from which they descend,
probably back into the garden (Womersley 2000: 16–18). Though this
may well have been Tuke's first and only play, he demonstrates a fine
understanding of how the modern theatre of the 1660s could support
spectacular staging.

Other plays from the early Restoration share the unequivocally
triumphalist ideology of *The Adventures of Five Hours*. In *Cutter of
Coleman-Street* (1661), Abraham Cowley, who had dabbled as a writer
of university drama in the years before the civil wars, reworked for the
Duke's Company *The Guardian*, first staged at Trinity College, Cambridge, in March 1642 as an entertainment for the visiting Charles,

Prince of Wales (Hughes 1996: 30–1; Corns 1992: 250–1). The original was premised on commonplace anti-Puritan stereotyping. Cowley revives it, locating it in the 1650s, in a world of indigence and disgrace for diehard cavaliers impoverished through compounding and confiscations. He develops, too, a more localized and specific satire, directed against the radical extremes of London sectaries, guying Anna Trapnel in the figure of Tabitha Barebottle, while Cutter, a fake Puritan, recounts his vision in which 'Major General *Harrison* is to come in Green sleeves from the North upon a Sky-colour'd Mule, which signifies heavenly Instruction' (Cowley 1663: 39). The latter allusion is pointed and contemporaneously pertinent. Harrison, regicide and Fifth Monarchist, had shown extraordinary equanimity at his execution (see below). The prophecy that he would rise from the dead to lead a new revolution of the saints may have inspired the short-lived but briefly alarming Fifth Monarchist rebellion, Venner's Rising, in the spring of 1661. Harrison had died over a year before the play was performed; since his dismembered head and quarters were still displayed, the prophecy of his resurrection was palpably unfulfilled.

Sir Robert Howard's *The Committee*, staged by the King's Company in 1662, shared some common ground with *Cutter of Coleman-Street*, in that it depicts cavalier diehards in the throes of the compounding process. Like Cowley, Howard returns to the old anti-Puritan stereotypes. Here, their hypocrisy and greed are stressed, and their lack of breeding. But its rehearsal of cavalier assumptions is clearer. The colonels not only get the better of the Puritans, they also marry heiresses who share their steadfastness and loyalty to the king. With a triumphalist flourish, Howard has Colonel Blunt tell his tormentor: 'The day may come, when those that suffer for their Consciences and honour may be rewarded' (Howard 1665: 93). In a straightforward way in 1662 Howard, a civil war veteran rewarded by Charles II after the Restoration (*DNB* 1975), may have thought that day had arrived.

Howard, a Whig in later life, developed a more complex political vision in *The Great Favourite, or The Duke of Lerma*, performed by the King's Company in 1668. The play postdates by about three months the fall and subsequent exile of the Earl of Clarendon. Howard has ingeniously constructed a dramatic world which both resembles contemporary court politics but also is at significant distance from it. The Duke of Lerma secures his position by placing his daughter as mistress to the King of Spain; Hyde's daughter had married the king's brother, by whom she was already pregnant. The play at once depicts the corrosive potential of a government swayed by sexual manipulation and offers a resolutely happy and even comic ending. Lerma is not executed, as his associates are, nor does he suffer impeachment like Clarendon, but he takes holy orders (as a cardinal, no less), and retires to a monastery of his choice, where 'I in my safe retreate may sit and smile'. The king actually marries his mistress (Womersley 2000: 70–1). Contemporaries recognized a political resonance. Of course, the most obvious target, Clarendon, was already in exile, the portrait of monarchy is ultimately a positive and even celebratory one, and the affairs of state end well. But the dangers and dynamics of court intrigue are certainly explored.

In a remarkable series of plays stretching from *The Indian Queen* (1664; co-authored with Sir Robert Howard), through *The Indian Emperor* (1665), the two parts of *The Conquest of Granada* (1670, 1671), to *Aureng-Zebe* (1675), Dryden produced another kind of drama thoroughly characteristic of the early part of the rule of Charles II. These 'heroic plays', the term he himself uses, are historical fantasies, usually relating only loosely to historical events, set in exotic locations, such as Mexico around the time of first contact with Spain or Spain itself in the last days of the Moorish empire. Typically, they depict ruling-class crises, coups, rebellions, civil wars, foreign incursions, the fall of dynasties, restorations and 'rebels', who generally come off badly. Their values chime with those of nostalgic cavalierism. The plot mechanism of the lost son newly found, so favoured in chivalric romance, sometimes drives the resolution. Thus, in *The Indian Queen*, Montezuma is recognized as the queen's lost son and acclaimed by the people:

> 3. Messen[ger] King *Montezuma* their loud shouts proclaim,
>   The city rings with their new Sovereigns name:
>   The banish'd Queen declares he is her Son,
>   And to his succor all the people run.
>   (V.i.192–5; Dryden 1956–2000: VIII, 226–7)

Almanzor, the Moorish cavalier whose heroism pervades all ten acts, is at the fall of Granada acclaimed by the most heroic Spaniard, the Duke of Arcos, as his lost son, still recognizable by a tattoo hastily applied in his infancy and some revered trinkets his dying mother had given him.

Dryden was not alone in writing in this mode, but he persisted with it more assiduously than others, showing considerable accomplishment in matching elevated diction and action to the possibilities of spectacular staging. *The Indian Queen* offers a probably innovative opening, synthesizing music and stage design in a new kind of prologue: 'As the Musick plays a soft Air, the Curtain rises softly, and discovers an *Indian* boy and Girl sleeping under two Plantain-Trees; and when the Curtain is almost up, the Musick turns into a Tune expressing an Alarm, at which the boy wakes and speaks' (Dryden 1956–2000: VIII, 184). Lavish and exotic spectacle characterizes the closing scene, depicting 'the Temple of the Sun all of Gold, and four Priests in habits of white and red Feathers attending by a bloody Altar' (ibid.: 220). Indeed, the epilogue makes explicit reference to 'the Show, / The Poets Scenes, nay, more, the Painters too' and to their cost: 'If all this fail, considering the cost, / 'Tis a true Voyage to the *Indies* lost' (ibid.: 231). *The Indian Emperor* may well not yet have been conceived when Dryden and Howard worked on its predecessor, *The Indian Queen*. This could explain why the earlier play contained so few characters and situations to be carried over to the later. But the sequel was certainly driven in part by the economics of theatre management, because it allowed the reuse of scenes, props and costumes, as the prologue acknowledges: 'The Scenes are old, the Habits are the same / We wore last year' (ibid.: IX, 29).

Derek Hughes's sensitive readings have demonstrated that Dryden's heroic plays are amenable to a sympathetic modern appreciation, even stripped of the spectacular staging of their early performances. He shows, too, that they address matters of serious philosophical interest. In Dryden's own age they were received with both admiration and disdain. Two issues, plausibility and the rhymed couplets in which they were written, predominate in the resulting debate.

The striving for dramatic effect, the use of exotic locations and romance-like plot mechanisms distance them from the kinds of mimesis recurrent in the mainstream of English early modern drama. These are characters unlike people we have ever met, responding in ways that we would not respond and behaving as we would not behave in settings that we have never visited in a remote historical period we can scarcely imagine, often represented as engaged in political activities that share very little constitutional similarity with political life in Stuart England. The most effective and insightful critique, surprisingly perhaps, came not in discursive prose but in a burlesque drama, *The Rehearsal* (1671), written by George Villiers, second Duke of Buckingham, in association with Martin Clifford, Samuel Butler and Thomas Sprat. As its principal character, Bayes, smugly remarks: 'I despise your *Johnson* [that is, Jonson] and *Beaumont,* that borrow'd all they writ from Nature; I am for fetching purely out of my own fancy' (II.i.67–71; Womersley 2000: 149). Its initial butt was Howard rather than Dryden, but in its final form the latter is plainly satirized in the figure of Bayes, while the hero of the play we see in rehearsal, Drawcansir, parodies the conduct, speech and manner of Almanzor. The political premise of the action is a conflict between the two kings of Brentford (*sic*) and their two rival usurpers, resolved with fitting absurdity by Drawcansir, who kills everybody: 'Others may boast a single man to kill; / But I, the blood of thousands daily spill' (V.i.343–4; Womersley 2000: 169).

Of course, all the characters in the play in rehearsal speak in couplets, though rather less eloquently than in Dryden's plays. It was a medium of which he was absolute master, but its role in drama proved controversial. After all, the Restoration stage presented revivals of many earlier play that were not in rhymed couplets, which Jonson, Beaumont and Fletcher and Shakespeare, for the most part, had eschewed, though Dryden himself argues in an exchange with Sir Robert Howard that, had Jonson's age been as accomplished in writing couplets as the Restoration, ''tis probable he would have used them in his more elevated dramas'. The attraction of couplets, for Dryden, is that they put a distance between heroic language and the everyday (Dryden 1956–2000: IX, 7). By 1675, however, the game had substantially been lost. *Aureng-Zebe* constitutes a kind of farewell to rhymed couplets in drama.

Dryden's best-known comedy, *Marriage A-la-Mode,* first performed by the King's Company in 1672, shares considerable common ground with his heroic dramas. It is set in an uncertain period in Sicily, though there is as little sense of place as of time. It depicts a bloodless restoration of a lost prince, Leonidas, which is followed by a generous reconciliation with the usurper and reward for those who changed sides at a late stage. Since the lost prince is a heroic and wholly admirable figure, a panegyric intention is very evident. But the play tells other stories. It has a matched set of seemingly ill-matched couples. Rhodophil is married to Doralice, but they have become disinterested in each other and he pursues Melantha. His friend, Palamede, is to marry Melantha at his father's insistence, but pursues Doralice. Both women encourage the advances and the relationships are often consummated but frustrated by comic coincidences and misunderstandings. In the end, all learn to love their legitimate partners. Situations are mildly risqué, as is their badinage, though the indecencies of Wycherley and

Etherege (see below) are assiduously avoided. Dryden achieves a comic idiom that does not compromise the decorum of the heroic story line. Indeed, he points this up in his epilogue:

> *But yet too far our Poet would not run,*
> *Though 'twas well offer'd, there was nothing done.*
> *He would not quite the Women's frailty bare,*
> *But stript 'em to the waste, and left 'em there.*
> (ll.11–14; Dryden 1956–2000: XI, 315)

That disconcerting image is arguably the most overtly erotic passage in the play.

The greatest comedic achievements of the rule of Charles II came in the 1670s in William Wycherley's *The Country Wife* (1675), staged by the King's Company, and Sir George Etherege's *The Man of Mode* (Duke's Company, 1676). Each depicts life among the young, rich and idle of the metropolis. Very few of the characters, except for the servants or lower professions (fiddlers, chaplains, 'quacks' and the like) do much apart from a daily round of play-going, promenading and socializing, all of which assist the process of sexual dalliance and promiscuity. Each play is quite distinctive, but both are premised on low expectations of human conduct: greed, lust and vanity make the world go round. There are hierarchies among the persons depicted, but they are neither social nor moral. The ranking characters are marked by verbal accomplishment, cunning, energy in pursuit of gratification, and by style; the losers are the would-be wits or dandies who are merely affected, and sometimes the naive, the old and the stupid.

The Country Wife presents the intersection of two plots. Horner pretends to have been rendered impotent by a botched medical procedure to cure syphilis in order to have freer access to married women (all of whom are deeply lustful for extramarital liaisons). Pinchwife, himself formerly a rake, takes a simple country girl as his wife and attempts to shield her from the kinds of familiarity with the city which would render her as promiscuous as other married women of her social status. 'Horner' is a fairly common surname in England, one of those derived from a craft, working in horn, but of course its rarer signification, 'cuckold-maker' (*OED*, sig. 3), is his vocation. An intense competition based on male sexual rivalry drives the play. The women Horner couples with present no challenge to the seducer once they have been separated from their husbands; the play, like Horner, simply works from the assumption that they will accede, and they do. But this is a depiction of aggressive competition about relative masculinity. Husbands, when they learn of Horner's alleged impairment, are unsparing in their contempt, and his seduction of their wives is an act of revenge perpetrated on them through their spouses. Indeed, in the most notorious scene, Lady Fidget leaves her husband, Sir Jaspar, who has ridiculed Horner as a eunuch throughout the play, enters his private chamber, supposedly to examine his china, and locks the door. Setting up an obvious double entendre, Horner exits 'to get into her the back way'. As Sir Jaspar is cuckolded while standing outside the locked chamber door, there is a strong suggestion that Horner begins the sexual encounter by sodomizing Lady Fidget, and thus, in the process, symbolically sodomizing her husband:

> SIR JAS. Wife, my Lady *Fidget*, Wife,
>   he is coming into you the back way.
> LA. FID. Let him come, and welcome, which way he will.
> SIR JAS. He'll catch you, and use you roughly, and
>   be too strong for you.
> LA. FID. Don't you trouble your self, let him if he can.
>   (IV.iii.163–70; Womersley 2000: 205)

This is a world in which received morality and its associated rhetoric are suspended, but is it endorsed or censured by the author? Certainly, some see a critique of sexual excess, viewing Horner as a depiction of madness, of 'monomania' (for example, Marshall 1993: 63–85). Yet the play shares the 'values' or perhaps the aspirations of rich, male nihilists, values probably held by the most influential element in the audience. Moreover, Wycherley passes over the opportunity afforded by the epilogue to point up the moral, if there were one. Instead, his epilogue, spoken by the actress who played Lady Fidget, merely warns males in the audience against confusing art with life and thinking they can play Horner's role because the women they bed or fail to bed will rate them on their sexual performance and find them lacking: 'men may still believe you Vigorous, / But then we Women – there's no cous'ning us' (ll.32–3; Womersley 2000: 222). Male sexual anxiety has driven the plot, and the play ends on a fitting note.

Etherege's *The Man of Mode or, Sir Fopling Flutter*, as the title page of the first edition calls it, shares much common ground with *The Country Wife*, and may well be perceived as the Duke's Company's rejoinder to their rivals' success of the previous year. Even more sharply, Dorimant, the rake hero, whose values remain unchallenged, is distinguished by his difference from the foppish, would-be wits that surround him. The play carries the name, not of Dorimant, but of the absurd man of fashion, newly returned from Paris and carrying wild affections of speech, manner and dress, 'the pattern of modern Foppery' (I.i.441–2; Womersley 2000: 295). Sir Fopling is the real comic interest; Dorimant's intrigues lack the brilliance and elan of Horner's, and approach closer to a discriminating depiction of contemporary society. In the course of the play, Dorimant pays off Molly, a whore ('I have no money and am very Mallicolly; pray send me a Guynie to see the Operies' – I.i.603–4; ibid.: 297); he discontinues a relationship with Mrs Loveit, a notorious gentlewoman, 'your *Pis aller* [last resort] as you call her', '*Dorimant*'s convenient' (I.i.21–3; ibid.: 292 and n.; III.iii.278; ibid.: 313); he debauches and then abandons Bellinda, a gentlewoman whose reputation is sufficiently intact to make it worth protecting through subterfuge; and he ends the play prepared to follow into the country and there to court Harriet, the heroine of the secondary plot. There is, perhaps, a regenerative schema of sorts here, though as W. B. Carnochan persuasively argues, the ending is purposefully 'tentative' (Etherege 1966: xviii). Certainly, Dorimant's last speech sounds smitten and perhaps redeemed: 'The first time I saw you, you left me with the pangs of Love upon me, and this day my soul has quite given up her liberty' (V.ii.507–9; Womersley 2000: 335). But Etherege does not take the simpler option of an explicit resolution; he could have married off Dorimant and Harriet alongside Emelia and Bellair, or he could have used the epilogue to point up a probable outcome. That, instead, deals wholly with the depiction of Sir Fopling Flutter and its relationship to the young men in the audience.

Etherege can write with pathos and a mimetic precision. The exchange between Bellinda and Dorimant after he has seduced her have a tenderness – and sense of the social consequences of sexual conduct – that Wycherley cannot aspire to:

BELLINDA I have a Thousand fears about me: have I not been
    seen think you?
DORIMANT By no body but my self and trusty *Handy* [his valet].
BELLINDA Where are all your people?
DORIMANT I have disperst 'em on sleeveless Errants [trifling errands].
    What does that sigh mean?

BELLINDA Can you be so unkind to ask me? – well –

Sighs.

Were it to do again –
DORIMANT We should do it, should we not?
BELLINDA I think we should: the wickeder man you to make me love so
well – will you be discreet now?

(IV.ii.5–16; ibid.: 321–2 and n.)

Wycherley's next play, *The Plain Dealer*, staged by the King's Company in 1676, was his last, a retirement from the theatre that coincided
with his own fall from favour with Charles II. This play has a spokesman for morality in the unflinching plain speaking of its hero, Manly,
whose name indicates his freedom from the sexual anxieties that per-
meate *The Country Wife*. Yet he is somewhat ingenuous, for he
entrusted Olivia, his former mistress, with his personal fortune before,
ruinously, serving in an Anglo-Dutch war; she has both betrayed him
by marrying his closest friend and embezzled his fortune, leaving him,
in Hughes's phrase, an 'almost tragic character' (Hughes 1996: 190).
Around his position at the still centre of a morally unstable world
evolves a broader satire, on litigiousness, on the legal trade, on for-
tune-hunting through the courtship of rich widows. Fidelia, a breeches
role, is his secret admirer, who, dressed as a man, has accompanied him
to the wars, with no great distinction, but whose loyalty wins his love,
albeit in a somewhat muted ending which does not actually marry
them off. Even Manly's morality has its limits, as when, in an act of
revenge, he plots to deceive Olivia into a sexual encounter. The episode is alarming conduct for a hero, compounded by Fidelia's albeit
reluctant complicity.

Restoration comedy often retained a dependence on cannibalizing
earlier plays. As editors note, *The Country Wife* owes much to Terence's *Eunuchus* and to Molière's *L'École des Femmes*; 'the esssential
conceit underpinning the plot [of *The Plain Dealer*] bears both general
and particular resemblances to Molière's *Le Misanthrope*', while 'the
character of Fidelia looks back to Viola in Shakespeare's *Twelfth Night*'
(Womersley 2000: 172, 224). Aphra Behn's most famous play, and the
one of which she first publicly acknowledged authorship, *The Rover*
(first performed by the Duke's Company in 1677), depends closely
and heavily on *Thomaso*, a work usually thought to have been written
towards the end of the Interregnum. Though it remained unper-
formed, Killigrew had published it in 1664 (Killigrew 1664). Killigrew

was an old friend and patron, probably her recruiter and perhaps her handler in her days as royalist spy (Todd 1996: 31), but the evident cooperation between the companies in his provision of the material for a play for the rival house points up the collusive nature of Restoration theatrical cartel.

Janet Todd concludes, 'So what did Behn lift from *Thomaso*? The answer is, most of the play, although the breaking up and reassigning of speeches makes *The Rover* something new' (ibid.: 215). There are, however, important shifts of emphasis, which involve the writing up of the female parts and adjusting the moral balance between the English characters, in James Grantham Turner's phrase, 'diminishing their glamour' (Hutner 1993b; Turner 2002: 236–8). Nevertheless, the play feels decidedly old-fashioned. Its plot bears a generic resemblance to those of *The Adventures of Five Hours*. Its heroes are drawn from the same ranks of broken diehard soldiery as people the stage of *The Committee* or *Cutter of Coleman-Street*. Maureen Duffy ingeniously and convincingly argues that this very outmodedness functions nostalgically to good polemical effect, as 'a rallying for the faithful when the first romance of the King's return had worn thin and the country was again divided into factions', and she notes that it was immediately popular in the highest circles, 'constantly called for at court' (1977: 144). Certainly one can appreciate the attractions of reflecting on simpler times for Charles and James as opposition to the latter's succession gathered strength.

The transposition of the play from Madrid, as in the original, to Naples underscores the carnivalesque quality, but this is less a world turned upside-down than a world in which those who should be dominant are respected and emerge triumphant. The events depict the arrival into the society of expatriate royalists of Willmore, a sea-captain, presumably commander of a ship from the squadron of Prince Rupert, which fitfully and ineffectually continued military action in the years following the debacle of the battle of Worcester; quite why he is in Naples remains unexplained. The royalists are joined by Ned Blunt, the son of someone who has not lost his fortune in the service of the king. Blunt is variously patronized and duped by his fellow-countrymen. Behn works hard to establish the exotic location; Willmore receives instruction on Neapolitan conduct, the characteristics of carnival, and how the more expensive prostitutes behave, all very pertinent, since Angellica Bianca, a newly arrived and pricey whore, attracts him and becomes enamoured of him. There is no choric criticism of

Willmore's conduct in taking money from Angellica and then desert-
ing her for an heiress, though her response, perhaps the only attempt
at depicting genuine affection within the play, shows a desperation of
near tragic potential. It is a critical commonplace that Behn has renamed this character from the original, giving to her her own initials,
an insight from which several critical avenues lead.

Bianca's failure represents some sort of exploration of the limitations
of female empowerment even in the world of carnival. Indeed, the
comic subplot peters out in a scene premised on the grossest manifestation of female powerlessness. Blunt is duped by a prostitute,
robbed of his trousers (which contain much of his ready money) and
dumped in a sewer to make his way home. He responds by a sexual
assault on Florinda, a gentlewoman loved by Belville, one of the
English royalists. Strikingly, Frederick, another expatriate diehard, is
prepared to join in the indecency until Florinda mentions his name:
'Stay, Sir, I have seen you with *Belvile*, an *English* Cavalier, for his sake
use me kindly; you know him, Sir' (IV.667–8; Behn 1992–6: V, 506).
Frederick's response is pragmatic, rather than moral; if they rape a
ruling-class virgin, 'a Maid of quality', they risk arrest, whereas they
assume they can 'ruffle a Harlot' with impunity. They desist for the
moment. Blunt's first response is to assure Florinda that, were Belville
present, he would join in the gang rape, and, in any case, she'll be kept
for him to violate later: 'he'd have a Limb or two of thee my Virgin
Pullet, but 'tis no matter, we'll leave him the bones to pick' (IV.682–4;
ibid.: 670–2). Perhaps most tellingly, Florinda, at the resolution of the
play, accepts their most perfunctory of apologies; yes, of course, if she
had not been a lady, then her violent gang rape would have been a
wholly appropriate way for young gentlemen to revenge the humiliation of one of their number by a whore. Indeed, were these real events
and were the setting London in the 1660s or 1670s, Frederick and
Blunt could have expected to complete the assault on Florinda with
impunity (Turner 2002: esp. ch. 6). Behn's own view remains morally
uncertain, though she is clear-eyed about the conduct of rich young
toughs, and here, as elsewhere in her oeuvre, shows a precise awareness
of class difference both in conduct and treatment.

The political turmoil of the late 1670s and early 1680s resonated
through the new drama of those years. Susan Owen calculates, 'During
the Exclusion Crisis some fifty-four new plays, or new versions of old
plays, were written', the large majority of which engage with the
political crisis, as dramatists 'strain every nerve to offer a royalism

which is nevertheless tormented and fractured; or offer a message of moderation which insists upon the need for royal temperance; or launch boldly into a rhetoric of outright Whiggery' (1996: 2–3). All concerned knew how easily the stage could be controlled, and this awareness surely shaped the conduct of both authors and the theatre companies. Indeed, of the three particularly rewarding plays I shall analyse in detail, one was banned shortly after its premiere and another was delayed till the battles of exclusion had been fought and won. None is ideologically unequivocal, and all work to distance the cultured reflections of the theatrical milieu from the cruder partisanships of the mob.

Lucius Junius Brutus by Nathaniel Lee was performed by the Duke's Company in December 1680, though it was quickly deemed defamatory of the government and banned. It depicts the republican revolution occasioned by Tarquin's rape of Lucrece and the subsequent suppression under the leadership of the eponymous hero of a royalist counter-revolution to restore Tarquin to the Roman throne. As we have noted, Charles himself had been associated with Tarquin since the earliest issues of *Mercurius Politicus*, and, in Derek Hughes's phrase, 'few subjects could have been more politically sensitive than that of republican rebellion against a tyrannical and lecherous ruling house' (1996: 295). However, I share Hughes's view that this is more than a mere exercise in Whig partisanship. Perhaps evasively, Lee does not depict Tarquin. The focus is elsewhere.

Lee places at the centre of the play the tragic love story of the star-crossed Titus, son of Brutus, and Teraminta, 'the blood of *Tarquin*, / The basest too' (II.i.40–1; Womersley 2000: 433). He flanks them with groups representing the extremes of the royalist and republican factions. The royalists have within their ranks young men whose conduct resembles the worst excesses of the rakish courtiers of Charles's court, 'your roaring Squires', who 'poke us [the citizens of Rome] in the night, beat the Watch, and deflower our Wives' (II.i.81–2; ibid.: 440). The rakes see an obvious advantage in monarchy in that the king's pardon secures their immunity from prosecution, whereas Brutus's republic would require equality before the law, 'Laws that are cruel, deaf, inexorable, / That cast the Vile and Noble altogether' (II.i.17–18; ibid.: 439). Yet the issues even here are not straightforward. Committing outrages and securing royal pardon had most spectacularly and sensationally characterized the conduct of the Dukes of Buckingham and Monmouth, both of whom lined up against the king on the exclusion issue. On the other side, the republicans, far from uniformly exhibiting high-principled civic duty, include firebrands and misfits who harbour disruptive and dangerous social prejudices. When Vinditius rouses the mob with 'look you, Sirs, I am a true Common-wealths-man, and do not naturally love Kings, tho they be good' (II.i.44–6; ibid.: 439), he speaks the language of the Good Old Cause, of Interregnum republicanism, and from his own mouth con-firms the Tory canard that the new Whigs were rebranded roundheads.

In this unrelievedly sombre tragedy, both sides behave badly and both also have their blameless victims. Lucrece's rape and suicide open the play; Teraminta, 'whooted like a common strumpet ... and drag'd about the streets', witnesses her lover's death wound before she, too, stabs herself (V.i.78–9, V.ii.158; ibid.: 459, 462). Titus, peripherally involved in the abortive counter-revolution to which his brother had lent himself, shares his gruesome and degrading execution, cut short by a kindly sword thrust from a republican partisan, to the horror of witnesses appalled by Brutus's stern intransigence that his sons must suffer to demonstrate the impartiality of republican justice as opposed to royalist caprice and favouritism. Extremism has brought about the tragedy. Of course, no society can tolerate a rapist ruler, or license rich, young thugs, who launch their failed coup by drinking the blood of cruelly slaughtered opponents in what is patently a parody of the Catholic mass (IV.i.1–121; ibid.: 452–3). Nor should the likes of Vinditius be given free rein. Brutus demonstrates the inappropriate-ness of inflexible action from abstract principles, which exclude all natural impulse, all human kindliness, from his decision-making, leav-ing him poignantly to kiss the 'trembling lips' of the dying son whose execution he had decreed (V.ii.174; ibid.: 463).

Thomas Otway's *Venice Preserv'd*, which depicts an abortive coup in the Venetian republic, was performed by the Duke's Company in February 1682, by which time the king and his supporters had plainly weathered the storm. It is topped and tailed by a prologue and epi-logue of transparent Tory partisanship, in triumphal mood. The con-cluding sentiment anticipates the 'Songs of Triumph' to greet the return of James, Duke of York, from Scotland, where he had been lying low since 1680 (Epilogue, l.34; ibid.: 502). Yet the play is as ideologically complex as *Lucius Junius Brutus*. Indeed, in its structural similarity it so closely resembles Lee's play as to invite interpretation as a pendant. It, too, has a tragic love story at its centre: Jaffeir has ruined himself through his marriage to Belvidera, without the approval of her father, the senator Priuli; he is drawn to the coup in desperation, only to betray it when one of its leaders tries to rape his wife; and he perishes by his own hand. Belvidera explicitly likens herself to Lucrece (II.i.8; ibid.: 480). The final scenes are again dominated by the cruel and unusual executions of captured conspirators, which, in the case of Jef-feir's friend Pierre, is shortened by a kindly dealt death wound, much as Titus's had been. Once more, both sides have dreadful villains among good men. The conspirators are led by a would-be rapist, and they anticipate releasing devastation on the state. Renault urges them, 'Shed blood enough, spare neither Sex nor Age, / Name nor Condition' (III.ii.334–5; ibid.: 485). The senators include the ghastly Antonio, who is depicted barking like a dog in the bedroom of his dominatrix, and more generally the distempers of the state, alluded to by the more honourable among the conspirators, are grave and pressing.

The complexity of the play finds reflection in the range of conflicting readings it has provoked (usefully summarized in Owen 1996: 236–7). Its location in an ancient republic places the issues it raises at some significant remove from the immediate crises of the kingdom. J. A. Downie perceptively suggests that Otway 'was consciously contribut-ing to the contemporary debate about the nature and origins of government which had been going on throughout the seventeenth century, because not everyone was prepared to accept the doctrine of the Divine Right theorists' (Downie 1994: 17). Indeed, the location precludes the divine right argument against rebellion. In its place come a horror at the insecurity, the threat to life and property, released by resort to direct action, and, in cautionary but not triumphalist fashion, an illustration of the personal tragedies that befall good men caught up in insurrectionary politics.

Nathaniel Lee collaborated with Dryden in writing *The Duke of Guise*, first performed in November 1682 by the newly formed United Company, though it had been written in the summer of that year, at which time its transparent attack on Monmouth 'offended his much tried but still protective father' (Hughes 1996: 307). Though it is a fiercely loyalist play – and marks a considerable ideological shift on Lee's part – its apparent prophecy of the Duke's assassination and its rehearsal of the obvious political advantages for the crown could well have been inflammatory had it been performed when it was first intended. It is not, however, simplistic. Rather, it transfers to the stage the subtleties of Dryden's *Absalom and Achitophel* (considered below). Like the poem, it makes a profound distinction between the worst of the Whigs and Monmouth himself. Within the play, Malicorne, who seems almost certain to be recognized as the Shaftesbury figure (Hughes 1996: 308), has signed a Faustian pact and his familiar devil eventually carries him down to hell in a surprisingly old-fashioned scene: '*a flash of Lightning, they sink together*' (Dryden and Lee 1683: 68). Guise, the Monmouth figure, has formerly shown great courage in fighting for the king, and within the play is restrained, honourable and brave. But he mistakes his place within a divinely ordained order. As Marmoutier, a woman courted both by the king and himself, cautions him, 'He's born to give you fear, not to receive it' (ibid.: 46). The play, like the poem, unequivocally endorses the divine status of kingship. Like David in the poem, the king is too passive, too slow to act, but is eventually decisive, though here the action is both a political counterattack, analogous to the dismissal of the Exclusion Parliament, and a bloody reprisal: 'Bid *Dugast* execute the Cardinal, / Seize all the Factious Leaders' (ibid.: 75). Similarly, the king, like David, relies on staunch and competent loyalists, depicted in some detail in a celebration of Tory grandees.

Hughes is scathing about the 'clear (and intellectually barren) parallel between the sedition of the Catholic League against Henri III and that of the Whigs against Charles' (Hughes 1996: 307). But is it so barren? In *Absalom and Achitophel* Dryden cleverly shifts the basis of the crisis away from religion to matters of personality and the central principles of divinely ordained monarchical government. *The Duke of Guise* frustrates the Whig argument from religion. In the events depicted, it is a conspiracy of Catholic fanatics who are trying to exclude the Protestant Henri of Navarre, the future Henri IV, from succession to Henri III. Ambition and insubordination drive the plot, and religious disagreements function as part of the mechanism to bewilder the common people. While this play lacks the challenging ambivalences of *Lucius Junius Brutus* and *Venice Preserv'd*, it shows guile and panache in bringing a sense of closure to theatrical engagements with the Exclusion Crisis.

Rochesterism

John Wilmot, second Earl of Rochester, achieved notoriety in both his own age and ours as the quintessence of Restoration libertinism, in life as in his art. Yet recent scholarship has done much to refine and correct that status, limiting his certain oeuvre, while modern critical readings suggest a philosophical depth and a political engagement and reposition him as a relatively complex interrogator of the sexual politics of his own age (see, especially, Thormählen 1993; Chernaik 1995; Turner 2002).

Rochester himself occupied a curious social position. The first earl, his father, had an active and distinguished career in the king's cause: he participated in the failed royalist coup of 1641, commanded at the battle of Copredy Bridge, a rare success for the royalists in the later stages of the first civil war, accompanied Charles II to Scotland and thence to the fateful battle of Worcester, from which he escaped with the young king, and he held a position of trust in the subsequent years of exile (*DNB* 1975). He died in 1658. He had been created earl in 1652. The Wilmot family, however, in terms of their property base (itself, of course, ravaged by the effects of exile and confiscation), had more affinities with the upper gentry than the established aristocracy. The second earl depended for his prosperity on the patronage of the king, whose evident initial good will towards the son of one of his closest and loyalist adherents was further confirmed by Rochester's own high-profile and distinguished conduct as a gentleman volunteer in the second Anglo-Dutch war (vividly narrated by Greene 1974: ch. 3). From 1666 he was a Gentleman of the King's Bedchamber, an office his father had held in exile, and from 1674 Keeper of Woodstock Park, both wealthy offices in the gift of the king, who also encouraged him in the formation of a lucrative marriage. Though royal displeasure from time to time led to his expulsion from the court, he retained royal patronage till his death (*DNB* 1975). Other alliances may well have been significant in the forming of the ideological orientation of his verse. He was certainly in the circle of George Villiers, second Duke of Buckingham, an immensely wealthy and destructively profligate grandee, though scarcely an office-broker on the scale of the first duke. Buckingham's own career was complex, vacillating and unstable, though by the mid-1670s he was broadly associated with country-party critics of the court and of James's succession. Again, the family associations of Rochester's mother included significant links to parliamentarians. Anne Wilmot, first Countess of Rochester, was cousin and friend of Lucy Hutchinson, knowing her well enough to possess a manuscript copy of her major verse work, *Order and Disorder* (see below; also Hutchinson 2001: xviii). The acerbity Rochester develops towards the king's promiscuity reflects the strictures of the outsider as well as the courtier's more intimate distaste, though his personal morality scarcely gave him the high ground.

Establishing the Rochester canon, for reasons to which we shall shortly turn, has proved immensely challenging. In Harold Love's recent edition (Rochester 1999) 'poems probably by Rochester' amount to scarcely more than 100 pages. They include fewer than than 50 short poems, the longer 'Tunbridge Wells', 'A Satyre against Reason and Mankind', 'A Letter from Artemiza in the Towne to Chloe in the Countrey', 'A Ramble in St. James's Park', 'A Satyr' ('In the Isle of Brittain'), and a score of other, generally less distinguished works.

Indeed, the quality is as uneven as the oeuvre is generically diverse. Rochester certainly knew well the court poetry of the Caroline era, and some of his less challenging verse could be mistaken for Carew's or Herrick's. His 'Dialogue' between 'Nymph' and 'Sheppard', each articulating uncertainty and resentment, finds resolution in a concluding chorus, 'Then Lett our flaming hearts be joyn't / While in that sacred fire, / e're thou prove falce or I unkind, / Together both expire' (ll.17–20: ibid.: 16). It is artfully written – the 'thou / I' pronouns, sung together, express their mutuality, and the joining of the voices mirrors the joining of their hearts. Had it been written 30 years earlier, Henry Lawes could have set it with facility. In the event, Louis Grabu, a French composer much patronized by Charles II, set it, no later than 1684 (ibid.: 521). Again, that restrained libertinism found in some of Suckling's lyrics also recurs. The song 'Phillis, be gentler I advise', though broadly in the tradition that adapts the *carpe diem* topos into a seduction routine, ends with a hard minatory edge: 'then if ... / You'll peevishly be coy, / Dye with the Scandall of a Whore, / And never know the joy' (ll.12–15; ibid.: 20).

Yet elsewhere Rochester insistently subverts the Caroline idiom. In 'A song' ('*Faire Cloris* in a Pigsty lay'), the shepherdess is displaced by a swine-girl, who, stimulated by the sounds of the pigs around her, dreams an erotic rape-fantasy, from which she wakes unsatisfied:

> Frighted shee wakes, and wakeing friggs:
>   Nature thus kindly eas'd
> In dreames raisd by her grunting Piggs
>   And her owne thumb betwixt her Leggs,
> Shees Innocent and pleas'd.
>
>   (ll.36–40; ibid.: 40)

The gender politics are as unsettling as the social perspective. Rochester seems to me, *pace* his more sympathetic modern critics, unrelenting in his sexist assumptions, and here the poem is premised on the related notions that women may find rape or the thought of rape stimulating and that women are in an undifferentiating way open to, desirous of, ready for sex. But the principal point of the poem is essentially literary. Rochester takes pastoralism from the idealizing conventions in which court ladies are represented as shepherdesses and places it in a real setting of animal husbandry, a pigsty; the heroine may have a name from classical pastoral, but she sleeps among her pigs and masturbates with her thumb. In a similar way the song 'By all *Loves* soft, yet mighty *Pow'rs*' has the stanzaic form of a Caroline lyric, it has nymphs and a heroine called Phillis, but the proposition it opposes is the decidedly unidealized notion 'that *Men* shou'd Fuck in time of *Flow'rs* [menstruation] / Or when the *Smock*'s beshit' (ll.3–4; ibid.: 37).

Rochester also picks away at the cocky assurance of the libertinism of the age of Suckling and Carew. 'The Imperfect Enjoyment', a poem on *ejaculatio praecox* and subsequent impotence, substitutes the swagger with something altogether more anxious and troubling. But once more, the principal point is literary. As the lovers embrace in an advanced stage of foreplay,

> Her nimble tongue (loves lesser lightning) plaied
> Within my Mouth; and to my thoughts conveyd
> Swift Orders, that I should prepare to throw
> The all dissolving Thunderbolt beloe.
> My fluttering soul, sprung with the pointed Kiss,
> Hangs hovering o're her balmy brinks of bliss;
> But whilst her buisy hand would guide that part
> Which shou'd convey my soul up to her heart
> In liquid raptures I dissolve all o're,
> Melt into sperm and spend at every pore.
>   (ll.7–16; ibid.: 14)

The thunderbolt momentarily associates the lover with Zeus, whose weapon of choice it was, and thus with his legendary and literally polymorphous sexual energy. But the mythic moment soon fades. Herrick had used the pouring of the soul as an elegant euphemism for the sexual act in his delicate little poem, 'The Night-piece, to Julia' (l.20; Herrick 1956: 217). Rochester subverts the conceit. What in Herrick had been a decorous periphrasis, in Rochester becomes something of a debasement of the concept itself of the soul, not a category that he esteems much, as we shall see. Again, though a gesture towards grandiloquence, albeit ironized, persists, a clear, precise description of the mechanics of human sexuality overwhelms it: 'Smileing she chides in a kind, murmring noise / And from her body wipes the clamy Joyes' (ll.19–20). 'Joyes' may have a Herrickian evasiveness: 'clamy' doesn't.

Rochester famously died in Christian penitence, but his most explicit poetic engagement with religion is his translation of a passage from Seneca, which asserts as its premise, 'After Death nothing is, and nothing Death'. Hell and its torments are dismissed as tendentious duplicities 'Devis'd by Rogues, dreaded by fools' ('Senec. Troas. Act. 2. Chor. Thus English'd by a Person of Honour', ll.1, 15; Rochester 1999: 45–46). Though 'Upon Nothinge' acknowledges that, somehow, the created world has been produced from nothing, its dissolution is anticipated not in terms of the apocalyptic transformation of Christian orthodoxy, but as a return to a state of nothingness, of nonbeing; existence 'Into thy [nothing's] boundless selfe must undistinguish'd fall' (l.9; ibid.: 46). Atheism in the modern sense of the word is a rare phenomenon among the educated classes in the seventeenth century; Rochester approaches very close to it.

It is a critical commonplace that Rochester's social psychology and political philosophy owe much to Thomas Hobbes, though the nature of that debt remains controversial (cf. Thormählen 1993: 174–9 with Chernaik 1995: ch. 1 *et passim*). At the least, he takes from Hobbes a notion that the human animal is prompted by potentially destructive individualism which tends against the common good, and that morality functions superstructurally (and in Rochester's version, hypocritically and ineffectually) to control those urges. 'A Satyre against Reason and Mankind', usually regarded as his most impressive longer poem, analyses the mismatch between the essential characteristics of the species and the assumption that rational behaviour, based on something other than the interpretation of data gathered by the senses, is achievable and appropriate:

> Your Reason hinders, mine helps to enjoy,
> Renewing appetites yours would destroy.
> My Reason is my friend, Yours is a cheat,
> Hunger calls out, my Reason bids me eat;

> Perversly yours your appetites does mock,
> They ask for food, that answers what's a clock.
>   (ll.104–9; Rochester 1999: 60)

Other species more completely fulfil their essential capabilities because they do not share the delusional aspirations of moralising rationalism; hence, 'I'de be a Dog, a Monky, or a Bear. / Or any thing but that vain Animal / Who is so proud of being Rational' (ll.5–7; ibid.: 57).

But this poem is scarcely typical of Rochester's 'satires', which engage, for the most part, with anti-social conduct. In some respects, they have an old-fashioned character when set against the satires of Marvell and of Dryden (see below), harking back to the opening years of the century, to the generalizing satirical mode that drew on the stereotyping tendency of character-writing. Here we meet the familiar roll call of jilts and jades, rakes and gulls, pimps and fops, perhaps best exemplified by 'A Letter from Artemiza in the Towne to Chloe in the Countrey', which concludes with an anecdote describing a young heir, coming to London, 'From Pedagogue, and Mother just sett free', who proves an easy target for a demimondaine (l.211; ibid.: 69).

At his strongest, Rochester adds obscenity, a disconcerting precision, and an inclination to fashion an image of himself as a man both sexually anxious and impervious to moral outrage, as in 'A Ramble in *St. James's Park*'. The park at night-time had achieved considerable notoriety, and with a breathless sweep the poet offers a sort of dance of death in which

> Unto this All-sin-sheltring *Grove*,
> *Whores* of the *Bulk*, and the *Alcove*,
> Great *Ladies*, *Chamber-Maids*, and *Drudges*,
> The *Rag-picker*, and the *Heiresse* trudges:
> *Carr-men*, *Divines*, great *Lords*, and *Taylors*,
> *Prentices*, *Poets*, *Pimps* and *Gaolers*;
> Foot-Men, fine *Fops*, do here arrive,
> And here promiscuously they swive.
>   (ll.25–33; ibid.: 77)

But the speaker is no disengaged observer. Unequivocally, he has entered the park in search of sexual adventure. He is surprised to notice Corinna, his mistress, evidently on the pick up, and is appalled when she goes off in a hackney carriage with three men, a possibly identifiable would-be courtier, an Inns of Court man, and a youthful would-be rake. The initial interpretation the reader is drawn to – that her mere disloyalty is the outrage – is quickly set aside. The poet's problem is not that his mistress is unfaithful and promiscuous ('There's something gen'rous in meer lust'), but that she shows such poor taste in her choice of partners. He represents himself as a sort of super-cuckold, who has waited for her return from other nocturnal adventures, 'Drencht with the Seed of half the *Town*', and, in an act of supreme self-abasement has added his own 'Dram of Sperme' to her 'spewing' genitalia (ll.98, 114–15). What we have is not a moral schema, but moral chaos, a world without inhibition where the only decorum is a perverse taste that permits the loved one to indulge herself with '*Porters Backs* and *Foot-mens Brawn*' (l.120), in a sort of inverted chic, while congress with those only two or three notches lower than Rochester's own class is a profanation.

Just as Herbert died before the high days of Laudianism which would have forced him to take sides on the major issues of ecclesiastical policy, so Rochester entered his terminal decline before the great watershed of the early 1680s. His more political verse clearly shows that he aligned himself with Buckingham against his known adversaries. Hence the exchange of poetic unpleasantries with John Sheffield, third Earl of Mulgrave, who, as Harold Love explains, 'in alliance with Dryden, worked during the later 1670s to assemble a patronage-group of Yorkist writers' (Rochester 1999: 424). Yet Rochester's verse attacks on the king rest squarely on the common prejudices and preferences which predominated among the English political nation. Indeed, the king is energetically promiscuous; hardly a surprise given the readiness with which he acknowledged his bastards. Generally, his English mistresses are preferable to the Duchess of Portsmouth, who is widely suspected of being a promoter of French interests. Hence poems like 'Dialogue L: R', which concludes with the 'People' praying, 'Now Heav'ns preserve our *Faiths Defendor* / From *Paris* Plotts, and Roman Cunt' (ll.13–14; ibid.: 91). Hence, too, the facile anti-Catholicism disclosed in asides about Jesuits' enthusiasm for 'the use of *Buggery*' ('A Ramble in *St James's Park*', l.146; ibid.: 80). But there is scarcely a mature, developed and sustained satirical purpose.

Establishing the Rochester oeuvre remains problematic, though his most recent editor, Harold Love, has carried numerous problems towards resolution. The reasons for the uncertainty are complex. Unlike some other poets who generally eschewed print in their lifetimes – Donne and Herbert, for example – Rochester did nothing to set his manuscripts in order before his death. Indeed, he compounded the confusion by ordering their destruction during the penitential days of his final illness, so the possibility of something approximating to an authorially endorsed posthumous collection never arose. In his lifetime, as the texts escaped, as he most surely knew they would (Love 1993: 81), from the narrow circle of court libertines for whom he represented himself as writing ('An allusion to Horace', ll.120–4; Rochester 1999: 74), they fell into a loose and unpredictable network of dissemination in which anonymous works were likely to be attributed to him. As the texts entered circulation in coffee-houses, Inns of Court, and thus through gentry-class networks linking London to the provinces, the class base of their audience surely widened. At the same time, a readership developed which was much further from the real circles of power and influences, for whom a satire or lampoon could serve much as a newsletter would, as an insight of sorts into those circles. The attribution 'Rochester' was in some ways perceived as authenticating such accounts. As Love remarks:

> That the name Rochester appears more frequently than any other in the [manuscript] collections of the 1680s is because it was a notorious one which might be added at a venture to any piece encountered in circulation, either through honest speculation or a desire to raise the value of a piece of poetical merchandise. . . . It was a short step from speculating on the authorship of an anonymous lampoon to adding the name of the supposed author to a transcript. (Rochester 1999: xxxvi–xxvii)

The early printing history of his work is instructive but unhelpful in establishing the canon. The collection published in 1680 after his death, *Poems on several occasions by the Right Honourable, the E. of R—*, 'was simply a surreptitious printing of a copy of a scribally published anthology of poems by Rochester and other writers of libertine verse'; it was reprinted at least 13 times. The editions of 1685 and 1691 'brought him within the pale of polite literature, but at the cost of much mutilation and exclusion' (Rochester 1999: xxxv, xv). While the first was perhaps published to take advantage both of the recent death of a celebrity and the lapse in the licensing order, and reflects the wild uncertainties of those months of crisis, the other is indicative of changes both in literary taste and public morality, reflecting a movement away from uncontrolled licentiousness to a new decorum (see below, chapter 7).

Works erroneously attributed to Rochester are often more unrelentingly obscene than the works he probably wrote. Thus, the 'song' that starts 'In the *Fields* of *Lincolns Inn*, / Underneath a tatter'd *Blanket*' offers an anatomically precise description of a troilist episode, while 'Advice to a Cuntmonger' pretty much lives up to its title (ibid.: 275–6, 269–70; Love argues that the latter may be authentic – ibid.: 489). Usually excluded from his oeuvre is the most extraordinary example of that already curious genre, the closet drama, *Sodom and Gomorah*, which mixes the obscenest of fantasy with a partially sustained parody of heroic drama and an implacably hostile critique of the court of Charles II. He is recognizable within the play as King Bolloxinian, whose arbitrary government takes the form of a decree requiring all intercourse henceforth to be sodomitical ('I do proclaim that Buggery may be vsd / O're all the land so C— shall not be abus'd'), an edict that a courtier immediately terms 'this indulgence', obviously linking it to Charles's Declaration of Indulgence, which is also echoed in the king's speech (I.i.69–70, 75; ibid.: 305, 499).

The Poetry of Dryden and Butler

John Dryden differed from Rochester socially, culturally and ideologically. His major poetry of 1660–85 displayed an awesome technical accomplishment, a mature and precise understanding of contemporary politics and a dedication to the role of laureate celebrant of restored majesty. Dryden, the child of a modestly propertied gentry family, had attempted to establish himself as a public poet in the closing years of the Interregnum (for his elegy on Cromwell, see chapter 5, above.) Though his prosperity in the 1660s and 1670s rested initially on his career as dramatist (see above), he rapidly transformed the high public style of his *Heroic Stanzas* on the late Protector into a neoclassical idiom well suited to hail Charles II in Virgilian mode as a new Augustus. Only in the case of *Mac Flecknoe*, a poem otherwise atypical of his poetic oeuvre, was a major work put into manuscript circulation. Dryden wrote for print publication. In the decade of the Restoration, Henry Herringman emerged as natural successor to the late Humphrey Moseley, who died early in 1661. Dryden reputedly lodged with him at the start of in his own career, and certainly cemented an important working relationship that lasted until 1678. He switched thereafter to the even more enterprising literary entrepreneur Jacob Tonson, with whom he remained despite apparent disagreements about payment (Winn 1987: 95; *DNB* 1975, s.n. Tonson, Jacob).

Among members of the respectable end of the publishing industry with whom Dryden dealt, authors were paid regularly for their copy and agreements were honoured. His aversion to manuscript circulation largely precluded piracy of his intellectual property. *Mac Flecknoe*, again exceptionally, 'reached print in a pirated text of no authority' (Dryden 1995–2005: I, 306).

While cash transactions for the text of his poems (like those for the text, rather than performing rights, of his plays) were, at the height of his earning power, a relatively minor income stream compared with his direct theatrical earnings, they ensured the circulation by prestigious publishing houses of the works on which both his current and his contemporary literary reputations most securely depend. They both secured for him the post of Poet Laureate on the death of Sir William Davenant in 1668 and constituted his major accomplishment in that role. For Dryden, the laureateship implied grander responsibilities than the production of birthday odes for coterie circulation, nothing short of the public celebration and defence both of the king and of James, Duke of York, the heir apparent and himself a significant patron of the poet.

He had already taken that role to himself in the opening months of the Restoration, though at the outset he had to elbow his way through a considerable crowd. The new regime had been greeted with a blizzard of poetic compliment. Coronation odes and related panegyrics for Charles II far outnumber those for James I and Charles I. Despite their profusion and the diversity of authorship as republican placemen jostled with diehard cavaliers, they showed a surprisingly uniformity of theme, ideology and strategy. None ignored the interruption to Stuart rule by the republic and all represented the new king as stronger because of his suffering (Corns 1999b: 18; Dryden 1995–2005: I, 36). In *Astrea Redux*, published by Herringman in the summer of 1660, Dryden repeats the emphases of his contemporaries, but fashions them into a consciously Virgilian project, which ends:

> O happy age! O times like those alone
> By Fate reserved for great Augustus' throne!
> When the joint growth of arms and arts foreshow
> The world a monarch, and that monarch *you*.
> (*Astrea Redux*, ll.320–3; Dryden 1995–2005: I, 54)

Dryden also tries out the Davidic topos that is to figure significantly in his later verse. Charles in exile was like 'banished David' driven from

Israel 'When to be God's anointed was his crime' (ll.79–80; ibid.: 42). Dryden's own complicity in the superseded regime is elided in the collective guilt of England. A bold personification metamorphoses the cliffs of Dover into a humiliated penitent: 'The land returns, and in the white it wears / The marks of penitence and sorrow bears' (ll.254–55; ibid.: 50). Of course, Dryden has everything to gain from incorporating his personal history into a national culpability.

Dryden's coronation ode, *To His Sacred Maiesty, A Panegyrick On His Coronation* (1661), was published, once more by Herringman, to coincide with the ceremony. It continued the penitential motif, and also made much of a new theme, England's potential as a maritime power. Thus, he took the most positive element of Cromwellian foreign policy and mapped it onto the new regime. In the 1650s it had plainly been demonstrated that an English navy, appropriately funded and competently led, could match the fleets of Spain or the United Provinces. Charles, too, recognized the potential. Dryden commemorates him in those terms: 'Born to command the mistress of the seas, / Your thoughts themselves in that blue empire please' (ll.99–100; ibid.: I, 59). The notion further informs his most ambitious poem of the 1660s, *Annus Mirabilis*, first published early in 1667.

This is a polemical poem of sorts. Popular prediction, seizing on '666' as the number of the beast of Revelation 13:18, had expected 1666 to be a year of singular, perhaps apocalyptic, ill omen. The bloody battles of the Second Anglo-Dutch War, following hard on the plague year of 1665, and in turn capped by the Great Fire of London, had certainly given credibility to the notion. Dryden works through the events towards a crowning vision of England as the new Rome, an *imperial* power founded on naval supremacy:

297

Now like a maiden queen she [London] will behold
From her high turrets hourly suitors come:
The east with incense and the west with gold
Will stand like suppliants to receive her doom

. . . .

303

Already we have conquered half the war,
And the less dangerous part is left behind:

> Our trouble now is but to make them [the Dutch] dare,
>   And not so great to vanquish as to find.
>
>   304
>   Thus to the eastern wealth through storms we go,
>   But now, the Cape once doubled, fear no more:
>   A constant trade-wind will securely blow,
>   And gently lay us on the spicy shore.
>   (ll.1185–8, 1209–16, ibid.: I, 200–1)

The aspirations anticipate the dreams of Victorian imperialism, of a trading nation imposing through naval might its order on the world. But Dryden's model, of course, is Augustan Rome, and drawing on the foundation myth underlying Virgil's *Aeneid*, he tropes the United Provinces as the doomed rival, Carthage:

>   5
>   Thus mighty in her ships stood Carthage long,
>   And swept the riches of the world from far;
>   Yet stooped to Rome, less wealthy but more strong:
>   And this may prove our second Punic War.
>   (l.17–20, ibid.: 131–2)

The idiom he develops is consciously and explicitly Virgilian. Though the poem takes its stanzaic form from the iconic cavalier romance, Davenant's *Gondibert* (see above, chapter 5), Virgilian allusion abounds, witnessed in the footnotes of scholarly editions and emphasized in Dryden's own occasional annotation. In a lengthy preface in the form of a letter to Sir Robert Howard, he observes:

> I must own the vanity to tell you, and by you the world, that he [Virgil] has been my master in this poem: I have followed him everywhere, I know not with what success, but I am sure with diligence enough: my images are many of them copied from him, and the rest are imitations of him. (Ibid.: 123)

Indeed, the poem has a pervasive grandeur, carried along by its high seriousness of theme, its stylistic decorum, and its persistent striving after the idiom of epic. Polemically, this functions in two ways. By representing current affairs as the epic encounters of ancient heroes, Dryden may pass over the troublesome details of the English naval campaign of 1666, which had been marked by missed opportunities, as in the fiasco of the Bergen expedition, and inconclusive or highly dubious victories. Secondly, the sustained panegyric to the king, particularly in his management of the aftermath of the fire, associates him with those virtues by which Virgil characterized Aeneas (and by implication Augustus), in the words of the preface, 'the piety and fatherly affection of our monarch to his suffering people' (ibid.: 114). Thus, the so-called '*King's Prayer*' for help over the fire has Charles speak with evident *pietas*: 'I since have laboured for my people's good, / To bind the bruises of a civil war' (ll.1050–1). Significantly, as Paul Hammond observes, the poem echoes David's prayer in time of pestilence, 1 Chronicles 21:17, and as such it rehearses Dryden's other favoured trope for Charles. James Anderson Winn sagely notes, 'Dryden's daring rhetoric here blunts the arguments of those who blamed the fire on the King's immorality; the Charles of his poem acknowledges that immorality but beseeches God to punish him alone, sparing the nation' (1987: 175). It calls for a special kind of creative courage to produce and celebrate *pius Carolus*.

But, not for the last time, Dryden was fashioning an epic vehicle for an unworthy subject. The English navy, far from subduing the fleets of the known world, suffered in the months following the publication of *Annus Mirabilis* probably its worst ever humiliation as the Dutch sailed up the Thames. Dryden had made the same blunder as Abraham Cowley in his poem on the first civil war, but Cowley at least stopped when the tide turned against the royalists and never published his poem; Dryden's was in the public domain as events demonstrated the incompetence and corruption of English military and political leadership, hurrying Clarendon onward to the fall of his administration, his flight and banishment.

Dryden's next great public poem was a long time coming, but with the passing of the crisis over the issue of the exclusion of James, Duke of York, for long a major patron, he produced in *Absalom and Achitophel*, published by Tonson in November 1681, the finest explicitly political poem of the century and arguably the finest in the English literary tradition.

Of course, it is by no means the first poem in that tradition to discuss contemporary politics through a kind of *roman à clef*. Indeed, Cowley had used the history of David in his own *Davideis* to similar purpose (see above, chapter 5), and drawing analogies between individual contemporaries and biblical figures was a commonplace of popular polemic at least since the 1640s. Pertinently, several pamphlets during the late 1670s and early 1680s had used the same story (Dryden 1995–2005: I, 447). But Dryden's project is more fully elaborated, more detailed and more complex. The main figures to be represented are plain enough. Absalom (Monmouth) is seduced by Achitophel (Shaftesbury), aided by Zimri (the second Duke of Buckingham), into rebelling against David (Charles), against a background of discontent fomented by Corah (Titus Oates, who initiated the activities around the Popish Plot). But minor figures are less certainly identified in the modern scholarly tradition. For example, Balaam, one of Achitophel's party, is only tentatively identified by Hammond: 'here probably Theophilus Hastings, seventh Earl of Huntingdon', while his associate, Caleb, is various interpreted (ibid.: I, 497–8nn.). Among contemporaries, finding the key was by no means universally straightforward and no doubt proved easier for insiders than for those more remote from the seats of power and conflict, which may explain why so many copies of the early editions are annotated with identifications of the characters and brief comments (ibid.: I, 448; Zwicker 1984: 57), the kinds of aids to memory and interpretation that modern readers frequently add.

Dryden's selection of this biblical analogue allows him to negotiate carefully the representation of Monmouth. The poem depicts Charles's dismissal of the parliament that met at Oxford. At the point at which Dryden writes, quite how or indeed whether Monmouth would be politically rehabilitated is uncertain, though he reflects the growing confidence of the Tory loyalists that Shaftesbury's challenge has been seen off. He interrupts the biblical story before its conclusion, the summary execution of Absalom by David's agent and the king's subsequent grief (2 Samuel 18–19), thus opening the avenue of reconciliation while leaving as a minatory edge recollection of the fate of the biblical Absalom. Monmouth persisted in his opposition to the king, as Dryden makes explicit in his introduction:

> Were I the inventor, who am only the historian, I should certainly conclude the piece with the reconcilement of Absalom to David. And who knows but this may come to pass? Things were not brought to an extremity where I left the story. There seems yet to be room left for composure; hereafter there may only be for pity. (Dryden 1995–2005: I, 452)

Dryden's portrait of Absalom is guilefully evasive, allowing his enemies to recognize, in the account of 'Amnon's murther', allusion to one or other of the vile acts of murderous violence perpetrated and pardoned in his youth: 'What faults he had (for who from faults is free?/ His father could not, or he would not see' (ll.35–6; ibid.: 457). All of postlapsarian humankind have faults; for most, they do not find expression in killing or maiming.

Dryden offers his readers two alternative prospects for England: as a place of inclusion and stability under a generous, forgiving and divinely endorsed monarch; or as a chaotic realm subject to random disorder and the inversion of social hierarchy. Once more, he vividly evokes recollection of the horrors of civil war: 'The Good Old Cause revived a plot requires; / Plots, true or false, are necessary things / To raise up commonwealths and ruin kings' (ll.82–4; ibid.: 461–2). Images of instability adhere to the leading Whigs. All Shaftesbury, 'with wealth and honour blessed', needed to do to enjoy a respected and prosperous life was nothing. Instead, 'Restless, unfixed in principles and place', he is driven to seek out random dangers: 'wild ambition loves to slide, not stand, / And fortune's ice prefers to virtue's land'. Buckingham, 'A man so various', 'Was everything by starts, and nothing long'. The English people, 'the giddy Jews', 'one in twenty years ... / By natural instinct ... change their lord' (ll.165, 154, 198–9, 545, 548, 216, 218–19; ibid.: 470, 467, 473,495, 474). Dryden's strategy is to convince readers, including moderate Whigs we may assume, that Charles offers a kind of stability and defence of order and property, which in turn implies, but does not explicitly argue for, the retention of due order in the matter of his successor. In a politic ploy, James, Duke of York, had spent the crisis out of the country; in Dryden's poem he is similarly marginalized, not even given a name (ll.353–60; ibid.: 482).

The brightest parts of the poem, aside from the ingenuity of its adaptation of the biblical narrative, for the modern reader and probably for his contemporaries rest in the most overtly satirical section, the pen portraits of the leading Whigs. But this poem defies the usual genre categories. Its overall thrust is away from denigration towards panegyric and perhaps epic. Charles is surrounded by a band of heroes closer to figures from the *Iliad* than the books of Samuel. Thus, Barzillai (James Butler, Duke of Ormonde), Zadok (William Sancroft, Archbishop of Canterbury), Hushai (Laurence Hyde, Clarendon's son) and other Tory grandees are unremittingly praised. The poem concludes with a stately reworking of the words with which Charles dismissed the Oxford parliament, an act which receives explicit divine endorsement: 'Th'Almighty, nodding, gave consent, / And peals of thunder shook the firmament' (ll.1026–7; ibid.: 532). Hutton summarizes the events rather differently:

> To avoid disorder, and also to humiliate the Whigs, the dissolution was sprung as a complete surprise. On the 28th [of March, 1681] Charles was carried to the Lords in a sedan-chair, his royal robes and crown concealed in it. He donned them in an antechamber and summoned the Commons as they gave the new Exclusion Bill a first reading. Stumbling up the narrow staircase to Christ Church hall, they were confronted by their monarch in his regalia, and heard him finish the Parliament with one sentence. He then lunched and drove away to Windsor, leaving the two Houses to disperse, watched by his Guards. (Hutton 1991: 401)

Dryden does not mention the guards.

The second part of *Absalom and Achitophel* was primarily the work of Nahum Tate within the template established by Dryden, though there is a critical consensus that Dryden wrote some passages. As a whole, the poem seems redundant. The ranks of those to be praised are increased and the Duke of York, who had by now returned from Scotland, appears prominently. Dryden contributed a further poem to the crisis, *The Medal*, written in response to the minting of a medal to commemorate Shaftesbury's acquittal from a charge of high treason. Battle lines, by then, were more clearly drawn and the moment for conciliation had passed. Dryden is unflinchingly partisan throughout, sometimes brutally so. Stephen Zwicker judges well the tone: this is 'a harsh and brilliant and momentary lapse into a flagrancy that the poet could nor would not long sustain' (Zwicker 1984: 104). The medal depicted on its obverse the portrait bust of Shaftesbury and on its reverse London and its bridge beneath a sun breaking through obscuring clouds (Dryden 1995–2005: II, facing page 196). Dryden, with measured venom, observes in his prefatory 'Epistle to the Whigs': 'the head would be seen to more advantage if it were placed on a spike of the Tower, a little nearer to the sun, which would then break out to better purpose' (ibid.: 10). The title page calls the poem 'a Satyre against Sedition'. Dryden's principal technique is to take the straightforwardly satirical components of *Absalom and Achitophel* and to expand them, suppressing the nuances and balances of the earlier work. Shaftesbury again appears 'wildy' steered by ambition (l.30; ibid.: 18). Once more, modern Whigs are driven on by the spirit that had brought chaos to the mid-century decades.

Dryden's poem, unsurprisingly, provoked numerous highly personal responses, among them, interestingly, a charge by Thomas Shadwell that Dryden had mistaken the difference between satire and libel, invoking the classical notion of satire as a form that tells the truth with a laugh (discussed by Paul Hammond in ibid.: II, 8). Shadwell himself had already felt Dryden's lash in a composition unique within his oeuvre as his only sustained attack on a creative writer and his only major poem to have circulated extensively in manuscript. It is uncertain when Dryden wrote it, but it probably predated print publication by about six years. Its eventual appearance in print was in a pirated version purposefully entitled *Mac Flecknoe, or a Satyr upon the True-Blew-Protestant Poet, T[homas] S[hadwell]*. As Hammond observes, the subtitle is 'the bookseller's attempt to make the poem politically topical in the light of the controversy between D[ryden] and Shadwell in 1682 over *The Medal*' (ibid.: I, 306). But there is little that is political about his critique, nor does his case against Shadwell as writer have much substance. Yet this is Dryden at his most playful, assured in his mastery of the witty couplet: 'The rest to some faint meaning make pretence, / But Shadwell never deviates into sense' (ll.19–20; ibid.: 315). The suburban coronation of Shadwell as king dunce, a bravura essay in mock heroic, anticipates in miniature the achievement of Alexander Pope's *Dunciad*, and in so doing points to a wealth of comic vision that Dryden in his poetry rarely exploited in his high-minded pursuit of the Virgilian idiom and his laureate mission as public celebrant of Charles's rule.

He wrote one further major poem before the death of the king, *Religio Laici or A Laymans Faith*, published by Tonson in November 1682. It contributes to the controversy occasioned by the publication *A Critical History of the Old Testament*, a translation of a challenging treatise by Richard Simon, a French Catholic, who saw in his critique of the transmission of the scriptures an argument against Protestants' privileging of the text over the authority of the interpretative tradition. In one of the most considerable philosophical poems in English, Dryden works towards a Protestant definition of saving faith that the Milton of his final prose work, *Of True Religion* (1673; see below), could probably have agreed with. Thus, 'the scriptures ... / Are uncorrupt, sufficient, clear, entire / In all things which our needful faith require'; 'Th'unlettered Christian, who believes in gross, / Plods on to heaven, and ne'er is at a loss' (ll.297–300, 322–3; Dryden 1995–2005: III, 126–7). Dryden, though, takes a very different view of the threat to order posed by such unlettered Christians engaging in controversial theology, linking it with the disorders of the mid-century decades when 'The tender page with horny fists was galled, / And he was gifted most that loudest bawled' (ll.404–5; ibid.: 131).

Dryden recalls, perhaps, the unlettered squabbling among the Puritan saints depicted in Samuel Butler's immensely successful poem, *Hudibras*, published in three parts, in late 1662, in 1664 and in 1677. The first part went through nine editions in its first year, and was read with enjoyment by Charles II and his courtiers (Butler 1967: xix). Its robust ridicule for the displaced Puritan ascendancy plainly recommended it to that readership, and it served to fix in the literary culture of the Restoration the old anti-parliamentarian stereotyping, inherited by Cleveland from Jonson and others. When Ralpho, the Presbyterian Hudibras's sectary squire, denounces bear-baiting as 'No less then worshipping of *Dagon*' (First Part, Canto I.814; ibid.: 25), the spirit of Zeal-of-the-Land Busy stirs again.

The assault on the displaced saints is unrelenting. Butler seems to be thinking primarily of the disparities between the aspirations of Puritans in local government and magistracy and the anarchic vitality of the communities they wished to control, though a long section in the final part satirizes the chaotic constitutional improvisation that followed the death of Cromwell, when

> Some were for setting up a King,
> But all the rest for no such thing,
> Unless King *Jesus*; others tamper'd
> For *Fleetwood*, *Desborough*, and *Lambard*.
> (Third Part, Canto II.267–70; ibid.: 241)

Yet Butler's poem has an energy, an expansiveness and generosity that overwhelms the narrow objectives of anti-Puritan satire. Cervantes is an acknowledged influence, and allusions to *Don Quixote* abound. Cervantes's hero develops from the peg on which to hang a parody of chivalric romance into a mythic figure of romantic overreaching and self-delusion. Hudibras, in his scuffles and brawls in an English provincial setting, develops a kind of preposterous heroism, while still gratifying an anti-Puritan reader with incidents that are humiliating and comic. In the process, Butler makes it extremely difficult for any contemporary poet drawn to writing epic. His rather curious prosodic choice, couplets of eight-syllabled lines, is variously rough and jaunty, quite distinct from Dryden's heroic couplets and Milton's blank verse. Yet his sustained send up of the most elevated of poetic idioms cuts the ground from under English attempts at Italianate, chivalric epic of the kind Milton apparently once intended (see below).

Marvell After 1660

Andrew Marvell, like Dryden, had walked with Milton in the funeral procession of Oliver Cromwell, in whose civil service he had served. Like Dryden, he made a relatively untroubled transition from republicanism to respectability at the Restoration, but unlike Dryden he remained active in political life. Creative writing assumed a far different role in his subsequent career. During the brief protectorate of Richard Cromwell he had become the Member of Parliament for Hull, the town where he grew up, and, elected again in 1660, served till his death in 1678.

He fashioned himself into an assiduous servant of his constituency. Almost 300 letters are extant, which he wrote to the corporation of Hull, informing them about developments in the capital which had possible significance for them and generally keeping them abreast of the affairs of state. Arguably, they show some commitment to opening up the process of government to wider scrutiny, certainly a theme in his polemical prose, though they show, too, a general wariness. Marvell rarely vouchsafes an oppositional value judgement on the events he reports. From his dry observations on the exhumation and gibbeting of Cromwell, Bradshaw and Ireton, one could not surmise his previous role in republican England. Again, his account of the second Anglo-Dutch War, seemingly accepting the official line, relates that 'The Dutch haue been fighting with us in the mouth of the river [Thames] but I think with more damage to themselves then us' (Marvell 1971: II, 7, 56). Of his republican poems, considered in chapter 5, only 'The First Anniversary of the Government under His Highness the Lord Protector' had been contemporaneously printed, and manuscript circulation of the others was, Nigel Smith concludes, at most limited to 'small, elite circles' (Marvell 2003a: 266, with specific reference to the 'Horatian Ode'). Apart from 'The First Anniversary', the Cromwellian panegyrics remained unprinted till the posthumous publication of his *Miscellaneous Poems* in 1681, itself 'part of a Whig propaganda campaign at the end of the Exclusion Crisis' (Marvell 2003a: xiii). Even then, they were excised from nearly all extant copies, no doubt because they offered such easy substantiation of the familiar Tory claim, present for example in *Absalom and Achitophel*, that the new Whigs were heirs to the old republicans.

But by then, remarkably for one so cautious in other aspects of his public life, Marvell had produced a considerable oeuvre of poetry and prose that was deeply critical of successive administrations; on this his early reputation was based. Indeed, stimulated by two immensely valuable editorial projects (Marvell 2003a, 2003b), there is an evident critical impetus towards 'a long-overdue corrective, shifting the centre of gravity so that Marvell's later writings ... can be seen as integral parts of ... his literary achievement' (Chernaik and Dzelzainis 1999b: 4).

Among the welter of anti-court lampoons and satires, numerous spurious items were attributed to Marvell in the manuscript collections of the late Stuart period, reflecting, though on a more modest scale, the effect of literary celebrity (or notoriety) that rendered so problematic the establishment of the Rochester canon (see above). In Marvell's case the process gathered pace as the century closed (von Maltzahn 1999: 63). Acute difficulties of attribution surround the cluster of poems stimulated by Edmund Waller's panegyric to the English war effort, *Instructions to a Painter, For the Drawing of the Postures and Progress of His Ma[jes]ties Forces at Sea*, 'published first in short form as a broadsheet in 1665 ... , then in 1666 as a thin folio volume' (Marvell 2003a: 321). Waller, like Dryden in *Annus Mirabilis*, had cheered too soon, since the victory he celebrates, the battle of Lowestoft, had been followed by disgraceful and humiliating reverses. By the time the Dutch were commanding the Thames estuary and burning the fleet in the Medway, Waller's confident panegyric and predictions were embarrassingly inappropriate:

> The Trembling *Dutch* th'approaching Prince behold
> As Sheep a Lion leaping tow'rds their Fold.
>
> . . .
>
> What Wonders may not *English* Valour work,
> Led by th'Example of Victorious YORK?
>
> (Waller 1666: 15)

The canonical status of *The Second Advice to a Painter* (?April 1666) and *The Third Advice* ('Late 1666–January 1667'; Marvell 2003a:

342) remains controversial. There is agreement about Marvell's authorship of *The Last Instructions to a Painter* (written 'between 31 August and 29 November 1667'; Marvell 2003a: 360), his finest post-Restoration poem and currently the subject of considerable critical and scholarly interest. Among Marvell's works, probably only 'Upon Appleton House' exceeds it in ambition. Its political orientation is transparently oppositional, though the argument, as we shall see, exhibits considerable guile and nuance. Nigel Smith plausibly surmises that 'it may be that the poem was written either for presentation to Buckingham, or for limited circulation among like-minded peers or MPs, as a new, hopefully uncorrupt and efficient, era of government dawned' (Marvell 2003a: 360). (Clarendon fled into exile in the aftermath of England's military disasters, leaving Buckingham, at the brief zenith of his political career, in effect as Charles's most influential minister.)

Like *Absalom and Achitophel, The Last Instructions* eludes easy genre categorization. It opens by parodying the idiom of Waller's poem ('Paint me ... ', 'Paint me ... ', 'Paint Castlemaine ... ' – ll.29, 49, 79; ibid.: 368–9), though what he offers are caricatures, not portraits, of a cluster of court figures, purposefully selected – Henry Jermyn, Earl of St Albans, the Duchess of York and Barbara Palmer, Countess of Castlemaine. The choice is purposeful and cunning. He surrounds the Duke of York and Charles himself with figures of bloated depravity. St Albans, currently ambassador to France, retained a notoriety dating from his days as Henrietta Maria's Vice-Chamberlain in the late 1620s. A contemporary anecdote – one among many – related how Thomas Carew (see above, chapter 4), lighting the king to the queen's chamber, 'saw Jermyn ... with his arm around her neck; – he stumbled, and put out the light; – Jermyn escaped' (quoted in Carew 1964: xxxv). The notoriety extended to doubts about the paternity of Henrietta Maria's children. Marvell's grotesque image represents Jermyn as 'The new court's pattern, stallion of the old' and 'Membered like mules' (ll.30, 34; Marvell 2003a: 368), a man promoted far beyond his political ability on account of his sexual prowess: 'Him neither wit nor courage did exalt, / But Fortune chose him for her pleasure salt' (ll.31–2). In his caricature of Anne Hyde, Duchess of York, he revives a cluster of scandals – the birth of her first born just two months after her marriage, her alleged murder of Lady Denham, one of the Duke's mistresses, and her own promiscuity. As in the portrait of St Albans, the commonplaces of popular lampoon are transformed

with consummate art. The steatopygous Anne becomes her own car-
oche as her grooms mistake her buttocks for the platform at the back
and hop aboard: 'so large a rump, / There (not behind the coach) her
pages jump' (ll.63–4; ibid.: 369), with a probable obscene play on
'jump'. The equine connections continue as the Countess of Castlemaine appears in pursuit of a servant whose bulging 'drawers' (l.81;
ibid.: 370) have caught her eye:

> Stripped to her skin, see how she stooping stands,
> Nor scorns to rub him down with those fair hands,
> And washing (lest the scent her crime disclose)
> His sweaty hooves, tickles him 'twixt the toes.
> (ll.93–6; ibid.: 370)

Bless thee, Bottom. Thou art translated. But Titania-Palmer actually
consummates the relationship. Once more in this opening sequence, a
bestial congress is implied. She 'stands stooping', offering herself like a
mare to be covered. She rubs her lover down like a horse, though
before, rather than after, exercise. 'Stooping' suggests social condes-
cension; more literally, it means bending over.

As James Grantham Turner observes, this poem 'draw[s] together a
whole network of sexual-political tropes from the clandestine subcul-
ture of libels and whispers' (Turner 1999: 227). But Marvell transforms them into one wing of a triptych; the corresponding wing holds
his depiction of the death of Archibald Douglas. Descriptively, the
passage is a *tour de force*, once more a metamorphosis, though
here, through a transfiguration of soldier into saintly icon, Douglas,
steadfast when all the English troops had deserted their post, remains
on the *Royal Oak*, torched by the Dutch at Chatham:

> Round the transparent fire about him glows,
> As the clear amber on the bee does close,
> And, as on angels' heads their glories shine,
> His burning locks adorn his face divine.
> (ll.681–4; Marvell 2003a: 386)

The sensibility of this passage, as critics often note, is baroque, resonating with the cultural assumptions and values of the Counter-Reformation. Douglas was not only Scottish, but also a Catholic, and, to the
knowing reader, the line 'His ship burns down, and with his relics

sinks' (l.691; ibid.: 386) surely functions as an acknowledgement of his denomination. Waller, like Dryden in *Annus Mirabilis*, had played on English patriotism. Indeed, he tropes the early victories of the war as Augustus Caesar's over Cleopatra, thus, like Dryden, playing on England's imperial aspirations to be the new Rome (Waller 1666: 16). Marvell, recognizing how the ideology of English patriotism serves to avert closer scrutiny of government conduct, opens his poem with a general lament for 'this race of drunkards, pimps, and fools' (l.12; Marvell 2003a: 367). Douglas's nationality further frustrates any facile schema that would oppose English heroism to a racial stereotype of the Dutch. Only a Scot, and a Catholic at that, stood fast.

Just as Douglas's conduct reproaches English cowardice, so his sexual morality opposes English lechery. Here Marvell plays more freely with the facts. As Martin Dzelzainis observes, 'He clearly regarded [Douglas] as malleable property' (1999: 299). Though Douglas was a married adult, Marvell turns him into a virginal, androgynous and unobtainable object of desire. Down covers his chin. 'Envious virgins hope he is a male' (l.652; ibid.: 385). Nymphs spy on 'his limbs, so soft, so white' as he river-bathes (l.655). But his only erotic encounter is with the fire: 'Like a glad lover, the fierce flames he meets, / And tries his first embraces in their sheets' (ll.677–8; ibid.: 386). Of course, the contrasts between his chastity and the lechery of Anne and Castlemaine and between his delicate beauty and the stallion masculinity of St Albans or Castlemaine's servant are clear. Yet, as sometimes in his lyric poetry, Marvell develops here a disorienting sexual sensibility, a delicacy, an ambivalence, strangely out of place in a poem that has leant so heavily on the easy certainties of satire, lampoon, and literary caricature:

> But when in his immortal mind he felt
> His altering form and soldered limbs to melt,
> Down on the deck he laid himself and died,
> With his dear sword reposing by his side ...
>   (ll.685–9; ibid.: 386)

This is a different kind of beauty and a new kind of heroism, intractable to incorporation into the pseudo-Virgilian and martial imperialism of Dryden and Waller.

Between Castlemaine and Douglas comes a long, detailed section on parliamentary politics, which flirts with the mock-heroic idiom.

Indeed, the allegorical representation of Excise (ll.131–46; ibid.: 371) plainly owes something to Milton's representation of Sin and Death in *Paradise Lost*, Book 2. Clarendon's placemen troop through parliament to do his bidding like Greeks and Trojans en route to battle. Marvell briefly holds aloof, seemingly hostile to 'the court and country' (l.107; ibid.: 370), though his account obviously endorses the latter in his praise for

> A gross of English gentry, nobly born,
> Of clear estates, and to no faction sworn;
> Dear lovers of their king, and death to meet
> For country's cause, that glorious think and sweet;
> To speak not forward, but in action brave,
> In giving generous, but in counsel grave ...
>   (ll.287–92; ibid.: 376)

Marvell's affiliation is not difficult to discern. But the insistent historical present of his narration gives it an air of actuality, of truth-telling, of memorializing the culpable idiocies that led to the catastrophe of the Dutch raid, as though Marvell were placing on record and in the public domain events concealed by parliamentary privilege and the obfuscation of government.

The final section, a sort of coda, is explicitly threatening. Charles himself figures for the most part peripherally in the densely peopled landscape of the rest of the poem. In the end, Marvell shows him in his chamber, 'in the calm horror all alone' (l.889; ibid.: 392). A female allegorical figure appears in a reverie – 'England or the Peace', 'Naked as born' (ll.906, 892). The reader perhaps anticipates a lewd incident, but she fades, to be replaced by the spectral forms of Charles's grandfather, the assassinated Henri IV of France, who 'in his open side / The grisly wound' reveals, and his own father, 'the ghastly Charles', who turns his collar down to show 'The purple thread about his neck' (ll.919–20, 922). They provide an immediate encounter with the grim reality that monarchies are fragile and monarchs as vulnerable as the next person.

The section on Douglas recurs in *The Loyal Scot*, probably Marvell's last major poem (though his sole authorship has been disputed). The poem playfully engages John Cleveland's 'The Rebell Scot' (see above, chapter 5), requiring Cleveland's ghost, 'as a favourable penance' (l.5; ibid.: 401) to narrate the story of Douglas's death. Cleveland, of

course, had shamelessly invoked an English nationalist stereotype of
the Scot in order to traduce the alliance against Charles I in the early
1640s. Marvell, as in *The Last Instructions*, works towards neutralizing
that stratagem, and in so doing he opens the way to reconstructing the
old alliance between English and Scottish dissent:

> Nation is all but name as shibboleth,
> Where a mistaken accent causes death.
> In paradise names only Nature showed,
> At Babel names from pride and discord flowed;
> And ever since men with a female spite
> First call each other names, and then they fight.
> Scotland and England! Cause of just uproar,
> Does 'man' and 'wife' signify 'rogue' and 'whore'?
> Say but 'a Scot', and straight we fall to sides,
> That syllable like a Pict's wall divides.
>   . . .
> One king, one faith, one language, and one isle;
> English and Scotch, 'tis but cross and pile.
> [That is, heads and tails, and by extension two sides of the same thing.]
>   (ll.262–72, 276–7; ibid.: 409 and n.)

'One faith', and indeed attitudes to that 'one king', are rather more
complex than the ringing assertion of the concluding formula.

Nigel Smith, who relates the poem with precision to the immediate
circumstances of Anglo-Scottish relations, observes, 'M[arvell] was . . . ,
as ever, writing strategically' (Marvell 2003a: 399). Yet his political
verse often has a curiously ambivalent status. So much of it, even in his
writing on the 1650s, remained unprinted in his lifetime and manuscript circulation was often closely constrained. *The Loyal Scot*, however
timely its contribution to political life in the late 1660s, was not
printed till the 1690s and only two extant manuscripts 'may belong
to the 1670s' (ibid.: 397); the rest are later. In general, Marvell seems
to have been very cautious in releasing his poetry, though those whose
opinion he most assiduously sought to shape and who had most to
gain from absorbing the guile and wisdom of his polemic, probably
had access to it. Who read his verse may well have meant far more to
Marvell than how many read it.

His prose works, a remarkable series of major tracts towards the end
of his life, were plainly intended for print publication, which, with
varying degrees of legality, they obtained. *The Rehearsal Transpros'd*

(1672) and *The Rehearsal Transpros'd: The Second Part* (1673) were published about the time of the Declaration of Indulgence, when government policy, veering suddenly towards toleration of dissent as a quid pro quo for toleration of Catholicism, wrong-footed its traditional supporters among the most repressive Anglicans. Sir Roger L'Estrange, in charge of press censorship, seems to have winked at their publication. Briefly. Marvell found himself in step with government (as arguably he had been at the point of Clarendon's fall). His remaining works were anonymous or pseudonymous, and were clandestinely printed. Early editions of *An Account of the Growth of Popery and Arbitrary Government in England* (1677) carried a spurious Amsterdam imprint, though editions following Marvell's death in 1678 bore his name. Those involved in this samizdat activity were vigorously and indeed sometimes successfully hunted out. Marvell, of course, could speak with impunity from the grave, and this, his last undisputed prose work, secured his place in the emerging Whig tradition (Marvell 2003b: I, xxiii–xxvii; II, 203–7).

The ideological significance of the title *The Rehearsal Transpros'd*, which alludes to Buckingham's then current success, *The Rehearsal* (1672; see above), has been well analysed by N. H. Keeble, who notes that it makes a play for an audience outside those who habitually read the graver sort of controversial prose: 'His implied reader is a man of the town, not a cleric, a coffee-house wit not a divine, still more a man impressed by Buckingham's circle and by the taste of the court' (Keeble 1999: 250). Just as Buckingham's play ridicules Dryden, celebrant of conservative court values, so Marvell's text dissects with sustained satirical panache the repressive Anglicanism of Samuel Parker's *Preface Shewing What Grounds there are of Fears and Jealousies of Popery*, prefixed to his edition of *Bishop Bramhall's Vindication of Himself and the Episcopal Clergy* (1672). Indirectly, Marvell aligns himself with Buckingham, who was, when not tormenting Dryden, the most influential advocate in court circles of the policy of Protestant toleration. Marvell's tract enjoyed immediate success and 'established Marvell's reputation as – in the first instance – a prose writer' (Martin Dzelzainis and Annabel Patterson in Marvell 2003b: I, 20). Timely though its arguments were, that success was essentially a triumph of wit and style, persistently rewarding the reader as Marvell tracks Parker over his discourse. An obvious point of comparison in the same polemical subgenre is Milton's *Animadversions* (1641; see above, chapter 5), which treats a tract by Bishop Joseph Hall much as Marvell treats

Parker's. But while Milton is brusque, relentless and brutal, Marvell is expansive, imaginative and genuinely witty. He plays much more freely around the text he confutes. Consider a characteristic passage:

> I sometimes could think that he [Parker] intends no harm either to Publick or Private, but onely rails contentedly to himself and his Muses; That he seeks onely his own diversion, and chargeth his Gun with Wind but to shoot at the Air. Or that, like boyes, so he may make a great Paper-Kite of his own *Letter* [an earlier work] of 850 pages, and his *Preface* of an hundred, he hath no further design upon the Poultry of the Village. But he takes care that I shall never be long deceived with that pleasing imagination: and though his Hyperboles and Impossibilities can have onely a ridiculous effect, he will be sure to manifest that he had a felonious intention. He would take it ill if we should not value him as an Enemy of mankind: and like a raging Indian (for in Europe it was never before practised) he runs a *Mucke* (as they call it there) stabbing every man he meets, till himself be knockt on the head.
>   (Marvell 2003b: I, 72–3)

Parker is provisionally exculpated – surely he must write without expectation of being read? He is diminished – firing blanks, a boy playing with a kite – albeit a kite made of 850 pages. But, no, he is in deadly earnest, though in an outlandish fashion, like an Indian running amok, and in need of a summary response. Here is a measured impudence, a reduction of a grave and, until very recently, dominant position to an object of mirth. Marvell establishes powerfully an authorial voice, which is undeferential, urbane and smart. Parker's defence of the magistrates' role in matters of conscience and his advocacy, in a phrase that becomes a recurrent motif in Marvell's tract, of 'the Pillories, Whipping-posts, Gallies, Rods, and Axes, (which are *Ratio ultima Cleri*, a Clergy-mans last Argument, ay and his first too;)' (ibid.: 147), sound antediluvian in a new age characterized by the rational civility implicit in the Marvellian voice and this most unfanatical defence of those whom Parker, in the anti-Puritan tradition, interminably terms fanatics.

Parker responded with a long, deeply personal attack, which Marvell met with *The Rehearsal; Transpros'd: The Second Part* (1673). Marvell now is commenting on Parker's reply to his reply to Parker, a kind of exchange usually more fascinating to its original readers than posterity. Marvell again is witty and cool, though the character assassination is sustained and has been widened to include Parker's father, a Puritan controversialist and 'a very ill sire' (ibid.: I, 260). By the end, the reader probably craves a plain exposition of the case for toleration argued from clearly stated principles, but that desire remains unsatisfied. Instead, Marvell ends with a gross anecdote, implying that he has ingested and excreted Parker and his texts, and with a pre-emptive admission that 'our sport is . . . unfit for serious Spectators' (ibid.: 438).

The twin volume, *Mr Smirke; Or, the Divine in Mode . . . Together with a Short Historical Essay* (1676), contributed to the revival of the toleration debate in the period that followed the withdrawal of the Declaration of Indulgence. The mid-decade years saw renewed vigour in the suppression of nonconformity. Marvell writes explicitly against 'this . . . Persecution . . . now on foot against the Dissenters' (ibid.: II, 165). *Mr Smirke*, a confutation of a confutation, technically marks little development from his earlier prose, and he concludes it with a sort of shrug: 'I am weary of such stuff, both mine own and his [his adversary's]' (ibid.: 113). The *Short Historical Essay*, however, marks a significant departure.

Formally, the text resembles Milton's *Of Reformation* (1641; see above, chapter 5). It offers a brief, rather tendentious, history designed to establish a basically simple thesis, that the enforcement of particular theological interpretations originated in the self-interest of early bishops and always provoked the schisms it notionally sought to suppress. Marvell is suave whereas Milton thunders, but they agree at several points. Both assert the primacy of the unadorned, unglossed gospel, though their idiom differs instructively. Thus, Marvell writes:

> Far be it from me in the event as it is from my Intention, to derogate from the just authority of any of those Creeds or Confessions of Faith that are receiv'd by our Church upon clear agreement with the Scriptures: nor shall I therefore, unless some mens impertinence and indiscretion hereafter oblige me, pretend to any further knowledge of what in those particulars appears in the ancient Histories. But certainly if any Creed had been Necessary, or at least necessary to have been Imposed, our Saviour himself would not have left his Church destitute in a thing of that moment. (Ibid.: 143)

The exposition is lucid, qualified, rational but unflamboyant. Contrast that with the following from *Of Reformation*:

> [T]he *Prelates* . . . comming from a meane, and Plebeyan *Life* on a sudden to be Lords of stately palaces, rich furniture, delicious fare,

and *Princely* attendance, thought the plaine and homespun verity of *Christs* Gospell unfit any longer to hold their Lordships acquaintance, unless the poore thred-bare Matron were put into better clothes; her chast and modest vaile surrounded with celestiall beames overla'd with wanton *tresses*, and in a flaring tire bespecckle'd with all the gaudy allurements of a Whore. (Milton 1953–82: I, 556–67)

By the 1670s – indeed, by the late 1650s – Milton himself had moved on from such stylistic exuberance; prose could be witty, refined, precise, but it was no longer expected to exhilarate, and certainly not to hector. Marvell's role model is not the tub-thumper but the urbane companion socialising in a coffee-house. He speaks to a new age, profoundly suspicious of overt rhetoric and of enthusiasm, and he seeks to engage the support of tolerationists who are not themselves Nonconformists. He is drawn, still, to the kinds of levity that characterized his earlier prose, but recognizes its incompatibilities with the high seriousness of principled argument.

An Account of the Growth of Popery and Arbitrary Government in England (1677) has far more to say about the latter than about Catholicism, though it underpins the proto-Whig campaign, which as it gathered momentum increasingly took advantage of the Duke of York's now open conversion to Rome. Stylistically, the tract is often starkly functional, and rests heavily of the reproduction of documents, many of which had had little or no currency outside parliamentary circles. Marvell's larger argument is that a conspiracy is at work that aims to advance French interests over English and Catholic interests over Protestant. Cautiously, he does not name the conspirators, nor does he inculpate the king. But he 'gives evidence to the Fact, and leaves the malefactors to those who have power of enquiry' (Marvell 2003b: II, 375). In a rare image of imaginative verve, he concludes that 'if any one delight in the Chase, he is an ill Woodman that knows not the size of the Beast by the proportion of his Excrement' (ibid.: 376), with a clear suggestion that the condition to which England's recent foreign and domestic policies have been reduced must have come from big beasts like Danby and the Duke.

Marvell's tract patiently logs the alleged facts, with dates, circumstances and documents. The 1620s had seen an English reading public hungry for news and frustrated by the constraints limiting the development of journalism (see above, chapter 3). Marvell's own letters to the corporation of Hull functioned as a customised version of the manuscript newsletter. But here Marvell pushes political discourse and the affairs of state much more emphatically into something approximating to a public sphere. Men of property, outside government, outside parliament, receive an account of how their money, raised through taxation, has been spent. Accountability is the key concept. Within the text, Marvell allows explicit enunciation of the alternative view, most memorably by quoting in full Charles's speech to adjourn parliament in May 1677, when he scolded MPs for presuming to advise him on foreign policy: '*I am confident it will appear in no Age ... that the Prerogative of making Peace and War hath been so dangerously invaded*' (ibid.: 367). Amid the rational and dispassionate exposition of apparent fact, once more the opposing position appears atavistic: this is the voice of James I, whereas Marvell's anticipates the idiom and values of John Locke and a new age.

Marvell's tract achieved iconic status in the Whig political and historiographic traditions, and it still seems almost uncannily modern, not least in those sections where he tries to prise open the hidden reasons why England went to war, for no advantage, on a specious pretext, and at the behest and in the interest of another nation (see, especially, ibid.: 259–62). The right to know is taken for granted.

Bunyan, Pepys and Sprat

John Bunyan matched the stereotypical description of the radical sectary almost perfectly. As he claims at the beginning of *Grace Abounding to the first of Sinners*, first published in 1666, 'for my descent then, it was, as is well known by many, of a low and inconsiderat generation; my fathers house being of that rank that is meanest, and most despised of all the families in the Land' (Bunyan 1962: 5). His other works frequently begin with similar assertions. In *The Holy City* (1665), for example, he declares, somewhat unpromisingly for an introduction to an exegetical treatise on the Book of Revelation, that 'Men of this World' will deride and 'laugh in conceit' at his plain, unlearned expression and his evident lack of formal scholarship (Bunyan 1976–94: III, 69–71).

As his modern biographers have generally observed, he exaggerates a little. The meanest sort in early modern England, after the destitute, were agricultural day labourers, whereas by trade Bunyan was an itinerant tinker, a skilled metal-worker and self-employed. He was, however, a remarkable figure to have entered the literary canon. In distinction from most prominent writers in the dissenting tradition, he was not university educated (unlike Marvell or Milton), independently wealthy (unlike Milton), a business man (unlike Winstanley) or London-based (unlike all of those).

He had been a rank-and-file soldier in the New Model Army, and by the Restoration he was an unordained minister to a Bedford congregation. Theologically, he seems a conservative figure, a Particular Baptist, committed to an unqualified belief in double predestination in an extreme manifestation of the Calvinist tradition. Radical versions of Arminianism, such as we find in Milton and among General Baptists, seemed abhorrent to him. He was similarly hostile to the privileging of the spirit within over the gospel text, a belief which characterized both Ranter and Quaker thinking. His writing does not explicitly engage with contemporary politics. He did not in print resist the Restoration; he did not attack the crown; nor did he join in the tolerationist and exclusion controversies of the 1670s and 1680s. Yet he was, in some ways, the purest manifestation of that interregnal world, a world turned upside-down: a proletarian writer; wholly undeferential to his social superiors; subscribing to a theology that was unceremonial and egalitarian; convinced of his own godliness; and wholly unpatronizing to the poor, the unlearned, even to children, in ways that reflect his own awareness of social and political disempowerment. Christopher Hill, who among modern critics best appreciated Bunyan's subversiveness, observes, 'The gentry knew their enemies' (1989: 107). Shortly after the Restoration he was arrested and imprisoned under anti-dissenter legislation, an incarceration surely prolonged by his own intransigent refusal to give undertakings to leave off preaching. He was not released till 1672 – 'Only regicides and outstanding political figures ... were treated with greater severity' (ibid.: 106) – and he subsequently endured a shorter period in gaol. Much of his finest work is prison writing.

Bunyan wrote for print circulation, albeit a considerable *Nachlass* remained to be published after his death. His earliest publications were works of controversial theology directed against Quakerism, and indeed much of his oeuvre belongs to genres generally unconsidered in this history. These include narrow controversy, works of theological interpretation, and improving and moralizing writing of a kind commonplace and much read throughout the century. Even to the least literary and most unpromising genres (from the point of view of readerly pleasure) he sometimes brings a verve, a felicity of expression, a shrewdness of observation and a distinctive voice. Thus, in the midst of a grim little tract, *The Strait Gate, or, Great Difficulty of Going to Heaven* (1676), we find:

> At this day [the last judgement] those things that now these *many* count sound and good will then shake like a quagmire, even all their naked knowledge, their feigned faith, pretended love, glorious shews of gravity in the face, their holy-day words and specious carriages will stand them in little stead: I call them holy day ones, for I perceive that some professors [that is, those who profess their own godliness] do with religion, just as people do with their best apparel, hang it against the wall all the week, and put them on on Sundays: for as some scarce ever put on a Sute, but when they go to a Fair or a Market, so little house-religion will do with some; they save religion till they go to a Meeting, or till they meet with a godly chapman. (Bunyan 1976–1994: III, 99)

'Quagmire' seems to transpose the apocalyptic scene to a muddy English field, though it is not the landscape that shakes but the confidence of the damned who stand upon it. The principal image, of false religion as Sunday clothes, familiarizes the issue and reduces it to a human scale; the detail of the suit hanging 'against the wall' shows an eye for the detail of domestic life. But radical social assumptions are pervasive and unmistakeable; the mighty, even those whose might is confined to the congregations of the godly, are subject to divine evaluation that sets human hierarchies at nothing.

Grace Abounding was the first text to bring Bunyan to a wide readership. The clearest indicator is its publishing history: it went through six lifetime editions, though two of these seem not to have survived. Generically, it is a typical spiritual autobiography, an account of personal salvation and regeneration, and as such commonplace within the broad tradition of popular theological writing and Puritan devotional practices. What distinguishes it is the vivid intensity with which it depicts extreme states of psychological anguish while retaining a strong sense of place and setting. Thus, he generates a remarkable tension between the seeming ordinariness of the world he moves through and the inner turmoil he describes:

> So one day I walked to a neighbouring Town, and sate down upon a Settle in the Street, and fell into a very deep pause about the most fearful state my sin had brought me to; and, after long musing, I lifted up my

head, but methought I saw as if the Sun that shineth in the Heavens did grudge to give me light, and as if the very stones in the street, and tiles upon the houses, did bend themselves against me, me-thought that they all combined together to banish me out of the World. (Bunyan 1962: 58–9)

Bunyan offers us a double image, of a working man sitting on a bench in the street of a provincial town, and of an anguished Christian, struggling for the salvation of his own soul, a soul as valuable in the eyes of God as that of the mightiest of the land. The informing theology is Calvinist, but a particularly difficult crux, a sort of algorithm of despair, is at the heart of his torment: if he believes himself saved, he manifests pride, which is a mark of the damned, whereas if he believes himself damned, he shows a want of faith, which is also a mark of the damned. The final crisis comes in prison, in a leap of faith that is simultaneously an imagined leap to his death. Hanging was a primitive and public business in the early modern period. A rope was passed over the crossbar of the gallows and tied around the victim's neck; he or she was pushed, pulled or prodded up a ladder placed against the gallows; and then obliged to jump or be kicked off, to be throttled. It was surely a difficult death to contemplate, even if one felt confident about the fate of one's soul. For someone in turmoil there was an added anxiety that a public display of fear would be interpreted as evidence of a want of faith or of the conviction of one's own sinfulness. Bunyan vividly recounts his own obsessive, haunted meditation: 'if I should make a scrabling shift to clamber up the Ladder, yet I should either with quaking or other symptoms of faintings, give occasion to the enemy to reproach the way of God and his People, for their time-rousness: ... I was ashamed to die with a pale face, and tottering knees' (ibid.: 100). As he muses, 'that word dropped upon me, *Doth Job serve God for nought?*' (ibid.: 101), which sudden revelation completes the leap of faith and brings comfort after despair.

Throughout the autobiography the social assumptions are clear. A vital stage in his spiritual development is triggered by conversation with 'three or four poor women sitting at a door in the Sun, and talking about the things of God' (ibid.: 14). His persecutors, vaguely sketched, are allegedly duplicitous, 'taking my plain dealing with them for a confession' (ibid.: 95); though prison brings a crisis of faith, they cannot really touch his mind and soul and the struggle within them. Yet Bunyan depicts himself brooding over the implications of imprisonment for a propertiless man. Leaving his family is 'as the pulling the flesh from my bones', not least because they are plunged into 'hardship, miseries and wants', which are particularly threatening to his blind daughter, 'who lay nearer to my heart than all I had besides' (ibid.: 98). For Lovelace, prison brought good fellowship and visits from the long-haired Althea; Bunyan offers a rather different perspective.

The Pilgrim's Progress from this World to That which is to come appeared first in 1678, and went into at least 11 lifetime editions. It enjoyed an immediate success, which continued through the century and beyond. The publisher of Bunyan's posthumous collected works, writing in 1692, observed that it '*hath been printed in* France, Holland, New-England, *and in* Welch, *and about a hundred thousand in England*' (Bunyan 1976–94: XII, 456; discussed in Spargo 2002: 87). If that figure were approximately accurate and if we posit a multiple readership for most copies, then we have an enormous proportion of the potential readership familiar with the work by the last decade of the century. Its appeal, no doubt, was in part genre-related, for this is a work of improving, practical theology of a familiar kind cast in a compelling narrative form. Its usefulness in Christian mission is reflected in its later history when it was translated into Tamil, Fanti, Ibo, Luo, Maori, Rarotonga, Inuit, Ganda, Tahiti and other languages of the British Empire. For early readers, the allegorical structure of a passage through time being represented as a passage through space may well have been very familiar. Though the issues are primarily concerned with individual salvation, Bunyan's Calvinism is largely obscured. Gordon Campbell argues that 'neither election nor reprobation touches Christian's own experience ... even though [the] journey is allegorically soterial' (Campbell 1980: 247). Perhaps, but there is an alternative perspective. For Bunyan, those predestined to be saved are predestined to go through the inner struggles that Christian, his hero, endures, and they persevere through all the temptations and pitfalls which a fallen world may throw at them. They persevere because they are saved; they are not saved because they persevere.

Once more, this is explicitly prison writing, though whether it was produced and held over from his early and long period in gaol which ended in 1672 or a second, shorter term later in the decade remains unclear (Bunyan 1960: xxi–xxiii). Certainly, it shares the angst-ridden sensibility of *Grace Abounding*. Christian runs from his wife and his 'sweet babes' with his fingers in his ears to shut out their calls, while 'crying, Life, Life, Eternal Life' (ibid.: 8, 10). He has faced a dilemma not much different from that Adam faces in *Paradise Lost* when confronted by the fallen Eve: does he die with her or obey the divine imperative? Christian chooses the correct course. Though the allegorical level is important, crucial scenes throughout the book seem grounded in the actualities of impoverished, provincial life; his neighbours pursue him, as, were this a low-mimetic account, they surely would, since his abandoned family would be a charge on the parish.

Indeed, many of the finer moments of the text retain this mimetic quality. Thus, as the critical tradition has long recognized, the treatment of Christian and Faithful at Vanity Fair recalls the rough justice and flawed judicial processes meted out to Nonconformists in provincial England, though to me the depiction seems closer to the experiences of early Quakers than those in the Baptist tradition. The trial of Christian and Faithful reflects the prejudice and hostility of the magistracy and packed juries, while the actual execution of Faithful, lanced and stoned and stabbed, seems closer to the spectacular punishment of some regicides (ibid.: 90–7).

The Pilgrim's Progress. From this World to That which is to come The Second Part appeared first in 1684 and went through two further lifetime editions. In terms of its religious sensibility, the anxieties of the first part have given way to a calmer and in some ways more generous soteriology. Christiana and her children, the family Christian had abandoned, make their way, with rather easier progress, to the world that is to come, aided by various guardians and champions along a route that has improved considerably since Christian passed through it. No doubt the changes reflect changes in the condition of Nonconformists from the early 1670s to the mid-1680s. By then ideological and physical survival was no longer at issue, and the terrors of the Clarendon code were significantly muted, despite something of a backlash in the wake of the Exclusion Crisis. Even in Vanity Fair, the inhabitants 'are much more moderate now then formerly' (ibid.: 275). Modern readers may prefer the psychological edginess of the first part, though that can hardly support a literary judgement. However, there are other changes of a more technical kind that mark a falling off. Within the allegory of the passage through time as a journey through space, Bunyan nests passages much closer to the allegorical figures of the emblem tradition. Thus, in part one, the House of the Interpreter describes a series of tableaux detached from that subtle interaction of symbolism and mimesis that characterizes the principal narrative. For example, Christian is shown a fire burning against a wall, which burns the more fiercely despite a man always throwing water on it, while another man behind the wall is secretly feeding the fire with oil (ibid.: 32). Of course, there is no narrative plausibility here: no one is 'always' doing any action. What we have, as the modern editors note, is an emblem adapted from Jesuit writers and probably mediated through Quarles (ibid.: 317; see above, chapter 4). This kind of writing is much more frequent in the second part.

Two other works by Bunyan often figure in literary histories, *The Holy War*, a late and quite elaborate allegory of the struggle for Mansoul, first published in 1682, and *The Life and Death of Mr. Badman*, first published in 1680. They are, as Michael Davies observes, 'difficult to read, overtly doctrinal, anti-narrative' (Davies 2002: 131). The latter, however, has sometimes been interpreted, at least in older accounts, as in some sense a precursor to the novels of Defoe. That position seems untenable. We see little of the interiority of the exemplary and eponymous 'bad man'. Rather, we encounter a litany of 'sins', for the most part the kinds of misdemeanours treated nowadays in the magistrates' courts: fiddling weights and measures, riding while under the influence of drink, inebriated disorderliness, domestic violence and so on. Motivation goes unexplored. There is no suspense – the protagonist is already dead and damned before the story begins. The narrative structure is remote from the vivid first person of *Grace Abounding* or the plain but sonorous voice of *Pilgrim's Progress* as Mr Wiseman moralizes on the case of Mr Badman to the duly attentive Mr Attentive. Into the primary narrative Bunyan inserts gossipy snippets about Dorothy Mately, who pinched tuppence, denied it with an oath that '*I would I might sink into the earth if it be not so*', and immediately sank into the earth (ibid.: 33), and so on.

At his best, Bunyan is an end, not a beginning. He transmutes with his intensity and his descriptive verve the received forms of popular theology, at the same time suffusing them with the values and the undeferential and feisty attitude of the radical sectaries. It is among the ironies of literary history that this late and glorious manifestation of the world turned upside-down should have been so comprehensively appropriated in the nineteenth century and later by a sort of evangelical Anglicanism.

Samuel Pepys's career fulfilled a familiar ambition among bright, educated but relatively unpropertied young men of early modern England, the sort of career John Donne or Thomas Carew had aspired to but had bungled. In his mid-20s, he secured employment in the household of Edward Mountagu, his father's cousin, in effect as a sort of personal assistant. Mountagu himself had a spectacular career spanning the late republic and early Restoration, both as a 'General-at-Sea' and as a political power-broker. He was prominent in the group that secured the return of Charles II, and he was rewarded with the continuity of high command in the navy and with a peerage. The fortunes of Pepys, his dependant, tracked his master's, and he secured a series of increasingly lucrative posts in naval administration, which brought with them very valuable perquisites. They also kept him quite close to the real seats of power in Restoration England (*DNB* 2004; Pepys 1970–83: I, xvii–xl).

For ten years, from 1660, Pepys kept a diary. He was near enough to the governmental process and intimate enough with Mountagu for his observations to have value for political historians, and his shrewd comments on London life and culture are often quoted in literary criticism. A diary, as a private document written artlessly for an audience of one, may seem to be of only dubious literary value in itself, whatever its other fascinations. Yet Pepys's is certainly an exception. It survived in a single holograph manuscript written in a fairly common form of shorthand, and had no currency whatsoever in Pepys's own age. But evidently he produced it with considerable care about issues of style and tone. The manuscript is plainly a fair copy, which in turn has received some later editing by Pepys. 'It was manifestly done far more carefully than was necessary simply for the writer's own reading' (ibid.: I, xliv). The idiom, too, seems to imply a wider readership. Pepys persistently tells us things we need to know but which seem redundant in a private journal. Thus, he notes 'At Dorsett-house I met with Mr. Kipps my old friend' (ibid.: I, 184). Surely, 'old friend' is too familiar a fact for Pepys to need to record it. Again, he visits 'our Landlord Vanly'; superfluous if the object is solely to record a business meeting (ibid.: I, 245).

Pepys, of course, tells an engagingly good tale, and he does so with irony, with control and with a careful management of the narrative voice. The key unit is the entry for a whole day, which is often carefully shaped. Consider one of the most frequently cited entries, that for 13 October 1660, the first day of regicide executions. C. V. Wedgwood, drawing on several contemporary sources, in her classic study describes the events with solemn eloquence:

[Major-General Thomas Harrison] went to his death with equanimity, the first of the Regicides to suffer. The crowd was hostile and derisive. 'Where is your Good Old Cause now?' they jeered. 'Here in my bosom,' said Harrison, 'and I shall seal it with my blood.' His courage astonished and impressed the onlookers, and a story later went round among the missionary prophets who still had their following in the poorer streets of London that he would shortly rise again, to judge his judges, and bring in the Rule of the Saints on earth. (Wedgwood 1966: 223)

This is Pepys's version of the day:

To my Lord's in the morning, where I met with Captain Cuttance. But my Lord not being up, I went out to Charing-cross to see Major-Generall Harrison hanged, drawn, and quartered – which was done there – he looking as cheerfully as any man could do in that condition. He was presently cut down and his head and his heart shown to the people, at which there was great shouts of joy. It is said that he said that he was sure to come shortly at the right hand of Christ to judge them that now have judged him. And that his wife doth expect his coming again.

   Thus it was my chance to see the King beheaded at White-hall and to see the first blood shed in revenge for the blood of the King at Charing-cross. From thence to my Lord's and took Captain Cuttance and Mr. Sheply to the Sun taverne and did give them some oysters. After that I went by water home, where I was angry with my wife for her things lying about, and in my passion kicked the little fine Baskett which I bought her in Holland and broke it, which troubled me after I had done it.

   Within all the afternoon, setting up shelfes in my study. At night to bed. (I, 265)

Pepys appears impressively detached in his observations. He goes almost accidentally to the place of execution; had Mountagu been up and stirring, he would not have been there. Harrison appears with his title of rank and without any evaluative epithet. His conduct is described with a tough irony that again evades judgement, though invites the question of how cheerful anyone can look on being strangled and eviscerated. The second paragraph, however, lets Pepys assume the role of witness to the great events of his age. But once the connection between the two executions is made, he turns again to everyday business, and the failure to articulate any sense of providentiality seems silently to signify a secular perspective on even regicide. He returns to the world of oysters, shelves and domestic discord.

The diary has another function, as a reflective evaluation of personal conduct. It shows some affinity with spiritual autobiography, particularly in the dissenter tradition. Not by chance do the journal sections of *Robinson Crusoe* come to mind as one reads Pepys, who shares Daniel Defoe's concerns with practical details and personal salvation.

Thomas Sprat's personal history through the 1660s bears some comparison with Pepys's. Two years his younger, he, too, had been a junior beneficiary of the Cromwellian ascendancy. His early career rested on the encouragement of John Wilkins, Warden of Wadham College, Oxford, and Oliver Cromwell's brother-in-law. In an initiative that owed much to Bacon's proselytizing for the advancement of scientific enquiry, Wilkins gathered around himself a talented array of young intellectuals, among them Christopher Wren. Sprat was part of this group, whose Oxford careers had been eased after the purging of the university which followed the surrender of the city to the parliamentary army. All rapidly accommodated themselves to the new regime, and gave to the newly formed Royal Society much of its intellectual energy and direction.

Sprat was already in holy orders by 1660, and his ecclesiastical career led to numerous preferments and his eventual appointment to the see of Rochester. In his later years, he was an influential ecclesiastical politician and a significant participant in the detailed interactions of church and state which followed the Williamite revolution (*DNB* 2004). Yet with Dryden and with Waller he had contributed a long and unflinchingly panegyric elegy to a collection commemorating Cromwell's death. For him, the Restoration required a significant rewriting of the history of the mid-century decades and in particular his own part in it.

The thinkers in the Wilkins group worked to associate sympathizers of impeccable royalist credentials with their nascent society and to secure the patronage of Charles II. Shortly after its formal foundation, Sprat was commissioned to write its official history and to defend its objectives. The project was delayed by the plague of 1665 and the Great Fire of London, and did not appear, as *The History of the Royal-Society of London, for the Improving of National Knowledge*, until 1667.

Sprat's strategy is to build an opposition between the discourse of theological controversy and that of scientific enquiry. To the former, tainted with fanaticism, he attributes an almost frenzied divisiveness, which produced 'the passions, and madness of that dismal Age [the mid-century]' (Sprat 1667: 53). The latter allows rational and constructive disagreement as a component in advancing the state of human knowledge. He describes the Oxford phase of the founding group of the society in terms that disguise the solid Cromwellian credentials of its leader:

> To have been eternally musing on *Civil business*, and the distresses of their Countrey, was too melancholy a reflexion: It was *Nature* alone, which could pleasantly entertain them, in that estate. The contemplation of that, draws our minds off from the past, or present misfortunes, and makes them conquerers over things, in the greatest publick unhappiness: while the consideration of *Men*, and *humane affairs*, may affect us, with a thousand various disquiets; *that* never separates us into mortal Factions; *that* gives us room to differ, without animosity; and permits us, to raise contrary imaginations upon it, without any danger of a *Civil War*. (Ibid.: 56)

The volume is prefaced by a poem 'To the Royal Society' from Abraham Cowley, himself no stranger to ideological repositioning in the 1650s and 1660s. Cowley's praise for Sprat's style points up his significance for the history of Restoration prose writing: he has 'vindicated Eloquence and Wit', purging them from the excrescent excesses of mid-century, tub-thumping rhetoric, and thus producing a style which 'has all the Beauties Nature can impart, / And all the comely Dress without the paint of Art' (ibi.: sig. B3v). Sprat can write with an extreme plainness, adapting the emerging idiom of scientific discourse, but more usually he aims at and achieves a certain stately sparseness, without rhetorical patterning and without an obtrusive use of similes and metaphors. He anticipates the elegant functionalism that characterizes high-culture prose in the years following the Williamite revolution (see below, chapter 7).

Milton, St Nicholas and Hutchinson

Milton observed a careful silence in the years immediately following the Restoration. Of course, he was no longer a well-paid public servant. But he retained enough to live without obvious hardship, and a support network evidently formed to allow him, despite his blindness, to continue to study and to write. *Paradise Lost* circulated in a very limited way in manuscript. The only evidence is the recollection of Thomas Ellwood, a young and talented Quaker, who was part of that network and who had read presumably a late draft in February 1666 (Ellwood 1714: 234), and an echo in Marvell's *Last Instructions to a Painter*, which probably preceded its publication (Campbell 1997: 206). Milton published the poem towards the end of 1667. The first edition was organized into ten books. Mary Simmons, its printer, contracted to pay Milton £15 in three tranches for an edition of up to 1,500 copies, 'then a reasonable remuneration', in Alastair Fowler's judgement (Milton 1999: 5). The sum can scarcely have changed Milton's material circumstances significantly. As Karl Marx observes, 'Milton produced *Paradise Lost* for the same reason as that which makes the silk-worm produce silk. It was an activity wholly natural to him' (quoted Prawer 1976: 310). For a work of demanding creative writing, it sold steadily, though the preliminaries were revised, and it was reissued with the 'Arguments' which now preface each book 'for the satisfaction of many that have desired it' (Milton 1999: 51; originally they were gathered in the front matter) and with the defence of its unusual metrical form, blank verse, all presumably written by Milton himself. By April 1669, eighteen months after publication, it had sold 1,300 copies. In 1674 a second edition appeared, in which Milton had reconfigured the ten books as twelve. Each book now had its own argument printed as a sort of headnote.

Milton had evidently long contemplated both writing an epic and writing an imaginative account of the fall. Early manuscript drafts and jottings gathered together in the Trinity Manuscript show him sketching out a tragedy called 'Paradise Lost' (Milton 1972: 35; see also the biographical digression in his *Reason of Church-Government*, Milton 1953–82: I, 812–14). Yet in the context of his published oeuvre, the work seems a remarkable development. Among his earlier vernacular verse, probably only 'Lycidas', fashioned as a pastoral elegy, followed scrupulously in the neoclassical manner the formal characteristics of a Latin or Greek genre. The ten-book first edition has been interpreted as in some sense invoking recollection of Lucan's *Pharsalia*, as a republican alternative to the Augustan imperialism of the *Aeneid* (see, most persuasively, Lewalski 2000: 448; 2001: 16; Norbrook 1999: 438–67). Although certainly the allusions to Lucan are ideologically significant, nevertheless allusions to Virgil's epic are pervasive. Changing the division of the text carried other implications. Indeed,

Maren-Sofie Røstvig has demonstrated that the change replaces a nuanced numerological structure with an altogether cruder schema (1994: 461–534). As Milton makes these sacrifices, he draws his work closer to Virgil, not, I suggest, as a tribute, but as a challenge, engaging the iconic Augustan text, in the assertion that an English and Protestant and radical epic may not simply rival but surpass a Latin, pagan and imperial work.

Other narrative poetry besides classical contextualizes and shapes his practice. The younger Milton had been a confirmed neo-Spenserian, and, in Fowler's view, '*The Faerie Queene* is the most important vernacular model [for *Paradise Lost*], even if not apparently so' (Milton 1999: 11–12). Certainly, Spenser demonstrated that complexities of argument and structure are compatible with writing English verse. Again, the editorial tradition has long recognized a debt to Joshua Sylvester's late Elizabethan and early Jacobean translation of *The Divine Weeks and Works of Guillaume de Saluste Sieur du Bartas* (1592–1608) (see above, chapter 2). Moreover, there was a vernacular tradition of retelling biblical narratives in verse, which offered significant precedents, albeit of a less ambitious kind, and pointed to the tastes and expectations of seventeenth-century readers.

Yet Virgil and to a lesser extent Homer remain the texts most plainly mirrored in *Paradise Lost*. For Ben Jonson, classical models, pre-eminently Martial but also Horace and Juvenal, defined for the poet a socializing role, correcting inappropriate, extravagant or immoral behaviour. For Dryden, writing in the Virgilian and imperial mode allowed him to figure Restoration England as a new Rome. But Milton explicitly seeks to transcend the classical models as Protestant Christianity, for him, transcends paganism.

Thus, at the start of book 9 Milton asserts the supremacy of his Christian muse:

> . . . sad task [to relate the fall and its immediate impact], yet argument
> Not less but more heroic than the wrath
> Of stern Achilles on his foe pursued
> Thrice fugitive about Troy wall; or rage
> Of Turnus for Lavinia disespoused,
> Or Neptune's ire or Juno's that so long
> Perplexed the Greek and Cytherea's son;
> If answerable style I can obtain
> Of my celestial patroness, who deigns

Her nightly visitation unimplored,
And dictates to me slumbering, or inspires
Easy my unpremeditated verse:
Since first this subject for heroic song
Pleased me long choosing, and beginning late;
Not sedulous by nature to indite
Wars, hitherto the only argument
Heroic deemed, chief mastery to dissect
With long and tedious havoc fabled knights
In battles feigned; the better fortitude
Of patience and heroic martyrdom
Unsung; or to describe races and games,
Or tilting furniture, emblazoned shields,
Impreses quaint, caparisons and steed;
Bases and tinsel trappings, gorgeous knights
At joust and tournament; then marshalled feast
Served up in hall with sewers, and seneschals;
The skill of artifice or office mean,
Not that which justly gives heroic name
To person or to poem.

                              (ll.13–41; Milton 1999: 468–70)

This complex passage constitutes a multifaceted cultural agenda. Milton makes some disparaging points about the subject matter of Homer and Virgil. In their poems, a plurality of pagan gods are motivated by depraved and human impulses, and the heroes are driven by murderous rage. 'Heroic' poetry was already a synonym for the epic (*OED*, s.v. 'Heroic', sig. 3.a.), but evidently the deeds it depicts fall short of the Christian heroism established in the conduct of Jesus and those who follow his example of patience and passive fortitude. But Milton is also making a point about class. As Fowler notes, 'joust and tournament' abound in the Italianate narrative poets, such as Boiardo, Ariosto and Tasso, who drew on Virgilian epic but gave it a chivalric dimension, as in English chivalric writers, including Spenser and Sidney. Chivalry was routinely appropriated into Christian allegory. Nevertheless, such tourneys represent the most exclusive social ritual of early modern Europe, the sport literally of princes, wholly unavailable to wayfaring Christians outside the highest court circles. (Spectators were widely drawn, but participation was narrowly limited.) Milton extends the account to embrace the wider depiction of court ritual, which of course seems to him contemptible, a waste of ingenuity and a waste of virtue. 'Office mean' echoes his late republican attack on monarchy's perversion of socially meritorious endeavour as courtiers' ambition is channelled into the pursuit of court offices, 'to be stewards, chamberlains, ushers, grooms, even of the close-stool' (Milton 1953–82: VII, 425–6).

By the time readers reach these lines, they have already traversed three-quarters of the poem, and Milton's perspective on earlier epic, though not explicit, has been plain enough. He does, in fact, depict both chivalric tourneys and the games of classical heroes, but only the fallen angels take part, while the bards among them 'sing . . . / Their own heroic deeds and hapless fall / By doom of battle' (2.531–8, 546–50; Milton 1999: 135–6). The unfallen angels do exercise themselves in unarmed 'heroic games' (4.551; Milton 1999: 253). Similarly, his account of the war in heaven depicts events not unlike those of *The Iliad* or the closing books of *The Aeneid*, but, however meritorious their conduct in that conflict may be for the good angels who take part, it is reduced to irrelevance in practical, military terms by the eventual appearance of the Son before whom the fallen angels drop 'their idle weapons' (6.839; ibid.: 382). No godly human throws a single blow within the poem.

Milton skilfully exploits the advantages offered by imitating the narratological complexities of classical epic. He disrupts the time line, starting not with the war in heaven, but with the debate in hell and Satan's subsequent escape. As a long critical tradition recognizes (Fish 1971 is seminal), Milton thus allows the naive reader an early opportunity to mistake Satan's heroic status, before book 3 shows his impotence and corruption as the godhead is partially revealed. Again, Milton nests the narrative of the war in heaven in the middle of the work, and in so doing he positions the transcendent figure of the Son at the symbolically important centre of the poem. Moreover, he allows Raphael to give Adam and Eve the information they need about the nature of evil in order for the subsequent test of their obedience to be fair. The poem ends not with the vision of futurity, but with the depiction of Adam and Eve stepping out into that postlapsarian world as the first exemplars of the steadfast godliness which that vision had foretold.

Milton's choice of unrhymed verse was not without precedent in a narrative context. But it certainly struck contemporaries as remarkable. Andrew Marvell and Samuel Barrow (attrib.), in the poems prefixed to the 1674 edition, draw particular attention to it, and the printer explains that the note on the verse form, added first to the fourth issue of the first edition, has been solicited, like the arguments, in response to readers' requests; it is 'a reason of that which stumbled many others, why the poem rhymes not' (2.5331–8; Milton 1999: 51–4). The note on the verse points to classical, Italian and Spanish precedents, and to 'our best English tragedies', and it gives the project a nostalgic republican air: it is 'an example set, the first in English, of ancient liberty recovered to heroic poem from the troublesome and modern bondage of rhyming' (ibid.: 55). That he links the choice to the prosodic preference of 'our *best* tragedies' – evidently excluding the rhymed heroic drama of Dryden and looking back to the age of Shakespeare – is highly pertinent, for not only was his earliest concept for a depiction of the fall a tragedy, but also a high proportion of *Paradise Lost* consists of dialogue, between humans, between humans and angels, between angels, between God and angels, and between the Father and the Son. Moreover, by stripping the verse of the constraint of rhyme Milton demonstrably opens up the possibilities for writing the kinds of long and complex sentences which, though commonplace contemporaneously in serious discursive prose (including his own), are unique to his late poetry. These sentences, while they share the grandeur and scale of Ciceronian periods, are wholly English in their syntax (Corns 1990b; 2001c).

Even in the mid-century decades, poetry on the whole received a lighter scrutiny from the censors than most prose genres and particularly journalism. But Milton in the 1660s was a notorious republican, who had effected no reconciliation with the restored monarchy, and an early biographer records how some passages caught the licenser's eye (Darbishire 1932: 189). But, though the early modern state could be brutal in its treatment of dissidents – John Twyn was hanged, drawn and quartered in 1663 for printing an incitement to rebellion (Keeble 2002a: 151) – it was not comprehensively repressive in the style of some modern totalitarian states. Charles II was unconcerned that many of his countrymen disliked him and spoke disparagingly of him; there were no gulags in Restoration England for thought criminals. Though *Paradise Lost* is replete with republican and anti-clerical sentiments, it is explicitly endorsed on its title page 'Licensed and Entred according to Order'.

Milton depicts Satan in the infernal kingdom as a figure of outlandish, barbaric extravagance:

High on a throne of royal state, which far
Outshone the wealth of Ormus and of Ind,
Or where the gorgeous East with richest hand
Showers on her kings barbaric pearl and gold,
Satan exalted sat, by merit raised
To that bad eminence ...
(2.1–6; Milton 1999: 110)

The ostentation perhaps recalls the plumed and jewel-encrusted splendour of Charles II's own coronation. Numerous such small-scale insinuations of republican judgement pervade the poem. So do its anti-clerical barbs: Belial, for example, establishes a special relationship with the professional clergy 'when the priest / Turns atheist', though 'In courts and palaces he also reigns'. The antics of the sons of Belial, 'flown with insolence and wine', suggest some of the worst anti-social excesses of loutish courtiers indulged by the king (1.490–502; ibid.: 90–1).

But a more serious political argument rests at the heart of the poem. Milton reneges on no previous point of political principle. But, though he reaffirms his values (he sings 'with mortal voice, unchanged / To hoarse or mute'), the Good Old Cause appears guarded, defensive and in obvious eclipse. Milton represents himself as 'fallen on evil days, / ... / In darkness, and with dangers compassed round', alone except for his godly muse. There is a certain defiance in his expressed intention to find his 'fit audience', though he plainly fears that the fate of Orpheus could be his own (7.23–39; ibid.: 390–2). Moreover, his own vulnerability characterizes the typical condition of the godly, who, in the vision of the future in the last two books, are almost always excluded from civil power as Milton now was. As Adam asks Michael, once the Son has returned to heaven, 'Will they [the enemies of truth] not deal / Worse with his followers than with him they dealt?'; 'Be sure they will', Michael replies (12.483–5; ibid.: 669). The problem of evil, how and why a just and omnipotent God allows the godly to suffer, is central to the poem, but its specific manifestation often takes a political form. Emphatically, this is the epic of 1660s nonconformity, a work of ideological perseverance in a world that is pervasively and potently threatening.

Milton's only other publication in the first decade of the restored monarchy was a children's primer, *Accedence Commenc't Grammar* (1669), chiefly interesting in that he uses English, rather than Latin, as the medium of instruction, since, against prevailing practice, it reflects some of the pedagogic principles expressed in his earlier treatise, *Of Education*. Thereafter, however, he published a diverse miscellany of works, including a Latin treatise on the art of logic (1672), adapted from an earlier commentary on Peter Ramus's work. His *History of Britain* (1670), while not conspicuous for its scholarship, is suffused with anti-monarchical and anticlerical assumptions. Indeed, when he lashes the clergy of early medieval Britain as 'suttle Prowlers, Pastors in Name, but indeed Wolves', he uses the language and images in which he characteristically spoke of the clergy of his own day (Milton 1953–82: 5.i.175). His posthumously published *Brief History of Moscovia* (1682) rests on a slight basis of research, but again shows some anticlerical flourishes, as he notes that, despite their ostentation of piety, 'for Whordom, Drunkenness and Extortion none [is] worse than the [Russian] clergy' (8.492). He comes close to overt political engagement in *A Declaration, or Letters Patents of the Election of this present King of Poland* (1674), a translation of a Latin account of the accession of John Sobieski. This constitutes an oblique contribution to the incipient controversy that would become the Exclusion Crisis, in that the Polish *elective* model for kingship not only demonstrates that there are constitutionally sophisticated alternatives to the ponderous assertions of the divine right of English monarchs, but also describes a procedure that would allow for the deselection of unsuitable candidates (by implication, such as James, Duke of York). His most controversial works, the state papers he had written for the republic and the heterodox theological treatise we know as *De Doctrina Christiana*, were carried posthumously to the United Provinces in search of a publisher, and editions of the former did appear. The manuscript of the latter, together with a transcription of the state papers, were confiscated by the government and only rediscovered in 1823.

Quite why Milton chose to publish such relatively undistinguished items as Latin exercises from his university days, his *Prolusiones*, remains uncertain; there is a certain sense of clearing his desk before his death, though both his notoriety and the impact of *Paradise Lost* probably made even these modest works vendible. In 1673 he published a new edition of his minor verse, adding to the poems printed in 1645 some political sonnets, though not the ones to Vane, Cromwell and Fairfax, together with some technically accomplished psalm translations. There is evidently a greater air of freedom and security about Milton in the 1670s, reflecting the improved circumstances in which

Nonconformists found themselves; the years of fiercest persecution had passed, and they had survived. Indeed, during the relaxation of press control around the time of the Declaration of Indulgence, Milton returned to overtly controversial writing with *Of True Religion, Haeresie, Schism, Toleration, And what best means may be us'd against the growth of Popery* (1673). It takes a typical anti-court line on the attempted quid pro quo of Catholic toleration in return for the toleration of dissent: the former is an outrage, the latter merely a recognition of diversity within the Protestant faith community. While the anti-Catholicism is commonplace and opportunistically applied, its vision of an otherwise tolerant society is striking. Milton, rather like Dryden in *Religio Laici* (see above), distinguishes between the simplicities of saving faith and the complexities of the finer points of controversial theology, which have their value but are irrelevant to salvation.

Much more interesting, and indeed much more puzzling, is the double volume, *Paradise Regain'd. A Poem in Four Books. To which is added Samson Agonistes*, published in 1671. In the former he selects an unusual episode on which to ground a depiction of the Son's triumph. In the western tradition, his resurrection from the grave, the harrowing of hell, the ascension and the second coming and last judgement are more typically represented as pivotal moments of divine victory. Milton here eschews for the most part events which miraculously transcend the physical laws of the created world, centring his account in the portrayal of a wholly human incarnation who feels variously hunger, cold, and a bewilderment at what is happening to him and at what he feels within:

> O what a multitude of thoughts at once
> Awakened in me swarm, while I consider
> What from within I feel myself, and hear
> What from without comes often to my ears,
> Ill sorting with my present state compared.
> (1.196–200; Milton 1997: 432)

The tests the Son faces are temptations analogous to those the godly habitually face, albeit in more spectacular form. The ordinary citizen is not offered the command of vast armies to impose his rule, but the possibilities of returning to positions of some power and influence were available to most who had been servants of the republican regime, and some, like Pepys or Dryden or Marchamont Nedham, chose to accept them. The conflict depicted is intimate and personal. The good angels sing in anticipation of the events that are to unfold, 'Victory and triumph to the Son of God / Now ent'ring his great duel, not of arms, / But to vanquish by wisdom hellish wiles' (1.173–5; ibid.: 431). Milton greatly supplements the temptations depicted in the gospel accounts. The Son explicitly rejects command over vast armies ('Much ostentation vain of fleshly arm, / And fragile arms' – 3.387–8; ibid.: 480) and the attractions of monarchic or imperial splendour ('Nor doth this grandeur and majestic show / Of luxury, though called magnificence, / More than of arms before, allure mine eye' – 4.110–12; ibid.: 488). It is within the power of anyone to say no. In a curious innovation which has vexed the critical tradition, Milton has the Son reject even the temptation posed by pagan (and thus, by implication, humanistic) culture: 'he who receives / Light from above, from the fountain of light, / No other doctrine needs' (4. 288–90; ibid.: 496). In the context of the Son's debate with Satan, the passage is an assertion of the superiority of holy texts in the Judaeo-Christian tradition over the specious accomplishment of Athens and Rome. In the context of seventeenth-century England, it is an assertion that saving faith no more needs the elite learning of the academy than the chivalric culture of the court.

In genre terms, *Paradise Regained* may seem puzzling to a modern readership whose notions of elevated narrative poetry are shaped by Virgil, Homer and indeed by *Paradise Lost*. However, Barbara Lewalski's seminal study (1966) locates it in the tradition of the Book of Job, which Milton had termed in *The Reason of Church-Government* 'a brief model' of 'that Epick form' (Milton 1953–82: 1, 183), and she relates it, too, to the work of vernacular imitators of that model, among them Quarles. I doubt that it would have seemed strange or unprecedented to any informed contemporary reader, though of course it is a singularly fine example of the genre.

To the modern reader, its companion piece, *Samson Agonistes*, may seem much more familiar. In its name, in its dramatic structure, even in its fine-grained detail, it appears, straightforwardly, to be a neoclassical, vernacular exercise in the formal characteristics of Athenian tragedy on the model of Sophocles and Euripides, while taking its subject matter from the biblical tradition. Indeed, it has a chorus, which occasionally splits to perform strophes and anti-strophes; its events occur in one place, within the time of a day, and actions take place off stage and are reported. Of course, Sophocles and, probably to a greater extent,

Euripides write challenging dramas that confront the seeming simplicity of received morality. Moreover, as Milton writes in evident imitation of them, he asserts that tragedy has been and may be 'the gravest, moralest, and most profitable of all other poems', as its introductory note claims (ibid.: 355). Thus, Milton tacitly confronts the theatre of his own age with the purity of a classically informed alternative. But, as Joseph Wittreich notes, there is another pertinent influence in the neo-Latin closet dramas of the humanist tradition, such as the plays of Hugo Grotius, George Buchanan and Daniel Heinsius, which are essentially problem plays opening up moral questions in 'the spirit of interrogation' (Wittreich 2002: 19).

Samson shares some common ground with the hero of the brief epic. Both are godly, isolated, initially bewildered and surrounded by physical forces more powerful than themselves, and neither seems remotely drawn to the temptations placed before them. Samson, however, is a fallen hero, who has sinned though loquacity: he has talked too much, revealed too much, to Dalila. The Son, of course, is singularly taciturn in his conversations with Satan. Samson's regeneration allows him to slaughter large numbers of unsuspecting and unarmed Philistines engaged in a recreational activity. The question his action raises is not really whether such violence may be justified – after all, to one who accepts the historicity of the source, it happened and seemingly had divine sanction – but how meritorious it is in comparison with other modes of godly action. Milton had spent the last decade of his political life in the service of armed saints who had killed their adversaries in, and indeed after, battles, in which they had identified themselves as the agents of a divine providence. The regicide General Thomas Harrison had asserted that, in signing the death warrant, 'I did what I did, as out of conscience to the Lord', which earned his judge's rebuke, 'will you make God the author of your treasons and murders?' (Wedgwood 1966: 222–3). Milton's Samson shows similar conviction at his end. Yet by 1660, the armed saints had achieved little at enormous cost and left the godly of England at the mercy of their enemies. After the slaughter of the Philistines and Samson's self-slaughter, Israel is not free, though, on his father's account, it has the potential for freedom if it follows Samson's example (ll.1714–16; Milton 1953–82: 412). In contrast, the Son's godly but passive witness liberates all humankind.

Scholarship in very recent years has brought two fascinating analogues to Milton's late publications to critical attention in the poetry of Thomas St Nicholas and Lucy Hutchinson. Both deserve critical engagement. The mid-century writings of the former we have considered above (chapter 5). His small but evocative Restoration oeuvre, retained in the same manuscript as his earlier work, shows the response of another republican public servant and activist to the experience of defeat as he views his precarious circumstances and the persecution of his friends. Once more, he is best when he is most specific, as in 'An officer of Dover Castle being at the George in Lydd upon public affairs, one spying me come in said, "There's old Mr St Nicholas come in". The officer replied, "Then there's an old Parliament dog come in". Thereupon *sic cogitavi* [*I have thought thus*]' (St Nicholas 2002: 144–5). The poet, in a mere 35 lines, moves from indignation, through an audit of his own moral standing ('Humour I men's lusts, / And fawn upon my masters for their crusts?' – ll.9–10), to the concluding echo of Revelation 22:11, 'If they [the likes of the abusive officer] will / Yet filthy be, let them be filthy still' (ll.34–45). In the process, he neatly turns the scoff into a homely, humble but resolute image of himself as a dog 'Fed with the crumbs that from thy [God's] table fall' (l.27). A similar dynamic runs through 'Upon Mr Benchkin, the curate of Ash, his presentment of me to the consistory court at Canterbury for helping to lay my poor old nurse, the widow Solly, in her grave as soon as she was brought thither and the coverings, without noise or disturbance, taken off. August 10, 1664' (ibid.: 99–100). Benchkin's deposition, which is extant, describes an ideologically charged scene in a country churchyard, as evidently St Nicholas sought to have the body placed in the grave without the reading of the office of the dead, thus following the practice of *The Directory for the Public Worship of God* adopted by the Long Parliament, while the clergyman insisted on following the Book of Common Prayer of 1662. The law, of course, was with the clergyman. St Nicholas's poem, while repeating familiar nonconformist accusations of the venality of the professional clergy, works towards a reconciliation of sorts. At its heart, however, is a carefully turned, intimate, personal and reflective image:

> My poor old nurse who now is dead and gone,
> And lived to see her year of ninety-one,
> A sober matron of good reputation
> For honest life and conversation,
> And sixty-two years since, when, helpless, I

> Could do nought else but suck and sleep and cry,
> Fed and preserved me with her breasts, and then
> Lulled me asleep, laid me to bed again,
> Could I do less for her than once, at last,
> For all her kindness, though so long time past,
> Help lay her aged bones to rest before
> I go from hence and shall be seen no more?
>
> (ll.29–40)

The sermon-acting priest has nothing of value to add to a transaction as delicate and as appropriate as this, the final decorum of the child, now himself grown old, laying the nurse to bed.

Lucy Hutchinson, until recently, had been read primarily as the biographer of Colonel John Hutchinson, her husband and a regicide, who died in prison in 1664. That text, *The Memoirs of the Life of Colonel Hutchinson*, remained in manuscript until 1806 (Hutchinson 1995: xxx). It has been quarried frequently by historians for its eloquent and detailed representation of a political perspective that is at once upper-gentry class, republican and Puritan. Nor is it a polemically naive document (see, especially, Keeble 1990). But since the publication of *Order and Disorder* (Hutchinson 2001), interest has grown in Hutchinson's achievements as a poet. Hutchinson, the wife of a senior figure in the Midlands gentry prominent on parliament's side in the Civil War, probably felt both gender and social inhibitions about print publication, concerns that may well have been exacerbated by a sense of the precarious status of the family of a regicide in Restoration England. Her most ambitious project remained unfinished at her death, though the first five cantos were printed, anonymously, in 1679, two years before she died. Its solitary manuscript, the sole source for the remaining fifteen cantos, carries the date '1664' though not adjacently to the poem itself, 'so that it is not entirely clear whether the date refers to the manuscript book or to the poem', in the view of David Norbrook, its modern editor (Hutchinson 2001: liii–liv). A secure dating would resolve current speculation that either *Paradise Lost* influenced *Order and Disorder*, or vice versa.

In the short term, critical interest inevitably has clustered around comparisons between the two poems. Hutchinson's view on salvation is unrelentingly Calvinist, and in the expanse of world history she depicts, the godly and the reprobates are sharply and straightforwardly distinguished within the paradigm of double predestination. Milton's

Arminianism allows for struggle, for limited but restored free will, and for synergy with grace within each soul. Narratologically, Hutchinson takes the simplest option, relating events in chronological order; Milton, of course, avoids such simplicity. Again, in an unpromising caveat in the preface to the printed version, she warns her readers, 'they will find nothing of fancy in it; no elevations of style, no charms of language, which I confess are gifts I have not, nor desire not in this occasion' (Hutchinson 2001: 5), while Milton assures his readers that he aims to surpass the work of other epic poets. Hutchinson's style is indeed plain though decorous; its imagery is scarce, though sometimes vivid, as we shall see. Moreover, in terms of transmuting and retelling biblical history, she proceeds conservatively, whereas Milton is imaginatively and speculatively creative in the ways he supplements his source.

Yet, outside the framework of such comparison, Hutchinson's poem appears in itself a considerable achievement of real critical interest. Her writing offers a sustained yet oblique restatement of republican and Puritan values, as David Norbrook's commentary persuasively demonstrates, and she ingeniously connects the events she describes to moral imperatives that apply transhistorically though with a particular urgency to Restoration England. Her treatment of the drunken Noah exemplifies this well. As Norbrook notes, 'For royalists Noah was the first post-Flood monarch and a pattern for all later government'. Hutchinson makes much of the episode of his drunken incapacity, 'in lewd plight found / Immodestly incovered on the ground' (canto 9.13–14). She avoids an allegorical gloss – 'the episode was mainly interpreted as a rebuke of irreverence [represented by the scoffing of his son Ham] towards the mysteries of the state' (2001: 136, n.256). Instead, she offers praise, in a surprising and apposite image, of the vine as a source of pleasure and support when used in moderation: 'None more abounds with blessings than the vine / In whose fair arms numberless bottles shine' (lines 17–18). After that, a long exposition of the evils of drunken excess resonates with criticisms fitting to the Restoration court and the licentious culture it indulged: 'Princes forget their ranks and great affairs, / Cast of their kingdoms' necessary cares / And revel in their drunken jollities' (lines 59–61; ibid.: 137). But that corruption trickles down through the society it supports, to the 'wanton and ridiculous like apes' and 'goats whose bloods hot lust doth fire' (ll.94, 97). We recall Sir Charles Sedley's obscene libation (see above).

Hutchinson's relation of the events of Genesis attempts no exculpation of Eve, though her account of the curse laid upon her occasions some of her most vivid writing:

> How painfully the fruit within them [pregnant women] grows,
> What tortures do their ripened births disclose,
> How great, how various, how uneasy are
> The breeding-sicknesses, pangs that prepare
> The violent openings of life's narrow door,
> Whose fatal issues we as oft deplore!
>
> (Canto 5.149–54)

The passage continues to review the agonies of parturition, the discomforts of lactation, the fatigue of nurturing and the anxieties of motherhood. It contrasts eloquently with the assessment Milton makes of Eve's curse, as expressed by Adam's curt reassurance that it threatens 'Pains only in child-bearing . . . / And bringing forth, soon recompensed with joy, / Fruit of thy womb' (10.1051–3; Milton 1999: 594). Hutchinson gave birth to eight children (Hutchinson 2001: 70, n.132).

Katherine Philips and Margaret Cavendish

Katherine Philips had much in common with Lucy Hutchinson and Thomas St Nicholas. Her family background was solidly Puritan. Indeed, Major-General Philip Skippon, her step-father, was not only a prominent parliamentary commander in the civil wars (most signally, he commanded the trained bands at Turnham Green), but also in effect military commander of the London region in the 1650s (*DNB* 1975). Colonel James Philips, her husband, like Colonel Hutchinson and St Nicholas, wielded considerable power and influence in support of parliament and the republic in his own region (in this case, South Wales). Her upbringing was on her own account Presbyterian. Her poetry, too, belonged initially to a manuscript culture, and her chosen genres share some of the formal characteristics of those favoured by St Nicholas. Her works are often occasional, and those occasions frequently relate to life-events of her own circle. Thus, a title like 'A sea voyage from Tenby to Bristol, 5 September 1652. Sent to Lucasia 8th September 1652' (Philips 1990: 88–90) would not be out of place in St Nicholas's works, except for Philips's adoption of a poetic soubriquet for a member of her circle (in this case, the daughter of an Anglesey squire – ibid.: 335; Philips styled herself 'Orinda').

But Philips differs from Hutchinson and St Nicholas in very significant ways. Despite her close family connections with the Interregnum establishment, she was plainly a royalist. Her poetic output was stimulated by the Restoration, the events of which she celebrated in occasional panegyric of a familiar kind. Moreover, in the 1650s she moved in royalist cultural circles. She knew Henry Vaughan and celebrated his work. Four of her poems were set by Henry Lawes, who had set much of the poetry of the Caroline court (see above, chapter 4). Moreover, rather in the manner of Lovelace's late poetry or Charles Cotton's (above, chapter five), her poetry frequently rehearses the royalist themes of friendship and retirement as strategies for negotiating political eclipse. In her case, fascinatingly, the company into which she withdraws is overwhelmingly female. The shared bottle and an enthusiasm for Anacreontic verse are unsurprisingly absent, and the activities associated with friendship as she conceived and practised it appear rather uncertain. Indeed, as the 90-line poem 'A Friend' observes, 'Friendship is abstract of this noble flame, / 'Tis love refin'd and purg'd from all its drosse' (ll.7–8; ibid.: 165).

The circumstances of literary production changed very significantly for Philips at the Restoration. Of course, she was now a celebrant of the new regime, though there were many such. Most crucially, in a fairly brief sojourn in Dublin, she translated a Corneille play, *La Mort de Pompée*, which was performed there in 1663 and shortly afterwards published in London. It may well have been staged subsequently in London (ibid.: 17–18). In a culture starved of new plays and attuned to welcoming literary endorsement of the restored monarchy, this woman dramatist achieved immediate celebrity; a pirated edition of most of her poetry appeared early in 1664. Her response was successfully to press the publisher to withdraw the publication, reflecting no doubt an anxiety about displaying herself in print, in which the imagined social stigma was compounded by a sense of what constituted decorous conduct for a respectable woman and possibly some concern about critical reception. An authorized edition appeared in 1667, three years after her death from smallpox.

Margaret Cavendish actively promoted the printing of her own works, starting with the first edition of her collected verse in 1653. Cavendish, too, was a royalist married to a soldier. Her husband William Cavendish, the Marquess of Newcastle (created a duke in

1665), had commanded the royalist army of the North. His poor judgement in disposing the battle line contributed pivotally to Cromwell's victory at Marston Moor, after which he lived abroad till the Restoration. He met his wife, who was a gentlewoman of Henrietta Maria, in exile. Margaret Cavendish's oeuvre is transparently partisan, and defences of her husband, whose biography she wrote (first published in 1667), appear digressively in her more imaginative writing.

Much of her poetry dates from the early 1650s. Her enthusiasm for print perhaps reflects her understanding of the dispersed readership for royalist texts once the royal courts were displaced abroad and many royalists had retired to their country properties. But she retained the practice of print publication even after 1660, a fact which significantly qualifies the familiar generalizations about the stigma of print among the propertied in general and women writers in particular.

A handful of her poems have become modern anthology pieces, though the selection imperfectly represents the predominant characteristics of her early verse. Much of the editions of 1653 and 1656 are taken up with philosophical poems. Many, in the tradition of Lucretius, explore atomic theories of the physical world. Others offer verse dialogues, typically between opposed abstractions. A group of poems describe a fairy world. Yet, however charming these seem, they are not simple-minded whimsy. Cavendish would go on to write huge prose engagements with many of the principal controversies of western European philosophy in the early modern period. 'The Fairies in the Brain may be the Causes of many Thoughts' (Cavendish 1653; anthologized in Cummings 2000: 466–7) represents the formation of emotions and desires as the reflections of the moods and actions of tiny inhabitants of the cranium:

> ... thus within the head may be a fair:
> And when our brain with amorous thoughts is stayed,
> Perhaps there is a bride and bridegroom made;
> And when our thoughts all merry be and gay,
> There may be dancing on their wedding day.
> (ll.20–4; Cummings 2000: 467)

Although Cavendish was regarded as eccentric by some contemporaries, the notion of fairies inhabiting the brain and determining its function is not literally intended. Rather, lightly, fancifully and wittily, she offers a contribution to contemporary philosophical controversy about the nature of the cognitive faculties. She challenges the notion of the human mind as a *tabula rasa*, a clean slate without innate notions, on which the senses inscribe ideas. Her 'fairies' function as impulses inherent to the human brain; to shift the metaphor, they are hard-wired into the human personality and human ratiocination. William Cavendish's circle while in exile 'included among others Hobbes, Mersenne, Descartes, and Pierre Gassendi' (*DNB* 2004, s.n. 'Cavendish, William'), a veritable roll-call of the most powerful European philosophers of the mid-century, and Margaret evidently moved confidently in that milieu.

She is a deeply philosophical writer, and her major works are philosophical and scientific disquisitions written in a functional prose. Her currently most widely considered creative writing, *The Description of a New World, Called The Blazing World*, was first published in 1666 as part of a double volume containing her *Observations Upon Experimental Philosophy.* Much of the more philosophical component of *The Blazing World* mirrors in a different mode and genre the concerns of its companion piece. But for the modern reader and perhaps for her contemporaries its primary interest lies elsewhere. Cavendish has picked up the traditions of prose romance and of the fantastic voyage as a medium for philosophical speculation, firmly established by Sir Thomas More's *Utopia* (1551), but pushed them with extraordinary creative power towards what is often discussed as a ground-breaking work of science fiction. Indeed, she imagines and represents a coherent universe inhabited by creatures that are only vaguely hominid, though of course that universe mirrors the real world, as she conceives it, in complex ways. The author confidently plays around the emergent conventions of fictional narrative. The heroine of the tale has a kindred spirit in the form of the character 'Margaret Cavendish', a figure introduced to advance the philosophical speculation and to rehearse the Duke of Newcastle's claims for compensation for revenues and properties lost in the civil wars, amounting to 'half his woods, besides many houses, land, and movable goods; so that all the loss ... did amount to half a million of pounds' (Cavendish 1992: 193).

In terms of gender ideology, Cavendish apparently poses problems. Certainly, she boldly intrudes into philosophical and scientific discourses that were contemporaneously perceived as wholly male preserves, even to the point of inviting herself to the Royal Society, while her use of 'the interdicted practices of writing and publishing ... challenge the negative consequences for women of patriarchal codes of femininity' (ibid.: xiv). But her politics are deeply conservative, reflecting her husband's commitment to monarchism and to social hierarchy.

7

From the Accession of James II: After February 1685

_____

James II and the Williamite Revolution

Charles II died on 6 February 1685, after a brief illness initiated by a cerebral haemorrhage. Before his death a priest was called, and he confessed according to the Catholic practice and received extreme unction. He died without legitimate offspring. His brother James, Duke of York, succeeded to the throne. James's own conversion to Catholicism was long standing and widely known. The Exclusion Crisis it had provoked in the late 1670s and early 1680s was unpropitious.

Yet at first the new regime enjoyed considerable success. James rapidly incorporated into government the predominantly aristocratic and Tory politicians on whom Charles, in the closing years of his reign, had relied, rehabilitating some whose fortunes had lately been in decline. But there was change as well as continuity at court. James was a womanizer, albeit more discreetly and on a more modest scale than his brother. Yet he attempted the sort of cultural transformation Charles I had made on his own accession: 'he declared that he would not employ drunkards, blasphemers, gamblers and men who did not pay their debts. He warned that anyone who came to court drunk would lose his place and admonished husbands to be faithful to their wives and sons to obey their fathers' (Miller 2000: 121). William III and Mary II made much of the reform of manners; arguably, James had already started that process.

Politically and economically, the new regime opened well. James worked assiduously to reduce the burden of debt Charles had accumulated, in part through bringing to government his own innate parsimony, and in part through attacking waste and corruption. Moreover, the parliament he called in February 1685 'showed itself generous' (ibid.: 137). Given the propertied classes' understandable aversion to civil disorder, James's position for a while seemed fairly secure. John Miller summarizes the issues thus:

> The danger of rebellion was virtually non-existent, Scotland and Ireland were quiet and the sea largely isolated England from the dynastic power politics of the continent. Once James's first Parliament had granted him an adequate revenue, he had little real need to call another, so there was little real danger of serious disputes there with his subjects. The Tories were still vociferously loyal. The Whigs, shattered and demoralized, lay low or crept to make their peace with the new King. James's position was thus so secure that he could make all kinds of mistakes without placing his regime in serious jeopardy. (Ibid.: 124)

Yet by the end of 1688 he was functionally finished in England, and by 1690 all his kingdoms were lost to him.

Religion lay at the root of the disaster. Almost certainly, James nursed neither hope nor expectation of winning England back to Catholicism. Yet, like his brother, he sought to remove the disadvantages under which his Catholic subjects laboured, which both hindered the open observation of their faith and precluded their participation in government, in parliament and in public office. Like his brother, he was prepared to associate that ambition with a general toleration that would have similarly emancipated Protestant dissenters. However, his boldness, stimulated by a powerful coterie of Catholics with whom he surrounded himself, proved widely alarming.

Three issues proved crucial. James admitted Catholics to public office by suspending the Test Act, which would have excluded them. Though he acted within the precedented privileges of the crown, his actions seemed a manifestation of the return to arbitrary government and caused particular concern when exercised in the area of military appointments in a newly expanded standing army. As J. A. Downie, quoting J. R. Jones, summarizes, 'Officered by Catholics in open defiance of the Test Act, the army was quartered in the provinces "so that by 1688 the whole kingdom was taking on the appearance of a country under military occupation"' (1994: 31). Secondly, James alienated the leadership of the Church of England. Toleration was never likely to find much support in such quarters. However, he sought confrontation, especially in the field of academic employment. Oxford and Cambridge were intended exclusively for those conforming to the Church of England. In high-profile cases, James imposed Catholic appointments. He was frustrated in imposing a Catholic President (that is, Master) on Magdalen College, Oxford, and responded by depriving the fellows of their fellowships and barring them from holding any benefice in the Church of England. The case proved very destructive to his standing: 'By his rigidity and vindictiveness, he put himself in the wrong and completed the alienation of the Anglicans' (Miller 2000: 171).

The third and final event, under other circumstances, would have been a support to the regime: in June 1688, the queen gave birth to a male heir, James Francis Edward, the future 'Old Pretender'. James already had two surviving children, the Princesses Mary and Anne. Till that point, the former was his heir. She was married to James's nephew, William, Prince of Orange, the strong man of the Dutch republic and since 1678 'an absolute monarch in all but name' (Ogg 1965: 434). William was perceived as Europe's leading Protestant prince. The Stuarts, hitherto, had proved relatively short-lived as English monarchs. Neither James I nor Charles II had survived to their seventh decade. James II was 52 at his accession. An optimist could reasonably have expected his to be a brief Catholic interlude before the restoration of a Protestant succession. But the young prince, born to a Catholic mother, to be educated as a Catholic, and probably to be subject to a Catholic-dominated regency should his father expire, took away that consolation.

James overcame with facility the Monmouth Uprising of July 1685. James Scott, Duke of Monmouth, launched in the West Country a doomed attempt to secure by arms what he had failed to secure through the Exclusion Crisis. The minatory edge of *Absalom and Achitophel* (see above, chapter 6) proved prophetic. Monmouth's irregulars were routed at the Battle of Sedgemoor. Monmouth was captured and decapitated. About 300 of his supporters were hanged, drawn and quartered in the marketplaces of their native counties, and many more were transported into virtual slavery. With the birth of James's son, a much sterner coalition formed against him. Respectable Whigs, who had been terrified by the judicial savagery that had followed the Rye House Plot and had avoided involvement in Monmouth's adventure, were radicalized by old anxieties over popery.

Tories who had not converted to the king's denomination both shared those concerns and were appalled by the apparent attack on such Anglican institutions as the universities. Moreover, William of Orange now saw that the waiting game, through which he expected access to England's resources on the eventual accession of his wife, was lost, and he possessed qualities of leadership, military experience and a disciplined army, all of which Monmouth, for the most part, lacked. On 5 November, that most resonant of dates in English Protestantism, he landed in the West Country with a substantial force.

James put an army in the field, but as it wavered in allegiance, he tried to flee, was captured in humiliating circumstances and returned to London. Once the city was in William's control, a second escape attempt was facilitated, and James fled to France, from where he organized resistance in Ireland, his one kingdom with a majority of Catholic subjects. But in 1690 at the Battle of the Boyne, his army was defeated, and he once more left for France. 'Jacobites', as his diehard supporters were termed, remained thereafter either associates of his increasingly impoverished court in exile or, in rather greater numbers, marginalized figures outside the significant arenas of English political life. The Williamite revolution was complete and irreversible. It withstood the death of Mary in 1694; Anne, strictly the immediate successor, complied with William's continuing rule, eventually acceding on his death in 1702.

The new regime brought with it immediate reforms. Since William intended to ally British resources to Dutch in resistance to Louis XIV and since he recognized that, constitutionally, supply depended on parliamentary resolutions, parliament remained in session throughout his reign. A legislative programme that shaped the English constitution into a parliamentary democracy and constitutional monarchy followed on from the Declaration of Rights, which asserted the errors of the reign of James II and pointed towards the obligation of monarchs to summon parliaments, the ascendancy of the Protestant faith and a degree of toleration for dissent. Legislation further disabled the Catholic community, though in effect they 'became what they had been under the Protectorate and in the earlier days of Charles II, a quiet body, not actively persecuted' (Clark 1955: 153). The Licensing Act, which in various earlier guises had governed the work of the press over the century, lapsed in 1695 and was not renewed. Religious controversy certainly does not disappear from the subject matter of English literature, though it loses its centrality.

By 1690, the ideological landscape of England – and with it its cultural life – had changed at least as drastically as in 1603. England became, in association with the United Provinces, a powerful presence in continental conflicts. Until the Treaty of Ryswick (1697), William retained a large English army in the field against France, setting a course of English foreign policy that was to continue to the twentieth century. Necessarily, since armies depended on votes of supply, a different relationship between parliament and government emerged. With that came a new kind of political writing. As Tony Claydon (1996) has carefully charted, William relied on a coordinated and highly effective propaganda machine. Through the early years Gilbert Burnet orchestrated the campaigns. He himself was a career clergyman, as were many of his ablest associates – men like John Tillotson, the Dean of Canterbury, and Simon Patrick, the Dean of St Paul's. Revolutionary independency had Milton and Nedham; the proto-Whigs had Marvell. Here we see a shift to writers, not of creative genius and vivid expression, but people of high competence, praised in their own age and subsequently for a calm and lucid eloquence (Williamson 1966: 358–9). Only around the close of the William's reign, in the figures of Daniel Defoe and Jonathan Swift, do creative writers of canonical status once more emerge in the context of explicit political engagement.

Aphra Behn: The Late Works

Aphra Behn's royalist partisanship was plainly evident in her earliest writing, and her currently most regarded play, *The Rover*, assiduously celebrates cavalier values in the nostalgic context of the Restoration (see above, chapter 6). Her Tory commitment allowed an easy transfer of her loyalties to James II. For his coronation, she produced and published a Drydenesque 'Pindarick Poem', though its lofty celebration of James's heroic status peters out in grandiloquent reportage of the event itself: 'And now the *Royal Robes* are on, / But oh! what numbers can express / The Glory of the Sacred Dress!' ('A Pindarick Poem on the Happy Coronation of His most Sacred Majesty James II', ll.465–7; Behn 1992–6: I, 212). She remained quick to praise the king throughout the reign. She wrote poems both on the news of the queen's pregnancy and on the birth of the Prince of Wales: 'No *MONARCH's Birth* was ever Usher'd in / With Signs so Fortunate as this hath been' ('A Congratulatory Poem to the King's Most Sacred Majesty, On the Happy Birth of the Prince of Wales', ll.15–16; ibid.: I, 297).

She poignantly claimed the latter was written 'with *Prophetick Fire*' (l.7). Five months later William landed. Behn died in 1689, though the final year of her life saw her at least considering a realignment with the new regime. Gilbert Burnet, director of William's propaganda system, evidently attempted to turn her, and was rewarded with another 'Pindaric poem', 'On the Honour he did me of Enquiring after me and my Muse' (ibid.: I, 307–10). In the event, she wrote and published only one overtly Williamite poem, 'A Congratulatory Poem to Her Sacred Majesty Queen Mary, Upon Her Arrival in England' (ibid.: I, 304–7). She shows considerable polemical ingenuity. As a well-known supporter of the ousted king, she must proceed with care. William goes unmentioned. James figures frequently as a melancholy figure of uncertain political standing. A solemn and rather funereal tone is gradually displaced by the arrival of Mary, who is hailed not as wife of William, but as daughter of James, which practically (though, in strictly constitutional terms, dubiously) lends some specious legitimacy to the regime change:

> And thou, Great Lord [James II], of all my Vows, permit
> My Muse who never fail'd Obedience yet,
> To pay her Tribute at *Maria's* Feet,
> *Maria* so Divine a part of You,
> Let me be Just – but Just with Honour too.
> (ll.54–8; ibid.: 305)

Honour is an elusive concept for Tory turncoats, and she moves on to the strongest argument for accepting the regime change: that it allows a new stability in which all parties (except for the diehard and predominately Catholic Jacobites) could live in orderly fashion: 'You Great Cesar's Off-spring blest our Isle, / The differing Multitudes to Reconcile' (ll.107–8; ibid.: 307).

If James noticed the poem, he may reasonably have felt that reconciliation had come a little early and a trifle cheaply. Yet Behn as a professional writer had only the alternative of honest poverty. Indeed, she may well have felt under financial pressure since 1682 when the formation through merger of the United Company reduced the demand for new plays, although she continued to write for the stage till her death. Her late political poetry was written for print publication and presumably was sold by her to publishers, though it had a secondary purpose of securing patronage and protection in a suddenly uncertain world. Janet Todd suggests that the same pressure may have prompted her in her final years to write a number of novellas of a disparate kind (Behn 1992–6: III, xi). Some draw on real events or on continental sources. Among them, the most remarkable, *Oroonoko: or, The Royal Slave. A True History*, first published in 1688, achieved some contemporary success and in recent times has reached canonical status. It was dramatized by Thomas Southerne in 1695. In recent years it has become an anthology piece (Abrams et al. 2000: I, 2170–215).

Yet it is a curiously conflicted work. In the aftermath of the Monmouth rebellion, its hero's misfortunes, enslavement, castration and dismemberment, were punishments meted out to captured rebels. Apart from about 300, who were spectacularly executed, 'Many others were transported, which meant that they were granted to courtiers who sold them into slavery in the colonies'. The going rate was £10–£15 each (Miller 2000: 141–2). The author of *Oroonoko* seems unconcerned about judicial cruelty and slavery per se. Oroonoko as a warrior prince has habitually sold captive enemies to white slave-dealers, a practice which receives no hostile authorial comment; presumably, it is his ruling-caste privilege, much like the courtiers who traded in Monmouth's men. Once in slavery, he attempts to negotiate his own release with the offer of 'a vast quantity of Slaves' (Behn 1992–6: III, 93).

Milton had argued that, if the race of princes were indeed superior to other men, as horses bred in Tutbury were superior to other horses, then kingship would be justifiable as a system of government (quoted above, chapter 5). Behn's celebration of the innate superiority of royalty takes no chances. Oroonoko is physically quite distinct from other Africans. Certainly he is black, in fact blacker than the others, 'not . . . that brown, rusty Black which most of that Nation are, but a perfect Ebony, or polish'd Jett'. But his physiognomy is distinctively European: 'His Nose was rising and *Roman*, instead of *African* and flat. His Mouth, the finest shap'd that cou'd be seen; far from those great turn'd Lips, which are so natural to the rest of the *Negroes*' (ibid.: 62–3). When the revolt he leads fails through the pusillanimity of his followers, he concludes that he erred 'in endeavoring to make those Free, who were by Nature *Slaves*' (ibid.: 109).

Ideologically, then, *Oroonoko* endorses slavery in general but exempts from it those who are genetically distinct, as of royal blood and disposition. The 'royal slave' of the secondary title is an oxymoronic term around which much of the narrative pivots. Yet the book has an appeal that is virtually independent of its principal argument. At the end of her career, Behn, an accomplished professional in other genres, showed herself to be a considerable writer of a fictional prose which was both evocative and sensational. Surinam is vividly depicted as at once a kind of earthly paradise and a place of danger for incomers, a land of voracious predators and deadly reptiles. Todd notes that the depiction 'looked forward to Defoe who in *Robinson Crusoe* located the hero's island somewhere near the mouth of Orinoco River and drew on Behn's slave for his own character Friday' (ibid.: xvi). But her narrative structure is arguably subtler than Defoe's. Whereas he favours a pseudo-autobiographical form, Behn has her tale told by a figure who witnesses the events mostly at a remove and who comments on them, not as royal or a slave, but as an intelligent and not uncompassionate observer. Her text stands, too, as an early ancestor of the novel of imperial adventure, a remote precursor of H. Rider Haggard. Behn invests her African scenes with a frisson of sexual strangeness that borders on the pornographic, not least in the unconsummated relationship between the king, Oroonoko's grandfather, and Imoinda, his beloved: 'he commanded [she] shou'd be brought to him, they [his servants] (after dis-robing her) led her to the Bath, and making fast the Doors, left her to descend. The King, without more Courtship, bade her throw of her Mantle, and come to his Arms' (ibid.: 66). Behn's sense of her market remained acute.

Dryden and James II

Dryden retained the post of poet laureate under James II, an appointment that proved more lucrative than in Charles's days since the new king's sounder financial management meant he was paid more regularly (*DNB* 2004). Dryden's support for James extended back through the days of the exclusion crisis to the Anglo-Dutch wars. He had shown a loyalty staunchly manifest at a time when his eventual succession seemed uncertain, and James himself had been a significant patron of the poet. The poetry he wrote during his reign shows ideological continuity and coherent development.

His earliest task was to commemorate the death of Charles. His *Threnodia Augustalis: A Funeral Pindaric Sacred to the Happy Memory of King Charles II* exhibits his accomplishment in the form of the freely structured ode he favoured for most of his late commemorative poems, a classical and elevated genre that admitted an effusive flow of panegyric associations. The poem works towards a concluding theme Dryden had established in his earliest Restoration poetry (see above, chapter 6), that Charles had established a navy that would extend British influence 'ev'n to remoter Shores' (1.510; Dryden 1995–2005: II, 420). En route, much of what had concerned him in his poetry of the last quarter century is reprised: Charles's forgiving nature, his commitment to the hereditary principle, his support for his brother, his tolerant endurance of 'senates, insolently loud, / (Those echoes of a thoughtless crowd)' (ll.319–20; ibid.: 409). An abrasively Tory poem, it reflects the confidence and triumphalism of the last years of the reign. This is not a poem to heal a nation but to reassure the new ruler and the factions closest to him.

Dryden shortly returned to considering authority and interpretation in matters of religion, issues which he had treated from a Protestant perspective in his *Religio Laici* (1682) (see above, chapter 6). At some point between its publication and the winter of 1686–7 Dryden converted to Roman Catholicism. In a spirit and with a motivation that cannot now be determined, but with a palpable honesty, he launched a sort of debate with his former self. *The Hind and the Panther* argues for the superiority of the Catholic faith in terms of the sure guidance the church gives in matters of interpretation. Dryden attributes to the Panther, the figure representing the Anglican perspective, attacks on authority which the Hind, representing Catholicism, traces back to Puritan arguments against the patristic tradition. Milton, for example, had made similar points against the episcopalian defences of prelatical church government which drew on evidence from the early church (see above, chapter 5). In *The Hind and the Panther* Dryden persistently nudges Anglicanism into a compromised position, too dependent on Catholic modes of thought to subscribe wholeheartedly to radical Protestant declarations of the coherence of the gospel independent of the interpretative tradition: 'For purging fires traditions must not fight, / But they must prove episcopacy's right' (Part II, ll.286–7; ibid.: III, 101).

Dryden takes up another argument, well worn in the controversies of the 1640s: that a true church must be capable of controlling schisms and sects. Episcopalians had raised the charge against Presbyterians and Independents. Dryden carefully surrounds the Panther with other beasts representative of nonconformity, and points to them, not simply as uncontrolled by the Church of England but nurtured as allies united by their opposition to Catholicism: 'No union they pretend but in non-popery' (Part II, l.462; ibid.: III, 108). To this he opposes a brilliant image of the indivisibility of Catholicism:

> One in herself, not rent by schism, but sound,
> Entire, one solid shining diamond,
> Not sparkles shattered into sects like you,
> One is the church, and must be to be true:
> One central principle of unity.
> (Part II, ll.526–30; ibid.: 111)

James's master plan to secure toleration for his co-religionarists, which culminated in his Declaration of Indulgence promulgated shortly before the poem was finished, rested on the strategy of securing broad support by extending toleration both to dissenters and to Catholics. It was an old game, first played by Charles II in the 1670s with no great success. While some Anglicans favoured tolerating some sectaries, most sectaries joined with Protestants within the national church in opposing toleration for Catholics. James, nevertheless, persevered, and indeed William Penn the Younger, a well-connected Quaker leader, had a growing influence on him through his reign (Miller 2000: 156). Among less radical groups, support for the crown was much less evident. In *The Hind and the Panther*, in his epistle to the reader, Dryden explicitly endorses the official policy: 'there are many of our sects, and more indeed than I could reasonably have hoped, who have withdrawn themselves from the communion of the Panther, and embraced this gracious indulgence of His Majesty in point of toleration' (ibid.: III, 40). His avowed target consists of those in the broad spectrum of Protestant belief who resist the irenic royal indulgence. But the poem seems much more belligerent. Besides the Panther, his beast fable extends to the Bear (Congregational Independents), the Hare (Quakers) and the Boar (Baptists), whom he represents with a satirical savagery in the opening lines of the poem. He associates them with the Panther as an indictment of its failure to control scandalous schism. Inevitably, too, since the poem is an oblique conversion narrative, Dryden finds much to say about what drew him to Catholicism. The result is fascinating, eloquent and, as a rehearsal of James's policy, flawed.

Steven Zwicker points to the curious silence within high literary culture with which the Williamite coup was received: 'It is hard to think of a political crisis in [the seventeenth] century so unremarked in literary form.' From this generalization he rightly exempts Dryden's heroic drama *Don Sebastian*, the 'only literary masterpiece' produced in response to the coup (Zwicker 1993: 174). The play was performed by the United Company after the Jacobite rout in England, 'sometime late in 1689' (Dryden 1956–2000: XV, 382), and it reflects in complex and sometimes tangential ways on the fall of a regime with which Dryden had been prominently associated.

Though he retains blank verse, rather than the couplets of his earliest heroic drama, the play in other ways has a retrospective and nostalgic air. As in *The Conquest of Granada*, the subject matter is a legendary interpretation of Iberian history. Its roots lie in the adventurous involvement of Sebastian II of Portugal in a bold intervention in the civil wars of Morocco, which ended in disastrous defeat at Alcazar in 1589. The king's body was never found, and several alternative legends arose about his fate. Dryden selects from those a version which has him survive, but end his days in eremitical seclusion (see ibid.: XV,383–91). He withdraws from the world after consummating his marriage to a Moroccan princess, who turns out to be his half-sister conceived through his father's adulterous relationship.

The events depicted cannot easily be read as a coded attack on William III or a lament for James II. Although Dryden could scarcely have anticipated this, the exiled James ended up living an increasingly devout and withdrawn life almost as austere as a hermit's: 'In his last years he scourged himself and wore around his thighs an iron chain studded with spikes' (Miller 2000: 234). Moreover, in post-revolutionary and Williamite London, no theatrical company could have engaged in open and hostile criticism of the new regime. Theatres could be closed; they could be devastated by riots; audiences could take direct action during performances perceived as disloyal. There is some safety in evasiveness, and Dryden and the company that performed the play, formerly the Duke of York's Company, came as close to recent events as prudence allowed.

Nevertheless, Dryden scores numerous hits on the Whigs and their allies. The play celebrates as openly as *Oroonoko* the notion of the innate nature of monarchy. Among the forces captured after Alcazar, the royal prisoners, though disguised, are immediately recognized as distinctively superior to the rank and file, much like Behn's African prince: 'these look like the Workmanship of Heav'n: / This is the porcelain clay of human kind' (I.i.239–40; Dryden 1956–2000: XV, 88).

Most of the negative points Dryden makes come in his depiction of the church and the mob. His Morocco has an established church, albeit an Islamic one, and it allows its leader, the Mufti, a platform to dabble very actively in the politics of the state. James's reign had been bedevilled by the leadership of the Church of England, who defied his designs for the toleration and promotion of Catholicism. The Mufti has a corrupt sense of how states may be manipulated, offering advice on rousing and directing the mob (III.1.373–56; ibid.: XV, 139). He admits his role as 'chief of my Religion' is 'to teach others what I neither know nor believe my self' (IV.ii.2–3; ibid.: XV, 161). The mob plays a crucial part in the resolution of the civil war. Mustapha, its leader, though a comic character, is sinister enough, a slave-dealer who humiliates a Christian prisoner by riding him round the stage, and he is a lord of misrule. The Mufti may claim 'The voice of the Mobile [that is, the mob] is the voice of Heaven' (IV.iii.219–20; ibid,: XV, 169), but their motivation is simpler. As the character designated 'Second Rabble' puts it: 'We are not bound to know who is to Live and Reign; our business is only to rise upon command, and plunder' (IV.iii.33–5; ibid.: XV, 170). Mustapha rallies them with recollection of their recent success:

> Do you remember the glorious Rapines and Robberies you have com-mitted? Your breaking open and gutting of Houses, your rummaging of Cellars, your demolishing of Christian Temples, and bearing off in triumph the superstitious Plate and Pictures, the Ornaments of their wicked Altars, when all rich Moveables were sentenc'd for idolatrous, and all that was idolatrous was seiz'd? (IV.iii.124–30; ibid.: XV, 173)

When the play was first performed, the most immediate recollection of riot was the recent sacking of Catholic homes and places of worship in the aftermath of James's flight. Dryden ridicules the avowed piety of the mob, and in so doing stirs among his propertied audience that old suspicion of the many-headed monster. But Mustapha's account links their activities not only with recent events but also with the routine sacking of churches by the Puritans in the 1640s, and thus it more subtly suggests the ancestry of popular support for William in the less glorious revolution of the mid-century.

Don Sebastian is a display of courage not only by Dryden but by the United Company. But it is not a call to arms. Rather, it rehearses a residual loyalty to a displaced ideology and a refusal to endorse the new regime at a time when its victory was still contested; the war continued in Ireland. Thereafter, Dryden's Jacobitism takes an ever more tangential, quiescent and nostalgic form.

After 1690

Periodization bedevils every attempt at literary history. Which are the cultural watersheds that should structure the endeavour? Even the major dynastic shift of 1603, with which this study effectively begins, may be challenged. After all, Shakespeare, Donne and Jonson, who arguably tower over the early Jacobean period, were already mature authors in the final decade of Elizabeth. Politically, the arrival of the Hanoverians with the accession of George I in 1714 both ended the Stuart dynasty and settled the constitutional changes initiated in 1688. Dryden died in 1700. So, too, did the sole surviving child of Queen Anne, on whom the possibilities for Stuart continuation rested. Otherwise, the mere change of the century was unremarkable.

Few major writers of the Restoration period lived on into the 1690s. Milton died in 1674, Marvell in 1678, Rochester in 1680, Otway in 1685, Bunyan in 1688, Behn in 1689. Etherege died in 1691, though Wycherley survived till 1716; both had long since quit the stage. Nor, except in the case of the stage, are the major writers of the next age already emerging. Joseph Addison published a little juvenilia and made a modest but significant contribution to the editorial material in Dryden's translation of Virgil (see below). There are a few works of non-fictional prose from Daniel Defoe. Jonathan Swift, Alexander Pope, John Gay published nothing till the 1700s. Arguably, in terms of its part in the English literary tradition, the 1690s produced less of abiding merit than any decade since the 1570s.

The best drama of the 1690s appears transitional in several ways. Drama in the brief reign of James II had been distinguished by late plays from Behn and Dryden. It had been reduced to near bankruptcy early in 1685 when the closure of theatres at the time of the Monmouth rising postponed the performance of the opera *Albion and Albanius*, scripted by Dryden, in which the United Company had heavily invested in props, stage machinery and costumes. In 1695, the monopoly of the established London stage by the United Company broke down. It was a move that anticipated by almost two and half centuries the foundation of United Artists by screen celebrities disenchanted with the established studios. Thomas Betterton, Elizabeth Barry and Anne Bracegirdle, the most prominent actors of their day, broke away to open a new theatre at Lincoln's Inn Fields. In a sense, that marks the coming of age of the star system, rudimentarily present in Elizabethan and Jacobean theatre, which had been developing since the earliest days of the Restoration stage. It carried theatre further away from its dependency on the protection of the mighty. The King's Men, in a sense, had finally become their own men, and women, too, took control of their own careers. The actors' confident initiative, in which Betterton emerged as leader, anticipated the rise of the actor-manager, the entrepreneur bred up in the profession, which reached maturity with David Garrick's mid-eighteenth-century career and which operated in many English theatres well into the twentieth century. However, at the same time, independence from the court came at a price. As Claydon notes, 'William disliked and disapproved of public entertainments. Reducing royal hospitality to a bare minimum, he gave every impression of having to force himself into what few social events he did offer to the English elite' (1996: 93). He did not need companies of actors to provide or supplement performances at court celebrations. No longer did royal protection shield the stage from its fiercest critics.

The new theatre opened with the premiere of William Congreve's *Love for Love* (1695). 'A Prologue for the opening of the new Play-House, Propos'd to be spoken by Mrs. *Bracegirdle* in Man's Cloaths' represents what was essentially a commercial venture in explicitly political terms:

> Freedom's of *English* growth, I think, alone;
> What for lost *English* Freedom can attone?
> A Freeborn Player loaths to be compell'd;
> Our Rulers Tyraniz'd, and We Rebell'd.
> (ll.22–5; Womersley 2000: 506)

As David Womersley observes, the idiom here resonates with recent political significance. It chimes, too, with an important theme in Whig thinking, most perfectly expressed in John Locke's *Two Treatises of Government*, first published in 1690, in which true freedom requires the freedom to use one's own property and apply one's own labour without the arbitrary control of others, much as Betterton and his consortium had claimed for themselves.

Congreve's major plays mark another kind of transition. They share some plot lines with the theatre of Wycherley and Etherege. These are often plays of courtship. They depict witty heroes and heroines. Often the generations are locked in conflict. Congreve resists sentimentalizing relationships overmuch, while avoiding the raw and aggressive eroticism of Restoration comedy. *The Way of the World* (1700) depicts a London where young men of the beau monde still keep and discard mistresses and where clandestine relationships are consummated. But it celebrates, too, a new kind of civility and a new contract between the sexes. Its principal couple, Mirabell and Millamant, establish a relationship that is both affectionate and rational. Her individuality and aspirations are respected, 'As liberty to pay and receive visits to and from whom I please, to write and receive Letters, without Interrogatories on your part. To wear what I please; and choose Conversations with regard only to my own taste', and so on (IV.i.244–8; Womersley 2000: 676). This exchange, crucial for the themes of the play, concludes with an image that embodies whiggish values: Mirabell observes, 'Shall I kiss your hand upon the Contract?' (ll.329–30; ibid.: 677). The word 'contract' reflects with Lockean concerns about freely entered engagements as a foundation of ordered society and shows a legalism that recognizes how the law should protect equally the rights of partners.

Congreve's major rival in the later 1690s was Sir John Vanbrugh, whose plays, arguably, retained a stronger affinity with Restoration comedy. Yet both wrote for a theatre that was increasingly aware of external pressures which were broadly aligned with the assertion of the alleged need to reform manners, which was at the core of Williamite propaganda. As Claydon (1996) has demonstrated, the decade was marked by a studied transformation in the ways in which the new regime represented itself and in the manner in which it sought to fashion the cultural life of the country. Combined with a new indifference to the well-being of the theatre, these developments exposed drama to a new onslaught. Early in 1695 the Lord Chamberlain had tightened up the procedures for licensing plays, requiring a full scrutiny before permitting performance. In 1699, Nahum Tate proposed new regulations in 'a clear belief that a total ban on the theatres was being considered if such reforms did not occur' (Bull 2001: 433). Against this background, Vanburgh and Congreve probably wrote more circumspectly than they would have done had they enjoyed the freedoms of Etherege and Wycherley. Yet, along with Dryden's *Don Sebastian*, *Love for Love* and Vanbrugh's *The Relapse* (1696) recur as targets for censure in *A Short View of the Immorality and Profaneness of the English Stage* by Jeremy Collier (1698).

Collier sits at the end of a long tradition of Puritan attacks on the stage, though he was far from the dissenters in his own religious beliefs. Indeed, despite focusing the moral crusade of Whig propaganda onto the contemporary stage, he was in other respects out of step with the Williamite ascendancy. Although he was in holy orders in the Church of England, he declined to swear allegiance to William, and had ministered on the scaffold to would-be assassins thwarted in an attempt on the king's life (*DNB* 2004). His presence among the detractors of the stage certainly indicates how widely that antipathy was shared. His book is quite learned, comparing contemporary plays disadvantageously with classical drama and with the theatre of Shakespeare and Jonson. Yet he does not acknowledge that a comparison of the plays of the 1670s with those of his own time plainly discloses a new self-restraint. There is ultimately a silliness about his project. He concludes with a series of rhetorical questions: 'How *many* of the Unwary have these *Syrens* [presumably, the attractions of the theatre] devour'd? And how often has the best Blood been tainted, with this Infection [presumably, enthusiastic theatre-going]? What Disappointment of Parents, what Confusion in Families, and What Beggary in Estates have been hence occasion'd? (Collier 1698: 287). We may not be sure, but I suspect the likeliest answer is 'none'. At least, none seduced by the texts he examines, though no doubt theatres remained, and would long remain, an easy place for quite rich young men to meet a better class of prostitute, a notion which underlies the imagery he selects and probably points to his deeper concerns.

One text towers over the publications of the decade, John Dryden's magisterial translation of the works of Virgil, published in 1697 by Jacob Tonson, with whom he had worked since 1678 and who retained a prominence among London booksellers (see plates 8 and 9). The work originated in Dryden's own indigence since 1688: he had lost the post of poet laureate to Thomas Shadwell, whose Whig credentials were irreproachable. Dryden had returned to drama,

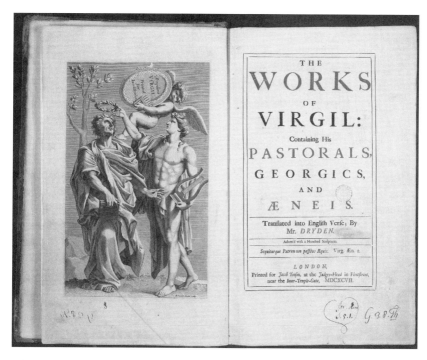

Plate 8 John Dryden, *The Works of Virgil* (1697), frontispiece and title page. Reproduced by permission of The Bodleian Library, University of Oxford. G.3.8. Th.

though abandoned it again in 1694 after *Love Triumphant*, a 'deliberately old-fashioned' piece that he evidently regarded as his valediction to a medium he had come to regard as unprofitable and to a public exposure which, in the eclipse of his ideological position, had evidently become wearisome (Winn 1987: 471–5). But the Virgil project broke new ground in terms of the economics of authorship and publishing. Dryden received from Tonson, in staged payments, advances, so-called 'copy money', that allowed him to live fairly comfortably while he was engaged on the task. The publication itself appeared in two versions, which carried the organization of subscription editions to a new level of complexity. Those who had subscribed at the higher rate of five guineas had their names and coats of arms incorporated into the illustrations in the book and received copies printed on superior paper. Those who subscribed to pay two guineas were merely listed but still received the de luxe edition. The net profit from the de luxe edition seems to have gone wholly to Dryden.

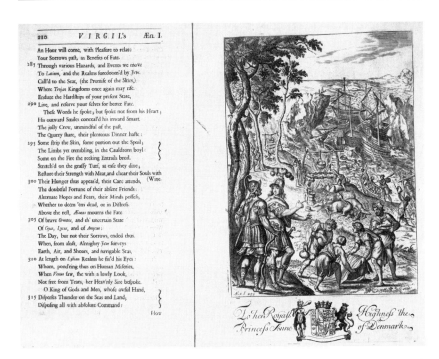

Plate 9 John Dryden, *The Works of Virgil* (1697), a plate from the *Aeneid*. Reproduced by permission of The Bodleian Library, University of Oxford, Page 210 and illustration opposite. G.3.8. Th.

Tonson kept the profit from the trade edition on ordinary paper (see ibid.: 475–8). Though Dryden and Tonson quarrelled over the details of the transaction, together they had found a way for an elite author of limited personal means and no patronage to produce a very substantial work of high literary merit.

That success marks the maturation of the London book trade. Analysis of both subscription lists show Dryden's accomplishment and celebrity had secured him a readership across the political spectrum. Princess Anne and her husband both subscribed five guineas. The book itself is, by the standards of London book production in the early modern period, a masterpiece, lavishly illustrated and effectively designed. It offers, too, a cornucopia of information of immense use to a modestly educated readership, in the form of biography, annotation and introductions. That in itself says something about shifts in high culture and its expectations. Of course, translation had for long a place in the English literary tradition.

The poem perhaps marks the emergence of a new political consensus. Superficially at least, it is a major text with no immediate engagement with issues of political and constitutional legitimacy, a sort of holiday from a world still carrying fresh wounds of recent and recurrent divisions. Since his earliest panegyrics, Dryden had simulated a Virgilian idiom for his praise, transiently, of Cromwell and, persistently, of Charles II and James II. Here, apparently, he puts the idiom to rest on less contentious ground.

Dryden's last publication, *Fables Ancient and Modern; Translated into Verse, from Homer, Ovid, Boccace, & Chaucer: with Original Poems* (1700), was published by Jacob Tonson very shortly before the poet's death. Its title indicates its decidedly miscellaneous quality. The original verse amounts to little more than three panegyric exercises. There is a delicately turned funeral elegy written for 'The Monument of a Fair Maiden Lady, Who dy'd at Bath, and is there Interr'd': 'A Female Softness, with a manly Mind: / A Daughter duteous, and a Sister kind: / In Sickness patient; and in Death resigned' (ll.34–6; Dryden 1956–2000: VII, 512). He addresses a long verse epistle to his cousin, 'To My Honour'd Kinsman, John Driden, of Chesterton in the County of Huntingdon, Esquire'. Driden was a minor politician, recently returned to parliament through a by-election. Dryden, no longer so clearly an anti-Williamite partisan, nevertheless returns to political engagement, urging steadfastness on an issue of recent significance. The Nine Years War, in which William had embroiled England on the side of the United Provinces against his old enemy France, had recently ended, and parliament had forced through a marked reduction in the English standing army. The concluding lines, arguing that 'Patriots, in Peace, assert the Peoples Right; / With noble Stubbornness resisting Might' (ll.184–5; ibid.: 201), surely restates the purposefulness of resisting William's martial enthusiasm. The verse epistle dedicatory is to the Duchess of Ormond, and it seconds the prose epistle to her husband, the second Duke, the grandson of the Ormond Milton had challenged in his *Observations* (see above, chapter 5). The second Duke was a Tory loyalist, but had accepted the settlement following the Williamite revolution. He would later resist the Hanoverian succession and thereafter live much of his life as an exiled Jacobite. Dryden has laid his last fruits at the feet of ideologically sympathetic recipients.

The bulk of the considerable volume – it runs to more than 12,000 lines – is made up of a curious range of translations, of tales from Boccaccio's *Decameron* and from *The Canterbury Tales* together with books and fragments from *The Iliad* and from Ovid's *Metamorphoses* and *The Flower and the Leaf*, contemporaneously and erroneously attributed to Chaucer. Dryden is attracted to working over some highlights from his sources, such as the sketch of the Parson from The General Prologue or 'The Speeches of Ajax and Ulysses' from *Metamorphoses*, book XV. The technical tasks Dryden has set himself are diverse and considerable. Turning Chaucer into modern English needs a careful attention that the Middle English idiom does not corrupt the contemporaneity of the language. Boccaccio requires the versifying of prose. Ovid and Homer are challenges closer to the ones he had so triumphantly met in his Virgil translation.

Indeed, the whole project according to Dryden had its origins in an initial attempt to produce a sample of Homer as a prospectus for a great new translation on the scale of his Virgil. He seems defensive about how the other texts accreted around that unrealized ambition. His own account describes the process of selection, and, while a coherence of sorts emerges, elements of serendipity are acknowledged. After translating 'the first of *Homer's Iliads*' he moved to the twelfth book of the *Metamorphoses* because it describes the beginning of the Trojan war, but he moves on to the speeches of Ajax and Ulysses for no better reasons than their proximity and the fact that they presented a 'pleasing Task' (ibid.: 24).

Dryden in a sense takes on his mighty precursors, but the whole preface exudes a respect for the wide and various achievement of great writers, with a touching assurance that they form fit company for the mature genius of the poet. His complete mastery of the heroic couplet remains undiminished. Like the Virgil translation, although on a more modest scale and with a more muted marketing strategy, this volume, too, was a publishing success, and a fitting conclusion to Dryden's part in the professionalizing of high-culture literary production. Tonson agreed an advance of 250 guineas, to be topped up to £300 to be paid to him or his heirs when it went into a second edition. Straightforward reward for literary dedication proved rare in the opening decades of our period, despite a myriad of panegyric epistles dedicatory. In sharp contrast, Dryden received a hefty present from the Duchess of Ormond – on one contemporary account as much as £500 (ibid.: 573). Literary celebrity, which would extend through Pope and Dr Johnson to our own age, had finally arrived as an element in English cultural production.

Bibliography

A Dogs Elegy, or Rupert's Tears (1644) London.

Academiæ Oxoniensis Funebria Sacra Æternæ Memoriæ Serenissimæ Reginæ Annæ (1619) Oxford.

An exact description of Prince Ruperts Malignant She-Monkey (1645) London.

The Bible and Holy Scriptures (1560) Geneva.

Cantabrigiensium Dolor et Solamen: seu Decessio Beatissimi Regis Jacobi Pacifici: et Successio Augustissimi Regis Caroli (1625) Cambridge.

Certain Verses Written by Several of the Author's Friends (1653) London.

Justa Edouardo King naufrago, ab Amicis moerentibus (1638) Cambridge.

Lacrymæ Cantabrigienses: In obitum Serenissimæ Reginæ Annæ (1619)

Abraham, Lyndy (1998) *A Dictionary of Alchemical Imagery.* Cambridge: Cambridge University Press.

Abrams, M. H. et al. (eds.) (2000) *The Norton Anthology of English Literature*, 7th edn. New York and London: Norton.

Adamson, J. S. A (1994), Chivalry and Political Culture in Caroline England. In Sharpe and Lake, eds. (1994), pp. 161–97.

Alberge, Dalya (2005) John Donne, 17th-Century Poet of Pop. *The Times*, 9 May 2005: 16.

Alciato, Andrea (1531) *Emblematum liber.* Augsburg.

Anne-son, James (n.d.) *Carolanna.* London.

Anselment, Raymond A. (1988) *Loyalist Resolve: Patient Fortitude in the English Civil War.* Newark: University of Delaware Press; London and Toronto: Associated University Presses.

Arber, Edward (1875–94) (ed.) *A Transcription of the Registers of the Company of Stationers.* London: private print.

Aristotle et al. (1965) *Classical Literary Criticism.* Translated with an introduction by T. S. Dorsch. Harmondsworth: Penguin.

Armitage, David, Armand Himy and Quentin Skinner (eds.) (1995) *Milton and Republicanism.* Cambridge: Cambridge University Press.

Ashton, Robert (ed.) (1969) *James I by his Contemporaries*. London: Hutchinson.

Bacon, Francis (1605) *Twoo Bookes of the Proficience and Advancement of Learning*. London.

Bacon, Francis (2000) *The Essays or Counsels, Civill and Morall*, ed. Michael Kiernan. The Oxford Francis Bacon, vol. 15. Oxford: Clarendon Press.

Bangs Carl (1971), *Arminius: A Study in the Dutch Reformation*. Nashville and New York: Abingdon.

Barnard, John and D. F. McKenzie, with Maureen Bell (2002) *The Cambridge History of the Book in Britain. Volume IV: 1557–1695*. Cambridge: Cambridge University Press.

Barroll, Leeds (2001) *Anna of Denmark, Queen of England: A Cultural Biography*. Philadelphia: University of Pennsylvania Press.

Bates, Catherine (2002) Shakespeare's Tragedies of Love. In McEachern, ed. (2002), pp. 182–203.

Bath, Michael (1994) *Speaking Pictures: English Emblem Books and Renaissance Culture*. London and New York: Longman.

Baumann, Gerd (ed.) (1986) *The Written Word: Literacy in Transition*. Oxford: Clarendon Press.

Beaumont, Francis (1967) *The Knight of the Burning Pestle*, ed. John Doebler. London: Arnold.

Beaumont, Francis and John Fletcher (1966–94) *The Dramatic Works in the Beaumont and Fletcher Canon*, ed. Fredson Bowers et al. Cambridge: Cambridge University Press.

Beaumont, Sir John (1629) *Bosworth-field: with a Taste of the Variety of other Poems*. London.

Bawcutt, N. W, (1996) *The Control and Censorship of Caroline Drama: The Records of Sir Henry Herbert, Master of the Revels 1623–73*. Oxford: Clarendon Press.

Beal, Peter (2002) John Donne and the Circulation of Manuscripts. In Barnard and McKenzie, eds. (2002), pp. 122–6.

Behn, Aphra (1992–1996), *The Works of Aphra Behn*, ed. Janet Todd. London: William Pickering.

Beier, A. L. (1986) Engine of Manufacture: The Trades of London. In Beier and Finlay (1986a), pp. 141–67.

Beier, A. L. and Roger Finlay (1986a) *London 1500–1700: The Making of the Metropolis*. London and New York: Longman.

Beier, A. L. and Roger Finlay (1986b) The Significance of the Metropolis. In Beier and Finlay (1986a), pp.1–33.

Beilin, Elaine V. (1996) *The Examinations of Anne Askew*. Oxford: Oxford University Press.

Bell, Ilona (1987) Herbert's Valdesian Vision. *English Literary Renaissance* 17: 303–28.

Bell, Maureen and John Barnard (1992) Provisional Count of STC Titles 1475–1640. *Publishing History* 31: 48–64.

Bell, Maureen and John Barnard (1998) Provisional Count of Wing Titles 1641–1700. *Publishing History* 44: 89–97.

Bennett, H. S. (1965) *English Books and Readers 1558 to 1603.* Cambridge: Cambridge University Press.

Bentley, Gerald Eades (1941–68) *The Jacobean and Caroline Stage.* Oxford: Clarendon Press.

Berry, Lloyd E. (ed.) (1969) *The Geneva Bible: A Facsimile of the 1560 Edition.* Madison, Milwaukee, and London: University of Wisconsin Press.

Bevington, David (2000) The Major Comedies. In Harp and Stewart, eds. (2000), pp. 72–89.

Binns, J. W. (1990) *Intellectual Culture in Elizabethan and Jacobean England: The Latin Writings of the Age.* Leeds: Francis Cairns.

Blagden, Cyprian (1958) The Stationers' Company in the English Civil War. *The Library,* 5th series, 13: 1–17.

Blagden, Cyprian (1960) *The Stationers' Company: A History, 1403–1959.* London: George Allen and Unwin.

Bond, Ronald B. (ed.) (1987) *Certain sermons or homilies (1547).* Toronto and London: University of Toronto Press.

Bradbrook, M. C. (1935) *Themes and Conventions in Elizabethan Tragedy.* Cambridge: Cambridge University Press.

Bradbrook, M. C. (1955) *The Growth and Structure of Elizabethan Comedy.* London: Chatto and Windus.

Bradstock, Andrew (1997) *Faith in the Revolution: The Political Theologies of Muentzer and Winstanley.* London: SPCK.

Brailsford, H. N. (1983) *The Levellers and the English Revolution.* Nottingham: Spokesman. First published 1961.

Brennan, Michael (1988) *Literary Patronage in the English Renaissance: The Pembroke Family.* London and New York: Routledge.

Brome, Richard (1980a) *A Critical Edition of Brome's The Northern Lasse*, ed. Harvey Fried. New York and London: Garland.

Brome, Richard (1980b) *A Critical Edition of Richard Brome's The weeding of Covent Garden and The Sparagus Garden*, ed. Donald S. McClure. New York and London: Garland.

Brown, Carleton, ed. (1939) *Religious Lyrics of the XVth Century.* Oxford: Clarendon Press.

Brown, Jonathan (1995) *Kings & Connoisseurs: Collecting Art in Seventeenth-Century Europe.* New Haven and London: Yale University Press.

Browne, Sir Thomas (1964) *Religio Medici and Other Works*, ed. L. C. Martin. Oxford: Clarendon Press.

Browne, Sir Thomas (1981) *Sir Thomas Browne's* Pseudodoxia Epidmica, ed. Robin Robbins. Oxford: Clarendon Press.

Browne, William (1613) *Britannia's Pastorals*. London.

Browne, William (1616) *Britannia's Pastorals*. London.

Bull, John (2001) Sir John Vanburgh and George Farquhar in the Post-Restoration Age. In Owen, ed. (2001), pp. 429–45.

Bunyan, John (1960) *The Pilgrim's Progress*, ed. James Wharey; 2nd edn, ed. Roger Sharrock. Oxford: Clarendon Press.

Bunyan, John (1962) *Grace Abounding to the Chief of Sinners*, ed. Roger Sharrock. Oxford: Clarendon Press.

Bunyan, John (1976–94) *Miscellaneous Works*, ed. Roger Sharrock et al. Oxford: Clarendon Press.

Bunyan, John (1988) *The Life and Death of Mr. Badman*, ed. Jams F. Forrest and Roger Sharrock. Oxford: Clarendon Press.

Burton, Robert (1989–2000) *The Anatomy of Melancholy*, ed. Thomas C. Faulkner et al. Oxford: Clarendon Press.

Butler, Martin (1987) *Theatre and Crisis 1632–1642*. Cambridge: Cambridge University Press. First published 1984.

Butler, Martin (2002) Literature and the Theatre to 1660. In Loewenstein and Mueller, eds. (2002), pp. 565–602.

Butler, Samuel (1967) *Hudibras*, ed. John Wilders. Oxford: Clarendon Press.

Campbell, Gordon (1980) The Theology of *The Pilgrim's Progress*. In Newey, ed. (1980), pp. 251–62.

Campbell, Gordon (1997) *A Milton Chronology*. Basingstoke and New York: Macmillan and St Martin's Press.

Capp, B. S. (1994) *The World of John Taylor the Water-Poet 1578–1653*. Oxford: Clarendon Press.

Carew, Thomas (1964) *The Poems of Thomas Carew with his Masque* Coelum Britannicum, ed. Rhodes Dunlap. Oxford: Clarendon Press. First published 1949.

Carlton, Charles (1995) *Charles I: The Personal Monarch*, 2nd edn. London and New York: Routledge.

Carey, John (1990) *John Donne: Life, Mind and Art*, 2nd edn. London: Faber and Faber.

Cavendish, Margaret, Duchess of Newcastle (1653) *Poems, & Fancies*. London.

Cavendish, Margaret, Duchess of Newcastle (1992) *A Description of a New World, Called the Blazing World, and Other Writings*, ed. Kate Lilley. London: Pickering.

Charles I (attrib.) (1649) *Eikon Basilike*. Many editions. London and elsewhere.

Charles, Amy M. (1977) *A Life of George Herbert*. Ithaca and London: Cornell University Press.

Chernaik, Warren (1995) *Sexual Freedom in Restoration Literature*. Cambridge: Cambridge University Press.

Chernaik, Warren and Martin Dzelzainis (eds.) (1999a) *Marvell and Liberty.* Basingstoke and New York: Macmillan and St Martin's Press.

Chernaik, Warren and Martic Dzelzainis (1999b) Introduction. In Chernaik and Dzelzainis, eds. (1999a), pp. 1–22.

Clark, Sir George (1955) *The Later Stuarts 1660–1714,* 2nd edn. Oxford: Clarendon Press.

Clark, Sandra, ed. (1997) *Shakespeare Made Fit: Restoration Adaptations of Shakespeare.* London and Vermont: Dent and Tuttle.

Clark, Sandra (2001) Shakespeare and Other Adaptations. In Owen, ed. (2001), pp. 274–90.

Claydon, Tony (1996) *William III and the Godly Revolution.* Cambridge: Cambridge University Press.

Cleveland, John (1967) *The Poems of John Cleveland*, ed. Brian Morris and Eleanor Withington. Oxford: Clarendon Press.

Cogswell, Thomas (1989) *The Blessed Revolution: English Politics and the Coming of War, 1621–1624.* Cambridge: Cambridge University Press.

Coiro, Ann Baynes (1999) 'A Ball of Strife': Caroline Poetry and Royal Marriage. In Corns (1999a), pp. 26–46.

Collier, Jeremy (1698) *A Short View of the Immorality and Profaness of the English Stage.* London.

Corns, Thomas N. (1982) *The Development of Milton's Prose Style.* Oxford: Clarendon Press.

Corns, Thomas N. (1986) Publication and Politics 1640–1661: An SPSS-Based Account of the Thomason Collection of Civil War Tracts. *Literary and Linguistic Computing* 1: 74–84.

Corns, Thomas N. (1990a) Milton's *Observations upon the Articles of Peace*: Ireland Under English Eyes. In Loewenstein and Turner, eds. (1990), pp. 123–34.

Corns, Thomas N. (1990b) *Milton's Language.* Oxford: Blackwell.

Corns, Thomas N. (1992) *Uncloistered Virtue: English Political Literature 1640–1660.* Oxford: Clarendon Press.

Corns, Thomas N., (1993a) (ed.) *The Cambridge Companion to English Poetry: Donne to Marvell.* Cambridge: Cambridge University Press.

Corns, Thomas N. (1993b) Thomas Carew, Sir John Suckling, and Richard Lovelace. In Corns, ed. (1993a), pp. 200–20.

Corns, Thomas N. (1995) Milton and the Characteristics of a Free Commonwealth. In Armitage, Himy and Skinner, eds. (1995), pp. 25–42.

Corns, Thomas N. (1998) The Poetry of the Caroline Court. *Proceedings of the British Academy* 97: 51–73.

Corns, Thomas N. (ed.) (1999a) *The Royal Image: Representations of Charles I.* Cambridge: Cambridge University Press.

Corns, Thomas N. (1999b) Duke, Prince and King. In Corns (1999a): 1–25.

Corns, Thomas N. (1999c) Milton's prose. In Danielson, ed. (1999), pp. 84–97.

Corns, Thomas N. (2000) The Early Modern Search Engine: Indices, Title Pages, Marginalia and Contents. In Rhodes and Sawday (2000), pp. 95–105.

Corns, Thomas N., ed. (2001a) *A Companion to Milton*. Oxford: Blackwell.

Corns, Thomas N. (2001b) 'On the Morning of Christ's Nativity', 'Upon the Circumcision' and 'The Passion'. In Corns, ed. (2001a), pp. 215–31.

Corns, Thomas N. (2001c) Milton's English. In Corns, ed. (2001a), pp. 90–106.

Corns, Thomas N. (2001d) Radical Pamphleteering. In Keeble, ed. (2001), pp. 71–86.

Corns, Thomas N. (2002a) Bunyan, Milton and the Diversity of Radical Protestant Writing. In Keeble, ed. (2002b), pp. 21–38.

Corns, Thomas N. (2002b) Milton before Lycidas. In Parry and Raymond, eds. (2002), pp. 23–36.

Corns, Thomas N. and David Loewenstein (eds.) (1995) *The Emergence of Quaker Writing: Dissenting Literature in Seventeenth-Century England*. London: Cass. (First published as a special issue of *Prose Studies*, 1994).

Cotton, Charles (1958) *Poems of Charles Cotton*, ed. John Buxton. London: Routledge and Kegan Paul.

Cotton, Priscilla and Mary Cole (1655) *To the Priests and People of England, we discharge our consciences, and give them warning*. London.

Coward, Barry (ed.) (2003) *A Companion to Stuart Britain*. Oxford: Blackwell.

Cowley, Abraham (1656) *Poems: I. Miscellanies. II. The Mistress, or Love Verses. III. Pindarique Odes. And IV. Davideis*. London.

Cowley, Abraham (1663) *Cutter of Coleman-Street*. London.

Cowley, Abraham (1905) *The Poems of Abraham Cowley*, ed. A. R. Waller. Cambridge: Cambridge University Press.

Cowley, Abraham (1989–) *The Collected Works of Abraham Cowley*, ed. Thomas O. Calhoun et al. Newark: University of Delaware Press; London and Toronto: Associated University Presses.

Crashaw, Richard (1957) *The Poems English Latin and Greek of Richard Crashaw*, ed. L. C. Martin. Oxford: Clarendon Press.

Crashaw, Richard (1972) *The Complete Poetry of Richard Crashaw*, ed. George Walton Williams. New York: New York University Press.

Cressy, David (1980) *Literary and the Social Order: Reading and Writing in Tudor and Stuart England*. Cambridge: Cambridge University Press.

Cressy, David and Lori Anne Ferrell (eds.) (1996) *Religion and Society in Early Modern England: A Sourcebook*. London and New York: Routledge.

Cummings, Robert (ed.) (2000) *Seventeenth-Century Poetry: An Annotated Anthology*. Oxford: Blackwell.

Cust, Richard (1986) News and Politics in Early Seventeenth-Century England, *Past & Present* 112: 60–90.

Danielson, Dennis (ed.) (1999) *The Cambridge Companion to Milton*, 2nd edn. Cambridge: Cambridge University Press.

Darbishire, Helen (1932) *The Early Lives of Milton*. London: Constable.

Davenant, Sir William (1638) *Madagascar: with Other Poems*. London.

Davenant, Sir William (1658) *The Cruelty of the Spaniards in Peru. Exprest by Instrumentall and Vocall Musick, and by the Art of Perspective in Scenes, &c.* London.

Davenant, Sir William (1665) *Two excellent plays: The Wits, a comedie: The Platonick Lovers, a tragi-comedie.* London.

Davenant, Sir William (1971) *Gondibert*, ed. David F. Gladish. Oxford: Clarendon Press.

Davenant, Sir William (1972) *The Shorter Poems, and Songs from the Plays and Masques*, ed. A. M. Gibbs. Oxford: Clarendon Press.

Davies, H. Neville (1975) Laid Artfully Together: Stanzaic Design in Milton's 'On the Morning of Christ's Nativity. In Maren-Sofie Røstvig, ed., *Fair Forms: Essays in English Literature from Spenser to Jane Austen*. Cambridge: D. S. Brewer, pp. 85–146.

Davies, J. C. (1986) *Fear, Myth and History: The Ranters and the Historians.* Cambridge: Cambridge University Press.

Davies, Julian (1992) *The Caroline Captivity of the Church: Charles I and the Remoulding of Anglicanism 1625–1641*. Oxford: Clarendon Press.

Davies, Michael (2002) 'Stout Valiant Champions for God': the Radical Reformation of Romance in *The Pilgrim's Progress*. In Keeble, ed. (2002b), pp. 103–32.

Dekker, Thomas (1604) *The Magnificent Entertainment*. London.

DNB (1975) *The Compact Edition of the Dictionary of National Biography.* Oxford: Oxford University Press.

DNB (2004) *Oxford Dictionary of National Biography: In Association with the British Academy: from the earliest times to the year 2000*, ed. H. C. G. Matthew and Brian Harrison. Oxford and New York: Oxford University Press.

Dobson, Michael (2000) Adaptations and revivals. In Fisk, ed. (2000), pp. 40–51.

Doerksen, Daniel W. (1997) *Conforming to the Word: Herbert, Donne, and the English Church Before Laud*. Lewisburg and London: Bucknell University Press and Associated University Presses.

Donne, John (1953–62) *The Sermons of John Donne*, ed. Evelyn M. Simpson and George R. Potter. Berkeley and Los Angeles: University of California Press.

Donne, John (1975) *Devotions Upon Emergent Occasions*, ed. Anthony Raspa. Montreal and London: McGill-Queen's University Press.

Donne, John (1978) *The Divine Poems*, ed. Helen Gardner, 2nd edn. Oxford: Clarendon Press.

Donne, John (1990) *John Donne*, ed. John Carey. Oxford: Oxford University Press.

Downie, J. A. (1994) *To Settle the Succession of the State: Literature and Politics, 1678–1750*. Houndmills: Macmillan.

Drayton, Michael (1931–41) *The Works of Michael Drayton*, ed. J. William Hebel. Oxford: Blackwell for the Shakespeare Head Press.

Dryden, John (1956–2000) *The Works of John Dryden*, ed. Edward Niles Hooker, H. T. Swedenberg, Jr. and Vinton A. Dearing. Berkeley: University of California Press.

Dryden, John (1995–2005) *The Poems of John Dryden*, ed. Paul Hammond. Harlow: Longman.

Dryden, John and Nathaniel Lee (1683) *The Duke of Guise*. London.

Duffy, Eamon (1992) *The Stripping of the Altars: Traditional Religion in England 1400–1580*. New Haven, CT: Yale University Press.

Duffy, Maureen (1977) *The Passionate Shepherdess: Aphra Behn, 1640–89*. London: Jonathan Cape.

Duncan-Jones, Katherine (2001) *Ungentle Shakespeare: Scenes from his Life*. London: The Arden Shakespeare.

Dzelzainis, Martin (1999) Marvell and the Earl of Castlemaine. In Chernaik and Dzelzainis, eds. (1999a), pp. 290–312.

Ellwood, Thomas (1714) *The History of the Life of T. E.* London.

Etherege, Sir George (1966) *The Man of Mode*, ed. W. B. Carnochan. Lincoln: University of Nebraska Press.

Fallon, Robert (1993) *Milton and Government*. University Park, PA: Pennsylvania State University Press.

Fane, Mildmay (2001) *The Poetry of Mildmay Fane, 2nd Earl of Westmorland*, ed. Tom Cain. Manchester and New York: Manchester University Press.

Fielding, John (1993) Arminianism in the Localities: Peterborough Diocese, 1603–1642. In Fincham, ed. (1993), pp. 93–113.

Fincham, Kenneth, ed. (1993) *The Early Stuart Church, 1603–1642*. Houndsmill, Basingstoke: Macmillan.

Fincham, Kenneth, and Peter Lake (1993) The Ecclesiastical Policies of James I and Charles I. In Fincham, ed. (1993), pp. 23–49.

Firth, C. H. and R. S. Rait (1911) *Acts and Ordinances of the Interregnum, 1642–1660*. London: HMSO.

Fish, Stanley (1971) *Surprised by Sin: The Reader in Paradise Lost*. Berkeley: University of California Press.

Fish, Stanley (1978) *The Living Temple: George Herbert and Catechizing*. Berkeley, Los Angeles and London: University of California Press.

Fisk, Deborah Payne (ed.) (2000) *The Cambridge Companion to English Restoration Theatre*. Cambridge: Cambridge University Press.

Fisk, Deborah Payne (2001) The Restoration Actress. In Owen, ed. (2001), pp. 69–91.

Ford, John (1965) *The Chronicle History of Perkin Warbeck*, ed. Peter Ure. London: Methuen.

Ford, John (1968) *The Broken Heart*, ed. Brian Morris. London: Ernest Benn.

Ford, John (1975) *'Tis Pity She's a Whore*, ed. Derek Roper. London: Methuen.

Fowler, Alastair (1970) *Triumphal Forms: Structural Patterns in Elizabethan Poetry.* Cambridge: Cambridge University Press.

Fowler, Alastair (1985) *Kinds of Literature: An Introduction to the Theory of Genres and Modes.* Oxford: Clarendon Press. First published 1982.

Fowler, Alastair (ed.) (1991) *The New Oxford Book of Seventeenth-Century Verse.* Oxford: Oxford University Press.

Fowler, Alastair (ed.) (1994) *The Country House Poem: A Cabinet of Seventeenth-Century Estate Poems and Related Items.* Edinburgh: Edinburgh University Press.

Fowler, Alastair (2003) *Renaissance Realism: Narrative Images in Literature and Art.* Oxford: Oxford University Press.

Fox, Alistair (1995) The Complaint of Poetry for the Death of Liberality: The Decline of Literary Patronage in the 1590s. In Guy, ed. (1995a), pp. 229–57.

Fox, George (1998) *The Journal*, ed. Nigel Smith. Harmondsworth: Penguin.

Frank, Joseph (1961) *The Beginnings of the English Newspaper 1620–1660.* Cambridge, MA: Harvard University Press.

Frank, Joseph (1980) *Cromwell's Press Agent: A Critical Biography of Marchamont Nedham, 1620–1678.* Lanham: University Press of America.

Freeman, Rosemary (1948) *English Emblem Books.* London: Chatto and Windus.

Gardiner, S. R. (1889) *History of the Great Civil War.* London: Longman, Greens, and Co,

Gardiner, S. R. (ed.) (1979) *The Constitutional Documents of the Puritan Revolution 1625–1660*, 3rd edn. Oxford: Clarendon Press. This edition first published 1906.

Goodwin, Thomas, Philip Nye, Sidrach Simpson, Jeremy Burroughs and William Bridge (1643) *An Apologeticall Narration, Humble Submitted to the Honourable Houses of Parliament.* London.

Greg, W. W. (1967), *A Companion to Arber.* Oxford: Clarendon Press.

Gowing, Laura (1998) *Domestic Dangers: Women, Words, and Sex in Early Modern London.* Oxford: Clarendon Press. First published 1996.

Greene, Graham (1974) *Lord Rochester's Monkey: Being the Life of John Wilmot, 2nd Earl of Rochester.* London: Bodley Head.

Guibbory, Achsah (1999) *Ceremony and Community from Herbert to Milton: Literature, Religion, and Cultural Conflict in Seventeenth-Century England.* Cambridge: Cambridge University Press. First published 1998.

Gurr, Andrew (1980) *The Shakespearean Stage 1574–1642*, 2nd edn. Cambridge: Cambridge University Press.

Gurr, Andrew (1996) *The Shakespearian Playing Companies*. Oxford: Clarendon Press.

Guy, John (ed.) (1995a) *The Reign of Elizabeth I: Court and Culture in the Last Decade*. Cambridge: Cambridge University Press.

Guy, John (1995b) The 1590s: The 2nd reign of Elizabeth I? In Guy, ed. (1995a), pp. 1–19.

Hammer, Paul E. J. (1995) Patronage at Court, Faction and the Earl of Essex. In Guy, ed. (1995a), pp. 87–108.

Hammer, Paul E. J. (1999) *The Polarisation of Elizabethan Politics: The Political Career of Robert Devereux, 2nd Earl of Essex, 1585–1597*. Cambridge: Cambridge University Press.

Hammond, Gerrald (1985) Richard Lovelace and the Uses of Obscurity. *Proceedings of the British Academy* 71: 203–34.

Hammond, Gerald (1990) *Fleeting Things: English Poets and Poems 1616–1660*. Cambridge, MA, and London: Harvard University Press.

Hardacre, Paul H. (1956) *The Royalists During the English Revolution*. The Hague: Mouton.

Harp, Richard (2000) Jonson's late plays. In Harp and Stewart, eds. (2000), pp. 90–102.

Harp, Richard and Stanley Stewart (eds.) (2000) *The Cambridge Companion to Ben Jonson*. Cambridge: Cambridge University Press.

Harrison, Stephen (1604) *The Arches of Triumph*. London.

Healy, Thomas F. (1986) *Richard Crawshaw*. Leiden: E. J. Brill.

Healy, Thomas and Jonathan Sawday (eds.) (1990) *Literature and the English Civil War*. Cambridge: Cambridge University Press.

Henslowe, Philip (1904–8) *Henslowe's Diary*, ed. W. W. Greg. London: Bullen.

Herbert, George (1633) *The Temple*. Cambridge.

Herbert, George (1652) *Herberts Remains or, Sundry Pieces*. London

Herbert, George (1941) *The Works of George Herbert*, ed. F. E. Hutchinson. Oxford: Clarendon Press.

Herrick, Robert (1956) *The Poetical Works of Robert Herrick*, ed. L. C. Martin. Oxford: Clarendon Press.

Hill, Christopher (1978) The Religion of Gerrard Winstanley. *Past and Present*, supplement 5.

Hill, Christopher (1989) *A Turbulent, Seditious, and Factious People: John Bunyan and his Church 1628–1688*. Oxford: Oxford University Press. First published 1988.

Hirst, Derek (1975) *The Representative of the People? Voters and Voting in England under the Early Stuarts*. Cambridge: Cambridge University Press.

Hobby, Elaine (1988) *Virtue of Necessity: English Women's Writing 1646–1688*. London: Virago.

Hobby, Elaine (1995) Handmaids of the Lord and Mothers in Israel: Early Vindications of Quaker Women's Prophecy. In Corns and Loewenstein, eds. (1995), pp. 88–98.

Holman, Peter (1993) *Four and Twenty Fiddlers: The Violin at the English Court, 1540–1690* Oxford: Oxford University Press.

Hoover, David and Thomas N. Corns (2004) The Authorship of the Post-script to *An Answer to a Booke Entituled, An Humble Remonstrance. Milton Quarterly*, 38, 59–75.

Houlbrooke, Ralph (2000) *Death, Religion and the Family in England 1480–1750*. Oxford: Oxford University Press. First published 1998.

Howard, Sir Robert (1665) *The Committee*. London

Howarth, David (1997) *Images of Rule: Art and Politics in the English Renaissance, 1485–1649*. Basingstoke: Macmillan.

Howe, Elizabeth (1992) *The First English Actresses: Women and Drama 1660–1700*. Cambridge: Cambridge University Press.

Hughes, Ann (1991) *The Causes of the English Civil War*. London: Macmillan.

Hughes, Derek (1996) *English Drama 1660–1700*. Oxford: Clarendon.

Hutchinson, Lucy (1995) *Memoirs of the Life of Colonel Hutchinson*, ed. N. H. Keeble. London and Vermont: Dent and Tuttle.

Hutchinson, Lucy (2001) *Order and Disorder*, ed. David Norbrook. Oxford: Blackwell.

Hutner, Heidi (ed.) (1993a) *Rereading Aphra Behn: History, Theory, and Criticism*. Charlottesville and London: University of Virginia Press.

Hutner, Heidi (1993b) Revisioning the Female Body: Aphra Behn's *The Rover*, Parts I and II. In Hutner, ed. (1993a), pp. 102–20.

Hutton, Ronald (1991) *Charles II*. Oxford: Oxford University Press. First published 1989.

Hughes, Ann (1991) *The Causes of the English Civil War*. Basingstoke: Macmillan.

James VI and I (1598) *Trew Law of Free Monarchies*. Edinburgh.

James VI and I (1599) *Basilikon Doron*. Edinburgh.

James VI and I (1994) *Political Writings*, ed. Johann P. Sommerville. Cambridge: Cambridge University Press.

Jardine, Lisa and Alan Stewart (1998) *Hostage to Fortune: The Troubled Life of Francis Bacon*. London: Gollancz.

Jensen, Kristian (1996), The Humanist Reform of Latin and Latin Teaching. In Kraye, ed. (1996), pp. 63–81.

Jonson, Ben (1604) *B. Ion: his part of King Iames his royall and magnificent entertainment*. London.

Jonson, Ben (1616) *The Workes of Benjamin Jonson*. London.

Jonson, Ben (1925–52) *Ben Jonson*, ed. C. H. Herford, Percy and Evelyn Simpson. Oxford: Clarendon Press.

Jonson, Ben (1965) *Sejanus*, ed. Jonas A. Barish. New Haven and London: Yale University Press.

Jonson, Ben (1976) *The Workes of Benjamin Jonson 1616*. Introduction by D. Heyward Brock. Ilkley: Scolar Press.

Jonson, Ben (1985) *Ben Jonson*, ed. Ian Donaldson. Oxford and New York: Oxford University Press.

Jonson, Ben, George Chapman and John Marston (1973) *Eastward Ho!* ed. C. G. Petter. Tonbridge: Benn.

Kastan, D. S. (1982) *Shakespeare and the Shapes of Time*. London: Macmillan.

Keeble. N. H. (1990) 'The Colonel's Shadow': Lucy Hutchinson, Women's Writing and the Civil War. In Healy and Sawday, eds. (1990), pp. 227–47.

Keeble, N. H. (1999) Why Transpose *the Rehearsal?* In Chernaik and Dzelzainis, eds. (1999a), pp. 249–66.

Keeble, N. H. (ed.) (2001) *The Cambridge Companion to Writing of the English Revolution*. Cambridge: Cambridge University Press.

Keeble, N. H. (2002a) *The Restoration: England in the 1660s*. Oxford: Blackwell.

Keeble, N. H. (ed.) (2002b) *John Bunyan: Reading Dissenting Writing*. Bern: Peter Lang.

Killigrew, Thomas (1664) *Thomaso*. London.

Kishlansky, Mark (1986) *Parliamentary Selection: Social and Political Choice in Early Modern England*. Cambridge: Cambridge University Press.

Knoppers, Laura Lunger (1994) *Historicizing Milton: Spectacle, Power, and Poetry in Restoration England*. Athens, Georgia, and London: University of Georgia Press.

Knoppers, Laura Lunger (1999) Reviving the Martyr King: Charles I as Jacobite Icon. In Corns, ed. (1999a), pp. 263–87.

Knoppers, Laura Lunger (2000) *Constructing Cromwell: Ceremony, Portrait, and Print, 1645–1661*. Cambridge: Cambridge University Press.

Kraye, Jill (ed.) (1996) *The Cambridge Companion to Renaissance Humanism*. Cambridge: Cambridge University Press.

Lake, Peter (1993) The Laudian Style: Order, Uniformity and the Pursuit of the Beauty of Holiness in the 1630s. In Fincham, ed. (1993), pp. 161–85.

Langhans, Edward A. (2000) The Theatre. In Fisk, ed. (2000), pp. 1–18.

Lawes, Henry (1669) *The Treasury of Musick: containing Ayres and Dialogues... composed by Mr Henry Lawes... and other Excellent Masters*. London.

Lawes, Henry (1988) *Sitting by the Streams*. Performed by the Consort of Musicke, directed by Anthony Rooley. Hyperion CDA66135.

Lawes, Henry (1993) *Goe, lovely rose*. Performed by Nigel Rogers, Paul O'Dette and Frances Kelly. Virgin VC5450042.

Lee, Maurice, Jr. (1990) *Great Britain's Solomon: James VI and I in His Three Kingdoms*. Urbana and Chicago: University of Illinois Press.

Levine, Laura (1994) *Men in Women's Clothing: Anti-Theatricality and Effeminization, 1579–1642.* Cambridge: Cambridge University Press.

Lewalski, Barbara K. (1966) *Milton's Brief Epic: the Genre, Meaning, and Art of Paradise Regained.* Providence, RI, and London: Brown University Press and Methuen.

Lewalski. Barbara K. (1979) *Protestant Poetics and the Seventeenth-Century Religious Lyric.* Princeton: Princeton University Press.

Lewalski, Barbara K. (1994) *Writing Women in Jacobean England.* Cambridge, MA: Harvard University Press. First published 1993.

Lewalski, Barbara K. (2000) *The Life of John Milton.* Oxford: Blackwell.

Lewalski, Barbara K. (2001) Genre. In Corns, ed. (2001a), pp. 3–21.

Lewalski, Barbara K. (2002) 'Literature and the Household.' In Loewenstein and Mueller, eds. (2002), pp. 603–32.

Lindley, David, ed. (1995) *Court Masques: Jacobean and Caroline Entertainments 1605–1640.* Oxford and New York: Oxford University Press.

Lockyer, Roger (1981) *Buckingham: The Life and Political Career of George Villiers, First Duke of Buckingham 1592–1628.* London and New York: Longman.

Loewenstein, David (1995) The War of the Lamb: George Fox and the Apocalyptic Discourse of Revolutionary Quakerism. In Corns and Loewenstein, eds. (1995), pp. 25–41.

Loewenstein, David (2001) *Representing Revolution in Milton and his Contemporaries.* Cambridge: Cambridge University Press.

Loewenstein, David and John Morrill (2002) Literature and Religion. In Loewenstein and Mueller, eds. (2002), pp. 664–713.

Loewenstein, David and Janel Mueller (eds.) (2002) *The Cambridge History of Early Modern English Literature.* Cambridge: Cambridge University Press.

Loewenstein, David and James Grantham Turner (1990) *Politics, Poetics, and Hermeneutics in Milton's Prose.* Cambridge: Cambridge University Press.

Loftis, John, ed. (1979) *The Memoirs of Anne, Lady Halkett and Ann, Lady Fanshawe.* Oxford: Clarendon Press.

Love, Harold (1993) *Scribal Publication in Seventeenth-Century England.* Oxford: Clarendon Press.

Love, Harold (2002) Oral and Scribal Texts in Early Modern England. In Barnard and McKenzie, eds. (2002), pp. 97–121.

Love, Harold and Arthur F. Marotti (2002) Manuscript Transmission and Circulation. In Loewenstein and Mueller, eds. (2002), pp. 55–80.

Lovelace, Richard (1930) *The Poems of Richard Lovelace,* ed. C. H. Wilkinson. Oxford: Clarendon Press.

Loxley, James (1997) *Royalism and Poetry in the English Civil Wars: The Drawn Sword.* Houndmills: Macmillan and New York: St Martin's Press.

McColley, Diane (1997) *Poetry and Music in Seventeenth-Century England.* Cambridge: Cambridge University Press.

McEachern, Claire, ed. (2002) *The Cambridge Companion to Shakespearean Tragedy.* Cambridge: Cambridge University Press.

McKenzie, D. F. (2002) Printing and Publishing 1557–1700: Constraints on the London Book Trades. In Barnard and McKenzie, eds. (2002), pp. 553–67.

Maclure, Millar (1958) *The Paul's Cross Sermons 1534–1642.* Toronto: University of Toronto Press.

McManus, Clare (2002) *Women on the Renaissance State: Anna of Denmark and Female Masquing in the Stuart Court.* Manchester and New York: Manchester University Press.

Malcolm, Noel (1984) *De Dominis (1560–1624): Venetian, Anglican, Ecumenist and Relapsed Heretic.* London: Strickland Scott.

Manley, Lawrence (1995) *Literature and Culture in Early Modern London.* Cambridge: Cambridge University Press.

Maltby, Judith (2000) *Prayer Book and People in Elizabethan and Early Stuart England.* Cambridge: Cambridge University Press. First published 1998.

Manning, Brian (1976) *The English People and the English Revolution 1640–49.* London: Heinemann.

Manning, John (2002) *The Emblem.* London: Reaktion.

Marotti, Arthur (1993) Manuscript, Print, and the Social History of the Lyric. In Corns, ed. (1993a), pp. 52–79.

Marshall, G. W. (1993) *A Great Stage of Fools: Theatricality and Madness in the Plays of William Wycherley.* New York: AMS Press.

Marston, John (1999) *The Malcontent*, ed. George K. Hunter. Manchester and New York: Manchester University Press. First published 1975.

Marvell, Andrew (1971) *The Poems and Letters of Andrew Marvell*, ed. H. M. Margoliouth. 3rd edn, revised by Pierre Legouis with E. E. Duncan-Jones. Oxford: Clarendon Press.

Marvell, Andrew (2003a) *The Poems of Andrew Marvell*, ed. Nigel Smith. London: Pearson Longman.

Marvell, Andrew (2003b) *The Prose Works of Andrew Marvell*, ed. Annabel Patterson et al. New Haven and London: Yale University Press.

Massinger, Philip (1964a) *A New Way to Pay Old Debts*, ed. T. W. Craik. London: Ernest Benn.

Massinger, Philip (1964b) *The City-Madam*, ed. T. W. Craik. London: Ernest Benn.

Masten, Jeff (1998) ' "Shall I turne blabb?"'; Circulation, Gender, and Subjectivity in Mary Wroth's Sonnets. In Pacheco ed. (1998), pp. 25–44.

Middleton, Thomas (1619) *The Triumphs of Love and Antiquity.* London.

Middleton, Thomas (1621) *The Sunne in Aries.* London.

Middleton, Thomas (1622) *The Triumphs of Honour and Virtue.* London.

Middleton, Thomas (1623) *The Triumphs of Integrity.* London.

Middleton, Thomas (1626) *The Triumphs of Health and Prosperity.* London.

Middleton, Thomas (1965) *A Mad World, My Masters*, ed. Standish Henning. London: Arnold.

Middleton, Thomas (1968) *A Chaste Maid in Cheapside*, ed. Alan Brissenden. London: Benn.

Middleton, Thomas and William Rowley (1964) *The Changeling*, ed. Patricia Thomson. London: Ernest Benn.

Middleton, Thomas (1975) *Women Beware Women*, ed. J. R. Mulryne. London: Methuen.

Middleton, Thomas (1993) *A Game at Chess*, ed. T. H. Howard-Hill. Manchester and New York: Manchester University Press.

Middleton, Thomas and William Rowley (2003) *Y Ffeirio* [*The Changeling*]. Translated and adapted by Nic Ros; performed Theatr Gwynedd, Bangor, 10–11 April 2003.

Miller, John (2000) *James II*. New Haven and London: Yale University Press. First published 1978.

Milton, Anthony (1995) *Catholic and Reformed: The Roman and Protestant Churches in English Protestant Thought 1600–1640*. Cambridge: Cambridge University Press.

Milton, John (1645) *The Poems of Mr John Milton, Both English and Latin, Compos'd at several times*. London

Milton, John (1953–82) *Complete Prose Works of John Milton*, ed. Don M. Wolfe et al. New Haven: Yale University Press.

Milton, John (1972) *Poems Reproduced in Facsimile from the Manuscript in Trinity College, Cambridge, with a Transcript*. Menston: Scolar.

Milton, John (1997) *Complete Shorter Poems*, ed. John Carey, 2nd edn. London and New York: Longman.

Milton, John (1999) *Paradise Lost*, ed. Alastair Fowler. 2nd edn. London and New York: Longman. First published 1998.

Milward, Peter (1977) *Religious Controversies of the Elizabethan Age: A Survey of Printed Sources*. London: Scolar.

Milward, Peter (1978) *Religious Controversies of the Jacobean Age: A Survey of Printed Sources*. London: Scolar.

Miner, Earl (1971) *The Cavalier Mode from Jonson to Cotton*. Princeton: Princeton University Press.

Morrill, John (1976) *The Revolt of the Provinces: Conservatives and Radicals in the English Civil War 1630–1650*. London: Allen and Unwin.

Morrill, John (1993) *The Nature of the English Revolution*. London and New York: Longman.

Moorman, F. W. (1910) *Robert Herrick: A Bibliographical and Critical Study*. London and New York: T. Nelson.

Morton, A. L. (1975) *Freedom in Arms: A Selection of Leveller Writings*. London: Lawrence and Wishart.

Nedham, Marchamont (1650–60) *Mercurius Politicus*. London.

Nedham, Marchamont (1659) *Interest will not Lie. Or, a View of England's True Interest.* London.

Nelson, Carolyn and Matthew Seccombe (2002) The Creation of the Periodical Press 1620–1695. In Barnard and McKenzie, eds. (2002), pp. 533–50.

Nethercot, Arthur H. (1931) *Abraham Cowley: The Muse's Hannibal.* London: Oxford University Press.

Newey, Vincent, ed. (1980) *The Pilgrim's Progress: Critical and Historical Views.* Liverpool: Liverpool University Press.

Nicholl, Charles (1984) *A Cup of News: The Life of Thomas Nashe.* London: Routledge and Kegan Paul.

Nichols, Philip (1626) *Sir Francis Drake Revived Calling on this dull and effeminate age, to follow his noble steps.* London.

Norbrook, David (1984) *Poetry and Politics in the English Renaissance.* London, Boston, Melbourne and Henley: Routledge & Kegan Paul.

Norbrook, David (1999) *Writing the English Republic: Poetry, Rhetoric and Politics, 1627–1660.* Cambridge: Cambridge University Press.

Norbrook, David (2002) *Poetry and Politics in the English Renaissance.* 2nd edn. Oxford and New York: Oxford University Press.

Nutall, A. D. (1980) *Overheard by God: Fiction and Prayer in Herbert, Milton, Dante and St John.* London and New York: Methuen.

Nyquist, Mary (1988) The Genesis of Gendered Subjectivity in the Divorce Tracts and in *Paradise Lost.* In Nyquist and Ferguson, eds. (1988), pp. 99–127.

Nyquist, Mary and Margaret W. Ferguson (eds.) (1988) *Remembering Milton: Essays on the Texts and Traditions.* London and New York: Methuen. First published 1987.

Ogg, David (1965) *Europe in the Seventeenth Century,* 9th edn. London: Adam and Charles Black.

O Hehir, Brendan (1968) *Harmony from Discords: A Life of Sir John Denham.* Berkeley and Los Angeles: University of California Press.

O Hehir, Brendan (1969) *Expans'd Hieroglyphicks: A Critical Edition of Sir John Denham's* Coopers Hill. Berkeley and Los Angeles: University of California Press.

Orgel, Stephen and Roy Strong (eds.) (1973) *Inigo Jones: The Theatre of the Stuart Court.* Berkeley and London: University of California Press and Sotheby Parke Bernet.

Orrell, John (1985) *The Theatres of Inigo Jones and John Webb.* Cambridge: Cambridge University Press.

Overbury, Sir Thomas (1890) *The Miscellaneous Works in Prose and Verse of Sir Thomas Overbury, Knt,* ed. Edward F. Rimbault. London: Reeves and Turner.

Owen, Susan J. (1996) *Restoration Theatre and Crisis.* Oxford: Clarendon Press.

Owen, Susan J. (ed.) (2001) *A Companion to Restoration Drama*. Oxford: Blackwell.

Pacheco, Anita (ed.) (1998) *Early Women Writers: 1600–1720*. London and New York: Longman.

Pacheco, Anita (ed.) (2002) *A Companion to Early Modern Women's Writing*. Oxford: Blackwell.

Palliser, D. M. (1983) *The Age of Elizabeth: England under the later Tudors 1547–1603*. London and New York: Longman.

Parker, William Riley (1968) *Milton: A Biography*. Oxford: Clarendon.

Parker, William Riley (1996) *Milton: A Biography*. 2nd edn, ed. Gordon Campbell. Oxford: Clarendon.

Parr, Anthony, ed. (1995) *Three Renaissance travel plays*. Manchester and New York: Manchester University Press.

Parry, Graham (1981) *The Golden Age Restor'd: The Culture of the Stuart Court*. Manchester: Manchester University Press.

Parry, Graham (1985) *Seventeenth-Century Poetry: The Social Context*. London: Hutchinson.

Parry, Graham (1995) *The Trophies of Time: English Antiquarians of the Seventeenth Century*. Oxford and New York: Oxford University Press.

Parry, Graham (2001) Literary Baroque and Literary Neoclassicism. In Corns, ed. (2001a), pp. 55–71.

Parry, Graham (2002) Literary patronage. In Loewenstein and Mueller, eds. (2002), pp. 117–40.

Parry, Graham and Joad Raymond, eds. (2002) *Milton and the Terms of Liberty*. Cambridge: Brewer.

Patrides, C. A. (ed.) (1983) *George Herbert: The Critical Heritage*. London: Routledge & Kegan Paul.

Peacock, John (1995) *The Stage Designs of Inigo Jones: The European Context*. Cambridge: Cambridge University Press.

Peacock, John (1999) The Visual Image of Charles I. In Corns, ed. (1999a), pp. 176–239.

Pennington, Donald and Keith Thomas (eds.) (1978) *Puritans and Revolutionaries*. Oxford: Clarendon Press.

Pepys, Samuel (1970–83) *The Diary*, ed. Robert Latham and William Matthews. Berkeley and Los Angeles: University of California Press.

Peters, Kate (1995) Patterns of Quaker Authorship, 1652–56. In Corns and Loewenstein, eds. (1995), pp. 6–24.

Philips, Katherine (1990) *The Collected Works of Katherine Philips The Matchless Orinda, volume I, The Poems*. Stump Cross: Stump Cross Books.

Pitcher, John (2002) Literature, the Playhouse and the Public. In Barnard and McKenzie, eds. (2002), pp. 351–75.

Polisensky, J. V. (1974) *The Thirty Years War*. trans. Robert Evans. London: New English Library. First published in Czech 1970; this translation 1971.

Post, Jonathan F. S. (1982) *Henry Vaughan: The Unfolding Vision.* Princeton: Princeton University Press.

Post, Jonathan F. S. (1999) *English Lyric Poetry: The Early Seventeenth Century.* London and New York: Routledge.

Potter, Lois (1989) *Secret Rites and Secret Writing: Royalist Literature, 1641–1660.* Cambridge: Cambridge University Press.

Potter, Lois (1999) The Royal Martyr in the Restoration. In Corns, ed. (1999a), pp. 240–62.

Prawer, S. S. (1976) *Karl Marx and World Literature.* Oxford: Clarendon Press.

Prest, Wilfrid R. (1972) *The Inns of Court under Elizabeth I and the Early Stuarts 1590–1640.* London: Longman.

Purkiss, Diane (ed.) (1994) *Renaissance Women: The Plays of Elizabeth Cary; The Poems of Aemilia Lanyer.* London: William Pickering.

Quarles, Francis (1620) *A Feast for Wormes.* London.

Quarles, Francis (1621) *Hadassa: or, The History of Queene Ester.* London.

Quarles, Francis (1624) *Iob Militant.* London.

Quarles, Francis (1631) *The Historie of Samson.* London.

Quarles, Francis (1635) *Emblemes.* London.

Quarles, Francis (1638) *Hieroglyphikes of the life of Man.* London.

Raymond, Joad (1993) *Making the News: An Anthology of the Newsbooks of Revolutionary England 1641–1660.* Moreton-in-Marsh: Windrush Press.

Raymond, Joad (1996) *The Invention of the Newspaper: English Newsbooks 1641–1649.* Oxford: Clarendon Press.

Reay, Barry (1985) *The Quakers and the English Revolution.* London: Temple Smith.

Reed, J. C. (1927–30) Humphrey Moseley, Publisher, *Oxford Bibliographical Society Proceedings and Papers*, 2: 57–142.

Richardson, R. C. (1977) *The Debate on the English Revolution.* London: Methuen.

Rhodes, Neil and Jonathan Sawday (2000) *The Renaissance Computer: Knowledge technology in the first age of print.* London and New York: Routledge.

Righter, Anne (1962) *Shakespeare and the Idea of the Play.* London: Chatto and Windus.

Riggs, David (1989) *Ben Jonson: A Life.* Cambridge, MA, and London: Harvard University Press.

Rivers, Isabel (2001) Prayer-Book Devotion: The Literature of the Proscribed Episcopal Church. In Keeble, ed. (2001), pp. 198–214.

Roach, Joseph (2000) The Performance. In Fisk, ed. (2000), pp. 19–39.

Rochester, John Wilmot, 2nd Earl of (1999) *The Works of John Wilmot, Earl of Rochester*, ed. Harold Love. Oxford: Oxford University Press.

Rooley, Anthony (1990) *John Blow,* Venus and Adonis *and Christopher Gibbons and Matthew Locke,* Cupid and Death. Performed by the Consort of Musicke under the direction of Anthony Rooley. Freiburg: Deutsche Harmonia Mundi. GD77117.

Røstvig, Maren-Sofie (1994) *Configurations: A Topomorphical Approach to Renaissance Poetry.* Oslo, Copenhagen and Stockholm: Scandinavian University Press.

Rowse, A. L. (1974) *Simon Forman: Sex and Society in Shakespeare's Age.* London: Weidenfeld and Nicolson.

Rowse, A. L. (1978) *The Poems of Shakespeare's Dark Lady: Salve Deus Rex Judeorum by Emilia Lanyer,* London: Cape.

Russell, Bertrand (1946) *History of Western Philosophy and its Connection with Political and Social Circumstances from the Earlist Times to the Present Day.* London: George Allen and Unwin.

Russell, Conrad, ed. (1973) *The Origins of the English Civil War.* London and Basingstoke: Macmillan.

Russell, Conrad (1995) *The Fall of the British Monarchies 1637–1642.* Oxford: Clarendon Press. First published 1991.

St Nicholas, Thomas (2002) *At Vacant Hours: Poems by Thomas St Nicholas and his Family,* ed. H. Neville Davies. Birmingham: Birmingham University Press.

Salzman, Paul (1985) *English Prose Fiction 1558–1700: A Critical History.* Oxford: Clarendon Press.

Schleiner, Louise (1976) Herrick's Songs and the Character of *Hesperides. ELR* 6: 77–91.

Schoenbaum, S. (1975) *William Shakespeare: A Documenatry Life.* Oxford: Clarendon Press.

Schoenfeldt, Michael C. (1991) *Prayer and Power: George Herbert and Renaissance Courtship.* Chicago and London: University of Chicago Press.

Scott, David (2003) The Wars of the Three Kingdoms. In Coward, ed. (2003), pp. 311–30.

Scott, Jonathan (1991) *Algernon Sidney and the Restoration Crisis, 1677– 1683.* Cambridge: Cambridge University Press.

Shakespeare, William (1623) *Mr. William Shakespeares Comedies, Histories, & Tragedies.* London.

Shakespeare, William (1989) *The Complete Works,* ed. Stanley Wells et al. Oxford: Clarendon Press. First published 1988.

Shakespeare, William (1997) *Cymbeline,* ed. Roger Warren. Oxford: Clarendon Press.

Shakespeare, William (1998) *Pericles,* ed. Doreen DelVecchio and Antony Hammond. Cambridge: Cambridge University Press.

Shakespeare, William (2002) *The Complete Sonnets and Poems,* ed. Colin Burrow. Oxford: Oxford University Press.

Sharpe, Jim (1995) 'Social Strain and Social Dislocation, 1585–1603. In Guy (1995a), pp. 192–211.

Sharpe, Kevin (1992) *The Personal Rule of Charles I.* New Haven and London: Yale University Press.

Sharpe, Kevin and Peter Lake (eds.) (1994) *Culture and Politics in Early Stuart England* Basingstoke and London: Macmillan.

Shirley, James (1637) *The Lady of Pleasure.* London.

Shirley, James (1973) *The Lady of Pleasure.* Introduced by John P. Turner, Jr. Menston and London: Scolar Press.

Shirley, James (1987), *Hyde Park,* ed. Simon Trussler. London: Methuen.

Siebert, Frederick S. (1952) *Freedom of the Press in England 1476–1776: The Rise and Decline of Government Controls.* Urbana: University of Illinois Press.

Slatier, William (1619) *Threnodia.* London.

Smith, Nigel (1983), ed., *A Collection of Ranter Writings from the 17th Century.* London: Junction.

Smith, Nigel (1989) *Perfection Proclaimed: Language and Literature in English Radical Religion 1640–1660.* Oxford: Clarendon Press.

Smith, Nigel (1994) *Literature and Revolution in England 1640–1660.* New Haven and London: Yale University Press.

Smith, Nigel (2002) Literature and London. In Loewenstein and Mueller, eds. (2002), pp. 714–36.

Smuts, R. Malcolm (ed.) (1996a) *The Stuart Court and Europe: Essays in Politics and Political Culture.* Cambridge: Cambridge University Press.

Smuts, R. Malcolm (1996b) Art and the Material Culture of Majesty in early Stuart England. In Smuts, ed. (1996a), pp. 86–112.

Spargo, Tamsin (2002) Bunyans Abounding, or the Names of the Author. In Keeble, ed. (2002b), pp. 79–102.

Spink, Ian (1986) *English Song: Dowland to Purcell.* London: Batsford. First published 1974.

Spufford, Margaret (1979) First Steps in Literacy: The Reading and Writing Experiences of the Humblest Seventeenth-Century Autobiographers. *Social History* 4: 407–35.

Spufford, Margaret (ed.) (1995) *The World of Rural Dissenters, 1520–1725.* Cambridge: Cambridge University Press.

Spurr, John (1991) *The Restoration Church of England, 1646–1689.* New Haven: Yale University Press.

Spurr, John (2000) *England in the 1670s: 'The Masquerading Age'.* Oxford: Blackwell.

Stearns, Raymond Phineas (1954) *The Strenuous Puritan: Hugh Peter 1598–1660.* Urbana: University of Illinois Press.

Stone, Lawrence (1979) *The Family, Sex and Marriage in England 1500–1800.* Abridged edn. Harmondsworth: Penguin.

Strier, Richard (1983) *Love Known: Theology and Experience in George Herbert's Poetry.* Chicago and London: University of Chicago Press.

Strong, Roy (1972) *Van Dyck: Charles I on Horseback.* London: Allen Lane The Penguin Press.

Strong, Roy (1986) *Henry, Prince of Wales and England's Lost Renaissance.* London: Thames and Hudson.

Suckling, Sir John (1638) *Aglaura.* London.

Suckling, Sir John (1971a) *The Works of Sir John Suckling: The Non-Dramatic Works,* ed. Thomas Clayton. Oxford: Clarendon Press.

Suckling, Sir John (1971b) *The Works of Sir John Suckling: The Plays,* ed. L. A. Beaurline. Oxford: Clarendon Press.

Sullivan, Ceri (2002) *The Rhetoric of Credit: Merchants in Early Modern Writing.* Cranbury, NJ, and London: Associated University Presses.

Sylvester, Josuah (1612) *Lachrimae Lachrimarum; or, The Distillation of Teares Shede for the Untimely Death of the Incomparable Prince Panaretus.* London.

Sylvester, Josuah (1979) *The Divine Weeks and Works of Guillaume de Saluste Sieur du Bartas,* trans. Josuah Sylvester, ed. Susan Snyder. Oxford: Clarendon Press.

Taylor, John (1644) *Crop-Eare Curried, or, Tom Nash His Ghost.* n.p.

Taylor, John (1645) *Rebells Anathematized, And anatomized: or, A Satyricall Salutation to the Rabble of seditous, pestiferous pulpit-praters, with their Brethren the Weekly Libellers.* Oxford.

Theophrastus (2002) *Characters,* ed. and trans. Jeffrey Ruston. Cambridge, MA: Harvard University Press.

Thomas, David and Arnold Hare (1989) *Restoration and Georgian England, 1660–88. Theatre in Europe: A Documentary History.* Cambridge: Cambridge University Press.

Thomas, Keith (1978) The Puritans and Adultery: The Act of 1650 Reconsidered. In Pennington and Thomas, eds. (1978), pp. 257–82.

Thomas, Keith (1986) The Meaning of Literacy in Early Modern England. In Baumann, ed. (1986), pp. 97–131.

Thormälen, Marianne (1993) *Rochester: The Poems in Context.* Cambridge: Cambridge University Press.

Todd, Janet (1996) *The Secret Life of Aphra Behn.* London: Andre Deutsch.

Tourneur, Cyril (1964) *The Atheist's Tragedy,* ed. Irving Ribner. London: Methuen.

Tourneur, Cyril (attrib.) (1966) *The Revenger's Tragedy,* ed. R. A. Foakes. London: Methuen.

Townsend, Aurelian (1983) *The Poems and Masques of Aurelian Townshend,* ed. Cedric C. Brown. Reading: Whiteknight Press.

Trevor-Roper, H. R. (1962) *Archbishop Laud 1573–1645.* 2nd edn. London: Macmillan.

Turner, James Grantham (1999) Libertine Abject: The 'Postures' of *The Last Instructions to a Painter.* In Chernaik and Dzelzainis, eds. (1999a), pp. 217–48.

Turner, James Grantham (2002) *Libertines and Radicals in Early Modern London: Sexuality, Politics and Literary Culture, 1630–1685.* Cambridge: Cambridge University Press.

Tyacke, Nicholas (1973) Puritanism, Arminianism and Counter-Reformation. In Russell, ed. (1973), pp. 119–43.

Tyacke, Nicholas (1987) *Anti-Calvinists: The Rise of English Arminianism, c.1590–1640.* Oxford: Clarendon Press.

Underdown, David E. (1960) *Royalist Conspiracy in England 1649–1660.* New Haven: Yale University Press.

Underdown, David E. (1985) *Revel, Riot, and Rebellion: Popular Politics and Culture in England 1603–1660.* Oxford: Clarendon Press.

Valdes, Juan de (1638) *The Hundred and Ten Considerations of Signior Iohn Valdesso*, trans. Nicholas Ferrar; epistle and notes by George Herbert. Oxford.

Van den Berg, Sara (2000) True Relation: The Life and Career of Ben Jonson. In Harp and Stewart (2000), pp. 1–14.

Van Lennep, William et al. (1965) *The London Stage 1660–1800*, ed. William Van Lennep, with a critical introduction by Emmett L. Avery and Arthur H. Scouten. Carbondale: Southern Illinois University Press.

Vaughan, Henry (1957) *The Works of Henry Vaughan*, ed. L. C. Martin. 2nd edn. Oxford: Clarendon Press.

Veevers, Erica (1989) *Images of Love and Religion: Queen Henrietta Maria and Court Entertainments.* Cambridge: Cambridge University Press.

Vendler, Helen (1975) *The Poetry of George Herbert.* Cambridge, MA, and London: Harvard University Press.

Vickers, Brian (2002) *Shakespeare, Co-Author: A Historical Study of Five Collaborative Plays.* Oxford: Oxford University Press.

Von Maltzahn, Nicholas (1999) Marvell's Ghosts. In Chernaik and Dzelzainis, eds. (1999a), pp. 50–74.

Wainwright, Jonathan P. (1999) The King's Music. In Corns, ed. (1999a), pp. 162–75.

Waller, Edmund (1645) *Poems, &c.* London.

Waller, Edmund (1655) *A Panegyrick to my Lord Protector.* London.

Waller, Edmund (1666) *Instructions to a Painter For the Drawing of the Postures and Progress of His Ma[jes]ties Forces at Sea.* London.

Walls, Peter (1996) *Music in the English Courtly Masque 1604–1640.* Oxford: Clarendon Press.

Walton, Izaak (1983) *The Compleat Angler 1653–1676*, ed. Jonquil Bevan. Oxford: Clarendon Press.

Watt, Tessa (1991) *Cheap Print and Popular Piety 1550–1640.* Cambridge: Cambridge University Press.

Watt, Tessa (1995) Piety in the Pedlar's Pack: Continuity and Change, 1578–1630. In Spufford, ed. (1995), pp. 235–72.

W[eaver], T[homas] (1654) *Songs and Poems of Love and Drollery.* n.p.

Webster, John (1972) *Three Plays.*, ed. D. C. Gunby. Harmondsworth: Penguin.

Wedgwood, C. V. (1966) *The Trial of Charles I.* London: The Reprint Society. First published 1964.

West, Anthony James (2001) *The Shakespeare First Folio: The History of the Book. Volume I: An Account of the First Folio Based on its Sales and Prices, 1623–2000.* Oxford: Oxford University Press.

Wheeler, Elizabeth Skerpan (1999) *Eikon Basilike* and the Rhetoric of Self-Representation. In Corns, ed. (1999a), pp. 122–40.

Wickham, Glynne, Herbert Berry and William Ingram (eds.) (2000) *English Professional Theatre, 1530–1660.* Cambridge: Cambridge University Press.

Wilcher, Robert (2001), *The Writing of Royalism 1628–1660.* Cambridge: Cambridge University Press.

Wilding, Michael (1987) *Dragons Teeth: Literature in the English Revolution.* Oxford: Clarendon Press.

Williams, John (1625) *Great Britains Salomon. A Sermon Preached at the Magnificent Funerall, of the most high and mighty King, James.* London.

Williamson, George (1966) *The Senecan Amble: Prose from Bacon to Collier.* Chicago: Phoenix Books. First published 1951.

Wilcher, Robert (2001) *The Writing of Royalism 1628–1660.* Cambridge: Cambridge

Winn, James Anderson (1987) *John Dryden and His World.* New Haven and London: Yale University Press.

Winstanley, Gerrard (1941) *The Works of Gerrard Winstanley,* ed. George H. Sabine. Ithaca, NY: Cornell University Press.

Wiseman, Susan (1998) *Drama and Politics in the English Civil War.* Cambridge: Cambridge University Press.

Wither, George (n.d.) *The Schollers Purgatory, discovered in the Stationers Common-wealth.* London.

Wither, George (1621) *Withers Motto. Nec Habeo, nec Careo, nec Curo.* 2nd edn. STC 25928.7. London.

Wither, George (1623) *The Hymnes and Songs of the Church.* London.

Wither, George (1635) *A Collection of Emblemes, Ancient and Moderne.* STC 25900b. London.

Wither, George (1643) *Campo-Musae, or The field-musings of Captain George Wither.* London.

Wither, George (1655) *The Protector.* London.

Wittreich, Joseph (2002) *Shifting Contexts: Reinterpreting* Samson Agonistes. Pittsburgh: Duquesne University Press.

Womersley, David (ed.) (2000) *Restoration Drama: an Anthology.* Oxford: Blackwell.

Woods, Susanne (2002) Aemilia Lanyer, *Salve Deus Rex Judaeorum*. In Pacheco, ed. (2002), pp. 125–35.

Woudhuysen, H. R. (1996) *Sir Philip Sidney and the Circulation of Manuscripts 1558–1640*. Oxford: Clarendon Press.

Wroth, Lady Mary (1621a) *The Countesse of Mountgomeries Urania*. London.

Wroth, Lady Mary (1621b) *Pamphilia to Amphilanthus*. Printed as an appendix to Wroth (1621a); non-continuous signature, but no title page.

Wroth, Lady Mary (1996) *The Early Modern Englishwoman: A Facsimile Library of Essential Works. Part 1: Printed Writings, 1500–1640. Volume 10: Mary Wroth*. With an introductory note by Josephine A. Roberts. Aldershot: Scolar Press.

Zwicker, Steven N. (1984) *Politics and Language in Dryden's Poetry: The Arts of Disguise*. Princeton: Princeton University Press.

Zwicker, Steven N. (1993) *Lines of Authority: Politics and English Literary Culture, 1649–1689*. Ithaca and London: Cornell University Press.

Zwicker, Steven N. (2002) Habits of Reading and Early Modern Literary Culture. In Loewenstein and Mueller, eds. (2002), pp. 170–98.

Index